Interdisciplinary Applications of Agent-Based Social Simulation and Modeling

Diana Francisca Adamatti
Universidade Federal do Rio Grande, Brasil

Graçaliz Pereira Dimuro
Universidade Federal do Rio Grande, Brasil

Helder Coelho
Universidade de Lisboa, Portugal

A volume in the Advances in Human and Social Aspects of Technology (AHSAT) Book Series

Managing Director:	Lindsay Johnston
Production Editor:	Jennifer Yoder
Development Editor:	Austin DeMarco
Acquisitions Editor:	Kayla Wolfe
Typesetter:	John Crodian
Cover Design:	Jason Mull

Published in the United States of America by
Information Science Reference (an imprint of IGI Global)
701 E. Chocolate Avenue
Hershey PA 17033
Tel: 717-533-8845
Fax: 717-533-8661
E-mail: cust@igi-global.com
Web site: http://www.igi-global.com

Library of Congress Cataloging-in-Publication Data

Interdisciplinary applications of agent-based social simulation and modeling / Diana Francisca Adamatti, Gracaliz Pereira Dimuro and Helder Coelho, editors.
   pages cm
 Includes bibliographical references and index. ISBN 978-1-4666-5954-4 (hardcover) -- ISBN 978-1-4666-5955-1 (ebook) -- ISBN 978-1-4666-5957-5 (print & perpetual access) 1. Social sciences--Computer simulation. 2. Multiagent systems. 3. Computer simulation. I. Adamatti, Diana Francisca. II. Dimuro, Gra?aliz Pereira. III. Coelho, Helder.
 H61.3.I58 2014
 300.285'63--dc23
                      2014001633

This book is published in the IGI Global book series Advances in Human and Social Aspects of Technology (AHSAT) (ISSN: 2328-1316; eISSN: 2328-1324)

Advances in Human and Social Aspects of Technology (AHSAT) Book Series

Ashish Dwivedi
The University of Hull, UK

ISSN: 2328-1316
EISSN: 2328-1324

Mission

In recent years, the societal impact of technology has been noted as we become increasingly more connected and are presented with more digital tools and devices. With the popularity of digital devices such as cell phones and tablets, it is crucial to consider the implications of our digital dependence and the presence of technology in our everyday lives.

The **Advances in Human and Social Aspects of Technology (AHSAT) Book Series** seeks to explore the ways in which society and human beings have been affected by technology and how the technological revolution has changed the way we conduct our lives as well as our behavior. The AHSAT book series aims to publish the most cutting-edge research on human behavior and interaction with technology and the ways in which the digital age is changing society.

Coverage

- Activism & ICTs
- Computer-Mediated Communication
- Cultural Influence of ICTs
- Cyber Behavior
- End-User Computing
- Gender & Technology
- Human-Computer Interaction
- Information Ethics
- Public Access to ICTs
- Technoself

IGI Global is currently accepting manuscripts for publication within this series. To submit a proposal for a volume in this series, please contact our Acquisition Editors at Acquisitions@igi-global.com or visit: http://www.igi-global.com/publish/.

Titles in this Series

For a list of additional titles in this series, please visit: www.igi-global.com

Gender Considerations and Influence in the Digital Media and Gaming Industry
Julie Prescott (University of Bolton, UK) and Julie Elizabeth McGurren (Codemasters, UK)
Information Science Reference • copyright 2014 • 313pp • H/C (ISBN: 9781466661424) • US $195.00 (our price)

Human-Computer Interfaces and Interactivity Emergent Research and Applications
Pedro Isaías (Universidade Aberta (Portuguese Open University), Portugal) and Katherine Blashki (Noroff University College, Norway)
Information Science Reference • copyright 2014 • 325pp • H/C (ISBN: 9781466662285) • US $200.00 (our price)

Interdisciplinary Applications of Agent-Based Social Simulation and Modeling
Diana Francisca Adamatti (Universidade Federal do Rio Grande, Brasil) Graçaliz Pereira Dimuro (Universidade Federal do Rio Grande, Brasil) and Helder Coelho (Universidade de Lisboa, Portugal)
Information Science Reference • copyright 2014 • 314pp • H/C (ISBN: 9781466659544) • US $195.00 (our price)

Global Issues and Ethical Considerations in Human Enhancement Technologies
Steven John Thompson (Johns Hopkins University, USA)
Medical Information Science Reference • copyright 2014 • 322pp • H/C (ISBN: 9781466660106) • US $215.00 (our price)

Exchanging Terrorism Oxygen for Media Airwaves The Age of Terroredia
Mahmoud Eid (University of Ottawa, Canada)
Information Science Reference • copyright 2014 • 347pp • H/C (ISBN: 9781466657762) • US $195.00 (our price)

Women in IT in the New Social Era A Critical Evidence-Based Review of Gender Inequality and the Potential for Change
Sonja Bernhardt (ThoughtWare, Australia)
Business Science Reference • copyright 2014 • 274pp • H/C (ISBN: 9781466658608) • US $195.00 (our price)

Gamification for Human Factors Integration Social, Education, and Psychological Issues
Jonathan Bishop (Centre for Research into Online Communities and E-Learning Systems, Belgium)
Information Science Reference • copyright 2014 • 362pp • H/C (ISBN: 9781466650718) • US $175.00 (our price)

Emerging Research and Trends in Interactivity and the Human-Computer Interface
Katherine Blashki (Noroff University College, Norway) and Pedro Isaias (Portuguese Open University, Portugal)
Information Science Reference • copyright 2014 • 580pp • H/C (ISBN: 9781466646230) • US $175.00 (our price)

www.igi-global.com

701 E. Chocolate Ave., Hershey, PA 17033
Order online at www.igi-global.com or call 717-533-8845 x100
To place a standing order for titles released in this series, contact: cust@igi-global.com
Mon-Fri 8:00 am - 5:00 pm (est) or fax 24 hours a day 717-533-8661

List of Reviewers

Table of Contents

Section 1
Current Discussions on Agent-Based Social Simulation and Modeling

Section 2
Research on Agent-Based Models for Social Simulation

Section 3
Developing Reliable Interdisciplinary Applications of Agent-Based Social Simulation and Modeling

Detailed Table of Contents

Section 1
Current Discussions on Agent-Based Social Simulation and Modeling

Chapter 1

Cristiano Castelfranchi, Institute of Cognitive Sciences and Technologies, Italy

Agent-based computer simulation is the central (revolutionary) challenge for the future of Social Sciences. The foundational issue of the Social Sciences is the micro-macro link, the relation between cognition and individual behavior and social self-organizing and complex structures. There are no approaches for understanding its (causal) mechanisms better than computer simulation. Special attention should be devoted to the "immergent" top-down feedback on the agent control system. This chapter also attempts to explain a techno-political revolution allowed by distributed computing, and in particular "agents"; agent-based simulation, agents embedded in the smart environment, and agents as representing and mediating in human negotiation and agreement. The social "planning" was doomed to fail for intrinsic political and cognitive limits. MAS and Social Simulation will provide a platform/instrument for social policies, for planning and decision-making; and for focused monitoring and participation. However the solution of the "problem" can never been merely "technical". The solution requires processes of political negotiation and decision.

Chapter 2

Helder Coelho, Universidade de Lisboa, Portugal
António Carlos da Rocha Costa, Universidade Federal do Rio Grande, Brazil
Paulo Trigo, Instituto Superior de Eng. de Lisboa, Portugal

Morality tells agents what they ought to do, and this defines their identity and character. This chapter deals with moral behaviour, following the classical view in Philosophy that defends character as a state concerned with choice, and able to direct the agent decision-taking. The authors also include new values regarding agent moral signature that may enhance the evaluation of agents, namely on reputation and satisfaction. So, the popularity of the agents can be measured with more depth, and not only for organizations but also for social networks.

Chapter 3

Luis G. Nardin, Universidade de São Paulo, Brazil

Luciano M. Rosset, Universidade de São Paulo, Brazil

Jaime S. Sichman, Universidade de São Paulo, Brazil

The exploitation of Agent-Based Social Simulation (ABSS) full capabilities often requires massive computing power and tools in order to support the achievement of breakthrough results in social sciences. Lately, this issue has being addressed by the release of several high-performance computing agent-based simulation tools; however, they have not been used for exploring critical issues, such as ABSS results invariance and universality. Hence, in order to advance this topic, this chapter provides an invariance analysis, considering scale and topology, of a model that incorporates the concepts of trust and coalition formation, in which agents are placed on a square lattice interacting locally with their neighbors and forming coalitions. By varying the environment size, its topology, as well as the neighborhood topology, it is identified in the experimental scenario that apparently the only parameter that affects the simulation dynamics is the neighborhood topology.

Chapter 4

Marcia R. Friesen, University of Manitoba, Canada

Richard Gordon, Gulf Specimen Marine Laboratory, USA & Wayne State University, USA

Robert D. McLeod, University of Manitoba, Canada

In this chapter, the authors examine manifestations of emergence or apparent emergence in agent based social modeling and simulation, and discuss the inherent challenges in building real world models and in defining, recognizing and validating emergence within these systems. The discussion is grounded in examples of research on emergence by others, with extensions from within our research group. The works cited and built upon are explicitly chosen as representative samples of agent-based models that involve social systems, where observation of emergent behavior is a sought-after outcome. The concept of the distinctiveness of social from abiotic emergence in terms of the use of global parameters by agents is introduced.

Chapter 5

Pablo Lucas, University of Essex, England

Diane Payne, Geary Institute, University College Dublin, Ireland

Political scientists seek to build more realistic Collective Decision-Making Models (henceforth CDMM) which are implemented as computer simulations. The starting point for this present chapter is the observation that efficient progress in this field may be being hampered by the fact that the implementation of these models as computer simulations may vary considerably and the code for these computer simulations is not usually made available. CDMM are mathematically deterministic formulations (i.e. without probabilistic inputs or outputs) and are aimed at explaining the behaviour of individuals involved in dynamic, collective negotiations with any number of policy decision-related issues. These CDMM differ from each other regarding the particular bargaining strategies implemented and tested in each model for how the individuals reach a collective binding policy agreement. The CDMM computer simulations are used to analyse the data and generate predictions of a collective decision. While the formal mathematical treatment of the models and empirical findings of CDMM are usually presented and discussed through peer-review journal publications, access to these CDMM implementations as computer simulations are often unavailable online nor easily accessed offline and this tends to dissuade cross fertilisation and learning in the field.

Chapter 6

Many papers on simulation in the social sciences come up with significance tests in which the authors describe the effect of a parameter on some simulation outcome as significant on some level of significance. This chapter discusses the question whether significance tests on simulation results are meaningful, and it argues that it is the effect size much more than the existence of the effect that matters and that it is the description of the distribution function of the stochastic process incorporated in the simulation model which is important, particularly when this distribution is far from normal — which is particularly often the case when the simulation model is nonlinear.

Advances on information technology in the past decades have provided new tools to assist scientists in the study of social and natural phenomena. Agent-based modeling techniques have flourished recently, encouraging the introduction of computer simulations to examine behavioral patterns in complex human and biological systems. Real-world social dynamics are very complex, containing billions of interacting individuals and an important amount of data (both spatial and social). Dealing with large-scale agent-based models is not an easy task and encounters several challenges. The design of strategies to overcome these challenges represents an opportunity for high performance parallel and distributed implementation. This chapter examines the most relevant aspects to deal with large-scale agent-based simulations in social sciences and revises the developments to confront technological issues.

Section 2
Research on Agent-Based Models for Social Simulation

This chapter discusses the way that three distinct fields, decision theory, game theory and computer science, can be successfully combined in order to optimally design economic experiments. Using an example of cooperative game theory (the Stag-Hunt game), the chapter presents how the introduction of ambiguous beliefs and attitudes towards ambiguity in the analysis can affect the predicted equilibrium. Based on agent-based simulation methods, the author is able to tackle similar theoretical problems and thus to design experiments in such a way that they will produce useful, unbiased and reliable data.

Policy diffusion needs to be studied as a complex phenomenon, since it involves interdependent relationships between autonomous and heterogeneous countries. This chapter aims at developing a simple computational model based on a theoretical model of policy diffusion (Braun & Gilardi, 2006) that helps to explain the emergence of diffusion in a complex system. Based on three simple conditions (ready, choose, change) and a few internal and external characteristics that define countries and their interactions, the model presented in this chapter shows that policies do diffuse and lead to local convergence and global divergence. Moreover, it takes time for a country to introduce the best-suited policy and for this policy to become very effective. To conclude, diffusion is a complex phenomenon and its outcomes, as ensued from the author's model, are in line with the theoretical expectations and the empirical evidence.

Chapter 10

The key motivation for this chapter is the perception that within the near future, markets will be composed of individuals that may simultaneously undertake the roles of consumers, producers and traders. Those individuals are economically motivated "prosumer" (producer-consumer) agents that not only consume, but can also produce, store and trade assets. This chapter describes the most relevant aspects of a simulation tool that provides (human and virtual) prosumer agents an interactive and real-time game-like environment where they can explore (long-term and short-term) strategic behaviour and experience the effects of social influence in their decision-making processes. The game-like environment is focused on the simulation of electricity markets, it is named ITEM-game ("Investment and Trading in Electricity Markets"), and it is publically available (ITEM-Game, 2013) for any player to explore the role of a prosumer agent.

Chapter 11

In the last sixty years of research, several models have been proposed to explain (i) the formation and (ii) the evolution of networks. However, because of the specialization required for the problems, most of the agent-based models are not general. On the other hand, many of the traditional network models focus on elementary interactions that are often part of several different processes. This phenomenon is especially evident in the field of models for social networks. Therefore, this chapter presents a unified conceptual framework to express both novel agent-based and traditional social network models. This conceptual framework is essentially a meta-model that acts as a template for other models. To support this meta-model, the chapter proposes a different kind of agent-based modeling tool that we specifically created for developing social network models. The tool the authors propose does not aim at being a general-purpose agent-based modeling tool, thus remaining a relatively simple software system, while it is extensible where it really matters. Eventually, the authors apply this toolkit to a novel problem coming from the domain of P2P social networking platforms.

Davide Nunes, University of Lisbon, Portugal

Luis Antunes, University of Lisbon, Portugal

In real world scenarios, the formation of consensus is a self-organisation process by which actors have to make a joint assessment about a target subject, be it a decision making problem or the formation of a collective opinion. In social simulation, models of opinion dynamics tackle the opinion formation phenomena. These models try to make an assessment, for instance, of the ideal conditions that lead an interacting group of agents to opinion consensus, polarisation or fragmentation. This chapter investigates the role of social relation structure in opinion dynamics and consensus formation. The authors present an agent-based model that defines social relations as multiple concomitant social networks and explore multiple interaction games in this structural set-up. They discuss the influence of complex social network topologies where actors interact in multiple distinct networks. The chapter builds on previous work about social space design with multiple social relations to determine the influence of such complex social structures in a process such as opinion formation.

Section 3
Developing Reliable Interdisciplinary Applications of Agent-Based Social Simulation and Modeling

Gabriel Franklin, Federal University of Ceará, Brazil

Tibérius O. Bonates, Federal University of Ceará, Brazil

This chapter describes an agent-based simulation of an incentive mechanism for scientific production. In the proposed framework, a central agency is responsible for devising and enforcing a policy consisting of performance-based incentives in an attempt to induce a global positive behavior of a group of researchers, in terms of number and type of scientific publications. The macro-level incentive mechanism triggers micro-level actions that, once intensified by social interactions, lead to certain patterns of behavior from individual agents (researchers). Positive reinforcement from receiving incentives (as well as negative reinforcement from not receiving them) shape the behavior of agents in the course of the simulation. The authors show, by means of computational experiments, that a policy devised to act at the individual level might induce a single global behavior that can, depending on the values of certain parameters, be distinct from the original target and have an overall negative effect. The agent-based simulation provides an objective way of assessing the quantitative effect that different policies might induce on the behavior of individual researchers when it comes to their preferences regarding scientific publications.

Chapter 14

Fernanda Mota, Furg, Brazil

Iverton Santos, Furg, Brazil

Graçaliz Dimuro, Furg, Brazil

Vagner Rosa, Furg, Brazil

Silvia Botelho, Furg, Brazil

The electric energy consumption is one of the main indicators of both the economic development and the quality of life of a society. However, the electric energy consumption data of individual home use is hard to obtain due to several reasons, such as privacy issues. In this sense, the social simulation based on multiagent systems comes as a promising option to deal with this difficulty through the production of synthetic electric energy consumption data. In a multiagent system the intelligent global behavior can be achieved from the behavior of the individual agents and their interactions. This chapter proposes a tool for simulation of electric energy consumers, based on multiagent systems concepts using the Net-Logo tool. The tool simulates the residential consumption during working days and presented as a result the synthetic data average monthly consumption of residences, which varies according to income. So, the analysis of the produced simulation results show that economic consumers of the income 1 in the summer season had the lowest consumption among all other consumers and consumers noneconomic income 6 in the winter season had the highest.

Chapter 15

Nuno Trindade Magessi, Universidade de Lisboa-LabMag, Portugal

Luis Antunes, Universidade de Lisboa-LabMag, Portugal

Tax evasion is a classic problem in the field of economics and has been intensively studied over the last few decades. So far, research has been focused, and reasonably followed, on extensions from the original model developed by Alligham and Sandmo (1972). This chapter has taken the initiative to analyse and discuss the behaviour of taxpayers and the relation with risk when they act strategically. In this sense, the authors propose to replicate and discuss the three main conceptual functions of the brain (expressed by Spinoza) when agents do their strategic options concerning tax evasion risk. Output results demonstrate a tendency for strategic taxpayers to first react in detriment of structured and complex reasoning. The assumption, commonly used in tax evasion literature, that taxpayers are exclusively rational, is liable of being refuted. Even the strategic taxpayers are reluctant to follow only their reason.

Chapter 16

Nunzia Carbonara, Politecnico di Bari, Italy

Agglomeration economies are positive externalities associated with the co-location of firms within a bounded geographic area. Traditionally, these agglomerative advantages have been expressed in terms of pecuniary externalities and they have been identified as one of the key sources of geographical cluster (GC) competitive advantage. However, in the last years the basics of competition are changed and the ability of firms to create new knowledge is more crucial for success rather than the efficiency in production. This has shifted the attention of scholars on the role of knowledge and learning in GCs. In line with these studies, this chapter suggests that agglomeration economies are related to both pecuniary externalities and knowledge-based externalities. The latter are benefits that co-located firms can gain in terms of development of knowledge. To investigate whether knowledge-based externalities affect geographical clustering of firms, an agent-based model is developed. By using this model, a simulation analysis is carried out.

Chapter 17

Flávia Santos, Universidade Federal do Rio Grande—Brasil

Thiago Rodrigues, Universidade Federal do Rio Grande—Brasil

Henrique Donancio, Universidade Federal do Rio Grande—Brasil

Iverton Santos, Universidade Federal do Rio Grande—Brasil

Diana F. Adamatti, Universidade Federal do Rio Grande—Brasil

Graçaliz P. Dimuro, Universidade Federal do Rio Grande—Brasil

Glenda Dimuro, Universidade de Sevilla—Spain

Esteban De Manuel Jerez, Universidade de Sevilla—Spain

The SJVG-MAS Project addresses, in an interdisciplinary approach, the development of MAS-based tools for the simulation of the social production and management processes observed in urban ecosystems, adopting as case study the social vegetable garden project conducted at the San Jerónimo Park (Seville/Spain), headed by the confederation "Ecologistas en Acción." The authors aim at the analysis of the current reality of the SJVG project, allowing discussions on the adopted social management processes, and also for investigating how possible changes in the social organization (e.g., roles assumed by the agents in the organization, actions, behaviors, (in)formal interaction/communication protocols, regulation norms), especially from the point of view of the agent's participation in the decision making processes, may transform this reality, from the social, environmental and economic point of view, then contributing for the sustainability of the project. The MAS was conceived as a multi-dimensional BDI-like agent social system, involving the development of five components: the agents' population, the system's organization, the system's environment, the set of interactions executed among agents playing organizational roles (e.g., communication protocols for reaching agreements) and the normative policy structure (internal regulation established by SJVG community). The aim of this chapter is to discuss the problems faced and to present the solution found for the modeling of SJVG social organization using JaCAMo framework. The chapter shows the integration of the considered dimensions, discussing the adopted methodology, which may be applied in several other contexts.

Chapter 18

Luca Arciero, Bank of Italy, Italy

Cristina Picillo, Bank of Italy, Italy

Sorin Solomon, Hebrew University of Jerusalem, Israel

Pietro Terna, University of Turin, Italy

Agent-based models (ABMs) are quite new in the modeling landscape; they emerged on the scene in the 1990s. ABMs have a clear advantage over other approaches: they create the capacity to manage learning processes in agents and discover novelties in their behavior. In addition to bounded rationality assumptions, ABMs share a number of peculiar characteristics: first of all, a bottom-up perspective is assumed where the properties of macro-dynamics are emergent properties of micro-dynamics involving individuals as heterogeneous agents who live in complex systems that evolve through time. To apply this framework to financial crisis analysis, a simplified implementation of the SWARM protocol (www.swarm.org), based on Python, is introduced. The result is the Swarm-Like Agent Protocol in Python (SLAPP). Using SLAPP, it is possible to focus on natural phenomena and social behavior. In the case of this chapter, the authors focus on the banking system, recreating the interactions of a community of financial institutions that act in the payment system and in the interbank market for short-term liquidity.

Foreword

The modelling of agents applied to the computational study of social phenomena has been around for at least a couple of decades. Readings (Gilbert & Doran, 1994; Gilbert & Conte, 1995; Conte et al., 1997; etc.) and monographs (Epstein & Axtell, 1996; Epstein, 2007; etc.) abound, and the field is now crowded with agent models.

Numbers of publications can measure the popularity of a field of science. Whether they indicate also scientific maturity and breakthroughs, is a totally different question. In social simulation, a lot is to be done yet. In particular, Agent Based Modelling is still in want of a strong and solid theoretical foundation. Agent models are often built up from scratch, assembling simple rules that are thought to generate expected macro-social effects. Thus constructed, agent models often entertain a one-to-one correspondence with the phenomena of interest, while lacking generality. Furthermore, they are almost *ad hoc* and rather arbitrary. Finally, and consequently, agent models are countless: one single phenomenon is often accounted for by different models, which obviously produce different results. Take the example of cooperation. From tit-for-tat strategies (Axelrod) to strong reciprocity (Bowles and Gintis, to cite but a few), and from image score (Nowak and Siegmund) to reputation-building, solutions to the puzzle of cooperation pop up every now and then, but no systematic conclusion as to the causes has yet been reached. In particular, we still miss an adequate account of the proximate causes of cooperation, i.e., the mechanisms internal to cooperative systems that generate their behaviours.

Not surprisingly, the field recently entered a phase of relative decline. Despite its success, the strong offensive launched by Epstein's book against inductive and deductive methodologies (see the first chapter in this volume) with the arm of ABM found a strong obstacle in inductive science, thanks to the powerful weapons of Big Data and statistical physics. Since the appearance of Lazer et al.'s paper in Science in 2009, the field of Computational Social Science (CSS) is threatening the scientific status and influence of ABM (see Conte et al., 2012). Far from generating phenomena to be observed *in silico*, CSS collects vast bodies of real-world data from which to extract correlational information. With the scaling up of its empirical bases, the heuristic and innovative power of the science of artificial goes down, at the same time challenging or at least strongly resizing the role of ABM. Once essential to feed generative science, ABM is now likely to be replaced by large scale Individual Based Modelling, where individuals are featured along the computational footprints left by the real people (Pastor-Satorras & Vespignani, 2001). By this means, however, the study of the behavioural mechanisms which account for social phenomena would be relinquished.

As a consequence, the appearance of a new book on Agent Based Social Simulation is always welcome. This is especially true in the case of the book by Adamatti, Dimuro and Coelho, which is written not (only) from within the social and behavioural sciences, but also from within the agent field of ICT. The cross-fertilization between social simulation and agent systems gave impulse to the long series of

Multi-Agent Based Simulation (MABS) workshops, one of the satellites of the ICMAS first, and later of the AAMAS conference on agent systems, which now appears as a mature and integrated field of study.

This is good for several reasons. First, it provides evidence, if still needed, of how vital and productive *agent-based* social simulation is (see the chapter by Nardin et al. in this volume). Second, it takes seriously and shows the potential of a really interdisciplinary approach (see Georgalos's chapter). This is a far from granted result. Interdisciplinary science is not always perceived as a plus. Some funding agencies, like Horizon 2020, especially under specific programs (see for example, Future Emergent Technologies) provide an incentive to interdisciplinary science. But on the other hand, interdisciplinary research is hard to publish, especially in high-impact journals. Consequently, interdisciplinary careers are often penalised. Still, the continuous interbreeding of scientific fields offers new frontiers and new opportunities for investigation and discovery, therefore attracting fresh task force. While respecting the disciplinary boundaries is a success-enhancing strategy at the individual level, it is poorly effective for scientific discovery, thus creating the scientific variant of a classic social dilemma. What is individually fit, is no use at the social level. Fortunately, however, scientists, much as other humans, not always behave according to the principles of economic rationality. Agent Based Social Simulators, evidently, do not.

Third, filling in the traditional gap between the science of society, on the one hand, and the science of nature and physical matter - including mathematics and computer science - on the other, agent based social simulation accounts for the proximate causes of social processes, for the mechanisms that generate social phenomena. Generative science, indeed, is the only efficacious measure against reductionism and the status of social and human sciences as Minor God children.

There is still more to this book, which deserves mentioning. For example, the geographical distribution of contributors. In the early nineties, social simulation was a European hunting land, launched by a handful of scientists put together by Nigel Gilbert in a series of symposia at the University of Surrey, UK. From the mid nineties, the success of SugarScape (Axtell & Epstein, 1996) imposed the field of artificial societies to a wider audience on both sides of the Atlantic ocean. Ever since, it sailed the seven seas. Still, this is perhaps the first collection of simulation studies, in which authors are so widely distributed geographically. I take this as another, if not the most convincing, marker of success of the field.

A pleasant surprise for the reader is to find out that the first part of the volume is dedicated to controversial issues. Rather than moving them to a final section about future works, the editors decided to open up the book with unanswered issues. Controversies concern not only social theory (see the first two chapters) and conceptual instruments (as social distance, too often confused with a topological notion, or emergence). They also invest methodological decisions (see the problem of validation in Troitzsch's chapter) and call into question the effective usefulness of social simulation as an instrument of investigation (see the problem of scale in Montañola et al.'s chapter). Analogously, no traditional boundary between fundamental and application-oriental research in social simulation is drawn. A policy-oriented application (see Luyet's chapter) of social simulation is included in the same part of the volume that contains chapters discussing interdisciplinary integration (Georgalos) or comparing agent-based and traditional social network analysis (Franchi).

Finally, the reader's expectations for inquiries into the domains of society and economy hassling social scientists no less than stakeholders, will not be disappointed. Part III of the volume includes research works showing the advantages of agent based social simulation in the study of incentive, energy consumption, tax evasion, industrial clusters, urban ecosystems, and last but not least, the emergence of crises. In a few words, the volume offers a rather dynamic and controversial view of the field, in need for and likely to engage in continuous confrontation with adjacent or complementary approaches. A portrait of the field as a vital, complex environment well-suited for scientific development.

Rosaria Conte
ISTC-CNR, Italy

Rosaria Conte *is Research Director, Head of the Laboratory of Agent Based Social Simulation at the ISTC-CNR in Rome and Vice President of the Scientific Council of the National Research Council of Italy. Former President of the Italian Cognitive Science Association, and of the European Social Simulation Society, she coordinated and participated to several research projects. She taught Cognitive Psychology and Social Psychology at the Univ. of Torino, the Univ. of Siena and Uninettuno International Telematic University. She is member of the Scientific Board of Sapienza University of Rome for the Social Science PhD course. She is member of several Management and Evaluation Committees and Journals Advisory Boards. She published more than 200 works. Her scientific activity aims to explain pro-social behaviour among intelligent autonomous systems and model the bidirectional dynamics of norms and norm-enforcement mechanisms through a highly interdisciplinary approach and a computational methodology (ABSS).*

REFERENCES

Conte, R., Gilbert, N., Bonelli, G., Cioffi-Revilla, C., Deffuant, G., & Kertesz, J. et al. (2012). Manifesto of computational social science. *European Physics Journal, 214*, 325–346.

Conte, R., Hegselmann, R., & Terna, P. (Eds.). (1997). *Simulating social phenomena (Lecture Notes in Economics and Mathematical Systems)*. Berlin: Springer.

Epstein, J. (1996). *Growing artificial societies: Social science from the bottom up*. Washington, DC: The Brooking Institution Press.

Epstein, J. (2007). *Generative social science: Studies in agent-based computational modeling*. Princeton, NJ: Princeton University Press.

Gilbert, N., & Conte, R. (Eds.). (1995). *Artificial societies. The computer simulation of social life*. London: UCL Press.

Gilbert, N., & Doran, J. (Eds.). (1994). *Simulating societies: The computer simulation of social phenomena*. London: UCL Press.

Lazer, D., Pentland, A., Adamic, L., Aral, S., Barabási, L., & Brewer, D. et al. (2009). Computational social science. *Science, 23*, 721–723. doi:10.1126/science.1167742 PMID:19197046

Pastor-Satorras, R., & Vespignani, A. (2001). Epidemic spreading in scale-free networks. *Physical Review Letters, 86*, 3200–3203. doi:10.1103/PhysRevLett.86.3200 PMID:11290142

Preface

The main topic of this book is social simulation and modeling, aiming at agent-based applications, which naturally refers to the term interdisciplinarity since several disciplines are involved.

Social simulation has a dialectical relationship to Artificial Intelligence (AI), in general, and to Autonomous Agents and Multi-agent Systems (MAS), in particular. It is both an area for the application of methods, techniques and technologies of AI and MAS, as well as a source of inspiration for new theories, as it draws upon the theories, models and methods of the social sciences, such as anthropology, sociology, political science, economy, government, and management.

Social modeling and simulation is a difficult activity, mainly because its interdisciplinary character. This book brings new insights on the whole discipline, looking through its dangers, pitfalls, deceits and challenges.

The book presents some current discussions on agent-based social simulation and modeling, addressing theoretical, methodological, technical and instrumental issues concerning the area of social simulation, mainly based on AI and MAS technology, and focusing on applications, so offering different kinds of models and tools that can help the reader to face complex developments.

The book is divided into 3 sectopms. Section 1, "Current Discussions on Agent-Based Social Simulation and Modeling", is a reflection on the tone of the book, by introducing the reader to the actual mission of Social Simulation, and the different challenges concerning the theme, such as morality aspects, the emergence issue, replication of models, the role of significance tests on simulation results, and large-scale problems and the effects of scale and topology.

Chapter 1, "Making Visible the Invisible Hand: The Mission of Social Simulation", by Castelfranchi, brings a discussion about the mission of Social Simulation, showing that computer-based simulation should be considered a third scientific approach, to be added to the traditional *inductive* and *deductive* ones. The chapter remarks that Social Simulation provides the social sciences with a truly "experimental" method for the validation and adjustment of the models. In particular, it shows its importance for the specification of working architectures. The chapter stresses that agent-based social simulation provides the social sciences with "a generative approach", and a synthetic, constructive approach – an operational approach.

Chapter 2, "On Agent Interactions Governed by Morality", by Coelho, Costa, and Trigo, deals with agent moral behavior, following the classical view in Philosophy that defends character as a state concerned with choice, and able to direct the agent decision-making. The authors analyze the values regarding the agent moral signature, showing that it may enhance the evaluation of agents, for example, on reputation and satisfaction, leading to a more consistent way for measuring agents' popularity in organizations and social networks at large.

Chapter 3, "Scale and Topology Effects on Agent-Based Simulation: A Trust-Based Coalition Formation Case Study", by Nardin, Rosset, and Sichman, provides an invariance analysis, considering scale and topology, of a model that incorporates the concepts of trust and coalition formation, in which agents are placed on a square lattice interacting locally with their neighbors and forming coalitions.

Chapter 4, "Exploring Emergence within Social Systems with Agent Based Models", by Friesen, Gordon, and McLeod, analyses manifestations of emergence or apparent emergence in agent based social modeling and simulation, discussing the inherent challenges in building real world models and in defining, recognizing and validating emergence within these systems.

Chapter 5, "Usefulness of Agent-Based Simulation in Testing Collective Decision-Making Models", by Lucas and Payne, discusses the importance of the specification and implementation of simulation assumptions and processes in the context of an agent-based model replication of a range of collective decision-making models (CDMM) that have been developed and established in political science.

Chapter 6, "Analysing Simulation Results Statistically: Does Significance Matter?", by Troitzsch, discusses the question whether significance tests on simulation results are meaningful, and argues that it is the effect size much more than the existence of the effect that matters and that it is the description of the distribution function of the stochastic process incorporated in the simulation model which is important.

Chapter 7, "Large-Scale Social Simulation, Dealing with Complexity Challenges in High Performance Environments", by Montañola-Sales, Rubio-Campillo, Casanovas-Garcia, Cela-Espín, and Kaplan-Marcusán, analyses the most relevant aspects to deal with large-scale agent-based simulations in social sciences and revises the developments to confront technological issues.

Section 2, "Research on Agent-Based Models for Social Simulation", provides a look on some new agent-based models for social simulation that constitute the focus of some current research in the theme, such as social networks, economic experiments, policy diffusion, and electricity market.

Chapter 8, "Playing with Ambiguity: An Agent-Based Model of Vague Beliefs in Games", by Georgalos, discusses the way that three distinct fields, decision theory, game theory and computer science, can be successfully combined in order to optimally design economic experiments, using agent-based simulation methods.

Chapter 9, "From Meso Decision to Macro Results: An Agent-Based Approach for Policy Diffusion", by Luyet, aims at developing a simple computational model based on a theoretical model of policy diffusion that helps to explain the emergence of diffusion in a complex system.

Chapter 10, "Multi-Agent Economically Motivated Decision-Making", by Trigo, describes the most relevant aspects of a simulation tool that provides (human and virtual) producer-consumer agents an interactive and real-time game-like environment where they can explore (long-term and short-term) strategic behavior and experience the effects of social influence in their decision-making processes. The game-like environment is focused on the simulation of electricity markets.

Chapter 11, "A Unified Framework for Traditional and Agent-Based Social Network Modeling", by Franchi, and Tomaiuolo, presents a unified conceptual framework to express both novel agent-based and traditional social network models. This conceptual framework is essentially a meta-model that acts as a template for other models. To support the meta-model, Franchi and Tomaiuolo also introduce a different kind of agent-based modeling tool for developing social network models.

Chapter 12, "Social Space in Simulation Models", by Nunes and Antunes, discusses the role of social relation structure in opinion dynamics and consensus formation. The chapter presents an agent-based model that defines social relations as multiple concomitant social networks and explores multiple interaction games in this structural set-up. The authors discuss the influence of complex social network topologies where actors interact in multiple distinct networks.

Section 3, "Developing Reliable Interdisciplinary Applications of Agent-based Social Simulation and Modeling", is the core of the book, presenting applications in different fields, such as an incentive for scientific production, energy usage in households, tax evasion risk, geographical clustering of firms, social production and management processes, and emergence of financial crisis.

Chapter 13, "Simulating an Incentive Framework for Scientific Production by Means of Adaptive Agents", by Franklin and Bonates, describes an agent-based simulation of an incentive mechanism for scientific production.

Chapter 14, "Agent-Based Simulation of Electric Energy Consumers: A NetLogo Tool", by Mota, Santos, Dimuro, Rosa and Botelho, discusses the energy usage in households, proposing a MAS-based simulating tool, implemented in NetLogo.

Chapter 15, "Agents' Risk Relations in a Strategic Tax Reporting", by Magessi and Antunes, analyses and discusses the behavior of taxpayers and its relation with risk, when they act strategically, by replicating the three main conceptual functions of the brain, when agents do their strategic options, concerning tax evasion risk task.

Chapter 16, "Knowledge-Based Externalities and Geographical Clusters: An Agent-Based Simulation Study", by Carbonara, presents an analysis of the role of knowledge and learning in geographical clusters, investigating whether knowledge-based externalities affect geographical clustering of firms, using an agent-based simulation tool.

Chapter 17, "Towards a Multi-Agent-Based Tool for the Analysis of the Social Production and Management Processes in a Urban Ecosystem: An Approach Based on the Integration of Organizational, Regulatory, Communication and Physical Artifacts in the JaCaMo Framework", by Santos, Fredes Rodrigues, Donâncio Rodrigues, Adamatti, Pereira Dimuro, Dimuro, and De Manuel Jerez, addresses the development of a MAS-based tool for the simulation of the social production and management processes observed in urban ecosystems, adopting as case study the social vegetable garden project conducted at the San Jerónimo Park (Seville, Spain). The authors discuss the use of JaCAMo framework, presenting the adopted multi-dimensional based methodology consisted by the integration of artifacts.

Chapter 18, "Building ABMs to Control the Emergence of Crisis Analyzing Agent's Behaviors", by Arciero, Picillo, Solomon, and Terna, apply agent-based modeling and simulation to the financial crisis analysis, adopting a simplified implementation of the SWARM protocol, based on Python, and presenting the Swarm-Like Agent Protocol in Python (SLAPP).

Finally, we attempted to provide a comprehensive and integrated view of the current discussions and investigations on agent-based social simulation and modeling, from a conceptual point of view to the development of models and applications, with an interdisciplinary character.

Diana Adamatti
Universidade Federal do Rio Grande, Brazil

Graçaliz Dimuro
Universidade Federal do Rio Grande, Brazil

Helder Coelho
Universidade de Lisboa, Portugal

Rio Grande and Lisboa, December, 2013

Acknowledgment

This book is the result of many efforts, not just of the editors, but of a lot of people and institutions.

Firstly, we thank the authors for believing in the book proposal and submitting their work, and for their time and interest in revising their chapters in order to accommodate all the suggestions and demands of the editorial advisory board.

Then, we would like to express our sincere thanks to the members of the editorial advisory board, for their cooperation in the reviewing process, offering their time and labor for reading the chapters carefully. We appreciate their efforts, suggestions and fast feedbacks very much, which guaranteed the quality of this publication.

Our very special thanks goes to Prof. Dr. Rosaria Conte, who wrote the foreword, and contributed to increase the book quality, with her expertise in the area.

Finally, we would like to thank IGI Global for all the help in the editing process, and to our institutions, for the continuous support during the organization of this book. So, many thanks to Centro de Ciencias Computacionais of Universidade Federal do Rio Grande (Brazil) and Faculdade de Ciencias of Universidade de Lisboa (Portugal).

This book was made possible by the financial support of the Brazilian funding agency CNPq, under the Process numbers 476234/2011-5, 560118/2010-4, 305131/2010-9, 481283/2013-7, 240181/2012-3.

Diana Adamatti
Universidade Federal do Rio Grande, Brazil

Graçaliz Dimuro
Universidade Federal do Rio Grande, Brazil

Helder Coelho
Universidade de Lisboa, Portugal

Rio Grande and Lisboa, December, 2013

Section 1
Current Discussions on Agent–Based Social Simulation and Modeling

Chapter 1
Making Visible "The Invisible Hand"
The Mission of Social Simulation[1]

Cristiano Castelfranchi
Institute of Cognitive Sciences and Technologies, Italy

ABSTRACT

Agent-based computer simulation is the central (revolutionary) challenge for the future of Social Sciences. The foundational issue of the Social Sciences is the micro-macro link, the relation between cognition and individual behavior and social self-organizing and complex structures. There are no approaches for understanding its (causal) mechanisms better than computer simulation. Special attention should be devoted to the "immergent" top-down feedback on the agent control system. This chapter also attempts to explain a techno-political revolution allowed by distributed computing, and in particular "agents"; agent-based simulation, agents embedded in the smart environment, and agents as representing and mediating in human negotiation and agreement. The social "planning" was doomed to fail for intrinsic political and cognitive limits. MAS and Social Simulation will provide a platform/instrument for social policies, for planning and decision-making; and for focused monitoring and participation. However the solution of the "problem" can never been merely "technical". The solution requires processes of political negotiation and decision.

1. THE *SCIENTIFIC REVOLUTION* OF COMPUTER-BASED SOCIAL SIMULATION[2]

Sometimes in the literature of Social Simulation it seems that the problem is just to provide new (kind of) data to the social sciences and policies, and that, in order to do so, one has to refer to classical cognitive or social theories, implement them, and run some experiment. In my view, this is a reductive and subordinated attitude, which in the end will offer only a limited contribution to the social sciences. Let me be a bit provocative on this. Do we realize that social theories have – in general - been built without any true experimental method? Do we realize that in many cases social theories have not been grounded on really operational or formal concepts?

DOI: 10.4018/978-1-4666-5954-4.ch001

It is true that Social Simulation is "the most promising approach to the social sciences"[3], provided that we conceive it in a more radical way.

As Axelrod claimed, computer-based simulation is a third scientific approach, which should be added to the traditional 'inductive' and 'deductive' ones (Axelrod 1997). Indeed, simulation is so important and crucial because it finally provides the social sciences with *a truly "experimental" method* for the validation and adjustment of the models and, in particular, for the specification of *working* architectures and not mere *formal* descriptions. As we will see later in this contribution, such experimental support is even more crucial for the development of new social policies and strategies than for social theory per se. After all, we cannot experiment in real social contexts with real people and their everyday life!

In particular we should stress the role of Agent-based social simulation (ABSS). It provides the social sciences with "a generative approach" (Epstein, 2006): "Generation is *necessary* for *explanation*", "if you do not grow x, you cannot explain it" (Epstein, 1996). Science in fact cannot be satisfied with just "laws" of the phenomenon under study; detecting regularities and describing their time course or expected outcomes is not enough, and neither is finding mere correlations. What about the *causal mechanism producing* that regularity, that outcome? An explicit modeling of proximate causes is a fundamental level of explanation and understanding, like the diachronic, historical, developmental, or evolutionary explanations[4].

However, ABSS is not simply a *generative* approach (that might just be useful for developing theories) but also a *synthetic*, constructive approach: a radically *operational* approach. When creating an ABSS model, the phenomenon is engineered and even re-produced. As a consequence, ABSS is fundamental in my view for studying two crucial issues:

- Combined and complex effects; emergence (the main social issue; see below - Gilbert, 1995; Castelfranchi, 1998, 2000, 2001; Sawyer, 2005; Axtell, 2007).[5]
- "Proximate" mechanisms, behind the phenomenon; hidden, underlying "causes" of the observable behavior.

In a sense, *computer simulation makes 'visible' and 'tangible' the hidden, background mechanisms* that are assumed behind an observable (not necessarily social) phenomenon. And in such a way it provides us with explicit and clear (operational) models.

1.1 Import-Export between Social Simulation and Social Sciences

In sum, Social Simulation is not just an "experimental method": it is a *modeling* method (synthetic approach; proximate mechanisms). The real challenge is much more serious: to develop *new theories* with cognitive and social scientists; to apply *formal modeling tools* to understand dynamic and complex phenomena; to introduce *new concepts* that will not be derived just from folk-science and common sense but should be well defined, formalized, and operational (computational); to define *new process-models*; to reveal *logical gaps* in the theories (Sawyer, 2003) and originate *new surprising* (dis-confirming) *evidence*.

True 'discoveries' will come from computer simulation of social phenomena (not just simulation of current social theories). It is just *the beginning of the new computational sciences* (computational economics, computational sociology, computational history, etc.). It is a revolution similar to the birth of the 'cognitive sciences', due to the impact of information and computer sciences (the "sciences of the artificial" of Herbert Simon) on the human sciences: psychology, linguistics, logics, philosophy of mind, ...

However the relation and exchange with the Social Sciences and their traditional methods and theories must be correctly set up. Taking advantage of existing social theories and models is obviously crucial (i.e. theories of norms, of membership, of organizations, game theory, market, etc.), but with a critical attitude.

It is a bilateral exchange and evolution, not an "application" of off-the-shelf theoretical frameworks. We have to change such attitudes and expectations from both sides.

The most productive exchange is not just new (real or simulated) data to the Social Sciences, which have the task of elaborating the theories and leave to Social Simulation the task of running experiments (Figure 1, the left cycle). On the contrary, Computer (Agent)-based simulation is for the social sciences a 'Trojan horse': traditional social scientists believe to just have a new platform for running their previous ideas, for having some experimental confirmation and additional data. They do not realize what they will in fact get: new conceptual tools! (Figure 1, the reversed arrows) especially for modeling the micro and macro processes; new models and theories; new hidden phenomena discovered, even directly from social data.

2. THE *THEORETICAL MISSION* OF SOCIAL SIMULATION

Agent-based computer simulation of social phenomena is the *central* (revolutionary) challenge for the future of social sciences. But why is it so?

In fact, von Hayek was just right: "This problem (of the unintentional emergence of order and of spontaneous institutions) is in no way specific to economics... *it is without doubt the core problem of the whole of social science*" (Hayek, 1988).

This is the *foundational* issue of the Social Sciences: the micro-macro link, the relation between cognition and individual behavior and social self-organizing phenomena or complex structures and organizations[6] and institutional actions/phenomena (the two faces of "social order": the "spontaneous" one and the organized or at least institutionalized one). This is the main reason for the existence of the social sciences, what they have to "explain", diachronically and synchronically, in its origin and dynamics.

There are no approaches or models for studying this complex phenomenon and eventually understanding its (causal) mechanisms that are better than computer simulation based on agents.

That is also why *Methodological Individualism,* although fundamental or better necessary, is not *sufficient* at all as a framework for explain-

Figure 1. The right collaborative model

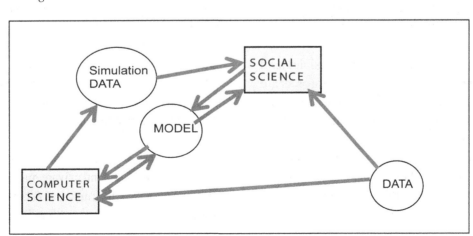

ing social interactions and phenomena (Conte & Castelfranchi, 1995).

In particular, given the perfect characterization of the socio-economic self-organization by Adam Smith[7] the problem is *"How"* the Invisible Hand does really work; finally in the end, we should (and could) explain the "mechanism" and its reproductive feedback on the agents' minds and behaviors. What does it means and how is it possible that this invisible hand pushed us to pursue some "end" or /"goal" which is not among our "intentions", is not intended? Aren't we purposive intentional agents, self-directed and autonomous? What kind of goals are these? What kind of teleology? The real problem is to understand how not only such process it coexists with intentional mental-driven action but also exploits it (Castelfranchi, 2013).

Thus special attention should be devoted not only to the "emergent" bottom-up processes but also to the "immergent" ones: the top-down feedback from emergent phenomena to on the agent control- system via by learning or by through understanding and intending (Conte et al., 2007).

Special attention should be devoted to identify on which one of the macro-level phenomena is or *has to be* mentally represented, understood, and even intended in order to reproduce itself and to work be effective (like norms), and to discriminate those that which are unintended and blind, and presupposes some form of alienation (like social functions or institutional powers).

2.1 The Spontaneous Order is neither Neutral nor Optimal

What we have to explain is how the Invisible Hand and spontaneous (self-organizing) social order are not so spontaneous and disinterested or optimal for the involved people but do systematically work for powerful agents.

What is needed is a criticism to von Hayek's theory[8] (or vulgate) about the spontaneous social order as the best *possible* outcome: the often implicit assumption that *no better result with any*

understanding of the social dynamics, deliberate planning, and intentionally pursue often non-individual outcomes cannot achieve better results.

The spontaneous social order is self-referential, "good" per se in itself but, not in relation to the goals of the agents, is not the best possible result, the best most balanced; there is are no collective "virtues" in it (there are several centuries that we have the fairy story that in contrast with the old Mandeville's motto that "private vices are public benefits", Mandeville). Why the spontaneous result is very often bad for the large part of the participants although everybody is choosing and acting for its his own good? The Because of the answer cannot but lie in the concentration, dynamics, and effects of powers. Neither the spontaneous "order" is egalitarian egalitarian nor it is fair, proportional to each individual contribution, effort, qualities or, ..merits. It strongly reflects and reproduces the preexisting or casual differences of power.

One of the major weaknesses of the anti-centralized ideology of society and superiority of open, distributed ""market"" of autonomous agents is the implicit presupposition that *THE the* problem is "knowledge": the timely and appropriate/relevant information for our adaptive and fast decisions. This of course is a central problem: (the crucial cognitive limit of centralization with respect to distributed and market-based adjustments). However, we shall not forget that the central issue of decisions (teleconomically regulating our conduct) are *goals*! And goals are nNot reducible to personal utility maximization of private preferences. We might have correct and complete information, knowledge about real and local circumstances, etc. but this doesn't is not enough to solve the decision problem: what we do we prefer? What does motivates (attracts, rejects) us more?

In principle, this is and can just be an individual level issue, a personal and private matter; not only nobody can decide for me what is better for me! (otherwise we are no longer "free"!), but preferences - by definition - can only be individualistic and self-interested. All that This view is simply false, and should be regarded as; mere ideology. The cognitive and social truth is quite in fact different, and open very serious moral and political problems. Especially due not only to our pro-social and even altruistic motives and behaviors but to the cognitive theory of "interests" and our possible *ignorance* of them, with the consequent need for "delegation" and trust in some authority (Conte & Castelfranchi, 1995; Castelfranchi et al., 1994).

2.2 Pseudo-Spontaneous Social Order

In sum, A part from the very important contribution of although the role of Social Simulation for in modeling and helping support into manage concrete economic, social and, cultural, demographic, environmental ... practical problems (see other chapters) is indeed crucial, in a sense the there is another often neglected practical (related) mission of the Social Simulation is which is to explain how the "spontaneous" social order is not so casual, but in fact *it is systematically biased, to favor and increase cumulated powers* (Castefranchi, 2000). As a consequence, this understanding will open the possibility to And thus to make better interfere with the spontaneous order itself, which although still being spontaneous and self-organizing, could be made more fairer. Or it is it "fair" that those who haves more (not because deservings it, by talent or effort, but for example by inheritance; Bowles, Gintis and and GintisOsborne, 20052) gets more? This is a very spontaneous view of "natural" order for bourgeoisie! Let's cite the fundamental and evident observation of Errico Malatesta and his critical remarks to the social "sciences" that do not even attempt to explain that: "If, say the theorists of the authoritarian school, the interests, tendencies, and desires of an individual are in opposition to those of another individual, or perhaps all society, who will have the right and the power to oblige the one to respect the interests of the other or others? Who will be able to prevent the individual citizen from offending the general will? The liberty of each, they say, has for its limit the liberty of others: but who will establish those limits, and who will cause them to be respected? The natural antagonism of interests and passions creates the necessity for government, and justifies authority. Authority intervenes as moderator of the social strife and defines the limits of the rights and duties of each.

This is the theory; *but to be sound the theory should be based upon an explanation of facts. We know well how in social economy theories are too often invented to justify facts, that is, to defend privilege* and cause it to be accepted tranquilly by those who are its victims. Let us here look at the facts themselves. In all the course of history, as in the present epoch, government is either brutal, violent, arbitrary domination of the few over the many, or it is an instrument devised to secure domination and privilege to those who, by force, or cunning, or inheritance, have taken to themselves all the means of life, first and foremost the soil, whereby they hold the people in servitude, making them work for their advantage" (L'Anarchia, 1891). See sections 3 and 4.

3. THE *PRACTICAL/ POLITICAL OPPORTUNITY* OF SOCIAL SIMULATION

In what follows, I try enlightening here a starting to identify the principles of a *techno-political revolution*, which will (might?) be precisely allowed enabled by distributed computing. The focus will be in particular on, and in particular "Agents"; both, ABSS (agent-based social simulation) and agents embedded in the smart environments, agents as that will representing and mediating in human negotiation and agreement, agents for or situated collective planning,; and the computational support for coordination, cooperation, conflict of future human societies, ... (that is, the theoretical and practical results of MAS research).

In this view, it will be necessary both to conceive and design, and to experiment: models, formalisms, technology, specifically for that designed for this aim. Here we are not talking of the focus in not so much on grounding and adjusting the simulations and the "models" on the basis of the empirical data of the a given domain. This unavoidable requirement holds even for the past: just for understanding and explaining past dynamics, historical processes.

What is of main importance here is that we are referring to "predictive" and imaginative simulations; running models in order to diagnose, anticipate, *possible* trends and effects of different policies or of current social movements. Computer modeling and running simulation for predicting the an observable phenomenon and for understanding (make explicit) the underlying psycho-social mechanisms; which all of this is crucial for an effective intervention policy (§ 3.5, 3.6).

However this is not enough: a fundamental challenge for the future is - in my view - the following one:

How can we systematically integrate the simulations of social phenomena with the real-time feedback coming from everyday social context the playground? (§ 3.2, 3.3)

3.1 Sometimes (Ideas) Return

In one decade (or a bit more) we will see a generalized and structural use of computer simulations (especially agent-based) as the required ground for all the decisions to be taken in relation to strategies or policies, in a number of different domains: from the military, to the environmental, economic, financial, urban, demographic, energetic, educational, health, logistic, ... domains. ones.

Indeed, *no political/managerial complex decision will be taken without a based grounding it on fine grain predictions of effects and possible* *developments and outcomes; precisely, which will be enabled by thanks to a computer modeling and simulation of the relevant phenomenon under intervention and of its long-term orientation unfolding and "governable" dynamics.*

But,.... isn't this the old, shameful, unmentionable "planning" of socialist memory?

Why can the big corporations could ""plan"" (planetary global) policies and interventions for a budget much higher than those of many nations, and for a horizon much extended than those of a government or of a national financial law, while those states it is better national states cannot do not talk of "planning", otherwise they have without being blamed for an "anachronistic, inefficient, anti-liberal" vision? It is it not perhaps the case that the dramatic limits of the ominous traditional "economic planning" of the "real socialism" also were in fact mainly *cognitive* limits?

That is,: it might be argued that the main limitation so far has been the lack of there wasn't a collective "brain" really apt (able and in condition)able to interpret, calculate and predict the extremely *complex* dynamics, and to take into account (in real time) the indicators any feedback from the field.[9] Thanks to up the advent of *responsive society* opportunity unleashed by should to offer their goals succeed due to, and, reliable; it will require fine-grained predictions based on, and the local of such predictions imagined themselves (Figure 2).

It is a dialectic spiral of increasing realism and fitting work on the that aims to match what is indeed happening in the field[10]. It is a designed cyclical and feedback based artifact, and not just a top-down solution; an "intelligence" that plans, decides, and *"accommodates"* (in Piaget's famous expression), but always on the basis of powerful models and the actual simulations of possible developments.

The traditional "Social Planning" was absurd also because, in a sense, it was a violation of the natural cognitive rules for planning/problem-solving: it was a planning (problem-solving)

Figure 2. The monitoring and adjusting cycle

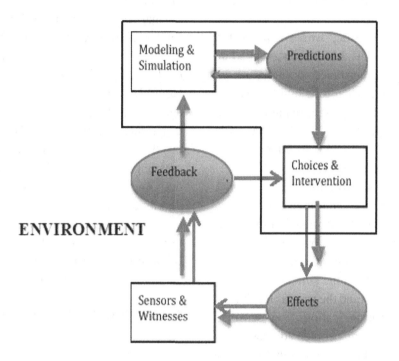

without "learning" (and negotiation). What is needed is the normal "cycle" of learning in/for problem-solving and ability acquisition:

Objective ==> hypothesis about possible actions (planning/problem-solving) ==> attempt and feedback ==> possible failures ==> interpretation/understanding ==> re-planning (new adjusted solution) ==> ....

No learning without possible (predicted) failures and their monitoring for revising models and re-planning behaviors. Babies do that; why not nations?

The actual information and computer technology create the tools and the cultural conditions for those run-time, decentralized, high qualified feedbacks. It might exploit different kinds of "agents":

1. Local sensors and detectors, of various kinds (possibly learning and adjusting), even interconnected and locally "cooperating" for a more reliable and global information;

2. Local computational, for primary elaboration and reaction (additional data, additional "agents", alarm smart systems, ...);

3. Active voluntary people communicating via sms, call centers, ...

4. Local or domain "group", communities, associations interested in monitoring and giving advice on the phenomenon: bloggers, consumers unions; elaboration of big-data, sentiment analysis, specific alert, …

5. Local professional in charge: policemen, medical staff, teachers, social assistants, observatories (economic, demographic, environmental, …)

6. local administrations, with their "research/ documentation centers" and their local officers.

(1) (3) (5) already hold for traffic information (and regulation), but without simulation and model-based predictions.

However, on the one side, "we need to consider the credibility of models. Models that worked in the past in many circumstances do not work in the future. The model should be highly flexible and adjustable to reflect current dynamics"[11]. It is a serious challenge for ABSS, which has very stimulating results, but is still in its infancy as far as robust solutions are concerned.

On the other side, the solution (and its design) cannot obviously be the same in every domain. For example, in traffic monitoring and planning (for example in view of a transportation strike or of a big political demonstration) one can imagine a fast interaction between the simulated "plans" (with their predictions) and the various feedbacks from the actual event: indications from sensors, telephonic advices from people; advices from policemen and toll booths; recommendations and requests from users' blogs, or consumers associations, or local authorities. Rather different feedbacks are required in case of an epidemic, or in case of an unforeseen leakage of toxic substances. Much less simple is the case of social policies and interventions on population health or welfare: *which stakeholders to privilege and which role/weight give them? Which (objective or subjective) wellbeing indicators to choose?* When one should verify the development of the situation? Which instruments to adopt for the surveys? (experts evaluations? interviews? groups? ...).

3.3 The Feedback Problem

Which information is locally needed for producing the resulting 'equilibrium' or 'order' or 'desired structure', and coming back from this emerging structure? Is it a *local* information or a *global* one?[12] A generic or specialized one for the "addressee"?

For example, in markets the price is the necessary local *information* about the spontaneous emergent equilibrium between supply and demand;

local feedback at the individual level from and for the *global* dynamics. This is the crucial *superiority* of "markets" in a broad sense, based on fast, local, self-interest distributed "decision" (adjustment to the output). However, what is needed are *different kinds and layers of feedback* and of indicators and parameters of the social dynamics and outcomes, depending on the competence of the stakeholders and its interests (personal and individual, or based on the "role") and on the combined, emerging meaning of the feedback: a single local information (one case of strange behavior) or a complex distributed one: a statistical data, or a Big Data to be computed and extracted, or a complex pattern to be interpreted? (Is there an epidemic? Is there some general trend? For example, is there an increase in school abandonment?).

3.4 What's the Real Meaning of That?

Simple: *also the simulative "cognition/mind" must be "situated" and "distributed" (externalized).* As we have said, computer modeling and simulation is a revolution of the *"collective" cognition*; and it must equally be "situated", that is, context-dependent and opportunistic, based on data "here" (not into the mind but in the environment) and "now", continuously adapted to the field, not fully and rigidly planned. Only in this way human plans work; this is an important lesson coming from of Cognitive Science and its recent developments.

This aritificial "cognition" must also be "distributed", with various subjects and local simulation sub-systems; whose criteria, ends, priorities and data will need to be complemented and integrated (not a trivial thing), in part a-priori (coordination, distribution, negotiation) in part a-posteriori, with very powerful and flexible computational instruments: unifying ontologies; factor models; etc.

This approach provides the "social simulation" with a *double experimental ground*:

- On the one side, the really "experimental" data of running the model, of simulation, with its results (expected and unexpected) (like in a "laboratory");
- On the other side the "field study" of what is really happening on the ground when applying a given (simulated) policy or observing a given (also simulated) phenomenon.

3.5 A Hybrid and Collective "Mind"

This is what we are building: a "mind". What is in fact a "mind"? Mind is a "simulation" device, for anticipation and virtual experiments. It is an escape from reality to master it better.

In a sense it is the application of the basic principles of natural selection, variation and selection, from the *material* (and very risky) reality to the material but *representational/symbolic* world. The cost of material variations and attempts and their selection and failure is in fact very high. In the material, "external" world, trials are costly and errors even more so. Creatures with a mind find solutions in their own "intelligence" (imagination), not by risky trial and errors in their overt behaviors. Also the explored possibilities are much broader, less limited by current material conditions; less guided by circumstances and the actual environment and more by goals. And we build on that by memorizing experiences, by specializing that activity.

These are some advantages of "unreality" and of virtual selection. Of course there also are disadvantages and risks; it might be that we formulate fully unrealistic hypotheses, which are impossible in practice, and that we choose something that in "reality" will fail. By direct experience we learn to adjust our simulative activity to reality.

I am suggesting that nowadays we are at the fringe of creating the technology for *building* such a "mental" activity at the collective level, combining natural minds and artificial ones (§ 5).

In other words, cognition is fighting against uncertainty, and the complexity and unpredict-ability of the world. But this is not just a passive epistemic attitude, it is a pragmatic attitude: we do not just "predict" the future, we actively and purposively build it. Not only we progress (cognitively and practically) by moving from mere uncertainty to "risk" calculation. This is a view of action just as a (rational) bet. It ignores the control (cybernetic, goal-oriented) view of conduct. We do not just bet on a given outcome, we "drive" our behavior toward that result.

3.6 Simulation for "Imagination" and "Interpretation"

So it is important to make clear that Social Simulation for possible social policies is not just a tool for "predicting" spontaneous trends and possible outcomes.

On the one side we need:

1. A new cognitive power for prediction and for *imagination* (not the same thing!) We need to "imagine" not just what is possible and probable and will probably happen. We have to imagine what is impossible, and what might be or become possible (since action consist in creating new conditions and modifying the possibility and probability of future events!), and we need "imagination" also for exploring creative solutions in problem solving, in "designing"; this cannot be well done in "reality", on the flesh of the people, but on representations, virtually (like architects on drawings and scale models). As Alan Kay once suggested, "the best way to predict the future ... is to invent it"; the "Artificial Collective Imagination" that we are building is for that too. Moreover, simulation is for *counter factual reasoning* (not about what is happening or will happen, but about what might have been!), a fundamental instrument for assigning "responsibility", but also for the *evaluation* of the results. We do not evaluate results in absolute but relatively

to our (possible) expectations; this is true also at the collective level. "Is this medical intervention on epidemic going well? A lot of people is actually dying" "Yes, but HOW the epidemic would have spread WITHOUT that intervention?!" This is the correct parameter, and this can just be simulated, or compared with other real data, if any.

2. We need a new cognitive power for local and timely information and *interpretation* and understanding "what *is* happening"; since the signals from sensors or the messages/alerts from witnesses must be interpreted, not just "believed", and coordinated. In fact, frequently the real meaning of what is *locally* happening is detected only thanks to the convergence with several distributed local events, globally; so we need MAS, network communication and coordination, global data, ... but also involving local expert (people) stakeholders. Moreover, interpretation frequently means a causal interpretation; and simulation will provide that.

3. We need cognitive complex artifacts for decision making, like in fact was public administration, politics[13] but now much more well informed, much more participatory and taking into account different interests, needs, views, not enough represented; giving voice to marginal groups, etc.

Simulation is not only, and not mainly, for "predictions" also because strict predictions are impossible in complex dynamics like social systems. We shouldn't forget that "predictions" are frequently imprecise and wrong and that *in principle* it is impossible to predict events especially due to complex dynamics. They are unpredictable, like earthquakes. That's right. However:

1. Is seismology a useless science since they cannot precisely and reliably predict a earthquakes? I don't think so. Also approximated and probabilistic predictions can be very useful (for example for prevention, proportional investments)

2. We need long-term and global predictions (very problematic), but also very short term and operational predictions in guiding and monitoring specific "actions" like motor-prediction in motor-action. And these predictions are there for immediate matching and for *immediate* adjustment of both the acting and the prediction. This is one basic function in embodied cognitive regulation of human action.

Human *imagination/simulation* guides both human executive actions and long-term decisions (Figure 3).

Figure 3. Anticipatory simulation in action control. Comparison between purely stimulus-response systems (a) and those endowed with anticipatory capabilities, which run an 'internal loop' on-line with action (b), or off-line (c) (Pezzulo 2011).

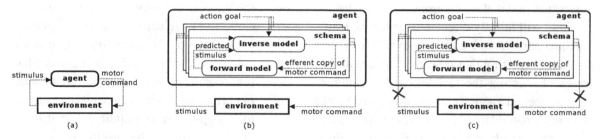

We have to build an analogous machinery at the collective action level.

What's the function of forecasting? Is it just the illusion of omnipotence and of controlling "natural" trends? We have explained the construction of the "future" and plans (and feedbacks compared with them) as anticipatory representations are essential in cognition related to action. But it is even more than that: the detailed comparison (match-mismatch) between what expected and what is actually there, between anticipated and perceptual information, allows us to systematically and quickly react to the "unexpected" (with its threats and opportunities). The cognitive integration of past and future and the interaction with the present allows us to discriminate (mentally and behaviorally) what is "normal", "predictable", from what is "strange" and requires special cognitive investments and resource; for example by orienting our "attention".

Do we have (and would we need) at the collective level an analogous process of "attention"? We need to build not only "imagination" but also artificial "attentional systems", not by pre-programmed inspections and controls (like tax authorities) but by timely signaling and focus changing in monitoring, interpreting, and predicting.

4. AN EVEN MORE ADVANCED FORMULA: EMPOWERING PEOPLE

It is not only a matter of *feedbacks* from the field and from people, from various signalers and indicators, and in different times, and of continuous readjusting of the model and of the simulation. A more (politically and technically) advanced model is conceivable on such technological bases, implying rooms for *negotiation* and *decisions*.

Since, for any given social phenomena there are always a variety of *stakeholders* with different interests, *the solution of the problem can never been merely "technical"* and predefined. It is a matter of new forms of "participatory *evaluation*"[14], but more than that. The solution requires

processes (and thus rooms, time, and modalities) of *political negotiation between the various subjects, interests, points of view.*

Social research and scientists not only cannot provide us strict "predictions", but they cannot provide us "recipes", solutions. They can just give us the evaluation of possible pros and cons of the various alternatives, and a critical attitude (doubts) about our certainties and preferences. The decision is always (overtly or hidden) "political" not technical.

Those "who have a say" should be inserted in the very "model" of the "social planning" (when, where, how?); which would not simply be feedback, re-simulation, re-planning (like in Figure 1); but a model including "re-decision" phases and places: *Who decides?* And – more importantly – *on the basis of what re-discussion and re-negotiation of the involved interests?* And how to give room, how to support, and how to *mediate* those agreement and decision processes?

To play such a role however computer Social Simulation must become stronger and much more reliable. Not biased by internal arbitrary parameters, that might produce whatever result we want, guided by the values of a given group of interest.

And perhaps we even will need a "participatory" simulation (like in scientific work) *with different stakeholders* providing and comparing their results.

Notice also how some issues currently discussed in "Ambient Intelligence" converge (but at a more collective level) with what we have just said. See for example the problem identified by Nigel Shadbolt[15]: *"Power, empowerment, and possibilities.*

It turns out that one of the real challenges for ambient intelligence is the perennial problem of power. How do you keep the myriad devices and the ever-present ubiquitous and pervasive infrastructure powered up? Aside from prosaic but fundamental problems of power, what about the users?. [I would add: "and their role?"].

Unfortunately, the correctly identified problem is then impoverished and reduced to the traditional dimension of user friendly interaction, of house or work environment, etc. [16]; without: (i) any understanding of the absolute centrality of "agents" and MAS ground; (ii) any socio-political view of the phenomena and of the role of people and of the distributed intelligences in the environment. While the conclusion of the reasoning remains correct: "But will these digital environments really empower people?" and collectivity?

Both Ambient Intelligent and the Computer Power for social simulation and modeling should be improved and complemented by an additional use of "Human Computing/Computation" with its brainpower (see for example Zittrain, 2008; Quinn and Bederson, 2011) and new opportunities for participation, transparency of political decisions, e-democracy.

Another crucial issue (that we cannot develop here) is *the need for norms and laws* also for Artificial Agents and their "society". See for example the classic work by Shoham and M. Tennenholtz (1995) where they reflect on the necessity of social laws in a computational environment. "Either due to the off line *design* of social laws, where we as designers must decide ahead of time on useful laws, or to the automatic synthesis of useful laws"[17]. Let me add that we also need room for emerging "social conventions". However, the issue is made quite complicated by the emerging "hybrid" society; not just a MAS to be regulated by norms or laws (designed or selected) but mixed organizations regulating at the same time the behavior of Agents and humans. Who has to "design" these laws? It is not just an engineering problem.

4.1 Other Functions of Social Simulation

In this perspective it is clear that other uses of computer simulation will also be important.

Such virtual environments can be used as a "laboratory" for experience and *understanding*:

problem-focused and data-based realistic sociological "serious games"; and an *educational* role of learning-by-doing, and understanding by looking and possible outcomes of our proposals and moves (note 7).

We cannot have a real participatory "discussion", project, and "decision" just based on spontaneous judgments, twitting, opinions, prejudices, group-psychology and even demagogy. It is crucial to circulate real information, and improve real understanding and knowledge. Networking and information circulation and discussion should serve also to educate, to argue, to increase our knowledge; and using simulations, by trial and errors, predictions and unexpected results can indeed be effective and useful.

Before decision and real feedback and readjusting, simulating hypothesis might be a very important instrument for bottom-up, participatory "proposals".

5. FINAL REMARKS: YOUTOPIA?

As for the question: ".. will these digital environments really empower people?" and collectivity? In our view the answer is: "Yes, this is a possibility; to be understood and *designed*". But it is not an issue of "users/consumers" and their "satisfaction"; it is a matter of demo-crazy, or at least of effective social governing. Now distributed and ubiquitous computing, agents, agent-based simulation, complexity models, internet of things, people connection, smart environments, and AmI, *provide us with the "externalized" cognition, the necessary powerful "intelligence" for collective planning, for regulating the needed self-organization social dynamics.*

And, in fact, this predicting and planning and simulating and deciding "mind", "intelligence", *cannot be centralized and fully hierarchical.* It must be "distributed": local, partially autonomous intelligences are needed, for interacting with local data, phenomena, models, and feedbacks;

elaborating and adjusting the local (simulated) process; connected and cooperating in a distributed computing platform for a "collective" distributed cognition (and action/experiments).

Computer scientists are building not just new technical systems (as they believe), but new socio-cognitive-technical systems: new forms of intelligence and of sociality.

What we really - unexpectedly - have is a *"hybrid" new society* where social interaction of any kind (information exchange and knowledge institution building; commerce; confidence and friendship; organization; political movement; sex; ...) is not just between humans but "mediated" by artificial supporting systems, is "hybrid": that is, there are "social" interactions (in full sense), social networks, and collective behaviors *between Humans and AI Agents, Human and Robots, between Agents, between Robots, between Agents and Robots,* and even *between humans themselves.* The system is radically hybrid, mixed, of "natural" intelligences (actually rather acculturated and artificialized) and "artificial" ones (actually rather acculturated and even affective). This will not be just the sum of all the components, but a new complex cognitive system.

A possible techno-political revolution is allowed by distributed computing, and in particular "agents": to effectively manage the distributed "signals" coming from (possibly intelligent and learning, more or less credible) active observers and signalers in the environment (not only physical but economic, social, demographic, ...); to simulate the trend of the process and its possible readjustment, and to readjust it by signaling on the territory; or mediating that readjustment by complex negotiations and agreement between the agents the stakeholders.

Will the "Invisible Hand" governing human society be implemented in the Emergent Intelligence of a Self-organizing open and hybrid MA systems? Will we have from ICT and AI not only tools but experimental theories for the "government of complex systems" (an oxymoron!)?

Will the hybrid socio-cognitive technical system we are building be useful for managing social life and realizing human objectives and values, or will *we* just be one (cognitive) gear of the new hybrid global machine[18]?

5.1 What is Mind for: The Dialectics between "Reality" and "Unreality"

As we have suggested before (§ 3.5), there is a dialectic link between mental representations (epistemic and motivational, knowledge and goals) and the world. On the one side, we have to adjust our beliefs to the world, to make them "true" and pragmatically adequate; but on the other side (for Goals) we change the world in order to realize our goals, that is, in order to make the world corresponding to our imagination, creative representation of what "is not (still) there".[19]

We cannot and should not just let that the world (too complex, ungovernable) goes in its unpredictable directions, and just adjust our schema, knowledge, and action to it; we can and want - at least in part - change the world following our "goal", to conform it to an idea, to "govern" it. That's why we need mental representations of unreality: of what might be, might have been, of what is possible or probable, of the future. Is this a delirium or self-deception? Only partially; it also is an effective adaptive tool. This is why the "mind" is there, and we do not just "react" to the external stimuli; it is intelligent, intentional action.

The opposition between a selectionist (evolutionary, Darwinian) model and a "projectual" mind and action is not fully correct. Also mind is a selectionist apparatus. However, the selection is both in reality, by failures, attempts, but also (with a great economic advantage) in "virtual reality", in imagination. The main difference is that the selection is not between possible candidates just due to mutations, random changes; they are not fully casual, they are produced following their relevance with the goals and the context, and on the basis of experience, memory, culture with several biases (not fully rational and representative).

What we are building is a new hybrid mind, preserving *both* its functions: not only empowered knowledge of the world, but also its intentional change.

5.2 Beyond the Pessimism of "Reason," Some Optimism of Will

In sum, the cognitive apparatus we were outlining

- Of a system able to simulate and imagine the *real* effects and processes (environmental, economics, social, cultural, psychological, educational) and to readjust on such basis the projects, the plans and measures; with a transparent mediation between subjects and interests in conflict, but with eyes wide open on the very serious power inequalities; and also

- Joined with a monitoring and real-time feedback of the real and local trends, not abstract and partial "indicators" (like PIL, inflation, ..) but measures of the real welfare and perspectives of people; and even signals and reactions from the involved subjects/groups;[20]

- As well as able to welcome protests and proposals, of "giving voice" and participation both in the formulation of projects and in the monitoring;

Such apparatus has a role. This knowledge and anticipation-based system of "governance" with exceptional cognitive and adaptation skills, if focalized not on norms and rules but on what they are *supposed* to achieve and protect, on the real effects (not on the ideological ones), might give rise to a new form of government, able to exist not "just" in a formal institutional sense (norm conformity) but in substantial sense (equity, welfare, opportunities).

Perhaps we have the tools and are in conditions (not yet the political ones) for a democracy, which is *global*, *participatory* and *liquid*, although implying delegation, representation, responsibility[21]. A democracy that is continuously evolving on the basis of conflicts, of ideas and views of the future, of bottom-up impulses, of a better *understanding*; continuously adjusting since it is focused on real conditions and effects, not on the stabilization and defense of the dominating powers, which remains there and maintains control and authority but is protective of subjects' interests, and, at the same time, is efficient and transparent; not self-referential.

Perhaps this is also the only way for overcoming (but not at the "national" level) the collapse of political power and its subordination to financial power and supra-national corporations.

REFERENCES

Axelrod, R. (1997). Advancing the art of simulation in the social sciences. In R. Conte, R. Hegselmann, & P. Terna (Eds.), *Simulating social phenomena* (pp. 21–40). Berlin: Springer-Verlag. doi:10.1007/978-3-662-03366-1_2

Axtell, R. L. (2007). What economic agents do: How cognition and interaction lead to emergence and complexity. *The Review of Austrian Economics*, *20*, 105–122. doi:10.1007/s11138-007-0021-5

Bishop, S., Helbing, D., Lukowicz, P., & Conte, R. (2011). FuturICT: FET flagship pilot project. *Procedia Computer Science*. Retrieved from http://papers.ssrn.com/sol3/papers.cfm?abstract_id=1895523

Bowles, S., Gintis, H., & Osborne, M. (2005). *Unequal chances: Family background and economic success*. Princeton, NJ: Princeton University Press.

Buckingham Shum, S., Aberer, K., Schmidt, A., Bishop, S., Lukowicz, P., Anderson, S., … Helbing, D. (2012). Towards a global participatory platform. Democratising open data, complexity science and collective intelligence. *The European Physical Journal, 214*(1).

Castelfranchi, C. (1993). Discredito dell'idea di piano e progetto e ruolo della scienza cognitive. *Il Mulino, 5*(1), 159–166.

Castelfranchi, C. (1998). *Simulating with cognitive agents: The importance of cognitive emergence multi-agent systems and agent-based simulation* (pp. 26–44). Lecture notes in computer science Berlin: Springer. doi:10.1007/10692956_3

Castelfranchi, C. (1998). Emergence and cognition: Towards a synthetic paradigm in AI and cognitive science. In H. Coelho (Ed.), *Progress in artificial intelligence - IBERAMIA 98* (pp. 13–26). Berlin: Springer. doi:10.1007/3-540-49795-1_2

Castelfranchi, C. (2000). Per una teoria pessimistica della mano invisibile e dell'ordine spontaneo. [For a pessimistic theory of the invisible hand and spontaneous social order] In S. Rizzello (Ed.), *Organizzazione, informazione e conoscenza. Saggi su F.A. von Hayek*. Torino, Italy: UTET.

Castelfranchi, C. (2000). The invisible (left) hand. For a pessimistic theory of the invisible hand and spontaneous social order: A critical homage to F. von Hayek (Invited talk). *Artificial Economics*. Retrieved from http://www.academia.edu/823483/For_a_Pessimistic_Theory_of_the_Invisible_Hand_and_Spontaneous_Order

Castelfranchi, C. (2001). The theory of social functions. Challenges for multi-agent-based social simulation and multi-agent learning. *Journal of Cognitive Systems Research, 2*, 5–38. doi:10.1016/S1389-0417(01)00013-4

Castelfranchi, C. (2012). *Simulation-based, reactive, and situated new social-planning. Hints for a manifesto*. (Preliminary version presented at ICAART 2012). Retrieved from http://www.academia.edu/1009698/Simulation-based_Reactive_and_Situated_new_Social-Planning._Hints_for_a_Manifesto

Castelfranchi, C. (2013). *Goaldirectness. Encyclopedia of philosophy and the social sciences*. Thousand Oask, CA: SAGE.

Castelfranchi, C., Conte, R., & Diani, M. (1994). Paradossi cognitivi della democrazia e limiti all'azione del cittadino. *Parolechiave, 5*, 33–63.

Conte, R., Andrighetto, G., Campennì, M., & Paolucci, M. (2007). Emergent and immergent effect in complex social systems. In *Proceedings of AAAI Symposium, Social and Organizational Aspects of Intelligence*. Washington.

Conte, R., & Castelfranchi, C. (1995). *Cognitive and social action*. London: UCL Press.

Conte, R., & Castelfranchi, C. (1996). Simulating multi-agent interdependencies. A two-way approach to the micro-macro link. In U. Mueller, & K. Troitzsch (Eds.), *Microsimulation and the social science (Lecture notes in economics)*. Berlin: Springer Verlag. doi:10.1007/978-3-662-03261-9_18

Conte, R., Gilbert, N,. Bonelli, G., Cioffi-Revilla, C., Deffuant, G., Kertesz, J. … Helbing, D. (2012). Manifesto of computational social science. *The European Physical Journal, 214*(1).

Cousins, J. B., & Earl, L. M. (1992). The case for participatory evaluation. *Educational Evaluation and Policy Analysis, 14*, 397–418.

Epstein, J. M. (2006). *Generative social science: Studies in agent-based computational modeling*. Princeton, NJ: Princeton University Press.

Epstein, J. M., & Axtell, R. (1996). *Growing artificial societies: Social science from the bottom up*. Washington, DC/Cambridge, MA: Brookings Institution Press/MIT Press.

Fosca, G., Pedreschi, D., Pentland, A., Lukowicz, P., Kossmann, D., Crowley, J., Helbing, D. (2012). A planetary nervous system for social mining and collective awareness. *The European Physical Journal, 214*(1).

Gelernter, D. H. (1992). *Mirror worlds: Or the day software puts the universe in a shoebox...how it will happen and what it will mean*. Oxford, UK: Oxford Univ. Press.

Gerritsen, C. (2011). *Using ambient intelligence to control aggression in crowds*. Retrieved from http://www.computer.org/csdl/proceedings/wi-iat/2011/4513/03/4513c053-abs.html

Gilbert, G. N. (1995). Emergence in social simulation. In G. N. Gilbert, & R. Conte (Eds.), *Artificial societies: The computer simulation of social life*. London: UCL Press.

Guba, E., & Lincoln, Y. (1989). Fourth generation evaluation. *Journal of Artificial Societies and Social Simulation*.

Hayek, F. (1988). *Conoscenza, Mercato, Pianificazione* (Anthology of Hayek's writings, including The Use of Knowledge in Society [). Bologna, Italy: Il Mulino.]. *The American Economic Review*, 1945.

Hayek, F. A. (1967). The result of human action but not of human design. In *Studies in philosophy, politics and economics*. London: Routledge & Kegan.

Malatesta, E. (1891). *L'Anarchia*. Retrieved from http://www.marxists.org/archive/malatesta/1891/xx/anarchy.htm

Paolucci, M., Kossman, D., Conte, R., Lukowicz, P., Argyrakis, P., Blandford, A., ... Helbing, D. (2012). Towards a living earth simulator. *The European Physical Journal, 214*(1).

Pezzulo, G. (2011). Grounding procedural and declarative knowledge in sensorimotor anticipation. *Mind & Language, 26*(1), 78–114. doi:10.1111/j.1468-0017.2010.01411.x

Prietula, M. J., Carley, K. M., & Gasser, L. (Eds.). (1998). *Simulating organizations: computational models of institutions and groups*. Cambridge, MA: MIT Press.

Quinn, A. J., & Bederson, B. B. (2011). Human computation: A survey and taxonomy of a growing field. In *CHI-2011, Proceedings of the SIGCHI Conference on Human Factors in Computing Systems* (pp. 1403-1412).

Sawyer, R. K. (2003, February). Artificial societies: Multi agent systems and the micro-macro link in sociological theory. *Sociological Methods & Research*. doi:10.1177/0049124102239079

Sawyer, R. K. (2005). *Social emergence: Societies as complex systems*. Cambridge, UK: Cambridge University Press. doi:10.1017/CBO9780511734892

Shadbolt, N.Y., Shoham, & Tennenholtz, M. (1995). On social laws for artificial agent societies: Offline design. *Journal of Artificial Intelligence, 73*(1-2).

The European Graduate School. (n. d.). *Carl Micham: Quotes*. Retrieved from http://www.egs.edu/faculty/carl-mitcham/quotes

Zittrain, J. (2008). *Ubiquitous human computing* (Oxford Legal Studies Research Paper No. 32/2008). Retrieved from http://papers.ssrn.com/sol3/papers.cfm?abstract_id=1140445

KEY TERMS AND DEFINITIONS

Agent-Based Social Simulation: The computer simulation of social phenomena, not just based on mathematical formula and statistical factors, but based on the implementation of independent "agents" (program entities able to acquire local information, or learn, or reason, or decide, or communicate with each other, or interact, or evolve, etc.; with some behavior repertoire, knowledge, acting in a common "word"). Thus a social simulation with a micro-level and a mental (although limited) counterpart.

Cognitive Anticipation: The ability of building and using a representation of possible or future events or outcomes; to "imagine" what might or will happen, and choosing on such a basis. Thus to build (also collectively) hypotheses, projects, intentions, utopias, .. and intelligently "design" the future.

Function: A specific effect/result of a given feature or behavior F/B that explains it existence in term of causal loop, feedback that reproduces and maintain it: its reason and "utility". "Function" in this sense is a self-referential notion; it doesn't imply that F/B and result is "good" for something else: for the agent, for the group, in relation to some goal or design. It is just good per sé, that is, self-reproducing. This means that "functional" behavior and outcomes - in this sense - can be very bad for people, can be "kako-functions".

Intelligence: The capability to solve problems not on the field by costly and risky trials and errors, but in a virtual reality, on mental or externalized representations of the world and of the problem. Only agent with a mind can be "intelligent" not simply adaptive and effective.

Invisible Hand: The force promoting, selecting, organizing an emergent social order, and distribution of roles and fortunes. "(The individual) - that does neither, in general, intend to pursue the public interest, nor is aware of the fact that he is pursuing it,... is conduced by an invisible hand

to pursue an end that is not among his intentions" (Adam Smith).

Mind: A "simulation" device, for acting in an "augmented" reality, that completes and interprets the external input; for building and working on "representations" (symbolic or sensory-motor), in particular anticipations and virtual experiments.

Spontaneous Order: The self-organizing social order, emergent from individual interaction, convergence and spreading of behaviors, evolution of habits, rules, conventions, and also statuses, groups, etc. It is not planned or designed, and not fully understood by the subjects.

Underlying Mechanisms: Those "proximate causes" of the observable phenomenon (in this case behind the behavior) not directly observable, hidden. Not only explaining that behavior in terms of general laws or statistics tendency and probabilities but in terms of the underlying devices and micro-process *producing* it. A fundamental level of explanation in behavioral sciences.

ENDNOTES

1. I have just accidentally discovered (because of the damned Internet) that I have stolen my beloved title from a very old paper by Antony Flew (*Social Science: Making Visible the Invisible Hands*. In The Journal of Libertarian Studies, Vol. VIII, 2, 1987!). It is a duty and a pleasure to me to acknowledge my rediscovering: it is well known that "All intelligent thoughts have already been thought; what is necessary is only to try to think them again" Johann Wolfgang von Goethe.

2. This work is also part of my contribution to the SintelNet Eu Project. A very preliminary version of these ideas in Castelfranchi, 1993 and 1998. A preliminary and partial version of this chapter was my paper "Manifesto", a contribution to the preparation of the FuturICT: FET Flagship Pilot Project; see

(Castelfranchi, 2012) and also invited talk at AAMAS 2013 (http://www.academia.edu/3564801/InMind_and_OutMind_Societal_Order_Cognition_and_Self-Organization_The_role_of_MAS). A special thanks to Luca Tummolini, for several discussions on these issues, and to the European Sintelnet Project. On FuturICT see Bishop, Helbing, Lukowicz, & Conte (2011), and *The European Physical Journal*, "Participatory Science and Computing for Our Complex World" Volume 214, Issue 1, November 2012. In particular R. Conte et al.; F. Giannotti et al.; S. Buckingham Shum et al.; M. Paolucci et al.

3. In 2001 Agent Based Modelling (ABM) and Social Simulation (ABSS) were presented at a Sackler Colloquium (Irvine, CA, Oct. 2001) as the most promising approach to the social sciences of the next 5/10 years (PNAS, 2001; http://www.pnas.org/site/aboutpnas/colloquia.xhtml).

4. This distinction is close to Weber's one between erlaken ("explaining" based on laws) and verstehen ("understanding").

5. In this book, see Ch. 18 by Pietro Terna, Luca Arciero, Cristina Picillo and Sorin Solomon; Ch. 7 "Large-scale social simulation, dealing with complexity challenges in high performance environments" by Cristina Montañola-Sales, Xavier Rubio-Campillo, Josep Casanovas, Jose Maria Cela-Espín and Adriana Kaplan-Marcusán; and Ch. 9 "From Meso Decisions to Macro Results: An Agent-based Approach of Policy Diffusion" by Stéphane Luyet.

6. See for example (with a more traditional approach) Prietula et al., 1998.

7. "(The individual) - that does neither, in general, intend to pursue the public interest, nor is aware of the fact that he is pursuing it,... is conduced by an invisible hand to pursue an end that is not among his intentions" (Adam Smith).

8. See also Hayek (1967).

9. And weren't the supposed feedbacks from the people and the "participation" via the "soviets" completely driven by the party, mainly top-down, very partial, and non-democratic at all?

10. This might possibly become also a partial remedial of the current deformation of democratic regimes in term of "survey", "public opinion" indicators, political decisions more aimed at public approval and suggestion (marketing) then at solving structural problems. etc. Here indicators would be more objectives, participation would be more active and organized (not just "opinions", suggestions), and with the experimental ground of simulation: "what would happen if....?", that is also enlightening and pedagogical (learning by -virtually - doing) for people and movements (§ 4.1).

11. An ICAART reviewer's suggestion.

12. Ex. in a line an approximate line (linear) structure (quite global information) and the position of the last guy (the one after whom I have to locate myself) (local information but determined by the global structure). Ex. Can blind people play circle? It is enough the very local information or we need the perception of the emergent gestalt?

13. For the use of Simulation also for "testing" collective decision making models see Ch. 5 in this book by Lucas & Payne.

14. See for example, Guba & Lincoln (1989); Cousins & Earl (1992).

15. "Power, empowerment, and possibilities". http://mami.uclm.es/jbravo/docencia/doctorado/Inteligencia_Ambiental/x4002.pdf

16. "What does the home dweller actually want? Systems that can recognize a friendly face or, more important, recognize an unfriendly

face, determine an unwanted intrusion, and inform the appropriate authorities seem compelling. Systems that adjust power and light levels according to external environmental conditions or the number, location, and activities of users sound good too. ..... . All these elements will be getting smarter and are deployable in contexts wider than the home".

[17.] See also Ch. 2 in this book.

[18.] Like Chaplin in the old mechanical factory.

[19.] " ... invention causes things to come into existence from ideas, makes world conform to thought; whereas science, by deriving ideas from observation, makes thought conform to existence." Carl Mitcham (quoted by The European Graduate School, n. d.).

[20.] Let's us put aside here the very serious problem of the ethical aspects of personal data acquisition and use, of surveillance, and so on. The awareness of these dangers and the discussion about moral and legal issues is quite high. For a more advanced approach introducing morality in the Agents see Ch. 2in this book: "On Agent Interactions Governed by Morality" by Helder Coelho, Antonio Costa and Paulo Trigo.

[21.] In this perspective there are interesting links with Gelernter' view (1992), the prophet of the WWW etc.- as suggested by a generous reviewer. In Gelernter' view for example computers can free users from being filing clerks by organizing their data, in an anti hierarchical way; or by moving all of human knowledge to online servers the in-person college experience can be replaced by user-driven self-education. However, for me his view is very individualistic, too "liberalism" inspired, and quite simplistic (both for educational, political issues, and also for the construction of our new "knowledge" institution) because of his ignoring the non-neutrality of the invisible end, the need for governing spontaneous collective trends, and for delegation and tutorial roles.

Chapter 2
On Agent Interactions Governed by Morality

Helder Coelho
Universidade de Lisboa, Portugal

António Carlos da Rocha Costa
Universidade Federal do Rio Grande, Brazil

Paulo Trigo
Instituto Superior de Eng. de Lisboa, Portugal

ABSTRACT

Morality tells agents what they ought to do, and this defines their identity and character. This chapter deals with moral behaviour, following the classical view in Philosophy that defends character as a state concerned with choice, and able to direct the agent decision-taking. The authors also include new values regarding agent moral signature that may enhance the evaluation of agents, namely on reputation and satisfaction. So, the popularity of the agents can be measured with more depth, and not only for organizations but also for social networks.

INTRODUCTION

Character is like a tree and reputation like its shadow. The shadow is what we think of it; the tree is the real thing (Abraham Lincoln)

Life in society may be studied with agent-based simulation experimentation, decision and game theory (Dehghani et al., 2008). Yet, simulation is epistemologically and ontologically different from empirical research, and it is a purely deduction activity. Also, the classical game theory is not sufficient to explain the fairness or the altruistic conducts of agents with qualitative manners (Dignum et al., 2001), along social interactions. Two other ideas, social preference theory and network structures were introduced later on with good results, but there is still a need to improve the systematic understanding of individual choice in parametric contexts, where an agent is always deliberating independently of the will of other agents (Castelfranchi et al., 2000, 2006; Casrelfranchi, 2014).

DOI: 10.4018/978-1-4666-5954-4.ch002

The use of game theory (GT) for modelling moral dynamics can be pursued by evolutionary GT, in biological contexts and by algorithmic GT, in social, psychological and economical contexts (Hegselmann, 2009). GT covers strategic interactions among rational players with a focus on preference over outcomes. An associated topic is moral dynamics, usually referred to processes by which moral behaviour and moral attitudes emerge. Attitudes regard the internal side of morality (internalized norms, moral dispositions, accepted values, guiding virtues, and feelings, such as guild, regret and shame). Moral behaviour regards the external side of morality.

In real life, and nowadays, there is a need of differentiation of intentions, decisions and actions between those that are good (right) and those that are bad (wrong). In a world with absence of ethics, agent character is an added value and simulation models are eager to incorporate it in order to promote trust, reputation, responsibility, and honesty. Agent characterization by preference rankings and beliefs is not enough to capture the real thing in society (Briot et al., 2008).

In our opinion, moral, strategy and power are the three key ingredients for fixing the qualities (differences in character), the preferences and the equality relationships of the members of societies (Greene et al., 2002). Therefore, the architecture of the agents is necessary to become explicit, and be crystal clear (far from a simple black box) in social simulation: moral agents are rational negotiators who never forget to choose the best alternative at each moment of choice by constrained maximization. Heuristic machinery is behind the idea of mutually beneficial bargaining and fair principles. Also, morality enables agents to cooperate and coordinate their actions in situations where the pursuit of self-interest prevents this. And the final consequence, morality is a kind of social regulator of choices ("needs as pushing motives"), driven by principles and axioms, and triggered by emotions and feelings to control

back and forward information flows under moral thinking (Dimuro et al., 2010).

Game theory has been adopted to understand the function of morality because it helps to construct thought experiments about the diverse conducts of agents. But, it may also be explored to explain, predict, and evaluate all agent behaviour in contexts where the outcome of the action depends on what several agents choose to do (in a dynamical manner) and where their choices depend on what others choose to do (Costa & Dimuro, 2007, 2009).

Along repeated interactions, stable equilibrium of exchanges may be reached by morality, where the behavioural issues of agents are determined by moral and/or social rules (e.g. "do to others as you want to be done by"). So, agents may be provided by an internal commitment capability, some sort of conscience (linked to motives and dispositions): the realization that it is unjust to take a free ride, or that it would be unfair not to do the right thing (Franco, 2008; Adamatti et al., 2009).

This paper presents a framework for the design of autonomous agents that have moral qualities and an implementation of part of this agent architecture, namely the machinery behind morality as a (stochastic) game. In the Intelligent Agents area of research it is common today to adopt very simple reactive agents (e.g. Social Simulation, MABS) or cognitive ones (e.g. Negotiation, Games), but only with thinking and decision abilities. Not so much mental states are requested (say, a BDI model as a maximum), emotion is not yet greatly considered, and morality is yet out of question (Macedo et al., 2012). Not very often, agents with qualities are necessary and relevant to some problem domain where they may face social situations and interactions, because those involved in thinking and reasoning are not sufficient. Very often, those in charge of specifying MAS simplify the problems, even when sociality is strongly mixed. In applications with organisations, obligations start to be mentioned (BOID and NBDI models) when norms are around (Andrighetto et al., 2007), emotions became interesting on account of exchanges with quality, but ethical concerns are discouraged and scientists are sceptical about their adoption (Coelho and Costa, 2009). The European EMIL (Emergent In the Loop: simulating the two way dynamics of norm innovation) project (2006-09) was a step ahead, not only regarding the research done, but also because it created a space for discussion.

We think reality is much more complex and we can be more keen in dealing with matters beyond those associated with cognition (Paglieri et al., 2012). The way an agent calculates what is right and wrong, and decides afterwards, illuminates the roles character (set of internal dispositions or mental skeleton) and personality (set of external dispositions acquired along existence) play. Therefore, there is much more to be considered beyond executing goals and acts. In society, we need to behave well, to take the other in respect, to be responsible and capable of forgiveness, and to get a distinctive mark such as the assemblage of good qualities (including the moral ones). Yet, it is not easy to design an agent to be gracious, merciful or respectful (Silva et al., 2009).

Acting in certain social situations (e.g., quarrel between husband and wife, or between two partners in a team) is not a simple matter of thinking, reasoning and negotiating. Character counts, and virtues (wisdom) play a definite role in formatting individual behaviours, aiding decision-making and animating verbal discussions via conflicts. The nature of the selected words may drive aggressiveness and the good manners.

MORALITY ISSUES

Morality, according to deontological theories, is viewed as a function of duties and obligations, regardless of the consequences of acting in accordance with those duties. Morality is a sort of push-pull converter, situated in concrete contexts, ruled by moral principles, axioms and maxims, and

triggered by emotions and feelings. Also, emotions are able to control back and forward flows behind moral thinking. If all the agent moral character traits are situation-specific rather than robust, what traits an agent manifests will depend on the situation that he finds himself in. But what situations an agent finds himself in is often beyond his control, and thus it is in fact a matter of (moral) luck. In the last decade, research was done in AI around rules and a universal moral grammar (Mikhail, 2007), moral reasoning (Pereira & Saptawijaya, 2007, 2009), in Cognitive Sciences (Hauser, 2006), in Social Psychology on moral profiles (Haidt & Kesebir, 2010), moral dilemmas (Horty, 1994), and on Neurosciences (Green at al., 2001) and, in particular, empathy (Churchland, 2011).

When designing an intelligent agent with character, we may include not only temperamental traits and dispositions, but also reflexive capacities for self-control and self-construction, i.e. agency and character merge together and are responsible for all the behaviours generated (Pereira et al., 2008). A virtue is a character trait, a quality valued by the culture as being always good in and of itself, a means for achieving moral ends. Personality is deeper than character and is connected with individuality.

Behaviour <- Character <- Personality

In those situations, each agent makes decisions which involve preferences and choices between different alternatives (e.g., a good and a bad, two "goods" or two "bads"). In the course of deliberating, each agent is forced to reflect (think about and think it through) before acting. A moral agent has a set of skills which allow to follow always a certain procedure within a social situation: 1) recognize a moral issue; 2) getting the facts; 3) evaluating alternative actions; 4) making a decision and testing it; 5) acting and reflecting on the outcome; 6) interpreting the answers obtained, and 7) behaving according to the detected meanings.

The agent moral judgment (Bentham, 2007) is associated to the calculus of the consequences involved and it is also a function of the different viewpoints and the values of the family/community (search of maximum utility for the majority).

Situation A: Clash in a Waiting Room

6.30 am in the waiting room of a health centre to get a blood test. The machine that delivers tickets to form queues of those attending is not yet operating. A civil servant informs all the patients still waiting the machine may start 6.45 am. Yet, several attendants tried to get a ticket without success. At 6.46, suddenly, a lady arrives, running, from the outside door and pushes the machine button. One ticket gets out and she picks it. A conflict is switched on. A discussion starts immediately about who owns that ticket, the first to arrive at the room or the lady that is the last one in the virtual queue. The result of the discussion (social exchanges through words and generation/solution of conflicts) depends heavily on the behaviour and character of those involved, aggressive or shy, and on qualities such as respect, gentleness, fairness, kindness, impartiality, self-control, selflessness, compassion, understanding, discernment, integrity, righteousness, courtesy, endurance, tolerance, say those qualities that make an agent be a complex entity.

The ticket machine serves to rank the attendees. But, it starts often with a delay comparing to those arriving. The order becomes the one related to press the button, and there is a mixture of objective and subjective criteria. Therefore, there are degrees of importance for different groups, those attending when the machine starts and the ones arriving without knowing what occurred before.

The discussion, behind situation A, is more than a social exchange (of sentences) which may attain an equilibrium or stay unbalanced, depending on the attached investment and satisfaction values. There are also exchanges of opinions about education, the importance that each one gives to the other, and game theory can translate what occurs when a dispute is activated. Opinions represent benefits (helpful opinions) and costs (unhelpful opinions) because they add a differential of weight to several rankings. Often, during the discussion agents exchange the weights attached to the possible orderings. Moral luck occurs when the moral judgment of an agent depends on factors beyond the agent´s control. Morality is connected to what society expected as the suitable solution for the problem, to the opinions of the other ones, and to the differences among all the involved agents.

Situation B: Couple Quarrel

One is joyful and get some pleasure to show it. The other is worried about some illness, become envious of that, and he tries to behave in "bad" ways and by saying "bad" words, which means having "bad" motives and interpersonal feelings such as anger, meekness and purposefulness. The final consequence of the dialogue is the two get a part of and annoyed with each other. Trust is destroyed, empathy becomes impossible, and love is in trouble. The ultimatum game can model such a situation (Macedo et al., 2012).

There is always a relationship between moral thought and action. The "bad" agent selects a viewpoint to annoy the partner, making jokes and humour, but provoking the rage of the other. Yet, he does not fully recognize that, and irony is also difficult to grasp by the other. Naturally, meanings are turn directly into aggressive acts and words. Everything gets confused, and both misinterpret what the other intends. The virtue of forgiveness, by excusing a mistake or offense, compassionate feelings that support a willingness to forgive, takes much time to be triggered because the quality of unselfish concern for the welfare of others is not always available and self-controlled, i.e. the trait of resolutely controlling your own behaviour and impulses, is often absent or disconnected. Therefore, certain behaviours occur by impulses and in a very fast mode. Agents with patience, with good-natured tolerance of delay, are still rare. Unhappily, goodness appears much less than badness!

AROUND THE BEHAVIOUR
OF A MORAL AGENT

In the past six years, we discovered that a moral agent has a hybrid architecture, where cognition, responsiveness, emotionality, aesthetics and morality are altogether mixed (Coelho et al., 2009 and 2010). However, the key, and central question, is not how many layers has the architecture (Wiegel, 2006), but how its decision policy is managed, because the environment is pro-active and it imposes a complexity of behaviours for an agent (Corrêa & Coelho, 1998 and 2010). Choice and preference reconsideration (action selection) is mandatory. Moral agents have different individual cultures (Mascarenhas, 2009), universal principles and values and they must be cautious and respectful in order to avoid inappropriate behaviours (generation of social conflicts). Behaviours are ruled by norms which depend on values (Cascalho, 2007). Norms are means in order behaviours be compatible to moral values. Therefore, a moral global behaviour is the result of many informed local decisions, taken by different modules and along n-layers, of feedback and feedforward moves, and the negotiation among those modules is often required to support the final decision (Pereira et al., 2008). The ability for anticipatory moral reasoning should be implied, in such moral global behaviour, since the moral assessment of actions is strongly determined by the effects they produce. Moral decisions, thus, should in part be based on the expectation of their results (Macedo et al., 2012).

Emotions and mental states are organized as unconscious layers. Very often, agents have feelings (and emotions) and are not aware of. They are emotionally confiscated and cannot exhibit very strict moral behaviour patterns. Therefore, each agent may learn how to balance among several polarities, emotional, rational and moral, in order to attain wisdom at last.

The moral-sense decision-making process clearly needs to incorporate both the agent's inner-world (e.g. sentiments, feelings) and its outer-world (e.g. a situation to act upon) along with the evaluation (e.g. radical utilitarian, moral) of the available outer-world scenarios. Those three components, <inner-world, outer-world, evaluation>, can be directly mapped into the general formulation of a partially observable Markov decision process or POMDP (Kaelbling et al., 1998), where both worlds are described, respectively, as a set of observations and states, and the evaluation is modelled as a reward function (see blocks of Figure 1). The POMDP, in charge of the choices, relates interpretation and state via the probability distribution.

The POMDP solver (Events in Figure 1) considers that at each time step, t, the world is assumed to be in state $s^t \in S$ which (stochastically) changes to $s^{t+1} \in S$ after the agent's execution of action $a^t \in A$. The essential POMDP assumption is that the agent does not direct access the world sates but instead receives an observation, $o^t \in \Omega$ which is some stochastic function of s^t (if $o^t = s^t$ then the POMDP reduces to a fully observed MDP). Additionally, the agent also receives a reward, R^t, signal which depends both on the action a^{t-1} and the state, s^t, being reached.

The moral-sense 3-tuple, <inner-world, outer-world, evaluation>, directly maps into the <Ω, S, R> components of a POMDP formulation where Ω is the set of observations, S is the set of states and R(s, a) is the reward function (Goals in Figure 1). But, how to map the actions of a POMDP into moral-sense domain independent components? Here, instead of looking at the actions that directly affect the outer-world, we consider the inner-world driving forces that will trigger the agent's behaviour. The moral-sense behaviour is closely related with the adherence to norms (social rules) in such a way that "norm

Figure 1. Proposal of a moral agent architecture

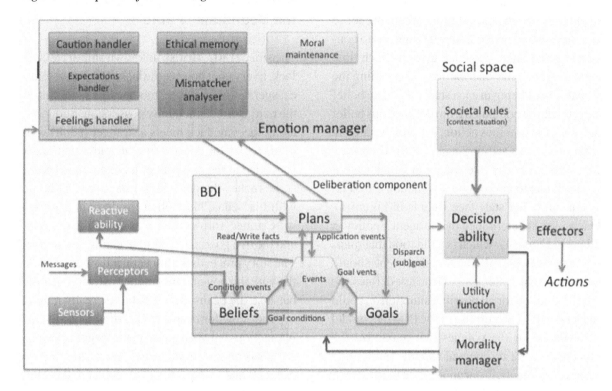

breaking" or "norm adherence" can be regarded as fundamental inner-world (meta) actions that will then enable a set of alternatives to act on the outer-world. Hence, we follow a "traffic light" metaphor and consider the POMDP actions as the set A = {Red_{norm}, $Yellow_{norm}$, $Green_{norm}$} of possible alternatives regarding each norm (Context in Figure1), where Red_{norm} and $Green_{norm}$ make reference, respectively, to violating and obeying norm and the $Yellow_{norm}$ is a midterm where the agent must call for an additional disambiguation decision process. The visual clue is that with Red_{norm} the norm "stops" fulfilment (i.e., the agent enters a "red zone of morality") and $Green_{norm}$ "keeps" norm fulfilment.

From the POMDP formulation, the outer-world dynamics is captured by the state transition function T(s, a, s') (associated to the Emotional Manager of Figure1) which gives the probability of ending in state s' if the agent performs action a in state s, i.e., it represents the conditional probability distribution Pr(s' | s, a) where s' ∈ S, s ∈ S, a ∈ A. Similarly, an observation function O(s', a, o) describes the inner-world dynamics as it gives the probability of observing o if action a is performed and the resulting state is s', i.e., it represents Pr(o | a, s') where o ∈ Ω, a ∈ A, s' ∈ S. From the moral-sense perspective, the observation function, O(s', a, o), describes the probability of an inner-world observation (perception) of sentiments, or feelings, o ∈ Ω given that action a was performed and the resulting state was s'. So, the observations refer to the internal agent states, i.e. they represent the agent´s perception as its own interpretation of an environment state.

This description (of function O) depends on each agent's individual characteristics. For example, the design of an agent that is respectful of elder people would lead the agent to feel bad (sentiment) whenever, e.g., it decides not to give his seat to an elder people that needs it, in a bus.

In a POMDP the states of the environment are not directly observable so the agent cannot choose its actions based on the states. It rather has to consider a belief state, b^t, which gives, at each time step t, a probability distribution, determining the probability of being in each state $s \in S$. The belief state, b^t, can be computed from the previous belief state, b^{t-1}, the previous action, a^{t-1}, and the current observation o^t (Kaelbling et al., 1998). Therefore, the agent has a way to estimate in which state it is, and it has to choose the next action based on its current belief state (see Beliefs in Figure 1). This action is determined by the agent's policy, π (Plans in Figure 1), which is a function that maps a belief state into the action the agent should execute in that belief state. Hence, π defines the agent's strategy for all possible situations it could be faced with. The purpose of the POMDP model is to search for the policies that maximize the expected sum of discounted rewards (utility and moral assessments, in our application) earned over some (finite or infinite) time horizon.

Therefore, in the moral-sense decision-making model, the POMDP policy represents a mapping of states of belief sets to "traffic light" actions ({Red_{norm}, $Yellow_{norm}$, $Green_{norm}$}, related to the (social) norms' compliance) that maximizes the agent's utilitarian and moral evaluation (via the reward, R, function) of the outer-world states.

A SCENARIO TO THINK ABOUT

The interplay of cognition, collective regulation and norm/value guidance is better described by taking the following situation C. The usual purpose of a fairy tale (fable) is to provide a context for some general moral interpretation. Although the global message is usually very clear, a deeper reading of some fable details (narrative) often reveals ambiguity even at the morality level interpretation.

Situation C: The "Jack and the Beanstalk" Fable

The story (1807, British unknown author) tells of Jack, a very poor boy, whose lack of common sense exasperates his widowed mother. She sends him to the market to sell their only possession, a cow, but along the way, Jack meets a stranger (adult) who offers to buy the cow for five "magic beans." Jack is thrilled at the prospect of having magic beans, so he makes the deal. When he arrives at home with his beans, his mother, in despair that they were ruined, throws the beans out of the window, and the two go to sleep without eating any supper. The story proceeds with several adventures but, in the end, the boy and his mother get very wealthy because the beans turned out to be really magic.

The "cow for beans' trade" illustrates diverse interactions between goals, plans, beliefs, desires, social norms and moral values. We named the two agents B and J, respectively, referring to the adult owner of the (magic) beans and to Jack (a child), so we have Ag = {B, J}. The set of available resources may be described by Rs = {cow, beans, money}. The "possess" relation, p: Ag → Rs, describes an agent's belongings, so initially we have p(B) = {beans, money} and p(J) = {cow}. Hence, the agents' outer-world is described by the tuple s = < p(B), p(J) >. For the POMDP formulation we consider three relevant states, i.e., S = {s_1, s_2, s_3}, where s_1 = <{beans, money}, {cow}>, s_2 = <{cow, money}, {beans}>, s_3 = <{beans, cow}, {money}>; for example, at t=0 the story assumes the state $s^0 = s_1$ = <{beans, money}, {cow}>. The outer-world dynamics is described by the POMDP transition T function, defined below.

One particular interpretation of the fable, that we took, identifies a social norm underlying the whole story, namely, that "an adult always *negotiates honestly* with a child." We designate this norm as norm-NH (in Context of Figure 1) so the POMDP action set is given by A = {a_1, a_2} where a_1 = Red$_{norm-NH}$, and a_2 = Green$_{norm-NH}$. Notice that the action Yellow$_{norm-NH}$ was omitted because it demands a second decision level which is beyond the scope of this example.

The norm-NH holds two important concepts: a) the negotiation (N), and b) the honesty (H). The "negotiation" calls for utility based evaluation and the "honesty" resorts to the moral interpretation of one's motivations. Honesty is the quality of being equitable, not deceptive or fraudulent, usually related with the perspective of good repute and respectable decision-making. The negotiation (N) utility evaluation is given by the reward function R(s, a). The honesty (H) interpretation of the agent's motivations is described by the POMDP observation set Ω = {o_1, o_2}, where o_1="greedy" and o_2="steady." For example an agent that favours honesty might raise high expectations of observing o_2 when performing a_2 to reach s_3. This inner-world dynamics contributes to define the agent's moral "signature" and it is fully described by the POMDP observation function O. We note that the "moral signature" concept is materialized simultaneously from two perspectives: a) the inner-world, throughout the observation function O, and b) the outer-world, via the reward function R. The inner-world "moral-signature" (function O) deals with sentiments (or feelings) while describing their expected distribution given the outer-world causal-effects. The outer-world "moral-signature" (function R) accounts for the valuation of concrete, and eventually achievable, situations. For example, the agent that is respectful of elder people may feel bad after sitting down on the last available bus seat while in the presence of elder people. Never-

theless, simultaneously that same agent may give high rewards to his own comfort (being seated). Those two perspectives, both "feeling bad" and "retaining comfort," contribute to characterize the agent's "moral signature."

RESULTS SO FAR

The previous illustrative scenario was formulated as a POMDP and we implemented a solver that follows an exact value iteration approach to search for an optimal policy (in a specified time horizon) using dynamic programming to compute increasingly more accurate values for each belief state. We analysed the ideas of the Witness algorithm (Littman, 1994) and implemented the technique of the Enumeration algorithm (Monahan, 1983). This approach serves our model's experimentation purposes because the POMDP design of this moral-sense decision-making scenario exhibits low dimension sets ($|S| \times |A| \times |\Omega| = 12$).

Table 1 shows the model of the outer-world dynamics, T(s, a, s'), where each action a $\in$ A is described separately, each s $\in$ S is represented as a line and each s' $\in$ S is a column.

.The transition function, T, indicates that s_2 and s_3 are absorbing states (no way out) where s_2 = <{cow, money}, {beans}> is highly probable from s_1 = <{beans, money},{cow}>, after performing a_1 = Red$_{norm-NH}$, the norm breaking action; and s_3 = <{beans, cow}, {money}>; is highly probable from s_1 = <{beans, money}, {cow}>, after performing a_2 = Green$_{norm-NH}$, the norm adherent action. This transition function describes a world that does not contain "magic

Table 1. Each action separately - on the left T(s, a_1, s'), on the right T(s, a_2, s')

a_1	s_1	s_2	s_3	a_2	s_1	s_2	s_3
s_1	0.1	0.8	0.1	s_1	0.1	0.1	0.8
s_2	0	1	0	s_2	0	1	0
s_3	0	0	1	s_3	0	0	1

beans" which benefit the owner with richness. Otherwise it would seem inconsistent for agent B to feel "greedy" (a_1) in state s_1 while being highly probable (0.8) to reach state s_2 (cf. Table 1 on the left). That is, if B feels greedy of J we do not expect B to benefit J, therefore "magic beans" are objects that do not exist within this formulation.

Table 2 shows the model of the inner-world dynamics, $O(s', a, o)$, where each action $a \in A$ is described separately, each $o \in \Omega$ is represented as a row and each $s \in S$ is a column.

The observation function, O, describes the agent's expectations about the causal effect of breaking, or adhering, to (social) norms. In this scenario, o_1 (i.e., a "greedy" feeling) is highly expected in state $s_1 = <\{beans, money\}, \{cow\}>$ after action $a_1 = Red_{norm-NH}$ (0.9, cf. Table 2 on the left) and o_2 (i.e., a "steady" feeling) is highly expected in state $s_1 = <\{beans, money\}, \{cow\}>$ after $a_2 = Green_{norm-NH}$ (0.9, cf. Table 2 on the right). The agent is indifferent in $s_2 = <\{cow, money\}, \{beans\}>$ and $s_3 = <\{beans, cow\}, \{money\}>$ because those are the absorbing states.

The reward function, R, represents the way an agent deals with the trade-off between opportunities (individual expected profit) and duties (socially expected behaviour). The Table 3 illustrates three types of agents: Type-1) ultimate ambitious agent that "disregards means to achieve ends," Type-2) fair negotiator agent that "negotiates fairly

independently of existing norms," and Type-3) norm follower agent that "always consider norms independently of achievable ends." We formulate the reward function as the case where the agent is trying to reach a specific set of absorbing goal states (as in classical planning) so we give a reward of -1 for each (s, a), $s \in S$, $a \in A$, pair except for those pairs that correspond to goal states.

The goal of the "ultimate ambitious" agent (Type-1) is to achieve the state where he owns both the money and the cow in exchange for the beans (i.e., $s2 = <\{cow, money\}, \{beans\}>$) regardless of any social norm (i.e., independently of the taken action being a1 or a2). An identical reasoning is followed by the "fair negotiator" agent (Type-2) only that his goal is get the cow but paying, for it, with "real" money instead of "magic beans" (i.e., achieve the state $s2 = <\{cow, beans\}, \{money\}>$). The goal of the "norm follower" agent (Type-1) is to achieve any state (s2 or s3) provided that he always follows the adopted social norm (i.e., he always chooses a2 as this is the norm adherent action).

Given the above $<S, A, \Omega, T, O, R>$ formulation we considered the initial (t=0) belief state $b(s^0) = <0.9, 0.1, 0>$ meaning that the agent is highly (0.9) confident that s_1 is the outer-world state. The POMDP solver computed the optimal policy and the Table 4 presents the best action to perform in the two first time steps (t=0 and t=1)

Table 2. Each action separately - on the left $O(s', a_1, o)$, on the right $O(s', a_2, o)$

a_1	s_1	s_2	s_3	a_2	s_1	s_2	s_3
o_1	0.9	0.5	0.5	o_1	0.1	0.5	0.5
o_2	0.1	0.5	0.5	o_2	0.9	0.5	0.5

Table 3. Three reward functions each representing a different type of agent

Type-1	a_1	a_2	Type-2	a_1	a_2	Type-3	a_1	a_2
s_1	-1	-1	s_1	-1	-1	s_1	-1	-1
s_2	0	0	s_2	-1	-1	s_2	-1	0
s_3	-1	-1	s_3	0	0	s_3	-1	0

Table 4. The belief state and best action for the three types of agents

		Type-1	Type-2	Type-3
$t = 0$	$b(s^0) =$	<0.9, 0.1, 0>	<0.9, 0.1, 0>	<0.9, 0.1, 0>
	$o^0 =$	o_1	o_1	o_1
best action =		$\mathbf{a_1}$	$\mathbf{a_2}$	$\mathbf{a_2}$
$t = 1$	$b(s^1) =$	<0.15, **0.76**, 0.08>	<0.01, 0.20, **0.77**>	<0.01, 0.20, **0.77**>
	$o^1 =$	o_1	o_1	o_1
best action =		$\mathbf{a_1}$	$\mathbf{a_2}$	$\mathbf{a_2}$

assuming the belief state $b(s^0)$ and, to simplify the presentation, we only show the o_1 observation sequence.

The results follow our initial intuition on the problem. Namely, the Type-1 agent will break the norm (i.e., execute $a_1 = \text{Red}_{\text{norm-NH}}$) and its updated belief state gives a high expectation (0.76) to state s_2. Both the Type-2 and Type-3 agents exhibit a similar behaviour as they will adhere to the norm (i.e., execute $a_1 = \text{Green}_{\text{norm-NH}}$) and get a higher expectation (0.77) to the belief about s_3. The above results illustrate the proposed POMDP formulation and evidence its applicability as a general method for a moral-sense agent to explore the "opportunity or duty" decision space.

DESIGN OF THE AGENT DECISION MACHINERY

The concept of morality tends to be better understood from humanism and qualitative appreciations than from technocracy and quantitative analysis. The absence of some formal characterization of morality forms makes it even harder to express such a concept as a specific combination of interrelated devices that own some formal or technological direct representation (see Hegselmann´s references). The design of a specific architecture aiming to model morality will always reduce the concept to a set of predefined dimensions. We can find morality projections (or interpretations) at least within four dimensions: a) social, b) personal, c)

temporal, and d) spatial. Briefly, the evidence of morality projection along those dimensions are shown in Table 5.

Is there a single computational architecture that can agglutinate, into functional components, such diversity of abstract concepts? Or, the best approach consists of focusing on some sketch (see Figure 1) and concentrating, on combining diverse models or mechanisms? One possible move towards an answer was to pick up existing models and to map them into those dimensions. The POMDP is founded in the decision theory and therefore satisfies the personal dimension. The model evaluates the current (world) state taking into account the result of past in order to achieve the future best option and, therefore, satisfies the temporal dimension.

The POMDP model has two layers: a) the world states and b) the internal observations. The world states are analyzed and transformed into internal observations. The idea of the world state analysis (and evaluation) is aligned with the satisfaction

Table 5. Space of 4 dimensions

Dimension	Morality Projection / Example
Social	Decision Making / e.g., hurt the group
Personal	Decision Making / e.g., offend the neighbour
Temporal	Generation Gap / e.g., use of offensive lyrics
Spatial	Geo-Political Context / e.g., war relations

of the spatial dimension. The transformation into internal observations informs the decision to take and therefore satisfies the social projection because it incorporates norms and the results of social exchanges. A first try was done by (Coelho, Costa, & Trigo, 2010). A different approach, based upon Piaget´s theory of social exchanges, was already tested by (Pereira et al., 2008; Dimuro et al., 2010). Therefore, POMDP emerges as a valuable framework to model a specific interpretation of morality. How to configure diverse moral perspectives within this same framework? And, how can we take into consideration the role of virtues to govern decision-taking and delay the impulses to act, i.e. are character issues advisable to be taken in care? May we try amalgamating several models, such as BDI (plans) with POMDP (policies)? These are still open questions for further research.

The POMPD design includes the specification of two probability distributions: a) the expected state given each action and current state, and b) the expected observation given each action and the current state. The first (a) distribution describes the world dynamics. The second (b) distribution configures each agent's moral perspective; e.g., one that gives high expectation to the act of competing in order to strip the other's ticket (cf. line ticket while in the medical waiting room) will most certainly exhibit such an "uncivilized" behaviour.

MORAL SIGNATURE

When we face applications of the Internet, namely via LinkedIn, Twitter, Flickr, MySpace and Facebook, it appears a need for better interaction modes through moral agents in social communities. The cultural consumption is activated by social networks and it requests good manners and natural dialogues. So, in the future a research direction around moral agents (reputation) will be required to increase the exploration of WWW.

The case of organisations at large, say electronic institutions (e-government) and electronic commerce (e-business and market places), supported more research on negotiation protocols and strategies and on reputation models and mechanisms (agreement technologies), because the use of MAS was increased (Lopes & Coelho, 2013). Trust is today a facet to be carefully followed. Our belief is the following: more social sharing of objects (e-books, newspaper articles, music and video clips, cultural agenda) may be activated by artificial agents, keen in social interactions where morality plays now an essential role. Therefore, agents with moral signature will be needed, and this means identity and character issues (e.g. those linked with moral strength) must be understood fully because they are connected with driving and regulating behaviour.

We call the agent's moral signature a set of ethical attributes of good character, manners, i.e. a sort of trace of (well or bad) behaviour, measured by confidence factors (m_value, to be aggregated later on to the so-called reputation value and in order to constitute the general opinion on some agent),

$$M\_value = m1\_value + m2\_value$$

where m1_value stands for the degree of moral consideration an agent obtains after using a service provided by another agent (a sort of image), and m2_value stands for the degree of moral consideration an agent obtains after asking for help about others to a third party (a sort of recognition). These values can be assigned automatically by collecting user complaints.

Moral signature can be designed to match the ideas brought about the research already done on reputation models (Silva et al., 2009). The decentralized and centralized mechanisms can be combined to evaluate the behaviour of agents, to store the values and reasons (degrees of good manners), and to allow later on the agents reason about the global values they receive. Such moral values may be combined with those regarding satisfaction, reputation and popularity, improving the quality of assessment on the ways these agents behave. No major changes are necessary in what concerns the architecture displayed in Figure 1, but more attention is required in order to articulate the emotional and moral managers with the planner, the action selection mechanisms, and the decision-making modules. Therefore, further work is still needed (March & Olsen, 2009).

CONCLUSION AND FURTHER RESEARCH

The present paper covers the kind of decision machinery that may be suitable for moral agents. In particular, we try to understand here how character issues may constrain behaviour, decision-making and choice. At large, ethical thinking and deliberating is about a certain mode of behaving, the one worried, not only about the own preferences, but also about the preferences of other agents in situation.

Although the POMDP seems to exhibit some well suited structure to describe a (flavour of) morality, the question remains: how can we explore the essential of the social exchange dimension along interactions? Certainly, a deeper insight is needed and standard approaches need to be considered. The FIPA effort around agent technology, as the most relevant reference in the standardization of the social exchange issue, needs to be amplified in order to cover morality themes. But, does FIPA remains in "the front line" given the current state of the art on social exchange models, techniques and interaction (agreement) technologies? Can we design a moral agent without the ability to generate agreements (through negotiation and argumentation)? The FIPA interaction protocols could be extended to provide the basis for a reputation (or fairness) knowledge base for agents and support the agents´ moral-based reasoning.

Otherwise, is it possible to apply mechanism design ideas to morality (Franco, 2008)? Can games support long sequences of ethical think-ing during conversations? And, what about using games to analyze and experiment on moral conducts issues instead of exploring stories? Games moves and interactions aid us to think about ethics, but it is necessary to separate the social dimension (with Game Theory) from the individual dimension (with Decision Theory), tackled along this paper. Namely, Game Theory is suitable to cover equilibrium defined as a function of the combination of the agent (the whole spectrum from good to bad) actions. Also, Game Theory helps to relate morality with rationality, and to discuss strategies and the negotiation issues among the layers of the moral agent architecture. Therefore, the use of games to support further inquiry about moral agents is mostly advisable, on account of providing small worlds with rules, strategies, relations, and conflict of interests. In these worlds, character plays also a key role on the agent choices and attitudes (Paglieri et al., 2012).

An instrumental approach to morality may recognize it as a social mechanism capable of regulating the interaction of multiple agents with opposing interests (Franco et al., 2009). Often, such interactions are taken from a (purely) personal perspective that reduces the evaluation of interests to the simple format of "me & everybody-but-me" rationality. This format simplifies our "daily" evaluation of interests thus enabling a prompt decision-making behaviour. Therefore, utilitarianism should be the expected convergence point of such behaviour; i.e., one aims to gain as much as possible while facing a skilful opponent who pursues an antithetical goal. Despite that expectation, our "daily" decision-making follows some sense of "fairness" that tends to balance the odds of the outcomes from the available decisions. Therefore, each "me & everybody-but-me" interaction can be modelled as a simple strategic game that owns an expected value (i.e., the payoff that good play will win for "me"); the expected value of a "fair" game is zero. Morality is a social mechanism that drives interaction games near to their "fair" payoff formulations so that we keep interacting with each other; often favouring the most "fair" opponents and avoiding encounters with previous "unfair" opponents.

Finally, the current version of this research shows different parts of the model are scattered throughout the paper, a complete conceptual model and the formal language would be desirable in separate sections. In our opinion, such criticism would destroy the way we composed the narrative of our inquiry, and we prefer to leave these elements for a follow-up paper.

ACKNOWLEDGMENT

We are greatly indebted to the anonymous reviewers for providing many comments, alarms and advices which help to improve the whole text. Following the European EMIL project (2006-09) was also a major drive, to open our own views on morality and to make us more demanding of agents with qualities.

REFERENCES

Adamatti, D., Sichman, J., & Coelho, H. (2009). An analysis of the insertion of virtual players in GMABS methodology using the Vip-JogoMan prototype. *Journal of Artificial Societies and Social Simulation*, *12*(3).

Andrighetto, G., Campenni, M., Conte, R., & Paolucci, M. (2007). On the immergence of norms: A normative agent architecture. In *Proceedings of AAAI Symposium, Social and Organizational Aspects of Artificial Intelligence,* Washington DC.

Bentham, J. (2007). *Introduction to the principles of morals and legislation*. New York: Dover Publications. (Original work published 1823)

Briot, J.-P., Vasconcelos, E., Adamatti, D., Sebba, V., Irving, M., Barbosa, S., et al. (2008, July). Computer-based support for participatory management of protected areas: The SimParc project. In *Proceedings of 28th Congress of Computation Brazilian Society (CSBC '08),* Belém, Brazil.

Cascalho, J. (2007). *The role of attributes for mental states architectures* (PhD Thesis) (in Portuguese). University of Açores, Portugal.

Castelfranchi, C. (in press). Making visible the invisible hand. The mission of social simulation. In D. Adanatti, G. Dimuro, & H. Coelho (Eds.), *Interdisciplinary applications of agent-based social simulation and modelling*. Hershey, PA: IGI Global.

Castelfranchi, C., Dignum, F., Jonker, C. M., & Treur, J. (2000). Deliberative normative agents: Principles and architectures. In *Proceedings of 6th ATAL Conference (1999), Intelligent Agents VI*, (LNCS 1757). Berlin: Springer.

Castelfranchi, C., Falcone, R., & Piunti, M. (2006). *Agents with anticipatory behaviours: To be cautious in a risky environment*. ECAI.

Churchland, P. (2011). *Braintrust: what neuroscience tells us about morality*. Princeton, NJ: Princeton University Press.

Coelho, H., & Costa, A. R. (2009). On the intelligence of moral agency. In L. S. Lopes, N. Lau, P. Mariano & L. M. Rocha (Eds.), *New trends in artificial intelligence: Proceedings of the Encontro Português de Inteligência Artificial (EPIA-2009)*, (pp. 439-450). Aveiro, Portugal.

Coelho, H., Costa, A. R., & Trigo, P. (2010). Decision taking for agent moral conducts. In *Proceedings of INFORUM2010*, University of Minho, Braga, Portugal.

Coelho, H., Costa, A. R., & Trigo, P. (2010). On the operationality of moral-sense decision making. In *Proceedings of the Brazilian Workshop on Social Simulation (BWSS2010), SBIA Congress*, São Bernardo, Brazil.

Corrêa, M., & Coelho, H. (1998). From mental states and architectures to agents´ programming. In *Proc. of the 7ᵗʰ Iberoamerican Congress on Artificial Intelligence (IBERAMIA98)*, Lisbon, Portugal (LNAI 1484, pp. 64-85). Berlin: Springer-Verlag.

Corrêa, M., & Coelho, H. (2010). Abstract mental descriptions for agent design. *Intelligent Decision Technologies, 4*(2), 115–131.

Costa, A. R., & Dimuro, G. (2007). A basis for an exchange value-based operational notion of morality for multiagent systems. In J. Neves, M. Santos & J. Machado (Eds.), *Proceedings of EPIA2007* (LNAI 4874, pp. 580-592). Berlin: Springer.

Costa, A. R., & Dimuro, G. (2009). *Moral values and the structural loop (Revisiting Piaget´s model of normative agents)*. PUC Pelotas Working Report.

Dehghani, M., Tomai, E., Forbus, K., & Klenk, M. (2008). An integrated reasoning approach to moral decision-making. In *Proceedings of 23th AAAI Conference on Artificial Intelligence* (pp. 1280-1286).

Dignum, F., Kinny, D., & Sonenberg, L. (2001). *From desires, obligations and norms to goals*. The Netherlands: Utrecht University.

Dimuro, G. P., Rocha, A. R., & Gonçalves, L. V. (2010). Recognizing and learning observable social exchange strategies in open societies. In *Proceedings of the Brazilian Workshop on Social Simulation (BWSS2010)*, São Bernardo do Campo, Brazil.

Franco, M. I. (2008). *Interaction mechanism among agents: Construction and evaluation of social exchanges*. Brazil: Universidade Federal do Rio Grande do Sul. (in Portuguese)

Franco, M. I., Costa, A. R., & Coelho, H. (2009). Exchange values and social power supporting the choice of partners. *Revista Pueblos y Fronteras Digital*, No. 9.

Green, J., & Haidt, J. (2002, December). How (and where) does moral judgment work? *Trends in Cognitive Sciences, 6*(12). PMID:12200171

Greene, J., Sommerville, R., Nystrom, L., & Darley, J. (2001). An fMRI investigation of emotional engagement in moral judgment. *Science, 293*(5537), 2105–2108. doi:10.1126/science.1062872 PMID:11557895

Haidt, J., & Kesebir, S. (2010). *Handbook of social psychology*. Hoboken, NJ: John Wiley.

Hauser, M. D. (2006). *Moral minds: How nature designed our sense of right and wrong*. New York: Ecco/Harper Collins.

Hegselmann, R. (2009). Moral dynamics. In R. A. Meyers (Ed.), *Encyclopedia of complexity and systems sciences* (pp. 5677–5692). Berlin: Springer. doi:10.1007/978-0-387-30440-3_338

Hegselmann, R., & Will, O. (2013). From small groups to large societies: How to construct a simulator? *Biological Theory, 8*(2), 185–194. doi:10.1007/s13752-013-0110-6

Horty, J. F. (1994, February). Moral dilemmas and non-monotonic logic. *Journal of Philosophical Logic, 23*(1), 35–65. doi:10.1007/BF01417957

Kaelbling, L. P., Littman, M. L., & Cassandra, A. R. (1998). Planning and acting in partially observable stochastic domains. *Artificial Intelligence, 101*(1-2), 99–134. doi:10.1016/S0004-3702(98)00023-X

Littman, M. L. (1994). *The witness algorithm: Solving partially observable Markov decision processes (Technical Report: CS-94-40)*. Providence, RI: Brown University.

Lopes, F., & Coelho, H. (Eds.). (in press). *Negotiation and argumentation in multi-agent systems, fundamentals, theories, systems and applications*. Bentham Books.

Macedo, L. F. K., Dimuro, G., Aguiar, M. S., Costa, A. C. R., Mattos, V. L. D., & Coelho, H. (2012, October). Analyzing the evolution of social exchanges strategies in social preference-based MAS through an evolutionary spatial approach of the ultimatum game. In *Proceedings of the Third Brazilian Workshop on Social Simulation*. Curitiba, Brazil: IEEE Press.

March, J. G., & Olsen, J. P. (2009). *The logic of appropriateness* (Arena Centre for European Studies Working Papers WP 04/09). University of Oslo, Norway.

Mascarenhas, S. F. (2009). *Creating social and cultural agents* (MS.C. Thesis). Instituto Superior Tecnico, Universidade Tecnica de Lisboa, Portugal.

Mikhail, J. (2007). Universal moral grammar: Theory, evidence and the future. *Trends in Cognitive Sciences*, *11*(4). doi:10.1016/j.tics.2006.12.007 PMID:17329147

Monahan, G. E. (1983). A survey of partially observable Markov decision processes: Theory, models and algorithms. *Management Science*, *28*, 1–16. doi:10.1287/mnsc.28.1.1

Paglieri, F., Tummolini, L., Falcone, R., & Miceli, M. (Eds.). (2012). *The goals of cognition: Essays in honour of Cristiano Castelfranchi*. College Publications.

Pereira, D. R., Gonçalves, L. V., Dimuro, G. P., & Rocha, A. R. (2008). Towards the self-regulation of personality-based social exchanges in multiagent systems. In G. Zaverucha & A. L. da Costa (Eds.), *Advances in AI, Proceedings of the Brazilian Workshop on Social Simulation (BWSS2008)*, Salvador (Baía) (LNAI 5249). Berlin: Springer.

Pereira, L. M., & Saptawijaya, A. (2007). Moral decision making with ACORDA. In *Proceedings from the 14th International Conference on Logic for Programming Artificial Intelligence and Reasoning (LPAR'07)*.

Pereira, L. M., & Saptawijaya, A. (2009). *Computational modelling of morality* (Working Report).

Silva, V. T., Hermoso, R., & Centeno, R. A. (2009). Hybrid reputation model based on the use of organizations. In J. F. Hubner, E. Matson, O. Boissier & V. Dignum (Eds.), Coordination, Organizations, Institutions and Norms (COIN2008) in Agent Systems IV, (LNCS 5428, pp. 111-125). Berlin: Springer.

Wiegel, V. (2006). Building blocks for artificial moral agents. In *Proceedings of EthicalALife06*. Workshop.

KEY TERMS AND DEFINITIONS

Agent Profile and Signature: Allow some kind of identity and differentiation, important to provide trust and responsibility along the transactions.

Behavior Regulation: Keeps the ongoing of a society either with simple rules, constraints, laws or norms.

Moral Agent Architecture, Mechanisms and Models: Needed To diversify properties, qualities and values. An agent can be described by a form, a structure, an organization, and by specific elements or means.

Morality: A sort of social mechanism capable of regulating the interactions of multiple agents with opposing interests.

Morality Reconsideration: Can be seen as a kind of belief revision.

Moral Judgment: Doing the right thing. Behind thinking we can also find several other operations, such as deliberation, judgment and decision taking.

Normative Governance: Achieved through different sorts of mechanisms.

POMDP Modeling: Ways of modeling partially observable markov decision taking processes of an agent with probability distributions over the set of possible states.

Sociality: Covers all the interactions. In some social situations, we require human (moral) judgment because it factors suitable information into decisions, it outweighs the costs, it involves ethical considerations, and it is able to measure any decision against the expected social (appropriate) behavior of users.

Stories and Games: Installations to describe narratives about social interactions among several agents or other courses of action.

Chapter 3
Scale and Topology Effects on Agent-Based Simulation:
A Trust-Based Coalition Formation Case Study

Luis G. Nardin
Universidade de São Paulo, Brazil

Luciano M. Rosset
Universidade de São Paulo, Brazil

Jaime S. Sichman
Universidade de São Paulo, Brazil

ABSTRACT

The exploitation of Agent-Based Social Simulation (ABSS) full capabilities often requires massive computing power and tools in order to support the achievement of breakthrough results in social sciences. Lately, this issue has being addressed by the release of several high-performance computing agent-based simulation tools; however, they have not been used for exploring critical issues, such as ABSS results invariance and universality. Hence, in order to advance this topic, this chapter provides an invariance analysis, considering scale and topology, of a model that incorporates the concepts of trust and coalition formation, in which agents are placed on a square lattice interacting locally with their neighbors and forming coalitions. By varying the environment size, its topology, as well as the neighborhood topology, it is identified in the experimental scenario that apparently the only parameter that affects the simulation dynamics is the neighborhood topology.

DOI: 10.4018/978-1-4666-5954-4.ch003

INTRODUCTION

Along the last decades, social sciences have been accepting gradually Agent-Based Social Simulation (ABSS) as an adequate approach for modeling social problems (Gilbert, 2008; Li et al., 2008). Although adequate, the exploitation of its full capabilities for facing the complexity of current social problems requires massive computing power and powerful tools endowed with features that allow the achievement of breakthrough results. The fulfillment of these requirements, for instance, would enable the simulation of large groups of agents rendering possible the study of more representative portions of the society. Additionally, it would enable the handling of the huge amounts of data recently made available by the increasing use of online tools in individuals' daily routines.

According to Murphy (2011), High-Performance Computing (HPC) is a good path to follow in order to fulfill such large-scale simulation needs. The term High-Performance Computing refers to any computational activity that aggregates computing resources in a way to deliver higher computing capabilities than one could get out of a single processor computer. HPC platforms are distributed systems composed of collections of independent processing units running in parallel. Their architectures are classified according to the coupling degree among their processing units. Some examples of HPC platforms are supercomputers, clusters, grids, clouds, and more recently GPU (Graphical Processing Units) computing (Fan et al., 2004). For an overview and a better understanding of the current HPC status, see (Dongarra & van der Steen, 2012).

Lately, several agent-based modeling and simulation (ABMS) tools, supporting different HPC platform architectures, have been freely released focused in fulfilling large-scale computing requirements: SWAGES (Scheutz, Schermerhorn, Connaughaton, & Dingler, 2006), D-MASON (Cordasco et al., 2011), Repast HPC (Collier &

North, 2012), Pandora (Wittek & Rubio-Campillo, 2012) and FLAME (Coakley et al., 2012). Since this work is not focused on reviewing ABMS HPC tools, for a comprehensive review see (Collier & North, 2012).

Regardless of the availability of these tools, currently only few simulation models have been implemented using them. Moreover, their primary purpose is the demonstration of ABMS HPC tools functionalities rather than to explore more critical issues, such as ABSS results robustness (Cioffi-Revilla, 2002). Hence, the main contribution of this chapter is an invariance analysis, considering changes in scale and topology, of an ABSS model proposed by Nardin and Sichman (2011). This model is based on a square lattice, in which agents interact locally with their neighbors and form coalitions. Additionally, this chapter provides some practical challenges and drawbacks faced during this model's implementation in a HPC environment using the Repast HPC toolkit.

The remainder of this chapter is organized as follows. In the next section, we describe some related work. In the sequence, we present the conceptual description as well as the implementation of our model. Then, we describe the experiments' design. Next, we present the main questions concerning the model invariance and their corresponding answers, considering the effects of scale and topology change in the dynamics of the system. Finally, we present our conclusions.

RELATED WORK

Among the few related work that approaches robustness, Flache and Hegselmann (2001) relaxed the assumption of rectangular grid structures and analyzed how the use of irregular (non-rectangular) structures, such as hexagonal or triangular cells, affects the migration and influence dynamics in cellular automaton models. They concluded that both dynamics are robust to structure variation.

Urbig et al. (2008) proposed an opinion dynamics model that allows the variation of the number of peers that meet at once in order to analyze changes on the speed of the opinions adaptation. They investigated the effect of such changes in different population sizes concluding that the number of meeting peers affects the tendency towards consensus.

Gotts and Polhill (2010) examined the effects of land-use convergence through the combination of pairs of land-use selection strategies in FEARLUS, a spatial-explicit agent model, in various environment sizes. They showed that the enlargement of the environment does not influence the winning strategy; nonetheless, they identified a delay in the land-use convergence as environment increases.

Finally, Murphy (2011) implemented the *Triangles* model (Sweeney & Meadows, 2010; Murphy, 2011) using the Repast HPC toolkit and performed some simulations that scale up to billions of agents. In his study, Murphy analyzed the influence of large-scale on the simulation dynamics. Despite not identifying any shift in the simulation dynamics as the scale was increased, he advocates that simulations with different structures and dynamics may be affected by such scale change. Thus, he suggests that a key point for future work is the identification of the kinds of simulations that may suffer such variation.

For a more comprehensive view of the main issues related to the use of HPC in ABSS, please refer to (Montañola-Sales et al., 2014).

TRUST AND COALITION MODEL

In this section, a brief conceptual description of the *Trust and Coalition* model is provided along with its interaction rules. In addition, we present some details and challenges faced during the model's implementation using the Repast HPC toolkit.

Conceptual Description

In the context of ABSS, Nardin and Sichman proposed an agent-based simulation model, named *Trust and Coalition* (or simply *T&C*), that integrates the notions of trust and coalition formation in order to understand how the former influences the procedure of coalition formation among autonomous agents (Nardin & Sichman, 2011).

The *T&C* model consists of a population of agents placed in a spatial structured environment, in which each agent interacts with its neighbors choosing either to cooperate or to defect. These agents may decide to play *independently*, or to join (or leave) a *coalition*. When an agent is independent, its action depends on its own strategy. On the other hand, when an agent belongs to a coalition, it cooperates with its own coalition members and defects with either independent neighbors or with those that belong to different coalitions. Our concept of coalition consists in a group of agents (subset of the population) that cooperate in order to obtain a certain utility. A coalition is formed by a mechanism that defines the arrangement of the group. A leader represents such a group, and it is responsible for evenly sharing the payoff accumulated by the coalition members after subtracting a tax percentage from it. The agents' decision to remain or to leave a coalition is based on *trust* information that they have gathered about their coalition leader. Such trust varies based on the payoff received from the leader in comparison to the neighbors' payoff.

Hence, the agents' decision to join a coalition is purely economic, while their action of remaining or leaving the coalition is based on the trust they have on their coalition leader. Trust refers to an estimate that an agent has about the actions to be taken by another agent, which directly affects itself, and is unknown at the time needed to decide which action should be taken (Dasgupta, 2000). Here, trust is used as a mechanism to postpone the agents' action of leaving the coalition, which may represent the tolerance that an agent has regarding unsatisfactory economic returns received from the group in comparison to other alternatives, i.e. playing independently or joining another coalition.

Interaction Rules

The *T&C* model is inspired on the spatial and iterative game approach proposed by Nowak and May (Nowak & May, 1992), in which interactions among agents consider the spatial structure of the population. For the spatial distribution, the model considers a two-dimensional square lattice composed of *N* cells (Figure 1). At each cell an agent A_i, belonging to an agent population $A = \{A_1, A_2, ..., A_N\}$, is placed. A subset of the agent population is considered a coalition, thus it is possible to have at most $(N / 2)$ coalitions since there is at least two agents to form a coalition.

Each agent A_i may only interact directly with its neighbors $NS_i = \{A_{1i}, ..., A_{ni}\}$, where the possible

Figure 1. Agent (A) with two neighborhood topologies: 4 cells {A_1, ..., A_4} and 8 cells {A_1, ..., A_8}

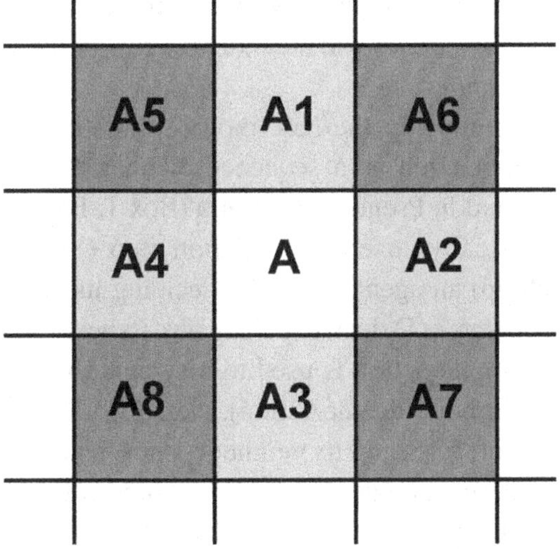

neighborhood topologies are Von Neumann (n = 4) and Moore (n = 8), as depicted in Figure 1.

Additionally to the neighborhood topology, the environment may be represented as a *grid* or a *torus*. While in the latter the left and right borders and the top and bottom borders are wrapped, in the former they are not. Therefore, in the *grid* environment topology, the agents on the borders have fewer neighbors than on the center, what is taken into consideration at the moment of the agents' payoff calculation.

Each agent has two options for acting when playing with any of its neighbors: Cooperate (C) or Defect (D). The outcome of an interaction depends on the actions chosen by the playing agents and it is represented by the standard PD payoff matrix presented in Table 1 that shows the payoff p_{ij} of an interaction between agents A_i and A_j.

Nonetheless, because the agent's interaction is modeled as an *n-person game*, in which each agent interacts with all its neighbors by playing independent 2-person games, the total agent's payoff is calculated as

$$p_i = \frac{\sum_{j=1}^{n} p_{ij}}{n}, \; i \in N, j \in NS_i$$

where *n* is the number of A_i's neighbors, p_{ij} is the payoff obtained in the interaction between A_i and A_j, and p_i is the A_i payoff.

An agent' interaction with its neighbors may follow different strategies depending on its role:

Table 1. Payoff matrix

$A_i \, A_j$	C	D
C	3 / 3	0 / 5
D	5 / 0	1 / 1

- **Independent:** The agent can either act as a cooperator or a defector with respect to its neighbors, depending on its own strategy, which is fixed for the whole simulation. The possible strategies used in this work are:
  - **Tit-for-Tat (TFT):** The agent mimics the last action performed by the majority of its opponents.
  - **Probabilistic Tit-for-Tat (pTFT):** The agent mimics the last action performed by the majority of its opponents according to a probabilistic approach.
  - **Random:** The agent chooses its action randomly.

  After each play, an *Independent* agent may join a coalition or remain independent. If it decides to join a coalition, the initial trust value on its new *Coalition Leader* is randomly assigned in a range from 0 to 100.

- **Coalition Member:** The agent cooperates with the neighbors belonging to its coalition and defects with the neighbors that are independent or with those belonging to other coalitions. A *Coalition Member* becomes *Independent* if its trust on the *Coalition Leader* drops below a specified threshold; otherwise, it updates its trust on the leader (increase or decrease), yet remaining a member of the coalition.

- **Coalition Leader:** The leader acts like its members; however, the leader cannot decide to become *Independent* at anytime. It becomes automatically *Independent* when there is no other *Coalition Member* in its coalition. In order to perform such leading role, it imposes a percentage on the payoff of the *Coalition Member* agents, denominated tax. An agent becomes a leader of a coalition whenever one of its neighbor agents selects it as such.

Each agent, when playing the role of *Coalition Member*, implements a simple trust model to evaluate its trust on its *Coalition Leader*. In such trust model, a single integer number ranging between 0 and 100 represents a trust value, where values close to 0 represent a low trust, and values close to 100 represent a high trust on the *Coalition Leader*. As the agents progress through the game, they update their trust value on their leader based on their experiences. Thus, by using such information, an agent can decide to remain in or to leave the coalition.

The Pseudo-Algorithm shown in Box 1 describes the procedure used by the agents to make a decision concerning joining, leaving or remaining in a coalition. When agent A_i is a *Coalition Member*, it checks whether its payoff is greater than or equal to the highest payoff achieved by its neighbors (A_m). If so, it increases its trust on its leader and remains on the coalition; otherwise, it decreases its trust on its leader and checks whether its trust value dropped below a specified threshold. If so, it becomes *Independent*. On the other hand, when the agent A_i is *Independent*, it checks whether its payoff is less than or equal to the worst payoff among its neighbors (A_k) and, if so, it joins the coalition of the neighbor with the highest payoff. Otherwise, it remains *Independent*. In the case the neighbor with highest payoff is also *Independent*, then they form a new coalition and the agent with higher payoff assumes the role of *Coalition Leader* and the other the role of *Coalition Member*.

Summing up, the *T&C* model simulation step is summarized as a sequence of operations as presented in Pseudo-Algorithm (Box 1, Box 2).

Basically, at each simulation step (SimulationStep) an agent begins by deciding its action (Cooperate or Defect) to play against its neighbors. Such single action is used to play against all of its neighbors (decideAction). Next, it calculates its payoff based on its neighbors chosen actions, considering the payoff matrix presented in Table 1 (calculatePayoff). Once calculated, the agent that

Box 1. Pseudo-Algorithm: Agent decision procedure related to joining/remaining/leaving coalitions

```
decideTrustBasedCoalition(A_i, A_m, A_k)
// A_i – Deciding agent
// A_m – Highest payoff agent
// A_k – Lowest payoff agent
if isCoalitionMember(A_i){
  if(Payoff(A_i) ≥ Payoff(A_m)){
  trustLeader = Min(100, (trustLeader + deltaTrust))
  }
  else {
  trustLeader = Max(0, (trustLeader - deltaTrust))
  if (trustLeader < trustThreshold){
  Independence(A_i)
  }
  }
  }
  // Is independent
  else {
  if(Payoff(A_i) ≤ Payoff(A_k)){
  JoinCoalition(A_m)
  }
  }
```

Box 2. Pseudo-Algorithm: T&C model sequence of operations

```
T&Csimulation
// M – simulation steps
for I = 1 to M{
  SimulationStep()
}

SimulationStep()
  for all A_i in N{
  decideAction (A_i)
  calculatePayoff (A_i)
  }
  for all Ai in N{
  if isCoalitionMember(A_i){
  sendPayoffLeader (A_i)
  }
  }
  for all Ai in N{
  if isCoalitionLeader(A_i){
  splitPayoff(A_i)
  }
  }
  A_m = neighbor with highest payoff agent
  A_k = neighbor with lowest payoff
  decideTrustBasedCoalition(A_i, A_m, A_k)
```

is member of a coalition sends its payoff to its *Coalition Leader*, which keeps for itself a percentage of the amount, correspondent to the tax, and split the remaining amount evenly among its members

(splitPayoff). Finally, the agent takes a decision with respect to the coalition (decideCoalition): an *Independent* agent decides to remain independent or join a coalition; a *Coalition Member* agent decides to remain in a coalition, increasing or decreasing its trust on the leader, or to leave it.

Implementation

The implementation of agent-based models in HPC environments imposes several infrastructure and modeling challenges. The former are related to software and hardware used to implement and execute the simulation in these environments, whilst the latter are mainly related to the agents' interdependence and interactions, and how to implement the model in a high-parallelized environment without losing its corresponding benefits.

In order to describe the *T&C* model implementation, we first provide a brief overview of the Repast HPC toolkit features that was used to implement it. For a detailed understanding of its capabilities and features, see (Collier & North, 2012).

It is worth noting that any large-scale ABMS HPC tool would support the main purposes of this chapter, which is not related to performance analysis or demonstration of tools' features, but aims to support an analysis of the simulation dynamics in different environment topologies. Nonetheless, our motivation to use the Repast HPC toolkit was based on several reasons: (i) its greatest advantages concerning flexibility and general use, due to its easy structure based on contexts and projections; (ii) its capability of handling transparently all required inter-process communication and agents status synchronization tasks; and (iii) its support for the Blue Gene/P supercomputer, which was the target machine for performing our large-scale experiments.

Repast HPC (Collier & North, 2012) (http://repast.sourceforge.net/repast_hpc.html) is a cross-platform C++ based environment to run large-scale agent models developed at Argonne

National Laboratory (http://www.anl.gov/). It is composed of five major architectural components:

- **Time Scheduler:** It coordinates and synchronizes the flow of agent activities (agent events) guaranteeing a consistent simulation execution.
- **Agent:** It represents a simulation element and holds its internal state information.
- **Context:** It is a simple container that groups *Agents* of the same type together.
- **Projection:** It imposes a structure to the *Agents* in a *Context*. The structure defines the *Agents* relationships by using the semantics of the projection. Three projection semantics are available: *Network*, *Grid*, and *Continuous Space*.
- **Data Collector:** It gathers agents' information and produces output files composed of aggregated or non-aggregated data from all simulation processes.

Repast HPC enables distributed simulation runs over multiple processes that communicate and share agents using Message Passing Interface (MPI). The processes run in parallel and memory is not shared across processes. Each individual process is responsible for executing a subset of all the agents in the simulation, called *local* agents. Copies of *non-local* agents (agents from other processes) may reside on a process, allowing agents to be shared among processes. However, these copies can only be accessed for reading purposes and status synchronization from the original agent to its copies shall be performed in order to have their status remotely updated.

All simulations in Repast HPC are managed by a set of controllers, which manage all architectural components described above. At the beginning of the simulation, the controllers create a set of *Agents* and associate them to *Contexts*. *Projections* are then created and associated to these *Contexts* with the purpose of establishing the *Agents* relationships. After this initial setup, *Agents* are triggered

and they create events, whose ordering and execution are respectively established and performed by the *Time Scheduler*. These events are generated in steps and the simulation runs until a predefined condition is met or a specified number of steps is reached. During the execution, aggregated or non-aggregated information may be gathered and written into files by the *Data Collector*.

In order to implement the *T&C* model using the Repast HPC, first a set of n agents of the same type are created and grouped into a single *Context*. The *Context* is associated to an $n_x \times n_y$ *Grid Projection*, where $n = n_x \times n_y$, in which the agents are positioned one at each cell of the grid. In order to parallelize the simulation, the grid is split into m processes, which must be a divisor of n. Therefore, each process becomes responsible to execute a subset of the agents. However, since each process executes in a different processor (with no shared memory) and coalition formation may require communication among agents under the management of different processes, every process must provide a read-only copy of its running agents in order to allow their information (i.e. payoffs) to be accessed.

The simulation proceeds with each process executing the sequence of operations described in the Pseudo-Algorithm shown in Box 2. Each process begins by executing the decideAction operation; however, due to the processes' parallel execution and the need for their synchronized continuation, after this operation execution two operations must be added: (1) a first operation (MPI_Barrier) that allows all processes to finish their execution before the simulation continues (support the simultaneous actions); and (2) a second operation (synchronization) operation that replicates the new agents' status among all processes.

Next, the agents calculate their payoff based on their neighbors action (calculatePayoff), and once again, the two extra operations, block and synchronization, must be performed.

Differently from the operation splitPayoff in the Pseudo-Algorithm shown in Box 2, in the parallelized version this operation must be divided in two: leadersCollectPayoff and memberCollectPayoff. In the leadersCollectPayoff operation, the leaders collect the payoff from its members and sum them up, subtract the tax, and calculate the member's payoff. Then, the memberCollectPayoff operation is executed in which the member agents gather from the leader such information. The reason for such division is due to the fact that the members cannot send their payoffs to their leader since they may be in different processes, thus not being allowed to update the leader internal payoff state and vice-versa.

Finally, the agents take a decision with respect to the coalition (decideCoalition) and their statuses are updated and synchronized among all the processes in order to begin a new simulation step.

Despite the simplicity of the sequential execution, the *T&C* model characteristics impose two main challenges when implemented in a parallel environment: *simultaneous actions* and *interaction among all the agents*. *Simultaneous actions* slow down the simulation because they require that all the processes execute synchronously; however, it does not cause great impact considering an environment composed of homogeneous processors and executing the same amount of agent operations. On the other hand, *interaction among all the agents* is more critical as it requires that all the agents access information from every other, for instance to check if some other agent picked it as a leader. Obviously, this fact causes high communication overhead and hence diminishes the simulation performance as a whole. Regardless of that, since our purpose here is the analysis of the model's behavior invariance with respect to scale and topology rather than how fast it performs, such drawback does not have a greater impact in this work.

EXPERIMENTS

In this section, we describe the experiments performed using the *T&C* model in order to analyze its invariance when scale and topology change. These experiments are a set of simulation scenarios formed as a combination of differing settings related to scale and topology. Basically, the former defines the *environment size* variable, which specifies the number of agents in the simulation. The topology is divided in two variables: *environment topology* and *neighborhood topology*. The *environment topology* specifies whether the simulation environment is a *grid* or a *torus*; while the *neighborhood topology* specifies how many and which are the interacting neighbors of an agent (*Moore and Von Neumann* neighborhoods). The sixteen scenarios created by combining these variables are summarized in Table 2.

The *environment size* variable values listed in Table 2 were chosen in order to enable the analysis of the simulation dynamics as the num-

Table 2. Experimental scenarios

Scenario	Environment Size	Environment Topology	Neighborhood Topology
1	484	Grid	Von Neumann
2	484	Grid	Moore
3	484	Torus	Von Neumann
4	484	Torus	Moore
5	1024	Grid	Von Neumann
6	1024	Grid	Moore
7	1024	Torus	Von Neumann
8	1024	Torus	Moore
9	16384	Grid	Von Neumann
10	16384	Grid	Moore
11	16384	Torus	Von Neumann
12	16384	Torus	Moore
13	102400	Grid	Von Neumann
14	102400	Grid	Moore
15	102400	Torus	Von Neumann
16	102400	Torus	Moore

ber of agents increase. The reason for beginning with 484 (22 x 22 agents) is due to its similarity to the *environment size* (21 x 21 agents) used in (Nardin & Sichman, 2011), allowing therefore a comparison for validation purposes. The other values escalate in the order of magnitude of 10, limited to 102400, since the time constraint imposed by our computing infrastructure is 48 hours; as scenarios of this size already consumes around 35 hours to run, we could not escalate the execution to larger scales or longer simulations.

In addition to the already described settings, the *T&C* model requires several other input parameters in order to execute the *T&C* model as listed in Table 3. They were fixed for all the simulation scenarios. These values were adopted based on the results we have obtained in (Nardin & Sichman, 2011); their actual values do not have a great impact in this work, since our goal is to analyze the invariance of the simulation dynamics by varying the scale and topology. In the experiments, all the agents consider trust to decide whether to join/remain/leave a coalition (Consider Trust = 100%), and all of them increase or decrease at each step their trust on their coalition leader by 15 (Delta Trust).

Each scenario was executed 10 times, and for each step the mean values of the following twelve metrics were calculated:

1. Number of coalitions (*numCoalitions*).

Table 3. Fixed input parameters

Parameter	Value
Steps	1000
Tax	25%
Consider Trust	100%
Delta Trust	15
Trust Threshold	50
Strategy	pTFT, TFT and Random

2. Number of created coalitions (*created Coalitions*).

3. Number of destroyed coalitions (*destroyed Coalitions*).

4. Number of agents that become *Coalition Members* (*numInChanges*).

5. Number of agents that become *Independent* (*numOutChanges*).

6. Number of *Coalition Member* or *Coalition Leader* agents (*numAgentsCoalitions*).

7. Number of *Independent* agents (*numAgentsIndependent*).

8. Number of TFT *Independent* agents (*numIndependentTFT*).

9. Number of pTFT *Independent* agents (*numIndependentpTFT*).

10. Number of Random *Independent* agents (*numIndependentRandom*).

11. *Coalition Member* or *Coalition Leader* agents' payoff (*coalitionPayoff*).

12. *Independent* agents' payoff (*independent Payoff*).

The experiments were developed using Repast for HPC version 1.0.1. Although the model could be executed in nearly any parallel environment, the *T&C* model was implemented for and executed on the Blue Gene/P supercomputer (BG/P) available at Rice University, since this University has an agreement with our University for sharing this HPC resource. All simulations were executed using the BGP/P DUAL mode, which divides each node composed of 4 GB RAM and 4 processors between 2 processes, thus giving a 2 GB RAM and 2 processors per process. For the full specifications of the BG/P supercomputing, see Research Computing Support Group (http://www.rcsg.rice.edu/sharecore/bluegenep/).

Despite not being the focus of this work, Table 4 presents the execution time of simulation scenarios using different number of processes, considering a *grid environment topology* and *Moore neighborhood topology*. As it may be observed, there is an advantage in executing the model in

Table 4. Simulation scenarios mean execution time

Environment Size	Number of Processes	Mean Time (Seconds)
484	01	464.850
484	04	214.282
484	121	192.084
1024	01	2003.869
1024	04	703.758
1024	16	380.923
1024	64	324.112
1024	256	408.382
16384	16	35319.700
16384	64	11930.700
102400	256	124062.800

parallel; however, in our experiments it seems to reach a saturation point in the *environment size* 1024, since the execution time begins to increase as more processes (256) are added.

ANALYSIS

This section provides an analysis of the simulation results obtained in the different scenarios and discusses the effects of scale and topology in the *T&C* model. The section is divided in three subsections; each one describing a characteristic effect in the *T&C* model dynamics.

Scale Effect

In this section, we aim to answer the following question:

Does a variation in the number of agents in the environment affect coalition formation dynamics in the T&C model?

Figure 2(a) and (b) displays, respectively, the evolution of two metrics collected in a *Grid* environment adopting *Moore* neighborhood: the mean coalition size and the number of coalitions. In this experiment, we varied the number of agents in the environment, presented in each quadrants

Figure 2. Evolution of the T&C model simulation dynamics in a Grid environment and Moore neighborhood, varying the environment size

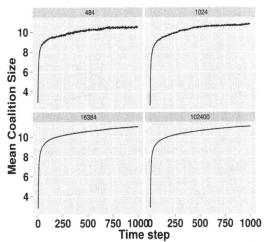

Figure 2(a). Mean coalition size

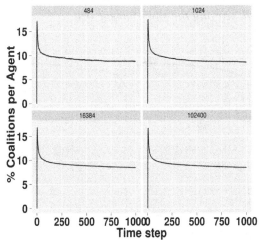

Figure 2(b). Number of coalitions normalized by the number of agents

label, and normalized the results. Analyzing these figures, it is possible to observe that even changing the environment size, the simulation dynamics regarding the coalition formation continues to be very similar concerning their curvature shape and scale. Figure 2(a) suggests that coalitions are rapidly formed at the beginning of the simulation with a size of around 10 agents on step 250 and presenting a slightly increase later on the simulation. Figure 2(b) indicates that in all the *environment sizes* the dynamic of coalition formation are similar.

Interestingly, we have also identified that for almost all the twelve collected metrics, the proportionality is very similar among different *environment sizes* scenarios. For example, the proportion of agents that are coalition members in the last 100 simulation steps was 92.56%, 92.76%, 93.37%, and 93.48%, respectively for *environment sizes* of 484, 1024, 16384, and 102400.

Based on these evidences, the answer to the question is that, in our experiments, the number of agents in the environment does not affect coalition formation dynamics in the *T&C* model.

Environment Topology Effect

Differently from the previous section, in this section we are interested to analyze the effect of changing the *environment topology* from *grid* to *torus*. Therefore, the question we aim to answer is the following:

Does a variation in the environment topology affect the coalition formation dynamics in the T&C model?

In order to answer this question, we have repeated the experiments, adopting now a *Torus* environment, presented in Figure 3(a) and (b). We compared these results with the simulation dynamics presented in Figure 2(a) and (b), where we used a *Grid* environment. This comparison is summarized in Table 5.

If we observe Figures 2 and 3, as well as Table 5, it is possible to identify that there is no dynamics change between the two environment topologies. Therefore, we may conclude that the environment topology does not affect *T&C* model coalition formation dynamics.

Figure 3. Evolution of the T&C model simulation dynamics in a Torus environment and Moore neighborhood, varying the environment size

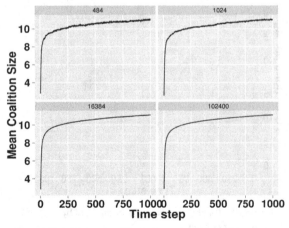

Figure 3(a). Mean coalition size

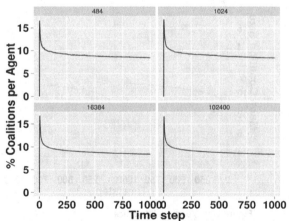

Figure 3(b). Number of coalitions normalized by the number of agents

Table 5. Comparison between the Mean Coalition Size and Normalized Coalitions in the Grid and Torus environment topology

Environment Size	Environment Topology			
	Grid		Torus	
	Mean Coalition Size	Normalized Coalitions*	Mean Coalition Size	Normalized Coalitions*
484	10.34	0.0894	11.03	0.0849
1024	10.74	0.0863	10.87	0.0960
16384	11.03	0.0846	11.09	0.0843
102400	11.03	0.0847	11.07	0.0844

* Number of coalitions divided by the number of agents.

Neighborhood Topology Effect

Finally, we in the final experiment we are interested to analyze the effect caused by changing the *neighborhood topology* (*Moore* and *Von Neumann* neighborhoods).in the T&C model coalition formation dynamics. Thus, the posed question is the following:

Does a variation in the neighborhood topology affect the coalition formation dynamics in the T&C model?

In order to answer this question, we have repeated the experiments represented in Figures 2 and 3, changing their *neighborhood topology*. Figures 4 and 5 respectively show the evolution of the mean coalition size and the number of coalitions, in a *Grid* and *Torus* environment, but

Figure 4. Evolution of the T&C model simulation dynamics in a Grid environment and Von Neumann neighborhood, varying the environment size

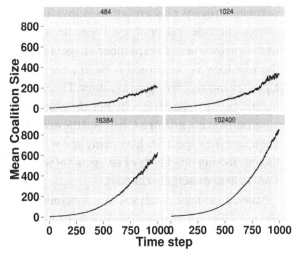

Figure 4(a). Mean coalition size

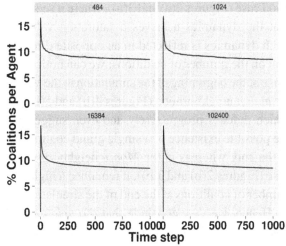

Figure 4(b). Number of coalitions normalized by the number of agents

Figure 5. Evolution of the T&C model simulation dynamics in a Torus environment and Von Neumann neighborhood, varying the environment size

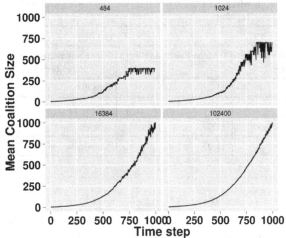

Figure 5(a). Mean coalition size

Figure 5(b). Number of coalitions normalized by the number of agents

adopting now in both experiments a *Von Neumann* neighborhood. By a simple visual comparison both between Figures 2 and 4, and between Figures 3 and 5, one can clearly identify that there is an important change on the simulation dynamics.

Concerning the coalition sizes, in the *Von Neumann* neighborhood (Figures 4(a) and 5(a)), the sizes are progressively increasing during the simulation, differently from the *Moore* neighborhood case (Figures 2(a) and 3(a)), where it seems that the dynamics achieves a saturation value. Such dynamics is reflected in an opposite direction on the number of coalitions: we can notice a spike at the beginning of the simulation in the *Von Neumann* neighborhood (Figures 4(b) and 5(b)), which reduces progressively and even suggests the possible existence of a single grand coalition at the end, whereas in the *Moore* neighborhood case (Figures 2(b) and 3(b)), it remained a higher number of coalitions at the end of the simulation.

Hence, we may conclude that the *neighborhood topology* affects the *T&C* model dynamics. However, we may not conclude at the moment whether such change is for worst or better; in order

to draw such conclusion, we must contextualize the model into a real scenario for evaluation.

CONCLUSION

In this work, we performed some experiments using the *Trust and Coalition* model implemented in the Repast HPC toolkit. We analyzed the experiments results concerning their invariance to changes in scale and topology. The scale is related to the *environment size* (number of agents) while the topology is concerned both to *environment topology* and *neighborhood topology*. The *environment topology* specifies whether the simulation environment is a *grid* or a *torus*; and the *neighborhood topology* specifies how many and which are the interacting neighbors of an agent (*Moore* and *Von Neumann* neighborhoods).

Based on such analysis, we concluded that the *environment size* and *environment topology* does not affect the coalition formation dynamics, while the *neighborhood topology* affects it significantly, causing the evolution and outcome to be completely different. A possible explanation for the invariance regarding the first two characteristics, and the variation regarding the *neighborhood topology,* is related to the fact that agents' interactions are local. We hypothesize that such agent's restricted view prevents them from being affected by some changes in the environment characteristics, consequently eliminating the variance on its outcomes. Yet, by changing their local interaction characteristic, represented by their neighborhood, there is a possible cause for the dynamics change.

Even though we have provided an analysis with respect to scale and topology variation, we know that further work is necessary to gain a better insight about the robustness of different models with respect to structural variations. First of all, we intend to repeat our experiments with input parameter values different from the ones adopted and shown in Table 3. Moreover, as future work, we intend to explore the model's robustness by, for instance, varying other structural properties or using other topologies, such as implementing the model using network topologies.

ACKNOWLEDGMENT

We would like to acknowledge the support of Laboratório de Computação Científica Avançada, LCCA/CCE (Universidade de São Paulo), which has an agreement with the Research Computing Support Group (Rice University), that enables us to use the needed computing time on the Blue Gene/P supercomputer. Jaime S. Sichman and Luciano M. Rosset are partially supported by CNPq/Brazil.

REFERENCES

Axelrod, R. (1997). Advancing the art of simulation in the social sciences. *Complexity, 3,* 16–22. doi:10.1002/(SICI)1099-0526(199711/12)3:2<16::AID-CPLX4>3.0.CO;2-K

Bonabeau, E. (2002). Agent-based modeling: methods and techniques for simulating human systems. *Proceedings of the National Academy of Sciences of the United States of America, 99,* 7280–7287. doi:10.1073/pnas.082080899 PMID:12011407

Cioffi-Revilla, C. (2002). Invariance and universality in social agent-based simulations. *Proceedings of the National Academy of Sciences of the United States of America, 99,* 7314–7316. doi:10.1073/pnas.082081499 PMID:12011412

Coakley, S., Gheorghe, M., Holcombe, M., Chin, S., Worth, D., & Greenough, C. (2012). Exploitation of high performance computing in the FLAME agent-based simulation framework. In *Proceedings of High Performance Computing and Communication 2012 IEEE 9th International Conference on Embedded Software and Systems (HPCC-ICESS),* (pp. 538-545).

Collier, N., & North, M. (2012). Parallel agent-based simulation with repast for high performance computing. *SIMULATION:Transactions of the Society for Modeling and Simulation International,* 1-21.

Cordasco, G., Chiara, R., Mancuso, A., Mazzeo, D., Scarano, V., & Spagnuolo, C. (2011). A framework for distributing agent-based simulations. Euro-Par 2011: Parallel Processing Workshops, 7155, 460-470. Berlin: Springer.

Dasgupta, P. (2000). Trust as a commodity? In D. Gambetta (Ed.), *Trust: Making and breaking cooperative relations* (pp. 49–72). Oxford, UK: Department of Sociology, University Oxford.

Dongarra, J. J., & van der Steen, A. J. (2012). High-performance computing systems: Status and outlook. *Acta Numerica, 21*, 379–474. doi:10.1017/S0962492912000050

Fan, Z., Qiu, F., Kaufman, A., & Yoakum-Stover, S. (2004). GPU cluster for high performance computing. In *Proceedings of the 2004 ACM/IEEE conference on Supercomputing (SC '04)* (pp. 47). IEEE Computer Society.

Flache, A., & Hegselmann, R. (2001). Do irregular grids make a difference? Relaxing the spatial regularity assumption in cellular models of social dynamics. *Journal of Artificial Societies and Social Simulation, 4*(4).

Gilbert, G. N. (2008). *Agent-based models*. Los Angeles, CA: Sage.

Gotts, N. M., & Polhill, J. G. (2010). Size matters: Large-scale replications of experiments with FEARLUS. *Advances in Complex Systems, 13*(4), 453–467. doi:10.1142/S0219525910002670

Li, X., Mao, W., Zeng, D., & Wang, F. (2008). Agent-based social simulation and modeling in social computing. In C. C. Yang, H. Chen, M. Chau, K. Chang, S. Lang, & P. S. Chen et al. (Eds.), *Intelligence and security informatics. LNCS 5075* (pp. 401–412). Berlin: Springer. doi:10.1007/978-3-540-69304-8_41

Montañola-Sales, C., Rubio-Campillo, X., Casanovas-Garcia, J., Cela-Espín, J. M., & Kaplan-Marcusán, A. (2014). Large-scale social simulation, dealing with complexity challenges in high performance environments. In D. F. Adamatti, G. P. Dimuro, & H. Coelho (Eds.), *Interdisciplinary applications of agent-based social simulation and modeling*. Hershey, PA: IGI Global.

Murphy, J. T. (2011). Computational social science and high performance computing: A case study of a simple model at large scales. In *Proceedings of the 2011 Computational Social Science Society of America Annual Conference*.

Nardin, L. G., & Sichman, J. S. (2011). Simulating the impact of trust in coalition formation: A preliminary analysis. In G. P. Dimuro, A. C. da Rocha Costa, J. Sichman, D. Adamatti, P. Tedesco, J. Balsa, & L. Antunes (Ed.), *Advances in Social Simulation, Post-Proceedings of the Brazilian Workshop on Social Simulation* (pp. 33-40). IEEE Computer Society.

Nowak, M. A., & May, R. M. (1992). Evolutionary games and spatial chaos. *Nature, 359*, 826–829. doi:10.1038/359826a0

Research Computing Support Group. (n. d.). *Website*. Retrieved from http://www.rcsg.rice.edu/sharecore/bluegenep/

Scheutz, M., Schermerhorn, P., Connaughaton, R., & Dingler, A. (2006). SWAGES: An extendable distributed experimentation system for large-scale agent-based ALife simulations. In *Proceedings of the 10th International Conference on the Simulation and Synthesis of Living Systems*.

Sweeney, L. B., & Meadows, D. (2010). *The systems thinking playbook*. White River Junction, VT: Chelsea Green Publishing.

Urbig, D., Lorenz, J., & Herzberg, H. (2008). Opinion dynamics: The effect of the number of peers met at once. *Journal of Artificial Societies and Social Simulation, 11*(2).

Wittek, P., & Rubio-Campillo, X. (2012). Scalable agent-based modelling with cloud HPC resources for social simulations. *Cloud Computing Technology and Science (CloudCom), 2012 IEEE 4th International Conference on* (pp. 355-362). IEEE Computer Society.

KEY TERMS AND DEFINITIONS

Agent-Based Social Simulation (ABSS): Agent-Based Social Simulation (ABSS) is the intersection among social science, computer simulation and agent-based computing whose main purpose is to provide models and tools for simulating social phenomena.

Coalition Formation: Coalition formation corresponds to mechanisms that allow the creation of alliances among agents. These coalitions usually have a specified time of duration or convenience in which the agents cooperate in order to benefit from such association.

High-Performance Computing: The term High-Performance Computing is any computational activity that aggregates computing resources in a way to deliver higher computing capabilities than one could get out of a single processor computer. HPC platforms are distributed systems composed of collections of independent processing units running in parallel. Their architectures are classified according to the coupling degree among their processing units.

Invariance: Invariance is a characteristic of agent-based simulation models in which the change of critical set of assumptions, parameters, or dimensions do not cause the change in the findings obtained through the model.

Large-Scale Simulation: Large-Scale Simulation means the execution of agent-based simulation models composed of a large number of agents.

Repast HPC: Repast HPC is Ana agent-based simulation platform that enables distributed runs over multiple processes that communicate and share agents using Message Passing Interface (MPI).

Trust: Trust is an estimate that an individual has about the actions to be taken by another individual, which directly affects himself, and is unknown at the time needed to decide which action should be taken.

Chapter 4
Exploring Emergence within Social Systems with Agent Based Models

Marcia R. Friesen
University of Manitoba, Canada

Richard Gordon
Gulf Specimen Marine Laboratory, USA & Wayne State University, USA

Robert D. McLeod
University of Manitoba, Canada

ABSTRACT

In this chapter, the authors examine manifestations of emergence or apparent emergence in agent based social modeling and simulation, and discuss the inherent challenges in building real world models and in defining, recognizing and validating emergence within these systems. The discussion is grounded in examples of research on emergence by others, with extensions from within our research group. The works cited and built upon are explicitly chosen as representative samples of agent-based models that involve social systems, where observation of emergent behavior is a sought-after outcome. The concept of the distinctiveness of social from abiotic emergence in terms of the use of global parameters by agents is introduced.

INTRODUCTION

This chapter explores agent based modeling (ABM) of social systems that involve or demonstrate aspects of emergence. Although many real world social systems display emergence, the modeling of an agent based social system that may demonstrate emergence is fraught with difficul-

ties, as emergence is inherently ethereal and/or ephemeral - that is, difficult to capture objectively. If one has explicitly coded for emergent behavior, then it is really *not* emergent as it is an expected or anticipated result. In this chapter, several instances of real and modeled emergence are illustrated and discussed, with a focus on the difficulties in identifying and defining true emergence that arises

DOI: 10.4018/978-1-4666-5954-4.ch004

unpredictably and not from modelers' decisions. In this work, emergences are conceptualized as agent- and/or group-level phenomena that are not specifically encoded by the modeler. While emergence is often thought of as a behavioral whole that is greater than the sum of its parts, in our conceptualization, emergence can manifest at large or small scales, may be a complex or a simple phenomenon, and may be counterintuitive or not. Emergence begins when the outcomes of a simulation cannot be tied back directly to the encoded agent behavioral rules and profiles.

Agent based modeling is 'bottom-up' systems modeling from the perspective of constituent parts. Systems are modeled as a collection of agents (in social systems, most often people) imbued with properties: characteristics, behaviors (actions), and interactions that attempt to capture actual properties of individuals. In the most general context, agents are both adaptive and autonomous entities who are able to assess their situation, make decisions, compete or cooperate with one another on the basis of a set of rules, and adapt future behaviors on the basis of past interactions. Agent properties may be conceived by the modeler or may be derived from actual data that reasonably describe agents' behaviors – i.e. their movements and their interactions with other agents. The emergence of a data culture, also called 'big data' and associated 'big data analytics', offers new opportunities to use real world data, even in real time, as inputs into ABMs. The modeler's task is to determine which data sources best govern agent profiles in a given ABM simulation. There are alternative ABM approaches that attempt to introduce even greater levels of agency, including other-regarding behaviors and social dilemmas (Goldstone & Janssen, 2005; Helbing, Yu, & Rauhut, 2011). The ABMs considered here are considerably simpler, but their interactivity in terms of agent contact and mobility is often more detailed.

The foundational premise and the conceptual depth of ABM is that simple rules of individual behavior will aggregate to illuminate complex and/or emergent group-level phenomena *that are not specifically encoded by the modeler*, and this is the key characteristic of emergence within an ABM. Emergent behavior may be counterintuitive, and may be a simple or complex behavioral whole that is greater than the sum of its parts (Swan, Gordon, & Seckbach, 2012). However, we do not regard "surprise" as an essential component of emergence (Ronald, Sipper, & Capcarrère, 1999; Gordon, 2000; Ronald & Sipper, 2001), if only because experience with emergent systems reduces one's sense of surprise.

There are a number of modeling efforts which imply or reference emergence within social systems. Often, the evidence for emergence is an observation that is unexpected, anecdotal, or circumstantial. As defined in (Wikipedia, 2013c): "In philosophy, systems theory, science, and art, emergence is the way complex systems and patterns arise out of a multiplicity of relatively simple interactions." While asserting that emergent behavior does not necessarily need to be complex, we propose that when it *is* complex, the complex behavior may also arise from relatively complex interactions, as would more likely be the case with biological systems. In either case, the modeling community likely displays a bias, tending to overload the term 'emergence' and/or to identify outcomes as emergent that are not truly emergent. Although not a bibliographic survey, a Google search of the phrase "modeling emergence" reports just over 5 million results. A Web of Knowledge search "Title=(model* emergen*) NOT Title=(emergency)" yielded nearly 1300 publications. We have also been guilty of this bias, and in this chapter we attempt to objectively add to the evolving modeling framework of emergent phenomena. More specifically, there is no doubt that there are considerable emergent phenomena; it is the modeling of such which is problematic or at least embryonic. Indeed, the phrase 'modeling emergence' is an oxymoron in that we are adhering to the premise that emergence cannot be explicitly modeled. The ability of system-level outcomes to elude simple prediction based on the known rules that govern agent behavior is a cornerstone of emergence.

Overall, the work in this chapter is grounded in the objective to explore social models at various combinations of scale, purpose, and input parameters. The scales range from less than 100 agents in a confined space to tens-of-thousands of agents over a wide geographic region and in a virtual space (social network). Purposes range from modeling memes in social media, to infection spread modeling for influenza outbreaks, to crowd movements for mass gatherings. Input parameters included published data, synthesized data, and real-world data such as cellular phone service records. Within this diversity and range in the work, the common thread is this chapter is the objective to trigger the manifestations of emergence from relatively simple frameworks, knowing that such emergence is elusive and – by definition – cannot be deliberately designed. The philosophy of this chapter aligns with the view that "emergence is much studied, but this does not mean it is well understood" (Conte et al., 2012).

First, a model of an ABM of an electronic social network extends the work of (Rand & Rust, 2011) who address how ABMs can illuminate emergence of complex marketing phenomena. The work is extended here to include electronic word-of-mouth as a marketing strategy, incorporating an ABM for modeling a Facebook post, with the objective to glean additional insights on potential emergence. Subsequently, three ABMs of crowd behaviors are demonstrated to explore unexpected behavior that may qualify as emergent behavior. The first ABM extends a simple parlor game recast as an ABM by (Bonabeau, 2002), with our extension to Bonabeau's work including modifications to input conditions. The second ABM is a model of agents exiting a building under an alarm condition, extending the work of Helbing, Farkas, and Vicsek (2000). With only simply agent behavior profiles, an emergent behavior was seen in the outcome of the simulation as agents aggregated and segregated

unexpectedly. The last crowd ABM is that of the Hajj mass gathering event and in particular the performing of Tawaf, with the objective to explore potential emergence within a large scale phenomenon. Glimpses of emergence were observed in pilgrim density variations. Finally, an ABM was developed to model human movement patterns within the context of infectious disease spread, using real-world data from cell phone subscribers as inputs to agent behaviors. This social model, highly tuned to agent proximity and contact, illustrated that infection spread demonstrated some spatial variation. In all of these explorations of social simulation, insights were gleaned relative to the ABM purposes, ranging from crowd movements, infection spread, and meme propagation. Instances of emergence were subtle and tenuous, but nonetheless provided insights into the phenomenon. Other ABMs (Helbing, Yu & Rauhut 2011) support the notion that mobility can play a significant role in demonstrating emergence, although those models are extremely simple and do not reflect real individuals and human movement pattern data.

Other authors in this volume hold complementary notions on the role ABMs may play in triggering, observing, or explaining emergence within social systems. In (Castelfranchi, 2014), the idea of an ABM shedding light on the "invisible hand" is explored, which is aligned with our position on the inherent nature of emergence as well as its elusive qualities that make it hard to definitively identify. (Montañola-Sales et al., 2014) argue that some ABMs may require high performance computing to create the potential to shed light on emergence, which we similarly demonstrate in our work in this chapter when agent populations become very large. (Arciero et al., 2014) aim at "integrating the multi-agent methods into the traditional macroeconomic thinking" as a means "of catching unexpected actions and behavior" in particular when markets go awry, and (Carbonara, 2014) investigates an agent-based model of the process of geographical clustering of firms (agents) as a form of emergent behavior. These works share some basic assumptions and approaches to our work in this chapter, and demonstrate the dangers of explicitly designing models for emergence.

EMERGENT BEHAVIOUR WITHIN AGENT BASED MODELS

Examples of emergence are often found in nature or natural systems (e.g. (Tyson, 2007; Swan, Gordon, & Seckbach, 2012)), although the agents in these examples are typically not people. Modelers have attempted to create ABMs that will replicate these known and observed emergent phenomena, without coding for them explicitly. These examples all have properties and behaviors that "emerge," with no one directing and no theory that predicts the new characteristics from knowledge of the constituents alone. The examples below implicitly involve human social systems, modeling people as agents. We discuss ABMs related to marketing, crowd behaviors, disease epidemic spreads, and traffic movement. These examples are given as prototypical social systems that are both easily modeled and also have the potential to display emergence.

Marketing

Marketing has a long and interesting history of observing and modifying social behavior, with the more interesting marketing strategies resulting in polar opposites of the intended results, such as the "Osborne Effect" where a pre-announcement of product release can have an extreme negative impact on its future sales (Osborne & Dvorak, 1984). In these situations, it is debatable whether any model would have been able to predict or anticipate agent reaction. In less extreme marketing scenarios, a company may be more interested in how to best deploy marketing resources to

optimize a product's adoption, which is an obvious opportunity for agent based models and simulations. For example, (Rand & Rust, 2011) examine production adoption via ABM with an emphasis on strategies to validate the ABM approach. Agents (simulated people) are exposed to a product through two forms of information processes. An adoption is made by the agent, formulated on a probabilistic decision based on mass media as well as a probabilistic decision based on the number of adopters within an agent's social neighborhood, modeled as a small world network parameterized by an increasing minimum vertex degree. Although the underlying network is highly abstracted, the ABM allows an experimenter to vary the connectivity associated with the small world network. This model has features of agent interaction, local communication, global communication, and a mild form of potential emergence. The phenomenon modeled exhibits similarities to a disease or infection spread model with familiar stylized S-curves of adoption.

ABM Extensions in Marketing

Our extensions to existing efforts include incorporating the role of social media (e.g. Facebook) in transmitting product information into the ABM. The research is similar to (Rand & Rust, 2011) although the distinction between word of mouth and mass media is blurred as the personal contact network is that of electronic social media. This is well-suited to an ABM as the underlying network and agent behaviors have data support. The tipping point at which a product adoption 'takes off' (where adoption becomes autocatalytic) can potentially be considered an emergent phenomenon. Conversely, if a tipping point is not reached, a product launch can be repeatedly simulated to find the threshold to going viral. Toward this objective, increasingly data are becoming available to allow more realistic modeling of electronic social networks where a word of mouth model of product spread or diffusion would be extended to a real electronic social network as opposed to a synthetic network model.

The fact that we live in a data culture is both good news and bad news. Gathering the datasets and tuning the input or agent parameters in an ABM is considered to be one of the most time-consuming and challenging – but critical - parts of making a realistic ABM. Complementary to the work of (Rand & Rust, 2011), our modeling efforts focus extensively on an ABM of an electronic social network based on Facebook with the objective of exploring potential emergence in a more formal manner.

The exploratory ABM was implemented in the Java-Based educational version of the Anylogic software toolkit (AnyLogic, 2013), which supports Agent-Based, Discrete Event and System Dynamics Modeling. Akin to real online social networks, the environment is a graph where each node represents a user/agent whose social friends are neighbor nodes in the graph. This graph is based on a real-world dataset of Facebook (Gjoka et al., 2010). The graph and its properties are described below.

The model consists of only one type of agent: Facebook users. In delineating the scope of the model, the following simplifying assumptions have to be made:

1. There are many different pieces of content, such as photos, links, status updates, event invites, notes, etc., which can be published on a Facebook Wall page. However, in this work, the word "post" or "note" is used to indicate generic content that is posted on a Wall page.

2. Users cannot send private messages to one another. They can neither make comments on any post nor share any note on somebody else's wall except for their own wall; in other words, they are only able to share something on their own wall.

3. The only possible relationship between users is the bidirectional friendship. This means subscriptions to Pages or Groups held in common between two or more agents, and any other similar features are ignored in the model.

4. Similar to the notification feature in the Facebook, when a user is online, if a friend of theirs shares a note, the user will receive a notification message within the model. As a result, considering Assumption 2, there is no way to receive or potentially save a notification for an offline user.

5. Users cannot make or remove any friendship connections, i.e., no change is allowed to the reality-based network graph.

These assumptions lead to a simplified model relative to the range of activities actually available in Facebook; however, the simplifying assumptions were necessary as a first attempt at a model of this social network. The model keeps an inner state for each user or agent, which controls their behavior. This stochastic hierarchical state machine is shown in Figure 1. All the users are in one of the two general states of Online or Offline. Every time the model restarts, a given so-called Login Rate for switching between these two general states is assigned to each user. The intervals when a user is in the Online state are drawn by an exponential distribution with the mean value of 1440 / (1440 – Login Rate) minutes per day (based on 1440 minutes = 1 day). For example, if the Login rate for a user is defined to be 23 minutes, they will be in the Online and Offline states for 23 and 1417 minutes, in every 24-hour day, respectively. However, since most people tend to check their Facebook profile more than once a day, this 23 minutes is divided into different intervals; and these intervals are drawn by an exponential distribution with the mean value of 1.02 minutes per a day. The choice of the exponential distribution is related to performance issues.

Figure 1. Agent-based state machine for users in an electronic social media

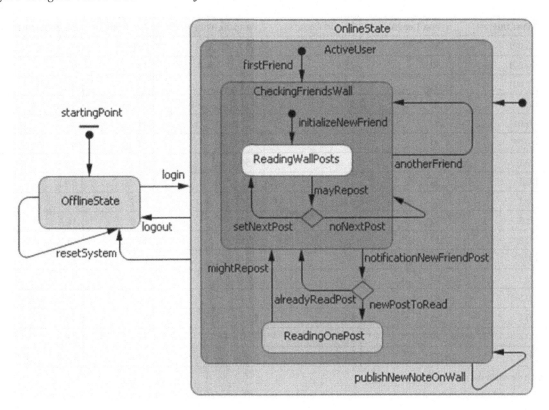

Since it is the default distribution for rate triggers in Anylogic, deploying another distribution would have decreased the speed of simulation.

Results are summarized in Table 1. Simulations were performed under several parameter variations, including the significance of the post or its interest (which affects probabilities of repeating the post), its time to be read, and the number of friends of the initial poster. As per (Rand & Rust, 2011), the model can be validated against real Facebook data as well as stylized behavior. When compared to Facebook, the distribution of the initial post behaves in a qualitatively similar manner (Figure 2) strongly depending on whether a post originates from a person with a small number of friends or from a person with a significantly larger number of friends. Moreover, the median value for most-recent post 'reach' is 19% of a poster's friends after an average 46.8 hours, which is comparable to Facebook's report (Bernstein et

al., 2013). According to this report, the median value for most-recent post 'reach' is 24% of a poster's friends, provided that post was at least 48 hours old.

These statistics build confidence in the model and allow further exploration. For the simulation IDs 1-9, where the post interest is relatively small, ANalysis Of VAriance (ANOVA) yielded a significant effect of *friend count* ($F_{7.53} = 25.07$, $p < 0.01$), no significant effect of *post interest* ($F_{7.53} = 0.22$, $p = 0.8$) and no significant interaction effect on *friend count* × *post interest* ($F_{5.12} = 0.23$, $p = 0.9$). In contrast, for the simulation IDs 9-15, ANOVA yielded a weak effect of *post interest* ($F_{4.88} = 6.29$, $p = 0.0029$), a bit stronger effect of *post length* ($F_{4.88} = 7.07$, $p = 0.0015$) and a significant interaction effect on *post interest* × *post length* ($F_{3.56} = 6.01$, $p < 0.001$).

When exploring the spread of a post, we found it somewhat intuitive that a post that tends to trend

Table 1. Average results of the spread of a post after one week

ID	Post Interest	Post Length	Friend Count	Post Life Time*	No. Read	No. of Repost
1	0.001	30	9	4.50	2.2	0
2	0.001	30	139	7.12	13	0
3	0.001	30	530	13.37	44.7	0
4	0.01	30	9	0.71	2	0
5	0.01	30	139	7.37	11	0
6	0.01	30	530	28.79	57	0.3
7	0.1	30	9	4.59	2	0.2
8	0.1	30	139	12.27	11.42	0.92
9	0.1	30	530	32.67	58.2	4.8
10	0.3	30	530	35.27	89.1	16.4
11	0.5	30	530	76.85	1892.2	640.2
12	0.1	60	530	50.79	34.4	2.3
13	0.3	60	530	52.81	39	7.1
14	0.5	60	530	45.17	56.5	19.1
13	0.1	90	530	29.39	9	0.30
14	0.3	90	530	32.05	11	2.9
15	0.5	90	530	63.79	17.6	3.4

* Last time when the post was read (in hours).

(be propagated) is one that is of short duration, of interest, and launched by a well-connected agent. In this case, the stylized adoption S-curve anticipated from (Rand & Rust, 2011) and from many scenarios of entity spread outside of the marketing field was not readily borne out in this work. For the simulations conducted here, the spread was monotonic as illustrated in Figure 3. Perhaps the absence of spread delay is attributable to characteristics of an electronic social network with greater vertex degrees when compared to

Figure 2. Distribution of audience size in the ABM (Left) and in Facebook (Right) as in (Bernstein 2013)

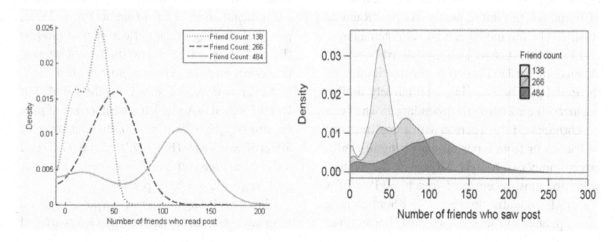

Figure 3. Post spread curve on a log-log scale

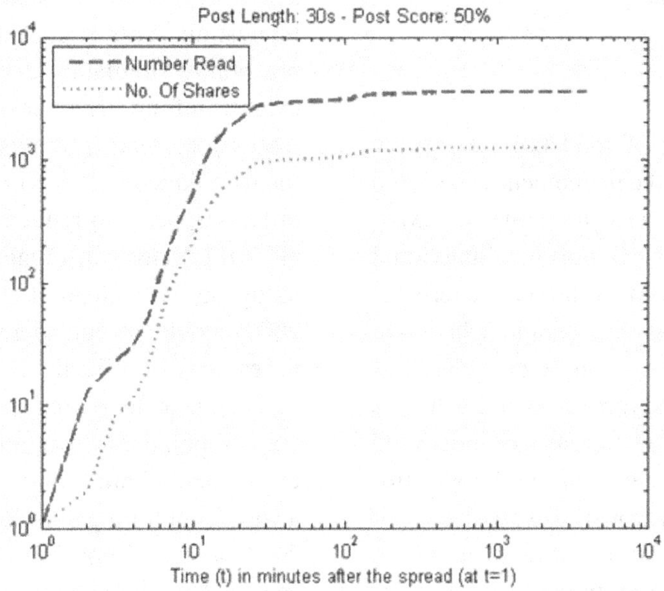

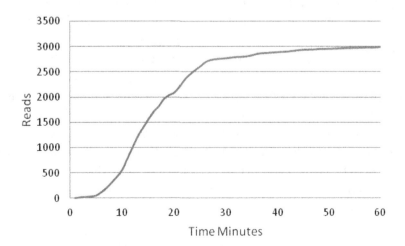

a physical social network augmented by a small number of very highly connected individuals.

An ABM affords the opportunity to explore root causes or critical factors associated with the spread, and such further investigation revealed that a stylized S type adoption curve is only evident for the first hour of a post for these simulations (Figure 4).

The sudden discontinuity associated with re-posting or adoption can be postulated to be one of two consequences. Either the post is reposted by a person with a large number of friends or alternatively a large number of people repost. In the preliminary simulations, the latter appeared to be the case. It may be argued that the adoption trend can be seen as an emergent phenomenon, and it would be difficult to determine this without utilizing an ABM. This may also have an analog in other models of product adoption or even disease / infection spread, as the cause of

Figure 4. Post spread curve S style

the phenomenon may not be readily apparent, intuitive, or identifiable.

Crowds

As a second example of modeling emergence within social systems, the phenomena associated with crowd behaviors were investigated. Existing research on crowds explores how individual behaviors are influenced by the characteristics and behaviors of surrounding people, which – in large enough quantities – can be considered as crowds, and how crowd formation and behavior are impacted by the characteristics of individual people in the crowd. For example, we know intuitively that the nature of crowds and experience of being in crowds varies from culture to culture in accordance with varying cultural rules and norms of personal space, interpersonal interaction, and socialization between sexes. Researchers have investigated pedestrian street crossings where individual agent decisions appear to create a filamentary flow (a group phenomenon). It is a slight extension of one's local information to include that of a person or persons they attempt to follow. This is often modeled by an ABM; however, the apparent emergence is often somewhat predestined by the programmed local decision rules which only make it *appear* that the stream flow is emerging. In fact, a pre-programmed social decision is made by an agent to follow another agent, provided that the opportunity to follow is deemed better than directly moving forward. For example, if one were to model movement in an analog to ant colony behavior where a pheromone trail was emulated, then one would likely induce filamentary flow. If, on the other hand, the program merely limited its agent direction to have the agent take the most direct route to their destination, and always to veer to the right if a head-on collision is imminent, and if a group phenomenon of stream flow were then observed out of these very elementary, agent-bounded rules then one may be able to say that filamentary flow phenomena "emerged" indepen-

dent of the simple rules of individual behavior. There are also swarm based models that generate interesting, if not emergent patterns of behavior, potentially simulating crowd movements. Ants exhibit milling behavior, i.e., continual circular motion for extended periods, which eventually kills them (Wikipedia, 2013b), whereas fish schooling in balls appears to reduce predation (Vaughn et al., 2011). This self-organized pattern, modeled as agents (Lukeman, Li, & Edelstein-Keshet, 2009), could be considered as emergent, if not necessarily beneficial.

Bonabeau explored several interesting examples of ABMs that attempt to demonstrate emergence within groups of people. The first is a simulation of a game (Icosystem Corporation, 2013) where "simple rules of individual behavior can lead to surprisingly coherent system level results" (Bonabeau, 2002). The game is stated as a parlor game, easily simulated, where each agent picks two other agents at random (labeled A and B). In the first instance, each agent is to move about, always keeping their respective agent B between themselves and their respective agent A. In a seemingly small and inconsequential change in the rules of behavior, each agent always attempts to position themselves between their respective chosen agents A and B. In the first instance, the people mill about in a more or less uniform manner, while in the second simulation, they immediately tend to cluster. At first, this appears to be a somewhat surprising or as unexpected collective behavior and, by extension, is possibly emergent. However, if it is easily predicted from the governing rules for agents, perhaps the agents and their interactions are not sophisticated or diverse enough to trigger a truly emergent phenomenon. It was also noticed in the simulation in (Bonabeau, 2002) that the agents have the ability to teleport across the room, making the simulation highly unrealistic as a parlor game and making model-matching with the real world difficult.

Extending Bonabeau's work, one can remove the agent teleportation ability and assign additional properties to the agents (for example, assign gender to each agent and explore the selection of agents A and B based on gender (same, opposite, one of each, etc.). Although this only adds one more level of specificity, it may be just enough to elude simple prediction, which is a cornerstone of the concept of emergence.

We developed an ABM to duplicate the model in (Bonabeau, 2002). Two modes were supported in the ABM: an agent could select two other agents either at random or an agent could select the other agent(s) based on similar gender. Figure 5 illustrates the outcomes, with Figure 5a) as the initial conditions. In Figure 5b), the agents select their A and B agents at random and the selecting agents attempt to position themselves between the agents they have selected. In Figure 5c), the agents select their A and B agents from the same gender and again attempt to position themselves between the agents they have selected. The simulation of Figure 5c) unexpectedly demonstrated the following stylized properties of social systems, without have designed them into the underlying model assumptions:

- Individuals with similar behavioral strategies tend to agglomerate.
- Individuals with different behavioral strategies tend to segregate.

Figure 6, illustrates the situation where the agent attempts to position itself such that its selected agent B is always between itself and its selected agent A. This does not result in "everyone in the room will mill about in a seemingly random fashion", as mentioned in (Bonabeau, 2002), but rather something that is unexpected: the agents systematically occupy the perimeter of the room.

Arguably Figures 5c) and 6 illustrate some form of potential emergence as the clusters formed are not obvious or predictable from the rules governing agent behavior, and the occupancy of agents along the perimeter is not as anticipated, given that one was expecting a more uniform movement pattern.

ABM Extensions in Crowds

In more complex scenarios more relevant to real life, we modeled crowds in two applications areas, the first area being models of pedestrian flow and building egress, which is itself a highly developed

Figure 5. a) Initial party-goers locations b) Homogeneous cluster and c) Segregated clusters

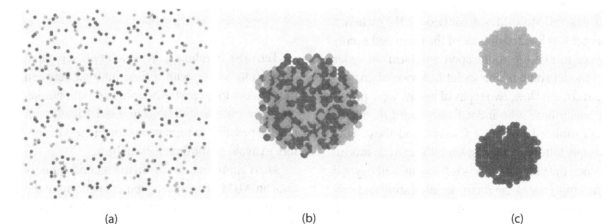

(a)   (b)   (c)

Figure 6. Potential emergent behavior

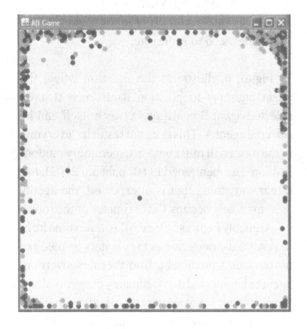

area of modeling. A non-obvious outcome already noted by others, which we attempted to duplicate, was that in the presence of a physical barrier in the pathway toward egress, more people were able to escape in a given period of time when compared to a simulation with no impediments to traffic flow. The second application area that we modeled was related to mass gathering events such as the Hajj pilgrimage.

Building Evacuations: An ABM was developed (Byagowi, Mohaddes, & McLeod, 2012), where a target was located outside of the room and agents were to exit the room upon an alarm. In order to model some of the social behavior of crowds and stream flow, two types of agents were provisioned: those who immediately heard the alarm and initiated their exit (aware), and those who simply followed others towards the exit (unaware). When the simulation was left to run well beyond the emptying of the room, an interesting and surprising pattern of agent interaction emerged. The agents who immediately heard the alarm clustered around the target, while the followers formed a

crescent around that group (Figure 7). This may be a manifestation of emergence, as it would have been difficult to explicitly code individual agent behavior for this outcome. The argument for emergence in this case is strengthened in that the rules governing agents related only to their decisions in finding the exit and did not include rules governing their behavior beyond the exit.

Figure 7a is a snapshot of the simulation when aware and unaware agents begin departing upon the sound of an alarm. Figure 7b is a snapshot of the simulation when agents form a bottleneck while exiting the room. In Figure 7c (zoomed in target area), the simulation is run well beyond the time of interest (room departure). Although simple, it clearly illustrates an unexpected and un-coded phenomenon, illustrating the potentially emergent pattern of the segregation of aware agents and unaware agents. This pattern was consistent in all simulations run and is unpredictable when considering the rules of agent interaction. An illustration can be seen at (Byagowi, 2012). In this ABM, the simulation again unexpectedly demonstrated the following stylized properties of social systems, without designing them into the underlying model assumptions:

- Individuals with similar behavioral strategies tend to agglomerate.
- Individuals with different behavioral strategies tend to segregate.

Terrorist bombings, in which two separated detonations occur with a time interval between them, seem to be partially designed with human behavior in these situations in mind. Likewise, it may be possible to train people or suggest behaviors to avoid to minimize casualties.

Mass gathering events: In the second application, an ABM of crowd movement patterns at the Hajj pilgrimage was undertaken (Khan & McLeod, 2012). One aspect of the Hajj is performing Tawaf (Figure 8), in which pilgrims circumambulate the Kaaba, i.e., form a human mill. There are distinct

Figure 7. The building evacuation ABM

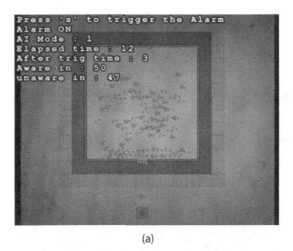

(a)

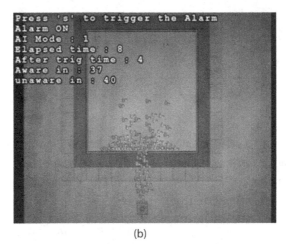

(b)

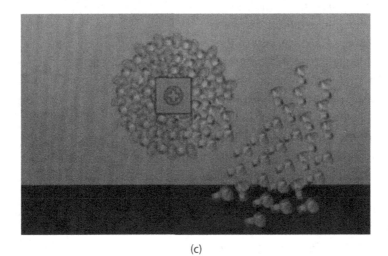

(c)

Figure 8. Pilgrims performing Tawaf in Mecca, Saudi Arabia

areas of density variation and, as a consequence, likely regions of greater and lesser concerns to Hajj organizers and policy makers.

Although many of the movement patterns from the model were as expected, some interesting phenomena emerged when the model included (as part of the governing rules) the demarcation line (a line that pilgrims are required to cross after circumambulating the Kaaba as part of the Tawaf ritual) and the demarcation of the ingress and egress areas. As TawafSIM simulates each scenario, it visually displays the crowd dynamics, some of which are potentially emergent. Figure 9 shows a snapshot of the Tawaf crowd, where the dots represent the pilgrims and the color indicates their spiraling status. The red pilgrims are spiraling inward from the edge of the crowd boundary to generally the outer one half of the circles. The green pilgrims are maintaining their radius at circles closest to the Kaaba, and the blue

pilgrims are spiraling outward, becoming black pilgrims when they complete the seven rounds and spiral outward to exit the crowd. The yellow

Figure 9. The TawafSIM ABM animation

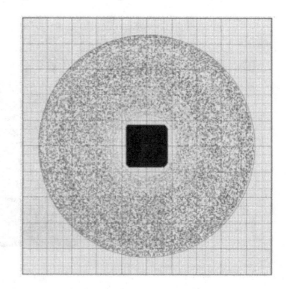

pilgrims are found throughout the crowd, which represent pilgrims that are distracted and have to change their desired macro-level spiral based trajectory due to other pilgrims and their preference for crowd aversion.

Although the crowd animation is interesting and provides a high level view of how the crowd behaves, it does not provide any details. The aggregate simulation data provides details with respect to throughput, satisfaction, and agent (pilgrim) health. Additionally, TawafSIM aggregates simulation data to generate a safety figure for various scenarios (Figure 10). The left plot shows the highest pilgrim density per grid while the right plot shows the percent of time each grid remains in high safety threat.

The results illustrate the patterns that can emerge from a simple model of interacting agents within a structured environment. The flow of a 'super cell' of pilgrims bound by language, custom, and nationality would likely elicit additional emergent behavior distinct from other mass gatherings.

Compared to more traditional ABMs, a technological advantage to modeling crowds may also be associated with available hardware platforms. Specifically, general-purpose computing on graphics processing units (GPGPUs) is amenable to modeling the agents within large crowds as a means of accelerating simulation. Agents within

crowds are particularly well suited as they are typically very simple agents with simple agency.

Epidemic Modeling

Epidemic modeling is one of the older areas of ABM and social simulation. In general, with anything that spreads, there are interesting associated phenomena – perhaps so familiar that it is difficult to cast as definitively emergent. In disease spread models, there is an opportunity to model infection intervention or mitigation strategies that may have unexpected effects. Also, there is an opportunity to model local and global interactions, particularly in the area of behavior modification, where an agent's local behavior is modified from information obtained globally (Gordon et al., 2009). In (Sahneh, Chowdhury, & Scoglio, 2012), a simple model is used to illustrate how preventive behavior may be adopted in light of "sensing infection". Global feedback was conjectured to modify an individual's behavior with the impact of suppressing and containing an infection. The emergent aspect is recognizing that individual agent behavior can be modified or influenced by data that an agent exposes itself to, via global feedback that can be mined and/or crowdsourced from social networks and search engines and conveyed by the electronic social media.

Figure 10. Safety metric for 40,000 maximum pilgrim capacity

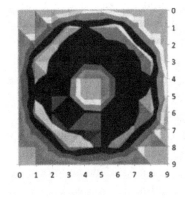  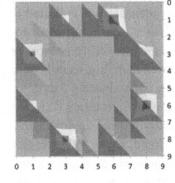 

ABM Extensions in Epidemic Modeling

Epidemiological modeling is a complex system and likely one that is computationally irreducible. The consequences are that there are likely no algorithmic or mathematical shortcuts that can be taken as alternatives to simulation. The ABM is a natural vehicle for disease modeling in light of the fact that the stochastic process (for example, the standard SIR model of disease spread (Wikipedia, 2013a)) can be made significantly more complex and tuned to individuals, and the ABM is amenable to significant data inclusion from sources that may initially appear unrelated to infection modeling.

The extensions in epidemic modeling which are well suited to ABM are the incorporation of real world data on people's mobility patterns to govern agent behaviors in the model. For example, cell phone trajectories are conjectured to proxy for an agent, and cell phone data are used to ultimately build improved models of geospatial disease spread. The incorporation of real data of people's mobility patterns extracted from cell phone data provides an ideal opportunity to demonstrate the multidisciplinary nature of ABM. In this work, cellular data were made available to us as anonymized records that represented approximately 20% of individuals within the Province of Manitoba.

Specifically, the cellular data included the geolocation and identification of the antenna sectors in use by mobile devices serviced by MTS (Manitoba Telecom Services) Allstream, as well as the date and anonymized user identification collected at 15-minute time intervals, which provided approximate location of the users of the network at a specific time. Just over 42 million records were obtained, representing approximately 5 days' of culled data, and the user trajectories collected from the sample data numbered approximately 180,000. These data would be used by the service provider to assist with network planning for future growth, load balancing, and usage patterns. While abstracted, visualization of cell phone trajectories allows for some perspective of movement patterns. In the near future, it is reasonable to assume that even more detailed spatial resolution would be available as people begin to use location-based services and/or share their cellular-assisted spatial location data.

An ABM implementing a standard disease spread model was developed (Wijedasa et al., 2013), utilizing the agent movement patterns extracted from cellular records. The ABM was built upon the Anylogic framework and reflected a parameterizable SEIR (Susceptible – Exposed – Infected – Recovered) individual disease spread model, a variant of a standard SIR (Susceptible – Infectious – Recovered) compartmentalized mathematical model of disease spread (Kermack & McKendrick, 1927; Wikipedia, 2013a).

Figure 11 illustrates the spread of infection within the lower part of the Province of Manitoba, Canada. The colors denote agent states, where blue denotes Susceptible agents, yellow denotes Exposed agents, red denotes Infected agents, and green denotes Recovered agents. In this simulation, the rural communities were less affected by the outbreak as a consequence of their isolation, thereby serving as an implicit form of social distancing. An animation illustrating the SEIR disease spread ABM can be found at (Gunasekara, 2012).

One of the greatest benefits of spatial models driven by actual data is that they provide a "plausible experimental system in which knowledge of the location of hosts and their typical movement patterns can be combined with a quantitative description of the infection process and disease natural history to investigate observed patterns and to evaluate alternative intervention options" (Riley, 2007). A spatial ABM driven by real data produces aggregate results (i.e., the recognized S-curve on the graphs of infection over time) qualitatively similar to those produced by ordinary differential equation versions of SEIR modeling. This adds credibility to the ABM methodology and the specific model developed in this work. Another

Figure 11. Illustration of the spatial spread of an infection in the Province of Manitoba, Canada

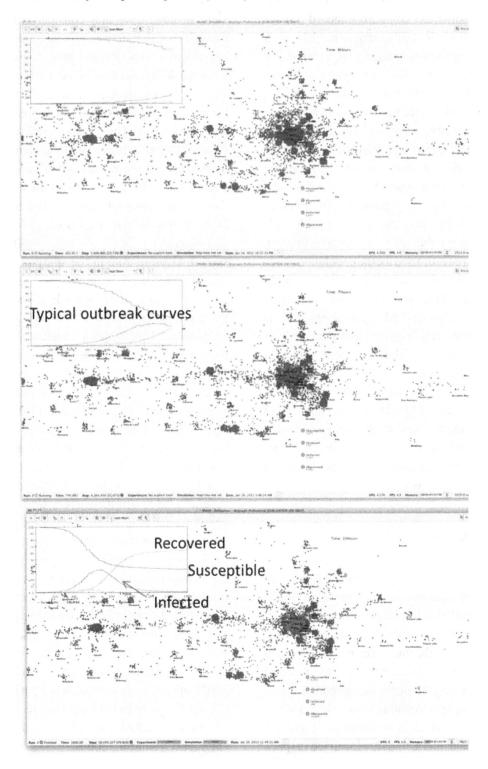

benefit of spatial ABMs driven by real data is the ability to resolve and compare standard disease characterizations in mathematical models, such as the basic reproduction number R_0 and force of infection F_{oi}, as a means of assessing the robustness and validity of the ABM model parameters.

In epidemiology, the basic reproduction number R_0 is the number of cases of infection that one case generates, on average over the course of its infectious period. When R_0 is less than one, the infection will die out; when R_0 is greater than one, it will spread within a population. The force of infection F_{oi} is the rate at which susceptible individuals become infected by an infectious disease. R_0 and F_{oi} can be estimated for the population. They both would be more useful metrics if they could be estimated as functions of both time and space, as geographically-caused delay of an epidemic is one of the main weapons in containing and managing serious outbreaks. This is an underexploited research area associated with data driven ABMs and an area where considerable value and insights could be gained. ABMs' level of complexity in terms of the many types of agents represented in a realistic ABM as well as the nuanced characteristics of the infection itself make it a rich field for potential emergence.

CONCLUSION

Emergence may be thought of as a macro-scale effect with unique and distinct qualities, which arises as a result of micro-scale interactions, independent of and unforeseeable from the modeling decisions made at the micro-scale in agent-based social simulation. The properties of an emergent phenomenon may be qualitatively and/or quantitatively unique from the micro-scale modeling decisions from which it is triggered. Typically, the micro-scale interactions are localized in space

and time, although this is not a requirement. In some instances, we may consider artificial long range interaction between social agents, if we allow electronic social networking to play a role in what we define as agent influence or interaction. Thus global parameters can alter the behavior of agents, a phenomenon usually not recognized in natural systems. This chapter reviewed current efforts in agent based modeling, some of which have demonstrated outcomes that hint at emergent phenomena. The work adds to the evidence for the continued maturation of agent based modeling as an interdisciplinary methodology for modeling and simulating social systems, with the goal to shed light on its role in the study of emergence within these social systems.

There is a hierarchy of kinds of emergence. In the inanimate, abiotic world, agents are regarded as passive. Despite this limitation, emergent phenomena occur, ranging from atomic nuclei to the structure of the universe, some of which is captured by cellular automata (Gordon & Drum, 1994; Wolfram, 2001). In a world filled with agents that have memories, make decisions, and act on these, the array of emergent phenomena increases. Furthermore, the ability of agents to take into account not only local, but global parameters, i.e., the emergent results themselves, leads to a further level of emergence well beyond that present in the abiotic world. Feedback to the individual of traffic patterns (Abdulhai & Abdelgawad, 2009), carbon emissions (Liu et al., 2012), weather, quorum sensing in bacteria (Goldstone et al., 2012), merging of flocks of birds, queue hopping (Shub, 1978), etc., are examples of the use of global, emergent parameters. The unsolved problems of the origin (Hazen, 2009) and evolution (Reid, 2007) of life, and our additions to it via human social organization enhanced by machines, may best be approached in terms of the emergence of emergence (Gordon, 2000).

ACKNOWLEDGMENT

The authors thank Hamid Reza Nasrinpour for his contribution of the ABM to marketing, Marc Friesen, Ahmad Byagowi and Imran Khan for ABM contributions to crowds, and Charith Gunasekara for his contribution to epidemic modeling.

REFERENCES

Abdulhai, B., & Abdelgawad, H. (2009). Towards fully integrated adaptive urban traffic control. In I. L. AlQadi, T. Sayed, A. Alnuaimi & E. Masad, (Eds.), *Efficient transportation and pavement systems: Characterization, mechanisms, simulation, and modeling: Proceedings of the 4th International Gulf Conference on Roads, Doha, Qatar,* (pp. 17-31).

AnyLogic. (2013). AnyLogic® multimethod simulation software. Retrieved from http://www.anylogic.com/

Arciero, L., Picillo, C., Solomon, S., & Terna, P. (2014in press). Building ABMs to control the emergence of crisis analyzing agents' behavior. In D. F. Adamatti, G. P. Dimuro, & H. Coelho (Eds.), *Interdisciplinary applications of agent-based social simulation and modeling.* Hershey, PA: IGI Global.

Bernstein, M. S., Bakshy, E., Burke, M., & Karrer, B. (2013). Quantifying the invisible audience in social networks. In *ACM SIGCHI Conference on Human Factors in Computing Systems (CHI 2013)* (in press).

Bonabeau, E. ((2002). Agent-based modeling: Methods and techniques for simulating human systems. *Proceedings of the National Academy of Sciences of the United States of America, 99*(Suppl. 3), 7280–7287. doi:10.1073/pnas.082080899 PMID:12011407

Byagowi, A. (2012). Agent based modeling project demonstration [Video]. Retrieved from https://http://www.youtube.com/watch?v=LS559iCNXjQ

Byagowi, A., Mohaddes, D., & McLeod, R. D. (2012). Accidental emergence within an agent based model simulation of agent interactions in an emergency situation. In Q. Mehdi, A. Elmaghraby, I. Marshall, R. Moreton, R. Ragade, B. G. Zapirain, J. Chariker, M. ElSaid, R. Yampolskiy & N.L. Zhigiang, (Eds.), *2012 17th International Conference on Computer Games (CGAMES)* (pp. 189-193). Los Alamitos, CA: IEEE Computer Society.

Carbonara, N. (2014in press). Knowledge-based externalities and geographical clusters: An agent-based simulation study. In D. F. Adamatti, G. P. Dimuro, & H. Coelho (Eds.), *Interdisciplinary applications of agent-based social simulation and modeling.* Hershey, PA: IGI Global.

Castelfranchi, C. (2014in press). Making visible the invisible hand. The mission of social simulation. In D. F. Adamatti, G. P. Dimuro, & H. Coelho (Eds.), *Interdisciplinary applications of agent-based social simulation and modeling.* Hershey, PA: IGI Global.

Conte, R., Gilbert, N., Bonelli, G., Cioffi-Revilla, C., Deffuant, G., & Kertesz, J. et al. (2012). Manifesto of computational social science. *The European Physical Journal. Special Topics, 214*(1), 325–346. doi:10.1140/epjst/e2012-01697-8

Gjoka, M., Kurant, M., Butts, C. T., & Markopoulou, A. (2010). Walking in Facebook: A case study of unbiased sampling of OSNs. In *2010 Proceedings IEEE INFOCOM.* New York: IEEE.

Goldstone, R. J., Popat, R., Fletcher, M. P., Crusz, S. A., & Diggle, S. P. (2012). Quorum sensing and social interactions in microbial biofilms. In G. Lear, & G. D. Lewis (Eds.), *Microbial biofilms: Current research and applications* (pp. 1–24). Norfolk, UK: Caister Academic Press.

Goldstone, R. L., & Janssen, M. A. (2005). Computational models of collective behavior. *Trends in Cognitive Sciences, 9*(9), 424–430. doi:10.1016/j.tics.2005.07.009 PMID:16085450

Gordon, R. (2000). The emergence of emergence: A critique of design, observation, surprise!. *Rivista di Biologia/Biology Forum, 93*(2), 349-356.

Gordon, R., Björklund, N. K., Smith, R. J., & Blyden, E. R. (2009). Halting HIV/AIDS with avatars and havatars: A virtual world approach to modelling epidemics. BMC Public Health, 9(Suppl 1: OptAIDS Special Issue), S13 (16 pages).

Gordon, R., & Drum, R. W. (1994). The chemical basis for diatom morphogenesis. *International Review of Cytology, 150*, 243–372, 421–422. doi:10.1016/S0074-7696(08)61544-2

Gunasekara, C. (2012). Mobile users' trajectory patterns in Manitoba Province. Retrieved from http://www.youtube.com/watch?v=cOJZKzy0XBY

Hazen, R. M. (2009). The emergence of patterning in life's origin and evolution. *The International Journal of Developmental Biology, 53*(5-6), 683-692

Helbing, D., Yu, W., & Rauhut, H. (2011). Self-organization and emergence in social systems: modeling the coevolution of social environments and cooperative behavior. *The Journal of Mathematical Sociology, 35*(1-3), 177–208. doi:10.1080/0022250X.2010.532258

Icosystem Corporation. (2013). *The game*. Retrieved from http://www.icosystem.com/labs-demos/the-game

Kermack, W. O., & McKendrick, A. G. (1927). Contribution to the mathematical theory of epidemics. In *Proceedings of the Royal Society of London Series a-Containing Papers of a Mathematical and Physical Character, 115*(772), 700-721.

Khan, I., & McLeod, R. D. (2012). Managing Hajj crowd complexity: Superior throughput, satisfaction, health, & safety. *Kuwait Chapter of Arabian Journal of Business and Management Review, 2*(4), 45–59.

Liu, B., Ghosal, D., Chuah, C.-N., & Zhang, H. M. (2012). Reducing greenhouse effects via fuel consumption-aware variable speed limit (FC-VSL). *IEEE Transactions on Vehicular Technology, 61*(1), 111–122. doi:10.1109/TVT.2011.2170595

Lukeman, R., Li, Y.-X., & Edelstein-Keshet, L. (2009). A conceptual model for milling formations in biological aggregates. *Bulletin of Mathematical Biology, 71*(2), 352–382. doi:10.1007/s11538-008-9365-7 PMID:18855072

Montañola-Sales, C., Rubio-Campillo, X., Casanovas-Garcia, J., Cela-Espín, J. M., & Kaplan-Marcusán, A. (2014in press). Large-scale social simulation, dealing with complexity challenges in high performance environments. In D. F. Adamatti, G. P. Dimuro, & H. Coelho (Eds.), *Interdisciplinary applications of agent-based social simulation and modeling*. Hershey, PA: IGI Global.

Osborne, A., & Dvorak, J. (1984). *Hypergrowth: The rise and fall of Osborne Computer Corporation*. Berkeley, CA: Idthekkethan Pub. Co.

Rand, W., & Rust, R. T. (2011). Agent-based modeling in marketing: Guidelines for rigor. *International Journal of Research in Marketing, 28*(3), 181–193. doi:10.1016/j.ijresmar.2011.04.002

Reid, R. G. B. (2007). *Biological emergences: Evolution by natural experiment*. Cambridge, MA: MIT Press.

Riley, S. (2007). Large-scale spatial-transmission models of infectious disease. *Science, 316*(5829), 1298–1301. doi:10.1126/science.1134695 PMID:17540894

Ronald, E. M. A., & Sipper, M. (2001). Surprise versus unsurprise: Implications of emergence in robotics. *Robotics and Autonomous Systems*, *37*(1), 19–24. doi:10.1016/S0921-8890(01)00149-X

Ronald, E. M. A., Sipper, M., & Capcarrère, M. S. (1999). Design, observation, surprise! A test of emergence. *Artificial Life*, *5*(3), 225–239. doi:10.1162/106454699568755 PMID:10648952

Sahneh, F. D., Chowdhury, F. N., & Scoglio, C. M. (2012). On the existence of a threshold for preventive behavioral responses to suppress epidemic spreading. *Scientific Reports, 2*.

Shub, C. M. (1978). On the relative merits of two major methodologies for simulation model construction. In *WSC '78 Proceedings of the 10th conference on Winter simulation, 1,* (pp. 257-264). IEEE Press.

Swan, L. S., Gordon, R., & Seckbach, J. (Eds.). (2012). *Origin(s) of design in nature: A Fresh, interdisciplinary look at how design emerges in complex systems, especially life*. Dordrecht, The Netherlands: Springer. doi:10.1007/978-94-007-4156-0

Tyson, P. (2007). Everyday examples of emergence. Retrieved from http://www.pbs.org/wgbh/nova/nature/emergence-examples.html

Vaughn, R. L., Muzi, E., Richardson, J. L., & Würsig, B. (2011). Dolphin bait-balling behaviors in relation to prey ball escape behaviors. *Ethology*, *117*(10), 859–871. doi:10.1111/j.1439-0310.2011.01939.x

Wijedasa, S., Gunasekara, C., Laskowsk, M., Friesen, M. R., & McLeod, R. D. (2013, 4 January). Smartphone and vehicular trajectories as data sources for agent-based infection spread modelling. *Health Systems*. doi:10.1057/hs.2012.1025

Wikipedia. (2013a). Compartmental models in epidemiology. Retrieved from http://en.wikipedia.org/wiki/Compartmental_models_in_epidemiology

Wikipedia. (2013b). Ant mill. Retrieved from http://en.wikipedia.org/wiki/Ant_mill

Wikipedia. (2013c). Emergence. Retrieved from http://en.wikipedia.org/wiki/Emergence

Wolfram, S. (2001). *A New kind of science*. Champaign, IL: Wolfram Media.

KEY TERMS AND DEFINITIONS

Emergence: The appearance of a new property or phenomenon in a simulation, apparent at the level of the individual agent, the sub-group, or the population as whole, derived from the interactions of agents within the model, but not explicitly programmed within the model.

Human Mobility Patterns: Patterns of people's movement (agent movement) extracted from real-world data.

Interacting Social Agents: Proxies for individuals (persons) in a model, who have agency.

Self-Organization: The formation of order, coordination, or categorization within the agent population, derived out of the local interactions between agents as an outcome of the simulation.

Chapter 5
Usefulness of Agent–Based Simulation in Testing Collective Decision–Making Models

Pablo Lucas
University of Essex, England

Diane Payne
Geary Institute, University College Dublin, Ireland

ABSTRACT

Political scientists seek to build more realistic Collective Decision-Making Models (henceforth CDMM) which are implemented as computer simulations. The starting point for this present chapter is the observation that efficient progress in this field may be being hampered by the fact that the implementation of these models as computer simulations may vary considerably and the code for these computer simulations is not usually made available. CDMM are mathematically deterministic formulations (i.e. without probabilistic inputs or outputs) and are aimed at explaining the behaviour of individuals involved in dynamic, collective negotiations with any number of policy decision-related issues. These CDMM differ from each other regarding the particular bargaining strategies implemented and tested in each model for how the individuals reach a collective binding policy agreement. The CDMM computer simulations are used to analyse the data and generate predictions of a collective decision. While the formal mathematical treatment of the models and empirical findings of CDMM are usually presented and discussed through peer-review journal publications, access to these CDMM implementations as computer simulations are often unavailable online nor easily accessed offline and this tends to dissuade cross fertilisation and learning in the field.

DOI: 10.4018/978-1-4666-5954-4.ch005

1. INTRODUCTION

In the discipline of political science, there is a range of Collective Decision Making Models (henceforth CDMM) developed to explain how individuals influence each other in a negotiation process to reach collective binding decisions, such as policy or legislative decisions (Thomson et al., 2003; Achen, 2006). The CDMM discussed in this research are based on the assumptions of rational choice theory and distinguished by their formal, mathematical description. The specifications of each CDMM aim to capture the essential features of interactions between individuals involved in political bargaining, where each actor's initial policy position may be modified in the process so that a collective decision is reached. Alongside developing the CDMM, researchers effectively implement these as computer simulations. These computer simulations are used to analyse the data and generate model predictions of the actual collective decisions and thus providing a measure of the accuracy of the CDMM. While the formal mathematical treatment of the models and empirical findings of the CDMM field are usually presented and discussed through peer-review journal publications, access to these CDMM implementations as computer simulations is often not publicly available online through open source code for example and/or easily accessed offline and this tends to dissuade rapid research cross fertilisation and learning in this field. The starting point for this present research is the observation that efficient progress in this field may be being hampered by the fact that the implementation of these models as computer simulations is not easily available.

Most purely textual specifications of simulation models do not provide a full and exact account of how these have been implemented. That is because discussions on a manuscript may not match the level of completeness and clarity that a computer language would require to accurately represent a model. Thus having access to the implementation source code is often *the* unequivocal way of assessing the proposed assumptions and processes. As CDMM are not readily accessible, these have been replicated into an agent-based model (henceforth ABM) to facilitate the understanding of CDMM via the design of experiments. The flexibility to develop ABM particularly highlights the need for modellers to adopt rigour throughout the specification and implementation of simulation assumptions and processes.

We discuss and demonstrate the importance of these issues in this chapter in the context of an ABM replication in NetLogo of four well-known CDMM from political science. We focus on three research challenges in this chapter. First, how can we generate a controlled environment for reproducible and flexible testing of CDMM hypotheses? Second, using our ABM replication approach, can we identify and explain which of the CDMM are most stable in terms of predicted outcomes? Third, can our ABM replication generate insights about the assumptions and dynamics of a CDMM?

In the following section, the replicated CDMM are reviewed and then the research design and empirical data used in this research are presented. Two case studies are selected for this research. The first case study and dataset discussed in Bennett and Payne (2001) introduces the United Kingdom (henceforth UK) Local and Regional Development Agencies' legislation, a policy intervention for enhancing opportunities for local and regional development. The second case study and dataset discussed in (Thomson, 2011) is a larger collection of policy decisions taken at the European Union level (henceforth EU). In this research, we systematically test the assumptions of these CDMM under different precision (rounding) floating-points (i.e. using different decimal points for performing the same mathematical calculations). Our ABM replication demonstrates how the underlying assumptions of these CDMM present adverse effects for interpreting the dynamics of each model. Our

ABM replication also demonstrates how we can explore a new CDMM implementation wherein individual model assumptions may interplay. Our contribution in this chapter is therefore twofold:

- A systematic testing, via replication, of the CDMM specified assumptions and processes along with their requisites for operation;
- Plus (2) a discussion of the gained insights, via the ABM, about the dynamics and precision (rounding) issues in CDMM when each is executed separately and how these interplay

2. COLLECTIVE DECISION-MAKING MODELS (CDMM)

CDMM are mathematically deterministic formulations (i.e. without probabilistic inputs or outputs) that are aimed at explaining the behaviour of individuals in negotiations given any number of issues, in which all the participants attempt to influence the outcome of a final and binding decision. Each model conceptualises the decision situation spatially, where political controversies are conceptualised as one or more issue continua (or scales) along which the agents' positions, can be placed (Thomson et al., 2006). Note that we can also place on each of these issue continua the actual issue outcome and the model predicted issue outcome. Each of the CDMM takes into account, per issue, three normalised input values for each agent that is involved in the negotiations.

First, as we have just mentioned, there is the initial position of the agent on each issue, where each issue is represented as a continuum or scale usually with a range from 1-100 and where at least one agent can be placed at each of the endpoints on the continuum at positions 1 and 100 respectively. The initial position of the agent for an issue is often referred to in the literature as the "most

preferred position," per issue and is treated as a single peaked preference function.

Second, the salience of an issue for the agent may be broadly understood as the importance attached to the issue by the agent and where the level of salience attached to an issue may differ across agents. Salience can be understood as the proportion of an agent's potential capabilities it is willing to mobilise to influence the decision outcome and is estimated as a value on a scale between 1 and 100 where for example the salience value of a 100 indicates an issue which is of the highest priority for that agent. It is worth noting that the concepts of position and salience are distinct in CDMM as for example an agent may take an extreme position on an issue but attach a very low level of salience to that issue.

Third, the CDMM require a measure of the agent's power and agents are ranked on a scale of 1-100, where the most powerful agent(s) is ranked 100. Power is also referred to in the literature as an agent's "resources" or "capabilities," which is immutable across issues.

There are different ways to measure an agent's power either by expert judgement or using an objective measurement such as the Shapley Shubik (henceforth SS) Index score, which is based on formal rules of decision making, for example the voting rules within the EU Council of Ministers (Thomson et al., 2006). We use expert judgements of agent power when we are interested in the concept of agent power as a measure of both formal (i.e. votes) and informal power, where an agent's informal power or influence may reflect the agent's access to informal resources such as leadership over many individuals, access to key stakeholders, financial resources or access bureaucratic expertise and efficiency. To summarise the CDMM require three input values for the agents involved in the collective decision making for each issue: position, salience and power and hereafter we refer to these *input variables* as *PSP*.

The CDMM differ from each other regarding the particular bargaining strategies implemented and tested in each model for how individuals reach collective binding agreements. The CDMM are aimed at producing a prediction of the outcome of an actual negotiation by processing, according to a CDMM algorithm, PSP values of each agent per issue. Thus it is crucial to understand the assumptions of and dynamics of each CDMM to gain insights about the processes underlying collective decision-making, including the following aspects:

- Amount of conflict, backing and acceptance between participants;
- Nature of the influence and implementation (i.e. compliance) processes;
- Stability of individual and collective outcomes, given the initial conditions;
- And strategic information about how agents may agree across any number of issues.

Both the data collection process and the interpretation of CDMM results require attention to the rather strict underlying assumptions in these models. This is important as one can process the same empirical dataset with different CDMM and analyse which result approximates best to the actual collective outcome, suggesting thus how individuals may have behaved. The data collection entails averaging the PSP input from, ideally at least three, experts by decomposing a collective decision into a number of independent issues, provided that each one is:

- An important element of the actual collective decision-making process;
- And on a continuum where every agent PSP value can be justifiably allocated.

Experts are selected on the basis of their indepth and detailed knowledge of the actual collective decisions being examined in the research.

Often these experts have participated in the decision making itself or have closely followed the negotiation in question.

2.1 The Compromise Model

This model is intended to perform best, prediction-wise, when there is a low polarisation of power and preferences across all the agents, implying that having abundant information –or expertise– in the matter is considered a key resource in this particular negotiation scenario. The mathematical simplicity of the Compromise model, along with the reporting of median and mean values across PSP values per issue, has been used extensively in the social science literature as a comparison yardstick with regards to how other CDMM perform.

The predicted outcome and expected utility for an agent in this model is calculated according to (Arregui et al., 2006), which consists of: dividing, per issue and per agent, the sum of all PSP values by the sum of power and saliencies. Once all compromise calculations are complete, the algorithm proceeds to provide the mean of all agents' positions per issue, weighted by their effective capabilities –which is defined as the individual power multiplied by salience in question (Arregui et al., 2006; Van den Bos, 1991; Stokman & Van den Bos, 1992).

The ABM replication of this model is straightforward so, unlike other more complex CDMM, the reader would not benefit from the provision of a pseudo-code to understand the algorithm in question. Instead the following description is sufficient to explain how the PSP values are processed: the ABM model calculates the aforementioned expected utilities, per agent and per issue of the dataset under analysis, and at the end of this process provides the expected outcomes per issue. The same structure is used to implement the median and mean models, as essentially all these three propositions do is to apply a single procedure to a range of values spread across issues.

It is worthwhile noticing that, to date, the most successful CDMM use some sort of mean amongst agent PSP values (Achen, 2006) and this finding has been reinforced through the robustness findings discussed in greater detail in Section 5. This suggests that the range of PSP values, which are spread over a number of issues as described in Section 2, can play a role in terms of how accurate these CDMM actually are to predict an outcome per issue.

2.2 The Challenge Model

This model is intended to represent the individual struggle of finding oneself in the process of pulling the collective decision outcome, per issue, closer to one's preferred position. Thus it explores the power hierarchy amongst agents in non-binding pair wise challenges, so that the agent's PSP values can change during the process and are carried into subsequent rounds, until each of the participants in the process has decided whether to challenge another. According to (Arregui et al., 2006), the assumptions about this model can be summarised as:

- The weighted median position is seen, by all agents, as the likely outcome per issue;
- In subsequent rounds of negotiations, agents deal with potentially new position values;
- Even if an agent shifted position values closer to another, this can later be reversed;
- And the rounds of negotiations are successive amongst all involved participants.

Power and salience of each agent remain unchanged during this process. From the original description of this model in Arregui et al. (2006), it is unclear whether the last assumption should be implemented using a fixed order of agents, or a random one every time the model is run. The replication was made using a fixed order, as no stochastic aspects about the model are discussed and the challenge process is described as only running once per dataset. The pseudo-algorithm of the Challenge model is described below and Figure 1 depicts how the decision-making process is construed according to the aforementioned assumptions:

Figure 1. The decision-tree, per agent and issue (Arregui et al., 2004)

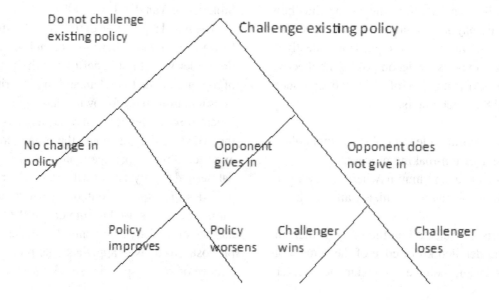

- Each agent identifies, sequentially and per issue, which is the biggest potential utility gain to be incurred by challenging another agent using the current-round PSP values;
- The challenging process stops when expected losses are higher than potential gains.

2.3 The Exchange Model

The proposition of this model is that agents can change their voting position in one issue by negotiating an exchange with another agent on another issue, provided that their gains in such a transaction are exactly the same (i.e. mutual). This model is also sometimes referred to in the literature as a log-rolling model. The model is intended to perform best, prediction-wise, when agents' saliencies are polarised across pair wise issues, involving any of the participants and the decision effectively depends on a number of related issues (i.e. where the agent's policy preferences differ across issues, there is an opportunity to exchange). The natural inference is then that this model would be less accurate, prediction-wise, when powerful agents face high negative externalities. As discussed in greater detail in Sections 4 and 5, based on Tables 1, 2, 5, and 6, one must consider the impact of how the precision (rounding) in calculations affect how many exchanges

Table 1. Summary means and standard deviations of all LRDA group of issues (ABC)

Data (σ)	A (8 issues)	B (5 issues)	C (5 issues)
Position	.476 (.386)	.435 (.349)	.206 (.294)
Salience	.260 (.256)	.248 (.215)	.162 (.222)
Power	.312 (.309)	.304 (.309)	.312 (309)
Obs.	248	155	155

can be realised and how that alters the deviation of the predicted outcome per dataset. In short, the main finding from replicating this model in an ABM framework is that: a higher accuracy in calculations leads to a reduction of how many pair wise exchanges can happen. Therefore it is worth bearing in mind this previously unknown aspect about the Exchange model when reviewing the pseudo-algorithm in Figure 2.

Once exchanges are over, every agent has then moved to a new position due to the pair wise mutual benefit. The Compromise model, described in Section 2.1, is used to transform the position values spread across all agents into the predicted decision outcome, per issue of the dataset in question. Along with this output, the replicated version of this model reports the total number of simulated potential exchanges, regardless of the criterion for agents to equally improve their PSP values, and the total number of simulated actual exchanges that happened.

3. INTEGRATING REPLICATIONS OF CDMM INTO AN ABM FRAMEWORK

The previously discussed CDMM, namely the Challenge, Compromise, Exchange, Mean and Median models, have been replicated verbatim and integrated into a single ABM. Replication is important for model verification and validation, as this allows a thorough inspection of how these models are specified and, ultimately, provides insights into their internal dynamics and how they were originally implemented. The replications in question were time-consuming due to the unavailability of the original source codes, lack of published details regarding some of the model assumptions and the algorithmic procedures necessary for the implementations. Nevertheless every CDMM model has been re-implemented according to the cited references.

Figure 2. Pseudo-code of the exchange model

```
REPEAT
   SET all pairwise issues, i.e. agents with PSP values in opposition
   SET, for each pairwise, the expected gains to each involved agent
   REPORT number of potential exchanges, regardless of gains criteria
UNTIL every agent has been processed

REPEAT
   SELECT the top pairwise (in case of ties, choose one at random)
   SET the new PSP values per agent per exchange
   REMOVE the currently selected exchange
UNTIL no more exchanges are possible
```

Another issue worth noting was the process of cleaning up the input data, so it could be read into the ABM in a standard form. The original data needed re-tabulation through new relational indexes for agents, issues and PSP values. This process also included the removing from the original data various special characters (such as trailing spaces and other invisible text markers) and normalisation of values. Both small and large CDMM datasets tend to contain the same issues and may also present missing PSP values. These can be treated as inexistent data entries or zeros, yet each has a different impact in the calculations of CDMM as respectively such entries will be either fully excluded or calculated with potential to nullify the participation of a particular agent in the decision-making process. As these issues have not yet been resolved at the CDMM level, the findings discussed in this chapter contain only the subsets that do not contain any missing value, so that every replicated CDMM could be processed as intended.

The ABM takes as input the indexes of agents, issues and PSP values. The output consists of: the predicted collective outcome (including final PSP values and losses), simulated potential challenges and simulated actual challenges (including a rank based on relative individual power and outcome) and matches within and across issues. The ABM

experimental setup designed for this chapter involved in running the following independent sequence of models (i.e. each run loaded the original PSP values, per dataset): Mean, Median, Challenge, and Exchange.

There are also two additional outputs: the Challenge-Exchange and the Exchange-Challenge composites. That is, for each of these setups, the output of the former model is used as the input of the latter. The intention of testing this combination is twofold: a) to observe whether a decision-making process may be best characterised as a shift from one CDMM to another (instead of being fully based on the assumptions of one CDMM only), and b) to analyse the effects that one CDMM model has on another in terms of processing the input PSP values.

Figure 3 depicts the structure of the implemented replications in the ABM framework. The structure of this ABM replication allows both the implementation of different experimental designs, such as the setup described above as well as the possibility for the user to run an individual CDMM with either a simulated or empirical dataset. As Figure 3 indicates, results are both displayed on the user interface and written to a text file to facilitate further analyses.

Figure 3. Pseudo-code of the ABM simulation

```
REPEAT

    SET a fixed random seed, zeroing the timer and control variables
    SET parameters for visualising the changes in network links

    WRITE all configured parameters in the simulation file
    PLOT initial actor positions, saliences and power

    IF a specific scenario is chosen
      LOAD  all scenario data (actors attributes and indexed issues)
      RUN   specified routine and order of chosen Decision-Making Model
    ELSE
      CREATE the number of chosen actors and issues
      LOAD   randomised values for Positions, Saliences and Power
      RUN    one the chosen Decion-Making Models
    END_IF

    WRITE results, per actor and issue, in the simulation file
    WRITE summary of predicted collective outcome, saliences and losses
    PLOT  final initial actor positions, saliences and power

UNTIL number of simulation runs is reached
```

4. RESEARCH DESIGN

In this research we apply the ABM replication of CDMM to two different case studies. Our first case study is discussed in Bennett and Payne (2001) and introduces the UK Local and Regional Development Agencies Initiative, a policy intervention for enhancing opportunities for local and regional development.

The other case study is discussed in Thomson (2011) and is a larger collection of policy decisions taken at the EU level. This data for this second case study differs in the sense that it contains a different number of agents in the EU, per group of decisions, depending on the year in which decision issues to be decided have been introduced to the union. This reflects the fact that the data collection covers three EU phases, where the number of EU member states increased from 15 in 1996 to 25 and then to 27 member states by 2008. The original dataset contains information regarding 331 decision issues proposed in 125 legislative proposals introduced between 1996 and 2008.

5. CASE STUDY: LOCAL AND REGIONAL DEVELOPMENT AGENCIES (LRDA)

Local and regional economic development has been a long-running concern of both central and local government in the UK. In May 1997 the Labour government introduced a range of measures which were hailed as positive policy initiatives concerned with the development of resources and wealth, employment and social opportunities at the sub-national level. The policy negotiations concerned various measures aimed at the reinvigoration of the regional level, a stronger role for local government and an overall emphasis on public-private partnerships (Bennett & Payne, 2001). In particular the policy negotiations in this case study concern proposals to establish a range of different types of Local and Regional Development agencies (LRDA) including these three initiatives:

- The development of the New Deal for long-term unemployment through partnerships;
- The replacement of Training and Enterprise Councils by Learning and Skills Councils;
- And the establishment of the Small Business Service for local businesses.

Each of these LRDA initiatives concerns a number of policy issues and Table 1 below provides the summary statistics of each set of issues (A, B and C). Overall 31 agents were involved in the negotiations and given the nature of data collection described in the Section 2, typically the range of overall PSP values tend to not vary much –although there can be significant differences per agent.

Furthermore the number of observations in CDMM datasets is given by the multiplication of the total number of issues by the total number of agents. Therefore the total size of an empirical dataset for CDMM depends largely on how many issues can be identified as relevant to a collective decision, along with how many agents were influential in it. Thus the researcher working on the data collection has to consider how many expert stakeholders can be interviewed, so that each data point can be justifiably positioned in the chosen scale.

5.1 Case Study: Obtained Findings from the LRDA Replication and Integration

The integration of the aforementioned CDMM into a single ABM framework allowed the flexible and systematic testing of assumptions and dynamics underlying each model. This provided key insights into understanding how these deterministic models operate, particularly with regards to whether the precision (rounding) of calculations affects the assumptions, internal dynamics and predicted outcomes per model. As can be observed in Tables 2 and 3, the Mean, Median and Challenge models remained largely unaffected by these tests. This finding in terms of robustness reinforces the analysis by (Achen, 2006) that the most successful models are those based on computing a type of mean amongst agent PSP values.

However Table 2 and Table 3 show that the Exchange model is significantly impacted by these changes in terms of how many pair wise exchanges can actually occur and how much the final predicted outcome diverges from the actual outcome –both per issue and across issues. One can observe a clear decrease of exchanges with the increase of precision in this model. The same effect occurs regarding when combining models (i.e. the setups where the output of one model becomes the input of another model). Both the Challenge-Exchange (CE) and the Exchange-Challenge (EC) tests incur differences driven by the precision issue observed in the Exchange model. An exception to that is the CE setup, where

Table 2. Potential exchanges (E.), Actual E. and Challenges per dataset per precision (P.)

Total / Dataset	A	B	C	P.
Actual Exchanges (AE)	216	29	8	1
	48	6	2	2
	6	0	6	3
	0	0	0	4
	0	0	0	5
AE Challenge Exchange	195	19	2	1
	58	6	4	2
	16	0	24	3
	4	0	0	4
	0	0	0	5
Challenges	285	305	287	all
Potential E.	1845	276	320	all

Table 3. Deviations from the actual outcome, per dataset (D) per rounding precision (P)

D	P	Mean	Median	Challenge	Exchange	CE	EC
A	01	-1.8	-2.4	-2.4	-2.6	-2.6	-3.3
A	02	-1.91	-2.45	-2.45	-2.3	-2.2	-3.01
A	03	-1.891	-2.45	-2.45	-1.963	-1.95	-2.45
A	04	-1.8919	-2.45	-2.45	-1.8919	-1.9757	-2.45
A	05	-1.89194	-2.45	-2.45	-1.89194	-1.97957	-2.45
B	01	0.6	0.6	0.6	1	1	0.6
B	02	0.63	0.65	0.65	0.7	0.91	0.9
B	03	0.627	0.65	0.65	0.627	0.809	0.65
B	04	0.6258	0.65	0.65	0.6258	0.8093	0.65
B	05	0.6258	0.65	0.65	0.6258	0.80927	0.65
C	01	0.2	-0.1	-0.1	0.2	0.2	-0.1
C	02	0.28	-0.05	-0.05	0.28	0.25	-0.05
C	03	0.276	-0.05	-0.05	0.26	0.269	-0.05
C	04	0.2758	-0.05	-0.05	0.2758	0.2682	-0.05
C	05	0.27581	-0.05	-0.05	0.27581	0.26812	-0.05

the Challenge model can cause an increase in the number of exchanges by realigning the PSP values of all agents per dataset.

Note that depending on the dataset group, there are instances where no exchanges happen at all if the precision of calculations is set between 2 and 4, depending on the dataset. This is a relevant and previously unknown finding about the dynamics of the Exchange model. It suggests that the number of exchanges depends directly on how strict are the requirements for both agents to accept equal gains, and this corroborates and further highlights the rigidness of the original CDMM assumption regarding the specification of which exchanges may happen.

Figure 4 depicts how each deviation differs, across precisions, per model setup. Note that, for most models, lower precisions yield greater differences in deviations. Dataset A is the only one that yields a significantly different dynamic when processed with the CE setup. All other models, for all tested datasets, yield stationary trends converging to one value or a range.

For dataset C, the results can be summarised as: (a) the EC setup performs almost identically to the Challenge model, with errors varying equally between -0.1 and -0.05; (b) all other models performances are similar, with errors varying between 0.2 and 0.27581. The floating point precision issue in the Exchange model is significant as, depending on the tested dataset, it can lead to deviations from the actual outcome of up to 0.85. That is a large difference in deviations, particularly when considering that most predicted outcomes deviate below 1 and that these variations arise only due to how precisely calculations are done in this CDMM.

Table 4 depict a minor, but nevertheless relevant, finding that the EC setup as the only model able to predict exactly the outcome of individual issues, even when the model is configured with different rounding precisions. These were issues 1 and 5, in datasets B and C, although one can also note that other runs were able to yield results very close to a perfect match per issue. This may be due to the little variability of PSP values per agent (see Table 1).

Figure 4. Matches across issues, per simulated rounded precision of two datasets (A) and (B)

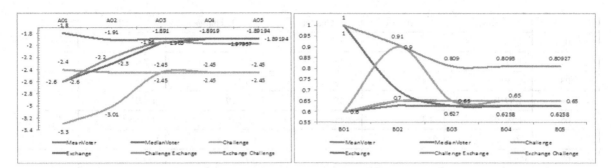

Table 4. Perfect matches within issues, per dataset per rounded precision

Issue	Dataset	Mean	Exchange	CE	EC
1	B01	0	0.1	0.1	0
5	B01	0.2	0.2	0.2	0
5	B02	0.17	0.19	0.27	0
5	B03	0.171	0.171	0.204	0
5	B04	0.171	0.171	0.2038	0
5	B05	0.17097	0.17097	0.20385	0
5	C01	0.1	0.1	0.1	0
5	C02	0.11	0.11	0.11	0
5	C03	0.11	0.097	0.118	0
5	C04	0.1097	0.1097	0.1179	0
5	C05	0.10968	0.10968	0.11786	0

The precision issue seen in the Exchange model is important, particularly due to the nature of the datasets used in CDMM. This is because these usually contain little value variability; given the small continuum range[1] used, for sake of simplicity, when collecting data. Given the precision of calculations and significant potential for repeated values across issues and agents, deterministic CDMM seem to effectively depend on the initial distribution of the PSP values.

6. CASE STUDY 2: EU DATASET

While the grand landmark EU decisions make good newspaper headlines, the vast majority of the EU legislation is decided and enacted on an incremental basis across a wide range of policy areas. This second case study is uniquely representative of these kinds of EU decisions and also covers a wide range of EU policy areas and policy sectors. Contrasting with the LRDA case study which contains the same number of agents and issues per decision, the EU dataset, contains a dif-

Table 5. Summary means and standard deviations of all EU {15, 25, 27} (proposals, issues)

Data (σ)	EU 15 (30, 81)	EU 25 (17, 48)	EU 27 (4, 13)
Position	.523 (.428)	.476 (.428)	.407 (.420)
Salience	.638 (.203)	.557 (.241)	.523 (.311)
Power	.066 (.351)	.041 (.028)	.038 (.024)
Obs.	1360	1196	364

ferent number of agents and issues per decision. This case study spans three phases of enlargement during the time period 1996-2008, so the number of agents involved in the negotiations will reflect this as well as formal decision rules for the policy issues concerned. For an in-depth discussion of the dataset, please refer to Thomson (2011).

The EU dataset also contains missing values, including agents without initial positions and/or salience values. The original dataset contains information regarding 331 issues proposed in 125 legislative proposals introduced between 1996 and 2008; each belonging to one of the EU stages: 15, 25 or 27 member states. Table 5 presents the final set of data selected for this ABM analysis, having excluded any policy negotiations wherein there was missing data for agents and/or issues.

6.1 Case Study: Obtained Findings from the EU Dataset Replication and Integration

Contrasting with Table 2, the results presented in Table 6 suggest that the Exchange model is impacted differently in terms of how many pair wise exchanges can actually occur given the dataset group. Only the smallest set –EU 27– remains unaffected throughout the experiment, which is further indication that results obtained in CDMM depend on the input dataset. It does also highlight that there is a likely interaction between the number of agents, number of issues and distribution of these values. As with the other dataset, the number of Challenges and Potential Exchanges remains the same throughout the experiment, regardless of the precision.

When comparing deviations to the actual outcome, the Mean model results approximate to the normal distribution and the other CDMM generated two categories of observed deviations:

- Distributions mainly on both tails (Challenge, ExchangeChallenge and Median);
- Skewed with a negative short tail (Median, ChallengeExchange and Exchange).

In this case study the authors did not find a clear stationary trend or convergence patterns that would allow a more robust discussion of the insights acquired about the CDMM. Proposals for further and more detailed research work in this area are elaborated in the next section of this chapter.

Table 6. Potential exchanges (E.), Actual E. And challenges per rounded precision (P.)

Total / Dataset	EU 15	EU 25	EU 27	P.
Actual Exchanges (AE)	64	30	2	1
AE Challenge Exchange	52	18	2	2
	66	24	2	3
	85	30	2	4
	62	18	2	5
	46	24	0	1
	35	12	0	2
	50	18	0	3
	60	22	0	4
	48	12	0	5
Challenges	42	133	76	all
Potential E.	5035	6663	1899	all

7. DISCUSSION AND RECOMMENDATIONS

The relevance of implementing CDMM in an ABM framework allowed for systematic testing of the Challenge and Exchange Models in a controlled environment that allows reproducible and flexible testing of hypotheses. The replication of CDMM is itself a worthwhile exercise and experiment, as during this process it was possible to identify issues of accuracy regarding the specification of CDMM algorithms that can impact the interpretation of their results.

Moreover, in doing so, a process for cleaning up (empirical or simulated) datasets for use in the ABM has been designed, so that the same framework can be used to process other data sources that follow the specifications for normalising values and flagging of missing entries. As the Challenge Model references contain no explicit specification of "marginal measure" and individual "risk taking," these were not implemented. Another aspect, also not discussed in the original references, is the processing order of agents and issues. This does not seem to matter due to the non-strategic, recursive nature of the Challenge model: once a challenge is won, the loser is assumed to subsequently adopt the position of the winner. With regards to the Exchange Model, the main finding discussed is that greater precision in the calculation of pair wise exchanges can reduce the number of exchanges which can occur in a given dataset.

The flexibility of developing agent-based models highlights the need for rigorously correct implementations, both in terms of the specification of simulation assumptions and processes. Experienced researchers using an ABM framework are aware that computational experiments must be clearly specified to appropriately test hypotheses, aimed at gaining insights about the actual phenomena and the model itself by analysing the simulation results. Thus one must ensure that results are indeed due to relationships in the model itself, and not an artefact (i.e. an observation that results from particular implementations) or error (i.e. a mismatch between the design and the implementation) (Polhill et al., 2005; Galan et al., 2009). The replications of the CDMM required a detailed scrutiny of their assumptions and procedural specifications. The difference in results observed due to the precision of calculations is not a model error per se, but rather an artefact in the model specification either because assumptions indeed did not originally account for the precision aspect or there was no clear specification regarding that.

8. FINAL REMARKS FOR FUTURE RESEARCH

The increasing demand to understand the processes driving collective decisions, including for instance policy-making and various socio-economic phenomena, is turning ABM simulations into a form of surrogate reasoning about the actual phenomenon in question. In this sense, our contribution through the ABM lens is the further understanding of how two CDMM work in terms of their assumptions and internal dynamics. By experimenting with the CDMM in the ABM framework, it was possible to identify differences in robustness between the Challenge and Exchange models and explore how these models interplay once combined in a setup where the output of one is used as the input of another. Further to this, should the reader wish to discuss the source code developed for this chapter, please contact the corresponding author.

The aforementioned findings provide insights that are helpful to improve the modelling of collective decision-making in future and the understanding as to why fundamentally different CDMM (i.e. strategic and non-strategic ones) can perform similarly. Due to the contrasting results obtained with both datasets, another line of follow-up research would be to test under which combination of conditions (i.e. number of agents, number of issues and distribution of PSP values) the CDMM models are sensitive to the precision of calculations. The replications have been made in an ABM framework due to the flexibility that it allows the authors to explore aspects of heterogeneity within and across the CDMM. Future research on this would allow setting up interaction between agents equipped with different CDMM, which can include agents equipped with different CDMM and interacting through the ABM framework.

REFERENCES

Achen, C. H. (2006). Evaluating political decision-making models. In R. Thomson, F. N. Stokman, C. Achen, & T. König (Eds.), *The European Union decides*. Cambridge, UK: Cambridge University Press. doi:10.1017/CBO9780511492082.011

Arregui, J., Stokman, F., & Thomson, R. (2004). Bargaining in the European Union and shifts in actors' policy positions. *European Union Politics*, 5(1), 47–72. doi:10.1177/1465116504040445

Arregui, J., Stokman, F. N., & Thomson, R. (2006). Compromise, exchange and challenge in the European Union. In R. Thomson, F. N. Stokman, C. H. Achen, & T. König (Eds.), *The European Union decides*. Cambridge, UK: Cambridge University Press. doi:10.1017/CBO9780511492082.006

Bennett, R. J., & Payne, D. (2000). *UK local and regional development agencies data: Renegotiating power under labour*. Aldershot, UK: Ashgate.

Bueno de Mesquita, B. (1994). Political forecasting: An expected utility method. In B. Bueno de Mesquita, & F. N. Stokman (Eds.), *European community decision making. Models, comparisons, and applications*. New Haven, CT: Yale University Press.

Galán, J. M., Izquierdo, L. R., Izquierdo, S. S., Santos, J. I., del Olmo, R., López-Paredes, A., & Edmonds, B. (2009). Errors and artefacts in agent-based modelling. *Journal of Artificial Societies and Social Simulation*, 12(1).

Polhill, G., Izquierdo, L. R., & Gotts, N. M. (2005). The ghost in the model (and other effects of floating point arithmetic). *Journal of Artificial Societies and Social Simulation*, 8(1).

Stokman, F. N., & Van den Bos, J. M. M. (1992). A two-stage model of policy making, the political consequences of social networks. In G. Moore, & J. A. Whitt (Eds.), *Research and Society* (Vol. 4). Greenwich, CT: JAI Press.

Stokman, F. N., & Van Oosten, R. (1994). The exchange of voting positions: An object-oriented model of policy networks. In B. Bueno de Mesquita, & F. N. Stokman (Eds.), *European Community decision making. Models, comparisons, and applications*. New Haven, CT: Yale University Press.

Thomson, R. (2011). *Resolving controversy in the European Union*. Cambridge, UK: Cambridge University Press. doi:10.1017/CBO9781139005357

Thomson, R., Stokman, F. N., Achen, C. H., & Konig, T. (2006). *The European Union decides*. Cambridge, UK: Cambridge University Press. doi:10.1017/CBO9780511492082

Thomson, R., Stokman, F. N., & Torenvlied, R. (2003). Models of collective decision-making: Introduction. *Rationality and Society*, 15(1), 5–14. doi:10.1177/1043463103015001037

Van den Bos, J. (1991). *Dutch EC policy making. A model-guided approach to coordination and negotiation*. Amsterdam, The Netherlands: Thela Thesis.

ADDITIONAL READING

Amadae, S. M., & Bueno de Mesquita, B. (2004). Decision-Making Models, Rigor and New Puzzles. *European Union Politics*, 5(1), 125–138. doi:10.1177/1465116504040448

Arrow, K. J. (1963). *Social Choice and Individual Values* (2nd ed.). New Haven: Yale University Press.

Axelrod, R. (1997). *The complexity of cooperation. Agent based models of competition and cooperation*. Princeton: Princeton University Press.

Axelrod, R. (1997). Advancing the Art of Simulation in the Social Sciences. In R. Conte, R. Hegselmann, & P. Terna (Eds.), *Simulating Social Phenomena*. Berlin: Springer. doi:10.1007/978-3-662-03366-1_2

Boero, R., & Squazzoni, F. (2005). Does Empirical Embeddedness Matter? Methodological Issues on Agent-Based Models for Analytical Social Science. *Journal of Artificial Societies and Social Simulation*, 8(4). Retrieved from http://jasss.soc.surrey.ac.uk/8/4/6.htm

Bonabeau, E. (2002). Agent-based modeling: Methods and techniques for simulating human systems [PNAS]. *Proceedings of the National Academy of Sciences of the United States of America*, 99(3), 7280–7287. doi:10.1073/pnas.082080899 PMID:12011407

Bueno de Mesquita, B. (1999). THE ROCHESTER SCHOOL: The Origins of Positive Political Theory. *Annual Review of Political Science*, 2, 269–295. doi:10.1146/annurev.polisci.2.1.269

Bueno de Mesquita, B. (2004). Decision Making Models, Rigor and New Puzzles. *European Union Politics*, 5, 125–138. doi:10.1177/1465116504040448

Caplin, A., & Nalebuff, B. J. (1991). Aggregation and Social Choice: A Mean Voter Theorem. *Econometrica*, 59, 1–23. doi:10.2307/2938238

Coen, D., & Richardson, J. (Eds.). (2009). *Lobbying EU Policy Making. Institutions, Actors and Issues*. Oxford: Oxford University Press.

Coleman, J. S. (1990) Foundations of Social Theory. Cambridge, M.A: The Belknap Press

Edmonds, B., & David Hales (2003) Replication, Replication and Replication: Some Hard Lessons from Model Alignment *Journal of Artificial Societies and Social Simulation* 6 (4). Retrieved from http://jasss.soc.surrey.ac.uk/6/4/11.html

Gilbert, N., & Terna, P. (2000). How to build and use agent based models in social science. *Mind and Society*, 1, 57–72. doi:10.1007/BF02512229

Gotts, N. M., Polhill, J. G., & Law, A. N. R. (2003)... *Agent-Based Simulation in the Study of Social Dilemmas Artificial Intelligence Review*, 19(1), 3–92. doi:10.1023/A:1022120928602

Hall, S., & Nevin, B. (1999). Continuity and Change: A review of English regeneration policy in the 1990s. *Regional Studies*, 35, 477–482. doi:10.1080/00343409950081310

Macal, C. M., & North, M. J. (2010). Tutorial on agent-based modelling and simulation. *Journal of Simulation*, 4, 151–162. doi:10.1057/jos.2010.3

Mokken, R. J., Payne, D., Stokman, F. N., & Wasseur, F. W. (2000). Decision context and policy effectuation: EU Structural reform in Ireland. *Irish Political Studies*, 15, 39–6. doi:10.1080/07907180008406613

Ormerod, P., & Rosewell, B. (2009). Validation and verification of agent-based models in the social sciences. Epistemological Aspects of Computer Simulation in the Social Sciences. *Lecture Notes in Computer Science*, 5466, 130–140. doi:10.1007/978-3-642-01109-2_10

Richiardi, M., Leombruni, R., Saam, N., & Sonnessa, M. (2006). A Common Protocol for Agent-Based Social Simulation. *Journal of Artificial Societies and Social Simulation*, *9*(1). Retrieved from http://jasss.soc.surrey.ac.uk/9/1/15.html

Robert, L., Goldstone, M., & Jannsen, A. (2005). Computational models of collective behaviour. *Trends in Cognitive Sciences*, *9*(9), 424–430. doi:10.1016/j.tics.2005.07.009 PMID:16085450

Sansores, C., & Pavón, J. (2005). Agent-based simulation replication: A model driven architecture approach. *Lecture Notes in Computer Science*, *3789*, 244–253. doi:10.1007/11579427_25

Stokman, F. N., Van Assen, M. A. L. M., Van der Knoop, J., & Van Oosten, R. (2000). Strategic Decision Making. *Advances in Group Processes*, *17*, 131–153. doi:10.1016/S0882-6145(00)17006-7

Wilensky, U., & Rand, W. (2007) Making Models Match: Replicating an Agent-Based Model *Journal of Artificial Societies and Social Simulation* 10,(4 2) Retrieved from http://jasss.soc.surrey.ac.uk/10/4/2.htm

KEY TERMS AND DEFINITIONS

Agent Based Model: A computational modelling approach which simulates the actions and interactions of autonomous agents (both individual or collective entities such as organizations or groups) with a view to assessing their both macro effects (on the system as a wholeon the whole system) and micro-level effects (on individuals).

Bargaining: The activity by which two or more parties try to reach agreement, settling how much each gives and takes, or what each performs and receives, in a transaction between them.

Collective Decision Making: A situation where a group of individuals make a decision for a set of alternatives before them and the decision taken is not attributable to any one individual in the group.

Experiment: An experiment is a controlled test or investigation to determine the validity of a hypothesis.

Policy: A principle or course of action adopted or proposed as desirable, advantageous, or expedient; *esp.* one formally advocated by a government, political party, etc (Oxford English Dictionary: http://www.oed.com/view/Entry/146842) Exchange.

Replication: The implementation (replicated model) by one group of scientists (model replicators or replicators) of a conceptual model described and already implemented (original model) by another group of scientists at a previous time (model builders or builders), where the process of the implementation of the replicated model must differ in some way from the original model building process (Wilensky and & Rand, 2007).

Simulation: The imitation modeling of the operation of a real-world process or system over time.

ENDNOTES

[1]   The datasets used increments either a) of 1 (from 0 to 10) or b) of 0.1 (from 0 to 1).

Chapter 6
Analysing Simulation Results Statistically:
Does Significance Matter?

Klaus G. Troitzsch
Universität Koblenz-Landau, Germany

ABSTRACT

Many papers on simulation in the social sciences come up with significance tests in which the authors describe the effect of a parameter on some simulation outcome as significant on some level of significance. This chapter discusses the question whether significance tests on simulation results are meaningful, and it argues that it is the effect size much more than the existence of the effect that matters and that it is the description of the distribution function of the stochastic process incorporated in the simulation model which is important, particularly when this distribution is far from normal — which is particularly often the case when the simulation model is nonlinear.

INTRODUCTION

Multiple runs of simulation models can be seen as samples from an unlimited universe of all possible runs executed by this simulation model for one single parameter combination. In empirical research one usually has only one sample at a time from a limited universe (typically, the population of a country), and this sample is usually biased by effects of the lack of precise information on the universe, low response rates and self-selection. Thus the situation of an empirically active researcher resembles the situation of a researcher running his or her simulation only once for each parameter combination. Thus simulation researchers are luckier than their empirically active colleagues, as the latter have to assume some probability distribution for the parameters they want to estimate from their empirical data, and usually they choose a normal distribution or some distribution derived from the normal distribution (such as the χ^2 distribution) or use some non-parametric analysis, whereas simulation researchers can construct an arbitrary large "sample of samples" from which they can at least visualise the form of the probability density function of the macro output parameter in question, as this resembles the histogram of the parameter estimates from the

DOI: 10.4018/978-1-4666-5954-4.ch006

individual simulation runs for an identical input parameter combination. And another advantage of simulation researchers is that they have full control of the input parameters of their simulation models whereas even the best controlled lab experiments with human test persons cannot avoid systematic bias (for the complementarity of real-world experiments and "simulation experiments" see also chapter 18).

If simulation serves the purpose of generating macrostructures from microspecifications (Axtell & Epstein, 1996)(Epstein, 2006, p. 8) then simulation is a deductive attempt(Epstein, 2006, p. xiv): trying to deduce macro behaviour from theoretical assumptions on micro behaviour — which more often than not is not directly observable, whereas the macro structure and the macro processes can often be easily observed. Thus one could argue that a simulation model can be used to test theories on the macro effect of micro assumptions: if the macrostructures predicted by a simulation model do not have empirical correlates then the micro assumptions are at least questionable (for more about the analysis of emergence in multilevel simulation models see also chapters 1 and 4).

The rest of this chapter gives several examples of multiple runs of some simulation models and argues that — unlike most empirical analyses — here the question is not whether a certain input parameter (the analogue of an independent variable) — has or has not an effect on a certain output parameter (the analogue of a dependent variable) but what is interesting in simulation research is the form of the relation between input and output parameters and the size of the effect. Sensitivity analysis, of course, is still interested in which input parameters have an effect on which output parameters, but mostly in order to eliminate input parameters whose effect is small.

The examples are taken from a well-published and relatively simple problem: the El Farol Problem (Arthur, 1994), and a much more complex one that extends the famous sugarscape model

(Axtell & Epstein, 1996) with an element of networks between agents (König, Möhring, & Troitzsch, 2003).

BACKGROUND

The Role of Simulation

Before we concentrate on stochastic simulation models (which seem to be a large majority among simulation models in the literature), a few words about simulations models and their role are in order. As argued decades ago by Thomas Ostrom, simulation models and the programming languages used to design and to implement them can be seen as a "third symbol system" beyond natural language and mathematics (Ostrom, 1988). All three symbol systems are used to derive new statements from statements already known. Thus, for instance, we use calculus to derive the function which describes the states of a system at arbitrarily many points of time from a differential equation which defines the relation between the state of the system and the change of this state:

$$\frac{dx}{dt} = f\left(x,t\right) \overset{yields}{\to} x = x\left(t\right), e.g.$$

$$\frac{dx\left(t\right)}{dt} = \lambda x\left(t\right) \overset{yields}{\to} x\left(t\right) = K \exp\left(\lambda t\right)$$

$$(1)$$

$$\frac{d\boldsymbol{x}}{dt} = \boldsymbol{f}\left(\boldsymbol{x},t\right) \overset{yields}{\to} \boldsymbol{x} = \boldsymbol{x}\left(t\right), e.g.$$

$$\begin{cases} \dfrac{dx}{dt} = x\left(a + bx + cy\right) \\ \dfrac{dy}{dt} = y\left(d + ex + fy\right) \end{cases} \overset{yields}{\to} \ ?$$

$$(2)$$

These are deterministic descriptions of systems whose states are determined by the time-dependent variable x (a scalar or a vector), and if it is possible to determine the function $x = x(t)$ in closed form (which is possible for Equation 1, but not for Equation 2), the symbol system of mathematics has delivered a deduction from the differential equation. If no such closed derivation is possible, a numerical solution is often used which is a more sophisticated version of a System Dynamics model (Forrester, 1968) and therefore a deterministic simulation. In principle, the same applies to stochastic systems which, in simple cases, can also be solved (perhaps only approximately) in closed form, as, for instance, a simple opinion dynamics model first described and discussed by Weidlich (Weidlich, 1972) and Weidlich and Haag (Weidlich & Haag, 1983) where the probability distribution of the percentage of proponents and opponents in a population is derived from assumptions about individual transition probability rates which in turn depend on this percentage. A simulation model describing the same system performs nothing else than the mathematical derivation (Izquierdo, Izquierdo, Galán, & Santos, 2013) and can therefore be labelled as a deductive technique, but with one exception: This simulation model will have to be executed several, perhaps many times with the same set of parameters, but with different seeds of the random number generator, and never yield a closed description of the resulting probability function, but only a large number of point estimates from which a probability function can be approximated.

Next we have to describe the role of stochastic simulation models shortly. Designing a stochastic simulation model has nothing to do with a possible belief on the modeller's side that the real world target system is controlled by random forces. Stochastic elements in simulation models rather reflect the uncertainty of the model assumptions, the inaccuracy of empirical measurement and/or the impossibility to quantify propensities and attitudes of real human beings in their social contexts.

The Role of Significance

Every textbook of statistics contains a definition of significance; some even distinguish between statistical significance, practical significance and substantive significance (Vogt, 1993, p. 210)(Bickman & Rog, 2009, p. xi)(Rudas, 2008, p. 84), some even criticise the "cult of statistical significance" claiming that everyday significance testing neglects effect sizes and is only interested in whether an effect exists (Ziliak & McCloskey, 2007). For our current discussion a textbook definition may suffice which says "*If* the null hypothesis is true ..., *then* the probability of an erroneous statistical conclusion is α ..."(Bickman & Rog, 2009, p. 46). In a frequentist interpretation, one could also say as a result of the analysis of one sample from a universe in which the null hypothesis is (assumed to be) true that the probability to find an even higher deviation from the null hypothesis in the next sample of the same size is α. And when this probability is low then we might believe that the deviation from the null hypothesis in our first sample is due to pure chance (Rudas, 2008, p. 83). No matter how α is calculated—usually assuming that the parameter estimated by our first sample is distributed according to some known distribution (usually a very courageous assumption!) — we only had this one sample.

The situation in the analysis of simulation results is entirely different: Here we always have a chance to draw the second sample and many more, such that we are not really interested in the test of significance derived from just one sample. Although we usually would not spend as much time and effort to calculate all possible samples from a simulation model (with the usual random number generators this would end up in 2^{64} samples, as a typical computer cannot generate more than 2^{64}

different random numbers) we can describe the distribution of sample estimates for parameters in much more detail than in the empirical case where we have one or very few samples and a questionable assumption of distributions.

This is also true in all cases where we want to compare an artificial economy or society to its real counterpart as for instance in the classical microanalytical simulation (Orcutt, Merz, & Quinke, 1986), Here we often use simulation input parameters estimated from empirical data (education-specific birth rates, life tables, propensities to move from one town district to another) and generate a hopefully large sample of large samples — say, 100 parallel runs of a census sample of, say, 100,000 real persons in real households — to deduce the distribution of some population feature — say, the percentage of mothers who give birth to their first children beyond the age of 35 (Hannappel & Troitzsch, 2012) or some specific segregation index in a town in Southern Brazil (de Fonseca Feitosa, Bao Le, & Vlek, 2011). In this case the research question is whether the distribution of the respective parameter calculated from the only available sample drawn from the real population a couple of years later is compatible with the distribution of this simulation output parameter deduced by means of the large sample of simulated samples (and it is here that considerations of statistical significance have their place).

EXAMPLES

The El Farol Problem

The El Farol Problem has often been discussed since it made its first appearance (Arthur, 1994). It represents inhabitants of Santa Fe who sometimes go to the El Farol bar which is famous for its Thursday evenings with Irish music. The artificial society of virtual El Farol consists of 100 people, and visiting the bar is most convenient when

60 persons attend. The potential visitors decide whether to go to the bar using the information about the attendance on previous Thursdays, trying to forecast with different forecasting strategies whether today the bar will have more or less than 60 visitors, abstaining from going there when more than 60 visitors can be expected and deciding to attend when less than 60 visitors can be expected. "… if there was an obvious model that all agents could use to forecast attendance and base their decisions on, then a deductive solution would be possible. But this is not the case. … So in what follows I will proceed with computer experiments" (Arthur, 1994, pp. 408–409) — as a surrogate of the impossible deductive solution. The model has been simulated several times, first by Arthur himself in his original paper (with a restricted evolutionary feature, later on, and perhaps most popular in (Rand & Wilensky, 2007), for an evolutionary extension see (Fogel, Chellapilla, & Angeline, 1999) and also treated analytically (Whitehead, 2008; Zambrano, 2004), just to mention a small part of the discussion in the literature.

We will use this model here for discussing the use or uselessness of a statistical treatment of this intrinsically deterministic model. It is deterministic as the decisions taken by the simulated agents are strictly deterministic. They use their memories to remember the attendance during w past weeks, they have s strategies which they can use to forecast the attendance on the upcoming Thursday (all of them weighted averages of the remembered past attendances) and among these they use the one which predicted the attendance of last Thursday best. The only random element lies in the initialisation when the agents get the weighting coefficients for their individual strategies.

Typically, e.g. in (Fogel, Chellapilla, & Angeline, 1999) the model is run several times with the same parameters — memory length and number of strategies — such that one can say each run is a sample of 100 agents drawn from a much larger population of potential bar visitors with randomly assigned weighting coefficient vectors. Therefore it is reasonable to use similar statistical techniques as in empirical research to describe the distributions of output variables depending on the random initialisation of weighting coefficients for different memory lengths and numbers of strategies.

For a first analysis we use the distribution of the individual number of attendances of the 100 agents during the last 500 Thursdays of a simulation of 600 Thursdays.

Figure 1 shows the histograms for five different parameter combinations (the case of memory size 6 and 12 strategies is used for two comparisons). The distributions in the two left comparisons are "significantly different" (Kolmogorov-Smirnov test, see Table 1), the distributions in the third comparison are not "significantly different" (i.e. the null hypothesis that that the two sample runs were taken from the same universe should not be rejected, moreover the two cases for a strategy number of 12 and memory sizes of 6 and 10 seem to be normally distributed with means 287.91 and 281.27, respectively, and standard deviations 180.92 and 147.42, respectively.

By the way, it is interesting to see that the Mann-Whitney U-test and a test just comparing the means of the number of attendances (instead of their complete distributions) yields entirely different values (which are not even "statistically significant" on a 0.05 level) — see Table 1.

Both the Mann-Whitney and the Kolmogorov-Smirnov test whether the two samples stem from the same population characterised by the distribution whose parameters are unused for the calculation of the test statistic, whereas the t-test only tests whether the population means of the samples from the two populations from which the samples were drawn are the same. Both the Mann-Whitney U-test (because of the extremely large number of rank ties) and the t-test (for the obvious bimodality at least of the sample comparison in the middle of Figure 1 are perhaps inappropriate; anyway the effect sizes (here the test statistics) are incommensurable, and perhaps one could use the α's for a comparison of effect sizes where these are incommensurable — after all there is a strict

Figure 1. Distribution of the individual number of attendances of the 100 agents during the last 500 steps of hundred 600-step simulation runs for five different parameter combinations (memory size 6 in the first graph and 10 in the second graph, number of strategies 12 for the third graph)

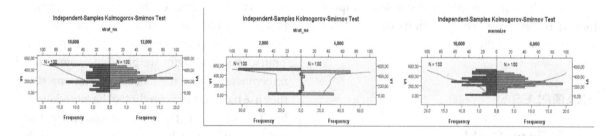

Table 1. Comparison of different test statistics for the distributions shown in Figure 1

Figure 1	Memory Length	Number of Strategies	Kolmogorov-Smirnov-Test		Mann-Whitney U-Test		T-Test	
			T	α	U	α	t	α
Left	6	10 / 12	*1.414*	*0.037*	4,884.5	0.778	0.083	0.934
Middle	10	2 / 4	*1.556*	*0.016*	4,367.0	0.088	0.983	0.327
Right	10 / 6	12	1.131	0.155	5,136.5	0.739	–0.326	0.745

functional dependence of α on the effect size for equal sample sizes.

But what can we learn from these calculations? The main result of these considerations is that the results generated by the simulation model are partly due to the parameter settings and partly due to the random allocation of weighting coefficients to the strategies which the individual agents use for making their decisions — as the process of decision making itself is strictly deterministic, the significance considerations can be used to find out whether the differences between particular runs are only due to random initialisation or whether the parameter settings play a role. From the five runs plotted in Figure 1 one could perhaps conclude that for a higher number of strategies (say 12) and a sufficiently long memory (6 or more) it is only the random initialisation that makes the difference. But the three comparisons are, of course, not sufficient.

As it is possible that under certain circumstances the agents within a sample make once-and-forever decisions (as in the two runs compared in the middle plot of Figure 1, where more than 50 per cent of the agents went to El Farol 500 times, and as already analytically predicted by (Whitehead, 2008) and (Farago, Greenwald, & Hall, 2002), but without going into the details of dependencies between memory size and number of strategies on

one hand and this effect on the other hand), the output variables used here are the amplitude of the attendance over time (measured as the range of the attendances during the last 100 out of 600 simulated weeks), and the mean of the numbers of individual attendance decision changes. For the figures, models were run with memory sizes of 2, 4, 6, 8, and 10 Thursdays and with strategy choices of 2, 4, 6, 8, 10, and 12.

As Figure 2 (left) shows, the amplitude is very small for a model where agents can only choose among two strategies, and it is highest for a wide choice of strategies for short memories. Long memories are also responsible for low amplitudes, but the main cause for large amplitudes is a short memory. The nonlinear function for the amplitude A, measured as the range of attendances during the last 100 steps,

$$A = \frac{\alpha \exp(\beta w)}{1 + \exp\left[-\gamma(s - \delta)\right]} \qquad (3)$$

approximates the data used for the histogram in Figure 2 (left) quite well with $\alpha \approx 156, \beta \approx -0.2, \gamma \approx 0.7, \delta \approx 5.3, (R^2 \approx 0.9)$ — but Equation (3) has no real justification for describing a macrostructure, as the arguments of function (3) are real numbers whereas the input

Figure 2. Behaviour of the El Farol model for different memory sizes and numbers of forecast strategies. Left: amplitude of the attendance over 100 ticks, middle: mean of individual attendance decision changes over all 600 ticks, right: correlation of the two output variables. Averages over 50 sample runs.

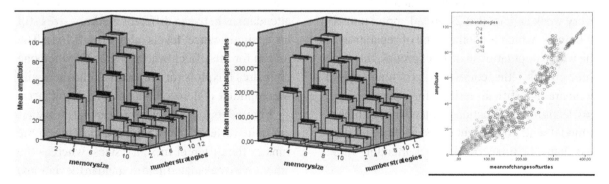

parameters of the simulation are integer numbers (such that A can be calculated for $s = 2.5$ and $w = 8.5$, but these input values do not make any sense).

The middle graph of Figure 2 shows how often, on an average, the agents change their minds between two Thursdays: with only two strategies they change their minds almost never after the first few weeks which leads to a separation of the agents into two distinct groups, which means that in most runs about 60 per cent of all agents attended the bar nearly 600 out of 600 times, while the other 40 per cent attended only occasionally, if at all. This also explains the nearly vanishing amplitude for these cases — nearly all agents made a once-and-for-all decision very early — and consequently the correlation between these two output variables of the model is extremely high ($R^2 = 0.934$). This correlation is particularly interesting, as the two variables — amplitude of the time series of overall attendances and number of individual attendance decision changes — can be observed empirically in real-world situations resembling the El Farol model, for instance likes and dislikes of Facebook items: If in such an empirical case a high correlation between the two observables can be shown, this would at least partly validate the El Farol model in terms of an unsuccessful refutation of the micro-behavioural conjectures of the theory underlying the El Farol model (in terms of (Popper, 1963)).

More than six strategies and memory of length 2 lead to a situation where a typical run ends up with sixty per cent of the agents attending approximately 400 out of 600 weeks, whereas 20 come every week and another 20 attend approximately 200 times, which is another kind of separation of the whole population in distinct groups, this time three groups. Other combinations of w and s yield comparably artificial results, for instance $w=10$ $s=6$ leads to a distribution of attendances which is bimodal with 30 per cent of the agents attending less than 112 times, 30 per cent attending more than 557 times and 40 per cent with attendances between 112 and 557.

The results show that the samples differ meaningfully for different parameter combinations, but does it matter whether the differences are statistically significant? Given that the relations between the two input parameters w and s on one hand and the output parameters depicted in Figure 2 are obviously nonlinear, only a nonparametric test can be applied. Keeping w constant, the independent samples median test for all three output variables against the number of strategies is "statistically significant" with $\alpha<0.0005$ for all levels of w, the other way round the independent samples median test for the three output variables against the memory size is also "statistically significant" with $\alpha<0.0005$ for all levels of $s>2$ (with only few exceptions where $0.0005<\alpha<0.02$). The same applies to the independent samples Jonckheere-Terpstra test (Lunneborg, 2005), and more or less the same applies to the independent samples Kruskal-Wallis test.

And this holds for 10 runs per parameter combination. It goes without saying that α can be further reduced to smaller and smaller values when the number of runs per parameter combination is increased.

When one runs the $s=2$ models for several w 100 times instead of only ten times, one finds that the differences between different memory sizes in the long term mean of the attendances and even the individual attendances (which were not "statistically significant" for 10 runs) now become "statistically significant" with $\alpha<0.0005$; only the difference of amplitudes of the long term attendances between different memory sizes still have significance levels above $\alpha>0.761$. The reason for this effect becomes graphic when one compares boxplots for the mean attendances and the amplitude of the oscillations of the attendances.

Figure 3 makes sufficiently clear that the means are quite different, both within and between the runs of the different memory sizes, whereas the amplitudes (calculated here as standard deviations) have more or less identical means between, but not within the runs for different memory size *w*. The same figure, by the way, shows that for short memory sizes the long term mean attendance lies far beyond the crowding threshold (quite opposite to Arthur's early findings (Arthur, 1994, p. 409). All differences of the distributions of the individual number of attendances between different memory sizes (for *s*=2) are "statistically significant" with $\alpha < 0.0005$, although with only three exceptions (for *s*=*w*=2) out of 500 runs the difference between the second and eighth deciles is 596 and more, and the median is always 597 and above. The differences only become visible (and "statistically significant") because of the transient phases at the beginning of each run. If one leaves the first 100 ticks out of the analysis, all "statistical significance" vanishes.

Sustainability in Structured Primordial Societies

The second example is about a sugarscape-like (Axtell & Epstein, 1996) society in which agents move around a virtual world of square fields on which some food grows, can be harvested and re-grows unless it is totally exhausted. This

model was first presented in (König, Möhring, & Troitzsch, 2003) and replicated in NetLogo (Troitzsch, 2013) for the purpose of this chapter. The main extension as compared to the various models presented in (Axtell & Epstein, 1996) is that agents can take several roles: the role of autonomous individuals who move around on their own, trying to survive, to gather provision, to breed, and to acquire additional information about food in their neighbourhoods; the role of coordinators who can additionally decide to collect and redistribute information about food in the neighbourhoods of their subordinates (who pay for this service) and who influence their subordinates; and finally the subordinates who, for some time, subordinate themselves to a coordinator. Both latter roles can be given up if they turn out to be unsatisfactory.

Figure 4 shows a screenshot of the running model showing sliders for the most interesting parameters on the left margin, the virtual world in the middle (with fields coloured white to dark green according to what can be harvested from them, white meaning a waste field, dark green meaning a promising one, and lighter and darker red triangles, inverted triangles and circles for more or less hungry coordinators, subordinates

Figure 3. Mean and amplitude of the history of attendances for the case with two strategies and various sizes of memory (100 runs each)

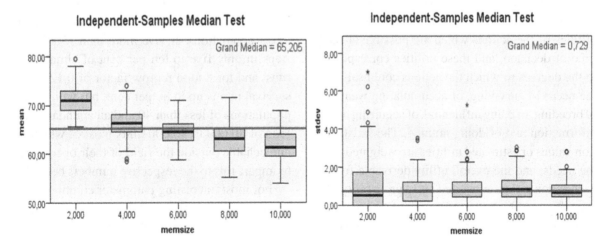

Figure 4. Sustainability in a structured primordial society: The virtual world (centre) and several plots describing the history of the virtual world

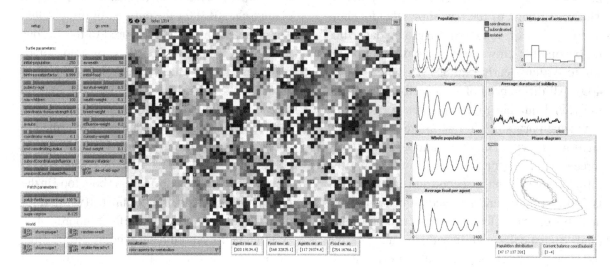

and autonomous agents) and several plots showing the change over time of the subpopulation sizes, the available worldwide food, the total population, the food per agent, the decisions taken, the average duration of subordination relations and, finally, the phase diagram of population size (horizontal) and overall food (vertical).

The simulation model describes a complex stochastic process which is initialised randomly, both for the fields and the agents. The stochasticity of the process stems mainly from the decisions taken by the agents — to move, to gather food, to breed, to enter and leave the roles of coordinator and subordinate. These decisions are made with probabilities which are derived from estimated utilities of the actions which are possible at the time of decision, and these utilities correspond to the degrees to which the actions could satisfy the needs of surviving, of accumulating wealth, of breeding, of being influential, of acquiring new information and of doing nothing. The satisfaction values or estimated utilities are weighted for the needs, and the overall utility derivable from each action is then converted into a probability of choosing exactly one out of these eight actions — where the probability of the action with the lowest

utility is set to zero; the algorithm resembles an algorithm used in da Fonseca Feitosa (2010) and de Fonseca Feitosa, Bao Le, and Vlek (2011) in a model of intra-urban migration and segregation and also that of LARA (Briegel, Ernst, Holzhauer, Klemm, Krebs, & Martínez Piñánez, 2012), in the latter case with the exception that in LARA the action with the highest utility is deterministically chosen.

Without coordination and subordination, populations die out soon or are restricted to small niches of patches with a medium yield whereas patches abundant of food are beyond their vision range and cannot be exploited by the few remaining agents (with a food regrow factor of 0.075 populations survive more than 1500 time steps in only five to ten per cent of simulation runs, and for a food regrow factor of 0.125 this survival rate is up to 80 per cent, but with agent populations of less than 40 and an abundance of food of 70,000 to 90,000 units most of which is unreachable outside the field of their operations (compare this to the respective numbers below!).

For most interesting parameter combinations — and these are the ones with coordination and subordination — the stochastic process is of the generalised Lotka-Volterra or predator-prey type, which is not a surprise as the agents can be seen as predators predating on the plants which yield the food. And indeed, from the phase diagram of Figure 4 the coefficients of a Lotka-Volterra system of differential equations (see Equation 2) can be estimated. This system of differential equations has a stable spiral point for approximately 211 agents and a food amount of approximately 24,163; the eigenvalues of the Jacobean of the system being −944.8392 ±19298.54i. A comparison between the simulation result and the numerical solution of the system of differential equations with the coefficients estimated from the simulation result can be found in Figure 5, for the coefficients see Equation 4.

$$\frac{dx}{dt} = x\left(a_{00} + a_{10}x + a_{01}y\right)$$
$$\frac{dy}{dt} = y\left(b_{00} + b_{10}x + b_{01}y\right)$$

(4)

with $a_{00} = -0.05620$, $a_{10} = 0.00008647$, $a_{01} = 0.00000157$, $b_{00} = 0.05564$, $b_{10} = -0.0001630$, $b_{01} = -0.0000008785$ for the solution of Equation 4 with the best fit to the simulation data, where

the coefficients are usually ascribed the following meaning: a_{00} and b_{00} are the intrinsic growth rates of agents and food (a_{00} is rather a death rate than a growth rate), $-a_{00} / a_{10} = 650$ and $-b_{00} / b_{01} = 63,340$ are the carrying capacities of agents and food, respectively, in the absence of the other population, and a_{01} and b_{10} are the coefficients describing the effect of agents "encountering" food on agents and food, respectively.

The distribution of the difference between the best possible numerical solution of Equation 4 and the simulation result are depicted in Figure 6 and show that the differences for both agents and food are not normally distributed (the Kolmogorv-Smirnov test yields test statistics of 1.628, α=0.01, and 2.836, α<0.0005), that their means are not 0 (but the sums of squared errors are at a minimum), such that one has to conjecture that a better fit could perhaps be arrived at with an even more generalised version of the Lotka-Volterra equation.

Runs for different parameter combinations show that the behaviour of the simulation model depends on parameters. Taking for instance the size of the initial agent population and the food regrowth factor as input parameters and the am-

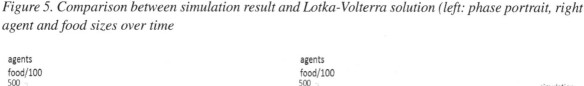

Figure 5. Comparison between simulation result and Lotka-Volterra solution (left: phase portrait, right agent and food sizes over time

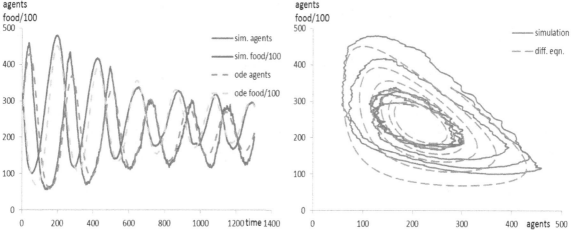

Figure 6. Estimation errors: Simulation against numerical solution of Equation 4

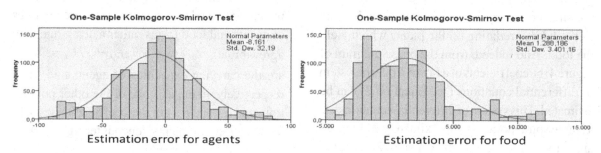

plitude of the last cycle as output parameter and running each of the combinations five times, we see that the former has little impact, whereas the latter has great impact on the amplitudes of the last cycle (see Table 2).

Significance (α) and effect (η^2) are, of course, correlated — the greater the effect, the smaller α for a fixed sample size —, but with an extremely small number of samples (i.e. simulation runs with fixed input parameter combination) the ef-

Table 2. Impact of selected input parameters on selected output parameters

	N Runs	Initial Population		Significance (α)	η^2
		150	250		
Agent amplitude	10	237.3	252.2	0.748	0.006
	50	248.0	258.54	0.586	0.003
Food amplitude	10	24802.355	29460.990	0.517	0.024
	50	26396.988	27728.61	0.631	0.002
		food regrowth factor			
		0.075	0.125		
Agent amplitude	10	326.70	162.80	0.000003	0.714
	50	332.02	174.52	<0.0000005	0.678
Food amplitude	10	40204.32	14059.025	0.000001	0.747
	50	39145.99	14979.61	<0.0000005	0.780
	n-runs=25	food regrowth factor			
	initial population	0.075	0.125		
Agent amplitude	150	338.80	157.20	<0.0000005	0.818
	250	325.24	191.84	<0.0000005	0.545
Significance (α)		0.433	0.010		
η^2		0.013	0.130		
Food amplitude	150	39300.85	13493.12	<0.0000005	0.830
	250	38991.12	16466.10	<0.0000005	0.734
Significance (α)		0.893	0.016		
η^2		0.00038	0.115		

fect of the food regrowth factor is not only high, but "significantly different from 0," whereas the effect of the size of the initial population is very low, and so is α. If we increase the number of runs, nothing much changes, the effect sizes are more or less the same (with 50 runs they are probably more exactly estimated than with 10 runs), and even the α's do not change considerably.

The two input parameters interact slightly, so from the lower half of Table 2 we can conclude that for the smaller initial population the effect of the food regrowth factor on the agent amplitude is considerably higher, whereas the difference in effects on the food amplitude is only a little higher. The other way round, the effect of the size of the initial population on both amplitudes is negligible (and not even "statistically significant" for 25 runs) for the low food regrowth factor, whereas it is still modest (but "statistically significant") for the high food regrowth factor.

Issues, Controversies, Problems

Both examples have shown that it is the effect of input parameters on output parameters generated by the respective simulation models — in terms of (Izquierdo, Izquierdo, Galán, & Santos, 2013, p. 241) "implementation[s] of a stochastic process, i.e. a function that transforms any given input into a certain probability distribution over the set of possible outputs" —, namely the form of the distributions shown in Figure 1 and Figure 6.

In the case of the first example it was useful to see that the output parameter "amplitude of the attendance over time" depended nonlinearly on the length of the agents' memories and the number of strategies available to them — and that a simple nonlinear function describing this dependence explained about nine tenths of the variance of this amplitude.

In the case of the second example it was also interesting to see that the microspecification-based model deviated a lot from the macro model, as only in the former the effect of the topography could become visible: The macro model assumes that food is everywhere and that the agents can move around their world without any limitations, whereas in the micro model an abundance of food at a place where currently no agents are moving shortens the effect of the coefficients of interaction between the two populations (a_{01} and b_{10} in the above equation), and the considerations about growth rate and carrying capacity are also influenced by the fact that both food and agents are not uniformly distributed over the world (this, for instance, is the reason why the input parameter "food regrowth rate" is different from the coefficient b_{00} in the macro equation).

Both examples showed that the main parameters describing the effect of the selected input parameters on the selected output parameters did not change considerably when the number of simulation runs was increased — although in nearly all cases an increase of the number of simulation runs led to "statistical significance" at least on the $\alpha=0.05$ level — which was not a surprise, but the material significance of the findings did not change at the same pace.

Comparing the examples, however, one might come to the conclusion that it is not always easy to compare effect sizes which were calculated on very different measures and measurement scales. The proportion of explained variance in η^2 or R^2 is incommensurable with the Kolmogorov-Smirnov test statistic or the test statistic of a comparison of medians. In these cases, α can be a convenient parameter to make differently calculated effect sizes comparable but, of course, only when the sample sizes are the same.

Solutions and Recommendations

The question remains under which conditions and how statistical analysis of simulation results should be done. It goes without saying that it is necessary to run a considerable number of simulations when a non-normal distribution of output parameters can be expected (which is usually the case when a model has nonlinear effects). To find out, for a trivial instance, whether a distribution is bimodal at least two simulation runs will be necessary as with only one simulation at best one of the two modes can be found. But beyond this, the general question "How many simulations must I run to be sure?" cannot be answered easily. To approach this problem, we return to the first example and estimate the parameters of the function shown

in Equation 3 for various numbers of simulation runs for each of 30 parameter combinations, i.e. for various numbers of samples drawn from 30 different universes of potential El Farol visitors, each of these universes characterised by the length of the memories of their individual members and the number of different strategies they can choose among. Figure 7 shows estimates and 95 per cent confidence intervals of the four parameters of the

Figure 7. Estimates of the parameters of Equation 3 approximating one of the output parameters (amplitude of attendances) in the El Farol example for various numbers of parallel runs (alpha-min, ... delta-max are the lower and upper bounds of the respective 95 per cent confidence intervals calculated from the nonlinear regression, the values for different numbers of samples start from the first simulation run, then the data of more and more simulation runs are included in the parameter estimation until the data of all 50 runs are included)

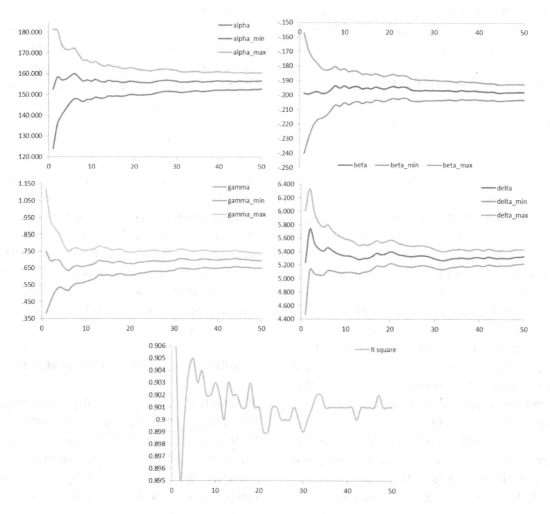

function described in Equation 3 as well as the variance shared with this function for 30 parameter combinations (s=2, 4, 6, 8, 10, w=2, 4, 6, 8, 10, 12) and various numbers of simulation runs per combination (from 1 to 50). The estimates themselves differ by 4.7, 3.0, 16.6, 9.3 and 1.2 per cent, respectively for α, β, γ, δ and R^2, from each other (calculated as the range, divided by the median), and the largest differences are found for the smallest numbers of runs. The confidence intervals have the shape of a funnel, as one would have expected, becoming narrower and narrower for increasing numbers of runs per combination and gives an indication which number of runs is satisfactory.

FUTURE RESEARCH DIRECTIONS

Given that this short chapter could not discuss all the analyses which are possible with respect to the two selected examples — let alone the analyses possible with other models — it could only touch some of the issues arising from simulation models with random initialisation (as the El Farol model) or stochastic decision making processes (as the Coordination and Sustainability model). Both models are open to various small extensions which lead to new questions. In the case of El Farol one could think of a population whose members have different sizes of memory and/or different repertoires of strategies — would the simulation reveal that in such an artificial society a selection of participants according to their capabilities would occur? In the case of the Coordination and Sustainability model one could think of a world in which — by some unrealistic miracle — the food available on each patch is equal at all times (such that the topology would not matter) — would the simulation reveal the effect of the unevenly distributed food on the emerging macrostructure? And, of course, as in the original publication (König, Möhring, & Troitzsch, 2003), is the fate of a society without coordination and

subordination — dying out after very few generations — inevitable, or can parameters be set which allow an unstructured artificial society with uncooperative individuals to survive, perhaps also oscillating around a stable spiral point?

Although many papers on simulation models contain discussion of the statistical properties of the macrostructures generated from the model's microspecification, this is still not standard, and perhaps the ODD protocol (Grimm, et al., 2006; Grimm, Berger, DeAngelis, Polhill, Giske, & Railsback, 2010) should be enlarged with an item describing the statistical properties of the model output.

This would also make a critical replication, evaluation and review of simulation results much easier, and it would also help those who apply the method of simulation to practical problems in economy and society to understand the role of prediction by simulation better—what we can predict (if we dare to do so at all) is distributions in the best case, never expected values.

CONCLUSION

The chapter was to show that simulation models are a means of deriving macrostructures from microspecification in the sense of (Axtell & Epstein, 1996) and thus a deductive procedure much like mathematical deduction (Beisbart & Norton, 2012) with the immense difference that they never yield closed solutions for the distribution of their output parameters but only estimates and confidence intervals for their parameters. As simulated and real macrostructures are much easier compared to each other than micro behaviours, as observing the latter is often impossible as the test persons themselves often cannot account for their propensities and decisions, at least replicative and predictive validity (Zeigler, 1976, p. 5) can better be judged with respect to macrostructures than with respect to micro behaviour. It is no problem to predict how many households will move from one district into another part of a large town next year, but it is nearly impossible to predict which household will move from district A to district B next year, to take an example from (da Fonseca Feitosa, 2010). Structural validity in the sense of Zeigler can only be judged with respect to micro behaviour, thus simulation and other deductive procedures can only sort out micro theory candidates which show macrostructures which are counterfactual and help us concentrate on those micro theories which yield realistic macrostructures. Statistical analysis will then allow us to estimate effect sizes which hopefully can be empirically validated, not only statistical significance that an effect exists.

ACKNOWLEDGMENT

The major programming work for the extended El Farol model was done on the base of (Rand & Wilensky, 2007) in Benjamin Leiberich's master thesis, whereas the replication of the Coordination and Sustainability model was mainly done by Florian Zink in his master thesis (both master theses were accepted by the Department of Computer Science of the University of Koblenz-Landau). The final versions of both NetLogo models were prepared by me. The final version of the paper profited from discussions with László Gulyás and other participants of the 4th ESSA Simulation Summer School (Hamburg, July 15-19, 2013) as well with participants of the Artificial Economics 2013 (Klagenfurt, August 29–30, 2013) where some of the results of this paper were first presented, and it profited from the suggestions of two anonymous referees.

REFERENCES

Arthur, W. B. (1994). Inductive Reasoning and Bounded Rationality. *The American Economic Review*, *84*(2), 406–411.

Axtell, R., & Epstein, J. M. (1996). *Growing Artificial Societies*. Cambridge, Mass.: MIT Press.

Beisbart, K., & Norton, J. D. (2012). Why Monte Carlo Simulations Are Inferences and Not Experiments. *International Studies in the Philosophy of Science*, *26*(4), 403–422. doi:10.1080/02698595 .2012.748497

Bickman, L., & Rog, D. J. (2009). *The Sage Handbook of Applied Social Research* (2nd ed.). Newbury Park: Sage.

Briegel, R., Ernst, A., Holzhauer, S., Klemm, D., Krebs, F., & Martínez Piñánez, A. (2012). Social-ecological modelling with LARA: A psychologically well-founded lightweight agent architecture. *International Congress on Environmental Modelling and Software 2012*. Leipzig.

da Fonseca Feitosa, F. (2010). Urban Segregation as a Complex System. An Agent-Based Simulation Approach. Bonn.

da Fonseca Feitosa, F., Bao Le, Q., & Vlek, P. L. (2011, March). Multi-agent simulator for urban segregation (MASUS): A tool to explore alternatives for promoting inclusive cities. *Computers, Environment and Urban Systems*, *35*, 104–115. doi:10.1016/j.compenvurbsys.2010.06.001

Epstein, J. M. (2006). *Generative Social Science. Studies in Agent-Based Computational Modeling*. Princeton, Oxford: Princeton University Press.

Farago, J., Greenwald, A., & Hall, K. (2002). Fair and Efficient Solutions to the Santa Fe Bar Problem. *Proceedings of the Grace Hopper Celebration of Women in Computing 2002.*

Fogel, D. B., Chellapilla, K., & Angeline, P. J. (1999, July). Inductive Reasoning and Bounded Rationality Reconsidered. *IEEE Transactions on Evolutionary Computation, 3*(2), 142–146. doi:10.1109/4235.771167

Forrester, J. W. (1968). Priciples of Systems (2nd preliminary ed.). Cambridge, Mass., and London: MIT Press/Wright Allen.

Grimm, V., Berger, U., Bastiansen, F., Eliassen, S., Ginot, V., & Giske, J. et al. (2006). A standard protocol for describing individual-based and agent-based models. *Ecological Modelling, 198*(1–2), 115–126. doi:10.1016/j.ecolmodel.2006.04.023

Grimm, V., Berger, U., DeAngelis, D. L., Polhill, J. G., Giske, J., & Railsback, S. F. (2010). The ODD protocol: A review and first update. *Ecological Modelling, 221*(23), 2760–2768. doi:10.1016/j.ecolmodel.2010.08.019

Hannappel, M., & Troitzsch, K. G. (2012). Demographic and educational projection. Building an event-oriented microsimulation model with CoMicS II. In K. G. Troitzsch, M. Möhring, & U. Lotzmann, *Shaping reality through simulation. 26th European Conference on Modelling and Simulation, May 29–June 1, 2012, Koblenz, Germany* (S. 613–618). Koblenz: ECMS.

Izquierdo, L. R., Izquierdo, S. S., Galán, J. M., & Santos, J. I. (2013). Combining Mathematical an Simulation Approaches to Understand the Dynamics of Computer Models. In B. Edmonds, & R. Meyer (Eds.), *Simulating Social Complexity. A Handbook* (pp. 235–271). Heidelberg: Springer. doi:10.1007/978-3-540-93813-2_11

König, A., Möhring, M., & Troitzsch, K. G. (2003). Agents, Hierarchies and Sustainability. In F. Billari, & A. Prskawetz (Eds.), *Agent-Based Computational Demography* (pp. 197–210). Heidelberg: Physica. doi:10.1007/978-3-7908-2715-6_11

Lunneborg, C. E. (2005). Jonckheere–Terpstra Test. In Encyclopedia of Statistics in Behavioral Science (S. DOI: doi:10.1002/0470013192.bsa324). New York: Wiley.

Orcutt, G. H., Merz, J., & Quinke, H. (1986). *Microanalytic Simulation Models to Support Social and Financial Policy. Information Research and Resource Reports* (Vol. 7). Amsterdam: North-Holland.

Ostrom, T. (1988). Computer Simulation: The Third Symbol System. *Journal of Experimental Social Psychology, 24*, 381–392. doi:10.1016/0022-1031(88)90027-3

Popper, K. R. (1963). *Conjectures and Refutations: the Growth of Scientific Knowledge.* London: Routledge.

Rand, W., & Wilensky, U. (2007). *NetLogo El Farol model.* Northwestern University, Center for Connected Learning and Computer-Based Modeling. Evanston, IL: http://ccl.northwestern.edu/netlogo/models/ElFarol.

Rudas, T. (2008). Probability Theory in Statistics. In T. Rudas (Ed.), *Handbook of Probability. Theory and Application* (pp. 69–84). Los Angeles: Sage. doi:10.4135/9781452226620.n5

Vogt, W. P. (1993). Dictionary of Statistics and Methodology. A Nontechnical Guide for the Social Sciences. Newbury Park: 1993.

Weidlich, W. (1972). The Use of Statistical Models in Sociology. *Collective Phenomena, 1*, 51–59.

Weidlich, W., & Haag, G. (1983). *Concepts and Models of a Quantitative Sociology. The Dynamics of Interacting Populations*. Berlin, Heidelberg: Springer. doi:10.1007/978-3-642-81789-2

Whitehead, D. (2008). The El Farol Bar Problem Revisited: Reinforcement Learning in a Potential Game. University of Edinburgh, Edinburgh School of Economics. ESE Discussion Papers 186.

Zambrano, E. (1. (2004, May). The Interplay between Analytics and Computation in the Study of Congestion Externalities: The Case of the El Farol Problem. *Journal of Public Economic Theory*, 6(2), 375–395. doi:10.1111/j.1467-9779.2004.00170.x

Zeigler, B. P. (1976). *Theory of Modelling and Simulation*. New York, London, Sydney, Toronto: John Wiley and Sons.

Ziliak, S. T., & McCloskey, D. N. (2007). *The Cult of Statistical Significance. How the Standard Error Costs Us Jobs, Justice and Lives*. Ann Arbor: University of Michigan Press.

ADDITIONAL READING

Casti, J. L. (1996). *Would-Be Worlds. How Simulation Is Changing the Frontiers of Science*. Chichester: Wiley.

Gilbert, N., & Troitzsch, K. G. (2005). *Simulation for the Social Scientist*. Maidenhead: Open University Press.

Hegselmann, R., Mueller, U., & Troitzsch, K. G. (1996). *Modelling and Simulation in the Social Sciences from the Philosophy of Science Point of View*. Dordrecht: Kluwer. doi:10.1007/978-94-015-8686-3

Squazzoni, F. (Ed.). (2009). *Epistemological Aspects of Computer Simulation in the Social Sciences*. Heidelberg: Springer. doi:10.1007/978-3-642-01109-2

Squazzoni, F. (2012). *Agent-Based Computational Sociology*. Chichester: Wiley. doi:10.1002/9781119954200

KEY TERMS AND DEFINITIONS

Deduction: The process of concluding a statement from something that was already known or believed to be true.

Microspecification: In a multilevel model, the description of rules which govern the behaviour of the entities of the lowest level on which features of entities of a higher level can be assumed to depend.

Multilevel Model: A mental, verbal, mathematical, or computer simulation model which models elements of a system and the system as a whole (and perhaps subsystems of the system as a whole) distinctly; agent-based social simulation models are necessarily multilevel models as they represent at least human individuals and their behavioural rules (lower level) or, instead, households or enterprises, alongside with the populations (higher level) which these lower level entities form, and often groups or subpopulations within these populations.

Random Number Generator: A physical device (rarely) that produces intrinsically random effects (e.g. counting decay events in radioactive matter) or an algorithm which produces a series of numbers which is sufficiently similar to the output of the former (currently, the Mersenne twister seems to be the most reliable pseudo-random number generator).

Statistical Significance Level α: As a result of the analysis of one sample from a universe in which the null hypothesis is (assumed to be) true: the probability to find an even higher deviation from the null hypothesis in the next sample of the same size.

Stochastic Process: A sequence of states of a system where the dependence of the system state at a later point of time depends not only and not exactly on the system state at an earlier point of time but also on some random effects where the latter either represent unknown deterministic influences or influences which are believed to be intrinsically random.

Validity: A model's property of delivering the same messages as the real-world target system it is designed to represent; one can distinguish between replicative validity (real-world data are already available at the time the model is being designed),

predictive validity (real-world data are collected only after the model has made predictions) and structural validity (the internal processes of the model can be shown to be sufficiently similar to the internal processes of the real-world target system); the latter is a sufficient, but not a necessary prerequisite for other two forms of validity (as structurally invalid models can make sufficiently correct and precise replications and predictions).

Chapter 7
Large–Scale Social Simulation, Dealing with Complexity Challenges in High Performance Environments

C. Montañola-Sales
Universitat Politècnica de Catalunya – Barcelona Supercomputing Center, Spain

J. Casanovas-Garcia
Universitat Politècnica de Catalunya – Barcelona Supercomputing Center, Spain

X. Rubio-Campillo
Barcelona Supercomputing Center, Spain

J. M. Cela-Espín
Universitat Politècnica de Catalunya – Barcelona Supercomputing Center, Spain

A. Kaplan-Marcusán
Universitat Autònoma de Barcelona, Spain

ABSTRACT

Advances on information technology in the past decades have provided new tools to assist scientists in the study of social and natural phenomena. Agent-based modeling techniques have flourished recently, encouraging the introduction of computer simulations to examine behavioral patterns in complex human and biological systems. Real-world social dynamics are very complex, containing billions of interacting individuals and an important amount of data (both spatial and social). Dealing with large-scale agent-based models is not an easy task and encounters several challenges. The design of strategies to overcome these challenges represents an opportunity for high performance parallel and distributed implementation. This chapter examines the most relevant aspects to deal with large-scale agent-based simulations in social sciences and revises the developments to confront technological issues.

DOI: 10.4018/978-1-4666-5954-4.ch007

INTRODUCTION

Computer modeling and complex systems simulation have dominated the scientific debate over the last decade, providing important outcomes in biology, geology and life sciences, and resulting in the birth of entirely new disciplines (e.g. bioinformatics, geoinformatics, health informatics, etc.). In social sciences research in this direction is increasing. The reason is the object of study in these disciplines, human society present or past, is difficult to analyze through classical analytical techniques. Social phenomena are unpredictable and changing (dynamic). Thus, other methodological techniques are needed to more adequately study this field. Computer simulation can actually be used as a virtual lab to explore different hypotheses capable of explaining patterns of phenomena and validate them.

In this context, Agent-Based Modeling (ABM) is one of the most widely used simulation techniques, from the physical sciences to the social sciences (Macal & North, 2007). ABM is particularly well suited with the concept of entities with individual decision-making processes interacting within a common environment which can show emergent behavior[12]. Given the inherent complexity of population dynamics and structures, agent-based simulation allows the implementation of experiments and studies that would not be feasible otherwise (Pavon et al., 2008). As a result, many agent-based simulation tools have been developed over the last years to explore the complexity of social systems. Agent-based simulation is recognized as one of the techniques which could contribute more to develop useful simulations of complex social interactions (Gilbert, 2008).

In the real-world social dynamics are very complex, containing billions of interacting individuals and an important amount of data (both spatial and social). That is the reason why a desktop computer or a small cluster might not have enough capacity to manage realistic models. For example, the study of past societies scientists may require an important number of simulations to validate their models against archaeological records (Rubio & Cela, 2010). One solution is to run simulation models on high performance distributed and parallel environments such as big computer clusters, supercomputers, clouds or grids. However, the performance analysis is a difficult task in parallel and distributed simulation (Fujimoto, 2000), especially when the system is as dynamic as human populations. Scalability (the capacity of a system to handle a higher amount of work as hardware grows) needs to be addressed, although there is no consensus on dealing with the difficulties it encounters on ABMs (Hybinette et al., 2006; Tesfatsion, 2002).

With this chapter we want to address some of the technological challenges social researchers could expect of the future of social simulation. Specifically, we explain the most relevant aspects on dealing with large-scale agent-based simulations in social sciences and humanities. The chapter approaches advanced computer science techniques to social researchers interested to take advantage of simulation for virtual experimentation of social phenomena. In the background section we will provide a general description of Parallel and Distributed Simulation (PADS) and the current computer architectures to run simulations. We will also discuss some advantages and challenges when dealing with High Performance Computing (HPC) systems. We will then point at some reasons why HPC are suitable for large social simulations. Later we will review specific challenges and solutions to perform social simulations in HPC architecture. After revising some of the available tools for large-scale agent-based simulations in social sciences, we will conclude our chapter discussing why technology advances matter and how social simulation community can get advantage of them.

BACKGROUND ON PARALLEL AND DISTRIBUTED SIMULATION

PADS deals with the distribution of simulation tasks and processes using multiple processors. While serial processing runs a simulation in sequence, PADS takes advantage of coupled computer systems (e.g. a supercomputer or a shared-memory multiprocessor) to reduce execution time or to execute large simulations. Figure 1 illustrates the difference between sequential simulation and parallel and distributed simulation. The simulation is composed by five tasks $(T_1 \ldots T_5)$ which are performed during simulation time. Tasks have dependencies between them. The figure shows a possible distribution of those tasks across three processors. By executing a simulation program in a set of processors it is hope that the simulation time can be reduced substantially, up to a factor equal to the number of processors (Law, 2007). In that way, the simulation is portioned somehow and its resulting partitions are mapped to processors. Through the combination of their results, the output of single simulation model is obtained.

PADS distinguish mainly by the computer architecture it uses. In parallel simulation computers are mostly connected with a high speed network and share the same physical space. Moreover, infrastructures are commonly composed by many homogeneous machines. Both characteristics make the delay in transmitting a message from one computer to other (known as *communication latency*) relatively low. Latency is a key element on performance studies since it determines how much time computers will spend on waiting for messages to be delivered. On the contrary, distribute architecture is composed by heterogeneous machines which are located in a broad geographic area. Therefore, communication latencies tend to be higher than in parallel architectures because they are affected by the distance between the two machines involved in the communication. Moreover, software protocols used to connect both computers tend to be complex and can also have an impact in the communication (Fujimoto, 2000).

Traditionally, PADS has been applied in military and network simulations. Today, we have seen an increase in the number of papers reporting on

Figure 1. Sequential versus parallel and distributed simulation example

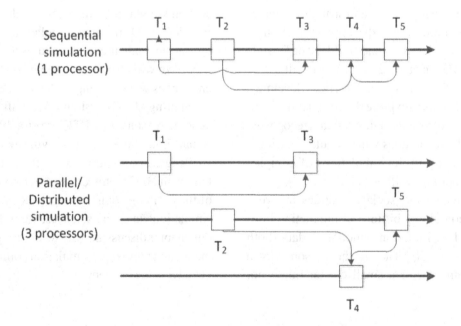

parallel simulation applications outside the traditional areas. Tang et al. (2005) conducted an initial study in applying parallel simulation to a plasma physics application. In the realm of biological science, Lobb et al. (2005) applied parallel simulation to a neuron model. Parker (2007) used distributed simulation to study an epidemic model. Lan and Pidd (2005) applied parallel simulation to simulate a quasi-continuous manufacturing process. Yoginath and Perumalla (2008) applied parallel simulation to a traffic simulation model. Rubio-Campillo et al. (2012) used parallel simulation to explore battlefield dynamics in archaeology. The situation is encouraging, although it is still far from ideal, since the number of applications of PADS in the social sciences is scarce.

There are two main schemes to divide the simulation: temporal or spatial[3]. Temporal partitioning consists on dividing the simulation along its time dimension. Therefore, each simulation time interval will be executed in a different processor. However, this scheme is atypical in social sciences applications since commonly past history shapes individual or societal behavior. In a spatial partitioning scheme the simulation is divided in different sections so each of them contains its corresponding part of the environment and its associated entities (agents in ABM). Furthermore, it is important to analyze the relation between time and space resolutions. Some problems need a specific time step (days, months, years) because

entities' dynamics do not have any sense at another time scale. For example, if we try to simulate a migration it is difficult to defining behavior at a daily time step rate, so we will use months, or years. For instance, Onggo et al. (2010) used month scale to simulate demographic changes in an agent-based model.

Simulation methodologies can be classified according to time advancement mechanisms. There are mainly two mechanisms: time-stepped and event-driven. In a time-stepped simulation all events are scheduled with a fixed time increment dt, and entities exchange their status updates via messages while simulation time advances from one time step to the next. Time-stepped simulations are efficient when events are frequent or dense. However, when events are less frequent (when compared to the size of time-steps) the performance of time-stepped simulations drop noticeably (Fujimoto, 2000). Event-driven simulations proceed in discrete time steps in which state updates are scheduled. In that way, entities state changes actually drive changes in the simulation. The difference of this approach is that entities exchange events (and not messages) for state updates. Those events are executed in time stamp order. Event-driven simulations have gained significant popularity because they can be effectively applied to a broad spectrum of systems (Fujimoto, 1990). Figure 2 shows the difference between time-step and event-driven simulation.

Figure 2. Difference between time-step simulation (left) and event-driven simulation (right). Inspired by (Fujimoto, 2000)

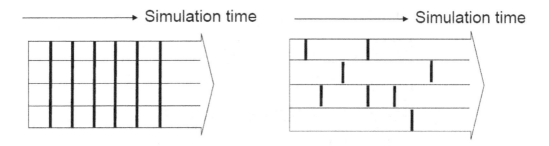

Computer Architectures for Simulation Studies

1. Simulation models can be run using the capacity of Core Processing Units (CPUs or cores), which are the atom of any computing system. CPU is responsible for calculating arithmetical and logistical operations. With the advances of computer technology, desktop computers went from one CPU to several cores with shared memory. The aggregation of computer nodes through a network is known as a HPC (High Performance Computing) infrastructure. There are three types of HPC systems that can be used to explore simulation problems: Internet

2. A set of computer nodes interconnected with high-speed networks offering HPC at a relatively low-cost (computer clusters),

3. Large sets of computers interconnected with high-speed networks and faster processing speeds thanks to their memory subsystems and interconnects (dedicated supercomputers),

4. Computers connected through a real-time communication network, typically the Internet, which provides dynamic and scalable resources as services to the end-user (clouds),

5. Computers connected through a real-time communication network as clouds, which require more control by the end user (grids)

An overview of distributed systems can be seen in Figure 3. Clusters and supercomputers are more oriented to the applications domain, whereas clouds are used in services-oriented applications. While supercomputers and clouds are used for large-scale studies, clusters and Web systems are used at small scale. Grid systems overlaps both with application and service oriented systems but is generally used at a lower scale than supercomputers and clouds.

The main advantage of HPC infrastructures is that they alleviate part of the computational demand by distributing the code among different computer nodes. Each desktop computer will typically have multi-core processors so user can

Figure 3. Overview of distributed systems (source (Foster, Zhao, Raicu, & Lu, 2008))

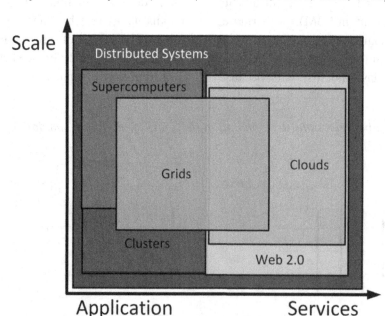

test their parallel applications in their desktop machines and later deploy them in a large system with little or no modification (Parry, 2012). A general architecture of an HPC computer cluster is shown in Figure 4. New increases in computer power are coming from embedding more cores in one node.

Whereas desktop machines and small computer cluster are affordable to many research groups, HPC clusters and supercomputers are expensive resources. Internet is an available network to parallelize and distribute simulation work through grids and clouds. Grids are heterogeneous, non-dedicated public systems useful to execute large-scale simulations (Zhang et al., 2005). They require the distribution of pieces of programs to a large set of computers. Cloud computing evolved out of grid computing and uses grid technologies as its infrastructure support (Foster et al., 2008). It provides to users an access to services which can use multiple servers anywhere on the globe without knowing which ones they are using and where they are located.

An alternative to CPU-based machines are Graphical Processing Units (GPU). Although GPU have traditionally been designed to handle intensive graphic tasks, recently they have been used to perform more general purpose calculations, including numerical computing (Owens et al., 2007). GPUs can quickly perform mathematical calculations because of their high bandwidth (rate of data transfer) (Parry, 2012). In ABMs they can be useful when the number of communications between agents is high or systems have high mobility. However implementing applications on GPUs clusters requires high-level skills and advance knowledge of the constraints imposed by the architecture. As a result, model implementation needs to be adjusted to GPU particularities. Despite this limitation, GPU can be used efficiently to implement some specific functions (for example to gather information of the environment or to calculate a shortest path). As an example, Wittek and Rubio-Campillo (2013) used GPUs for accelerating the update of knowledge of agents distributed in a GIS. They showed the impact of

Figure 4. General architecture of an HPC computer cluster

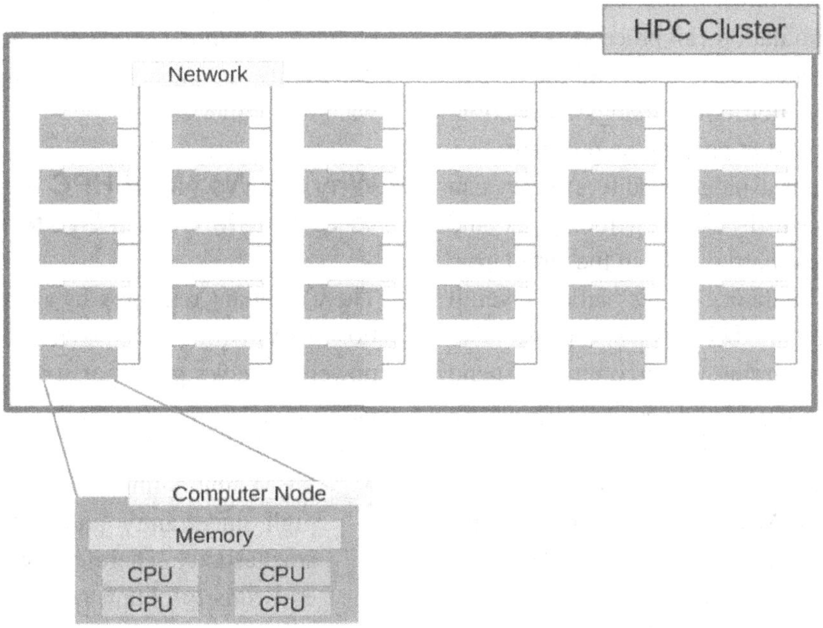

running the simulation in a GPU cluster had on the implementation of the model. GPUs have also limitations on memory use. Therefore, large-scale scenarios might require distributing simulations between independent GPU cores and subsequently incorporating message passing techniques. In that case multi-core graphic systems limitations on high latency will need to be taken into account.

Advantages and Challenges of Parallel and Distributed Simulation

PADS is useful in many ways (Fujimoto, 2000). First, parallel and distribution techniques can help to complete the simulation faster, using a number of processors to distribute the work. Reduction of computer time is critical in applications where simulation is used as a decision aid tool, for example in emergencies that affect air traffic management. It is also interesting in virtual environments for training where participants are located in distant geographical areas. Moreover, it can help handling large or complex systems where the execution is very time-consuming. Second, distributing the simulation workload in different processors makes the system more tolerant to failures. Therefore if a processors goes down others can pick up the work and the simulation can proceed as normal. Third, PADS makes possible to combine several proprietary simulation tools in a single simulation. In that way, the cost of porting the programs to a common system is avoided. And fourth they can combine geographically distributed computers and integrate different participants in the simulation (e.g. in flight simulators for air battle). Overall these advantages, PADS can make possible to simulate larger scenarios, which commonly spend a lot of resources and memory such as large nodes in computer networks or ABMs with a large number of individuals (Perumalla, 2006).

Nevertheless, PADS encounters some difficulties on its application. They are mainly due to the architecture of computer HPC systems which are being used. They include load balancing between computer cores, synchronization of events to ensure local causality constraint, management of communications between nodes, monitoring the distributed simulation time and dynamic resource allocation (Timm, 2005). Among them, good load balancing and inter-node communications with synchronization of events are central to parallel simulation (Parry, 2012). In order to ensure good performance of a simulation it is important to divide equitable the initial load of the simulation model among nodes. In that way, we will avoid situations of having a computer idle as others are working due to the initial workload unbalance. Pacheco (1997) gives some examples to solve it. However, if there is mobility in the system and computational demands change, techniques of dynamic load balancing will need to be considered. Although there are some solutions to deal with that (Jang & Agha, 2006; Jang & Agha, 2005), they also represent an additional overhead. Therefore, it will only be worth in cases where either some agents communicate with others with more intensity than others or communication patterns are constantly changing (Parry, 2012). Communications between nodes can slow down substantially the simulation execution time. Therefore, the way the simulation is split between nodes is an important element to obtain a good performance. However, this highly depends on the simulation model we want to parallelize.

Why Do We Need HPC Systems to Simulate Social Systems?

There are many reasons why agent-based simulations may require a considerable computational power. Here we point out some of them, partly based on (Helbing, 2012):

- ABM are nonlinear, dynamic systems with high uncertainty and notably degree of stochasticity. Therefore, we will need several runs to obtain results. With parametric sweep we can run multiple instances of the same program on different sets of input data. HPC infrastructures can minimize the time needed to achieve this task.

- Moreover, parametric sweep can solve the exploration of the model's parameter space[4]. However, determining the number of runs a given case scenario should be executed is not an easy task and the problem needs to be further explored.

- Large-scale scenarios of ABM might involve a very large number of agents. This might require access to a big infrastructure of computing nodes. Although most of the ABMs in the literature are barely large-scale, advances in the field could make the simulation of these scenarios more necessary.

- Realistic scenarios often include realistic decision-making processes[5]. Enriched models for agents, where a rational behavior or cognitive and psychological processes take place, require higher computing demands.

- Emergence is a property of many ABMs. In most studies it can be explored with small scale simulations. However, there are cases where that is not possible to achieve (Mithen & Reed, 2002). For example (Rubio-Campillo et al., 2012) showed how the typical linear warfare cannot be correctly modeled while trying to simulate few individuals. They proved it is not possible to simplify the simulation using fewer agents, as the behavior to explore is linked to the number of them that interact at a given time step.

LARGE-SCALE SOCIAL SIMULATION

Although there have been some attempts to define protocols for describing ABMs (Gilbert, 2008; Grimm et al., 2006), there is no common methodology for developing them. Neither it is defined how users should handle large-scale scenarios of ABMs. Parry (2012) states there are several ways to enlarge larger scale agent simulations: increase computer hardware (using vectorization techniques (Chandak & Browne, 1983) or processors dedicated to specific simulation functions (Comfort, 1984)), reduce the number of agents or revert to simpler modeling, work with aggregates of agents sharing similar characteristics and reprogram the model in parallel. Parry and Bithell (2012) describe the potential solutions to implement large-scale ABMs. The one that has fewer shortcomings is to modify the model to a parallel environment. This solution has been applied successfully to simulate particles on massive parallel computer systems in the physical sciences of fluid dynamics, materials sciences and meteorology. However, it might be monetary expensive and require advanced computational skills.

In this section we will describe the elements that affect agent-based simulations performance and we will briefly see some agent-based simulations platforms that are suite for large-scale scenarios.

Dealing with Simulation of Large-Scale Social Systems

There are several aspects which particularly affect the scalability of agent-based simulations. First, the complexity of the ABM has an impact on simulation performance. The overall complexity of an ABM depends on the number of agents and the behavior complexity of each of them. Artificial intelligence has long explored agents complexity, with approaches like the *Belief, Desires, Intentions* (BDI) scheme to model agents (Bratman, 1999), which has its roots in cognitive science and comes from a model of human reasoning[6]. Advanced approaches to human modeling of this kind require a high demand on computer power. Therefore, large-scale simulations with complex agents will most of the time require computer power of a HPC system.

Second, complexity and topology of communications between agents have a high effect on simulation speed. The number of communications in the system depends mainly on the distribution of space in the implementation of the ABM and the number of movements of agents across the environment scheme. Commonly large ABMs use spatial partitioning, where each computer node owns a section of the entire simulated scenario. This spatial partitioning is decided due to the interacting topology of agents, which can be either static or dynamic[7]. While there might be social mechanisms where space is not important (e.g., the evolution of paternal care), in other cases the logic of the model should be understand to divide efficiently the environment across computer processors (e.g., in migration flows studies)[8].

Third, environment can be as simple as dividing the model in different parts (regions) or being as complex as a Graphical Information System (GIS). A GIS consist of a set of tools which allow users to interact and understand spatial information. A GIS can not only deal with data at a geographical scale but also with alternative data such as culture, political ideology or religion. A good revision of GIS techniques and capabilities can be found in (Castle & Crooks, 2006). In agent-based systems, each agent needs to gather knowledge from environment, as well as from other agents in order to execute its decision making processes. Moreover, agents may modify the environment so environmental data and agents will be shared. The design of the solution for this kind of systems is model dependent. If the environment is rather simple we can have the same information in all nodes and distribute agents across processors. For example, Parry (2012) used this scheme with an ABM of aphid population dynamics in agricultural landscapes of the UK. However, if the agents are complex and have numerous interactions between them it will be costly to have them residing in different processors. Although there have been some initiatives to automatize the parallelization of agent-based simulations (Coakley et al.,

2012; Kurowski et al., 2009), overall, the nature of the problem and the properties of the computer platform will often guide the method to split the simulation execution.

Finally, the computational consideration of resolving time advancement mechanisms should be taken into account. The synchronously or asynchronously update of time determines how agents change during the simulation. Most social simulations commonly use a time-stepped execution, in which time advances at a fixed interval and agents are updated at each time step. However, there might be cases where the nature of agent updates is inherently asynchronous or asynchronous update of time might be an alternative to increase performance (Perumalla, 2010). However, in the parallel execution context it adds additional complexity since the mapping of asynchronous simulations is not so obvious. If there is communication between nodes, an asynchronous update is a problem since some nodes will have to wait for others to finish processes before communication can take place. To ensure simulation results are correct, research in PADS has produced a number of synchronization protocols. Perumalla (2006) provides a good summary on these techniques.

Furthermore, the duration of an ABM simulation is affected by technical characteristic of computer architecture. Network speed of different platforms (cluster, grids, clouds, supercomputers) may vary and cause differences on latency of message transmission. This will greatly affect communications of agents and thus simulation performance (Wang et al., 2005). Moreover, users should be aware that running agent-based simulation in heterogeneous computer infrastructure (such as grid or clouds) can result in unexpected unbalances and delay the execution time. There exists some mechanisms to profit shared-memory capacities of processors with libraries such as OpenMP which allow to parallelize the execution of agents' actions within a single computer node (Massaioli et al., 2005). However, there might be contexts where this is not possible to do due to conflicts on accessing and modifying the same data at the same time (for instance, when agents modify the same portion of space). Finally, output requirements or data storage can cause trouble in the implementation of agent-based simulations. For example, imagine that we need to get data at the micro-scale of each individual story. Reprogramming the model might affect to the output handling and decrease simulation performance.

Tools for Large-Scale Agent-Based Models in Social Sciences

There is a lot of interest in developing ABM as a general technique to be applied to the study of societies. A number of platforms exist to provide the means to study social phenomena. However, they are essentially discrete-event tools designed to execute serially on CPUs and have limited scalability (Lysenko & D'Souza, 2008). In the context of PADS, several frameworks have been recently developed. They range from parallel, distributed approach to the GPU/many-cores or tools to automatize parallel ABM simulation code. In this section, we will briefly describe some of them and compare them in terms of software capacity and architecture. All of them take advantage in different ways of HPC architecture to deal with either big or very complex simulations of social phenomena. The purpose of this chapter is not to fully revise these tools but introduce some of them to the reader.

Repast-HPC is the most popular tool for tightly-coupled, large computing clusters and supercomputers (Collier & North, 2012). It is based on the tool Repast for sequentially execute ABMs. Repast-HPC is intended for users with basic C++ expertise and access to high-performance computers. Repast-HPC implements a dynamic discrete-event scheduler with conservative synchronization. It offers useful features such as data collection, specifying agent interactions by space and networks or automatic management of agent interactions across processes. Repast-HPC

allocates a region of space to multiple processors and manages the boundaries by copying them (and their agents) in the adjoin region. In Collier and North (2011), the authors show an example of applying Repast-HPC to the spread of rumors through a networked population.

Pandora is an framework designed to implement ABMs and to execute them in HPC environments (Rubio-Campillo, 2013). Pandora is currently being used to simulate ancient societies and their relationship with environmental transformations in the project *"SimulPast."* Pandora implements a time-stepped scheduler and defines the environment where agents live as a set of layers containing raster map structures, following GIS standards. As in Repast-HPC, in Pandora the user is responsible for writing the agent-based code (in C++ or Python) and the world of the simulation is evenly divided among computer nodes. This layout is depicted in Figure 5 where simulation landscape is divided in four main sections which are executed in four different processors. Data and agents located in the border between adjacent nodes will be copied and sent to neighbors every time step, in order to keep data up-to-date in the entire scenario.

This solution for space partitioning is highly scalable, given the fact that every computer node

Figure 5. Space scheme distribution in Pandora

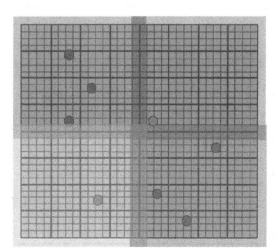

will need to communicate, at most, with 8 neighbor nodes, independently of the total size of the simulation. To solve collision between agent's actions, Pandora splits the section of every computer node in 4 equal parts, numbering 0 to 3, as it can be seen in Figure 6. The agents contained in all 0 sections will be executed simultaneously without the possibility of conflicts. When they finish, modified border data is sent to the neighbors, and a new section will begin its execution (1, 2 and finally 3). Once all of them are done, the entire state of the simulation is serialized and a new time step can be evaluated.

DMASON is the Distributed Multi-agents simulation toolkit, based on *Mason*. As in Repast-HPC, users can create an ABM in MASON and then use the framework to easily distribute it over many machines. It provides a partitioning functionality that self-balances regions and requires and all-to-all communication. As opposite to Pandora and Repast-HPC, partitioning of the field is decided by the user in advance and, in our opinion, may cause an additional unbalance. Agents can migrate from one region to other and, therefore, it does not guarantee load balancing. However, it implements a simple balancing mechanism: when

Figure 6. Space distribution to solve collisions in Pandora

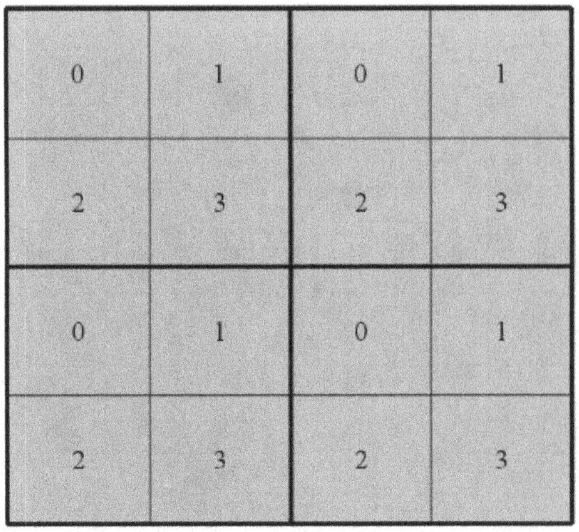

a region is overloaded it decides to split itself in smaller regions, dividing consequently the amount of agents in each of these regions (see Figure 7). To deal with boundaries problems, neighboring regions communicate before each simulation step. DMASON is developed in Java and uses Java Message Service (JMS) for communication between workers, so it is not meant for Java beginners.

Using grid technology, the open source project GridABM (Szemes & de Back, 2010) provides a set of templates to enable researchers to run ABMs in computing clusters and computational grids. It is based on Repast and depending on the topology of communication of agents it allow user to choose the appropriate schema and run their simulations in different PADS platforms. The programming is very similar to developing Repast sequential applications.

There are also proposed solutions that take advantage of GPU technology to perform large agent-based simulations. Examples of that can be seen in Lysenko and D'Souza (2008) and Perumalla and Aaby (2008). In their solutions, all agent data is stored in large multi-dimensional arrays where each element holds the complete state of an agent. In that way, GPU computer architecture is profited to faster several orders of magnitude ABM toolkits. However, the programming of GPUS is counter-intuitive. Moreover, these perspectives do not display well complex behaviors at interactive rates. There have been other approaches to simulate complex ABMs (Pelechano et al., 2007; Treuille et al., 2006) but they are far from scaling the number of agents. Vigueras et al. (2008) proposed a scalable architecture to manage large crowds of agents. They later apply it to a real case scenario (Vigueras et al., 2010).

There exist tools which automatically generate parallel agent-based simulation code. An example is FLAME (Richmond et al., 2010). In FLAME, agents are modeled as finite state machines which consist on a set of finite states, transition functions, and input and output messages. The state of each agent is determined by its internal memory.

Figure 7. Load balance policy in DMASON (source Cordasco et al., 2011)

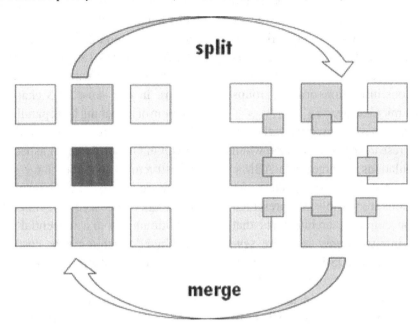

Agents communicate through messages that can be produced by themselves or can receive from others, similarly to Repast (Collier & North, 2011). FLAME takes the model definition of the ABM and the C-code to implement agent actions and state changes to automatize the generation of the user application. The resulting code can run either in a serial or in a parallel environment. It is available for both CPU-based and GPU-based systems. Although FLAME is meant to free the user from parallelism complexity, agent model must contain that parallelism at a task level. The advantage of this platform is that it distributes the computational load over the processing elements to achieve computational load balance.

Previous described tools have focused on the distribution of one simulation over several nodes and require high-programming computational skills. However, it would also be interesting to explore the distribution of a set of experiments over a HPC infrastructure. In that case, a single simulation is executed on one node and several simulations are launched in parallel. An example of this approach are the tools OpenMole (Reuillon

et al., 2013) and EPIS (Blanchart et al., 2011). OpenMole is a cloud approach for large-scale model exploration of complex systems, which distributes experiments on a HPC environment transparently. It uses a Domain Specific Language to design experiments for simulation models to perform their sensitivity analysis. EPIS also allows the deployment of lots of simulation runs over a cluster of nodes to explore the solution space of agent-based simulations. EPIS uses grid computing to distribute the experiments on a cluster. The advantage of both frameworks is the possibility to profit HPC architecture to explore parameter space without having HPC skills.

CONCLUSION

In the last years many disciplines have profited computer advances to deal with large-scale simulations of ABMs such as molecular physics, telecommunications, ecology or military research. The work done on the social field is not very substantial although the community of social simulation is expanding. Despite being quite new compared to other interdisciplinary fields like geoinformatics or bioinformatics, social simulation can profit from the technological advances to boost its results and examine large-scale social phenomena going beyond organizations, institutions or small groups without losing its micro-scale.

In this chapter, we have revised the technical challenges social researchers need to face when dealing with simulations of large-scale ABMs. One of the motivations was to show the reader that large simulations are feasible. We presented the most common computer architectures that encompass HPC infrastructures and gave several arguments to prove PADS is interesting for social models. Although most common tools for agent-based simulation are not meant to deal with large scale scenarios, we presented some that can actually help to overcome this problem. In order to parallelize large simulation models, it is interesting for modelers to know the difference between CPU and GPU or between parallel simulation in multicore clusters and grids or clouds. Technical characteristics of such systems can not only affect simulation performance but also may require significant changes on program restructuring. The debate about which system is better is far from the aim of this chapter, but it is important to note that they can serve for different purposes within a social perspective. On one hand, cloud and grid computing can be an affordable solution to run large social simulation when no high-speed cluster computing is available. On the other hand, the best solution for models with intensive communication is supercomputing (Wittek & Rubio-Campillo, 2013).

Scalability of social ABMs is not a trivial matter and requires an interdisciplinary effort. On one hand, computer scientists need to know certain aspects of the application domain to suc-

cessfully participate in the model design. On the other hand, social researchers should be aware of the computational challenges the model generates at different layers (availability of computational resources, experiment design, model scale, and so on). In this sense, this chapter explores the problem of launching large parallel and distributed simulations in the context of an interdisciplinary research. One of the main aspects of using HPC infrastructures to launch large simulations is to ensure we obtain the same results as the equivalent sequential execution. Since the process of transitioning from a sequential to a parallel and distributed version can be costly, it is worth to explore different options and study simulation needs at first. Moreover, there might be cases where parallel simulation is less efficient than the single processor implementation. Parry (2012) showed that, sometimes, a population size should be large enough to compensate overheads due to message passing and extra calculations required. Beyond that, we discussed the most important aspects that affect social agent-based simulations. We also described some of the currently available tool to simulate large-scale social ABMs. With this chapter we hope to guide social modelers through the possibilities parallel and distributed architectures can offer.

ACKNOWLEDGMENT

Xavier Rubio-Campillo and Cristina Monta-ñola-Sales are part of the SimulPast Project (CSD2010-00034) funded by the CONSOLIDER-INGENIO2010 program of the Spanish Ministry of Science and Innovation. We thank the two anonymous reviewers whose comments and suggestions served to improve the manuscript.

REFERENCES

Blanchart, E., Cambier, C., Canape, C., Gaudou, B., Ho, T.-N., & Ho, T.-V. et al. (2011). EPIS: A grid platform to ease and optimize multi-agent simulators running. In Y. Demazeau, M. Pechoucek, J. M. Corchado, & J. Bajo P'erez (Eds.), *Advances on practical applications of agents and multiagent systems* (Vol. 88, pp. 129–134). Berlin, Heidelberg, Germany: Springer. doi:10.1007/978-3-642-19875-5_17

Bratman, M. E. (1999). *Intention, plans, and practical reason*. Stanford, CA: Center for the Study of Language and Information.

Castle, C. J. E., & Crooks, A. T. (2006). *Principles and concepts of agent-based modelling for developing geospatial simulations* (Working Paper Series, 110). University College London. Retrieved from http://discovery.ucl.ac.uk/3342/

Chandak, A., & Browne, J. C. (1983). Vectorization of discrete event simulation. In *Proceedings of the 1983 International Conference on Parallel Processing* (pp. 359).

Coakley, S., Gheorghe, M., Holcombe, M., Chin, S., Worth, D., & Greenough, C. (2012). Exploitation of high performance computing in the FLAME agent-based simulation framework. In *IEEE 14th International Conference on High Performance Computing and Communication 2012 (HPCC-ICESS)* (pp. 538–545). doi:10.1109/HPCC.2012.79

Collier, N., & North, M. (2011). Repast HPC: A platform for large-scale agent-based modeling. In W. Dubitzky, K. Kurowski, & B. Schott (Eds.), *Large-scale computing* (pp. 81–109). Hoboken, NJ: John Wiley & Sons, Inc. doi:10.1002/9781118130506.ch5

Collier, N., & North, M. (2012). Parallel agent-based simulation with repast for high performance computing. *Simulation*, *89*, 1215–1235. doi:10.1177/0037549712462620

Comfort, J. C. (1984). The simulation of a master-slave event set processor. *Simulation*, *42*(3), 117–124. doi:10.1177/003754978404200304

Cordasco, G., De Chiara, R., Scarano, V., Carillo, M., Mancuso, A., Mazzeo, D., et al. (2011). *D-Mason: Distributed multi-agent based simulations toolkit*. Retrieved from https://sites.google.com/site/distributedmason/

Foster, I., Zhao, Y., Raicu, I., & Lu, S. (2008). Cloud computing and grid computing 360-degree compared. In *Grid Computing Environments Workshop, 2008. GCE'08* (pp. 1–10). doi:10.1109/GCE.2008.4738445

Fujimoto, R. M. (1990). Parallel discrete event simulation. *Communications of the ACM*, *33*(10), 30–53. doi:10.1145/84537.84545

Fujimoto, R. M. (2000). *Parallel and distributed simulation systems*. Hoboken, NJ: John Wiley & Sons.

Gilbert, G. N. (2008). *Agent-based models*. Thousand Oaks, CA: Sage Publications, Inc.

Grimm, V., Berger, U., Bastiansen, F., Eliassen, S., Ginot, V., & Giske, J. et al. (2006). A standard protocol for describing individual-based and agent-based models. *Ecological Modelling*, *198*(1-2), 115–126. doi:10.1016/j.ecolmodel.2006.04.023

Helbing, D. (2012). Agent-based modeling. In D. Helbing (Ed.), Social self-organization (Understanding complex systems). (pp. 25–70). Berlin: Springer-Verlag. doi: doi:10.1007/978-3-642-24004-1 2

Hybinette, M., Kraemer, E., Xiong, Y., Matthews, G., & Ahmed, J. (2006). SASSY: A design for a scalable agent- based simulation system using a distributed discrete event infrastructure. In *Proceedings of the 36th Conference on Winter Simulation (Monterey, California)* (pp. 926–933).

Jang, M.-W., & Agha, G. (2005). Adaptive agent allocation for massively multi-agent applications. In T. Ishida, L. Gasser, & H. Nakashima (Eds.), *Massively Multi-Agent Systems I: First International Workshop MMAS 2004* (pp. 25–39). Kyoto, Japan: Springer, Berlin.

Jang, M.-W., & Agha, G. (2006). Agent framework services to reduce agent communication overhead in large-scale agent-based simulations. *Simulation Modelling Practice and Theory, 14*(6), 679–694. doi:10.1016/j.simpat.2005.10.002

Kurowski, K., de Back, W., Dubitzky, W., Gulyás, L., Kampis, G., & Mamonski, M. et al. (2009). Complex system simulations with qoscosgrid. In *Computational Science--ICCS 2009* (pp. 387–396). Berlin: Springer. doi:10.1007/978-3-642-01970-8_38

Lan, C., & Pidd, M. (2005). High performance simulation in quasi-continuous manufacturing plants. In M. E. Kuhl, N. M. Steiger, F. B. Armstrong, & J. A. Joines (Eds.), *Proceedings of the 2005 Winter Simulation Conference* (pp. 1367–1372). Picataway, NJ.: IEEE Computer Society Press.

Law, A. M. (2007). *Simulation modeling and analysis* (4th ed.). New York: McGraw-Hill.

Lobb, C. J., Chao, Z., Fujimoto, R. M., & Potter, S. M. (2005). Parallel event-driven neural network simulations using the Hodgkin-Huxler neuron model. In *Proceedings of the 19th Workshop on Principles of Advanced and Distributed SImulation* (pp. 16–25). New York, NY: ACM Press.

Lysenko, M., & D'Souza, R. M. (2008). A framework for megascale agent based model simulations on graphics processing units. *Journal of Artificial Societies and Social Simulation, 11*(4), 10.

Macal, C. M., & North, M. J. (2007). Agent-based modeling and simulation: Desktop ABMS. In *Proceedings of the 39th Conference on Winter Simulation: 40 years! The best is yet to come* (pp. 95–106). Piscataway, NJ: IEEE Press. Retrieved from http://portal.acm.org/citation.cfm?id=1351542.1351564

Mason. (n.d.). Retrieved from http://cs.gmu.edu/~eclab/projects/mason/

Massaioli, F., Castiglione, F., & Bernaschi, M. (2005). OpenMP parallelization of agent-based models. *Parallel Computing, 31*(10), 1066–1081. doi:10.1016/j.parco.2005.03.012

Mithen, S., & Reed, M. (2002). Stepping out: A computer simulation of hominid dispersal from Africa. *Journal of Human Evolution, 43*(4), 433–462. doi: doi:10.1006/jhev.2002.0584 PMID:12393003

Onggo, B., Montañola-Sales, C., & Casanovas-Garcia, J. (2010). Performance analysis of parallel demographic simulation. In *Proceedings of the 24th European Simulation and Modelling Conference,* (pp. 142-148). Hasselt, Belgium: Eurosis-ETI.

Owens, J. D., Luebke, D., Govindaraju, N., Harris, M., Krüger, J., Lefohn, A. E., & Purcell, T. J. (2007). A survey of general-purpose computation on graphics hardware. *Computer Graphics Forum, 26,* 80–113. doi:10.1111/j.1467-8659.2007.01012.x

Pacheco, P. S. (1997). *Parallel programming with MPI.* San Francisco: Morgan Kaufmann Publishers Inc.

Parker, J. (2007). A flexible, large-scale, distributed agent based epidemic model. In S. G. Henderson, B. Biller, M.-H. Hsieh, J. Shortle, J. D. Tew, & R. R. Barton (Eds.), *Proceedings of the 39th Conference on Winter Simulation, Washington, DC,* (pp. 1543–1547). Piscataway, NJ, USA: IEEE Press.

Parry, H. (2012). Agent based modeling, large scale simulations. In R. A. Meyers (Ed.), *Computational complexity* (pp. 76–87). New York: Springer. doi:10.1007/978-1-4614-1800-9_5

Parry, H. R., & Bithell, M. (2012). Large scale agent-based modelling: A review and guidelines for model scaling. In *Agent-based models of geographical systems* (pp. 271–308). Berlin: Springer. doi:10.1007/978-90-481-8927-4_14

Pavon, J., Arroyo, M., Hassan, S., & Sansores, C. (2008). Agent-based modelling and simulation for the analysis of social patterns. *Pattern Recognition Letters*, 29(8), 1039–1048. doi:10.1016/j.patrec.2007.06.021

Pelechano, N., Allbeck, J. M., & Badler, N. I. (2007). Controlling individual agents in high-density crowd simulation. In *Proceedings of the 2007 ACM SIGGRAPH/Eurographics Symposium on Computer Animation* (pp. 99–108). Aire-la-Ville, Switzerland.

Perumalla, K. (2010). Computational spectrum of agent model simulation. In S. Cakaj (Ed.), *Modeling simulation and optimization - Focus on applications* (pp. 185–204). InTech.

Perumalla, K. S. (2006). Parallel and distributed simulation: Traditional techniques and recent advances. In *Simulation Conference, 2006. WSC 06. Proceedings of the Winter* (pp. 84–95).

Perumalla, K. S., & Aaby, B. G. (2008). Data parallel execution challenges and runtime performance of agent simulations on GPUs. In *Proceedings of the 2008 Spring Simulation Multiconference* (pp. 116–123).

Reuillon, R., Leclaire, M., & Rey, S. (2013). OpenMOLE, a workflow engine specifically tailored for the distributed exploration of simulation models. *Future Generation Computer Systems*, 29(8), 1981–1990. doi:10.1016/j.future.2013.05.003

Richmond, P., Walker, D., Coakley, S., & Romano, D. (2010). High performance cellular level agent-based simulation with FLAME for the GPU. *Briefings in Bioinformatics*, 11(3), 334–347. doi:10.1093/bib/bbp073 PMID:20123941

Rubio, X., & Cela, J. M. (2010). Large-scale agent-based simulation in archaeology: An approach using high-performance computing. In *Proceedings of the 38th Annual Conference on Computer Applications and Quantitative Methods in Archaeology,* (pp. 153-159). Granada, Spain.

Rubio-Campillo, Xavier, Cela, J. M., & Hernández-Cardona, F. X. (2012). Simulating archaeologists? Using agent-based modelling to improve battlefield excavations. *Journal of Archaeological Science*, 39(2), 347–356. doi:10.1016/j.jas.2011.09.020

Rubio-Campillo, X. (2013). *Pandora: An hpc agent-based modelling framework.* Retrieved from https://github.com/xrubio/pandora/

Simulating the past to understand human behavior (SimulPast). (n.d.). Retrieved from http://www.simulpast.es

Szemes, G. L. G. G. K., & de Back, W. (2010). GridABM - templates for distributed agent based simulation. In *Open Grid Forum 28*. Munich, Germany.

Tang, Y., Perumalla, K. S., Fujimoto, R. M., Karimabadi, H., Driscoll, J., & Omelchenko, Y. (2005). Optimistic parallel discrete event simulations of physical systems using reverse computation. In *Proceedings of the 19th Workshop on Principles of Advanced and Distributed Simulation* (pp. 26–35). New York, NY: ACM Press.

Tesfatsion, L. (2002). Agent-based computational economics: Growing economies from the bottom up. *Artificial Life*, 8(1), 55–82. doi:10.1162/106454602753694765 PMID:12020421

Timm, I. J. (2005). Large scale multiagent simulation on the grid. In *Proceedings of 5th IEEE International Symposium on Cluster Computing and the Grid* (pp. 334–341). IEEE Computer Society. doi:10.1.1.90.2116

Treuille, A., Cooper, S., & Popović, Z. (2006). Continuum crowds. *ACM Transactions on Graphics (TOG) - Proceedings of ACM SIGGRAPH 2006, 25*(3), 1160–1168.

Vigueras, G., Lozano, M., Perez, C., & Ordua, J. M. (2008). A scalable architecture for crowd simulation: Implementing a parallel action server. In *Proceedings of the 37th International Conference on Parallel Processing (ICPP. 2008)* (pp. 430–437). doi:10.1109/ICPP.2008.20

Vigueras, G., Orduña, J., & Lozano, M. (2010). A GPU-based multi-agent system for real-time simulations. In Y. Demazeau, F. Dignum, J. Corchado, & J. Pérez (Eds.), *Advances in practical applications of agents and multiagent systems* (Vol. 70, pp. 15–24). Berlin: Springer. doi:10.1007/978-3-642-12384-9_3

Wang, F., Turner, S., & Wang, L. (2005). Agent communication in distributed simulations. In P. Davidsson, B. Logan, & K. Takadama (Eds.), *Multi-agent and multi-agent-based simulation* (Vol. 3415, pp. 11–24). Berlin: Springer. doi:10.1007/978-3-540-32243-6_2

Wittek, P., & Rubio-Campillo, X. (2013). Social simulations accelerated: Large-scale agent-based modeling on a gpu cluster. In *GPU Technology Conference*. San Diego, CA.

Yoginath, S. B., & Perumalla, K. S. (2008). Parallel vehicular traffic simulation using reverse computation-based optimistic execution. In *Proceedings of the 22nd Workshop on Principles of Advanced and Distributed Simulation* (pp. 145–152). Piscataway, NJ.

Zhang, Y., Theodoropoulos, G., Minson, R., Turner, S., Cai, W., Xie, Y., & Logan, B. (2005). Grid-aware large scale distributed simulation of agent-based systems. In *Proceedings of the 2005 European Simulation Interoperability Workshop*.

ADDITIONAL READING

Axelrod, R. (1997). Advancing the art of simulation in the social sciences. *Complexity, 3*, 16–22. doi:10.1002/(SICI)1099-0526(199711/12)3:2<16::AID-CPLX4>3.0.CO;2-K

Fujimoto, R. M. (2000). *Parallel and distributed simulation systems*. Hoboken, New Jersey: John Wiley & Sons.

Gilbert, N., & Conte, R. (1995). *Artificial Societies: The Computer Simulation of Social Life*. Bristol, PA, USA: Taylor & Francis, Inc.

Greenough, C., Chin, S., Worth, D., Coakley, S., Holcombe, M., & Kiran, M. (2010). An Approach to the Parallelisation of Agent-Based Applications. *ERCIM News, 81*, 42–43.

Montañola-Sales, C., Rubio-Campillo, X., Cela-Espín, J. M., Casanovas-Garcia, J., & Kaplan-Marcusan, A. (2014). Overview on Agent-Based Social Modelling and the use of formal languages. In P. Fonseca (Ed.), *Formal Languages for Computer Simulation: Transdisciplinary Models and Applications* (pp. 333–377). Hershey, PA, US: IGI Global.

Parry, H. R., & Bithell, M. (2012). *Large scale agent-based modelling: A review and guidelines for model scaling. Agent-based models of geographical systems* (pp. 271–308). Springer. doi:10.1007/978-90-481-8927-4_14

Perumalla, K. (2010). In S. Cakaj (Ed.), *Modeling Simulation and Optimization - Focus on Applications* (pp. 185–204). InTech.

KEY TERMS AND DEFINITIONS

Agent-Based Models: Models that are formed by a set of autonomous agents that interact with their environment (including other agents) through a set of internal rules to achieve their objectives.

Distributed Simulation: A simulation where processes are assigned to a set of heterogeneous processors to be executed asynchronously in parallel. Each processor has its own private memory and exchanges information with others through passing messages techniques.

High-Performance Computing: Aggregation of a large set of computer facilities in order to provide a higher performance that could be obtained by desktop computers in order to solve large problems of science or engineering.

Parallel Simulation: A simulation where processes are assigned to a set of processors to be executed asynchronously in parallel. All processors have access to a shared memoreymemory and exchange information with others through passing messages techniques.

Simulation: The process of making a model that represents a portion of the reality to evolve through time with the purpose of understand its behaviourbehavior or to evaluate the impact of a set of strategies on it.

ENDNOTES

1. An extended explanation of emergency properties in social systems can be found in the chapter of this book written by Friesen, Gordon & McLeod (2014).

2. In the chapter in this book written by Luyet (2014), the reader can find an example of agent-based simulation to study emergence of diffusion.

3. For further analysis on scale and topology variation of agent-based social simulation in large scenarios see the chapter in this book by Nardin, Rosset & Sichman (2014).

4. In the chapter in this book written by Troitzsch (2014) the reader can find some interesting issues about analyzing the parameter space of a simulation model and how to acquire statistical significance.

5. An example of an agent-based model where agents exhibit strategic behavior and experience the effects of social influence in their decisions can be found in the chapter of this book written by Trigo (2014).

6. In this book, Santos, Rodrigues, Donancio, Santos, Adamatti, Dimuro, Dimuro & De Manuel Jerez (2014) extend the explanation on this scheme and uses it to model a multi-agent system of the social production and management processes in urban ecosystems.

7. In fact, in this book, Franchi & Tomaiuolo (2014) show how formation and evolution of networks differs in agent-based models and propose a unified conceptual framework to overcome them.

8. An example of that can be found in the chapter of this book written by Nunes & Antunes (2014).

Section 2
Research on Agent–Based Models for Social Simulation

Chapter 8
Playing with Ambiguity:
An Agent Based Model of Vague Beliefs in Games

Konstantinos Georgalos
University of York, UK

ABSTRACT

This chapter discusses the way that three distinct fields, decision theory, game theory and computer science, can be successfully combined in order to optimally design economic experiments. Using an example of cooperative game theory (the Stag-Hunt game), the chapter presents how the introduction of ambiguous beliefs and attitudes towards ambiguity in the analysis can affect the predicted equilibrium. Based on agent-based simulation methods, the author is able to tackle similar theoretical problems and thus to design experiments in such a way that they will produce useful, unbiased and reliable data.

INTRODUCTION

In this chapter, our aim is to explore how Agent-Based Simulation techniques can act as a complement to a relatively new field of the experimental economics literature, that of preferences towards ambiguity. As experimental techniques in economics constitute an indispensable part of the applied and empirical research, with scholarly research getting published in the top journals of the profession, it is of paramount significance for the implemented experimental protocols to be carefully designed so as to provide by minimizing the number of possible flaws. Moreover, advances in the field of decision theory, combined with the numerous available datasets of experimental observations,

pose a huge challenge to the 'rational' agent paradigm[1]. As a result, empirics have rendered the use of more realistic modelling of human behaviour as well as the interdisciplinary research to be more than necessary. Due to this, several new scientific fields have emerged such as the field of 'Behavioral' economics (where elements from psychology and biology are coalesced with the economic theory) or the field of neuroeconomics (where advances of neuroscience are applied) to name but a few. In addition to the latter, crucial improvements have been made to the literature of decision making under ambiguity, or stating it in a different way, improvements on how to model agents' behaviour in situations where they lack useful information. This fact can be explained

DOI: 10.4018/978-1-4666-5954-4.ch008

by the increased frequency of research papers published that either focus on similar theoretical issues or on the application of theory to real life. Consequently, every single field in economics now takes advantage of these advances augmenting the ability to explain data and behaviour in a more realistic way (e.g. macroeconomics, game theory, environmental economics). Similar applications can be found in the present volume by Trindade, Magessi, and Antunes (2014) and Arciero et al. (2014).

In this chapter, we show how three distinct fields can be brought together enabling us to design and conduct more effective experiments that will generate useful and unbiased data. Our aim is to use advances of the literature of decision making under ambiguity that centres on individual choice, in order to predict behaviour in strategic interaction environments. The commonest way to model interaction in economics is game theory. There are several other different ways to model social interaction such as using the public choice approach (for a similar approach, see Lucas and Payne (2014) and Trigo (2014) or principal-agent models to name but a few. Incorporating the theoretical advances into the game theoretical models enables us, on the one hand, to solve puzzles that the standard assumption of the rational choice produces and, on the other, to obtain better predictions of how agents will react in similar interactions. The next step, after having derived the theoretical predictions, is to test this theory in the lab. The role of agent-based simulation becomes apparent at the step before entering the lab. Thus, what we provide is an intuition of how decision theory, game theory and computer science can be combined for the optimum design of economic experiments. As this chapter is addressed to readers of multifarious scientific backgrounds, careful consideration has been taken as regards the fact that they may not be familiar with the tools and methods that are employed in economic analysis to model individual behaviour. Henceforth, effort has been made to keep mathematics and definitions to the lowest formal level possible. A mathematical as well as a technical appendix with the code for the simulation is attached at the end of this chapter.

Agent-Based Simulation in Economics

As was described in the introduction, we focus on the use of agent based modelling in order to design and implement economic experiments. Before proceeding to this, it is instructive to outline other cases as well in which agent-based modelling can be useful in economic research. It is well-known that economics is a science heavily based on mathematics, making it one of the most essential tasks when conducting research. The range of applications is enormous. Starting from complex optimization programs that need to be solved, testing theoretical models or writing estimation routines to simulate evolutionary systems, agent-based modelling can be proved to be the optimal way to do so. Tesfatsion (2006) provides a nice definition of Agent Based Computational Economics (ACE) as the "computational study of economic processes modelled as dynamic systems of interacting agents."

In economics, there are various reasons where simulation techniques can be exploited for research. Van Dinther (2008) discusses one of the major benefits in agent based modelling, namely that of controlling all the parameters of interest in order to adapt them to the specific problem under investigation. This offers to the researcher a unique flexibility in the modelling process that allows comparative statics analysis but also is a powerful prediction and testing tool.

Why should one use agent-based models in economics? Starting with the most simple, the main reason to program the behaviour of agents is to tackle complex mathematical problems that the theoretical model under consideration demands. When the mathematics allows, closed form expressions that represent the optimal decisions that a decision maker takes can be derived.

In a similar case, agent-based models are useful for conducting comparative statics exercises and seeing how the results change when some of the key variables fluctuate. But as the complexity of the problems increases and as more variables are added in order to capture extra elements of the reality (e.g. extend model to dynamic dimension), it becomes harder and harder to obtain analytical solutions in an efficient way. In addition, there are cases where an analytical solution is impossible to be calculated and, thus, the researcher seeks assistance to numerical methods that make extensive use of simulations (e.g. Monte Carlo simulations).

Van Dinther (2008) lists the most common approaches that are used in economics for carrying out simulations. More analytically, these include:

- Pure agent-based simulations
- Monte-Carlo techniques
- Evolutionary approaches
- Reinforcement learning techniques

Epstein (1996, 2008) has extensively described the alternative modelling opportunities that the agent based simulations offer. More specifically, he provides 16 reasons of why ABM is helpful not only for predictions but also for explanation, to seek new questions and to support decision analysis, to name but a few. Another field in economics where simulation plays a significant role is that of experimental economics. Duffy (2006) perfectly illustrates the connections between agent-based models and human-subject experiments by stating that the two methodologies should be complementary rather than rival as the one can compensate for the weaknesses of the other. Yet, most of the effort has been devoted to how simulations can be used so as to interpret behaviour and analyze the data of an already completed experiment. A role of agent-based modelling that is often omitted is its usefulness as a tool to design the experiments. As mentioned earlier, in order to guarantee the reliability of the data, an experimenter should be quite careful when designing the experiment. As

the decisions are made by human beings, noise in the data should not be taken for granted and appropriate assumptions should be imposed. Consequently, to minimize the biases, extensive simulations can be carried out to pick up the suitable tasks that the subjects are asked to undergo. Hauser et al. (2009) present the weaknesses of both scientific approaches. On the one hand, there are the restrictions that simulation models impose on agents' behaviour that usually depart from reality. On the other hand, it is vagueness that characterizes experimental methods. The latter is a common problem in experimental methods as the participation time is limited and does not allow for sufficient learning and adaptation, the use of simple and interesting experimental frameworks becomes obligatory. These difficulties can be bypassed by making the best use of both methods.

Hommes (2006) gives an account of the various benefits of the agent-based modelling. The most significant seems to be the ability to model agents that have heterogeneous preferences. In economics, and especially in fields that try to deviate from the mainstream analysis (e.g. Behavioural Economics), the latter is of outmost significance. Accepting that "people are different" in many aspects such as preferences, experience or culture to name but a few, it is crucial to capture similar differences in the analysis.

Decision Making under Ambiguity

Traditional decision theory, and thus game theory analysis as well, dogmatically rely on the mainstream microeconomic model that is used in the literature, that of the *homo economicus*. This is a well-established theory on how people make decisions which is based on the 'rational' agent model of the individual that maximizes her own utility subject to the various constraints[2]. Nevertheless, in the last decades, the extensive use of experimental methods has provided rich evidence on why this model cannot always capture the way people behave. Using experiments in the same manner as physics scientists do (by isolating the environment where agents act and observe only the parameters of interest), economists have obtained important input on how people make decisions and whether they abide by the neoclassical model of economic behaviour or not. As expected, most of the evidence shows that participants in these experiments often violate the rationality criteria that are imposed by the theoretical models. As a result, a new field of economics has been emerged, that of Behavioural Economics. In this alternative field of economic theory, researchers aspire to conduct interdisciplinary research and combine findings from distinct at first sight sciences (some characteristic examples include evolutionary economics and neuroeconomics). The importance of all this evidence lies in that it buttresses the power of experimental methods leading to an excessive demand for more robust protocols in both the design of experiments and the high quality of experimental data.

Extending this model to more complex situations such as in cases of risk, the famous Expected Utility model is set into action. However, in order to be able to represent the preferences in the way that the theory predicts, there is a number of axioms than need to be satisfied[3], an issue that in the recent years has started to be seriously challenged. Before introducing ambiguous beliefs, it would be useful to sketch some key decision theory elements that enable us to understand the main concepts of economic modelling. Additionally, this is a crucial issue in economic theory as it constitutes the main criticism against the mainstream 'rational' way of modelling economic behaviour.

Firstly, it is useful to discriminate between risk and ambiguity as it is a common mistake that many researchers not acquainted with the decision literature make when they model similar situations. Risk refers to the case where the possible probabilities for the future state of the world are well-defined, are known ex-ante and sum up always to 1. A standard illustration of risk in all introductory courses of statistics is that of throwing a die. The possible states of the world are six and assuming that this is a fair die, then the probability of receiving each state of the world, is the same for each side and equal to 1/6. Moreover, these probabilities are well-known to the decision maker and she is also fully aware of them. On the contrary, in the case of ambiguity, as Knight (1921) described it, the probabilities for the future states of the world are not well-defined, or at least the decision maker is not fully aware of the real chances, and do not necessarily add-up to 1 (we will return to this issue later on). Finally, another typical mistake that is usually made is to use the terms ambiguity and uncertainty interchangeably. Even though the essence of these two terms resembles in nature, we could think of uncertainty as being a subset of ambiguity. If we can think the probability space as an interval, where on the one extreme there is uncertainty and on the other risk, then ambiguity is somewhere in the middle. In Figure 1, A conceptual map presents the relationship among the three.

In our case, we are going to focus on ambiguity for two reasons. Firstly, a practical reason for testing experimentally similar assumptions is that ambiguity must be implemented in the lab and this must be done using some suitable device. On the other hand, it is quite reasonable to think of ambiguity as a more realistic characteristic of the daily economic life, where probabilities can be attached to the various events albeit with no accuracy.

In the cases of decision making under risk, the standard model employed by the literature is the Expected Utility model. This is simply the probability weighted sum of the utilities that an agent receives. Imagine, for instance, that we are offered two options. Either we can win for sure $50 or we can flip a coin where if it lands heads, we win $100 otherwise zero. Making the assumption that we are risk neutral[4]. In this case, the expected Utility from flipping the coin is $\Pr\left(Heads\right)U\left(50\right) + \Pr\left(Tails\right)U\left(0\right)$ and this

Figure 1. Relationship among risk, ambiguity, and uncertainty

amount is the compared to $U(50)$. In ambiguous situations where the formation of beliefs is not quite straightforward, Savage (1954) showed that the decision makers can always formulate subjective beliefs, which are always additive and precise. This notion is quite appealing and furthermore offers mathematical elegance. However, Ellsberg (1961) showed that this is not always true and that agents do not form correct beliefs for the various effects (Table 1). He suggested a simple thought experiment, the main idea of which was that due to the presence of ambiguity aversion, the subjects experience preference reversals. The Ellsberg's three-colour urn paradox suggests:

There is an urn with 90 balls of which 30 are black (B) and the rest 60 are red (R) and yellow (Y) (unknown proportions) and could be any number between 0 and 60. A ball is drawn from the urn and the decision maker has to bet on the colour she thinks it is, based on the amounts below (let us say in dollars):

Table 1.Ellsberg paradox

Bet	RED	BLACK	YELLOW
f	100	0	0
g	0	100	0
f'	100	0	100
g'	0	100	100

This means that if she chooses f and a Red ball is drawn, she wins $100 otherwise 0. The decision maker firstly has to choose between the bets f and g and then between f' and g'. Empirically, subjects prefer f to g and g' to f' which is a violation of the axioms that Subjective Expected Utility (SEU) assumes[5]. If f is preferred to g, then this shows that the subject believes that Prob(Red)>Prob(Black). Similarly, if g' is preferred to f', this shows that the subject thinks that Prob(Red)+Prob((Yellow)<Prob(Yellow)+Prob(Black) which leads Prob(Red)<Prob(Black) and apparently results lead to a contradiction and thus to decisions incompatible with the SEU.

Camerer (1992, 1995) summarizes the main experimental results that show deviation from Expected Utility preferences. Following this line of research, there is a considerable amount of experimental evidence that confirms that human subjects do not conform to the behaviour that the rational agent model requires. Nevertheless, in the literature there are plenty of alternative ways that one can use in order to model ambiguous beliefs. Ranging from simple heuristics to fancy mathematical objects, still there is no consensus on which model is the most suitable. For our example, we are going to use the Choquet Expected Utility model, which is based on Choquet integrals (Choquet, 1953) and was axiomatized as a theoretical model by Gilboa (1987) and Sarin and Wakker (1992). This model is appealing as it has some nice descriptive properties. Beliefs are not represented by subjective probabilities anymore but by capacities. This allows the incorporation of ambiguity aversion in the analysis. Imagine, for example, that someone is offered a bet by flipping a coin and wins one dollar if it comes heads or pays one dollar otherwise. When the agent is sure that the coin is a fair one, then there is no reason to believe that one of the sides has more chances to turn out than the other. In that case, the agent is indifferent to which one to choose and plays each with probability 50% which is exactly the probability that she attaches to each of the outcomes. Imagine now a situation where the agent does not trust that the coin is unbiased. In this case, she is not able to attach 50-50 chances. And since she is ambiguity averse, she attaches probabilities 40% to each side. This is exactly the notion of non-additive capacities, as, according to this definition, $p(tales) + p(heads) = 0.8 \neq 1$. There is a 0.2 missing, which in this model expresses the lack of confidence in the subjective probabilities. Contrary to expected utility, this model is a rank-dependent model which means that the agent ranks the several different outcomes and attaches different weights according to her preferences[6]. In the experimental literature of testing choices under ambiguity, there is robust empirical evidence that the Choquet Expected Utility performs considerably better than Subjective Expected Utility and thus outperforms as a model of ambiguous beliefs (Hey et al., 2010, 2011; Hanany, 2007).

Game Theory with Strategic Ambiguity

A standard way to extend individual decision making to interactive environments with two or more participants is game theory. In this extension, it does not suffice to assume that each player behaves in the same way as in the individual decision making model but we need to take into consideration that the actions of the one player affect the decisions of the other. The notion of Nash equilibrium constitutes a cornerstone for game theory and this is why thousands of papers and books cite the idea of the 'Beautiful Mind', John Nash. This idea is quite attractive in both normative and positive aspects. As an informal definition, Nash equilibrium shows all those combinations of strategies that players have at their disposal that make them lose any incentive from deviating of playing such strategies. The latter requires that agents satisfy two requirements at the same time. On the one hand, they always play their best strategy and, on the other, they hold firm beliefs about the opponent.

Camerer (2003) introduces the idea of Behavioural game theory by collecting a series of experiments that show deviation from the Nash equilibrium and effort is made to find the psychological reasons that can explain this. In our example, we are going to use a standard game with known equilibria and see how they can be affected by introducing ambiguous beliefs.

The Game

As an example we will use a standard cooperative game that was inspired by Jean Jacques Rousseau (1755). The idea of cooperative game theory, in contrast to the non-cooperative, is that the players of the game are better off when they cooperate. A variation of such a game is the *Stag* Hunt game. The story is quite simple. Two hunters meet in the woods. There are also only two kinds of preys that they can look for, Stags and Rabbits. Stags are the big preys and catching one suffices to feed both hunters. Rabbits, conversely, can be captured one at a time and are adequate only for one person. As the Stag is quite strong, more than one person are needed to catch it. On the contrary, a Rabbit is much easier to catch, so only one person is needed. Both hunters are hungry so it is to their benefit to leave the woods in a successful way. They start discussing and they conclude that they can cooperate and focus on catching the Stag. In this case both will receive the maximum payoff. Although, since this decision it is not binding, each of the hunters may be indulged, and when a Rabbit passes by, they can forget their mission to catch the Stag and go for a Rabbit. In this case, one of the hunters takes a payoff which is lower than what she would get by catching the Stag and the other gets zero. Finally, it is likely that both go for the Rabbit and each results with positive payoffs but always less than the payoff that the Stag offers. In this kind of games, the optimal result is obtained when both of the players coordinate. Having each player to choose between two available strategies {cooperate, defect} or {c, d}, we can represent this game using a payoff matrix which states the returns of each of the strategies. The payoffs are show in Table 2.

This game depicts the beliefs that each player attaches on the other player's strategy. It has two Nash equilibria, one when both cooperate (c, c) and one when both defect (d, d). So if Player 1 thinks that Player 2 is going to cooperate for sure, then the optimal thing to do is to cooperate as well. On the contrary, if we expect that the other player is going to defect, then in order to avoid the zero outcome, it is better to defect as well. When the players are sure about the behaviour of the fellow player, then the two Nash equilibrium will emerge. If we want to think this in terms of probabilities, it is as if we have two different types (cooperative, non cooperative) and we attach prior probability equal to 1 to the type on which we are sure. This leads us to the notion of mixed-Nash equilibrium.

In this case, we are not sure on the type of each player so we need to form some beliefs. In the appendix, we show that when Player 1 attaches probability 7/8 or more to the fact that Player 2 is cooperative type, then she always cooperates. If her beliefs are less than 7/8, then it is better for her to defect and go for the Rabbit.

In order to illustrate the previous result, we run a series of simulations. Using the payoff matrix given by table(payoff 1), we simulate a 2x2 game (2 players, 2 strategies). We assume that both players are identical in their preferences and are risk neutral. Nonetheless, they differ in the subjective beliefs each holds on the strategies of each player. As it holds in lab experiments and even more in real life, there are legitimate reasons why one can hold diverse beliefs. Past experiences, cultural background, social status, religious motives, anything can affect the way that agents form their subjective beliefs on others. As our scope is to examine how different beliefs affect the equilibrium, we will not focus on any of these "environmental variables" as Myerson (1991) calls them[7]. Hence, in order to model the beliefs of the agents, we use a random number generator that generates numbers from a uniform distribution in the space [0,1]. We range the number of iterations from 10 to 1000 and we simulate three different rounds with 10, 100 and 1000 iterations. The results are summarized in Table 3.

In this example, roughly 75% of the games resulted in the Pareto dominated[8] equilibrium and each of the players gained on average something less than 6.5 units of utility when they could have

Table 2. Payoff matrix 1

		Player 2	
		c	d
Player 1	C	9, 9	0, 8
	D	8, 0	7, 7

Table 3. Simulation game 1

Strategy	N_iter=10	N_iter=100	N_iter=1000
(c, c)	0.00%	0.02%	0.01%
(c, d)	0.10%	0.16%	0.10%
(d, c)	0.20%	0.13%	0.12%
(d, d)	0.70%	0.69%	0.77%
Avg Pay	6.50, 5.70	6.05, 6.29	6.44, 6.30

Table 4. Payoff matrix 2

		Player 2	
		C	D
Player 1	C	3, 3	0, 2
	D	2, 0	1, 1

won 9 units each. In this game, Rousseau wanted to show how attitudes inside a group affect the result. In other words, depending on the beliefs of the players and whether the player is optimistic or pessimistic, we may have cooperation or not.

A crucial issue here is the payoff matrix. Playing the same game but with a different payoff matrix, which keeps the same form of the game (coordination always gives the best outcome), may produce significantly different results. Consider now the payoff matrix in Table 4.

Solving for the Mixed Strategies Nash Equilibrium, it is easy to show that the probability where we observe a switch in the beliefs is ½. So if Player 1 believes that there is more than 0.5 chances that Player 2 will cooperate, she cooperates as well, otherwise she defects. The same holds for Player 2 regarding his beliefs for Player1. Running again three different simulations with 10, 100 and 1000 iterations, we obtain the results shown in Table 5.

Changing the payoff matrix and keeping the same game structure, the impact on the way that the game is played is significant. In Figure 1, the relative frequency of the strategies is depicted. The difference in the two equilibria is apparent due to the change in the payoffs.

As interesting it may be a similar result, it is still quite restrictive on the assumptions that standard decision making makes. In the examples above, it is required that the players have full information and they always form the correct probabilities on the strategies that the other player is going to play. Nevertheless, in real life, similar occasions are very rare, hence we need to extend the analysis to incomplete information.

In the analysis before, we made two explicit assumptions. We required that both the players are rational and identical concerning their attitudes towards ambiguity and we also assumed that they can always form subjective beliefs that are always precise and additive (agents are always able to set p and $1-p$ for each of the other player's strategies). In the remainder of the chapter we introduce the same game but with capacities instead of probabilities. In this case the chances that the other player, let's say Player B, will coordinate or defect are not anymore p and $1-p$ but $v_B(c)$ and $v_B(d)$ which are not necessarily additive (they do not sum up to 1). The advantage of using capacities is that now we can count for ambiguity as well. Furthermore, the use of ambiguity attitudes helps us to distinguish between different types of agents. In this case, we can define as an *optimistic* agent the one that always focuses on the biggest payoffs, while the *pessimist* type always focuses on the lowest payoff (Marinacci, 2000). In the appendix we provide the ways that each of the agents behave.

Table 5. Simulation game 2

Strategy	N_iter=10	N_iter=100	N_iter=1000
(c, c)	0.1%	0.26%	0.242%
(c, d)	0.3%	0.2%	0.241%
(d, c)	0.2%	0.25%	0.25%
(d, d)	0.4%	0.29%	0.267%
Avg Pay	1.1, 1.3	1.57, 1.47	1.49, 1.47

Let us now see how the results change when we allow for non-additive beliefs. Prior to this, we need to define a new term, the *measure of vagueness* which differentiates the additive and non-additive beliefs. Let Ψ to represent this measure. Let also $v_B(c)$ and $v_B(d)$ the beliefs that Player A attaches to each of the strategies of player B. Then the measure of vagueness is simply given by $\psi = 1 - v_B(c) - v_B(d)$. It is easy to show that in the case of additive beliefs, $\psi = 1$. Let us now introduce different levels of vagueness (in a lab experiment this can be done by using a random device and virtual players. The subjects are playing against a virtual player whose strategies are defined by this device). As is illustrated in the appendix, the two different types focus on different parameters. The pessimistic player cares for her beliefs that the other player will cooperate while the optimistic in the beliefs that the other will defect. This means that in our simulation we need again two different sources of ambiguity, each that represents the vague beliefs of each player. In the simulation we are running 1000 games in three different treatments, two optimistic players, two optimistic players and one optimistic against one pessimistic. We assume that both players face the same ambiguity and attach the same beliefs to each of the strategies. Using the payoffs of Table 2, as was stated earlier, we know that each player cooperates when the probability that the other player will cooperate is more than 0.5. Let us assume that each player attaches

beliefs equal to 0.45 at each strategy, creating in this case a measure of vagueness equal to 0.1. The results are summarized in Table 6.

Defining the two different types of behaviour is exactly the idea that Rousseau wanted to support when he was talking for optimism in the group. According to this idea, coordination maybe the equilibrium if there are optimistic types in the game. Three observations emerge from the results of the simulation. Firstly, when the population consists only of optimistic agents, then the most frequent equilibrium we observe is the coordination. The opposite holds for the pessimistic agents. In addition, when the level of vagueness (Ψ) increases, this result becomes more robust. So as ambiguity goes up, the optimistic agent always coordinate while the pessimistic defects. In the case of mixed players, the result converges to the pure strategy of each of the players. Lastly, we obtain different results in the case we allow for different types compared to the ones we obtained in simulating the game using expected utility and additive beliefs (simulation 2). It is easy to deduce that the results changed not only due to the different payoff matrix, but also due to the introduction of ambiguous beliefs to the modelling process.

Issues, Controversies, Problems

The literature is dispersed with several explanations on why we see different equilibrium to emerge.. Two of those focus on the payoff-

Table 6. Simulation 3

Strategy	Optimistic Vs Optimistic			Pessimistic Vs Pessimistic			Optimistic Vs Pessimistic		
Ψ	.10	.30	.70	.10	.30	.70	.10	.30	.70
(c, c)	0.293%	0.423%	**0.719%**	0.218%	0.11%	0.031%	0.239%	0.227%	0.115%
(c, d)	0.254%	0.213%	0.132%	0.229%	0.228%	0.111%	0.323%	0.447%	0.731%
(d, c)	0.268%	0.227%	0.121%	0.241%	0.224%	0.125%	0.197%	0.108%	0.02%
(d, d)	0.185%	0.137%	0.028%	0.312%	0.438%	**0.733%**	0.241%	0.218%	0.134%
Avg Pay	1.6, 1.572	1.86, 1.832	2.427, 2.449	1.448, 1.424	1.216, 1.224	1.076, 1.048	1.352, 1.604	1.115, 1.793	0.519, 1.941

dominant equilibrium (Harsanyi & Selten, 1988; Andrenlini, 1999) and the risk-dominant equilibrium (Carlsson & Van Damme, 1993; Harsanyi & Selten, 1995)[9]. In our experiment, we diverge from this line of research and suggest both the introduction of ambiguity in the strategies played and also the introduction of ambiguity attitudes. These results have not been tested experimentally yet, so using agent-based modelling is a quite useful way to design an appropriate experiment[10].

These simulations remained only to a simple level. We cannot reach fully-fledged conclusions with only these examples. Our objective, is to show how simulations can be helpful and, in fact, should constitute an indispensable part during the design of an economic experiment. From the examples described above, if someone remained on the assumption that different payoffs lead to different equilibrium, by incorporating ambiguity it can be easy to refute her.. When designing an experiment, it is vital to choose the payoff matrices as well as the questions that the subjects will be asked, in such a way that the experimenter will be sure that they cover all the possible aspects that can unpredictably affect behaviour. Then, on the basis of these observations, we will be able to both design the experiment in an optimal way and to provide the subjects with the suitable incentives that will lead to the elicitation of preferences and beliefs. Then, after having obtained the data from the experiment, a new model can be created that will assist the replication of the subjects' strategies and will simultaneously provide insights of human behaviour that can contribute to the refinements of the theory (Duffy, 2006).

FUTURE RESEARCH DIRECTIONS

The previous examples focus on a series of one shot games. This can be thought as a tournament where each player plays once against another player and they never meet again. This game has been extended to its repeated form, where players have the chance to learn and adapt from past experience. This kind of problems requires the introduction of learning models. In the game theory literature, one can find several models that have been suggested such as the fictitious play, the partial best response dynamic, the replicator dynamic, reinforcement learning, belief based learning (Camerer, 2003, pp. 235-365; Fudenberg & Levine, 1998). However, none of them involves the existence of ambiguous beliefs. Since similar models are an ideal candidate for agent-based modelling methods, a natural way to extend the previous experiments is to combine learning models, cooperation and ambiguous beliefs, an issue that seriously challenges the standard model, based on Bayesian updating and maximization of Expected Utility.

CONCLUSION

In this chapter, we focused on the formation of ambiguous beliefs and how the possession of non-additive beliefs can change the equilibrium during game play. As the objective was to show how the introduction of subjective beliefs can affect the results, all the simulations remained simple and focused only on the one-shot games where the individuals played once and did not have any opportunity to learn and adapt their behaviour. As most of the problems include time dimensions, we can benefit from the power the agent-based modelling gives and extend the models to their dynamic form. In addition, as the literature in decision making under ambiguity has been developed quite satisfactorily, it is more than imperative to include these advances in most of economic research. This has a cost in the difficulty that it adds but the payoff of getting more realistic and accurate predictions and models does compensate well.

REFERENCES

Andrelini, L. (1999). Communication, computability and common interest games. *Journal of Games and Economic Behaviour*, *27*, 1–37. doi:10.1006/game.1998.0652

Arciero, L., Picillo, C., Solomon, S., & Terna, P. (2014). Building ABMs to control the emergence of crisis analyzing agents' behavior. In D. Adamatti, G. Dimuro, & H. Coelho (Eds.), *Interdisciplinary applications of agent-based social simulation and modeling*. Hershey, PA: IGI-Global.

Binmore, K. (2009). *Rational Decisions. Gorman Lectures in Economics*. Princeton, N.J.: Princeton University Press.

Camerer, K. (1995). Individual decision making. In J. H. Kagel, & A. E. Ross (Eds.), *Handbook of experimental economics*. Princeton, NJ: Princeton University Press.

Camerer, K. (2003). *Behavioural game theory: Experiment in strategic interaction*. Princeton, NJ: Princeton University Press.

Camerer, K., & Weber, M. (1992). Recent developments in modelling preferences: Uncertainty and ambiguity. *Journal of Risk and Uncertainty*, *5*(4), 325–370. doi:10.1007/BF00122575

Carlsson, H., & Van Damme, E. (1993). Global games and equilibrium selection. *Econometrica*, *61*, 989–1018. doi:10.2307/2951491

Choquet, G. (1953). Theory of capacities. *Ann. Inst. Fourier (Grenoble)*, *5*, 131–295. doi:10.5802/aif.53

Coehlo, H., Rocha Costa, A. C., & Trigo, P. (2014). On agent interactions governed by morality. In D. Adamatti, G. Dimuro, & H. Coelho (Eds.), *Interdisciplinary applications of agent-based social simulation and modeling*. Hershey, PA: IGI-Global.

Dubois, D., Willinger, M., & Van Nguyen, P. (2011). Optimization incentive and relative riskiness in experimental stag-hunt games. *International Journal of Game Theory*, *41*, 369–380. doi:10.1007/s00182-011-0290-x

Duffy, J. (2006). Agent-based models and human subject experiments. In L. Tesfatsion, & K. Judd (Eds.), *Handbook of computational economics* (Vol. 2). Amsterdam, The Netherlands: Elsevier.

Eichberger, J., & Kelsey, D. (2011). Are the treasures of game theory ambiguous? *Economic Theory*, *48*, 313–339. doi:10.1007/s00199-011-0636-4

Ellsberg, D. (1961). Risk, ambiguity and the savage axioms. *The Quarterly Journal of Economics*, *75*, 643–669. doi:10.2307/1884324

Epstein, J. M. (2008). Why model? *Journal of Artificial Societies and Social Simulation*, *11*(4), 12.

Epstein, J. M., & Axtell, R. (1996). *Growing artificial societies*. Cambridge, MA: MIT Press.

Fudenberg, D., & Levine, D. (1998). *The theory of learning in games*. London: MIT Press.

Gibbons, R. (1992). *Game theory for applied economists*. Princeton, NJ: Princeton University Press.

Gilboa, I. (1987). Expected utility with purely subjective non-additive probabilities. *Journal of Mathematical Economics*, *16*, 65–88. doi:10.1016/0304-4068(87)90022-X

Gilboa, I. (2009). *Theory of decision under uncertainty (Econometric Society Monograph Series)*. New York: Cambridge University Press. doi:10.1017/CBO9780511840203

Halevy, Y. (2007). Ellsberg revisited: An experimental study. *Econometrica*, *75*(2), 503–536. doi:10.1111/j.1468-0262.2006.00755.x

Harsanyi, J., & Selten, R. (1995). *A general theory of equilibrium selection for games.* Cambridge, MA: MIT Press.

Harsanyi, J., & Selten, R. (1998). A general theory of equilibrium selection for games with complete information. *Journal of Games and Economic Behavior*, *8*, 91–122. doi:10.1016/S0899-8256(05)80018-1

Hauser, F., Huber, J., & Kirchler, M. (2009). Comparing laboratory experiments and agent-based simulations: The value of information and market efficiency in a market with asymmetric information. In C. Hernández, M. Posada, & A. López-Paredes (Eds.), *Artificial economics: The generative method in economics* (pp. 199–210). Berlin: Springer-Verlag. doi:10.1007/978-3-642-02956-1_16

Helbing, D., & Balietti, S. (2012). Agent-based modeling. In D. Helbing (Ed.), *social self-organization (Understanding complex systems)* (pp. 25–70). Berlin: Springer. doi:10.1007/978-3-642-24004-1_2

Hey, J. D., Lotito, G., & Maffioletti, A. (2010). The descriptive and predictive adequacy of theories of decision making under uncertainty/ambiguity. *Journal of Risk and Uncertainty*, *41*(2), 81–111. doi:10.1007/s11166-010-9102-0

Hey, J. D., & Pace, N. (2011). *The explanatory and predictive power of non two-stage-probability theories of decision making under ambiguity (Discussion Papers 11/22).* Department of Economics, University of York.

Hommes, C. H. (2006). Heterogeneous agent models in economics and finance. In L. Tesfatsion, & K. Judd (Eds.), *Handbook of computational economics* (Vol. 2). Amsterdam, The Netherlands: Elsevier.

Isaak, A. G. (2008). Simulating evolutionary games: A Python-based introduction. *Journal of Artificial Societies and Social Simulation*, *11*(3), 8.

Knight, F. H. (1921). Risks, uncertainty and profit. Boston: Houghton-Mifflin.

Lucas, P., & Payne, D. (2014). Usefulness of agent-based simulation to test collective decision-making models. In D. Adamatti, G. Dimuro, & H. Coelho (Eds.), *Interdisciplinary applications of agent-based social simulation and modeling.* Hershey, PA: IGI-Global.

Macal, C. M., & North, M. J. (2010). Tutorial on agent-based modeling and simulation. *Journal of Simulation*, *4*, 151–162. doi:10.1057/jos.2010.3

Marinacci, M. (2000). Ambiguous games. *Games and Economic Behavior*, *31*(2), 191–219. doi:10.1006/game.1999.0739

Myerson, R. B. (1991). *Game theory.* Cambridge, MA: Harvard University Press.

Rousseau, J. J. (1755). *Discourse on inequality.* Holland: Marc-Michel Rey.

Sarin, R., & Wakker, P. (1992). A simple axiomatization of nonadditive expected utility. *Econometrica*, *60*, 1255–1272. doi:10.2307/2951521

Savage, L. J. (1954). *The foundations of statistics.* New York: Wiley.

Shoham, Y., & Leyton-Brown, K. (2009). *Multiagent systems.* New York: Cambridge University Press.

Tesfatsion, L. (2006). Agent based computational economics: A constructive approach to economic theory. In L. Tesfatsion, & K. Judd (Eds.), *Handbook of computational economics* (Vol. 2). Amsterdam, The Netherlands: Elsevier. doi:10.1016/S1574-0021(05)02016-2

Trigo, P. (2014). Multi-agent economically motivated decision-making. In D. Adamatti, G. Dimuro, & H. Coelho (Eds.), *Interdisciplinary applications of agent-based social simulation and modeling.* Hershey, PA: IGI-Global.

Trindade Magessi, N., & Antunes, L. (2014). Agent's risk relation on strategic tax reporting game. In D. Adamatti, G. Dimuro, & H. Coelho (Eds.), *Interdisciplinary applications of agent-based social simulation and modeling*. Hershey, PA: IGI-Global.

Van Dinther, C. (2008). Agent-based simulation for research in economics handbook on information technology. In S. Detlef, C. Weinhardt, & F. Schlottmann (Eds.), *Finance international handbooks information system*. Berlin: Springer. doi:10.1007/978-3-540-49487-4_18

ADDITIONAL READING

Fudenberg, D., & Tirole, J. (1991). *Game Theory*. Cambridge, Mass.: MIT Press.

Game Theory Binmore. Ken. 1992. Fun and Games: A Text on Game Theory. Lexington, Mass.: D. C. Heath.

Gibbons, R. (1992). *Game Theory for Applied Economists*. Princeton, N.J.: Princeton University Press.

Gilboa, I. (2010). *Rational choice*. Cambridge, Massachusetts: MIT Press.

Hernández, C., Posada, M., & López-Paredes, A. (Eds.). (2009). *Artificial Economics: the Generative Method in Economics. Springer-Verlag Berlin Heidelberg*. Springer. doi:10.1007/978-3-642-02956-1

Kreps, D. M. (1988). *Notes on the Theory of Choice*. Boulder, Colo: Westview Press.

Matthieu, P., Beaufils, B., & Brandouy, O. (Eds.). (2006). *Artificial Economics. Agent-Based Methods in Finance, Game Theory and their Applications. Springer-Verlag Berlin Heidelberg*. Springer.

Myerson, R. B. (1991). *Game Theory: Analysis of Conflict*. Cambridge, Mass.: Harvard University Press.

Osborne, M. J., & Rubinstein, A. (1994). *A Course in Game Theory*. Cambridge, Mass.: MIT Press.

Tesfatsion, L., & Judd, K. (Eds.). (2006). *Handbook of Computational Economics* (Vol. 2). Netherlands: Elsevier.

KEY TERMS AND DEFINITIONS

Ambiguity: The case where there are no available exact measures of the probability that some events will happen.

Games: A methodology used in social sciences in order to model strategic interaction among agents.

Non-Additive Additive Capacities: When our beliefs on the probabilities that some events will happen do not add up to unit.

Optimism: When an agent focuses on the high payments of the payoffs.

Pessimism: When an agent focuses on the low payments of the payoffs.

Stag Hunt: A game that Rousseau used to explain social cooperation and optimism.

ENDNOTES

[1]   According to rational choice theory, an agent always has well-defined preferences and always maximizes her utility with respect to these preferences subject to the various constraints in her environment (income, institutional, etc).

[2]   A familiarity of the reader with basic economic theory is assumed. For more information on choice theory and utility maximization, see Binmore (2009).

[3] In order to represent the agent's preferences with a utility function, there are several axioms that must be satisfied. These axioms are either behavioral or axioms that guarantee the existence of such preferences. Most of the times they are normative axioms (what people should do).

[4] This means that the agent faces no risks.

[5] For more on decision making under ambiguity see Gilboa (2009).

[6] The main properties of capacities are presented in the appendix.

[7] Similar issues are discussed in the present volume by Coelho et al. (2014).

[8] Pareto dominated outcome is one which is reached when another outcome that makes at least one of the two players better off without hurting the other is available.

[9] For an extended literature review and experimental results, see Dubois et al. (2001).

[10] For further references on the issue, see Eichberger and Kelsey (2011).

[11] For an excellent tutorial on how to write Python programs for simulations in games, see Isaak (2008).

APPENDIX

Mixed Strategies Nash Equilibrium (MSNE)

In order to find the MSNE, we attach probabilities to the various strategies of the players. For example, we assume that Player 1 plays c with probability p and d with probability 1-p. Similarly, for player 2 we assume that she plays c with probability q and d with 1-q. In order to calculate the level of the probabilities where agents switch strategies, we use the following procedure:

For Player 1, we want to find the reaction of the opponent that makes her to be indifferent to playing either strategy. The expected utility of Player when she cooperates is:

$$EU_1\left(c\right) = qU_1\left(c,c\right) + \left(1-q\right)U_1\left(c,d\right) = 9q$$

Similarly, when she decides to defect:

$$EU_1\left(d\right) = qU_1\left(d,c\right) + \left(1-q\right)U_1\left(d,d\right) = 8q - \left(1-q\right)7 = q - 7$$

Player 1 is indifferent to either strategies when $EU_1\left(c\right) = EU_1\left(d\right)$ which leads to $q = \dfrac{7}{8}$

This gives three different cases:

- When $q < \dfrac{7}{8}$ Player 1 always defects

- When $q = \dfrac{7}{8}$ Player 1 is indifferent between cooperating and defecting

- When $q > \dfrac{7}{8}$ Player 1 always cooperate

Choquet Expected Utility (CEU)

Let X be a finite set and 2^X its power set. Then a capacity v on 2^X which satisfies:
$$v\left(\varnothing\right) = 0, v\left(X\right) = 1, v\left(A\right) \le v\left(B\right) \, if \, A \subset B\,.$$ A capacity v is convex if $v\left(A\right) + v\left(B\right) \le v\left(A\bigcup B\right) + v\left(A\bigcap B\right)$. As this model is a Rank Dependent Model, contrary to the Expected Utility model, in CEU the ranking of the outcomes plays significant role. If we assume that we have three different events $\{\, s_1, s_2, s_3 \,\}$ which respectively lead to consequences $\{\, x_1, x_2, x_3 \,\}$, then the decision maker makes a rank of the utility that she obtains from the three consequences. So if, for example, $u\left(x_1\right) > u\left(x_2\right) > u\left(x_3\right)$, then the decision maker maximizes the weighted expected utility. Thus, instead of probability, now the agent uses capacities which are weighted depending on the ranking. So in this case the Choquet Expected Utility to be maximized can be written as:

$$v_1 u\left(x_1\right) + \left(v_{12} - v_1\right) u\left(x_2\right) + \left(1 - v_{12}\right) u\left(x_3\right)$$

In the case of additive beliefs, this equation is simply the Expected Utility. Marinacci (2000) shows that when the capacities are convex (agent is ambiguity averse), then more weight is out on the worst outcome. This is exactly the way that a pessimistic agent forms her CEU. On the contrary, an optimistic decision maker maximizes the following:

$$\left(1 - v_{23}\right) u\left(x_1\right) + \left(v_{23} - v_3\right) u\left(x_2\right) + v_3 u\left(x_3\right)$$

Pessimistic Player: A pessimistic player focuses on the 'bad' outcome. Take, for example, the payoff matrix of game 2. In this case, the pessimistic player focuses on the payoff when she and the opponent both defect, thus 1. This is the outcome that is overweight. When she decides which strategy to play, she solves:

$$U_1\left(c\right) = 3 v_b\left(c\right)$$

$$U_1\left(d\right) = 1 + v_b\left(c\right)$$

Player 1 decides to cooperate when $U_1\left(c\right) > U_1\left(d\right)$ and this holds when $v_b\left(c\right) > 1/2$

Optimistic Player: Similarly, an optimistic player decides as:

$$U_1\left(c\right) = 3 - 3 v_b\left(d\right)$$

$$U_1\left(d\right) = 2 - v_b\left(d\right)$$

Player 1 decides to cooperate when $U_1\left(c\right) > U_1\left(d\right)$ and this holds when $v_b\left(d\right) < 1/2$

Figure 2. Simulation code 1[11]

```python
#Stag Hunt Simulation
#author georgalos, June 2013
#This version provides the equilibria for pure and mixed
#strategies depending on the beliefs each player attaches to the other
from __future__ import division
from random import*

#this is the payoff matrix
pay1=[[[9,9],[0,8]],
    [[8,0],[7,7]]]

pay2=[[[3,3],[0,2]],
    [[2,0],[1,1]]]

class game:
    def __init__(self,player1,player2,pay,p,q,ps,qs):
        self.player1=player1
        self.player2=player2
        self.pay=pay
        self.p=p;self.q=q
        self.ps=ps;self.qs=qs
        self.l=[0,0,0,0]
    def run(self):
        #pessimistic
        if self.p==self.ps:
            self.player2=randint(0,1)
        elif self.p>self.ps:
            self.player2=0
        elif self.p<self.ps:
            self.player2=1
        #optimistic
        if self.q==self.qs:
            self.player1=randint(0,1)
        elif self.q>self.qs:
            self.player1=0
        elif self.q<self.qs:
            self.player1=1
        self.payment1,self.payment2=self.pay[self.player1][self.player2]
        print 'the payoff is',self.pay[self.player1][self.player2]
        self.freq()
    def sums(self):
        k=[self.payment1,self.payment2]
        return k
    def freq(self):
        if self.pay[self.player1][self.player2]==self.pay[0][0]:
            self.l[0]=1
        elif self.pay[self.player1][self.player2]==self.pay[0][1]:
            self.l[1]=1
        elif self.pay[self.player1][self.player2]==self.pay[1][0]:
            self.l[2]=1
        else:
            self.l[3]=1
        return self.l
player1=0;player2=0

#game(player1,player2,pay,p=random(),q=random())
sum1=0;sum2=0
n_iter=1000
freq=[0,0,0,0]
for i in range(n_iter):
    play=game(player1,player2,pay2,p=random(),q=random(),qs=.45,ps=.45)
    play.run()
    pays=play.sums()
    sum1+=pays[0];sum2+=pays[1]
    l=play.freq()
    if l[0]==1:freq[0]+=1
    if l[1]==1:freq[1]+=1
    if l[2]==1:freq[2]+=1
    if l[3]==1:freq[3]+=1
    print freq, freq[0]/n_iter,freq[1]/n_iter,freq[2]/n_iter,freq[3]/n_iter
```

Figure 3. Simulation code 2[11]

```
#Stag Hunt Simulation
#author georgalos, June 2013
#This version provides the equilibria for pure and mixed
#strategies depending on the beliefs each player attaches to the other
from __future__ import division
from random import*

#this is the payoff matrix
pay1=[[[9,9],[0,8]],
    [[8,0],[7,7]]]
pay2=[[[3,3],[0,2]],
    [[2,0],[1,1]]]

class game:
    def __init__(self,player1,player2,pay,p,q,ps,qs):
        self.player1=player1
        self.player2=player2
        self.pay=pay
        self.p=p;self.q=q
        self.ps=ps;self.qs=qs
        self.l=[0,0,0,0]
    def run(self):
        if self.p==self.ps:
            self.player2=randint(0,1)
        elif self.p>self.ps:
            self.player2=0
        elif self.p<self.ps:
            self.player2=1
        if self.q==self.qs:
            self.player1=randint(0,1)
        elif self.q>self.qs:
            self.player1=0
        elif self.q<self.qs:
            self.player1=1
        self.payment1,self.payment2=self.pay[self.player1][self.player2]
        print 'the payoff is',self.pay[self.player1][self.player2]
        self.freq()
    def sums(self):
        k=[self.payment1,self.payment2]
        return k
    def freq(self):
        if self.pay[self.player1][self.player2]==self.pay[0][0]:
            self.l[0]=1
        elif self.pay[self.player1][self.player2]==self.pay[0][1]:
            self.l[1]=1
        elif self.pay[self.player1][self.player2]==self.pay[1][0]:
            self.l[2]=1
        else:
            self.l[3]=1
        return self.l
player1=0;player2=0
#game(player1,player2,pay,p=random(),q=random())
sum1=0;sum2=0
n_iter=1000

freq=[0,0,0,0]
for i in range(n_iter):
    play=game(player1,player2,pay1,p=random(),q=random(),qs=1/2,ps=1/2)
    play.run()
    pays=play.sums()
    sum1+=pays[0];sum2+=pays[1]
    l=play.freq()
    if l[0]==1:freq[0]+=1
    if l[1]==1:freq[1]+=1
    if l[2]==1:freq[2]+=1
    if l[3]==1:freq[3]+=1
    print freq, freq[0]/n_iter,freq[1]/n_iter,freq[2]/n_iter,freq[3]/n_iter
```

Chapter 9
From Meso Decisions to Macro Results:
An Agent-Based Approach of Policy Diffusion

Stéphane Luyet
Lausanne University Hospital, Switzerland

ABSTRACT

Policy diffusion needs to be studied as a complex phenomenon, since it involves interdependent relationships between autonomous and heterogeneous countries. This chapter aims at developing a simple computational model based on a theoretical model of policy diffusion (Braun & Gilardi, 2006) that helps to explain the emergence of diffusion in a complex system. Based on three simple conditions (ready, choose, change) and a few internal and external characteristics that define countries and their interactions, the model presented in this chapter shows that policies do diffuse and lead to local convergence and global divergence. Moreover, it takes time for a country to introduce the best-suited policy and for this policy to become very effective. To conclude, diffusion is a complex phenomenon and its outcomes, as ensued from the author's model, are in line with the theoretical expectations and the empirical evidence.

1. INTRODUCTION

Social sciences in general and political science in particular study phenomena of interest as complicated but not complex systems. Policy diffusion is a good example of the increasing complication at the methodological level that still cannot explain the process as a whole.[1] In other words, despite their sophistication, most studies are biased toward correlational accounts, and little is said about the process by which policies diffuse. Consequently, the non-linearity that results from the different interdependencies is not taken into account.

Moreover, what is generally missing is an explanatory model that comprehends factors that are internal and external to a country, since both determine the possible interactions in the process. Therefore, based on a largely accepted definition that diffusion is an interdependent process of policy choices between countries (Simmons, Dobbin, & Garrett, 2006), diffusion should be seen as a phenomenon that emerges be-

DOI: 10.4018/978-1-4666-5954-4.ch009

tween heterogeneous, adaptive, and autonomous[2] countries characterized by temporal and spatial features. Furthermore, diffusion processes are in play in complex adaptive systems (CAS), which are nonlinear systems composed of interacting agents (Rogers, Medina, Rivera, & Wiley, 2005).

To take into account the non-linearity of the policy diffusion process, methodologically, a computational agent-based model of policy diffusion has been developed, as it is a powerful tool for developing and testing new theories (Davis, Eisenhardt, & Bingham, 2007) and a well-suited tool for the study of non-linear processes (Axelrod, 2003; Bonabeau, 2002; Gilbert, 1998).

The aims of this chapter are twofold. First, the building of a computational agent-based model will be highlighted. More precisely, theoretical underpinnings that lie behind the choice of the parameters to "create" agents/countries and the rules they follow to progress within the world are emphasized. Second, diffusion as an emergent phenomenon will be stressed. In sum, based on the idea that diffusion can be explained as policy change driven by interdependencies (Braun & Gilardi, 2006), "in silico" countries based on a few parameters and conditions for interactions are created.

This chapter is structured as follows. Section 2 gives a definition of computational agent-based modeling and puts some emphasis on existing models that studied diffusion in social and political science. Section 3, policy diffusion will be defined and the theoretical choice of the different parameters will be discussed. With Section 4, the computational implementation of the theoretical factors and the different rules of interactions that shape the interdependencies between agents will be explained, as well as how the model works. Section 5 discusses the main findings. Future research directions and a conclusion will close this chapter.

2. COMPUTATIONAL AGENT-BASED MODELS AND DIFFUSION

Computational agent-based models (CABMs) have several uses. The first that comes to mind is prediction[3]. For our purpose, to demonstrate the emergence of complex behavior arising from simple rules is a more interesting use. For instance, Schelling's segregation model (Schelling 1978) shows that segregated neighborhoods can appear due to simple "thoughts" ("I want 30% of my neighborhood to be composed of neighbors who are like me").

After defining what we mean by computational agent-based modeling (Section 2.1), we will explain some of the significant examples of CABMs developed in social and political science (Section 2.2).

2.1 A Definition of Computational Agent-Based Models

Computational agent-based modeling can be defined as follows:

A computational agent-based model is a system whose dynamics and evolution is fully determined by the set of acceptable initial conditions and transformations rules, rendered as computer programs that specify all formal relationships algorithmically and discover solutions computing algorithms (Luyet, 2011, p. 66).

A computer program basically consists of instructions that can be read by a computer. Furthermore, the strength of a programmed computer lies in its capacity to execute repetitive action (Holland, 1998), since a program consists of a set (or sequence) of instructions that a computer executes indefinitely until a certain condition is satisfied.

Computational models can represent different things, such as a video game, or the evolution of the interest rate. Computational agent-based models can be applied to a variety of interacting systems, such as international relationships, ecosystems, immune systems, and so on. At this point, the social interactions are not taken into account. When we develop a computational (agent-based) model, we create a mathematical abstraction of the phenomenon we want to study in a computer, as already mentioned, and it is the act of interpretation, the injection of semantics, so to speak, that allows these electronic worlds to be the virtual counterparts of real-world observations (Casti, 1997). Thus, agents that are created within this world are only bits (that is, strings of 0s and 1s), but we give them the needed appearance by our interpretation of the different parameters.

Agent-based models can be developed without the computational help: Schelling has developed its segregation model on a checkerboard with two populations of agents (i.e., dimes and coins) (Schelling, 1978; see Section 3.2 below). When the number of agents increases, it is nearly impossible to solve the problem of complex interactions without the help of computers (Holland, 1998).

CABMs produce no outputs corresponding to the real world, since the world we see in reality is clearly different from a computational world. This means that we consider the model as the real world. While letting the agents interact, CABMs allow us to highlight the emergence that lies behind the complexity attached to the interactions that characterize every relationship in our society.

The next section will present several examples of computational agent-based models that highlight diffusion in the social science field in general and in political science in particular.

2.2 Examples of Computational Agent-Based Models Studying Diffusion

Computational agent-based models in social science in general and in political sciences in particular are mainly based on two concepts, namely threshold and bandwagon pressures. The idea of threshold is best expressed by the already mentioned segregation model. In his best-selling book *"Micromotives and Macrobehavior,"* Schelling (Schelling, 1978) attempts to explain the segregation that has taken place in big U.S. cities by assigning a threshold of similar neighbors that the people agree to support for staying in that particular neighborhood.

This idea of threshold is strongly linked with the notion of bandwagon pressures as emphasized by Abrahamson and Rosenkopf (1997) in their study of diffusion of innovation. When a defined threshold has been overcome, an agent adopts the innovations. Hence, the more adopters, the more information is available; thus, the stronger bandwagon pressure, the greater the incentive for a change (Abrahamson & Rosenkopf, 1997; Deffuant, Huet, & Amblard, 2005).

In political science, the combination of these two concepts has been applied notably to study the diffusion of democracy. For instance, Elkink (2011) highlights the diffusion of democracy as an emergent phenomenon from interactions between micro-level, that is the definition of a threshold (the individual political life, i.e. voting, debating, protesting...), and macro-level (geographical patterns of democratization) patterns. More precisely, diffusion of democracy results from the interactions between cross-borders democracy promotion of democratic regimes and "in-borders" democracy promotion of groups of citizens.

Moreover, by linking micro- and macro-level processes in the case of diffusion of democracy, Cederman and Gleditsch (2004) stress the emergence of a collective-security process, i.e. a cooperative defense arrangement. This process results in the development of "democratic clusters" that help protect democracies in a nondemocratic environment.

The emergence of clusters–partial convergence–has been emphasized by Axelrod (1997) in his well known model of the dissemination of culture. In order to investigate why differences between agents still persist despite the fact that "people tend to become more alike (. . .) when they interact" (Axelrod, 1997, 203), Axelrod has developed an agent-based model, based on the idea that the probability that two agents interact–the threshold for starting a communication, increases with their similarity, and is proportional to the number of cultural features[4] they have in common. The logical conclusion of this simulation should be convergence, because multiplying interactions with similar neighbors increases the similarity, as underlined by the bandwagon theory. However, a first result of the model is that local convergence is compatible with global polarization.

Rousseau and van der Veen (2005) use the same idea as Axelrod's to study the process leading to the emergence of a shared identity at the international level; i.e. repertoires of possible identities defined as a list of possible values. Their model shows that the probability that a shared identity emerges increases as the size of the repertoire decreases, as the range of the global bias increases, and when leaders are less powerful.

In sum, based on agent's threshold that generates bandwagon pressure and composed of heterogeneous and autonomous agents that interact on simple rules, these models show emerging results that are quite unexpected. The next section puts emphasis on the theoretical underpinnings of policy diffusion processes. Let us now turn to the explanation of the building of our policy diffusion CABMs.

3. A CONCEPTUAL FRAMEWORK OF POLICY DIFFUSION

Based on a largely accepted definition, policy diffusion will be explained (Section 3.1). The understanding of this process depends not only on the characterization of the interdependencies that exist among countries, as expressed by three main mechanisms of diffusion (horizontal diffusion), namely, learning, competition, and emulation (Section 3.2), but also on internal factors (Section 3.3).

3.1 A Definition of Diffusion

We can define international policy diffusion as follows:

International policy diffusion occurs when government policy decisions in a given country are systematically conditioned by prior policy choices made in other countries (Simmons, et al., 2006).

Policy diffusion is therefore characterized by interdependencies between countries. It is also a self-reinforcing, backward-looking process, because countries look at what has been done in other countries before deciding whether or not to introduce a policy change. Moreover, time has an influence on the evolution of the process (Hacker, 2004), with the consequence being that the percentage of adopters tends to follow an S-shaped curve, as shown in Figure 1 (Berry & Berry, 2006; Gray, 1973; Rogers, 2003).

Such a curve shows us that at the beginning of the process, there are only a few adopters; therefore, the curve stays near 0 until a point where the number of adopters is sufficiently high to induce countries that hesitated or were not really interested in changing their policy to start taking into account the eventuality of change, causing this sharp increase in the slope. This drastic change in the slope of the curve is driven by bandwagon pressure, defined as a process

Figure 1. The cumulative proportion of adopters. Source: Berry and Berry (2006, p. 227).

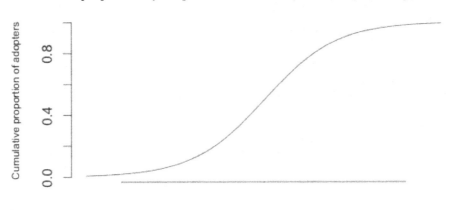

where the more countries that have changed their policy the higher the incentive (the pressure) to change (Abrahamson & Rosenkopf, 1993, 1997; Rosenkopf & Abrahamson, 1999). For instance, the introduction of a prospective payment system for hospital financing in OECD countries follows an S-curve as a result of the influence of prior experience of such system made in other countries (Gilardi, Fueglister, & Luyet, 2009).

As diffusion occurs between countries, space is also an important dimension to take into account. Thus, the conjunction of these interactions and the S-shaped curve results in the creation of political regions; i.e clusters that share the same policy, as can be seen in the context of the diffusion of democracies (Figure 2).

However, space needs not be only geographical/physical; it can also be cultural (Levi-Faur, 2005; Meseguer, 2005), economical—specifically, trade (Martin, 2009), ideological (Grossback, Nicholson-Crotty, & Peterson, 2004), or demographic (Volden, 2006). Consequently, in modern democracies, decisions in policy change are internal processes; however, they may be influenced by policy choices made elsewhere (Braun & Gilardi, 2006). These two sets of influence are explained in the next sections

3.2 The Mechanisms of Diffusion

As we have just seen, diffusion corresponds to an interdependent process of policy choice between countries, and these interdependencies can take several forms. In other words, several mechanisms can cause policy to diffuse, namely, learning, competition, and emulation.[5]

Learning: Learning is defined as a process whereby the experience of policymakers in other countries supply relevant information about the results of a policy and permit the update of policymakers' beliefs on the consequences of this policy (Braun, Gilardi, Fueglister, & Luyet, 2007; Dobbin, Simmons, & Garrett, 2007; Gilardi, et al., 2009; Meseguer, 2004, 2005, 2006b; Simmons, et al., 2006). In the theory of policy diffusion, scholars usually distinguish between purely rational learning and bounded learning. This latter form of learning is of interest in our purposes, since we cannot assume perfect access to information. These bounds exist due to, among other things, the prevalence of outstanding performers (often defined as leaders) and the importance of the geographical proximity (Boschma, 2005) and/or the availability of information. Moreover, these bounds provide cognitive shortcuts that facilitate the learning (Meseguer, 2005; Simmons & Elkins,

Figure 2. The diffusion of democracies, 1945-2009. Adapted from Gleditsch and Ward (2006, 915).

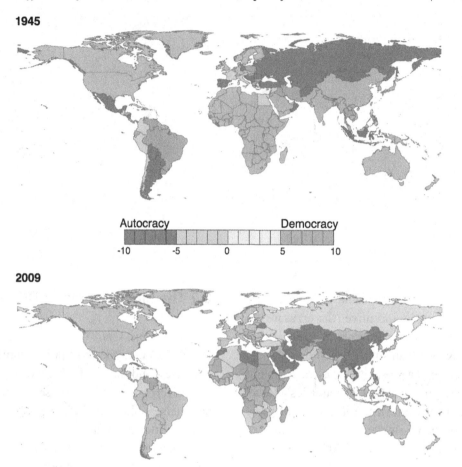

2004). It is worth stressing here that actors of the process of diffusion tend to learn from the most successful adopters (Gilardi, 2010; Gilardi, et al., 2009; Shipan & Volden, 2006; Volden, 2006).

Competition: This mechanism is primarily an economically driven mechanism. The introduction of a policy change can give a country a gain in competitiveness (Simmons, et al., 2006). Thus, facing the relative scarcity of resources, a country tends to adopt the political changes of its close competitors, in order not to lose their market share and/or economical power (Dobbin, et al., 2007). For instance, Swank (2005) argues that welfare state retrenchments are the results of diffusion of neoliberal policies due to competitive pressures. For instance, Denmark, whose close competitors

on the international markets of goods and services are Sweden and Britain, has strong incentive to introduce welfare state reforms that have been initiated in those countries (Swank, 2005).

Emulation: Emulation can be defined as a process through which the countries adopt a policy change because it is an accepted norm (Simmons, et al., 2006). More precisely, emulation, as a mechanism of diffusion, is mainly driven by social constructivism, that is, "the social construction of appropriate behavior" (Kil Lee & Strang, 2006). For example, Independent Regulatory Agencies (IRAs) have increasingly become the norm in the organization of regulatory policy (Gilardi, 2005). Consequently, countries that want to change their policy may imitate peer countries "simply because they are peers" (Meseguer, 2005, p. 73).

Of course, not only the influence of other countries plays a significant role in such process, but internal factors also influence the decision a country has to make for/against a change. At the individual level, each country has its own incentive toward a change, as assumed in Granovetter's threshold model (Granovetter, 1978), in which each actor has a different incentive to join a riot. Following this, each country has its own threshold that guides its decision to join the process of diffusion.

3.3 The Country Specific Factors

This section explains the key theoretical factors at play that define the threshold or the incentive a country has to join a process of diffusion. Here, four internal components of a political change have been identified, namely, political insecurity, ideology, policy effectiveness, and institutional constraints. They are briefly described below.

Ideology: The preference for a policy corresponds to the ideology. For example, leftist parties are supposed to introduce policies that are more state-oriented and rightist parties are in favor of more market-oriented policies. In the context of the diffusion of unemployment benefits retrenchment for instance, rightist governments are more prone to cut unemployment benefits, even if it is a bad solution (Gilardi, 2010). In other words, a government may introduce an ineffective policy because it is in line with the preference of the decision makers. Thus, the ideological position may be an important factor for driving diffusion (Volden, Ting, & Carpenter, 2008). Moreover, ideology is subject to change when elections and voting are taking place.

Political insecurity: Political insecurity competes with ideology for the introduction of a policy change. In other words, in democracies, when elections are near, and to keep the reins of power, governments[6] in place are more prone to

accept policy change supported by the majority of the population even if it is not in line with their dominant ideology. In their competition for votes, parties adapt their electoral platform in order to satisfy most of the citizens (Kollman, Miller, & Page, 1992, 1998). Thus, the fear of losing power may be an important internal driver for policy change.

Policy effectiveness: A policy is designed in order to attain a certain goal. For example, the aging policies that most developed countries introduced after World War II and during the Baby Boom aimed at replacing part of one's wage after one's active life, in an era characterized by economic and demographic growth, as well as a shorter life expectancy and the expansion of welfare state policies. However, these policies are no more effective in today's era challenged by "post-industrial pressures" (Pierson, 2001). Consequently, to face these new challenges, most governments have to find a more effective policy. As a result of this quest, reforms of pension systems have spread among countries (Brooks, 2005, 2007). Hence, when a country changes its current policy, it usually introduces a policy that is supposed to be more effective (Elkins, Guzman, & Simmons, 2006; Gilardi, 2010; Volden, 2006).

Institutional constraints: The idea of institutional constraints is approximated here with the notion of veto players (Bonoli, 2001; Tsebelis, 2002). More precisely, if actors have some veto power, they will introduce some rigidities (or constraints) into the process of change and use it in the political context to block decisions that go against their preferences (Ganghof, 2003). Consequently, the probability for a policy change to be voted into law gets lower. The assumed role of veto players is consistent with empirical research on their role and importance as, for example, in the context of capital control policies (Kastener & Rector, 2003), or in the context of the spread of income tax policies (Hallerberg & Basinger, 1998).

Therefore, for a process of policy diffusion to occur, not only must the countries look at what the others do by evaluating the effectiveness of their neighbors' policy change, but they also should be ready for the change. Thus, diffusion can be explained as policy change driven by interdependences (Braun & Gilardi, 2006). In other words, a country that is not satisfied with its current policy–because it is ineffective or of a majority change for example–should decide whether or not it is looking at having an acceptable policy, and in turn, introduce this policy, according to internal rules, that is, the political and institutional conditions for a change to occur.

4. A COMPUTATIONAL MODEL OF POLICY DIFFUSION

The aim of this section is to highlight how "in silico" countries are created—that is, transformed—into a computational program based on the theory of policy diffusion expressed in Section 3. More precisely, the country parameters (Section 4.1) and the conditions of interactions (Section 4.2) are explained.

Note that, since it is difficult to disentangle the influence of the different mechanisms throughout the process of diffusion (see, for instance, the attempts of Volden et al., 2008, and Gilardi, 2010), we assume that learning is in play, as agents learn from the past.

4.1 The Different Parameters

With a few exceptions (see, e.g., Swank & Steinmo, 2002), most studies rely either on the internal (domestic) factors explained in Section 3.3—policy effectiveness, ideology, political insecurity and/or institutional constraints—or on external (international) factors, as expressed by bandwagon pressures, to explain diffusion. Thus, Table 1 shows the main internal and external factors that define an agent and are briefly explained below.

Here below is explained the operationalization of these internal factors, whose interactions define the different thresholds a country must go through

Table 1. Internal and external factors that define an agent

Threshold	Bandwagon pressures
Policy Preference	Share of neighbors
Political insecurity	that have changed
Policy Effectiveness	their policy
Political Constraints	Proximity array
Policy (current and alternative)	

in order to introduce an alternative policy on the one hand, and, on the other, external determinants – interactions of neighbors entering the process of political change.

The preference for the policy: Each country is driven by a government, characterized by an ideology; i.e. a political preference, moving on the left-right axis (Swank, 2006). This ideal ideological point is not fixed forever, since it moves following the results of elections and/or voting, which roughly represent the political insecurity. Thus, each agent is modeled as having specific preferences over the current policy. Furthermore, at the beginning of the simulation, preferences are drawn randomly from a normal distribution with a mean 0.0 and standard deviation 0.2, truncated at 1.0 and -1.0. "1.0" means that the agent has extremely strong preferences for the current policy, while "-1.0" means that preferences are entirely against it. The preference for the current policy can be either fixed for a period of five time steps or for a period randomly chosen in a uniform distribution, evolving with the time of the simulation. To fix preference is supposed to reflect the fact that policy-makers' preferences change principally when elections and/or voting are close, as noted in Subsection 3.3.

The effectiveness of the policy: Governmental measures are characterized by policy implementations, and each policy is associated with a specific effectiveness that can be defined as the attainment of the desired outcome (Braun & Gilardi, 2006). Thus, in this model, a policy is represented by its effectiveness level. At the beginning of a run, each country has its own policy effectiveness, which is drawn randomly from a normal distribution with mean 0.0 and standard deviation 0.4, truncated at 1.0 and -1.0. "1.0" means that the policy is entirely effective, while "-1.0" means that it is entirely ineffective. Policy effectiveness has a rather large standard deviation throughout the world, meaning that the effectiveness difference between the countries is quite wide. At each time step, a variable randomly drawn from a normal distribution with a mean of −0.01 and a standard deviation of 0.03 is added to the policy effectiveness. Therefore, the effectiveness is likely to decrease through time, which is in line with what is observed in reality, as shown, for instance, by employment politics (Haeusermann & Palier, 2008).

The institutional constraints: This feature expresses the strength of veto players. Thus, agents face specific institutional constraints, which determine the probability with which a law can be passed. At the beginning of the simulation, institutional constraints are drawn randomly from a normal distribution with a mean of 0.0 and standard deviation of 0.3, truncated at 1.0 and -1.0. "1.0" means that there are no institutional constraints and, therefore, that a policy proposal faces no obstacles to be voted into law. We develop here two types of institutional constraints. Firstly, they are fixed throughout the entire simulation. This shows the institutional stability of the different countries. Second, this parameter is re-calculated each time there are elections in the world, leading to institutional instability.

Below, we briefly explain the theoretical pertinence and operationalization of the external characteristics.

The share of neighbors: This feature corresponds to the geographical neighborhood. Thus, the more neighbors that have changed their policy, the higher the chance is for a country to introduce the alternative policy. The substantial weight of the different neighbors in the process of diffusion is a well-known pressure that affects diffusion (see Sections 3.2). Hence, to be precise, we integrate into the model the share of neighbors that have

changed their policy. We take into account the Moore neighborhood—the eight adjacent cells—and the Von Neumann neighborhood—cells at the four cardinal points.

The proximity array: The neighborhood is defined not only as purely geographical but also as taking into account several other dimensions, such as the culture, the economic proximity, and so forth. Thus, sharing a border is a necessary but not a sufficient condition to define a neighborhood (Beck, Gleditsch, & Beardsley, 2006; Randolph & Tasto, 2012). Therefore, besides the geographical border, the neighborhood is defined as a proximity array with several dimensions, each representing a possible common feature that countries may share. Furthermore, computationally, this proximity array is based on the definition of culture as expressed in the model of the dissemination of culture (Axelrod, 1997; see also Section 3.2).

Now that the different parameters have been theoretically defined and computationally expressed, in the next section, the different conditions that define the interactions between the countries will be addressed.

4.2 The Conditions of Change

Diffusion enters the model by influencing how countries learn about an alternative policy and introduce it. Since a policy is here expressed by its effectiveness, learning allows a comparison between the effectiveness of the different alternatives (Braun & Gilardi, 2006). And, for a change to occur, a country must respect the three following conditions:

1. **The country is ready for change:** An agent is ready for changes when its effectiveness (e) is lower than its preference for the current policy (p). This means that if the policy becomes ineffective, the agent starts looking at its neighbors to get an idea of their current situation. Thus, policy-makers will accept high levels of ineffectiveness since they are ideologically (or electorally) biased

in its favor. By contrast, policy-makers who have lesser preferences for the policy will be willing to abandon it at lower levels of ineffectiveness. Formally, this can be expressed as follows:

$$e \prec p \tag{1}$$

2. **The choice:** When a country is ready for a change, it will choose an alternative policy by looking at what its neighbors that have already changed their policy do. In so doing, the agent can learn whether the substitute policy is more (or less) effective by comparing the average effectiveness of the neighbors that already have changed their policy

$$\left(\frac{\sum_{c=1}^{n} Ec}{Nc} \right)$$

to their current one (e). Then, the share of neighbors who have already changed their policy is taken into account. This corresponds to bandwagon pressure (Abrahamson & Rosenkopf, 1997), mathematically expressed by the following expression:

$$CV = \left| \left(\frac{\sum_{c=1}^{n} Ec}{Nc} - e \right) \left(\frac{Nc}{N} \right) \right| \tag{2}$$

The condition for a choice to occur is given by the following expression:

$$CV \succ threshold \tag{3}$$

In Equation 3, this threshold variable[7] is randomly chosen in a uniform distribution truncated at 2.0 and -2.0,[8] which represents

the point from which countries start looking at their neighbors.

3. **The change:** When the country has learned from the policy of its most effective neighbor(s), this policy is introduced if the following conditions for <u>change</u> are respected. The change variable comprises three parts:

a. **A baseline probability:** The baseline probability is arbitrarily fixed at 0.05 since there is a small number of diligent agents in the process of diffusion that will introduce the policy even if no one else does so (Simmons & Elkins, 2004).

b. **The average effectiveness among the similar neighbors:** This is introduced to take into account the fact that an ineffective policy can be introduced if it is in line with the preference of the policymakers (Braun & Gilardi, 2006). Therefore, the country calculates the difference between the average effectiveness of similar neighbors who have changed their policy

$$\frac{\sum_{s=1}^{c} E_{c}^{s}}{N_{c}^{s}}$$

and the current effectiveness (e). Here, by comparing itself with similar neighbors, it has acquired the conviction that the introduction of the chosen policy is the best solution, and, at this point, since the two interacting countries have been influenced by their shared information, they become more similar.

c. **The weighted institutional constraints:** The institutional constraints, as expressed by the veto players (Tsebelis, 2002), must be overcome for an alternative policy to be introduced. This institutional constraints parameter is then weighted with the share of neighbors who have already changed their policy

$(\frac{Nc}{N})$.

This expresses the fact that the internal political game is influenced by the information found in other countries.

Thus, the change variable can be formally expressed as follows:

$$change = \left(\begin{array}{c} 0.05 + \left(\dfrac{\displaystyle\sum_{s=1}^{c} E_c^s}{N_c^c} - e \right) + \\ \left(\left(\text{institutional constraints} \right) \left(\dfrac{Nc}{N} \right) \right) \end{array} \right) \quad (4)$$

Equation 4 is transformed as a logit

$$p(\text{change}) = \frac{e^{(change)}}{1 + e^{(change)}}.$$

Consequently, the change variable is now transformed as a probability and is bounded toward 0.0 and 1.0. Therefore, in this model, the change is seen as a success (x = 1 in Equation 5). For that reason, at each time step, each country that has chosen its alternative policy—the most effective policy among those of the similar neighbors—experiences a Bernoulli trial, where the probability of success (p) equals the change variable. And when a success occurs, a country introduces this best effectiveness, which represents the alternative policy. The probability function of the Bernoulli distribution is expressed as follows:

$$f(x;p) = \begin{cases} p & \text{if } x = 1; \\ 1 - p & \text{if } x = 0; \\ 0 & \text{otherwise.} \end{cases} \quad (5)$$

In sum, at each time step, the conditions for a change to occur are evaluated and if they are respected the country introduces the most effective policy of its most similar neighbor that has already changed his policy. If these conditions are not overcome, the different variables evolve randomly as stated in Section 4.1. In the next section, the main results, while letting agents in this model interact, are explained.

5. RESULTS

The parameters and conditions described in Section 4 have been computationally developed in Eclipse 4.2.2 (Juno version) using RePastJ as a toolbox. After letting the agents interact for 250 time steps,[9] the model shows the emergence of some interesting results that are explained in the following subsections.

More specifically, using the MEME module,[10] the values of the main parameters, shown on Figure 3, are changed as follow: The size of the world (WorldSize) is changed by 5 units from 14 to 24; the size of the proximity array (NumProximity) as well as the number of traits (NumTraits) is changed by 5 units from 5 to 15; the random seeds (RandomSeed) are changed by 1 unit from 0 to 9; and the following dichotomous variables vary between their different values, that is two types of topologies (Topology)—the torus-like world and the bounded world, and two neighborhoods (Neighborhood), the Moore (i.e., the eight adjacent cells) and the Von Neumann (the cells at the four cardinal points), as well as two types of political constraints (Constancy) (i.e. this parameter either is fixed for the entire simulation run or it can change at every elections time) and two kinds of electoral

Figure 3. The RePastJ's control panel of the model, with default values

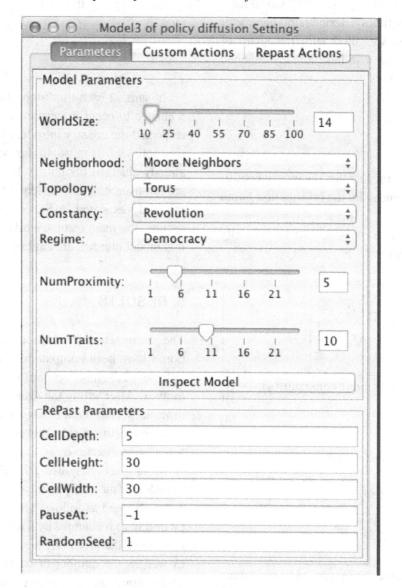

regimes (Regime) (i.e. this parameter either is fixed for a defined or a variable period). Thus, we perform 4320 runs[11] and analyze the evolution of the average effectiveness and number of regions.

5.1 Diffusion at the Conditional Level

Graphics a to c on Figure 4, 5, 6 and 7 highlight the fact that the average effectiveness decreases early in the process of diffusion up to a point where the number of effective policies is enough to favor the introduction of a more effective policy. The shape of the curves is not surprising for at least two reasons. First, for each country, effectiveness is likely to decrease. Second, the change condition assumes that countries do not learn from the best policy per se, but from the best policy among the (similar) neighbors who have changed their policy.[12]

Figure 4. Evolution of the average effectiveness and the number of regions for different neighborhoods and sizes of the world

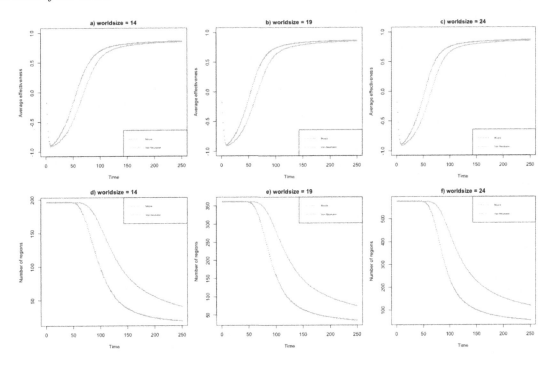

Figure 5. Evolution of the average effectiveness and the number of regions for different topologies and sizes of the world

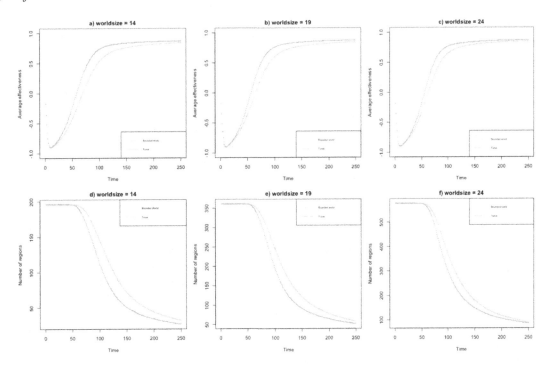

Figure 6. Evolution of the average effectiveness and the number of regions for different political constraints

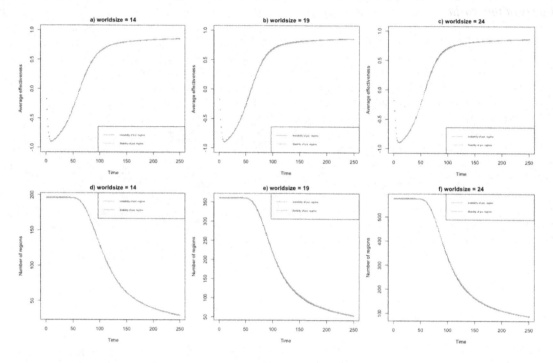

Figure 7. Evolution of the average effectiveness and the number of regions for different political regimes

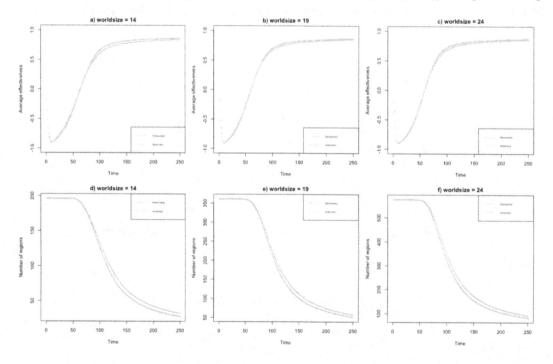

However, what is striking here is that despite this bias toward ineffectiveness, we assist with the emergence of a rather maximal average effectiveness, meaning that time is needed not only for a country to introduce the best-suited policy but also for a policy to become very effective.

Moreover, when facing different internal factors, the countries learn differently from their neighborhood. As a result, the average effectiveness in the world tends to follow a J-shaped curve, which seems to better correspond with what can be observed after the introduction of a new policy, as the transition from an old policy to a new policy seems to disadvantage the new one, thus increasing the current policy ineffectiveness (Meseguer, 2006a).

5.2 Diffusion at the Temporal and Spatial Level

The proportion of adopters over time follows an S-shaped curve. In the model presented here, as we concentrate not on countries, but on policies, the result of the process is an inverted S-shaped curve, as shown in Graphics d to f on Figure 4, 5, 6 and 7. In these graphics, we see that the number of regions—that is, groups of countries characterized by the same policy—decreases over time. This means that some policies are spreading, whereas others, supposedly less effective, simply disappear.

Moreover, after a slow takeoff at the beginning, the process of diffusion accelerates; that is, the number of policies is decreasing sharply while, conversely, the number of changing countries is increasing sharply. This is consistent with the consequences of bandwagon pressures, as defined in Section 3.1. Thus, as shown by Gilardi, et al. (2009) in the case of the diffusion of hospital financing reforms, learning is strongly influenced by the experience of others.

Furthermore, the number of regions diminishes, but never hits "1." Thus, the world is politically clustered, that is characterized by partial convergence – global divergence and local

convergence. The main point to pay attention to is the definition of the neighborhood. Since interactive learning takes place between proximate countries (Boschma, 2005), the consideration of dimensions other than the geographical, such as culture or trade, results in the emergence of similar political regions.

This result is in line with several real-world phenomena that have been theoretically and empirically studied. For instance, the development of welfare states, as shown by the famous "three worlds" typology (Esping-Andersen, 1990) is characterized by significant geographical clustering, as well as the diffusion of democracies that spread under the force of bandwagon pressures (Elkink, 2011; Gleditsch & Ward, 2006), or the development of different healthcare systems. Moreover, the existence of some main types, such as NHS or the liberal type in the healthcare domain does not mean that countries with the same healthcare type are totally identical, as, for instance, in Scandinavian countries.

Further, Figure 4 highlights the importance of neighborhood. Greater effectiveness and faster spreading are observed when countries take into account more neighbors, i.e. the Moore, instead of the Von Neumann, neighborhood. Moreover, Figure 5 shows that the more open a world is, the more effective policies are and the faster they spread. In sum, bandwagon pressures play stronger at the conditional, temporal and spatial level when countries, as well as their interacting space, are more open.

However, results for different political constraints and different political regimes as expressed on Figures 6 and 7 show great similarities. This suggests that which neighbor(s) a country interacts with—where a country takes its information—is more important in the process of diffusion than the internal political games. In other words, political constraints effects and/or time between elections are less important in the process of policy diffusion than the number of interacting neighbors and/or the openness of the world.

6. FUTURE RESEARCH DIRECTIONS

This model is a first attempt to develop a comprehensive agent-based model for the study of policy diffusion. However, several points still need to be addressed.

First, since the *choose* (*change*) condition assumes that countries do not learn from the best policy *per se*, but from the best policy *among the (similar) neighbors that have changed their policy*, the world goes toward some kind of stabilization, characterized by partial clustering. To break this equilibrium, policy innovation needs to be introduced, after a preference change for instance.

Second, to determine whether one's own computational model is empirical, the external validity of the model should be tested (see Chapter 3 in this book). Since studying "in silico" and "real-world" phenomena using same methods seems to be very weak (Elkink, 2011), an interesting strategy can be to study the two levels of analysis, micro and macro, separately and then put them together to highlight the main pieces of evidence that corroborate the main mechanisms. Furthermore, few studies have tried to disentangle the different mechanisms of diffusion (Boehmke & Witmer, 2004; Gilardi, 2010; Shipan & Volden, 2008).

At the theoretical level, which mechanism is in play and when remains open questions. "Playing" with the impact of the several thresholds of the model and bandwagon pressures—that is, the evolution of the weight of the neighbors who have changed their policy—are essential in explaining the transition from learning to emulation.[13] Another approach that is promising here is the development of dynamic networks. For instance, using network analysis, Cao (2010) shows that the diffusion of capital tax policy comes partly from competition between key actors at the country level and partly from learning and emulation between countries (for a useful tool, see Chapter 9 in this book).

Finally, the fact that the slope of the curve gets very sharp at the beginning of the process comes from the countries' strong interconnection, which facilitates the spread of the change (Rogers, 2003). Thereby, as is the case with cellular automata, the regular types of neighborhood used here are "far too idealized, to be an appropriate tool for modeling social processes" (Flache & Hegselmann, 2001, 2). Therefore, the development of a Voronoi neighborhood seems to be a very interesting way to break this regularity and extend the analysis of policy diffusion (see Chapter 11 in this book).[14]

7. CONCLUSION

Years of quantitative research in this field have brought a large set of results, such as the fact that diffusion follows an S-shaped curve and is a conditional phenomenon. However, based on three simple conditions (*ready, choose, and change*), the model presented in this chapter highlights policy diffusion as an emergent phenomenon from agents' interdependences in a complex system, whether this system is the world, the European Union, or a federal state such as Switzerland.

As a result, diffusion follows an inverted S-curve, which leads to partial convergence—global divergence and local convergence—that triggers the emergence of political clusters—i.e., the creation of regions with the same policy. Furthermore, the J-shaped curve of the average effectiveness means that not only time is needed for a policy to deploy its effects but also that it takes time for a country to find the best-suited policy. Moreover, where a country takes its information is more important in the process of diffusion than the internal political games.

Thus, computational agent-based models are useful tools for studying non-linear and/or threshold models. Its main advantages are threefold:

1. The flexibility of the model in the sense that is the researcher has total control over the simulated world and its parameter

2. The model produces no missing data

3. Each simulation can be considered as a laboratory that can be explored on its own.

Finally, the strength of such a model is that it can be applied to a wider range of diffusion phenomena. For instance, in the context of diffusion of democracy (Cederman & Gleditsch, 2004; Elkink, 2011), measures of its effectiveness may also follow a J-shaped curve, meaning that time is needed to fully understand its principles and use its tools. Consequently, the passage from autocracy to democracy may be tumultuous, as observed in Arabic countries since the Arabic Spring revolutions.

ACKNOWLEDGMENT

A slightly different version of the model developed in this chapter was presented at the 7th European Social Simulation Association Conference (essa2011), September 19-23 2011, Agropolis International, Montpellier, France. I gratefully acknowledge the participants in this conference, as well as two anonymous referees for helpful comments that allow the improvements presented here. The arguments presented here are developed more in detail in my Ph.D. dissertation (Luyet 2011). The financial support of the Swiss National Science Foundation (grant no. PBLA11-119660) and the Swiss Academy of Humanities and Social Sciences is also gratefully acknowledged. The usual disclaimer applies.

REFERENCES

Abrahamson, E., & Rosenkopf, L. (1993). Institutional and competitive band wagons: Using mathematical modeling as a tool to explore innovation diffusion. *Academy of Management Review*, *21*(1), 254–285. doi:10.5465/AMR.1996.9602161572

Abrahamson, E., & Rosenkopf, L. (1997). Social network effects on the extent of innovation diffusion: A computer simulation. *Organization Science*, *8*(3), 289–309. doi:10.1287/orsc.8.3.289

Axelrod, R. (1997). The dissemination of culture: A model with local convergence and global polarization. *The Journal of Conflict Resolution*, *41*(2), 203–226. doi:10.1177/0022002797041002001

Axelrod, R. (2003). Advancing the art of simulation in the social sciences. *Journal of the Japanese Society for Management Information System*, *12*(3), 16–22.

Beck, N., Gleditsch, K. S., & Beardsley, K. (2006). Space is more than geography: Using spatial econometrics in the study of political economy. *International Studies Quarterly*, *50*(1), 27–44. doi:10.1111/j.1468-2478.2006.00391.x

Berry, F. S., & Berry, W. D. (2006). Innovation and diffusion models in policy diffusion. In P. A. Sabatier (Ed.), *Theories of the policy process* (pp. 223–260). Boulder, CO: Westview Press.

Boehmke, F. J., & Witmer, R. (2004). Disentangling diffusion: The effects of social learning and economic competition on state policy innovation and expansion. *Political Research Quarterly*, *57*(1), 39–51.

Bonabeau, E. (2002). Agent-based modeling: Methods and techniques for simulating human systems. *Proceedings of the National Academy of Sciences of the United States of America, 99*(3), 7280–7287. doi:10.1073/pnas.082080899 PMID:12011407

Bonoli, G. (2001). Political institutions, veto points, and the process of welfare state adaptation. In P. Pierson (Ed.), *The new politics of the welfare state* (pp. 238–264). Oxford, UK: Oxford University Press. doi:10.1093/0198297564.003.0009

Boschma, R. A. (2005). Proximity and innovation: A critical assessment. *Regional Studies, 39*(1), 61–74. doi:10.1080/0034340052000320887

Braun, D., & Gilardi, F. (2006). Taking Galton's problem seriously. Towards a theory of policy diffusion. *Journal of Theoretical Politics, 18*(3), 298–322. doi:10.1177/0951629806064351

Braun, D., Gilardi, F., Fueglister, K., & Luyet, S. (2007). Ex pluribus unum: Integrating the different strands of policy diffusion theory. *Politische Vierteljahresschrift, 38*, 39–55.

Brooks, S. M. (2005). Interdependent and domestic foundations of policy change: The diffusion of pension privatization around the world. *International Studies Quarterly, 49*(2), 273–294. doi:10.1111/j.0020-8833.2005.00345.x

Brooks, S. M. (2007). When does diffusion matter? Explaining the spread of structural pension reforms across nations. *The Journal of Politics, 69*(3), 701–715. doi:10.1111/j.1468-2508.2007.00569.x

Cao, X. (2010). Networks as channels of policy diffusion: Explaining worldwide changes in capital taxation, 1998-2006. *International Studies Quarterly, 54*(3), 823–854. doi:10.1111/j.1468-2478.2010.00611.x

Casti, J. L. (1997). *Would-be worlds: How simulation is changing the frontiers of science*. New York: John Wiley & Sons, Inc.

Cederman, L.-E., & Gleditsch, K. S. (2004). Conquest and regime change: An evolutionary model of the spread of democracy and peace. *International Studies Quarterly, 48*(3), 603–629. doi:10.1111/j.0020-8833.2004.00317.x

Davis, J. P., Eisenhardt, K., & Bingham, C. B. (2007). Developing theory through simulation methods. *Academy of Management Review, 32*(2), 480–499. doi:10.5465/AMR.2007.24351453

Deffuant, G., Huet, S., & Amblard, F. (2005). An individual-based model of innovation diffusion mixing social value and individual benefit. *American Journal of Sociology, 110*(4), 1041–1069. doi:10.1086/430220

Dobbin, F., Simmons, B., & Garrett, G. (2007). The global diffusion of public policies: Social construction, corecion, competition or learning? *Annual Review of Sociology, 33*, 449–472. doi:10.1146/annurev.soc.33.090106.142507

Elkink, J. A. (2011). The international diffusion of democracy. *Comparative Political Studies, 44*(12), 1651–1674. doi:10.1177/0010414011407474

Elkins, Z., Guzman, A. T., & Simmons, B. (2006). Competing for capital: The diffusion of bilateral investment treaties, 1960$,Äì$2000. *International Organization, 60*(4), 811–846. doi:10.1017/S0020818306060279

Esping-Andersen, G. (1990). *The three worlds of welfare capitalism*. Princeton, NJ: Princeton University Press.

Flache, A., & Hegselmann, R. (2001). Do irregular grids make a difference? Relaxing the spatial regularity assumption in cellular models of social dynamics. *Journal of Artificial Societies and Social Simulation, 4*(4), 1–26.

Ganghof, S. (2003). Promises and pitfalls of veto player analysis. *Swiss Political Science Review, 9*(2), 1–25. doi:10.1002/j.1662-6370.2003.tb00411.x

Gilardi, F. (2005). The institutional foundations of regulatory capitalism: The diffusion of independent regulatory agencies in Western Europe. *The Annals of the American Academy of Political and Social Science*, *598*(1), 84–101. doi:10.1177/0002716204271833

Gilardi, F. (2010). Who learns from what in policy diffusion processes? *American Journal of Political Science*, *54*(3), 650–666. doi:10.1111/j.1540-5907.2010.00452.x

Gilardi, F., Fueglister, K., & Luyet, S. (2009). Learning from others: The diffusion of hospital financing reforms in OECD countries. *Comparative Political Studies*, *42*(4), 549–573. doi:10.1177/0010414008327428

Gilbert, N. (1998). *The simulation of social processes* (Unpublished).

Gleditsch, K. S., & Ward, M. D. (2006). Diffusion in the international context of democratization. *International Organization*, *60*(4), 911–933. doi:10.1017/S0020818306060309

Granovetter, M. (1978). Threshold models in collective behavior. *American Journal of Sociology*, *83*(6), 1420–1443. doi:10.1086/226707

Gray, V. (1973). Innovation in the states: A diffusion study. *The American Political Science Review*, *67*(4), 1174–1185. doi:10.2307/1956539

Grossback, L. J., Nicholson-Crotty, S., & Peterson, D. A. M. (2004). Ideology and learning in policy diffusion. *American Politics Research*, *32*(5), 521–545. doi:10.1177/1532673X04263801

Hacker, J. S. (2004). Review article: Dismantling the health care state? Political institutions, public policies and the comparative politics of health reform. *British Journal of Political Science*, *34*, 693–724. doi:10.1017/S0007123404000250

Haeusermann, S., & Palier, B. (2008). The politics of employment-friendly welfare reforms in post-industrial economies. *Socio-economic Review*, *6*(3), 559–586. doi:10.1093/ser/mwn011

Hallerberg, M., & Basinger, S. (1998). Internationalization and changes in tax policy in OECD countries: The importance of domestic veto players. *Comparative Political Studies*, *31*(3), 321–352. doi:10.1177/0010414098031003003

Holland, J. (1998). *Emergence: From chaos to order*. Cambridge, MA: Perseus Books.

Kastener, S. L., & Rector, C. (2003). International regimes, domestic veto-players, and capital controls policy stability. *International Studies Quarterly*, *47*(1), 1–22. doi:10.1111/1468-2478.4701001

Kil Lee, C., & Strang, D. (2006). The international diffusion of public-sector downsizing: Network emulation and theory-driven learning. *International Organization*, *60*(4), 883–909.

Kollman, K., Miller, J. H., & Page, S. E. (1992). Adaptive parties in spatial elections. *The American Political Science Review*, *86*(4), 929–937. doi:10.2307/1964345

Kollman, K., Miller, J. H., & Page, S. E. (1998). Political parties and electoral landscapes. *British Journal of Political Science*, *28*, 139–158. doi:10.1017/S0007123498000131

Levi-Faur, D. (2005). The global diffusion of regulatory capitalism. *The Annals of the American Academy of Political and Social Science*, *598*(1), 12–32. doi:10.1177/0002716204272371

Luyet, S. (2011). *Policy diffusion: An agent-based approach*. Lausanne, Switzerland: University Of Lausanne.

Martin, C. W. (2009). *Conditional diffusion: Smoke free air legislation and tobacco taxation policies in the United States 1970-2006*. Retrieved from http://www.polsci.org/martin/downloads/Martin_ConditionalDiffusion.pdf

Meseguer, C. (2004). What role for learning? The diffusion of privatisation in OECD and Latin American countries. *Journal of Public Policy*, 24(3), 299–325. doi:10.1017/S0143814X04000182

Meseguer, C. (2005). Policy learning, policy diffusion, and the making of a new order. *The Annals of the American Academy of Political and Social Science*, 598(1), 67–82. doi:10.1177/0002716204272372

Meseguer, C. (2006a). Learning and economic policy choices. *European Journal of Political Economy*, 22, 156–178. doi:10.1016/j.ejpoleco.2005.06.002

Meseguer, C. (2006b). Rational learning and bounded learning in the diffusion of policy innovations. *Rationality and Society*, 18(1), 35–66. doi:10.1177/1043463106060152

Meseguer, C., & Gilardi, F. (2009). What is new in the study of policy diffusion? A critical review. *Review of International Political Economy*, 16(3), 527–543. doi:10.1080/09692290802409236

Pierson, P. (2001). Post-industrial pressures on the mature welfare states. In P. Pierson (Ed.), *The new politics of the welfare state* (pp. 80–104). Oxford, UK: Oxford University Press. doi:10.1093/0198297564.003.0004

Randolph, G. M., & Tasto, M. T. (2012). Special interest group formation in the United States: Do special interest groups mirror the success of their spatial neighbors? *Economics and Politics*, 24(2), 119–134. doi:10.1111/j.1468-0343.2012.00394.x

Rogers, E. M. (2003). Diffusion of Innovations (5th Ed.). New-York: Free Press.

Rogers, E. M., Medina, U. E., Rivera, M. A., & Wiley, C. J. (2005). Complex adaptive systems and the diffusion of innovations. *The Innovation Journal: The Public Sector Innovation Journal*, 10(3), Article 29.

Rosenkopf, L., & Abrahamson, E. (1999). modeling reputational and informational influences in threshold models of bandwagon innovation diffusion. *Computational & Mathematical Organization Theory*, 5(4), 361–384. doi:10.1023/A:1009620618662

Rousseau, D., & Van Der Veen, A. M. (2005). The emergence of shared identity. *The Journal of Conflict Resolution*, 49(5), 686–712. doi:10.1177/0022002705279336

Schelling, T. C. (1978). *Micromotives and macrobehavior*. New York: W. W. Norton.

Shipan, C. R., & Volden, C. (2006). Bottom-up federalism: The diffusion of antismoking policies from U.S. Cities to states. *American Journal of Political Science*, 50(4), 825–843. doi:10.1111/j.1540-5907.2006.00218.x

Shipan, C. R., & Volden, C. (2008). The mechanisms of policy diffusion. *American Journal of Political Science*, 52(4), 840–857. doi:10.1111/j.1540-5907.2008.00346.x

Simmons, B., Dobbin, F., & Garrett, G. (2006). Introduction: The international diffusion of liberalism. *International Organization*, 60(4), 781–810. doi:10.1017/S0020818306060267

Simmons, B., & Elkins, Z. (2004). The globalization of liberalization: policy diffusion in the international political economy. *The American Political Science Review*, 98(1), 171–189. doi:10.1017/S0003055404001078

Swank, D. (2005). Policy diffusion, globalization, and welfare state retrenchment in 18 capitalist countries, 1976-2001. Paper presented at the American Political Science Association Annual Meeting, Washington, DC.

Swank, D. (2006). Tax policy in an era of internationalization: Explaining the spread of neoliberalism. *International Organization, 60*(4), 847–882. doi:10.1017/S0020818306060280

Swank, D., & Steinmo, S. (2002). The new political economy of taxation in advanced capitalist democracies. *American Journal of Political Science, 46*(3), 642–655. doi:10.2307/3088405

Tsebelis, G. (2002). *Veto players: How political institutions work*. Princeton, NJ: Princeton University Press.

Volden, C. (2006). States as policy laboratories: Emulating success in the children's health insurance program. *American Journal of Political Science, 50*(2), 294–312. doi:10.1111/j.1540-5907.2006.00185.x

Volden, C., Ting, M. M., & Carpenter, D. P. (2008). A formal model of learning and policy diffusion. *The American Political Science Review, 102*(3), 319–332. doi:10.1017/S0003055408080271

ADDITIONAL READING

Ball, P. (2004). *Critical Mass: How One Thing Leads To Another. New-York: Farrar*. Straus And Giroux.

Barabasi, A.-L. (2003). *How Everything Is Connected To Everything Else And What It Means For Business, Science, And Everyday Life*. Plume.

Bishop, B. (2009). *The Big Sort: Why The Clustering Of Like-Minded America Is Tearing Us Apart*. Mariner Books.

Crichton, M. (2002). *Prey. New-York*. Harper.

De Marchi, S. (2005). Computational And Mathematical Modeling. In *The Social Sciences*. Cambridge University Press.

Gilbert, N., & Troitzsch, K. G. (2005). *Simulation For The Social Scientist*. Maidenhead: Open University Press.

Watts, D. (2003). *Six Degrees: The Science Of A Connected Age. New-York*. Norton.

Zwirn, H. P. (2006). *Les Systèmes Complexes: Mathematiques Et Biologie*. Paris: Odile Jacob.

KEY TERMS AND DEFINITIONS

Bandwagon Pressure: A process where the more countries that have changed their policy the higher the incentive (the pressure) to change.

Computational Agent Based Modeling: Agent-based models developed using computer programs based on a set of clearly defined conditions that state the interactions between autonomous agents, with a view to assessing their effects on the system as a whole.

Policy Diffusion: Policy choices in one country are influenced by policy choices made in other countries.

S-Shaped Curve: The curve that results from the bandwagon pressure. This curve shows the cumulative proportion of adopters.

ENDNOTES

[1]   For a methodological review, see (Meseguer & Gilardi, 2009).

[2]   By autonomous, we mean that there is no central authority. At the international level, this may appear as a rather strong assumption. However, even if supranational organizations, such as the European Union (EU) for instance, remove some autonomy at the country level, they rely more on soft

coercion (see Section 3.2), that is not taken into account here. Nevertheless, European countries remain autonomous as regards the development of some policies, social policies for instance.

[3] Prediction it is a very difficult goal to achieve in social sciences due to the huge number of parameters that simultaneously play a role (see Chapter 5 in this book).

[4] A cultural feature is defined as a list of cultural traits, such as religion and language for instance.

[5] Coercion can be considered as a fourth mechanism. This mechanism implies that powerful actors (international organizations or powerful countries) constrain policy change in other countries. A difference can be traced between "hard" and "soft" coercion. The former, imposed by strength and threat, cannot be considered as a mechanism of diffusion, contrary to the latter, operating through persuasion.

[6] In the context of this study, the country will be the level of analysis; that is, the actors, in the model and it corresponds to a meso level, since we concentrate on countries and not on individual politicians. In other words, country becomes here a synonym of government.

[7] As Granovetter (1978) argues, threshold models are well suited for studying the diffusion of innovations, because it takes into account the cost-benefit analysis. Moreover, these models are also well suited for dichotomous dependent variables: In our model, each agent can have either its current policy or an alternative policy.

[8] -2 and 2 correspond to the extreme results of the Equation 2.

[9] This number of time steps is arbitrarily fixed and is sufficiently high to let interesting patterns emerge.

[10] The MEME module is a well-suited tool to use with RePastJ and provides facilities for collecting and organizing datasets, since it comes with the ability to export datasets as CSV files that can be used with other statistical softwares. For more information: http://mass.aitia.ai/intro/meme.

[11] Formally, we have: $3*3*3*10*2*2*2*2=4320$.

[12] Thus, even an ineffective policy can be introduced if it is the best policy among the neighbors that have changed their policy.

[13] For instance, we can imagine that learning characterizes the interactions when the number of neighbors with a new policy is less than 3, meaning that the weight of the comparison of the different effectiveness is more important, and emulation when the number of neighbors with an alternative policy is greater than four, because the weight of the social conformism is greater.

[14] RePastJ does not provide a class with already defined irregular neighborhoods. More time is needed to program such an evolution. However, mixing RePastJ and ReLogo (a NetLogo based "dialect" for repast) can help overcome this situation, but, as far as I know, no attempt for developing models using ReLogo exists. For more information, see the following Website: http://repast.sourceforge.net.

Chapter 10
Multi–Agent Economically Motivated Decision–Making

Paulo Trigo
ISEL, LabMAg – Instituto Superior de Engenharia de Lisboa, Portugal

ABSTRACT

The key motivation for this chapter is the perception that within the near future, markets will be composed of individuals that may simultaneously undertake the roles of consumers, producers and traders. Those individuals are economically motivated "prosumer" (producer-consumer) agents that not only consume, but can also produce, store and trade assets. This chapter describes the most relevant aspects of a simulation tool that provides (human and virtual) prosumer agents an interactive and real-time game-like environment where they can explore (long-term and short-term) strategic behaviour and experience the effects of social influence in their decision-making processes. The game-like environment is focused on the simulation of electricity markets, it is named ITEM-game ("Investment and Trading in Electricity Markets"), and it is publically available (ITEM-Game, 2013) for any player to explore the role of a prosumer agent.

1. INTRODUCTION

This chapter describes the perspective of agents with the ability to take the roles of consumers, producers and traders under the same market-context. This "multi-role" ability is named as the "prosumer" perspective of an agent (or simply prosumer agent). In this chapter the prosumer agent is characterized from a problem-oriented (specific domain) approach with emphasis to the liberalized electricity market environment and its relation with the emergence of prosumer agents.

There is a world-wide shift towards a low carbon economy where electric motors (free from internal fuel combustion) pervade the transportation industry (e.g., personal vehicles, high speed trains) and the increasing demand for renewable power generation calls for a huge amount of such generators, distributed across both the transmission and distribution networks. The current scenario of a grid where electricity flows one-way from producers to consumers is making the first moves towards a distributed network of prosumer agents that both produce and consume electricity according to their individual profiles, thus giving

DOI: 10.4018/978-1-4666-5954-4.ch010

rise to flows of electricity that continuously vary in magnitude and direction (Ramchurn et al., 2012). Each prosumer agent continuously makes decisions and evaluates its own position in respect to all other prosumers. The combination of both the prosumer and the market perspectives opens a space for those companies and individuals that intend to make long-term investment decisions (e.g., acquire generation or storage capacity) and to explore short-term strategies on trading (e.g., selling or buying) the electricity asset. Hence, prosumers will be able to act (sell and buy) in the market not simply either as producer or a (close to price agnostic) consumer, but also aiming for the profit.

A major economic rationale for the liberalization of the electricity industry was the vision of lower prices and more efficient power generation (and consumption) through market competition. A key assumption behind such rationale was that the power generation (after being separated from the power distribution) would endow competitive markets, rather than markets in which a small numbers of firms exercise market power. The foundational directives for an energy market where competition is to be achieved within a fair and transparent environment were settled by current European Directive (EC, 2009).

Usually the behaviour of markets depends on the participants' economical motivation, but often the market environment is too complex for the analytical game-theoretic analysis. Therefore it is of utmost importance to develop simulation and prediction tools where the observations of all the agents' plays are used to compute estimates for the utility of their strategies. This follows the "empirical game simulation" approach where, despite the lack of an analytic game formulation, agents evolve within a strategic scenario, at a practical level of abstraction, such that the analysis is computationally feasible and the game-theoretic concepts can still be explored.

A special concern with the market power concept guides this research. Although a company's market share is often correlated with market power, this is not always the case. Additional factors, apart from the number and size of companies in a market, impact the degree of competition within an industry. These factors include the price-responsiveness (elasticity) of both the demand and the production. In markets where customers can easily choose not to consume a product, or to consume a substitute instead, producers cannot raise prices far above costs without significantly reducing sales. Also, just as a producer with very price responsive customers cannot exercise much market power, neither can a producer faced with many price-responsive competitors. The market competition is driven by each stakeholder's search for means of influencing others' decisions in order to achieve (or increase) its own exercise of market power. The basic measure of the exercise of market power is the price-cost margin, which measures the degree to which prices exceed marginal costs. Both the price-cost margin and the elasticity of demand and production will be used to describe and to (graphically) represent, at each decision epoch, the power and influence relations among agents.

This chapter describes a game-like market simulator, named ITEM-game ("Investment and Trading in Electricity Markets"), where human and virtual agents can explore the investment and trading strategies for the electricity market. The ITEM-game was implemented as a derivation from the previous TEMMAS ("The Electricity Market Multi-agent Simulator") simulator (Trigo et al., 2010). The main difference between both simulators (TEMMAS and ITEM-game) is that, the TEMMAS follows a machine (reinforcement learning method to autonomously search for a (near optimal) competitive trading (pool bidding) strategy, while the ITEM-game is designed for humans to explore investment and trading strategies. Thus, the ITEM-game is an interactive tool and has already been played several times in classroom competitions with (human) participants organized in teams, each representing a power company, that compete in a simulated market environment where investment and trading decisions are made interactively (Sousa et al., 2012; Sousa & Trigo, 2011). This chapter also describes the initial ideas on extending the ITEM-game with the concepts of inter-agent (social) relations. The integration of quantitative metrics of social relations can be used (by players) to foster strategic coalitions.

Section 2 frames this chapter within related work. Section 3 broadly frames the prosumer agent's within the multi-agent based simulation (MABS) approach and presents the essential aspects of the ITEM-game's investment and trading perspectives. Section 4 presents both a general and a market interpretation for the influence and coalition concepts along the proposal of concrete metrics and an illustrative example. Section 5 provides the major conclusions and future perspectives from this work.

2. RELATED WORK

The research on multi-agent systems for electricity markets can be grouped in three main categories: 1) market design analysis, 2) modelling of the agents' decision-making processes, and 3) a mixture of the two previous categories.

The "market design analysis" aims to describe a market through the behavioural correlations among agents. A pioneer work (Day & Bunn, 2001) simulates a uniform price market clearing model where generation companies are profit maximizers who assume that competitors bid the same supply function as in the previous day. The model is explored in a case study (Bunn and Oliveira, 2003), to analyse whether two generation companies can increase their profits by manipulating market prices above marginal cost; results showed that to profitably manipulate prices both companies would have to act together. Another

work (Visudhiphan & Ilic, 2002) distinguishes between market power from situations where technical constraints might have raised prices. Some recent work explores the social simulation perspective (Castelfranchi, 2013) and its relation to the field of experimental economics, integrating the decision and game theory with computer science (Georgalos, 2013; Terna et al., 2013), in the design of agents with simple behavioural rules (that govern decisions and inter-agent influence) and search for the emergence of global phenomena (Friesen et al., 2013), such as the outbreak of large-scale power failures (blackouts) due to peak-increase of electricity consumption (Mota et al., 2013).

The "modeling of the agents' decision-making processes" early research (Richter & Sheble, 1998) describes the use of a genetic algorithm to optimize multiple bidding rounds for a one-time period of electricity deliveries. Another work (Koesrindartoto, 2002), simulates buyers and sellers bidding on a double-auction market to analyze the impact of agent learning of market outcomes for bidding at marginal cost or revenue. Additional work on agent's decision making includes the evaluation of coalitions as a means to exercise power (Nardin et al., 2013), the notion of risk management (Magessi & Antunes, 2013) and the evaluation ethics (or morality) (Coelho et al., 2013) within games with repeated decision-making encounters among multiple agents.

Research on both the "market design analysis" and the "modeling of the agents' decision-making processes" are complementary to ours; they provide results and methods to explore and (possibly) extend and incorporate in the ITEM-game simulator. The approaches that embrace both "market design analysis" and "modeling of the agents' decision-making processes" are usually described as market simulation frameworks.

The AMES (Agent-based Modeling of Electricity Systems) (Koesrindartoto et al., 2005) is targeted to small and medium markets and uses learning agents (Variant Roth-Erev algorithm

(Roth & Erev, 1995). The user can choose whether to use the learning agents but cannot choose (neither define) any bidding strategies. The AMES is implemented in Repast (Recursive Porous Agent Simulation Toolkit) (North et al., 2006), which does not support physically distributed virtual agents with goals, communicative needs and behavioural capabilities.

Another simulator is the PowerWeb (Zimmerman et al., 1999) that assumes a fixed demand and the bid-ding companies can only own a single generating unit. The bidder agent can either define a price-quantity energy block or choose from a set of predefined available strategies (e.g., bid all zero or marginal cost, increase or decrease the cost of previous day, respectively, sold or non-sold blocks, bid randomly); the system provides Web-based interaction but only supports human sellers, i.e.,, there are no autonomous bid-der agents, there is no notion of investment there are no repeated decision epochs.

The most adopted simulator is the EMCAS (Electricity Market Complex Adaptive System) (Conzelmann et al., 2004) that incorporates spot and bilateral markets and different levels of reserve for grid regulation. The consumer agents can switch their supplier or change their demand. The supply (power plants owners) decides on bidding strategies. Agents are maximizers of a multi-objective utility function that includes risk preferences, profit and market share; the goals are represented by a minimum and maximum expected value, and a risk preference. The EMCAS generates a price forecast based on data imported from external providers (electric system and historical prices); this information is used to calculate the expected utility of a given strategy. We remark that the commercial EMCAS system is being used, by EDP ("Electricidade de Portugal"), to analyse the Iberian Electricity Market (MIBEL) (Thimmapuram et al., 2008).

The EMCAS is a commercial system and it is implemented in Repast, which is a stand-alone simulation environment (tailored to analyze the evolution of simulation parameters), where all agents reside in the same memory space. Hence, Repast is non-FIPA compliant as agent communication is based on memory sharing. Additionally, Repast is not suited for dynamically integrating human interaction during the simulation.

The most recent power simulation environment, PowerTAC (Ketter et al., 2011), was launched (in 2012) as a competition where teams implement trading agents to act as self-interested "brokers" that aggregate energy supply and demand aiming for profit. Brokers compete to attract customers by offering tariff contracts to a population of anonymous small customers (households, small businesses), and by negotiating individual contracts with larger customers. Simulation "timeslots" take nominally 5 seconds of real (computer) time corresponding to 1 hour of simulated time. There are several differences between PowerTAC and our ITEM-game proposal. PowerTAC is targeted only for virtual agents; ITEM-game is designed for human agents and aims to incorporate virtual agents. PowerTAC is targeted for trading agents; ITEM-game incorporates both long-term investment and short-term trading decisions; we remark that "only trade" approach is a special case of "invest-and-trade" where the investment is a-priori defined. PowerTAC agents are traders that compete against a predefined market setting; ITEM-game agents are both investors and traders that compete among themselves.

The ITEM-game agents are both investors and traders that compete among themselves within a time-scale (usually) configured to simulate 1 year for each decision-epoch and such perspective of a yearly-defined time-scale is essential for the long-term investment concept.

3. THE ITEM-GAME AGENCY

The strategic interactions among market participants (e.g., prosumers) are usually described by game theoretic approaches based on the determination of equilibrium points against which to compare the actual market performance (Berry et al., 1999; Gabriel et al., 2004; Poza et al., 2010). However, those approaches find it difficult to incorporate the ability of market participants to repeatedly probe markets and adapt their strategies. Usually, the problem of finding the equilibria strategies is relaxed (simplified) both in terms of: 1) the agents' investment and trading policies, and 2) the technical and economical operation of the power system.

As an alternative to the equilibrium approaches, the multi-agent based simulation (MABS) comes forth as being particularly well fitted to analyze dynamic and adaptive systems with complex interactions among constituents (Schuster & Gilbert, 2004; Helleboogh et al., 2007; Santos et al., 2013) involving both individual and collective decision-making (Lucas & Payne, 2013, Nunes & Antunes, 2013) along with the resulting emergence and interpretation of macro-level behaviours (Luyet, 2013; Troitzsch, 2013).

3.1 The MABS Modelling of the ITEM-Game

Here we take the MABS approach and describe its structural constituents by means of two modelling concepts: 1) the *environmental entity*, which owns a distinct existence in the real environment, e.g. a resource such as an electricity producer, or a decision-making agent such as a market bidder generator company, and 2) the *environmental property*, which is a measurable aspect of the real environment, e.g. the price of a bid or the demand for electricity. The *set of environmental entities*, E_T, is often clustered in different classes, or types, thus partitioning it into disjoint subsets, each containing entities that belong to the same class. The

partitioning may be used to distinguish between decision-making agents and available resources; e.g. a company that decides the bidding strategy to pursue or a plant that provides the demanded power. The *set of environmental properties*, E_Y, can also be clustered, in a similar way as for the environmental entities, thus grouping properties that are related. Such partitioning may be used to express distinct categories, e.g. economical, electrical, ecological or social aspects (another, more technical usage, is to separate constant parameters from dynamic state variables). Hence, the whole simulated environment is the union of its entities and properties: $E = E_T \cup E_Y$. Each state of the environment is implicitly defined by the state of all its *environmental entities* and *environmental properties*. We follow a factored representation (Boutilier et al., 1995) that describes the state space as a set of discrete state variables. Finally, given that the embodiment is central in describing the relation between the entities and the environment (Clark, 1998), each *environmental entity* can be seen as a body, possibly with the capability to influence the environmental properties. Based on this idea of embodiment, two higher-level concepts (decoupled from the environment characterization) are considered: 1) agent, owning reasoning and decision-making capabilities, and 2) resource, without any reasoning capability. Thus, given a set of agents, Y, we define an association function, *embody*: $Y \rightarrow E_T$, which connects an agent to its physical entity. Similarly, given a set of resources, Φ, we define the mapping function *identity*: $\Phi \rightarrow E_Y$. We consider that $|E| = |Y| + |\Phi|$, thus each entity is either mapped to an agent or to a resource; there is no third category.

3.2 The ITEM-Game Environment, Agents and Resources

Those modeling concepts were exploited to capture the behaviour of the electricity market and to build the ITEM-game simulator which enables a (human) prosumer to play the role of a generator company (GenCo) operator, with distinct power generating units (GenUnit), while a (simulated) market operator (Pool) computes the hourly market price (driven by the electricity demand). Therefore, GenCo is embodied by an agent and represented by a (human) player. Each GenCo contains its own set of GenUnits that are resources described by properties such as "production cost" and "generation capacity." The Pool is also an agent with the capability to evaluate bids and to settle the market price.

Each ITEM-game agent owns an initial budget and takes decisions regarding the investment (i.e., buying generating units) and the trading (i.e., sending bids to the Pool) of the production capacity of its own generating units. Such decision-making is repeated throughout time, thus yielding, for each agent, an assets' portfolio that sustains the agent's gathered power to influence others (or to get influenced by others).

The ITEM-game agents exhibit bounded rationality, i.e., each agent's decision is based on its local information (partial knowledge) of the system and of other agents. The ITEM-game purpose is not to explicitly search for equilibria points, but rather to reveal and assist to understand the complex and aggregate behaviours that emerge from the interactions among the market agents.

3.3 The ITEM-Game Architecture

The ITEM-game explores the main features of liberalized electricity markets and the challenges faced by the agents in their long-term investment decisions and in their short-term trading strategies. Each ITEM-game player represents a generator company that pursues a profit maximization strategy. The investment and trading decisions are made interactively among players using a market simulator platform. The results of the game are based on the profit of each player, which results from the income of selling the electricity (produced by their generating units) in the power Pool and the costs associated with the generation, including variable costs (fuel, CO_2 emissions) and fixed costs (investment) (ITEM-game, 2013).

The Figure 1 presents an overview of the capabilities provided by the ITEM-game agents organized within three main groups: a) the "Player Agents," b) the "Monitor Agent," and c) the "Simulator Agents."

Figure 1. The architecture of the ITEM-game simulator

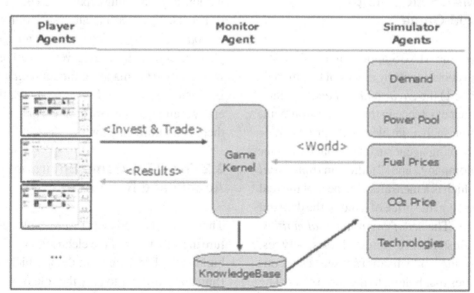

The "Player Agents" submit, at each decision epoch, their "Invest & Trade" decisions based on the perceived "Results" (from each previous decision epoch). A human player may embody those agents (by means of a graphical user-interface); additionally, the ITEM-game also provides a knowledge representation format (OWL-based (Ding & Khandelwal, 2012) ontology representation (Trigo & Coelho, 2009) for automatic submission of decisions and for the perception of the corresponding results. The "Monitor Agent" is designed to execute continuously and ensures that the time-dependent actions (e.g., decision-epoch evolution) are synchronized between player and simulation agents and that the knowledge persistence is guaranteed. The "Simulator Agents" are several simple reactive threads that provide specific contributions to the overall simulation. The "Demand" simulates the system's total demand for electricity and follows a growing pattern (e.g., a linear growth). The "Power Pool" implements the mechanism to set the market price based on the customers' demand and the power generators' (players') offers. Other agents include those that implement the dynamics of fuel price (that increases with demand) and the CO_2 price (which is related with the fuel consumption). The "Technologies" capture the evolution of generation technology such as the emergence of power generators with increased efficiency or towards the decrease of CO_2 emissions.

3.4 The Long-Term Investment

The ITEM-game supports long-term investment on generating units from a set of technologies, such as, nuclear, coal, and gas thermal power plants; hydro (not including pumping), wind and photovoltaic renewable power plants.

Each generating unit's technology is described both by its price and its technical properties, such as, its total generation capacity, efficiency (ratio between energy production and fuel consumption)

and CO_2 specific emissions. Each generating unit follows a 3-stage life cycle:

1. **Construction:** The period (e.g., number of years) that goes from the investment decision until the effective electricity production; this stage starts immediately after the agent's decision to invest,
2. **Operation:** The period (e.g., number of years) of effective electricity production; this stage starts immediately after the ending of the previous (construction) stage,
3. **Decommission:** The date (e.g., year) from which the unit finishes producing electricity; this stage starts immediately after the ending of the previous (operation) stage.

The Figure 2 presents (in the top) a hydro generating unit with a total generation capacity of 100 MW, efficiency is 35%, the specific emissions is 0 ton CO_2/MWh and the price is 50 M€. The Figure 2 also depicts (in the middle) the hydro 3-stage life cycle; starting from investment decision we have 3 years (including the investment's one) for construction, followed by 8 operational years and finally, at the 11th year after the investment decision, the unit is decommissioned.

An investment is a long-term decision, e.g., the hydro's 11 years life cycle (cf., Figure 2). Its purchase price represents a fixed cost (amortized) during all the opera stage's duration. Additionally, during the unit's operation stage its generation capacity is available for trading.

3.5 The Short-Term Trading

The trading involves short-term decisions (when compared to investment). The ITEM-game supports short-term trading (of the electricity asset) through a spot market, which is operated via a Pool institutional power entity. Each (human) agent plays the role of a generator company, GenCo, and submits (to Pool) how much energy, each

Figure 2. The life cycle of a (hydro) generating unit

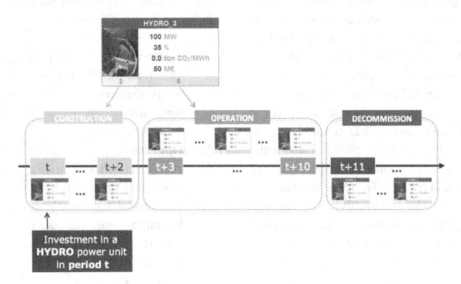

of its generating unit, GenUnit$_{GenCo}$, is willing to produce and at what price. Therefore, we have:

- The power supply system comprises a set, EGenCo, of GenCos, EGenCo,
- Each GenCo is embodied by an agent and represented by a (human) player,
- Each GenCo contains its own set, EGenUnitGenCo, of generating units, EGenUnitGenCo,
- Each GenUnit$_{GenCo}$ is described by a set, Ep(GenUnitGenCo), of properties, Ep(GenUnitGenCo),
- Each p(GenUnit$_{GenCo}$) always includes cost and capacity information,
- The market operator, Pool, evaluates the bids and settles the market price..

The submission of bids (to Pool) conforms to the so-called "block bids" approach (OMIP, 2013), where a block represents a quantity (MW) of energy being bided for a certain price (€/MWh). Also, there usually exists a regulatory price cap constraint (i.e., maximum allowed price), so that any bid price is always kept below a predefined cap value. Thus, a bid, b, is described by the vector,

$$b = <\text{GenUnit}_{GenCo}, \text{quantity}, \text{price}>, \text{where price} \leq cap \qquad (1)$$

The Figure 3 shows the ITEM-game graphical interface that (human) players may use to submit their bids. The example shows two CCGT (Combined Cycle Gas Turbine) block bids (200 MW and 100 MW) and, possibly, a third bid (of 900 MW) being "prepared" to join the other two bids.

Each supplier (GenCo) submits bids to the Pool to sell electricity (cf. expression 1). The Pool aggregates the quantities (MW) of equal-price (€/MWh) bids and forms a non-decreasing incremental price curve. The market clears (accepts) the lowest price bids that are sufficient to satisfy the demand. The market price, mkP, corresponds to the highest price accepted in the market. All GenCo in the market (i.e., with cleared bids) will sell their energy at the mkP value.

Therefore, the market supply essential measurable aspects are the generating unit's generation capacity and its marginal cost. Thus, we have,

$$E_T = \{ \text{Pool} \} \cup E_{GenCo} \cup_{g \in EGenCo} E_{GenUnit\ g} \qquad (2)$$

$$E_Y = \{ \text{quantity, price, marginalCost} \} \qquad (3)$$

Figure 3. The bid submission (from the ITEM-game graphical interface)

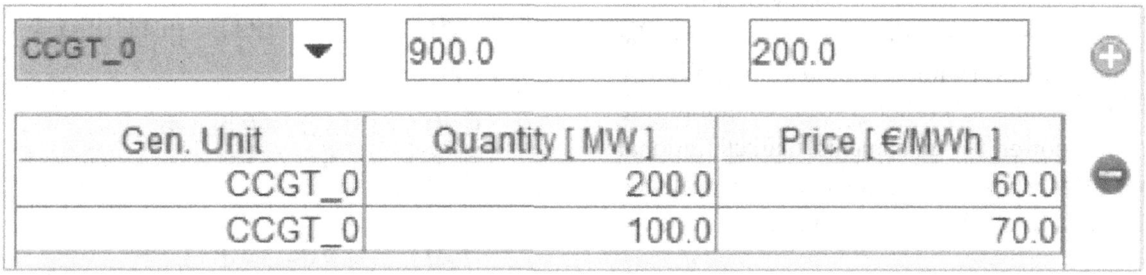

The quantity refers both to the supply and demand sides of the market. The demand (consumer) side of the market is mainly described by the quantity of demanded energy; we assume that there is no price elasticity of demand (i.e., no demand-side market bidding). The price refers both to the supply bided values and to the market settled (by Pool) value. The marginalCost refers to the marginal cost as defined by each GenUnit$_{GenCo}$.

The Pool is a reactive agent that always applies the same predefined auction rules in order to determine the market price and hence the block bids that clear the market. The E$_{GenCo}$ contains the decision-making agents. Each EGenUnitGenCo represents the GenCo's set of available resources.

4. ECONOMICALLY-MOTIVATED (INDIVIDUAL AND SOCIAL) DECISION-MAKING

A game environment may be described as a kind of institution where the social and organizational aspects that emerge, from the multitude of strategies being played, can reveal forms of power among agents. The power concept expresses an ubiquitous societal phenomenon that basically refers to the relationship between an agent, its goals and its abilities and resources (Castelfranchi, 2003).

A simple economic interpretation of the power concept is the ability to set price above marginal cost, usually ascribed as "market power," which is traditionally quantified, by the "Lerner index" (Lerner, 1934), as the proportional deviation of price, P, at the firm's profit-maximizing output from the firm's marginal cost, mgC, at that same output (given by (P – mgC) / P); a bigger wedge between P and mgC means greater monopoly power. The most important limitation of the Lerner index is that it "does not recognize that some of the deviation of P from mgC comes from either efficient use of scaling factors or the need to cover fixed costs" (Lindenberg & Ross, 1981). This is a significant limitation because few firms fit the textbook description of perfect competition. For example, the cost structure of firms in many technology-driven industries (e.g., software, pharmaceuticals and power industry) is markedly front-loaded (i.e., high cost are concentrated in the firm's early stages) and therefore marginal cost pricing, in those industries, is not feasible (and possibly not desirable) (Elzinga & Mills, 2011).

The impact of the Lerner index has been greater in coalition (merger) enforcement. Here, the relevant question is not whether a firm has market power, but whether a proposed coalition would increase the firm's market power. The predicted change in post-coalition price-cost margins used in conjunction with the Lerner index "can be the most important source of evidence on market power" and their use "can be expected to be a common occurrence" (Werden, 1998).

Intuitively, the market power (or monopolistic-path) perspective refers the ability of a firm, or a coalition of firms, to raise prices above the competitive level without a rapid loss of an ability to sell (Landes & Posner, 1981). Therefore, the "market power" is a fundamental market's rational tool that agents can use to define, or evaluate, strategies for coalitions' (re)formation.

4.1 The Social Welfare and the Marginal Costs

We follow the Lerner's general assumption that, within perfect competition, social welfare is (asymptotically) reached at marginal costs. We also assume that the market clearing mechanism intends to maximize social welfare. Under those assumptions, and given that suppliers (GenCos) are not required to bid at real costs, if the suppliers all bid their marginal cost, then social welfare maximization is achieved (Song et al., 1999).

The marginal costs' valuations are usually kept as a "private business" affair that incorporates the econometric and technical GenCos's knowledge. Although being undisclosed formulations, a common approach is to incorporate variable costs such as the fuel costs and the CO_2 specific emissions costs. Here we assume that fixed costs (e.g., investment amortization, maintenance) are not incorporated in the marginal costs' valuation.

4.2 Portfolio and Marginal Market Price-Making

To simplify the notation we describe a portfolio as a set that encloses classes of distinct quantities (MW) such that all the quantities that belong to a class have the same marginal cost (€/MWh). The Code 1 (Figure 4) describes an implementation (as a Python dictionary) of a portfolio, ptf_1, with 4 marginal costs (3.0, 6.0, 7.0 and 9.0) each related to a class; e.g., the 3.0 €/MWh marginal cost, of ptf_1, is related to a class with two blocks, one block of 25 MW and another of 15 MW. The

Figure 4. Code 1

Code 1. The "ptf1" portfolio

```
ptf1 =
{ 6.0:  [ 40, 25,  5 ],
  3.0:  [ 25, 15 ],
  7.0:  [ 10 ],
  9.0:  [ 50, 20 ] }
```

Code 2 (Figure 5) represents another portfolio, ptf_2, where 3 marginal costs (3.0, 6.0 and 7.0) are the same, as in ptf_1, and the 8.5 is specific to ptf_2.

Each portfolio is owned by an agent (GenCo) and contains the primary data for an agent to reason about the resources ($GenUnit_{GenCo}$) it needs to manage.

The Code 3 in Figure 6 describes the "portfolio to agent" assignment; the portfolio ptf_1 is assigned to agent ag_1 and ptf_2 to ag_2.

A portfolio distribution (among GenCo agents) implicitly defines an ordered (from lowest to highest) list of marginal cost bids. The Code 4 (Figure 7) shows the bidList generated after the ag_1 and ag_2 portfolios. We recall that each bid follows the structure given by expression 1; e.g., the bidList lowest bid is a 3.0 €/MWh offered for the 25 MW from the generating unit u_1 of generator company ag_1.

Figure 5. Code 2

Code 2. The "ptf2" portfolio

```
ptf2 =
{ 3.0:  [  5 ],
  6.0:  [  5, 15 ],
  7.0:  [ 10, 15 ],
  8.5:  [ 15,  5 ] }
```

Figure 6. Code 3

Code 3. Agents' portfolio

```
ag1 = Agent( ptf1 )
ag2 = Agent( ptf2 )
```

Figure 7. Code 4

Code 4. The ag_1 and ag_2 bids

```
bidList =
[ [ 3.0 , 25 , u1_ag1 ]
  [ 3.0 , 15 , u1_ag1 ]
  [ 3.0 , 5 , u1_ag2 ]
  [ 6.0 , 40 , u2_ag1 ]
  [ 6.0 , 25 , u2_ag1 ]
  [ 6.0 , 5 , u2_ag1 ]
  [ 6.0 , 5 , u2_ag2 ]
  [ 6.0 , 15 , u2_ag2 ]
  [ 7.0 , 10 , u3_ag1 ]
  [ 7.0 , 10 , u3_ag2 ]
  [ 7.0 , 15 , u3_ag2 ]
  [ 8.5 , 15 , u4_ag2 ]
  [ 8.5 , 5 , u4_ag2 ]
  [ 9.0 , 50 , u5_ag1 ]
  [ 9.0 , 20 , u5_ag1 ] ] ]
```

To simplify the approach we consider that there is there is no demand-side market bidding. Therefore, given a bidList and a demand value Q the market price is the minimum price offer that satisfies the demand, described as,

$$mkP = \min \{ p \in P(bidList) \mid ((\Sigma_{i \le p} \Sigma_{q \in quantity:i} q) \ge Q) \} \quad (4)$$

where, P(bidList) is a set that contains all the price offers in bidList and quantity:$_i$ is a set with all the i-priced quantities in bidList. As an example,

considering the code 4, bidList, and a demand Q = 100 we have mkP = 6.0.

The market clears (accepts) any bid, b, such that price(b) $\le$ mkP (where price(b) is the bid's b price). Any bid, b, such that price(b) = mkP is rated; this means that only a portion (price(b) / $\Sigma_{q \in quantity:mkP}$ q) of the quantity required at mkP is cleared from the b bid.

4.3. Coalitions and Decision-Making Metrics

Given a marginal market price, mkP (i.e., the market price computed from marginal cost bids), a strict evaluation of the Lerner index gives a positive value for bids below mkP and a zero value for the mkP bids. We take such strict evaluation to argument that mkP bids have a high motivation to increase the mkP value (and thus augment their market power). By doing so they will also increment the market power of the lower marginal cost bids, which calls for an equilibria analysis to be taken from each agent's (bid aggregation) perspective. Nevertheless, we take the bid's basic motivation (depart from zero Lerner index) as we intend to identify and develop the primary tools that will enable to achieve more sophisticated analysis.

Coalitions. Assuming that all agents, with at least one zero-valued Lerner index bid, have the goal to increase the mkP, they need to evaluate the possible coalitions that provide the power (quantity) required to achieve that goal.

Definition 1 ("redundant" bid): Given a set of bids, S, and a minimum quantity, q_{min}, we say that a bid, b $\notin$ S, is "redundant," with respect to S and q_{min}, if there exists a bid, b' $\in$ S, such that ((S \ {b'}) $\cup$ {b}) yields a set of bids such that their total quantity is not inferior to q_{min}. Otherwise, we say that the bid b is "non-redundant" with respect to S and q_{min}. Any bid is always "non-redundant" with respect to any set S such that |S| $\le$ 1 (i.e., empty and one element sets). The (above) "redundant" bid idea is used to describe the coalition concept.

Definition 2 (coalition): Given a set of bids, B, and a quantity, q_{min}, a coalition, C, is constructively described as follows: take a set of bids, S (possibly empty), such that their total quantity is inferior to q_{min}, and take a bid, b, not in S, i.e., $b \in B \setminus S$,

if b is "non-redundant" in respect to S and q_{min}, then add b to S, i.e., $S \leftarrow \{b\} \cup S$,

if the sum of all the bids in S is not inferior to q_{min}, then S is a coalition, i.e., C = S; else get another $b \in B \setminus S$ and repeat the previous step,

if all the bids such that $b \in B \setminus S$ and S did not evolve into a coalition, then no coalition can be built from S.

Definition 3 (k-coalition): Given a coalition, C, and a $k > 0$ ($k \in N$) we say that C is a k-coalition iff $|C| = k$.

Given a set of zero-valued Lerner index bids and the common intention to augment the market price (thus, the market power) there are two possible "power-of scenarios" (that may coexist):

- At least one bid has the power-of to increment the market price,
- At least one bid does not have the power-of to increment the market price.

Each bid, b, that has the power-of to increment the market price yields a 1-coalition. A bid that does not have the power-of to increment the market price is a member of a k-coalition, for $k \geq 2$, and depends on the remaining coalition member(s) in order to jointly achieve a collective-power-of. We remark that the 1-coalition bid may also participate in several 2-coalition (to complement the lack of power-of of the other bid).

The exhaustive construction of coalitions (given a set of bids, B, and a minimum quantity, q_{min}) enables to classify each bid (within each coalition) according to its power-of scenario.

Influence Metrics: The influence of a bid, b, is a measure of the dependence of all the other bids regarding b; i.e., the influence of b increases as more coalitions depend on b. Therefore, given a set of coalitions, SoC, a simple metric to express the influence of a bid, b, is its coalition frequency, cf(b, SoC), described as,

$$cf(b, SoC) = (\Sigma_{C \in SoC} I(b, C)) / |SoC|, \text{ where } I(b, C) = 1 \text{ if } b \in C; 0 \text{ otherwise} \quad (5)$$

The influence of the 1-coalition bid, b, is described as the inverse of the total number of such coalitions and corresponds to the special case, of cf, given by.

$$cf_1(b, SoC) = cf(b, H), \text{ where } H = \{ C \in SoC \mid |C| = 1 \} \quad (6)$$

Both the cf and cf_1 metrics are computed from each bid's perspective. An agent aggregates several bids and therefore an agent's, ag, overall influence may be simply evaluated as the average of cf (or cf_1) of the bids generated from ag's own portfolio.

4.4 An Example of the Decision-Making Metrics' Evaluation

As an illustrative example, consider the previous bidList (from Code 4) along with a demand $Q = 100$ MW. The code 5 (evaluation output in Figure 8), shows that $Q = 100$ MW implies a market price $mkP = 6.0$ €/MWh. The aggregate quantity of all the cleared bids is given by $q_{agg} = 135$ MW and therefore the minimum quantity that motivates a joint intention (to increase mkP) is given by $q_{min} = q_{agg} - Q = 35$ MW. The code 6 (Figure 9) shows the detail of all bids that will get involved in the coalition evaluation process; i.e., each bid, b, such that price(b) = mkP.

Figure 8. Code 5

Code 5. Demand and q_{min}

```
Q    = 100  [MW]
=>
mkP = 6.0  [euro/MWh]

q_agg = 135  [MW]
=>
q_min = 35   [MW]
```

Figure 9. Code 6

Code 6. The mkP bids

```
[
    [ 6.0,  40,  u2_ag1 ]
    [ 6.0,  25,  u2_ag1 ]
    [ 6.0,  5,   u2_ag1 ]
    [ 6.0,  5,   u2_ag2 ]
    [ 6.0,  15,  u2_ag2 ]
]
```

Figure 10. Code 7

Code 7. Coalitions' set (1 of 2)

```
[ [  6.0,  40,  u2_ag1 ] ]


[ [  6.0,  25,  u2_ag1 ]
  [  6.0,  15,  u2_ag2 ] ]


[ [  6.0,  25,  u2_ag1 ]
  [  6.0,  5,   u2_ag1 ]
  [  6.0,  5,   u2_ag2 ] ]
```

Figure 11. Code 8

Code 8. Coalitions' set (2 of 2)

```
[ [  6.0,  5,   u2_ag1 ]
  [  6.0,  40,  u2_ag1 ] ]


[ [  6.0,  5,   u2_ag2 ]
  [  6.0,  40,  u2_ag1 ] ]


[ [  6.0,  15,  u2_ag2 ]
  [  6.0,  40,  u2_ag1 ] ]


[ [  6.0,  25,  u2_ag1 ]
  [  6.0,  40,  u2_ag1 ] ]
```

The codes 7 and 8 (Figures 10 and 11) show the set of coalitions, SoC, that are generated (cf., definition 2) given the mkP bids (cf., code 6) and the q_{min} value (cf., code 5); each coalition is (graphically) framed by an upper and a lower horizontal lines. For example, in code 7 the second coalition considers 25 MW from $u2_{ag1}$ and 15 MW from $u2_{ag2}$. There are 7 possible coalitions; the bid <6.0, 40, $u2_{ag1}$> is the only one with the power-of to increment the market price.

The code 9 (Figure 12) shows the cf and cf_1 evaluation of the influence metrics (cf., respectively, expressions 5 and 6). For example, the bid

Figure 12. Code 9

Code 9. The cf and cf_1 influence metrics

```
[ 6.0,  40,  u2_ag1 ]  cf = 71.4%  |  cf1 = 100.0%
[ 6.0,  25,  u2_ag1 ]  cf = 42.9%  |  cf1 =   0.0%
[ 6.0,  15,  u2_ag2 ]  cf = 28.6%  |  cf1 =   0.0%
[ 6.0,  5,   u2_ag1 ]  cf = 28.6%  |  cf1 =   0.0%
[ 6.0,  5,   u2_ag2 ]  cf = 28.6%  |  cf1 =   0.0%
```

<6.0, 40, $u2_{ag1}$> has both the power-of to increment the market price and the highest influence value (i.e., cf = 71.4%) regarding all the others' bids perspective on possible coalitions. Also, the 15 MW bid is as influential as the lowest-quantity bids (5 MW).

The code 10 (Figure 13) shows an overall perspective of each agent's influence. An agent, ag, aggregates a set of bids; hence, we take the subset of bids that belong to ag and consider such set's cf average as the estimated value for the ag's influence. This overall influence metric gives a simple ranking criterion for agents to reason about possible coalitions and their position in the negotiation processes.

This illustrative example details each step of our approach taking the electricity market motivation. The approach is not confined to the electricity market case study; for example, the "bid-quantity" value is an immediate extension point that can be generalized to any agent-specific quantitative evaluation function. Despite that, we

Figure 13. Code 10

Code 10. Influence

$$ag1 = 47.6\%$$
$$ag2 = 28.6\%$$

intend to deepen our research (validate our assumptions) using this case study domain and to extend the ITEM-game platform to the inter-agent negotiation context prior to further generalization of the model.

Remarks and extensions: This preliminary work aims to identify and describe the primary concepts and assumptions that can be used to achieve some more sophisticated metrics of power and influence.

In this work the influence metric derives from a direct interpretation of the Lerner index; also, the metric is taken independently of any agent's perspective. Therefore, those two aspects deserve further extensions, namely:

- Each possible market price increase needs an utility evaluation that incorporates the income from such an increase; i.e., "what is an agent's effective motivation to trigger a coalition formation to increase the market price?,"

- Each possible coalition needs to be evaluated taking into account each participant's perspective and search for equilibria points (or Pareto efficient points), i.e., "what is each agent's incentive to participate in a given coalition?."

An important motivation to increase the marginal market price is to accommodate fixed costs (we assumed that the marginal value excludes fixed costs). Another agent's motivation is to improve its global position in the market. Both motivations are taken from an agent's, ag, perspective and therefore they must be evaluated as a function of the cumulative income gathered from all its bids. Both motivations need to consider the position of all other agents in respect to the ag's perspective. The position of an agent in respect to another can be described as the income difference between both agents. A position deviation in respect to a market price change is the ratio between the positions' difference and the prices' difference.

The motivation for an agent, ag, to cover fixed costs is likely to be "well accepted" by all agents that will get a positive deviation after moving from their initial position (marginal market price) to the position that corresponds to the ag's market price increase. Those are the "best" candidates for ag to initiate (a possible) coalition negotiation.

The motivation for an agent, ag, to improve its global position is more complex to follow. The agents that achieve a positive deviation are likely to "welcome" the ag's effort but they will also improve their position in respect to ag.

Thus, it is necessary to find the set of agents that will lose their position (in respect to ag) and to decide if the positions' improvement of the remaining agents is acceptable from the ag's perspective.

These main extensions, of our current model, resort to the power and influence model and metrics described in this paper.

5. CONCLUSION AND FUTURE WORK

This paper describes our work in the construction of a MABS framework to describe and explore the investment and trading dynamics of the electric power market. We used the proposed MABS framework to support the construction of the ITEM-game agent-based electricity market simulator.

The ITEM-game along with the "coalition scenario" simulator, described in this paper, is publically available (cf., (ITEM-game, 2013)) to be explored for "hands-on" experiences. The available implementation is being continuously improved and open to general (users') feedback and specific (technical) contributions. The ITEM-game also incorporates the feedback gathered after being used as the "hands-on" support for a tutorial training course (each year since (Sousa & Trigo, 2011)) in electricity markets.

The MABS framework was extended to include the social power concepts (ascribed as power-of and collective-power-of) along with a quantitative interpretation of such abstract concepts. Those concepts and the related quantitative metrics are the primary tools that agents can use to define (or re-evaluate) strategies for coalitions' (re)formation. The market's rational for a coalition is often related with the market power (or monopolistic-path) perspective. Therefore, the combined integration of those elements (power, dependence, coalition) aims for a highly realistic game-like market simulator. This high-realism goal is a key guideline within our research effort and clearly distinguishes our proposal from the "would-be world" (or "toy-model") approaches.

Additionally, the quantitative interpretation of the individual power concept provides the tool for an agent to execute a prospective (i.e., what-if) reasoning to evaluate different (possible) coalition formations and to establish the parameters (bidding prices and quantities) to use for the negotiation process to establish the most desirable (from each agent's perspective) coalition. Such capability of conceiving a prospective reasoning and being able to properly negotiate with others and drive them to overtake one's individual limitation reveals some attributes of "agent leadership" that we intend to further explore in future research.

Additionally we also notice that the disruptive concept of additive manufacturing (or 3D printing) is arriving at a mature stage where low-cost production of unique "one-offs" will give raise to new markets and therefore we intend to explore ways of integrating those arriving new business models into the prosumer agents' perspective.

Our overall goal is to research new ways of augmenting the agent's individual decision-making model with tools that foster everyone's negotiation capabilities and thus contribute to disseminate the collective-intelligence perspective within electricity markets.

REFERENCES

Berry, C., Hobbs, B., Meroney, W., O'Neill, R., & Stewart, W. R. Jr. (1999). Understanding how market power can arise in network competition: a game theoretic approach. *Utilities Policy, 8*(3), 139–158. doi:10.1016/S0957-1787(99)00016-8

Boutilier, C., Dearden, R., & Goldszmidt, M. (1995). Exploiting structure in policy construction. *Proceedings of the, IJCAI-95*, 1104–1111.

Bunn, D., & Oliveira, F. (2003). Evaluating individual market power in electricity markets via agent-based simulation. *Annals of Operations Research, 19*(2), 57–77. doi:10.1023/A:1023399017816

Castelfranchi, C. (2003). The micro-macro constitution of power. *Understanding the Social II: Philosophy of Sociality. ProtoSociology Journal, 18*, 208–265.

Castelfranchi, C. (2013). Making visible the invisible hand - The mission of social simulation. In Interdisciplinary applications of agent-based social simulation and modeling. Open Agent Based Modeling (OpenABM) Consortium.

Clark, A. (1998). *Being there: Putting brain, body, and world together again*. Cambridge, MA: The MIT Press.

Coelho, H., Costa, A., & Trigo, P. (2013). On agent interactions governed by morality. In Interdisciplinary applications of agent-based social simulation and modeling. Open Agent Based Modeling (OpenABM) Consortium.

Conzelmann, G., North, M., Boyd, G., Cirillo, R., Koritarov, V., Macal, C., et al. (2004). Agent-based power market modeling: Simulating strategic market behaviour using an agent-based modeling approach. In *Proceedings of the 6th IAEE European Conference on Modeling in Energy Economics and Policy*, Zurich, Switzerland.

Day, C., & Bunn, D. (2001). Divestiture of generation assets in the electricity pool of England and Wales: A computational approach to analyzing market power. *Journal of Regulatory Economics, 19*(2), 123–141. doi:10.1023/A:1011141105371

Deffeyes, K. S. (2010). *When oil peaked*. New York: Hill and Wang Press.

Ding, L., & Khandelwal, A. (2012). OWL 2 Web ontology language – Quick reference guide (2nd Ed.). W3C Recommendation, W3C.

EC. (2009). *European directive, 2009/72/EC (EUR-Lex.europa.eu)*. Retrieved from http://eur-lex.europa.eu/

Elzinga, K., & Mills, D. (2011). The Lerner index of monopoly power: Origins and uses. *The American Economic Review, 101*(3). doi:10.1257/aer.101.3.558

Friedman, T. L. (2008). *Hot, flat, and crowded: Why we need a green revolution and how it can renew America*. New York: Farrar, Straus and Giroux Press.

Friesen, M., Gordon, R., & McLeod, B. (2013). Exploring emergence within social systems with agent based models. In Interdisciplinary applications of agent-based social simulation and modeling. Open Agent Based Modeling (OpenABM) Consortium.

Gabriel, S., Zhuang, J., & Kiet, S. (2004). A Nash-Cournot model for the North American natural gas market. *In Proceedings of the 6th IAEE European Conference: Modelling in Energy Economics and Policy.*

Georgalos, K. (2013). *Playing with ambiguity: An agent based model of vague beliefs in games. Interdisciplinary applications of agent-based social simulation and modeling. Open Agent Based Modeling (OpenABM).* Consortium.

Helleboogh, A., Vizzari, G., Uhrmacher, A., & Michel, F. (2007). Modeling dynamic environments in multi-agent simulation. *Journal of Autonomous Agents and Multi-Agent Systems, 14*(1), 87–116. doi:10.1007/s10458-006-0014-y

ITEM-game. (2013). *Investment and trading in electricity markets.* Retrieved from http://www.item-game.org/

Ketter, W., Collins, J., Reddy, P., Flath, C., & de Weerdt, M. (2011). The power trading agent competition. In ERIM Report Series No. ERS-2011-011-LIS, (Vol. 2). SSRN.

Koesrindartoto, D. (2002). *Discrete double auctions with artificial adaptive agents: A case study of an electricity market using a double auction simulator (Technical report). Dep. of Economics.* Iowa University.

Koesrindartoto, D., Sun, J., & Tesfatsion, L. (2005). An agent-based computational laboratory for testing the economic reliability of wholesale power market designs. In *Proceedings of the IEEE Power Engineering Conference* (pp. 931–936). San Francisco, CA.

Landes, W., & Posner, R. (1981). Market power in antitrust cases. *Harvard Law Review, 94*(5), 937–996. doi:10.2307/1340687

Lerner, A. (1934). Concept of monopoly and the measurement of monopoly power. *The Review of Economic Studies, 14*(1), 157–175. doi:10.2307/2967480

Lindenberg, E. B., & Ross, S. A. (1981). Tobin's q ratio and industrial organization. *The Journal of Business, 54,* 1–31. doi:10.1086/296120

Lucas, P., & Payne, D. (2013). Usefulness of agent-based simulation to test collective decision-making models. In Interdisciplinary applications of agent-based social simulation and modeling. Open Agent Based Modeling (OpenABM) Consortium.

Luyet, S. (2013). From meso decisions to macro results: An agent-based approach of policy diffusion. In Interdisciplinary applications of agent-based social simulation and modeling. Open Agent Based Modeling (OpenABM) Consortium.

Magessi, N. T., & Antunes, L. (2013). Agent's risk relation on strategic tax reporting game. In Interdisciplinary applications of agent-based social simulation and modeling. Open Agent Based Modeling (OpenABM) Consortium.

Mota, F., Santos, I., Dimuro, G., & Rosa, V. (2013). Agent-based simulation of electric energy consumers: The NetLogo tool approach. In Interdisciplinary applications of agent-based social simulation and modeling. Open Agent Based Modeling (OpenABM) Consortium.

Nardin, L. G., Rosset, L., & Sichman, J. (2013). Scale and topology effects on agent-based simulation: A trust-based coalition formation case study. In Interdisciplinary applications of agent-based social simulation and modeling. Open Agent Based Modeling (OpenABM) Consortium.

North, M., Collier, N., & Vos, J. (2006). Experiences creating three implementations of the Repast agent modeling toolkit. *ACM Transactions on Modeling and Computer Simulation, 16,* 1–25. doi:10.1145/1122012.1122013

Nunes, D., & Antunes, L. (2013). Social space in simulation models. In Interdisciplinary applications of agent-based social simulation and modeling. Open Agent Based Modeling (OpenABM) Consortium.

OMIP. (2013). *Iberian electricity market operator*. Retrieved from www.omip.pt

Poza, D., Galán, J. M., Santos, J. I., & López-Paredes, A. (2010). An agent based model of the Nash demand game in regular lattices. In Balanced automation systems for future manufacturing networks (IFIP Advances in Information and Communication Technology, vol. 322), (pp. 243–250). Berlin: Springer.

Ramchurn, S., Vytelingum, P., Rogers, A., & Jennings, N. R. (2012). Putting the 'smarts' into the smart grid: A grand challenge for artificial intelligence. *Communications of the ACM, 55*(4), 86–97. doi:10.1145/2133806.2133825

Richter, C., & Sheble, G. (1998). Genetic algorithm evolution of utility biding strategies for the competitive market price. *IEEE Transactions on Power Systems, 13*(1), 256–261. doi:10.1109/59.651644

Roth, A., & Erev, I. (1995). Learning in extensive-form games: Experimental data and simple dynamic models in the intermediate term. *Games and Economic Behavior, 8,* 164–212. doi:10.1016/S0899-8256(05)80020-X

Santos, F., Rodrigues, H., Rodrigues, T., Dimuro, G., Jerez, E., Adamatti, D., et al. (2013). Multi-agent-based simulation of the social production and management processes in a urban ecosystem: An approach based on the integration of organizational, regulatory, communication and physical artifacts in the JaCaMo framework. In Interdisciplinary applications of agent-based social simulation and modeling. Open Agent Based Modeling (OpenABM) Consortium.

Schuster, S., & Gilbert, N. (2004). Simulating online business models. In *Proceedings of the 5th Workshop on Agent-Based Simulation (ABS-04)* (pp. 55–61).

Song, H., Liu, C. C., & Lawarrée, J. (1999). Decision making of an electricity supplier's bid in a spot market. In *Proceedings of the Power Engineering Society Summer Meeting, vol. 2* (pp. 692–696). IEEExplore.

Sousa, J., & Trigo, P. (2011). Investment and trading in electricity markets. Tutorial training course. In *Proceedings of the 8th International Conference on the European Energy Market (EEM'11)*.

Sousa, J., Trigo, P., & Marques, P. (2012). Investment and trading in electricity markets (ITEM). Seminar course. In *Proceedings of the 9th International Conference on the European Energy Market (EEM'12)*.

Terna, P., Arciero, L., Picillo, C., & Solomon, S. (2013). Building ABMs to control the emergence of crisis analyzing agents' behaviour. In Interdisciplinary applications of agent-based social simulation and modeling. Open Agent Based Modeling (OpenABM) Consortium.

Thimmapuram, P., Veselka, T., Vilela, S., Pereira, R., & Silva, R. (2008). Modeling hydro power plants in deregulated electricity markets: Integration and application of EMCAS to VALORAGUA. In *Proceedings of the 4th International Conference on the European Electricity Market (EEM-08)*.

Trigo, P., & Coelho, H. (2009). Agent inferencing meets the Semantic Web. In Progress in Artificial Intelligence, EPIA-09 (Lecture Notes in Artificial Intelligence, vol. 5816, pp. 497–507). Berlin: Springer-Verlag.

Trigo, P., Marques, P., & Coelho, H. (2010). (Virtual) agents for running electricity markets. *Journal of Simulation Modelling Practice and Theory, 18*(10), 1442–1452. doi:10.1016/j.simpat.2010.04.003

Troitzsch, K. (2013). Analysing simulation results statistically: Does significance matter? In Interdisciplinary applications of agent-based social simulation and modeling. Open Agent Based Modeling (OpenABM) Consortium.

Visudhiphan, P., & Ilic, M. (2002). On the necessity of an agent-based approach to assessing market power in the electricity markets. In *Proceedings of the International Symposium on Dynamic Games and Applications*, Saint- Petersburg, Russia.

Wellman, M. (2006). Methods for empirical game-theoretic analysis. In *Proceedings of the 21st national conference on Artificial Intelligence, vol. 2 of AAAI'06* (pp. 1552–1555). Boston, MA.

Werden, G. (1998). Demand elasticities in antitrust analysis. *Antitrust Law Journal, 66*, 363–414.

Zimmerman, R. D., Thomas, R. J., Gan, D., & Murillo-Sánchez, C. (1999). A Web-based platform for experimental investigation of electric power auctions. *Decision Support Systems, 24*, 193–205. doi:10.1016/S0167-9236(98)00083-9

KEY TERMS AND DEFINITIONS

Decision-Making and Gamification: Engage users, in the reasoning that leads to decisions, using game elements and game design techniques within a non-game context (i.e., a context where the goal is other than just the success in the game).

Electricity Market Multiagent Modeling: Characterization of the components of interest to exploit the dynamics of the electricity (commodity) with special emphasis to the investment and trading undertaken by competing agents that can negotiate while being physically distributed.

Empirical Game Simulation: Application of the incomplete information games' foundation to auctions and search for offer-and-bid strategies within a bounded-rationality constraint.

Experimental Economics: Integration of the decision and game theory foundations with computer science in order to simulated and explore phenomena that are difficult to observe directly in naturally occurring economic contexts.

Long-Term and Short-Term Decision-Making: Exploit the causal effect (cause-and-effect) relation between the broad vision (long-term) and the immediate reaction (short-term) when having the opportunity to take decisions that may encompass both those temporal dimensions.

Multiagent Market Simulation: The effort to replicate, within a controlled environment, some characteristics of the offer-demand dynamics using a computational approach of distributed and interacting software agents.

Social Metrics for Coalition-Based Reasoning: Take into account the qualitative social concepts such as "influence" and "power" and derive quantitative metrics that can be explored as the rational for coalitions among agents with (possibly) conflicting goals.

Chapter 11
A Unified Framework for Traditional and Agent-Based Social Network Modeling

Enrico Franchi
University of Parma, Italy

Michele Tomaiuolo
University of Parma, Italy

ABSTRACT

In the last sixty years of research, several models have been proposed to explain (i) the formation and (ii) the evolution of networks. However, because of the specialization required for the problems, most of the agent-based models are not general. On the other hand, many of the traditional network models focus on elementary interactions that are often part of several different processes. This phenomenon is especially evident in the field of models for social networks. Therefore, this chapter presents a unified conceptual framework to express both novel agent-based and traditional social network models. This conceptual framework is essentially a meta-model that acts as a template for other models. To support this meta-model, the chapter proposes a different kind of agent-based modeling tool that we specifically created for developing social network models. The tool the authors propose does not aim at being a general-purpose agent-based modeling tool, thus remaining a relatively simple software system, while it is extensible where it really matters. Eventually, the authors apply this toolkit to a novel problem coming from the domain of P2P social networking platforms.

INTRODUCTION

In the last sixty years of research, several models have been proposed to explain (*i*) the formation and (*ii*) the evolution of networks, or, more in general, (*iii*) various kinds of processes over networks.

Such models have been developed and studied by researchers coming from many different areas, such as computer science, economics, natural sciences, meteorology, medicine, pure or applied mathematics, sociology and statistics. As a consequence, a lot of material exists on the subject and it is beyond the scope of this work to review

DOI: 10.4018/978-1-4666-5954-4.ch011

and analyze it thoroughly (Bergenti et al., 2012; Franchi & Poggi, 2011); we refer to Jackson (2010) for the economic and game-theoretic point of view, and to Snijders (2011) for a complete review of the state of art of statistical models. Newman (2010) provides an accurate presentation of the approach developed in the computer, natural and physical sciences.

Several agent-based models have also been successfully developed in order to study specific problems that, because of either (*i*) the complexity of the agent to agent interactions, or (*ii*) the richness of the underlying environment, were relatively impervious to analysis using traditional techniques (Arthur, 1996; Axtel et al., 2004; Bagni et al., 2002; Carley et al., 2006; Dean et al., 2000; Epstein & Axtell, 1996; Folcik et al., 2007; Hill et al., 2006; Ilachinski, 2000; Kohler et al., 2005; Moffat et al., 2006; North et al., 2010; Lucas & Payne, 2014).

However, most agent-based models address very specific phenomena and, as a consequence, they have relatively low reusability. On the other hand, many traditional models focus on elementary interactions that are often part of several different processes, and, consequently, the effects of these elementary interactions have been thoroughly studied. Nardin, Rosset and Sichman (2014) present a more detailed discussion regarding how to obtain more universal conclusions from agent-based modeling.

We believe that such interactions should be introduced as basic building blocks even for agent-based models, enriched with more "agent-ness" when it is the case. However, several assumptions that are perfectly legitimate in a stochastic process are not well rendered in an agent-based model. Moreover, many considerations that we derive from the conversion from traditional stochastic to agent-based models are similar to the ones that should be made by implementing the stochastic model in a generic non agent-based concurrent environment.

Considering the relevance that social networking platforms have gained in our lives, either directly or indirectly, one of the most interesting applications of agent-based models for social networks is to social networking platforms.

The structure of this Chapter is as follows: (*i*) some considerations over the epistemology of agent-based modeling are given; (*ii*) our proposal for a meta-model for social network processes is described, and also a working toolkit built over such ideas is presented; (*iii*) as an example, our platform is used to model a problem coming from the implementation of P2P social networking platforms.

AGENT BASED MODELING FOR SOCIAL SCIENCES

ABM is a very powerful technique that has been applied increasingly often in the last years in a variety of different contexts. Examples of those contexts are (*i*) social sciences (Axelrod, 2003; Axelrod & Tesfatsion, 2006; Epstein, 1999, 2002, 2006; Kohler & Gumerman, 2000; Castelfranchi, 2014), (*ii*) economy (Arthur et al., 1997; Axtel et al., 2004; Epstein & Axtell, 1996; Arciero et al., 2014; Carbonara, 2013; Magessi & Antunes, 2014; Santos et al., 2014; Trigo, 2014), and marketing (North et al., 2010), (*iii*) epidemics and medicine (Bagni et al., 2002; Carley et al., 2006; Folcik et al., 2007), (*iv*) archeology (Dean et al., 2000; Kohler et al., 2005), (*v*) Philosophy (Coelho, da Rocha Costa & Trigo, 2014), (*vi*) energy distribution (Mota, Santos, Dimuro & Rosa, 2014), (*vii*) Game Theory (Georgalos, 2014) and (*viii*) warfare (Hill et al., 2006; Ilachinski, 2000; Moffat et al., 2006).

In ABM the subject of the modeling is described in terms of a collection of autonomous decision-making units, called agents, that are grouped together to form an agent-based model. Each agent individually assesses the situation and makes its own decision. A model consists of a group of agents, their individual behaviors and their mutual relationships.

The ideas behind agent-based modeling are rather simple: the decision process is decentralized and distributed among the simulated units, which are basically given the same information their real counterparts have. Moreover, the interactions among the agents tend to be simple and somewhat limited. Simpler interactions are usually easier to factor out from the system to model and, moreover, often agents formally act under the hypothesis of bounded rationality (Simon, 1955a), i.e., they are limited (*i*) by the information they have, (*ii*) by their cognitive abilities, and (*iii*) by the finite amount of time available to reach a decision.

Nonetheless, self-organization, patterns, structures and behaviors that have not been explicitly programmed arise from the individual interactions. In fact, emergence is one of the most peculiar features of ABM (Frisen, Gordon & McLeod, 2014). Essentially, the whole point of ABM is studying the emergence of the macro-level features of interest from the explicitly programmed micro-level interactions.

The intuitive notion of emergence, i.e., the manifestation of some property that seems to appear spontaneously in the system, is not hard to grasp and is quite a fascinating idea. Consequently, the notion has been often abused in contexts where it is not appropriate and, most of the times, is not defined at all. Researchers, such as Epstein and Axtell (1996), and Axerlrod (2007) frame the context of emergence defining an emergent phenomenon as a stable macroscopic pattern arising from the local interactions of the agents.

Another important consideration with emergence is that perfect knowledge of the micro-level interactions does not allow to predict macroscopic structure, so emergence cannot be usually predicted. However, agent-based models specified in terms of micro-level interactions can be executed so that the macro-level structure can be actually observed.

In fact, agent-based modeling is more than just a modeling and simulation technique. Agent-based modeling is an epistemological paradigm shift in the way science is done. Traditional sciences usually follow (*i*) a deductive approach, where phenomena explanations are deduced from more general rules, assumed correct, (*ii*) an inductive approach, where the explanations are inferred from repeated observations, or, perhaps, (*iii*) a combination of the two.

On the other hand, the question of the scientist using ABM is:

How could the decentralized local interactions of heterogeneous autonomous agents generate the given regularity? (Epstein, 1999)

Epstein proposes to use the term generative to characterize this approach. He also discusses the epistemological soundness of the proposed approach (Epstein, 1999). A full discussion of the subject, even if fascinating, is beyond the scope of this work. For our purposes, it is sufficient to say that in the generative method, demonstration obtained with ABM is taken as a necessary condition. In other words, if the agent-based model did not generate the desired phenomenon, then the modeled interactions do not explain the phenomenon itself. However, if the modeled interactions generate the expected emergent behavior, then they are only a candidate explanation. If more than one candidate explanations exist, additional care should be exercised to determine which explanation is the most tenable, typically considering the plausibility of the explanation and resorting to the same ideas used when proposing a hypothesis in inductive science, e.g., Ockham's razor. In this book, Castelfranchi (2014) discusses the epistemological issues of ABM to a larger extent.

AGENT BASED MODELING FOR SOCIAL NETWORK SIMULATIONS

Each agent-based model tends to be an *ad-hoc* product with the purpose of studying a precise and restricted family of phenomena. The sheer variety of domains where ABM has been a successfully applied prevents any sound possibility of standardization, as the price would be the flexibility that is so coveted by agent-based modelers. However, limiting ourselves to the domain of simulations of social networks, we can standardize the methodologies to specify models and simulations, so that they are easier to compare and evaluate. Moreover, in the context of social network models, several non-agent based models are extremely popular and agent-based variants of them could be important elements of more complex agent-based processes.

As a consequence, in order to simplify (*i*) the creation of new agent-based models and (*ii*) the adaptation of traditional models into agent-based ones, we designed a conceptual framework that separates the various concerns and allows to write simulations with few lines of code (Bergenti et al., 2013; Franchi, 2012b).

Analyzing the traditional models (Barabasi & Albert, 1999; Watts & Strogatz, 1998; Holme & Kim, 2002; Kumar et al., 2006), as well as some other non-generative network processes, such as the infection diffusion models described by

Pastor-Satorras and Vespignani (2001), we singled out a meta-model that is suitable to implement said models as agent-based models (Franchi, 2012a; Franchi, 2012b; Bergenti et al., 2011). The meta-model also allows for features typical of agent-based models to be introduced gradually and to added to the agent-based variants of the traditional models.

Since in many simulations the nodes do not have a pro-active, goal-directed behavior, but, instead, perform actions when required by the model, we provide the meta-model with a Clock and a special agent called Activator. The Clock beats the time, which is discrete. At each step, the Activator (*i*) selects which nodes to activate, and (*ii*) decides whether nodes shall be destroyed, or (*iii*) created, negotiating the eventuality with the NodeManager. The nodes execute actions after receiving the activation message. However, if the model is fully agent-oriented, they can also perform actions autonomously, without waiting for activation. The nodes can also leave the simulation, require the creation of other agents, and send messages to the other nodes. The general structure of the execution phase is presented in Figure 1.

In essence, a simulation is fully described providing the specifications of: (*i*) the selection process of the groups of nodes to create, activate or destroy, which is performed by the Activator agent; (*ii*) the behavior of the nodes themselves.

Figure 1. Interaction diagram of the main agents in the meta-model

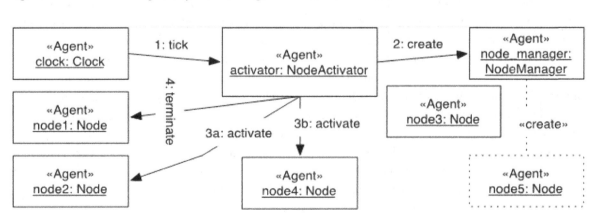

Notice that the general structure does not change significantly even when introducing some agentness in the simulations, e.g., introducing goal-directed behavior. For example, an agent can send messages to itself, starting from its initialization, so that, effectively autonomous behavior is obtained.

The social network simulation system we propose, PyNetSYM (PYthon NETwork Simulation-analYsis-Method), has an elaborate runtime system that supports the execution of simulations providing only brief specifications. Franchi (2012a) provides a more thorough description of the framework, and also presents some examples of how the framework can be used to develop agent-based models.

Design and Implementation of PyNetSYM

After more than 20 years of ABM for social sciences, several tools have been developed to ease the task of running the simulations; among these the most popular are Swarm (Minar et al., 1996), Mason (Luke et al., 2005), RePast (North et al., 2007) and NetLogo (Tisue & Wilensky, 2004), which, however, are not specifically tailored for social network simulations.

In this Chapter, instead, we introduce a different kind of ABM tool that we specifically created for network generation and general processes over networks (Franchi, 2012a). The tool we propose does not aim at being a general-purpose agent-based modeling tool, thus remaining a relatively simple software system, whereas it is extensible where it really matters (e.g., supporting different representations for networks, from simple memory-based ones to pure disk-based storage for huge simulations). Its theoretical foundations lie deep in the generative approach to science that we discussed in the previous section.

From a more practical point of view, the social network simulation system we propose has the following defining goals: (*i*) it must support both small and large networks; (*ii*) simulations shall be effortlessly run on remote machines; (*iii*) it must be easy to use, even for people without a strong programming background; (*iv*) deploying a large simulation should not be significantly harder than deploying a small one.

In our approach, the simulation system has four main components that can be modified independently: (*i*) the user interface, (*ii*) the simulation engine, (*iii*) the simulation model and (*iv*) the network database. The simulation model needs to be specified for each simulation and is the only part that has to be completely written by the user. Its specification is partly declarative and partly object-oriented. The user interface is responsible for taking input from the user, e.g., simulation parameters or information on the analysis to perform, and is specified declaratively. The simulation engine defines the concurrency model of the simulation, the scheduling strategies of the agents and the communication model among the agents. The network database actually holds a representation of the social network; it may be in-memory or on persistent storage, depending on the size of the simulation. Multiple network database implementations are provided and the framework can be extended with additional ones.

Large-scale simulations typically require more resources than those available on a desktop-class machine and, consequently, need to be deployed on external more powerful machines or clusters. In order to simplify the operation, we designed our system so that a simulation can be entirely specified in a single file that can be easily copied or even sent by email.

Considering that the simulations are frequently run on remote machines, we opted for a command line interface, because a traditional GUI becomes more complex in this scenario. An added benefit is that batch executions are also greatly simplified. We also support read-eval-print-loop (REPL) interaction to dynamically interact with the simulation.

In order to allow people without a strong programming background to easily write simulations, we decided to create a Domain-Specific Language (DSL). A Domain-Specific Language (DSL) is a language providing syntactic constructs over a semantic model tailored towards a specific domain (e.g., building software). The idea is that DSLs offer significant gains in productivity, because they allow the developers to write code that looks more natural with respect to the problem at hand than the code written in a general-purpose language with a suitable library.

The central element of the runtime system is the agent, since the elements under simulations and several infrastructure components of the runtime system are implemented as agents. In the following we describe the design characteristics of PyNetSYM agents.

For our purposes an agent is a bounded unit with its own thread of execution. All the communication among the agents occurs through message passing; each agent has a mailbox where the incoming messages are stored, and a unique identifier that is used to address the messages.

Agents also perceive and modify the environment. Our agents are not necessarily autonomic or goal-directed. Since they are used as a computational primitive, we need a lower-level specification that can be enriched to provide "real" agents but which does not place unnecessary overhead on the system.

Another important design decision regarding the system semantics is whether to implement cooperative or preemptive multi-tasking. Several popular languages and platform chose preemptive multi-tasking because in general purpose systems the probability and the risks of a misbehaving application consuming all the CPU time is too high. However, for a simulation oriented platform, such risks are minimal and we opted for cooperative multi-tasking because it allows a more deterministic control of complex time sequences.

As a consequence, in PyNetSYM a method handling a message can only voluntarily "give up"

the execution for a while, either explicitly going to sleep or by requesting a blocking operation. In all other situations, when an agent starts processing a message, it continues until termination. This property is analogue to the semantics of the Actor Model (Agha, 1986) and simplifies formal reasoning on the system. Moreover, from the point of view of the emergent properties of the simulation it has little impact (Bergenti et al., 2013).

When an agent has an empty mailbox, it can choose to be removed from main memory and have its state saved on secondary storage. If the stored agent is subsequently sent a message, it is restored in main memory from the saved state. This behavior is extremely convenient considering that for most social network topologies, a small fraction of agents is responsible for the vast majority of the links. Since in most processes over networks the agents with few links are seldom activated, we can save memory keeping them in secondary storage and do not lose much CPU time.

Another important memory-related issue is the storage of the network itself. A possible solution is completely distributing the knowledge of the network among the agents, so that each agent only knows its neighbors and the network must be reconstructed from their interactions. In order to allow for more efficient implementation of network processes, we provide a global view of the network that is accessible by the agents. From the point of view of ABM, the decision is consistent with the interpretation of the network as the environment, as: (*i*) agents can interact with it by creating or destroying links, and (*ii*) the agents behavior is influenced by the network in several process dependent ways.

This view is presented as a software component that we call network database. The network database provides a unified interface that agents can use to modify and query the network state. We provide multiple implementations in order to be able to balance the various trade-offs. Some implementations are RAM based, and their main advantage a more efficient access when the network is not excessively large; others are backed with various secondary-storage based solutions, which results in slower operations, but they allow for simulations on larger networks.

Structure of the Simulation

The actual simulation is divided in two distinct phases (*i*) setup and (*ii*) execution. During the first phase (setup), the system is initialized so that it reaches the initial configuration specified by the simulation. First, various infrastructural agents (e.g., Activator, NodeManager) are created and started, so that they are ready to receive messages, and the Clock (if present) is also created, but not started.

Later during this phase, the Configurator agent instructs the NodeManager (*i*) to create the initial nodes in the network, (*ii*) to give them instructions to establish the connections they are meant to have at t0, and (*iii*) to provide them with any other initial information that the simulation may require .

The NodeManager is generally responsible for (*i*) creating the new agent-nodes, passing them the appropriate initialization parameters and (*ii*) monitoring them, so that their termination (exceptional or not) is managed.

We created different Configurator agents for the most frequent needs, that are (*i*) reading an initial network specification from disk and setting the system up accordingly, or (*ii*) creating n node-agents of a given kind. When reading network specifications from file, we support (*i*) popular file formats for exchanging networks, such as GraphML or Pajek, (*ii*) networks saved as sparse matrices in HDF5 files, and (*iii*) networks stored in various DBMSs, such as MongoDB.

After configuring the simulation, (*i*) the Configurator agent terminates, and (*ii*) if present, the Clock agent starts, marking the transition to the execution phase, or (*iii*) the node-agents are otherwise notified that the simulation begins.

During the execution phase (second phase) the node-agents perform the simulation according to their behavior. Although from a theoretical point of view such behavior can be completely autonomous and it does not rely on an external time schedule, in practice most network generation models and generic processes over networks can be described in terms of a relatively simple meta-model as the one previously described.

SOCIAL NETWORKING PLATFORMS

Although in the last ten years the pervasive adoption of social networking sites has deeply changed the web, and such sites became an unprecedented social phenomenon (Boyd & Ellison, 2008), clear boundaries regarding the rights and responsibilities of service providers have not been established. Moreover, according to Stroud (2008), web sites have attracted users with very weak interest in technology, including people who, before the social networking revolution, were not even regular users of either popular Internet services or computers in general.

While most users are aware that their profile and the information they publish is essentially public, they usually harden their privacy settings only after problems arise and tend to overlook the actual impact of the information they disclose. Apparently harmless information can be exploited, and the more information the attacker has, the more severe and sophisticated the attack can be.

Privacy in online social networks is always intended as user-to-user privacy: even when the relative settings are set correctly, so that no other user in the system can access information not intended for his eyes, the system itself has full access to information. In fact, in most online social networks, the system owners actually rely on such information to make a profit, for example to improve the accuracy of target advertisement. Unfortunately, as long as they have full access to the information – i.e., the information is stored in the system without cryptography – any security issue or naivety results in privacy violations.

From a technological perspective, online social networks are mostly based on sets of web-based services that allow people to present themselves through a profile, to establish connections with other users in the system and to publish resources. Moreover, these systems use common interests and the natural transitivity of some human relationships to suggest new contacts with whom to establish a connection. Some of these aspects already appeared in other systems, but the unceasing flow of information that users pour in such systems, and their overwhelming intent to increase the number of their virtual friends and acquaintances, are unprecedented.

In other words, what sets social networking sites apart from other services is the *scale* and not the *architecture*. Distribution is used as mean for redundancy and is always *internal*: from the point of view of the users, the social networking system is a centralized system which does not behave differently from a regular website. In fact, these systems are monolithic entities owned by a single company.

As a consequence, service providers are in the position to effectively perform a-priori or a-posteriori censorship, or to disclose all the information they have, no matter how private, to other entities. They can perform such actions either motivated by selfish interests or forced under legal terms and other forms of pressure.

Considering that: (*i*) no single centralized entity can withstand the operative costs of a large scale social networking system without a solid business-plan; (*ii*) most business plans are based on targeted advertisement; and (*iii*) even if a service provider would be fair with its user's data, it would remain vulnerable to legal requests to disclose such data, we favor a P2P approach.

In the first place, P2P systems essentially achieve automatic resource scalability, in the sense that the availability of resources is proportional to the number of users. This property is especially desirable for media sharing social networking systems, considering the exceptionally high amount of resources needed.

Moreover, regarding censorship issues, a P2P system essentially solves them by design. Without a central entity, nobody is in the position of censoring data systematically, nor may be held legally responsible for the diffusion of censorable data: the sole owners and responsible of the data are the users themselves.

Building a P2P social networking platform is an open research challenge, because several simplifying assumptions that centralized platforms make cease to be valid, especially regarding the availability of the data. However, the importance of the problem is such that several researchers have proposed solutions either for full stack platforms (Buchegger & Datta 2009; Buchegger et al. 2009; Cutillo et al., 2009; Graffi et al., 2010) or to allow the distribution of certain aspects of a platform (Xu et al., 2010; Xu et al. 2010b; Perfitt & Englert, 2010)

Blogracy

Blogracy (Franchi & Tomaiuolo, 2013) is our own implementation of a P2P social networking platform. More specifically, it is an anonymous microblogging platform, built incrementally over BitTorrent (Cohen, 2003), a popular and resilient file-sharing service. The architecture of the platform is modular and is built around a module for basic file sharing and DHT operations, possibly exploiting an existing implementation, and another module providing a set of social services to the local user through a Web interface. Moreover, the platform provides two additional agent based modules respectively providing a set of pervasive services and a set of information retrieval and pushing services. In particular, the current prototype of Blogracy takes advantage of; (*i*) Vuze (Vuze, 2012), a popular BitTorrent client implemented in Java and available as open source software, for implementing the file sharing and

DHT operations, and (*ii*) Open Social (OpenSocial and Gadgets Specification Group, 2012), a set of APIs supporting the sharing of social data, for implementing the social services (Figure 2).

For its basic operation, Blogracy uses a P2P file-sharing mechanism and two logically separated DHTs. Users have a profile and a semantically meaningful activity stream, which contains their actions in the system (e.g., add a post, tag a picture, comment). One DHT maps the user's identifier with his activity stream, which also contains a reference to the user's profile and references to user's generated resources (e.g., posts, comments). These references are keys of the second DHT, which are then resolved to the actual files. The files are delivered using the underlying P2P file-sharing mechanism. For more details on Blogracy implementation, we refer to (Franchi & Tomaiuolo, 2013)

The most fundamental problem in a P2P social network is data availability, i.e., the problem to ensure that content placed on the network is accessible after the publisher disconnected. In fact, although popular content rapidly gains lots of seeds, resources published by peripheral users, with few contacts and sparse online presence, can instead suffer poor availability to the extent that the publisher may remain the only seed for his own posts. This issue is strongly related to the churn phenomenon in P2P networks, i.e., the fact that nodes can leave and join the network at arbitrary times.

The availability of a new resource mostly depends on the connection pattern of the source node and its followers. Having a larger number of followers who share the new resources increases the availability of the data itself, especially if some of the followers have an elevated online presence. A single follower with very high availability can guarantee a very good diffusion of data, since every follower in the social graph is also a seed in the file sharing application..

Essentially, low resource availability is especially troublesome for new users with few contacts. For users in these situations, it is relatively hard to enlarge their personal social network, both in terms of (*i*) adding more followees and (*ii*) receiving the attention of new potential followers. Unfortunately, while the solution is straightforward in centralized social platforms, in a distributed setting more care is required.

Since frequent problems regarding data availability may completely doom a social networking platform, because the users would not get the desired content, we started modeling the issues accurately to gather insight from simulations.

Data Availability Simulations

The problem of data availability for badly connected nodes is that some resources may not be available at a given time, and the follower experiences delays in the moment when he is able to actually get the resource. In this Section,

Figure 2. The architecture of the micro-blogging social networking system Blogracy

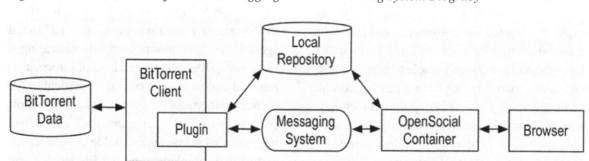

we describe some simulations that we performed in order to quantitatively measure such delays. Wang et al. (2009) and Mega et al. (2012) dealt with accurately modeling the effects of churn in a generic P2P network or in a P2P network with social networks. However, our situation is slightly different, because we do not intend to measure the low level performance of the P2P network. Instead we are interested in the delays perceived by the social networking platform users as a macroscopic phenomenon. As a consequence, less sophisticated models of churn suffice as long as they capture the behavior of social networking users.

More formally, the average notification delay is measured as the average lag between the reception of a new message with respect to the optimal reception time. If a follower is online at the instant when a new message is published, then the optimal reception time is the instant of publication. Otherwise, the optimal reception time is the first time the node goes online again, after the publication. We consider two kinds of nodes: (*I*) nodes connecting occasionally (twice a day, for half an hour); and (*ii*) more stable nodes, which simulate usage in a collaborative work scenario (connecting for 8 hours a day). The intervals are normally distributed around the average values.

In our experiment, each user is modeled as an agent. The agents have "follows" relationships according to an input social network. For the purpose of the simulation, we make the simplifying assumption that the social network is static, because the exchange of messages occurs on a much shorter time scale than modifications to the social network.

At each step of the simulation, some agents are considered online, and a fraction of them also creates new messages. Both newly created and older non-received messages are then exchanged among online agents. Offline followers will receive the messages in successive steps when (and if) they are simultaneously online with another agent that has already received said messages.

Such model can be easily fitted to the meta-model that we described in the previous sections. The Activator decides which agents are to be activated at each step and whether they shall be online as "occasional" users or as "stable" users. Activated agents are online for that step, and if "stable" for some successive steps as well.

At each step, an online agent (*i*) has some tunable probability (in our case 0.01) of creating a new message and (*ii*) receives the messages from its online followees. The step timestamp is then compared to the creation timestamp to determine the lag that occurred before the message was actually received, that is our main measure of system performance.

We performed the experiments simulating communities of different size, from 50 to 350 agents. The plot in Figure 3 represents the notification delays due to churn as a function of the number of followers, for different percentages (0%-25%) of stable nodes. The plot in Figure 4 shows the average notification delay due to churn as a function of the ratio of stable agents for different numbers of followers (50-300).

The delays are quite severe for small communities with few stable agents, however, with 350 nodes the delay is 0 even assuming no stable nodes. On the other hand, for communities larger than 150 agents the delays are negligible with just 5% of stable nodes. Considering that in 2012 an active Twitter user has on average 235 followers and that we expect a non-null ratio of stable users, the results are encouraging (Basch, 2012). An active user is someone who created at least post in the previous 30 days.

CONCLUSION

In this Chapter, we have presented PyNetSYM, a novel language and runtime for network specific simulations. PyNetSYM is built for the generative approach (Epstein, 1999) to science typical of agent-based modeling (ABM). We believe there

Figure 3. Notification delay due to churn as a function of the number of followers, for different percentages (0%-25%) of stable nodes. A stable node is a node connected for ~8h a day. The solid lines are guides for the eye.

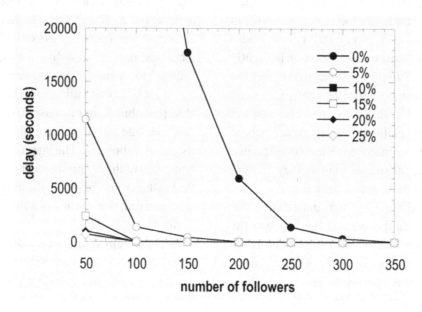

Figure 4. Notification delay due to churn as a function of the ratio of stable nodes for different numbers of followers (50-300). A stable node is a node connected for ~8h a day. The solid lines are guides for the eye.

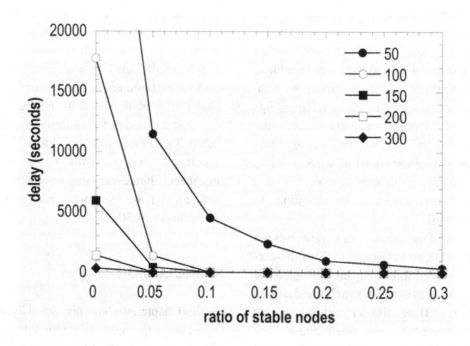

is a strong need for tools that are both: (*i*) easy to use (especially for people with little programming background but with a significant expertise in other disciplines, such as social sciences) and (*ii*) able to tackle large scale simulations, using remote high-performance machines and potentially distributing the computation on multiple servers. Therefore, while our primary goal is maintaining our toolkit simple and easy to use, efficiency is our second priority, since nowadays there is a wide interest on networks of huge size.

Specifically, we created PyNetSYM: (*i*) to easily support both small and huge networks, using either in-memory and on-disk network representations, and (*ii*) to be as easy to be used both on personal machines or on remote servers.

We also used PyNetSYM to simulate the behavior of users in Blogracy, a novel fully distributed social networking platform. Our goal was to understand the condition under which the information propagates to the intended recipients. These experiments confirm our confidence on the soundness of Blogracy architectural design and its realization over solid and widespread technologies, which are meant to provide a relatively large user-base. The results we obtained through simulation show that either (*i*) with small numbers of users (300) and no stable users or (*ii*) with some stable users and very few users the system is still expected to work. Considering that real systems have number of users orders of magnitude larger than the one simulated and that increasing the size of the network the performance improves, we expect it to be a viable option.

Moreover, the simplicity in creating simulations for novel domains shows that our approach is successful in providing a friendly and easy to use environment to perform agent-based simulations over social networks. Agent-based simulation is a powerful conceptual modeling tool for social network simulations and with the present work we contribute a natural and expressive way to specify social network simulations using a DSL.

REFERENCES

Agha, G. (1986). *Actors: A model of concurrent computation in distributed systems*. Cambridge, MA: MIT Press.

Arciero, L., Picillo, C., Solomon, S., & Terna, P. (2014). Building ABMs to control the emergence of crisis analyzing agents' behavior. In *Interdisciplinary applications of agent-based social simulation and modeling*. Hershey, PA: IGI Global.

Arthur, W. B. (1996). *Asset pricing under endogenous expectations in an artificial stock market* (Doctoral dissertation). Brunel University, London.

Arthur, W. B., Durlauf, S., & Lane, D. (1997). *The economy as a complex evolving system II*. Menlo Park, CA: Addison-Wesley.

Axelrod, R. (2003). Advancing the art of simulation in the social sciences. *Japanese Journal for Management Information System*, *12*(3), 1–19.

Axelrod, R. (2007). Simulation in social sciences. In J. Rennard (Ed.), *Handbook of research on nature-inspired computing for economics and management*. Hershey, PA: IGI Global.

Axelrod, R., & Tesfatsion, L. (2006). *A guide for newcomers to agent-based modeling in the social sciences. Handbook of computational economics* (Vol. 2, pp. 1647–1659). Amsterdam, The Netherlands: Elsevier.

Axtel, R., Epstein, J. M., & Young, H. P. (2004). Social dynamics. In *Social dynamics, economic learning and social evolution series*. Cambridge, MA: MIT Press.

Bagni, R., Berchi, R., & Cariello, P. (2002). A comparison of simulation models applied to epidemics. *Journal of Artificial Societies and Social Simulation*, *5*(3).

Barabási, A. L., & Albert, R. (1999). Emergence of scaling in random net- works. *Science, 286*, 509–512. doi:10.1126/science.286.5439.509 PMID:10521342

Basch, D. (2012). *Some fresh Twitter stats (as of July 2012, dataset included)*. Retrieved from http://diegobasch.com/some-fresh-twitter-stats-as-of-july-2012

Bergenti, F., Franchi, E., & Poggi, A. (2011). Selected models for agent-based simulation of social networks. In *3rd Symposium on Social Networks and Multiagent Systems (SNAMAS 2011)* (pp. 27-32).

Bergenti, F., Franchi, E., & Poggi, A. (2012). *Enhancing social networks with agent and Semantic Web technologies. Collaboration and the Semantic Web: Social networks, knowledge networks, and knowledge resources* (pp. 83–100). Hershey, PA: IGI Global. doi:10.4018/978-1-4666-0894-8.ch005

Bergenti, F., Franchi, E., & Poggi, A. (2013). Agent-based interpretations of classic network models. *Computational & Mathematical Organization Theory, 19*(2), 105–127. doi:10.1007/s10588-012-9150-x

Boyd, D. M., & Ellison, N. B. (2008). Social network sites: Definition, history, and scholarship. *Journal of Computer-Mediated Communication, 13*(1), 210–230. doi:10.1111/j.1083-6101.2007.00393.x

Buchegger, S., & Datta, A. (2009, February). A case for P2P infrastructure for social networks-opportunities & challenges. In *Wireless On-Demand Network Systems and Services, 2009. WONS 2009. Sixth International Conference on* (pp. 161-168). IEEE.

Buchegger, S., Schiöberg, D., Vu, L. H., & Datta, A. (2009, March). PeerSoN: P2P social networking: Early experiences and insights. In *Proceedings of the Second ACM EuroSys Workshop on Social Network Systems* (pp. 46-52). ACM.

Burkhart, R., Langton, C., & Askenazi, M. (1996, June). The swarm simulation system: A toolkit for building multi-agent simulations. Santa Fe, AZ: Santa Fe Institute.

Carbonara, N. (2014). Knowledge-based externalities and geographical clusters: An agent-based simulation study. In *Interdisciplinary applications of agent-based social simulation and modeling*. Hershey, PA: IGI Global.

Carley, K. M., Fridsma, D. B., Casman, E., Yahja, A., & Altman, N., C., L.-C., Kaminsky, B., & Nave, D. (2006). Biowar: Scalable agent-based model of bioattacks. *IEEE Transactions on Systems, Man, and Cybernetics. Part A, Systems and Humans, 36*(2), 252–265. doi:10.1109/TSMCA.2005.851291

Castelfranchi, C. (2014). Making visible the invisible hand. The mission of social simulation. In *Interdisciplinary applications of agent-based social simulation and modeling*. Hershey, PA: IGI Global.

Coelho, H., da Rocha Costa, A. C., & Trigo, P. (2014). On agent interactions governed by morality. In *Interdisciplinary applications of agent-based social simulation and modeling*. Hershey, PA: IGI Global.

Cohen, B. (2008). *The bittorrent protocol specification*. Retrieved from http://www.bittorrent.org/beps/bep_0003.html

Cutillo, L. A., Molva, R., & Strufe, T. (2009). Safebook: A privacy-preserving online social network leveraging on real-life trust. *Communications Magazine, 47*(12), 94–101. doi:10.1109/MCOM.2009.5350374

Dean, J. S., Gumerman, G. J., Epstein, J. M., Axtell, R. L., Swedlund, A. C., Parker, M. T., & McCarroll, S. (2000). Understanding Anasazi culture change through agent-based modeling. In T. A. Kohler, & G. G. Gumerman (Eds.), *Dynamics in human and primate societies: Agent-based modeling of social and spatial processes* (pp. 179–205). New York: Oxford University Press, USA.

Epstein, J. M. (1996). *Growing artificial societies: Social science from the bottom up*. Washington, DC: Brookings Institution Press.

Epstein, J. M. (1999). Agent-based computational models and generative social science. *Complexity*, *4*(5), 41–60. doi:10.1002/(SICI)1099-0526(199905/06)4:5<41::AID-CPLX9>3.0.CO;2-F

Epstein, J. M. (2002). Modeling civil violence: An agent-based computational approach. *Proceedings of the National Academy of Sciences of the United States of America*, *99*(Suppl 3), 7243–7250. doi:10.1073/pnas.092080199 PMID:11997450

Epstein, J. M. (2006). *Generative social science: Studies in agent-based computational modeling*. Princeton, NJ: Princeton University Press.

Erdos, P., & Rényi, A. (1959). On random graphs. *Publicationes Mathematicae*, *6*(26), 290–297.

Folcik, V., An, G., & Orosz, C. (2007). The basic immune simulator: An agent-based model to study the interactions between innate and adaptive immunity. *Theoretical Biology & Medical Modelling*, *4*(1), 39. doi:10.1186/1742-4682-4-39 PMID:17900357

Franchi, E. (2012a, August). A domain specific language approach for agent-based social network modeling. In *Advances in Social Networks Analysis and Mining (ASONAM), 2012 IEEE/ACM International Conference on* (pp. 607-612). IEEE.

Franchi, E. (2012b). Towards agent-based models for synthetic social network generation. In *Virtual and networked organizations, emergent technologies and tools* (pp. 18–27). Berlin: Springer. doi:10.1007/978-3-642-31800-9_3

Franchi, E., & Poggi, A. (2011). Multi-agent systems and social networks. In *Business social networking: Organizational, managerial, and technological dimensions* (pp. 84–97). Hershey, PA: IGI Global. doi:10.4018/978-1-61350-168-9.ch005

Franchi, E., & Tomaiuolo, M. (2013). Distributed social platforms for confidentiality and resilience. In L. Caviglione, M. Coccoli, & A. Merlo (Eds.), *Social network engineering for secure Web data and services* (pp. 88–114). Hershey, PA: IGI Global. doi:10.4018/978-1-4666-3926-3.ch006

Friesen, M. R., Gordon, R., & McLeod, R. D. (2014). Exploring emergence within social systems with agent based models. In *Interdisciplinary applications of agent-based social simulation and modeling*. Hershey, PA: IGI Global.

Georgalos, K. (2014). Playing with ambiguity: An agent based model of vague beliefs in games. In *Interdisciplinary applications of agent-based social simulation and modeling*. Hershey, PA: IGI Global.

Graffi, K., Gross, C., Mukherjee, P., Kovacevic, A., & Steinmetz, R. (2010, August). LifeSocial. KOM: A P2P-based platform for secure online social networks. In *2010 IEEE Tenth International Conference on Peer-to-Peer Computing (P2P)*, (pp. 1-2). IEEE.

Hill, R., Carl, R., & Champagne, L. (2006). Using agent simulation models to examine and investigate search theory against a historical case study. *Journal of Simulation*, *1*(1), 29–38. doi:10.1057/palgrave.jos.4250003

Holme, P., & Kim, B. (2002). Growing scale-free networks with tunable clustering. *Physical Review E: Statistical, Nonlinear, and Soft Matter Physics*, 65(2), 2–5. doi:10.1103/PhysRevE.65.026107

Ilachinski, A. (2000). Irreducible semi-autonomous adaptive combat (ISAAC): An artificial-life approach to land combat. *Military Operations Research*, 5(3), 29–46. doi:10.5711/morj.5.3.29

Jackson, M. O. (2010). *Social and economic networks*. Princeton, NJ: Princeton University Press.

Kohler, T. A., Gumerman, G. J., & Reynolds, R. J. (2005). Simulating ancient societies. *Scientific American*, 293, 76–84. doi:10.1038/scientificamerican0705-76 PMID:16008305

Kohler, T. A., & Gummerman, G. J. (Eds.). (2001). *Dynamics of human and primate societies: agent-based modeling of social and spatial processes*. New York: Oxford University Press.

Kumar, R., Novak, J., & Tomkins, A. (2010). Structure and evolution of online social networks. In *Link mining: Models, algorithms, and applications* (pp. 337–357). New York: Springer. doi:10.1007/978-1-4419-6515-8_13

Lucas, P., & Payne, D. (2014). Usefulness of agent-based simulation to test collective decision-making models. In *Interdisciplinary applications of agent-based social simulation and modeling*. Hershey, PA: IGI Global.

Luke, S., Cioffi-Revilla, C., Panait, L., Sullivan, K., & Balan, G. (2005). Mason: A multiagent simulation environment. *Simulation*, 81(7), 517–527. doi:10.1177/0037549705058073

Magessi, N. T., & Antunes, L. (2014). Agent's risk relation on strategic tax reporting game. In *Interdisciplinary applications of agent-based social simulation and modeling*. Herhsey, PA: IGI Global.

Moffat, J., Smith, J., & Witty, S. (2006). Emergent behaviour: Theory and experimentation using the MANA model. *Journal of Applied Mathematics and Decision Sciences*, 2006, 13. doi:10.1155/JAMDS/2006/54846

Mota, F., Santos, I., Dimuro, G., & Rosa, V. (2014). Agent-based simulation of electric energy consumers: The NetLogo tool approach. In *Interdisciplinary applications of agent-based social simulation and modeling*. Hershey, PA: IGI Global.

Nardin, L. G., Rosset, L. M., & Sichman, J. S. (2014). Scale and topology effects on agent-based simulation: A trust-based coalition formation case study. In *Interdisciplinary applications of agent-based social simulation and modeling*. Hershey, PA: IGI Global.

Newman, M. E. J. (2010). *Networks: An introduction. New York*. USA: Oxford University Press. doi:10.1093/acprof:oso/9780199206650.001.0001

North, M. J., Howe, T. R., Collier, N. T., & Vos, J. R. (2007, January). A declarative model assembly infrastructure for verification and validation. In *Advancing social simulation: The first world congress* (pp. 129-140). Japan: Springer.

North, M. J., Macal, C. M., Aubin, J. S., Thimmapuram, P., Bragen, M., & Hahn, J. et al. (2010). Multiscale agent-based consumer market modeling. *Complexity*, 15(5), 37–47.

OpenSocial and Gadgets Specification Group. (2012). *Open social specifications*. Retrieved from http://docs.opensocial.org/display/OSD/Specs

Pastor-Satorras, R., & Vespignani, A. (2001). Epidemic spreading in scale-free networks. *Physical Review Letters*, 86(14), 3200. doi:10.1103/PhysRevLett.86.3200 PMID:11290142

Perfitt, T., & Englert, B. (2010, May). Megaphone: Fault tolerant, scalable, and trustworthy p2p microblogging. In *2010 Fifth International Conference on Internet and Web Applications and Services (ICIW),* (pp. 469-477). IEEE.

Santos, F., Rodrigues, T., Donancio, H., Santos, I., Adamatti, D. F., & Dimuro, G. P. et al. (2014). Multi-agent-based simulation of the social production and management processes in a urban ecosystem: An approach based on the integration of organizational, regulatory, communication and physical artifacts in the JaCaMo framework. In *Interdisciplinary applications of agent-based social simulation and modeling.* Hershey, PA: IGI Global.

Simon, H. A. (1955a). A behavioral model of rational choice. *The Quarterly Journal of Economics, 69*(1). doi:10.2307/1884852

Snijders, T. A. B. (2011). Statistical models for social networks. *Annual Review of Sociology, 37*(1), 131–153. doi:10.1146/annurev.soc.012809.102709

Stroud, D. (2008). Social networking: An age-neutral commodity — Social networking becomes a mature web application. *Journal of Direct. Data and Digital Marketing Practice, 9*(3), 278–292. doi:10.1057/palgrave.dddmp.4350099

Tisue, S., & Wilensky, U. (2004, May). Netlogo: A simple environment for modeling complexity. In *International Conference on Complex Systems* (pp. 16-21).

Trigo, P. (2014). Multi-agent economically motivated decision-making. In *Interdisciplinary applications of agent-based social simulation and modeling.* Hershey, PA: IGI Global.

Vuze. (2012). *Vuze software.* Retrieved from http://www.vuze.com/.

Wang, X., Yao, Z., & Loguinov, D. (2009). Residual-based estimation of peer and link lifetimes in P2P networks. [TON]. *IEEE/ACM Transactions on Networking, 17*(3), 726–739. doi:10.1109/TNET.2008.2001727

Watts, D. J., & Strogatz, S. (1998). Collective dynamics of small-world networks. *Nature, 393*(6684), 440–442. doi:10.1038/30918 PMID:9623998

Xu, T., Chen, Y., Fu, X., & Hui, P. (2011). Twittering by cuckoo: Decentralized and socio-aware online microblogging services. *ACM SIGCOMM Computer Communication Review, 41*(4), 473–474.

Xu, T., Chen, Y., Zhao, J., & Fu, X. (2010, June). Cuckoo: Towards decentralized, socio-aware online microblogging services and data measurements. In *Proceedings of the 2nd ACM International Workshop on Hot Topics in Planet-scale Measurement* (pp. 4). ACM.

KEY TERMS AND DEFINITIONS

Agent-Based Model: A class of computational models for simulating interacting agents.

Multi-Agent System: A loosely coupled network of software agents that interact to solve problems that are beyond the individual capacities or knowledge of each software agent.

Peer-to-Peer System: A network based system in which each node can act as both client and server for the other ones of the system.

Social Networking System: A network based system facilitating the building of social networks.

Software Agent: A computer program that is situated in some environment and capable of autonomous action in order to meet.

Chapter 12
Social Space in Simulation Models

Davide Nunes
University of Lisbon, Portugal

Luis Antunes
University of Lisbon, Portugal

ABSTRACT

In real world scenarios, the formation of consensus is a self-organisation process by which actors have to make a joint assessment about a target subject, be it a decision making problem or the formation of a collective opinion. In social simulation, models of opinion dynamics tackle the opinion formation phenomena. These models try to make an assessment, for instance, of the ideal conditions that lead an interacting group of agents to opinion consensus, polarisation or fragmentation. This chapter investigates the role of social relation structure in opinion dynamics and consensus formation. The authors present an agent-based model that defines social relations as multiple concomitant social networks and explore multiple interaction games in this structural set-up. They discuss the influence of complex social network topologies where actors interact in multiple distinct networks. The chapter builds on previous work about social space design with multiple social relations to determine the influence of such complex social structures in a process such as opinion formation.

INTRODUCTION

In social simulation, the way one defines social spaces is determinant to construct relevant scenarios to target problems. Moreover, such spaces have a deep influence in results of the simulations by imposing restrictions that guide or filter agent interactions. In this chapter, we discuss the connection between models of social structures and phenomena observed in simulations at a macro level. We conduct a series of experiments to highlight the relevance of proper social space design considerations, when creating social simulation models.

In agent-based social simulation models, the way we deal with social structure varies according to multiple factors. These models may span across multiple levels of abstraction and are usually targeted for specific phenomena in order to shed light on some complex process that follows

DOI: 10.4018/978-1-4666-5954-4.ch012

a set of observed properties. Examples of social space models include: the usage of discrete grids or lattices in which agent interaction is restricted to certain neighbourhoods. Cellular automata (CA) models make use of such regular grids and are increasingly used to study a variety of social dynamics (Flache & Hegselmann, 2001). Other common approach, is the usage of generative procedures to create random network structures exhibiting real-world properties such as the celebrated Barabási-Albert model of preferential attachment (Barabási & Albert, 1999). The preferential attachment mechanism generates network models with scale-free properties, these properties can be observed in real-world structures such as the World Wide Web (Barabási, Albert, & Jeong, 2000). Other existing models try to describe aspects of real-world social networks. The work in (Hamill & Gilbert, 2009) for instance, gets inspiration from the notion of social circles to model key aspects of large real social networks such as low density, high clustering and preferential-attachment-like behaviour of degree of connectivity.

In this chapter we aim to present and discuss available modelling methodologies to design social spaces for simulation models; we also discuss the need for more complex social space designs, presenting our approach to model multiple concurrent social relations; finally we aim to discuss the influence of social networks in self-organisation phenomena such as consensus and opinion formation. We describe a model of opinion dynamics with multiple social networks and compare our work with existing literature on opinion dynamics and diffusion models.

One of the main subjects of this chapter is the study of models of social networks and how they affect social phenomena. It is important to notice that the study of models of social structure and their impact on simulation models is valuable not only as a contribution to complexity sciences, but also to develop new managerial tools and systems that can be used to deal with real problems. Complexity theory didn't deliver a *general theory of complex*

organisations yet, but the efforts in the last couple of decades generated many useful components such as modelling methodologies and simulation at different levels of abstraction. While these tools do not capture the complete set of properties from the world they mirror, the study of hierarchical structures, networks of interaction, non-linearity and emergence (see chapter 1) generated useful and in some cases practical understanding about observable properties (Cilliers, 2001). Simulation in general and social simulation in particular have allowed us to build bridges between the micro components of complex systems (that we know as facts or conjecture about its existence) and the macro effects of the processes being studied.

Taking the random models of complex networks as an example, while these are built based on known properties of real complex systems, this does not mean that they incorporate all the known properties of these systems (Hamill & Gilbert, 2009). Notwithstanding their limitations, their simplicity allows us to better understand the properties being modelled and take advantage of this knowledge to create solutions for complex problems. Models such as the Watts & Strogatz model (Watts & Strogatz, 1998), generate networks with low diameter and high clustering coefficient. Such properties are desirable for the construction of large-scale peer-to-peer networks because these make the topologies extremely robust. As such, these types of networks have been used to engineer peer-to-peer systems (Liu, Mackin, & Antonopoulos, 2006). While most of the models are simplified descriptions of the real-world, many models constitute complex systems themselves and thus the necessity of tools like simulation to explore their properties. In (Emmeche, 1997), Emmeche makes a distinctions between two types of complexity. Simply put, he characterises the complexity of real systems as *"ontological complexity"* and the complexity of models as "descriptive complexity." When using social network models as social spaces for social simulation, even thought, these models are characterised as *complex,* real social networks display a level of complexity much higher than their respective *descriptions.* Social network models, capture particular properties of the real world but these properties are just portrayals of different aspects of real network topologies. Moreover, our work tries to *describe* the complexity of real social relations by considering multiple social networks at the same time. We explore how different properties of different models influence the outcomes of our simulations. We aim to take the existing social space design methodologies and scale-up their descriptive complexity without compromising the analysis of our models.

The second subject of the chapter is consensus formation. Understanding trends, opinions and consensus within a population can help us to construct coherent views or possible explanations for real-world mechanisms such as the joint assessments of a policy, the impact of viral marketing or voting behaviours. We use a simple game of consensus (Antunes et al., 2009; Nunes & Antunes, 2012) and a model of continuous opinion dynamics to test the influence of our social space design approach on different social dynamics models (Nunes, Antunes, & Amblard, 2013).

The chapter is organised as follows. In the related work section, we review the state-of-the-art in social space modelling methodologies. We also describe the current literature on opinion dynamics and consensus formation models and discuss the connection between abstract social space models and real-world structures with similar properties. We also contextualise the research here presented by trying to create a connection to existing theories of social identity and formation of social networks. In a following section, we present our approach to model complex social simulation scenarios in which agents interact in multiple social networks. We then present a series of experiments designed to explore the influence of different social structures in a self-organisation process of consensus formation. Finally, we conclude by discussing

the simulation results and pointing out future research directions for social space modelling methodologies.

RELATED WORK

In this section, first we briefly discuss the work related to models of social structure. We review the literature dealing with models of social networks, bi-dimensional grids and other approaches such as probabilistic mechanisms to select pair-wise interactions. We then present the work related to models of consensus formation, dissemination phenomena and models of continuous and discrete opinion dynamics.

Models of Social Structure

One of the paradigmatic approaches to represent interaction spaces in abstract social simulation models is the usage of regular bi-dimensional grids. This approach stemmed from the first "checkerboard" models introduced in computational social sciences by Schelling (Schelling, 1971) and Sakoda (Sakoda, 1971). Another famous example that uses bi-dimensional grids as social structure is the social simulation model of dissemination of culture from Axelrod (Axelrod, 1997).

Cellular automata (CA) also make use of bi-dimensional structures to model neighbourhood interactions. While these models are simple (idealised) frameworks, the exploration of simple computational models can bring us deeper insights than models with high levels *descriptive complexity* which would render their analysis, very difficult. The work of Flache and Hegselmann (Flache & Hegselmann, 2001) relaxes the standard CA assumptions about the regular bi-dimensional grids by considering irregular grid structures (Voronoi diagrams). This work presents results on the robustness of some important general properties in relation to variations in the typical grid structure.

Bi-dimensional grids are just one of the idealistic models to represent neighbourhood structures. Going beyond the typical techniques to structure CA, we can find approaches that can incorporate both the complexity of random graph / network model structures and the behaviour of dynamic processes. One example of this combination is the work in (O'Sullivan, 2000) which explores a *graph-based cellular automaton* to study the relationship between spatial form of urban systems and the robustness of different process dynamics under spatial change. Moreover this allows for the integration of real geographical information to construct the graph-cellular automata. This fact makes so that while the models of dynamic processes are relatively abstract, they are tested in spatial structures based on data from real complex structures and thus making a connection between purely abstract models and data-driven models.

Previously, we briefly mentioned another type social network models; random graph / network models. Each complex network or class of complex networks, presents specific topological features which characterise its connectivity and the influence on processes that depend on their topology. One of the first complex network model is *the random graph model* from Erdős and Renyi (1959). Other examples include the already referred model of preferential attachment (Barabási & Albert, 1999) and the small-world network models (Watts & Strogatz, 1998). One common problem of these models is the fact that once generated, the network structure is static so these models are not really suitable for the description of highly dynamic groups or communities. An example of a model that takes these dynamics into account is the model of team formation (Gaston & desJardins, 2005). A more in-depth review of network models and their properties is given in (Nunes, 2012).

Finally, there are examples of interaction models that do not use explicit representations of social relationships. Instead, the interaction mechanism can be purely probabilistic and select agents from a population to perform pair-wise interactions. In these methodologies, agents do not make decisions of which products to buy, which technology to adopt, whether or not to become educated, whether to learn a language or how to vote, and so forth based on their explicit social network. Agents rather accumulate experience through the simulation conditioned by the probabilistic mechanism. An example of this approach is the model of Pesendorfer (1995), where he describes the spread of a new fashion as well as its decay over time using different probabilistic matching mechanisms. Some approaches of selecting the agents then generate fashion cycles and thus this approach could be valuable to ask questions such as: in what way does a population of agents need to be connected in order to exhibit a specific matching pattern? The reader is referred to Yariv and Jackson (2008) for a review on multiple diffusion models and how these incorporate social structure.

While idealistic models have their advantages, in real-world scenarios, actors engage in a multitude of social relations. These relations are different in kind and, while some network models display interesting properties that can be found in real systems, it is very unlikely that these properties reflect the complexity of the multiple social relations one actor engages in. In this chapter we present our modelling approach that uses multiple network models and explores the relationship between each social network. This methodology allows to explore different scenarios where agents can have different levels of dedication to different social relations and even behave differently in different contexts. Note that when we talk about contexts, we refer to a particular set of social relations that one agent maintains, family, friends or co-workers. These contexts are represented in our model as the neighbourhoods each agent has in the different networks.

Most simulation models don't explore social space designs that take into account the differentiation between *coexisting social structures*. Modelling multiple concomitant social relations was an idea pioneered by Peter Albin (1975) but it was never explored much beyond the original proposal. This configuration allows for the comprehension of a variety of real-world dynamics such as, e.g., the impact of on-line social media political campaigns or what is the impact of online social networks in decision making process of an individual. Furthermore, such complex social structures are the basis for the formation of social identity (Ellemers et al., 2002; Roccas & Brewer, 2002). Although we don't deal with the micro Psychological constructs of social identity directly, our model of multiple social relations tries to model this from a macro perspective. By engaging in multiple social networks simultaneously, each agent accesses a network topology that results from the entanglement of different social contexts. These multiple of social relations characterise the agent social identity and can be seen as ego network constructed by combining multiple networks.

In the context of social network analysis (SNA), an ego network is a network consisting of a single actor (ego) together with the actors they are connected to (*alters*). From an empirical point of view, these types of networks are attractive because of the ease of data collection compared with collecting data on whole networks. Information on the *alters*, including how they are connected, is usually obtained entirely from ego. Such structures can be sampled from large populations and can be used to make statistically significant conclusions about the whole population (Everett & Borgatti, 2005). For a detailed discussion on the statistical significance of social simulation model results see chapter 3.

Opinion Dynamics and Consensus

In social simulation, models of opinion formation try to make an assessment of the ideal conditions that lead a group of agents to opinion consensus, polarisation or fragmentation for example. One of the first concerns for the modelling of these

subjects was found in the context of economics and political science, the voting problem. The issues surrounding voting behaviour modelling were investigated in an early model proposed by Herbert Simon (1954).

Opinion dynamics models provide an understanding of opinion formation processes. An early formulation of these types of models was designed to analyse complex phenomena found empirically in groups (French, 1956). In particular, the work on consensus formation in the context of decision-making was first explored by DeGroot (DeGroot, 1974) and Lehrer (Lehrer, 1975). Empirical studies of opinion formation in large populations have methodological limitations. Simulation, in particular Multi-Agent Simulation (MAS), provides a methodological framework to study such phenomena in a larger scale. While this framework is useful, we should not forget that we cannot observe or analyse real-world opinion formation in these computational models, what we are doing is creating what-if-scenarios to test assumptions about real-world opinion formation processes. Modelling can be useful to gain insight about the target process and can even be used as a tool to guide an empirical study, but it does not replace it.

The majority of the opinion dynamics simulation models represent opinions of agents either as binary values (Antunes et al., 2009; Galam, 1997) or continuous opinion values (Deffuant, Neau, Amblard, & Weisbuch, 2000; Hegselmann & Krause, 2002). Agents update their opinions either under social influence or according to their own experience. A review on opinion dynamics model analytical and simulation results can be found in (Hegselmann & Krause, 2002).

Weisbuch's bounded confidence model (Weisbuch, 2004) uses random social network models to structure agent interactions and analyses the influence of different network topologies in the outcome of the opinion formation process. A first definition of opinion dynamics with bounded confidence was given by Krause in (Krause, 1997).

The experiments and models presented in this chapter build on previous work by applying the construction of social spaces with social networks to a model of continuous opinion dynamics, the relative agreement (RA) model (Deffuant et al., 2002). This model is an extension of the bounded confidence model (BC) (Weisbuch, 2004) by exploring the influence of the multiple networks in the formation of consensus. While Deffuant and Weisbuch explored their models with multiple networks, our work explores social structures with multiple social networks at the same time and compares the results with the single network approaches.

The work in (Antunes et al., 2009; Nunes & Antunes, 2012a) studies the influence of the multiple network design by applying a simple game of consensus formation that can be treated as a binary opinion dynamics model in which agents want to reach consensus about two possible opinion values and use a simple rule of majority to decide which opinion to take based on their neighbour opinions at a given time in the simulation. This model with be defined in the next section. The multi network social space is tested in terms of robustness using two different opinion dynamics models. In (Antunes et al., 2010; Antunes et al., 2009) it is found that by considering coexisting social relations, the agent population converges to a global consensus both faster and more often

under certain circumstances. Like with the previous discussion about models of social structure the review of the literature in (Yariv & Jackson, 2008) contains insights about both social structure modelling and different processes of diffusion ranging from models of epidemics to marketing, trends and innovation.

MULTI-LAYER SOCIAL SPACES AND INTERACTION MODELS

In this section we present and discuss our model of multiple social relationships as well as the opinion dynamics models used to test our social space design in terms of robustness. We analyse how different compositions of networks allow for consensus to be reached faster or more often and what are the structural properties of the multiple networks that allow this to happen.

The multi-context approach (Antunes et al., 2010, 2009) considers a multitude of concomitant social relations to represent the complex social space of an agent. This setting can be seen in a simulation as a n-dimensional set-up where each dimension represents a different social relations (see Figure 1) modelled with a social network generated using a model like the Barabási-Albert (BA) model (Barabási & Albert, 1999) or the Watts & Strogatz model (Watts & Strogatz, 1998). Agents

Figure 1. Multiplex social network structure forming the social space for our models of multiple concurrent social relations. In our models a set of agents is assigned to a node on each network leading to possible overlaps in their neighbourhoods.

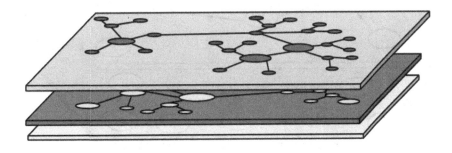

belong to distinct neighbourhoods which we call contexts. Some neighbourhoods may overlap over the multiple dimensions and this is what we call context permeability (Antunes et al., 2010).

Within this multi-layer scenario we experimented with multiple mechanisms to deal with how agents engage in the various networks. The first approach (Antunes et al., 2010) considered was one in which the agents populate the several views on social reality and interact simultaneously (see Figure 2). This becomes very restrictive if you consider distinct contexts in scenarios such as going home, spending time with your friends or travelling to a new country. The current results for this modelling approach (Antunes et al., 2009; Nunes et al., 2013) are promising and show that this allows consensus to be reached faster and more often. Agent reactiveness and the simplicity of the interaction game is intended to focus on the emergence of consensus and opinion formation processes. Other approaches in social simulation might explore different aspects for instance cognition or decision making of agents in certain situations. See chapter 15 for instance, in which moral behaviour of agents is the focus of the simulation models. Chapter 17 on the other hand, describes the simulation and modelling of collective decision making processes.

Context Switching Model

The next mechanism we adopted to study the influence of multiple networks was the context switching model (Antunes et al., 2009). In this model, similarly to the previous one, a population of N agents populates multiple social networks. The difference is that in this model each agent is active only in one context at a time. In each simulation step, the agents select a neighbour from their current context (neighbourhood in the current social network) and update their opinion according to some rule. At the end of each interaction an agent switches to a different network with a probability ζ_c in which c is the current context / network (see Figure 3). The ζ_c probability is a parameter associated with each social network and it is valid for all the agents in that network. This allows for modelling of time spent in each context, in an abstract way. We can think of context switching as a temporary deployment in another place, such as what happens with temporary immigration. This mechanism of switching *from* a particular network with a probability is what is explored in the results presented in this chapter.

One limitation that can be pointed out in this model, is the fact that we don't model context switching as a structured action. What we mean with this is that, in real world scenarios, actors

Figure 2. Different relations for the same agents

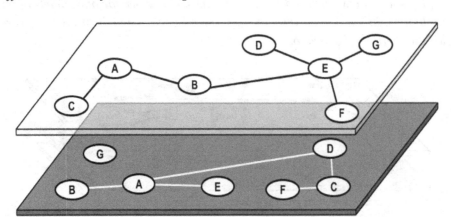

Figure 3. Example of context switching (Antunes et al., 2009) considering two contexts (belonging to two different networks) for a social agent denoted by the number 1. In this case, these contexts are created by two distinct physical spaces. Common nodes in both neighbourhoods (like agent 2) represent the same social actor being able to travel between both distinct contexts, representing an acquaintance of actor 1 in both of them. The dashed circle represents the scope of each context in the network.

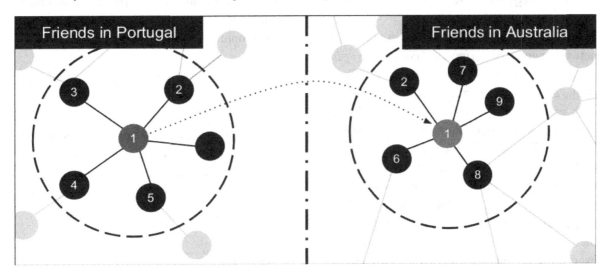

might not only dedicate different amounts of time to different contexts but also be engaged in different groups and communities that dictate local dynamics for this process. While this is true, modelling these processes requires more in-depth knowledge about their dynamics and adequate empirical evidence to characterise them. Moreover, the study of such dynamics is not the current target of study and thus our decision to keep this mechanism abstract. Our objective is to observe the influence of the multi-relational modelling approach in social dynamics focusing on the entanglement between multiple social networks.

Binary Consensus by Majority

We conducted experiments with two different interaction models of opinion dynamics. In the first model, the agents have to decide between two possible values. The objective of the game is to analyse under what circumstances the agent society reaches total consensus (all agents with the same opinion value). In this first consensus game, the agents update their opinion values as follows:

1. Choose an available neighbour from the current context randomly (neighbourhood of the network structure where the agent is currently located);
2. check the selected interaction partner current choice and increment the memory for the number of individuals "seen" with that choice;
3. check for the choice that has the majority and switch to it if the current opinion differs;

At the end of each interaction, an agent in a context C_i switches to a random distinct context C_j (in a different network) with a probability ζ_{Ci} (switching probability associated with the context / network C_i). It follows that one agent can only be active in one network at each time in the simulation and agents can only select agents that are active in their current context to interact.

For clarification, we designate this process as *consensus by majority*.

Continuous Opinions with Relative Agreement

The second model that was tested in our multi-network scenario was a model of *continuous opinion dynamics with relative agreement* (Deffuant et al., 2002; Nunes et al., 2013). In this model, each agent i is characterised by two variables, its opinion x_i and its uncertainty u_i both being real numbers. The opinion values are drawn from a uniform distribution between -1 and 1. This model can be seen as an extension of the Bounded Confidence (BC) model (Weisbuch, 2004). In the BC model, the agents have continuous opinions and the interactions are non-linear. The agents only exert influence on each other if their opinions are within a certain fixed threshold. The threshold can be interpreted as an uncertainty, or a bounded confidence, around the opinion. It is assumed that agents do not take into account opinions out of their range of uncertainty.

The RA model differs from the BC model in the fact that the change in an opinion x_j of an agent j under the influence of an agent i, is proportional to the overlap between the agent opinion segments (the agreement), divided by the uncertainty of the influencing agent uncertainty u_i. Another difference is that the uncertainty is not fixed, the value of u_j is also updated using the same mechanism. The opinion and uncertainty updates are illustrated in Figure 4.

The opinion overlap h_{ij} is given by:

$$h_{ij} = \min(x_i + u_i, x_j + u_j) - \max\left(x_i - u_i, x_j - u_j\right) \quad (1)$$

The opinion and uncertainty values are updated according to the following equations. As an example, the opinion x_j and the uncertainty u_j of agent j is updated according to equation 2 and 3 respectively, if $h_{ij} > u_i$.

$$x_j' = x_j + \mu\left(\frac{h_{ij}}{u_i} - 1\right)\left(x_i - x_j\right) \quad (2)$$

$$u_j' = u_j + \mu\left(\frac{h_{ij}}{u_i} - 1\right)\left(u_i - u_j\right) \quad (3)$$

where μ is a constant parameter that controls the speed of the dynamics.

Figure 4. Agent i (with the opinion xi and the uncertainty ui) influences agent j (with the opinion x_j and the uncertainty u_j). In this case, h_{ij} is the overlap between the agents and $2_{ui} - h_{ij}$ is the non-overlapping part. On the left is the representation of the opinion and uncertainty of agent j, on the right, the dashed lines represent the position of the segment before the interaction and the plain lines, the final values for the these two properties.

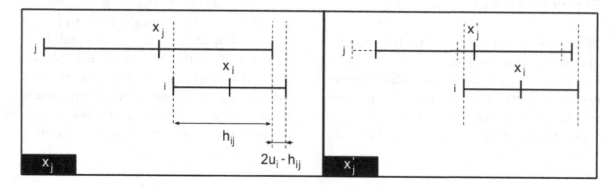

The agent population is initialised with an initial uncertainty value U. Similarly to the previous consensus by majority, the agents update their opinion values as follows:

1. Choose an available neighbour from the current context randomly (neighbourhood of the network structure where the agent is currently located);
2. Update agent i and j opinions and uncertainties according to the equations 2 and 3.

Like in the previous consensus model, the agents switch from a network according to the same switching probability mechanism. In the following section we present our results and discuss the robustness of our model against these two distinct interaction behaviours that generate different dynamics.

MODEL OF EXPERIMENTS AND RESULTS

In this section we present our experiment design, the important results for each game of consensus under our design of social space with multiple social networks. We discuss the results comparing the models both in terms macro phenomena observed and in terms of differences that lead to different outcomes.

The simulation model was created using MASON (Luke et al., 2005) and executed in a grid environment described in (Nunes & Antunes, 2012b). In each experiment, a population of 300 agents interacts until 3000 cycles pass or the opinion values stabilise. We perform 30 simulation runs for each parameter combination considered in all the results presented in this chapter. While a grid is not necessarily a priority when constructing social simulation models, we use it to reduce the time necessary to explore the parameter space resulting from multiple network configurations and context switching probability combinations

with multiple networks. The computational model is very simple but the exhaustive exploration of the parameters to generate response surfaces is very time consuming.

The results that follow are focused on the analysis of the dynamics induced by the context switching mechanism. We spanned the switching parameter (ζ_{Ci}) from 0 to 1 in intervals of 0.05 with two contexts. With this, we obtained a response surface with the average number of encounters necessary to achieve consensus for the multiple configurations of switching values attributed to each network. We also vary the network topologies in these contexts. In summary the objective is to analyse how different combinations of context switching probabilities and network structures affect the speed of convergence to stable opinion values with both the *binary consensus by majority* and the *relative agreement* model.

For the *relative agreement* model we set the initial uncertainty parameter to $U = 1.4$ as previous work (Deffuant et al., 2002) with single networks suggested that this value guaranteed the convergence in one central opinion value instead of polarisation. What we aim to achieve with this is to prevent the interactions from being filtered by the uncertainty levels while the opinion values do not stabilise. The models were tested using three standard models for networks: *k-regular networks*, providing a uniform connectivity (same number of connections) for each agent; *scale-free networks*, generated using the Barabási-Albert (BA) model (Barabási & Albert, 1999); and *small-world network*, generated using the Watts & Strogatz (WS) model (Watts & Strogatz, 1998).

Model Verification and the Effects of Connectivity

To validate the models and compare the results with previous work we performed a series of experiments with single networks. Using a parameter k (that controls the network connectivity) with the values $k = \{1, 2, 3, 4, 5, 10, 20, 30, 40, 50\}$. Figure

Figure 5. Average number of meetings necessary to achieve convergence to stable opinion values with a single network context (without switching). Results for k-regular, WS small-world with p = 0.1 and BA scale-free networks.

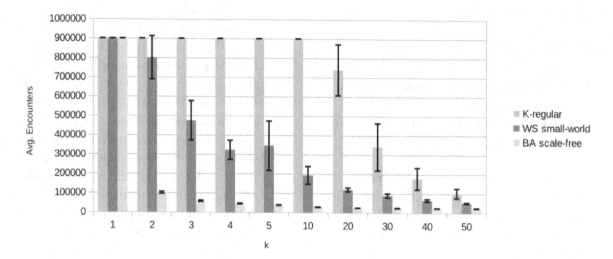

5 shows the results of these experiments single *k-regular*, *WS small-world* and *BA scale-free* networks applied to the model of continuous opinion dynamics with relative agreement (Nunes et al., 2013). For the result on the model of *consensus by majority* the reader is referred to (Antunes et al., 2009). For the regular networks the parameter k controls the connectivity with each agent having $2k$ neighbours. For the *small-world* networks, this parameter is used to construct an initial *k-regular* structure from which each connection is rewired with a probability $p = 0.1$ to shorten then average path length while maintaining the high clustering. For the *scale-free networks* the k is the minimum degree for each node.

We can see that the maximum value of encounters is limited by the maximum number of simulation cycles allowed. In this particular case, the models that display the maximum number of encounters did not converge to stable opinion values. Here we are trying to analyse the conditions in which the simulation converges to stable opinion clusters rather than total consensus. This model includes an additional interaction filter mechanism that progressively restricts the neighbours from

which an agent can be influence. Although in most cases we reach total consensus, with the model of relative agreement, the values of uncertainty decrease over time (and with it the number of agents that update their opinion). Moreover, this may lead to situations where agents converge to multiple opinion clusters (Deffuant et al., 2002).

We can also see that for $k \geq 2$, *scale-free* networks seem to outperform the other models in terms of convergence speed. We will see in following results that the approach with multiple networks allows the opinion formation process to converge both faster and more often because agents are exposed to multiple networks which creates a certain permeability for the diffusion of opinions.

Regular Networks

We first we focus on the analysis of how the switching probabilities affect the opinion formation game with a social structure built by two *k-regular* networks. We span the context switching values from *0* to *1* in intervals of *0.05*. Figure 6 depicts the landscapes for this parameter span for relative agreement model. We create two layers

Figure 6. Meetings to achieve convergence to stable opinion values with ζ ∈ [0.2, 1] and two 30-regular networks.

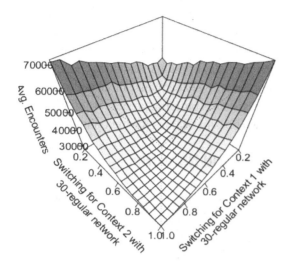

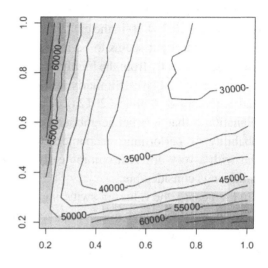

each one with a k-regular network with *k = 30*. Regular networks offer an easy way to model highly clustered populations of agents. Regular networks also provide a convenient way to observe the influence of neighbourhood size in the opinion stabilisation process, as the connectivity structure is equal for all the agents. Note that whenever we show the results for the values *ζ ∈ [0.2, 1]*, it is because for *ζ < 0.2*, the simulation does not converge to stable opinion values (similarly to what

happens in Figure 11) so we choose this region as the region of interest.

In the next experiment, we created a scenario to observe the effects of different connectivity levels for each context. Figure 7 depicts the span of the switching probability within the values ζ ∈ [0.2, 1]. The first context is now a 10-regular network (each agent has 20 neighbours) while the second is a 50-regular network (each agent having a total of 100 neighbours). As we can

Figure 7. Meetings to achieve convergence to stable opinion values with for ζ ∈ [0.2, 1]. In this case, we use a 10-regular and a 50-regular for context 1 and 2 respectively.

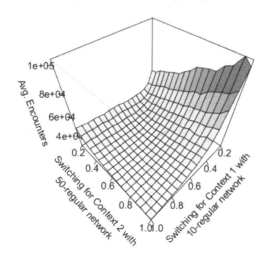

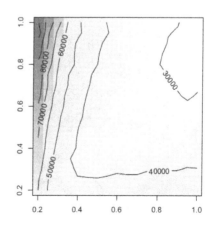

see the asymmetry in the connectivity has clear effects in the convergence to stable opinion values. In this case, we find that if an agent stays more time ($\zeta \in [0.2, 0.3]$) in the context with the lowest connectivity it seems to be important to switch less frequently from the highly connected and clustered social layer. Similarly results were found in (Nunes & Antunes, 2012a). A possible explanation is that in larger neighbourhoods, the probability of performing encounters with an agent with a very different opinion early in the simulation is considerable.

In both cases, the values of switching $\zeta \in [0, 0.2]$ result in either a high number of encounters necessary to achieve table opinion values, or this stabilisation never happens. The results are the same for the game of *consensus by majority* with a binary opinion value (Antunes et al., 2009).

Comparing these results with the analysis for the game of *consensus by majority* we observe some differences in the patterns that emerge. The effects of the switching probability are still more regular than those we will discuss for the other types of networks, the effects of switching with a

binary opinion game result in switching more often being bad for the convergence to consensus (see Figure 8). This happens because of the differences in the binary opinion game. The opinion updates in the *relative agreement* model are much smoother than with binary opinions. A sudden change of an opinion for an agent can cause more perturbations in the consensus building process when you only have two possible values for the opinions.

Small-World Networks

We then conducted a series of experiments with WA small-world networks (Watts & Strogatz, 1998). These topologies are constructed by re-wiring regular networks, introducing increasing amounts of disorder. Moreover, we can construct highly clustered networks, like k-regular networks or bi-dimensional grids or lattices, yet with small characteristic path lengths, like random graphs. They are called small-world by analogy with the phenomenon (Travers & Milgram, 1969), popularly known as six degrees of separation. This phenomena refers to the idea that everyone is on

Figure 8. Average number of encounters to achieve consensus for two 10-regular networks and $\zeta \in [0.2,1]$ (Antunes et al., 2009) in a majority game with binary opinions.

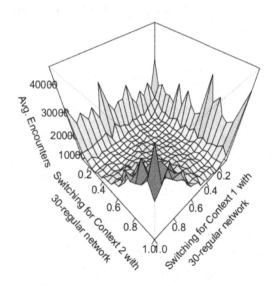
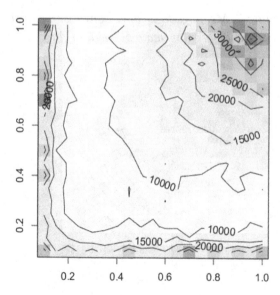

average approximately six steps away, by way of introduction, from any other person on Earth. Figure 9 and 10 show the results for a set-up with two WS networks with $k = 30$ and a rewiring probability of $p = 0.1$ and $p = 0.6$ respectively. The value of $p = 0.1$ for the rewiring, introduces enough disorder in the network to lower the average path length without sacrificing the clustering coefficient too much. In Figure 9, we can see that the influence is very similar to the previous results with regular networks (see Figure 6) but the reduction in the path length causes the model to converge more rapidly for higher switching probabilities.

Although the switching probability seems to cause greater disturbance on the response surface for $p=0.6$, the number of encounters seem to be almost homogeneous throughout the switching vales $\zeta_{Ci} > 0.3$. Also, as the number of necessary

encounters is a slightly lower, it seems that high values of switching are more important when the networks possesses highly clustered nodes.

Scale-Free Networks

For the experiments with scale-free networks, we used network with a minimum connectivity of $k = 1$. They maintain their properties while being very sparse networks. This allowed us to compare the results with the model with binary opinions and to make other observation. With the relative agreement model, while we didn't get convergence with a single *scale-free* network, adding a second network enabled both stable opinion values and consensus to be reached. Figure 11 shows the response surface for this scenario.

Figure 9. Average number of encounters to achieve convergence to stable opinion values for two Watts & Strogatz small-world networks generated with initial degree k = 30 and rewiring probability p = 0.1. The switching values are spanned across ζ ∈ [0.2, 1].

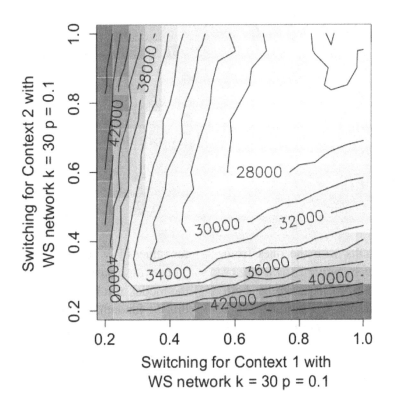

Figure 10. Average number of encounters to achieve convergence to stable opinion values for two Watts & Strogatz small-world networks generated with initial degree k = 30 and rewiring probability p = 0.6.The switching values are spanned across ζ ∈ [0.2, 1].

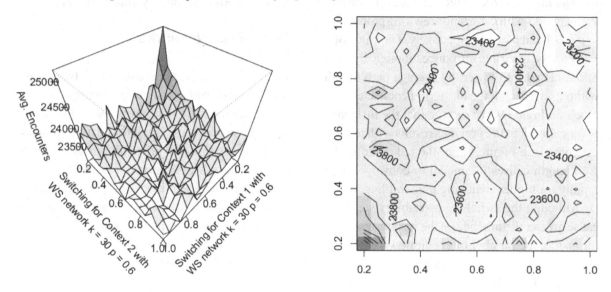

Figure 11. Average number of encounters to achieve convergence to stable opinion values for two scale-free networks with minimum degree k = 1. The switching values are spanned from ζ ∈ [0, 1].

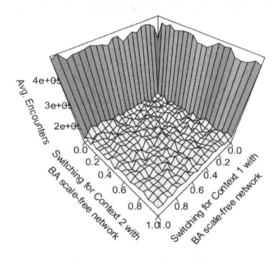
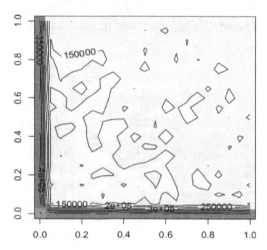

Comparing the results with the ones from the model of consensus by *majority with binary opinions* (see Figure 12), we observe that both interaction games cause perturbations in the response surface and still present better results for values of switching ζ > 0.2, proximately. The game with binary opinions seems to outperform the model of relative agreement. The reason for this the fundamental differences of the games.

CONCLUSION AND FUTURE RESEARCH DIRECTIONS

This chapter shows that the usage of different network model structures plays an important role when modelling opinion or consensus formation processes. This is a key point discussed both in the work of

Antunes et al. (Antunes et al., 2009) and Amblard et al. (Deffuant et al., 2002; Jager & Amblard, 2004) from which this work originates. Also, multi-network models seem to unveil interesting phenomena resulting from the interplay of different social dimensions. This methodology seems a promising approach to complement the existing paradigms. This modelling approach for social scenarios still needs more exploration and a more explicit connection to complex real-world scenarios. A final note on the previous work should go to the comparison between scenarios with multiple networks and scenarios with a single network. While we did not perform this comparison in this chapter, a deeper discussion is provided in (Antunes et al., 2010, 2009) in which a fair comparison is made. The purpose of the presented discussion was not focused on this as-

pect, but rather on the exploration of the dynamics induced by the different network models and the different consensus games or opinion dynamics.

In terms of research directions, we identify one major necessity to advance the current state-of-the-art in modelling social structures. The current literature on social simulation that considers random network models seems stagnated around the usage of the usual scale-free, random and small-world graph models. Numerous new models have been developed such as the one in (Hamill & Gilbert, 2009), and should be compared with the more commonly used ones to assess their usefulness.

Another possibility for the extension of the work here presented is for instance the exploration of the question: what is the influence of individuals with high centrality in a network in the final opinion values. We also intend to perform more in-depth experiments with our model of multiple networks and support this model with data from real online social networks. This can create a bridge between a model that is now purely abstract and real-world structures, allowing insights in the model to be used to understand how this new layer of social interaction created in the Web is influencing social behaviours.

Figure 12. Average number of encounters to achieve consensus for two scale-free networks and $\zeta \in [0.2, 1]$ in a majority game with binary opinions.

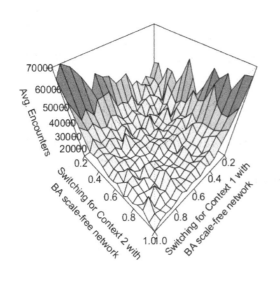
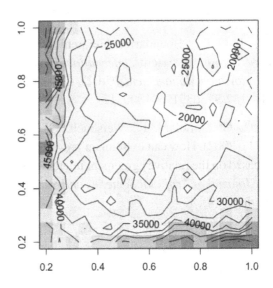

REFERENCES

Albin, P. S. (1975). *The analysis of complex socioeconomic systems*. Lexington, MA: Lexington Books.

Antunes, L., Balsa, J., Urbano, P., & Coelho, H. (2010). Exploring Context permeability in multiple social networks. In K. Takadama, C. Cioffi-Revilla, & G. Deffuant (Eds.), *Simulating Interacting agents and social phenomena* (Vol. 7, pp. 77–87). Japan: Springer. doi:10.1007/978-4-431-99781-8_6

Antunes, L., Nunes, D., Coelho, H., Balsa, J., & Urbano, P. (2009). Context switching versus context permeability in multiple social networks. *Progress in Artificial Intelligence, 5816*, 547–559. doi:10.1007/978-3-642-04686-5_45

Axelrod, R. (1997). The dissemination of culture. *The Journal of Conflict Resolution, 41*(2), 203–226. doi:10.1177/0022002797041002001

Barabási, A.-L., & Albert, R. (1999). Emergence of scaling in random networks. *Science, 286*(5439), 509–512. doi:10.1126/science.286.5439.509 PMID:10521342

Barabási, A.-L., Albert, R., & Jeong, H. (2000). Scale-free characteristics of random networks: The topology of the world-wide Web. *Physica A: Statistical Mechanics and its Applications, 281*(1-4), 69–77. doi:10.1016/S0378-4371(00)00018-2

Cilliers, P. (2001). Boundaries, hierarchies and networks in complex systems. *International Journal of Innovation Management, 05*(02), 135–147. doi:10.1142/S1363919601000312

Deffuant, G., Amblard, F., Weisbuch, G., & Faure, T. (2002). How can extremism prevail? A study based on the relative agreement interaction model. *Journal of Artificial Societies and Social Simulation, 5*(4), 1.

Deffuant, G., Neau, D., Amblard, F., & Weisbuch, G. (2000). Mixing beliefs among interacting agents. *Advances in Complex Systems, 3*(01n04), 87–98.

DeGroot, M. H. (1974). Reaching a consensus. *Journal of the American Statistical Association, 69*(345), 118–121. doi:10.1080/01621459.1974.10480137

Ellemers, N., Spears, R., & Doosje, B. (2002). Self and social identity. *Annual Review of Psychology, 53*(1), 161–186. doi:10.1146/annurev.psych.53.100901.135228 PMID:11752483

Emmeche, C. (1997). Aspects of complexity in life and science. *Philosophica, 59*(1), 41–68.

Erdős, P., & Rényi, A. (1959). On random graphs. *Publ. Math. Debrecen, 6*, 290–297.

Everett, M., & Borgatti, S. P. (2005). Ego network betweenness. *Social Networks, 27*(1), 31–38. doi:10.1016/j.socnet.2004.11.007

Flache, A., & Hegselmann, R. (2001). Do irregular grids make a difference? Relaxing the spatial regularity assumption in cellular models of social dynamics. *Journal of Artificial Societies and Social Simulation, 4*(4), 6.

French, J. P. R. J. (1956). A formal theory of social power. *Psychological Review, 63*, 181–194. doi:10.1037/h0046123 PMID:13323174

Galam, S. (1997). Rational group decision making: A random field Ising model T = 0. *Physica A: Statistical Mechanics and its Applications, 238*(1), 66–80.

Gaston, M. E., & desJardins, M. (2005). Agent-organized networks for dynamic team formation. In *Proceedings of the Fourth International Joint Conference on Autonomous Agents and Multiagent Sytems* (pp. 230–237).

Hamill, L., & Gilbert, N. (2009). Social circles: A simple structure for agent-based social network models. *Journal of Artificial Societies and Social Simulation*, *12*(2), 3.

Hegselmann, R., & Krause, U. (2002). Opinion dynamics and bounded confidence: Models, analysis and simulation. *Journal of Artificial Societies and Social Simulation*, *5*(3), 2.

Jager, W., & Amblard, F. (2004). Uniformity, bipolarization and pluriformity captured as generic stylized behavior with an agent-based simulation model of attitude change. *Computational & Mathematical Organization Theory*, *10*, 295–303. doi:10.1007/s10588-005-6282-2

Krause, U. (1997). In U. Krause, & M. Stöckler (Eds.), *Soziale Dynamiken mit vielen Interakteuren. Eine Problemskizze in Modellierung und {S}imulation von {D}ynamiken mit {V}ielen {I}nteragierenden {A}kteuren* (pp. 37–51). Modus, Universität Bremen.

Lehrer, K. (1975). Social consensus and rational agnoiology. *Synthese*, *31*(1), 141–160. doi:10.1007/BF00869475

Liu, L., Mackin, S., & Antonopoulos, N. (2006). Small world architecture for peer-to-peer networks. In *Proceedings of the 2006 IEEE/WIC/ACM international Conference on Web Intelligence and Intelligent Agent Technology* (pp. 451–454). Washington, DC: IEEE Computer Society. doi:10.1109/WI-IATW.2006.123

Luke, S., Cioffi-Revilla, C., Panait, L., Sullivan, K., & Balan, G. (2005). MASON: A multiagent simulation environment. *Simulation*, *81*(7), 517–527. doi:10.1177/0037549705058073

Nunes, D. (2012). *Exploration, design and analysis of social spaces for social simulation models* (MSc Dissertation). University of Lisbon, Portugal.

Nunes, D., & Antunes, L. (2012a). Consensus by segregation - The formation of local consensus within context switching dynamics. In *Proceedings of the 4th World Congress on Social Simulation, WCSS 2012*.

Nunes, D., & Antunes, L. (2012b). Parallel execution of social simulation models in a grid environment. In *Proceedings of the 13th International Workshop on Multi-Agent Based Simulation, MABS 2012*. Retrieved from http://www.Webcitation.org/67vbjSGuB

Nunes, D., Antunes, L., & Amblard, F. (2013). Dynamics of relative agreement in multiple social contexts. In L. M. Correia, L. P. Reis, & J. M. Cascalho (Ed.), *Proceedings of the 16th Portuguese Conference on Artificial Intelligence* (pp. 456–467). Berlin: Springer. doi:10.1007/978-3-642-40669-0_39

O'Sullivan, D. B. (2000). *Graph-based cellular automaton models of urban spatial processes* (PhD Dissertation). University of London.

Pesendorfer, W. (1995). Design innovation and fashion cycles. *The American Economic Review*, 771–792.

Roccas, S., & Brewer, M. B. (2002). Social identity complexity. *Personality and Social Psychology Review*, *6*(2), 88–106. doi:10.1207/S15327957PSPR0602_01

Sakoda, J. M. (1971). The checkerboard model of social interaction. *The Journal of Mathematical Sociology*, *1*(1), 119–132. doi:10.1080/0022250X.1971.9989791

Schelling, T. C. (1971). Dynamic models of segregation. *The Journal of Mathematical Sociology*, *59*(2), 143–186. doi:10.1080/0022250X.1971.9989794

Simon, H. A. (1954). Bandwagon and underdog effects and the possibility of election predictions. *Public Opinion Quarterly, 18*(3), 245–253. doi:10.1086/266513

Travers, J., & Milgram, S. (1969). An experimental study of the small world problem. *Sociometry, 32*(4), 425–443. doi:10.2307/2786545

Watts, D. J., & Strogatz, S. H. (1998). Collective dynamics of small-world networks. *Nature, 393*(6684), 440–442. doi:10.1038/30918 PMID:9623998

Weisbuch, G. (2004). Bounded confidence and social networks. *The European Physical Journal B - Condensed Matter and Complex Systems, 38*(2), 339–343.

Yariv, L., & Jackson, M. O. (2008). Diffusion, strategic interaction, and social structure. In Benhabib, Bisin, & Jackson (Eds.), *Handbook of social economics*. Elsevier. Retrieved from http://www.hss.caltech.edu/~lyariv/Papers/DiffusionChapter.pdf

Edmonds, B. (2010). Bootstrapping knowledge about social phenomena using simulation models. *Journal of Artificial Societies and Social Simulation, 13*(1), 8.

Epstein, J. M. (2006). *Generative social science: Studies in agent-based computational modelling.* Princeton University Press.

Fagiolo, G., Valente, M., & Vriend, N. J. (2007). Segregation in networks. *Journal of Economic Behavior & Organization, 64*(3), 316–336. doi:10.1016/j.jebo.2006.09.003

Granovetter, M. S. (1973). The strength of weak ties. *American Journal of Sociology,* 1360–1380. doi:10.1086/225469

Lorscheid, I., Heine, B. O., & Meyer, M. (2012). Opening the 'black box' of simulations: increased transparency and effective communication through the systematic design of experiments. *Computational & Mathematical Organization Theory, 18*(1), 22–62. doi:10.1007/s10588-011-9097-3

ADDITIONAL READING

Axelrod, R. (2006). Advancing the art of simulation in the social sciences. In *Simulating Social Phenomena, volume 456 of LNEMS. Springer, 1997. João Balsa, Luis Antunes, Ana Respício, and Helder Coelho. Autonomous inspectors in tax compliance simulation. In Proc. 18th European Meeting on Cybernetics and Systems Research.*

Borgatti, S. P., Mehra, A., Brass, D. J., & Labianca, G. (2009). Network analysis in the social sciences. *science, 323*(5916), 892-895.

KEY TERMS AND DEFINITIONS

Agent: Software entity with independent component behaviour that can range from primitive reactive decision rules to complex adaptive intelligence.

Agent-Based Modelling and Simulation: Is a computationally demanding technique having its origins in discrete event simulation and cellular automata. The systems are modelled using autonomous, interacting agents.

Simulation Model: Technique to represent or abstract a process or behaviour for analytical, decision support or learning purposes.

Social Network Model: Description that characterises a network intended to capture some properties from real-network structures. Random network models can be viewed as algorithms to generate a network structures with a given set of properties based on a stochastic method.

Social Space: A social space is physical or virtual space where individuals interact being a physical space or a virtual one like an online social network.

Section 3
Developing Reliable Interdisciplinary Applications of Agent–Based Social Simulation and Modeling

Chapter 13
Simulating an Incentive Framework for Scientific Production by Means of Adaptive Agents

Gabriel Franklin
Federal University of Ceará, Brazil

Tibérius O. Bonates
Federal University of Ceará, Brazil

ABSTRACT

This chapter describes an agent-based simulation of an incentive mechanism for scientific production. In the proposed framework, a central agency is responsible for devising and enforcing a policy consisting of performance-based incentives in an attempt to induce a global positive behavior of a group of researchers, in terms of number and type of scientific publications. The macro-level incentive mechanism triggers micro-level actions that, once intensified by social interactions, lead to certain patterns of behavior from individual agents (researchers). Positive reinforcement from receiving incentives (as well as negative reinforcement from not receiving them) shape the behavior of agents in the course of the simulation. The authors show, by means of computational experiments, that a policy devised to act at the individual level might induce a single global behavior that can, depending on the values of certain parameters, be distinct from the original target and have an overall negative effect. The agent-based simulation provides an objective way of assessing the quantitative effect that different policies might induce on the behavior of individual researchers when it comes to their preferences regarding scientific publications.

INTRODUCTION

The saddest aspect of life right now is that science gathers knowledge faster than society gathers wisdom. (Isaac Asimov)

It can be argued that one of the main differences between social and natural sciences lies in the methods used to assess their results. While natural sciences can rely on empirical procedures for evaluating their hypotheses, social sciences are seldom in a position to use such an approach,

DOI: 10.4018/978-1-4666-5954-4.ch013

mostly due to ethical questions and to the absence of instrumental conditions for allowing the construction of a reasonable experimental environment.

Agent-based models for social simulation provide an alternative to overcome those difficulties. They both rule out the ethical concerns – after all, no human subjects are involved in the experiments – and accomplish the necessary instrumental conditions, by means of proper computational modeling of the simulated environment.

A generally accepted statement is that our organizations (whether we are talking about government agencies or private companies) fairly regulate the distribution of rewards/recognition to high-performance individuals by means of incentive mechanisms. In most aspects of life, one is encouraged to pursue ever higher standards of performance, which are often arbitrarily set by a central agency, such as the government or the upper management of an organization. In order to reach this goal, one is typically "led by example," in such a way as to replicate (or, at least, approximate) the behaviors of a few examples of successful individuals, or prototypical models of success.

In this chapter we model an incentive framework for scientific production, in which agents are individual researchers that take decisions regarding what type of scientific journals they should target as potential vehicles for publicizing their work. A central agency is responsible for evaluating the performance of each researcher (in terms of published work) and providing an incentive that temporarily increases the researcher's productivity. The framework's policies regarding how to evaluate scientific publications and how to define rules for providing incentives are parameters of the simulation. Agents interact in a non-deterministic way, adjusting their preferences for scientific journals as they see fit, in light of the observed successes of their peers, as well as their own.

While decision-makers responsible for defining the framework's policies might have the best collective interests of the scientific community in mind, it is possible that certain choices of parameters of the framework lead to undesirable results. Specifically, it is possible that the aggregate numbers obtained at the macro level reflect a scenario of increased productivity that is not accompanied by an effort from individual researchers to engage in high-quality scientific investigation. Different policies might induce different behaviors from researchers and journals, some of which can be negative, as recently reported by Van Noorden and Tollefson (2013). Therefore, using agent-based models to simulate certain aspects of research incentive policies might be a useful way to assess potential risks.

The remainder of this chapter is organized as follows. First, we present the operant behavior theory (Skinner, 1965) and its presence in the institutions' (governmental or private) praxes. In addition, we discuss some recent studies about aspects of human behavior dynamics in academia. Next, we present the details of our social simulation model, specifying its parameters and the rules that control and induce agent behavior. Finally, we discuss the results obtained via simulation of different scenarios, tracing a parallel between B. F. Skinner's operant conditioning (Skinner, 1965) and Thomas Schelling's micromotives and macrobehavior (Schelling, 2006). We will argue that these two theories can be combined in order to better capture human behavior dynamics, whether individually or collectively.

OPERANT CONDITIONING AND HUMAN BEHAVIOR DYNAMICS

On Human Behavior

Human behavior is a highly unpredictable phenomenon. While the behavior of markets, gene regulatory networks and other natural, complex phenomena can be analyzed and understood to a certain extent, human behavior remains unpredictable and indomitable. Despite being unpredictable, human beings can be induced to present certain patterns of behavior, i.e., it is possible to increase the probability of a certain kind of behavior from an individual.

There are several ways of obtaining a specific kind of behavior from an individual. Perhaps the most ethically sound way, though not the most effective one, is inducing *behavioral mimetism*, a term we introduce here to denote the disposition of an individual to follow the examples of their peers. It is in the very nature of human beings to emulate behaviors that result in benefits.

Inducing behavioral mimetism might be an inefficient way of obtaining a specific behavior due to the time needed for a response. Depending on the scenario considered, it might take a long time before one has enough observation data to define success/failure parameters and, thus, the intended behavior might take an excessive time to be detected.

Operant conditioning (Skinner, 1965) is a typically more efficient way of obtaining a behavior than behavioral mimetism. It is based on a reinforcement scheme to promote the occurrence of the intended outcome. Reinforcements can be positive or negative and are associated with the presence or absence of a certain behavior, respectively. In operant conditioning, specific behavior is encouraged by offering prizes (positive reinforcement) or discouraged by means of punishments (negative reinforcements).

"The principal technique employed in the control of the individual by any group of people who have lived together for a sufficient length of time is as follows. The behavior of the individual is classified as 'good' or 'bad' or, to the same effect, 'right' or 'wrong' and is reinforced or punished accordingly" (Skinner, 1965).

Operant conditioning is very common in our daily lives, despite our inability to perceive all of its manifestations. Moreover, usually when we are aware of being subject to operant conditioning, our reaction is often one of repelling such practice, regarding it as abusive, arbitrary, or even oppressive. Nevertheless, operant conditioning is used by governmental institutions and private institutions alike. After all, in practice, the actions of both types of organizations are equivalent with respect to the intention of eliciting certain behaviors[1].

Human Behavior Dynamics in Academia

Watts and Gilbert (2011) proposed an agent-based simulation in which scientific publications are generated with data such as authors, reference and contents. A collective learning strategy is employed to guide the choice of such data by the authors of each paper. Papers are then analyzed by reviewers and accepted or rejected for publication. The model is used to analyze practices that lead to the cumulative advantage reported by previous studies (Merton, 1988), in which a new paper usually refers to papers that already have large numbers of citations. This phenomenon leads to a minority of papers and authors being cited very frequently, while the majority of papers and authors are rarely cited. Watts and Gilbert (2011) report that "practices leading to cumulative advantage in citations […] do not improve scientists' ability to find good solutions to scientific problems, compared to those practices that ignore past citations."

Ozel (2012) proposes a "conceptual framework to study diffusion of knowledge via collaborative social interactions." The framework examines mechanisms of knowledge diffusion and collaboration structure within an academic social network. The framework is applied to analyze knowledge diffusion and collaboration structures in the management science academic community in Turkey. Among other findings, the study reports on the detection of cohesive collaborating teams, as a result of a demand for publishing in citation indexed journals.

Both studies discussed above address important issues associated with the dynamics of human behavior in aspects related to academic activities. While the approaches pursued in those articles are significantly distinct from the one described in this chapter, there are aspects, such as information diffusion, article contents and authorship, that are present in each of the three studies. We also remark that the policy diffusion study in Chapter 7 of this volume can be related to the model we propose in this chapter. Indeed, if we consider the emphasis of a researcher as a manifestation of his/her own policy regarding scientific production, then long-term exposure to a researcher's policy might influence other researchers.

SIMULATING INCENTIVES

In this section we present a novel computational model developed for studying the dynamics of preferences of researchers in an arbitrary field of study, with respect to which scientific journals they choose for publicizing their work, and in presence of positive reinforcements in the form of financial incentives.

By means of a computational simulation (see, e.g., Gilbert (2005), Gilbert (2008) and Miller and Page (2009)), we show that a policy devised to act at the individual level might induce a single global behavior that can be distinct from the original target and have an overall negative effect, even though the individual behavior being reinforced is one of a desirable nature. The simulated environment is one of a governmental institution that manages and supports scientific research activity within a certain territory.

Publications, Agents and the Simulation Environment

We assume that the institution in question manages a system of incentive to research based on the publication of academic articles in specialized media. In order to do so, it uses operant conditioning mechanisms to achieve its results, offering prizes (in the form of monetary incentives) to researchers that achieve a certain level of performance

within a given period, and punishments (absence of incentive until the next period) to those who were out of the profile pattern.

To preserve democratic principles, and to avoid that the entire system be regarded as "arbitrary," the institution establishes a ranking of scientific journals that defines a partition of journals into three groups or strata, according to the quality and importance of each journal, as perceived by the academic community and measured by citation indices (see, e.g., Gilbert (1997)). The published work of a researcher is evaluated with respect to the relevance of individual articles, as judged according to the group to which the article belongs.

By means of this score and prize system the expectation is that of an increase in the number of scientific publications with high quality in the territory, fomenting high quality scientific activity. This outcome can be projected as an extrapolation of the individual behavior of researchers as they engage in research that might produce enough results to warrant the publication of articles belonging to the highest level stratum. However, we show that the outcome achieved may be different from the one expected, suggesting that a superficial analysis of human behavior dynamics might lead to an incorrect forecast.

In the remainder of this section we describe the three main components of our social model: scientific publications, researchers (agents), and the environment. Scientific publications correspond to sets of scientific journals with similar characteristics, such as: rejection rates (i.e., the rate of articles rejected to the total number of articles submitted within a given period), impact factors, and perceived reputation. Researchers have a direct correspondence with individual scholars that are expected to engage into scientific publishing, in an effort to both divulge their work and attract financial support to further their research agenda. The environment component encapsulates the policies implemented by a central agency, as well as the relationships between agents and between agents and scientific publications. The simulation is conducted iteratively over the course of several epochs, called *evaluation cycles*.

Scientific Publications

We consider a simplified scenario in which scientific journals are partitioned into three strata or types (say, A, B and C, in decreasing order of reputation), that we refer to simply as *scientific publications*. Rather than modeling the details of a specific group of journals, we only assume that any two journals belonging to a given stratum have approximately the same likelihood of accepting any given article. By assuming such a partition, we avoid modeling the probability distribution of rejection rates, what would constitute a challenge, given that rejection rates are usually not publicly available and cannot be objectively estimated, in general (see Schultz (2010) and Freyne et al. (2010)). Impact factor is also not unanimously regarded as an accurate indicator of the quality of a journal, although it is acknowledged as an important factor (see Freyne et al. (2010)). Therefore, we believe that assuming a three-way reputation-based partition of the spectrum of scientific journals in a specific field is a reasonable simplification of journal rankings. Moreover, such a simplification is unlikely to introduce more arbitrary modeling artifacts than any of the standard approaches for distinguishing individual journals.

Each stratum has two features: *acceptance probability* and *reputation score*. Acceptance probability is a value between 0.0 and 1.0 that corresponds to the likelihood that an arbitrary article submitted to a journal in that stratum is accepted (this value is directly related to the rejection rate of a journal or conference, a measure that is usually associated with the quality of that journal/conference). The reputation score of a journal is a positive integer value that is roughly proportional to the average reputation of a journal in that stratum. It is used as a way of determining how many articles of each stratum a researcher can produce during a single evaluation cycle.

Researchers

Each researcher (an agent in our framework) is endowed with four features, that are discussed below: intrinsic productivity, productivity coefficient, publication emphasis and neighborhood size.

The *intrinsic productivity* of a researcher is a fixed amount of points that is randomly and independently assigned to each researcher at the beginning of the simulation. The points of a researcher can be invested by the researcher during each evaluation cycle with the objective of producing scientific articles. This number is constant throughout the entire simulation and is uniformly distributed between two parameters of the simulation: MinPointsPerAgent and MaxPointsPerAgent.

The *productivity coefficient* of a researcher is a real value between 1.0 and 2.0, which is multiplied by the researcher's intrinsic productivity, in order to obtain their *true productivity*, or simply, their *productivity*. Each point in a researcher productivity corresponds to one score in a scientific publication's reputation score. Therefore, if a scientific publication has a reputation score of 10, any researcher must use 10 points out of its productivity in order to produce an article that qualifies for submission to a journal in that group. Note that qualifying for submission to a given scientific publication is not equivalent to acceptance for any given article. The criterion for qualifying for submission is a device for modeling the amount of work that a researcher typically must invest in order to produce an article of a certain caliber. In the next subsection we describe how the productivity coefficient is related to incentives and operant conditioning.

The *publication emphasis* of a researcher specifies on which types of scientific publication the researcher prefers to invest their true productivity. The emphasis of researcher r is defined as the tuple $E(r)=(E_A, E_B, E_C)$, where E_i specifies the priority of the scientific publication i, for i in

{A,B,C}. Each tuple contains positive real numbers and must sum up to 1.0. Thus, each value in *E(r)* corresponds to the percentage of points in the researcher productivity that is assigned to the associated scientific publication. If this number of points is fractional, the number is rounded up, whenever this rounding does not exceed the researcher's productivity.

The *neighborhood size* of a researcher is a number that specifies how many fellow scholars the researcher observes in order to assess their own performance relative to the average performance of their peers. The actual neighborhood of a researcher is randomly assigned at the end of each evaluation cycle, but the size of the researcher's neighborhood is determined at the beginning of the simulation and remains constant. Its actual value is randomly determined in the interval from 1 to MaxNumberOfNeighbors. This value is used to model the fact that certain researchers are more likely than others to adjust their own publication emphasis based on the emphasis of their colleagues, especially in view of evidence that certain publication emphases are more prone to lead to positive performance evaluations than others.

Environment and Agent Dynamics

In our social model the environment encapsulates the policies of a central agency, as well as the relationships between the other components of the model: researchers and scientific publications.

At the beginning of the simulation, a number of values are determined which influence the development of the simulation. The reputation scores of scientific publications, as well as their acceptances probabilities, are parameters of the simulation. So are the minimum and maximum number of points assigned to each researcher (MinPointsPerAgent and MaxPointsPerAgent) and the maximum number of neighbors a researcher might have (MaxNumberOfNeighbors). Each researcher receives an initial value of 1.0 for their productivity

coefficient, while random values are assigned to their emphasis tuple (ensuring that the sum of the values in the emphasis tuple equals 1.0).

The central agency is responsible for:

1. Assigning neighbors to each researcher at the end of each evaluation cycle;
2. Deciding which researchers are deemed productive during each evaluation cycle; and
3. Providing incentives to productive researchers, in the form of increments to their respective productivity coefficients.

In the remainder of this section we discuss the relationship between a researcher *r* and their neighbors, the criterion for deciding whether or not *r* was productive during a given evaluation cycle, and how changes in *r*'s emphasis are carried out.

Researcher-Publication Interactions

The reputation score of each scientific publication determines both the number of points a researcher must invest in order to produce an article in that stratum and the number of points earned by the researcher in return for the acceptance of such an article. Below we describe how a researcher invests and earns points in our framework.

A researcher earns points in a probabilistic way, according to the acceptance probability (AP) of the scientific publication to which the researcher made a submission. Let us assume, for instance, that the AP of stratum B is 70%. Then, for each article submitted to a journal in that stratum, a random decision is made by the simulation environment regarding the acceptance of the article, with a 70% chance of acceptance. The decisions regarding the acceptance of articles are independent and uniformly distributed. At the end of each evaluation cycle, every researcher might have submitted a number of articles, with this number being dependent on the researcher's emphasis, intrinsic productivity and productivity coefficient. Obviously, a researcher can only earn as many points as they have invested in scientific publications.

Every researcher that earns points in excess of a certain number (which we shall call the *qualifying threshold*) is assigned a "prize," consisting of a relative increase in their productivity during the subsequent evaluation cycle. This relative increase in productivity is implemented as a multiplication of the researcher's productivity coefficient by 1.2, i.e., an increase of 20% in its value. Whenever a researcher is assigned a prize at the end of an evaluation cycle, we say that the researcher was *successful* or *productive* during that evaluation cycle. If a researcher was not considered productive during the current evaluation cycle, the value of their productivity coefficient is reset to 1.0 before the following evaluation cycle begins.

This mechanism of productivity increase is intended to capture the potential boost in future academic performance that results of a researcher receiving funding from a governmental or private agency on the basis of its current academic performance, or on the basis of the merits of a research proposal (Freyne et al., 2010). Regardless of the criterion used for granting financial benefit to a researcher, it is reasonable to consider that additional funding fuels scientific production, which in turn is likely to sponsor more innovation and to increase the chances of the researcher receiving extra funding. In the event that the researcher remains productive for a number of evaluation cycles, the upper bound of 2.0 for the productivity coefficient enforces a realistic limit on the researcher's productivity, with respect to the baseline of a non-productive researcher.

A simple procedure is carried out by each researcher in order to determine how many scientific publications of each group he/she will attempt to publish in the current cycle. We illustrate the procedure by means of a small example, in which we show how a researcher r invests their true productivity in order to produce scientific publications, according to the priorities dictated by their publication emphasis. Let us consider that researcher r has intrinsic productivity 25,

productivity coefficient of 1.2 (as a result of being productive in the previous evaluation cycle) and the following publication emphasis tuple: $E(r)=(E_A, E_B, E_C)=(0.25, 0.45, 0.3)$. Let us also assume that the qualifying threshold of the simulation is 22 and that the three scientific publication strata have the following characteristics:

- **Stratum A:** Acceptance probability = 20%, reputation score = 10;
- **Stratum B:** Acceptance probability = 50%, reputation score = 8;
- **Stratum C:** Acceptance probability = 80%, reputation score = 4;

The true productivity of r is given by the product between their intrinsic productivity and their productivity coefficient: $25 \times 1.2 = 30$. Thus, in principle, r's true productivity is enough to produce a set of articles that, if accepted, would qualify r as productive in the current cycle. Starting from stratum A, we determine how many points the researcher will devote to producing articles in that stratum. Thus, $0.25 \times 30 = 7.5$. This value is rounded up to 8, since there is enough points in the researcher's productivity to allow for such rounding to take place. Since 8 is less than the reputation score of scientific publication A, then no A-type articles are produced by r in the current cycle. Next, stratum B is considered: $0.45 \times 30 = 13.5$ points are reserved for B-type articles. This value is also rounded up, since there are still $30 - 8 = 22$ points available to be invested by the researcher. Since stratum B has a reputation score of 8, r can produce only one article in that stratum. Finally, the remaining number of points that can be used to produced articles in stratum C is $30 - 8 - 14 = 8$. That amounts to two articles in that stratum. Therefore, researcher r will engage into the production of one article in stratum B and two articles in stratum C during the current cycle. In the event that all three articles are accepted for publication, only 16 points will be achieved by r, meaning that r has no chance of being regarded as productive in the current cycle.

Researcher-Researcher Interactions

After productive researchers have been determined at the end of an evaluation cycle, the environment assigns to each researcher r a number of distinct researchers that equals r's neighborhood size. We shall denote this set by $C(r)$, and refer to the elements of this set as the neighbors of r during the current cycle. Prior to the end of the cycle, r observes the emphasis of each member of $C(r)$, as well as the fact of whether or not each member of $C(r)$ qualified as a productive researcher in the current cycle.

Based on this information, researcher r can decide on updating their own emphasis. If there is an imbalance between r's emphasis and the emphases of successful colleagues in $C(r)$, then an update on r's emphasis is justified. Moreover, this update should be more pronounced if r was not productive in the current cycle. To compute this update, r must compare the emphasis of each productive neighbor in $C(r)$ to their own, recording the difference vector between them, i.e., the tuple resulting from taking the difference between r's emphasis and that of the productive neighbor. Summing up all those difference vectors, and multiplying this sum by $1/M(r)$, where $M(r)$ is the number of successful neighbors in $C(r)$, provides a direction D along which the emphasis tuple of r should be updated.

If r was successful in the current cycle, a minor change is applied to r's emphasis. If r was not successful, a larger adjustment is made to r's emphasis, as a way of bringing it closer to the emphases of those successful colleagues in $C(r)$ and hopefully increasing the chances of r being productive during the forthcoming evaluation cycle. Thus, operant conditioning takes place both in case of a positive and of a negative outcome. Indeed, a minor change in r's emphasis is indicative of a positive reinforcement, since r is induced to maintain its current publication emphasis. On the other hand, a negative reinforcement can be associated with the larger changes to r's emphasis that result from r being unsuccessful in the current evaluation cycle.

The actual change applied to r's emphasis is dictated by two additional parameters of the simulation: MinUpdatingCoefficient and Max-UpdatingCoefficient. If r was successful in the current cycle, then the direction of change D is multiplied by MinUpdatingCoefficient, and the result is added to r's emphasis tuple. If r was unsuccessful, a similar update to r's emphasis takes place, but the multiplying factor is Max-UpdatingCoefficient.

In order to illustrate the procedure for updating a researcher's emphasis based on the emphases and the success, or lack thereof, or fellow researchers, we provide a small example. Let us consider an unsuccessful researcher r, with neighborhood size 3, and let us assume that the value of the simulation parameter MaxUpdatingCoefficient is 0.1 and that the publication emphasis of r is given by the following tuple: $E(r) = (E_A, E_B, E_C) = (0.25, 0.45, 0.3)$. We shall denote the three neighbors of r by $n1$, $n2$ and $n3$, and let their respective emphases be $E(n1) = (0.31, 0.35, 0.34)$, $E(n2) = (0.29, 0.38, 0.33)$ and $E(n3) = (0.22, 0.40, 0.38)$. Furthermore, let us assume that $n1$ and $n2$ were successful in the current cycle and that $n3$ was not.

The emphasis of r will be updated, according to the deviation between r's emphasis and that of their successful neighbors, $n1$ and $n2$. The difference between r's and $n1$'s emphasis tuples is given by $E(r) - E(n1) = (0.25, 0.45, 0.3) - (0.31, 0.35, 0.34) = (-0.06, 0.10, -0.04)$. Similarly, $E(r) - E(n2) = (-0.04, 0.07, -0.03)$. Summing up those two difference vectors, and dividing the result by 2 (the number of successful neighbors of r) results in $D = (-0.050, 0.085, -0.035)$. Multiplying D by MaxUpdatingCoefficient results in $0.1 \times D = (-0.0050, 0.0085, -0.0035)$. Then, adding this vector to $E(r)$ results in $(0.2450, 0.4585, 0.2965)$, which is the new value of r's publication emphasis $E(r)$. Note that it is guaranteed that the sum of the coordinates of the new tuple $E(r)$ equals 1.

EXPERIMENTAL RESULTS

We implemented the social simulation model described in the previous section using the C++ programming language. We were able to run a typical simulation involving 100-500 agents and 200 evaluation cycles in approximately one minute, using a computer equipped with an Intel i7 CPU at 3.2 GHz, with 16GB of RAM memory, running under Windows 7 64bits. Thus, different scenarios can be run with a small setup time for changing parameters before re-running the application.

Simulations have shown that agents are prone to convergence to a single point within the spectrum defined by the emphasis vectors. That is, given enough evaluation cycles, it is to be expected that most researchers will converge to a single emphasis profile: one that reflects a high likelihood of reaching the qualifying threshold. This convergence phenomenon seems to prevail under a reasonably large set of conditions, with a high level of sensitivity to the qualifying threshold,

to the relative reputation scores assigned to each publication stratum, and to the number of neighbors controlled by the MaxNumberOfNeighbors parameter. It is important to remark that in each one of our experiments the number of successful researchers grew steadily from one evaluation cycle to the next, typically doubling after 10-20 cycles and stabilizing after approximately 30 cycles, with only small fluctuations from that point and on.

The higher the number $C(r)$ of colleagues that are observed at the end of each evaluation cycle, the faster the convergence takes place. This can be expected, since the adjustments of each researcher will be influenced by a larger number of colleagues, meaning that there is a larger chance of successful researchers being pooled and observed. Thus, each researcher has an increased chance of adjusting his/her emphasis in a way to follow a successful example. Figures 1 and 2 show the emphases of researchers plotted in a 3-dimensional graph, whose axes correspond to the value of the

Figure 1. Setting MaxNumberOfNeighbors=1 causes a slow convergence of researchers and a distribution with large spread around a certain region associated with high likelihood of reaching the qualifying threshold.

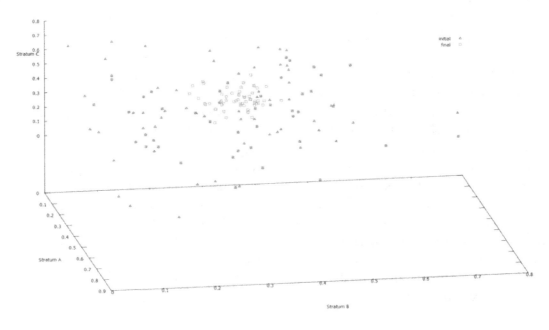

Figure 2. Setting MaxNumberOfNeighbors=10 causes a faster convergence of researchers and a distribution in which most researchers place themselves within a small region associated with high likelihood of reaching the qualifying threshold.

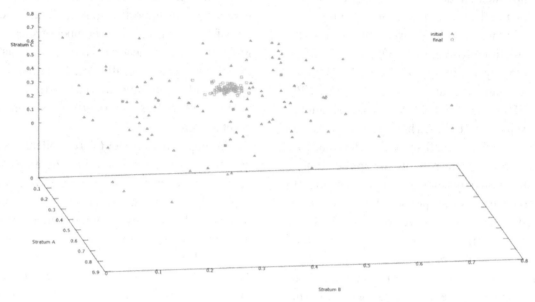

emphasis for each stratum. Red points correspond to initial positions of researchers, while green points corresponding to their final positions. The figures clearly show the influence of considering a larger set of colleagues observed by the end of each cycle. The number of evaluation cycles was the same in both cases.

An alternative way of speeding up convergence is to increase the values of the two parameters that affect the update of a researcher's emphasis: MinUpdatingCoefficient and MaxUpdatingCoefficient. If those values are increased, larger adjustments are made at each step and the overall tendency is that researchers will rapidly move to a region of the emphasis spectrum where chances are higher of reaching the qualifying threshold. From that point and on, it is likely that smaller adjustments are made, since researchers will often be successful and will use the MinUpdatingCoefficient parameter to weight their updates.

Obviously, very large values of those parameters might cause some level of instability or divergence, as researchers will frequently over-

shoot their adjustments. To prevent a misuse of those two parameters, a solution is to employ an adaptive adjustment as the simulation progresses: both values are decreased, down to a fixed value, as the number of evaluation cycles increase. We did not pursue this line of work, but rather kept the values of the MinUpdatingCoefficient and MaxUpdatingCoefficient parameters at 0.1 and 0.05, respectively.

In Figure 3 we show the trajectories, in the emphasis space, of three agents during a typical run of the simulation. The changes in emphasis are more pronounced during early stages of the simulation, and tend to become very small as the simulation progresses. This is in agreement with other observed measurements that suggest a convergence of a large group of researchers to one region in the emphasis space. As the emphasis of a specific researcher approaches the convergence region, i.e. a region where it is more likely to reach the qualifying threshold, smaller adjustments are made to his/her emphasis.

Figure 3. Changes in the emphases of 3 randomly selected researchers over the course of 200 evaluation cycles.

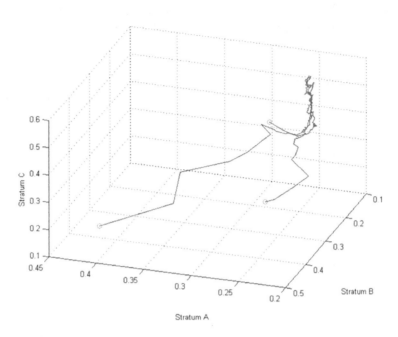

The influence of the qualifying threshold in the convergence is related to how many researchers reach or exceed the qualifying threshold in each evaluation cycle. The higher the number of successful researchers, the larger the adjustments to the emphasis vectors at each evaluation cycle and, therefore, the faster the convergence. Figures 4, 5 and 6 illustrate the changes observed in the emphases of researchers as the simulation progresses. The figures show the preference for publishing in each stratum, averaged over the entire set of researchers. With higher values for the qualifying threshold, a faster convergence is observed. Clearly, very high values of this parameter can lead to problems: a very large value of the qualifying threshold will make it impossible (or nearly impossible) for any researcher to succeed in any evaluation cycle, causing the entire simulation to become stale. Defining a upper bound on the qualifying threshold equal to a fraction of the MaxPointsPerAgent parameter can prevent this situation.

The reputation scores of the three strata also play an influential role in the speed of convergence of the simulation. Those parameters must be set in accordance with the corresponding acceptance probabilities, since the combination of those two values are important for defining which strata can be considered attractive from the researchers point of view. For instance, even if strata A has a good probability of acceptance, say 50%, the fact that its reputation score is very close to the maximum number of points each researcher receives (MaxPointsPerAgent) might prevent any researcher from moving towards an emphasis that reflects a preference for that strata. Similarly, a stratum with low probability of acceptance will only be attractive to researchers if its reputation score is relatively low, justifying the risk of submitting a paper to a journal in that stratum. Since acceptance probabilities are often an important criterion for ranking and grouping scientific publications, such probabilities are expected to be fixed in most scenarios. Thus, the information that is really subject to change and fine tuning by policy-makers is the

Figure 4. Raising the bar: A higher qualifying threshold results in faster convergence and a more pronounced polarizing effect. The figure shows the changes in average emphases for the three strata with a qualifying threshold of 20. The red curve corresponds to stratum A, while the green and blue curves correspond to strata B and C, respectively.

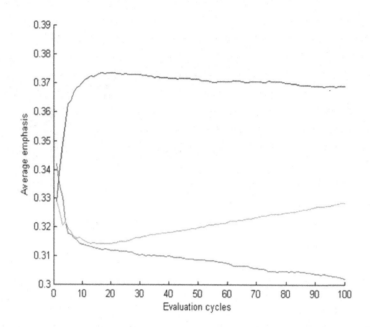

Figure 5. Changes in average emphases for the three strata with a qualifying threshold of 25.

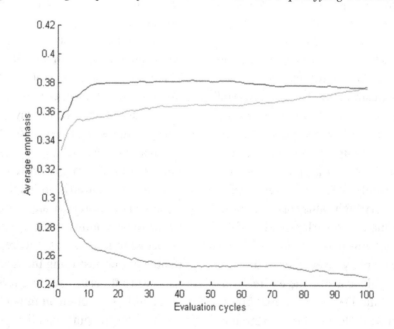

Figure 6. Changes in average emphases for the three strata with a qualifying threshold of 30.

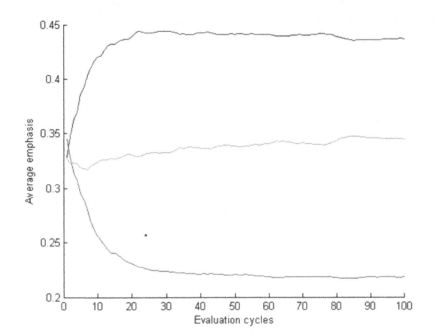

set of reputation scores, which reflect the number of points earned by researchers.

In Figures 7, 8 and 9 we illustrate the tendency of researchers to group within a small region of the emphasis spectrum. This convergence amounts to the ability of individual researchers to emulate successful behavior, a feature also present in humans. In real life, the tendency is justified by the financial incentive (additional funding) as well as by the acquired status, within the academic community, that results from qualifying as a productive researcher.

Analysis of Results

It is well-known that many institutions use, in different ways, operant conditioning techniques to induce people's behavior toward an aimed result. However, the expected result is not always achieved, mostly due to the fact that human behavior is still a highly unpredictable phenomenon. This unpredictability is amplified when human behavior is affected by social interactions. In such

a scenario, our ability to anticipate changes in individual and social behavior is further reduced.

There are two ways of analyzing human behavior: the individual and the group behavior. In fact, these two categories are intimately related, since one cannot exist without the other. We say that because the human being is a social animal, its behavior being connected to the behavior of its peers, forming a group behavior. We may say that from the interaction of several micromotives we have a single macrobehavior associated with the group (Schelling, 2006). In many cases, however, this macrobehavior is not an easily recognizable consequence of the individual microbehaviors or micromotives. This can be seen in the convergence that was observed in our experiments.

The analysis of the relationship between these two aspects of behavior is very important, because this is the precise point where the analysis of certain policies might fail when forecasting human behavior. Indeed, the predictions of an institution regarding a certain conditioning policy can amply diverge from the actual outcome because of the

Figure 7. Emphases of researchers in three moments during the simulation. Blue dots represent initial values of emphases, green dots represent emphases values at iteration 20, while red dots correspond to the final emphases at iteration 40. Distribution of emphasis are shown in terms of strata A and B.

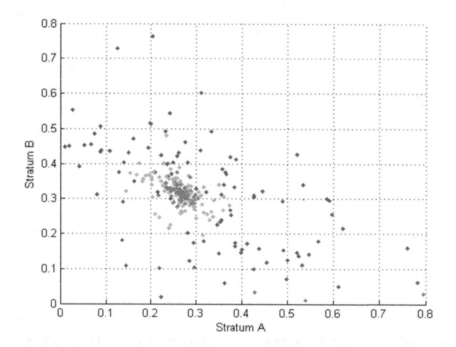

Figure 8. Emphases of researchers in three moments during the simulation. Distribution of emphasis are shown in terms of strata A and C.

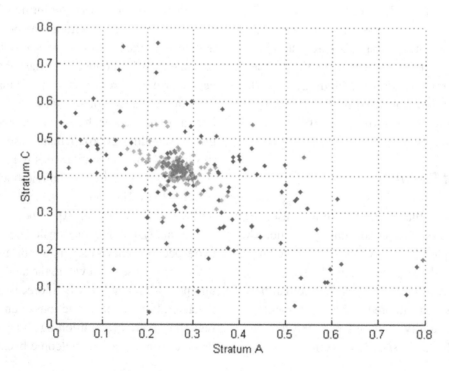

Figure 9. Emphases of researchers in three moments during the simulation. Distribution of emphasis are shown in terms of strata B and C.

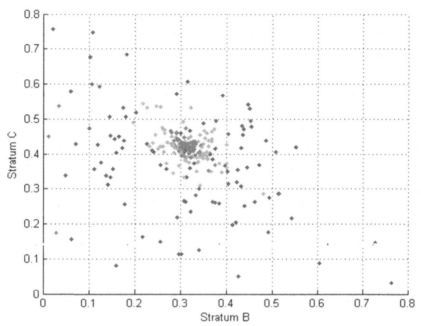

failure to take into account how individual and social behavior can influence each other.

Since an individual is, in most cases, highly influenced by its peers, his/her behavior must not be considered isolated from the group behavior. This additional variable is very important to the success of a planning that involves human action. Despite one's efforts to condition a behavior through reinforcements in order to achieve a desired outcome, the reinforcement of the intended behavior might, in fact, lead to an outcome that is quite diverse from the one originally intended. In the previous section we noticed that, while promoting an overall increase in the number of published articles, the policies are prone to induce a long-term migration of researchers to a single behavior in term of articles prepared for publication in the three strata, something that can be interpreted as an undesirable behavior.

Thus, we argue that a bias in the policy towards certain types of scientific publications can be associated with a qualitative shift in research focus

that leads, in the long run, to the production of research of diminished relevance. Indeed, depending on the definition of strata (and, therefore, their acceptance probabilities) and reputations scores, the society of researchers can display a single behavior in which a large number of individuals seek to publish in scientific journals of modest impact-factor and with low standards for accepting scientific articles. On the other hand, certain sets of parameter values might bring about changes that cause most agents to engage in high-quality research, while maintaining an elevated level of productivity.

The results suggest that, as time goes by, a single (or, maybe, a few) prevailing behavior tends to evolve, as the majority of agents converge to relatively safe *modus operandi* that frequently allows them to receive incentives. Since different high-level policies might induce different such safe profiles for individual agents, we believe that this type of simulation can be valuable for guiding the choice of parameters of real-life policies.

FUTURE RESEARCH DIRECTIONS

The space of parameters of the proposed agent-based simulation model is relatively large: there are several parameters, some of which can vary significantly, including the reputation scores. Therefore, an automatic calibration of parameters could prove beneficial in a real-life scenario.

In this setting, an agency could fix some of the basic parameters that are harder to calibrate (for instance, acceptance probabilities) and perform an automatic search for optimal values of the remaining parameters, e.g., reputation scores that prevent convergence to undesired regions of the emphasis space. Meta-heuristic strategies, including genetic algorithms, simulated annealing, among others, seem to be well suited to perform the required search.

In our model, articles are rejected according to some probability. Moreover, the effort invested in producing an article that is rejected in the current evaluation cycle is not taken into account during the next cycle. In an actual scenario, articles can be modified and re-submitted, sometimes to a journal in a lower stratum. Modifying the proposed model to account for such a fact would render it more realistic, while increasing its complexity, since the inclusion of a new parameter (or a new random factor) would be necessary.

FINAL REMARKS

We proposed a social simulation model based on adaptive agents for studying the dynamics of an incentive framework for scientific production. The model contains elements that allow for the reproduction of the main mechanisms concerning the policy of an agency that supports and fosters research activity within a given territory. Agents in the model corresponds to researchers. Resources are represented in the form of financial incentives (research funding) that can be obtained depending on the way that an agent is positioned in a so-called *emphasis space*, a three-dimensional space associated with the preference of researchers for publishing in scientific journals ranked into three strata.

The simulations carried out using the proposed model show a tendency of convergence of agents in the long run, meaning the researchers are induced to emulate a single behavior with respect to the types of journals targeted for publication. It is noteworthy that the only parameters of the simulation that are directly related to the actual quality of a publication are its reputation score and its acceptance probability, the latter being a measure closely related to the rejection rate of a journal. The reputation score of a journal is a less objective measure than its acceptance probability. Thus, it is fair to say that the convergence behavior of researchers can lead to a prevailing behavior, in terms of publication emphasis, that is partly related to the actual quality of the research being published, and partly related to the choice of parameters by policy-makers. This can lead to the convergence of researchers around an area of the emphasis spectrum that might reflect an emphasis on low reputation and high acceptance probability, as long as the simulation parameters are calibrated in a way to favor such a choice. This fact highlights the importance of carefully calibrating the reputation score by means of extensive simulation, as a way to prevent a choice of parameters that does not necessarily produce the originally intended behavior.

REFERENCES

Freyne, J., Coyle, L., Smyth, B., & Cunningham, P. (2010). Relative status of journal and conference publications in computer science. *Communications of the ACM*, *53*(11), 124–132. doi:10.1145/1839676.1839701

Gilbert, N. (1997). A simulation of the structure of academic science. *Sociological Research Online*, *2*(2). doi:10.5153/sro.85

Gilbert, N. (2008). *Agent-based models (No. 153)*. London: Sage.

Gilbert, N., & Troitzsch, K. G. (2005). *Simulation for the social scientist*. New York, NY: McGraw-Hill International.

Merton, R. K. (1988). The Matthew effect in science, II. Cumulative advantage and the symbolism of intellectual property. *Isis*, *79*, 606–623. doi:10.1086/354848

Miller, J. H., & Page, S. E. (2009). *Complex adaptive systems: An introduction to computational models of social life*. Princeton, NJ: Princeton University Press.

Ozel, B. (2012). Collaboration structure and knowledge diffusion in Turkish management academia. *Scientometrics*, *93*(1), 183–206. doi:10.1007/s11192-012-0641-9

Schelling, T. C. (2006). *Micromotives and macrobehavior*. London: Norton & Company.

Schultz, D. M. (2010). Rejection rates for journals publishing in the atmospheric sciences. *Bulletin of the American Meteorological Society*, *91*(2), 231–243. doi:10.1175/2009BAMS2908.1

Skinner, B. F. (1965). *Science and human behavior*. New York, NY: Free Press.

Van Noorden, R., & Tollefson, J. (2013). Brazilian citation scheme outed. *Nature*, *500*(7464), 510–511. doi:10.1038/500510a PMID:23985850

Watts, C., & Gilbert, N. (2011). Does cumulative advantage affect collective learning in science? An agent-based simulation. *Scientometrics*, *89*, 437–463. doi:10.1007/s11192-011-0432-8

KEY TERMS AND DEFINITIONS

Agent-Based Social Simulation: A computer simulation of a social phenomenon, in which the behavior of each individual is simulated by a software component, referred to as an agent.

Behavioral Mimetism: Modification of an individual's behavior resulting from him/her observing the reinforcement or punishing received by other individuals.

Behaviorism: From a psychological point of view, Behaviorism is concerned with the idea that behavior can be described and explained on the basis of external factors only, without resorting to considerations on the mental events or the internal psychological state of an individual.

Micromotives and Macrobehavior: In Thomas Schelling's book "Micromotives and Macrobehavior", the two terms are used to distinguish between the original intentions of individuals in a society (the micromotives), and the resulting effects of the individuals' actions at the level of the entire society. Individual actions (fueled by micromotives) can have a cumulative effect, and also inhibit or promote, further actions, thus making up a macrobehavior that might be quite different from what one could expect by analyzing micromotives at the individual level.

Operant Conditioning: Concept proposed by B. F. Skinner to describe the modification of voluntary behavior. Operant conditioning is based on reinforcement (or rewarding) and punishing as tools for modifying behavior.

Publication Stratum: A set of scientific journals enjoying a similar reputation among academic researchers, or having similar performance scores, which are in turn measured on the basis of factors such as the relative frequency of citations of its articles and the numbers of views and downloads of articles from the journals' websites.

Scientific Journal: Periodical publication specialized in scientific publications. The main purposes of a scientific journal are to help divulge recent scientific findings and to serve as a repository for bibliographical research. Scientific journals are typically published with a fixed number of issues per year, each including a limited number of articles.

Scientific Production: The set of all scientific publications produced by individuals belonging to a particular society during a given time frame.

Scientific Publication: A particular article or research paper reporting on scientific findings, published by a specialized publishing house and usually written by scholars associated with a university or research center.

ENDNOTES

[1]   In the same way that a governmental organization promotes tax reduction or exemption to stimulate the hiring of people with special needs, a private company creates pecuniary mechanisms to stimulate its employees to increase their productivity. Both examples are of positive reinforcements to obtain a certain kind of behavior from the individuals, which will lead to the aimed result (in the first case it leads to the social inclusion of people with special needs; in the second, it leads to higher profit for the company).

Chapter 14
Agent–Based Simulation of Electric Energy Consumers:
The NetLogo Tool

Fernanda Mota
Furg, Brazil

Graçaliz Dimuro
Furg, Brazil

Iverton Santos
Furg, Brazil

Vagner Rosa
Furg, Brazil

Silvia Botelho
Furg, Brazil

ABSTRACT

The electric energy consumption is one of the main indicators of both the economic development and the quality of life of a society. However, the electric energy consumption data of individual home use is hard to obtain due to several reasons, such as privacy issues. In this sense, the social simulation based on multiagent systems comes as a promising option to deal with this difficulty through the production of synthetic electric energy consumption data. In a multiagent system the intelligent global behavior can be achieved from the behavior of the individual agents and their interactions. This chapter proposes a tool for simulation of electric energy consumers, based on multiagent systems concepts using the NetLogo tool. The tool simulates the residential consumption during working days and presented as a result the synthetic data average monthly consumption of residences, which varies according to income. So, the analysis of the produced simulation results show that economic consumers of the income 1 in the summer season had the lowest consumption among all other consumers and consumers noneconomic income 6 in the winter season had the highest.

DOI: 10.4018/978-1-4666-5954-4.ch014

INTRODUCTION

The simulated patterns of consumption for Consumer Units individual is of paramount importance to provide data relating to the distribution of electricity to studies and research, since the actual data is difficult to obtain for privacy of service users electricity distribution and because the data available are scarce and outdated. Furthermore, the marked expansion of energy consumption has some negative aspects such as the possibility of exhaustion of resources used for energy production and environmental impact produced by this activity, although it may reflect warming economic and improving the quality of life of the population. Because of this, high investments in research of new energy sources and construction of new plants are being conducted by researchers around the world, (Castro, 2004). It should be noted that the factors linked to the growth of electricity demand in the residential sector are extremely complex and varied, because it involves variables that range from the type of user, his or her social class, type of equipment used, until the time of use and consumption habits, constraints often difficult to define. The knowledge, understanding and verification of their relationship are of utmost importance for the planning of activities, both aiming to supply this market, and for those who seek to optimize the use of electricity (Hansen, 2000).

An important aspect to be studied concerns the influence of climate on electricity consumption. It is known that in southern Brazil, and more specifically in the city of Porto Alegre, are recorded very adverse conditions of temperature, humidity and temperatures associated with equally high in summer and low in winter. Furthermore, we believe that all these investigations listed above can be of great value for both the planning area of the energy sector as well as for the planning of urban development (Hansen, 2000).

Unfortunately household energy consumption sources are a mystery for most of the people. This is due to the lack or scarce data of peoples' habits on the use of home appliances. Modeling the relationship of people with electric goods is very difficult due to the absolute absence of in-house data. One of the possible approaches is use of the average data available from Brazilian's Family Organization Program (a government initiative to generate data of population behavior in several aspects – also known as POF) (POF, 2010) to build a behavioral model of consumer's energy usage. The work developed in this chapter is focused on providing standards for synthetic data that approximate the actual patterns of Consumer Units by the technique of simulation-based multi-agent systems with NetLogo framework support. Finally, this chapter also describes a technique to simulate variations according to seasons.

BACKGROUND

Agents, Multi-Agent Systems, and NetLogo

Agents, according to (Wooldridge, 2002), are able to sense the environment extensively or partially and take actions that can modify it. They are endowed with certain autonomy to these actions, unlike procedural programs. Multi-agent Systems (MAS) offer a computing environment where programs that has a certain degree of autonomy (agents) interact with each other in the fulfillment of individual and collective goals (Wooldridge, 2002), (Singh, 1999).

The simulation model "agent" is based on the idea that agents exhibit the behavior described by its internal mechanisms, i.e., their instructions. An individual agent can simulate a world inhabited by artificial processes (programs) interacting. The simulation should carry a population of an artificial ecosystem for real world scenarios, where hypothesis can be explored by repeating the experiments in the same way as in a real laboratory or field conditions, but easier and without the cost, risks and time associated with them. Each individual in the population is represented by an agent whose behavior is programmed by a set of rules.

Thus, the agent-based simulation can model situations which individuals have different and complex behaviors, may take into account both quantitative properties (numerical parameters) and qualitative (individual behavior) of the system represented in the model. The computer simulation is then used to discover properties of the model and gain understanding in a dynamic process, which would be very difficult to model with standard mathematical techniques.

NetLogo (Wilensky, 1999) is a programmable modeling environment for exploring the behavior of decentralized systems and complex systems. It is particularly well suited for modeling and simulating complex systems over time. The NetLogo provides an easy way to get the agent-based modeling, even for those who do not have advanced programming skills and mathematics. The NetLogo environment consists of three types of agents: turtles, patches and observer. Modelers may give instructions to hundreds or thousands of independent agents working in parallel, making it possible to explore connections between the behavior of micro-level models and macro-level which emerge from the interactions of many individuals.

The NetLogo programming consists basically of assigning actions to three groups of entities: the observer (observer) and agents (turtles and patches) that are the creatures (turtles) and the environment (patches). The observer is a "creator" that specifies the conditions of operation and gives control to the other elements.

The tool allows you to set different species (breeds) for agents, which is one important feature, because once species has been defined, it becomes possible to schedule those having differ-

ent behaviors. For example, a simulation of prey / predator can be defined as two defined species called "sheep" and "wolf" that allows to writing a rule that makes the "wolf" eat the "sheep". Differentiation of species also makes the model becomes visually attractive and informative, as they can be assigned different ways to different species.

More recently, one has used a simulation based on agents, which is characterized by the use of a large number of agents interacting with each other, with little or no centralized coordination. Furthermore, it allows the observation of how individual agents (people, bacteria, insects, nations or organizations) interact with each other and with their environment. Getting to it, an approach that allows the understanding of system behavior - artificial societies. This approach has been shown to be very promising, especially in the understanding of complex systems (Azevedo & Menezes, 2007).

Related Work on Energy Simulation

Most related work focuses on energy simulations of buildings or offices. This section is a brief study of the application of multi-agent systems in electricity consumption. In (Abushakra & Claridge, 2001), it was presented a library of schedules and diversity factors based on data from electricity consumption that were measured by simulations and calculations considering the electricity in peak cooling load in commercial buildings. They derived several sets of diversity factors from measured data in 32 commercial buildings. The work in (Abushakra & Claridge, 2001) used the occupation and lighting diversity profiles to find a strong correlation between these two variables using linear regression. However, in (Degelman, 20010), it was modeled lighting and occupancy in buildings using a Monte Carlo approach based on statistics and research of how people use office spaces. (Le et al., 2010) suggested that more attention should be given to the occupant behavior in order to increase the accuracy of model building thermal insulation in commercial buildings.

Simulations based on profiles or static based on the behavior of a single user are unrealistic. Usually in building simulators only thermal variation generated by appliances and occupants is considered. Furthermore, the occupants are considered only as present or absent, without consider how they behave when they are consuming energy. In simulations of energy, just the analysis of simple curves for the presence or absence of people are considered, instead of taking into account the real behavior of humans that affect energy consumption. This can help in building a project more realistically.

Many of the factors that influence energy consumption are reported as problem of supply and energy efficiency, linking the personal interests, characteristics of origin, social norms and lack of knowledge about energy use (Raaij & Verhallen, 1983), [Jinlong & Kazunori, 2009]. The authors (Seryak & Kissock, 2000) conducted a study on university residential houses and demonstrated that occupation of the same house for 2 academic years for different occupants got different energy consumption due to behavioral differences. In (Masoso & Grobler, 2010), the authors conducted an energy audit and the results showed that more energy is consumed during the hours that people are at home than in the period in which they are working. This is due to the behavior of the occupant that leaves the lights and other equipment connected at the end of the day (Kashif et al., 2011).

In (Klein et al., 2011), it was presented and implemented a multi-agent simulation of energy consumption, evaluating the level of comfort of residents and energy consumption (MACES - Confort Multiagent Simulation and Energy) for management, control and construction of alternative models of behavior of occupants. This work used computational agents and humans to explore current trends in electricity consumption. Additionally, they applied a predictive control and reactive

agents in an attempt to reduce energy consumption, however, maintaining occupant comfort, thus implementing a simulation tool compatible with the real world to instigate the behavior of occupants and motivate conscious control of energy. From this study, it can be concluded that preliminary results demonstrate promising improvements to building energy management and comfort of occupants. The article showed a 17% reduction in energy and about 85% of the occupants were satisfied. Thus, the work presented in this article differs from other scenarios that utilize predefined static because changes in the thermal model of the house or the weather condition in the simulation also affect the beliefs of the inhabitants, which ultimately affects their decisions to act according to certain objects apparatus and the environment.

SIMULATION TOOL

A MAS (Multi-agent System) based model was implemented in NetLogo framework to produce a tool to simulate the electric energy consumption in homes.

For this model, two seasons (winter and summer) were considered, with different equipment patterns used in these seasons (defined by the user). The MAS will use various monetary monthly incomes, making it possible to build different consumer profiles according to this data. The tool will generate different energy consumption for each consumer, based on income and on the season, allowing the construction of different types of consumers, according to Figure 1. Finally, the number of households in each income as well as the total number of households of all income is defined by the user.

The simulation model of energy consumption, based on the agent paradigm and implemented in NetLogo tool, has probabilistic behavior, yet uses the abstractions specific to this metaphor. Thus, it can be said that:

Figure 1. Model of the multiagent simulation system

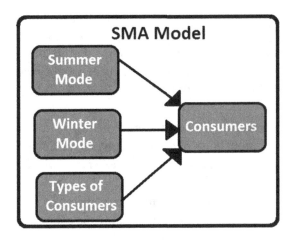

- User profiles, as well as the appliances, are modeled as computational agents. They are modeled through the creation of different breeds. These species represent the idea of agents, each of which incorporates a different set of instructions to be executed, such as the simulation of honeycomb agents, working species having different behaviors of the species queen.
- The environment also supports the situation where agents are not at home.
- Industrial and commercial consumers are not modeled.

The tool allows interaction between the consumer agents that inhabit the same house, as they share the equipment and generate an average consumption for each residence. The output is the energy consumption per household per minute. It can be observed the total consumption by income or the total consumption of all incomes. The output can be in minutes, hours or days, and can be observed in both graphical and files logs that can be copied to a text file for further analysis.

Were also created seven types of incomes and two types of consumers (economic and non-economic). Equipment vary according to the income of households, the higher the income the greater the number of devices. Each device has a variable number of times to be connected. Each device has a control variable for defining if the equipment is connected or not. Consumers remain some time away from home (8 hours) and can also sleep (for a period of up to 8 hours).

The interaction occurs inter-residences, that is, the interaction happens only among the habitants of the same household; there is no communication between neighbors.

The consumers are active agents. They can walk through the scenario, since the residences are passive agents that react only when consumers are at home, connecting any equipment, or when they forget an equipment connected when leaving home or going to sleep.

The tool has controls to allow the user to set which station will be simulated, and one can define what type of consumer (economic, non-economic) is to be simulated. The number of households and the percentage of income that will be simulated can also be defined by the user. One can change the unit (minutes, hours or days) being simulated, and the time is controlled by ticks (each tick corresponds to one minute).

Thus, an expert will make the decision based on the simulated socio-economic region, thus simulating the behavior of small regions that can generate consumer anomalies (peaks or valleys). To help to understand the behavior of inter - residential consumers, one can simulate other scenarios of consumptions by the introduction of new types of home appliances (replacing the refrigerator, for example), in order to verify the impact of public policies that encourage the exchange of home appliances.

The greatest difficulty in validating the tool was the lack of data to compare and validate the model. Another difficulty was the impossibility of having generic functions that accept parameters as input, so we had to repeat several times code snippets in order to perform different runs.

In addition, there were problems regarding the behavior space that was used to make controlled simulations. However, this code and the variables are dynamic, changing at run time. Therefore, it was impossible to use it to validate the tool, and it was necessary to build scripts to alter and control NetLogo in order to make possible to perform the simulations.

We need to consider some abstractions of the real world, such as:

- The number of times that the equipment are connected range from 1 to 50 times, except for the shower, for which we consider at most 15 times. Furthermore, since we consider limited types of equipment, all consumers of each income have the same type of equipment. For example, consumer income 1 has a refrigerator of 400 watts. There is also a maximum number of devices for each income. For example, income 1 may has at least 3 and at most 10 (9) equipment in the summer (winter).

- Households and consumers are considered agents: consumers are active agents, they interact among themselves in the same residences, and that is, there is no interaction between neighbors. In contrast, equipment is passive agents, since they do not move and just react. When an agent is at home or forgets certain equipment on, it generates energy consumption.

Consumers

Each residence has one to three people, with a period of up to eight hours for sleeping and exactly eight hours to be away from home. Furthermore, the agents can share the equipment and they can be of one of two types:

- **Economic consumer:** When it has a 70% probability of disconnecting the equipment while the consumer is sleeping or when is away from home.

- **Non-Economic consumer:** there is a 30% probability of disconnecting the equipment while the consumer is sleeping or when is away from home.

We modeled seven kinds of consumers (the colors of the residences and of the persons varies according to the kinds of incomes, as shown in Figure 2) according to the characteristics presented in Figure 3.

- **Income 1:** The residences of this group have family income up to R$ 830.00. This income has the following equipment (POF, 2010) (Table 1).

- **Income 2:** The residences of this group have family income varying from R$830.00 to R$ 1245.00. This income has the following equipment (POF, 2010) (Table 2).

Figure 2. Interface model that simulates the electrical power consumption of the four types of consumers

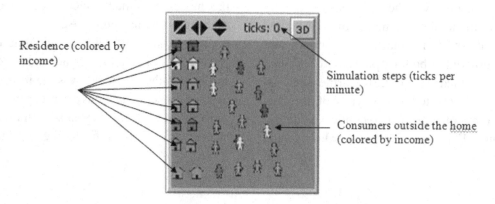

Figure 3. Consumer diagram

Figure 3. Consumer diagram

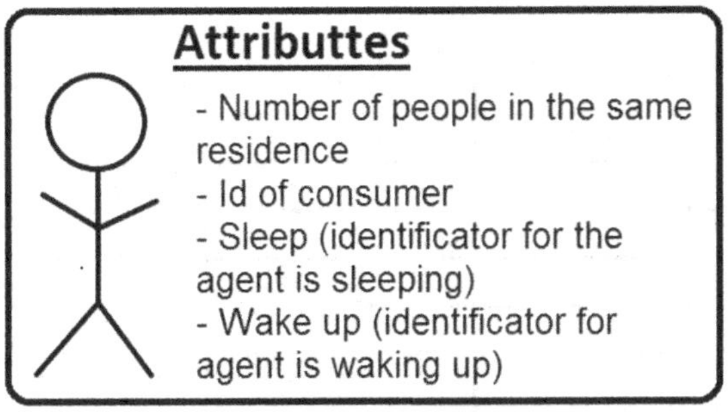

- **Income 3:** The residences of this group have family income varying from R$ 1245.00 to R$ 2490.00. This income has the following equipment (POF, 2010) (Table 3).
- **Income 4:** The residences of this group have family income varying from R$2490.00 to R$ 4150.00. This income has the following equipment (POF, 2010) (Table 4).
- **Income 5:** The residences of this group have family income varying from R$ 4150.00 to R$ 6225.00. This income has the following equipment (POF, 2010) (Table 5).
- **Income 6:** The residences of this group have family income varying from R$ 6225.00 to R$ 10375.00. This income has the following equipment (POF, 2010) (Table 6).
- **Income 7:** The residences of this group have family income greater than R$830 .00 up to R$ 1245.00. This income has the following equipment (POF, 2010) (Table 7).

Table 1. Features and consumptions of the equipment of the Income 1

Equipaments	Power (watts)	Wmin		Equipaments	Power (watts)	Wmin
Refrigerator - Summer	400	2.08		Electric Iron	1000	16.67
Refrigerator - Winter	200	1.04		Washing Machine	500	8.33
Microwave	1200	20		PC + Monitor	80	2.67
Incandescent Lamp	60	1		TV 14"	60	1
Shower- Summer	2000	33.33		Fan	65	1.08
Shower- winter	3000	50		Stereo System	20	0.33

Table 2. Features and consumptions of the equipment of the Income 2

Equipments	Power (watts)	Wmin		Equipments	Power (watts)	Wmin
Refrigerator	400	2.08		TV 19" LCD	80	1.33
Microwave	1200	20		Fan		1.94
Incandescent Lamp	60	1		Slow Cooker	1100	12.22
Incandescent Lamp	100	1.67		Coffee Machine	600	10
Shower	2000	33.33		Stereo System	20	0.33
Electric Iron	1000	16.67		Stove	60	1
Washing Machine	500	8.33		Clothes Dryer	1000	16.67
PC + Monitor	80	2.67		Laser Printer	180	3

Table 3. Features and consumptions of the equipment of the Income 3

Equipments	Power (watts)	Wmin		Equipments	Power (watts)	Wmin
Refrigerator	400	2.08		PC + Monitor	80	2,67
Freezer	400	3.70		TV 32" LCD	150	2.50
Microwave	1200	20		Air Circulator	90	1.50
Incandescent Lamp	60	1		Slow Cooker	1100	12.22
Incandescent Lamp	100	1.67		Coffee Machine	600	10
Shower	3000	50		Stereo System	45	0.75
Clothes Dryer	1000	16.67		Stove	60	1
Electric Iron	2000	33.33		Laser Printer	180	3
Washing Machine	700	11.67				

Table 4. Features and consumptions of the equipment of the Income 4

Equipments	Power (watts)	Wmin		Equipments	Power	Wmin
Duplex Refrigerator	400	2.11		PC + Monitor	100 watts	3.33
Freezer	400	3.70		TV 42" LCD	210 watts	3.50
Microwave	1400	23.33		Air Conditioning	7500 BTUs	16.67
Incandescent Lamp	60	1		Slow Cooker	1100 watts	12.22
Incandescent Lamp	100	1.67		Coffee Machine	600 watts	10
Shower	3000	50		Home Theater	350 watts	5.83
Clothes Dryer	3500	58.33		Stove	60 watts	1
Electric Iron	2000	33.33		Laser Printer	180 watts	3
Washing Machine	700	11.67				

Table 5. Features and consumptions of the equipment of the Income 5

Equipments	Power (watts)	Wmin		Equipments	Power	Wmin
Duplex Refrigerator	400	2.11		TV 46" LCD	260 watts	4.33
Freezer	400	3.70		Air Conditioning	12000BTUs	24.17
Microwave	1400	23.33		Slow Cooker	1100 watts	12.22
Incandescent Lamp	60	1		Coffee Machine	600 watts	10
Incandescent Lamp	100	1.67		Home Theater	350 watts	5.83
Shower	4000	66.67		Stove	60 watts	1
Clothes Dryer	3500	58.33		Laser Printer	180 watts	3
Electric Iron	3000	50		Grill	900 watts	15
Washing Machine	700	16.67		Multiprocessor	420 watts	7
PC + Monitor	100	4		Dishwasher	1500 watts	25

Table 6. Features and consumptions of the equipment of Income 6

Equipments	Power	Wmin	Equipment	Power	Wmin
Duplex Refrigerator	500	2.63	TV 52" LCD	310	5
Freezer	400	3.70	Air Conditioning	15000BTUs	33.30
Microwaver	1400	23.33	Slow Cooker	1100	12.22
Fluorescent Lamp	11	0.92	Coffee Machine	600	10
Fluorescent Lamp	15	1.25	Home Theater	350	5.83
Shower	5000	83.33	Stove	60	1
Clothes Dryer	3500	58.33	Laser Printer	180	3
Electric Iron	3000	50	Grill	900	15
Washing Machine	1000	16.67	Multiprocessor	420	7
PC + Monitor	120	4	Dishwasher	1500	25

Table 7. Features and consumptions of the equipment of Income 7

Equipaments	Power (watts)	Wmin	Equipaments	Power	Wmin
Duplex Refrigerator	500	2.63	TV 55" LED	210 watts	3.50
Freezer	600	5.56	Slow Cooker	1100 watts	12.22
Microwave	1400	23.33	Coffee Machine	600 watts	10
Fluorescent Lamp	15	1.25	Home Theater	350 watts	5.83
Fluorescent Lamp	23	1.92	Stove	60 watts	1
Shower	5000	83.33	Laser Printer	180 watts	3
Clothes Dryer	3500	58.33	Grill	900 watts	15
Electric Iron	3000	50	Multiprocessor	420 watts	7
Washing Machine	1000	16.67	Dishwasher	1500 watts	25
PC + Monitor	140	4.67	Air Conditioning	18000BTUs	35

Equipment

Each device has its kWmin (a minute is the tick of the simulation, so this unit was used instead of kWh). Figure 4 shows the considered house attributes. All devices have the same probability of being selected / connected. There is a list of the maximum and the minimum number of devices according to the income, as can be seen in Table 8:

Another aspect of the model is that the number of equipment is chosen randomly for each family income, and each equipment in a house can be used by the agents a random number of times. Furthermore, each device can be powered up a variable (random) time. The shower is the only equipment that cannot be turned on when the all the agents in a house are sleeping or not at home.

Figure 4. Residence diagram

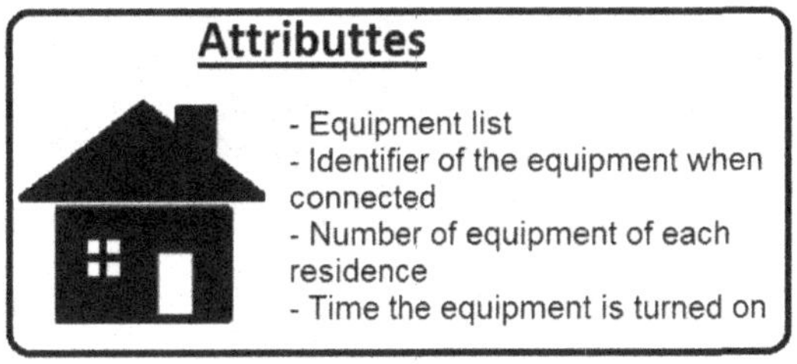

Attributtes

- Equipment list
- Identifier of the equipment when connected
- Number of equipment of each residence
- Time the equipment is turned on

Table 8. List of the maximum and the minimum number of devices according to the income

Incomes	Maximum	Minimum
1	10 (winter); 9 (summer)	3
2	16	3
3	17	4
4	17	4
5	20	4
6	20	4
7	20	4

Finally, the refrigerator and the freezer are the only devices that are always powered on.

Solutions and Recommendations

Two seasons (winter and summer) were evaluated by simulation considering two types of consumers (economic and non-economic) for the seven user profiles, forming a 2x4x7 simulation matrix. Further, ten-simulation days were made for each type of consumer in every season of the year, that is, we performed four types of simulation (economic consumer in summer, non-economic consumer in summer, economic consumer in winter, uneconomic consumer in winter), as can be seen below:

- **Economic consumers in summer:** As presented in Figure 5 and Table 9, incomes had the following means and standard deviations. As expected, income 1 had the lowest average consumption (15.70 kWh) and income 6 had the highest average consumption (51.38 kWh).
- **Economic consumer in winter:** As shown in Figure 6 and Table 10, incomes had the following means and standard deviations. As expected, income 1 had the lowest average consumption (kWh 18.50) and income 7 had the highest average consumption (58.58 kWh).
- **Non-Economic consumers in summer:** As shown in Figure 7 and Table 11, incomes had the following means and standard deviations. As expected, income 1 had the lowest average consumption (43 kWh) and income 7 had the highest average consumption (363 kWh).

Figure 5. Simulation result of the economic consumers in summer season. This figure shows the variations in the consumption of each income for each simulated day

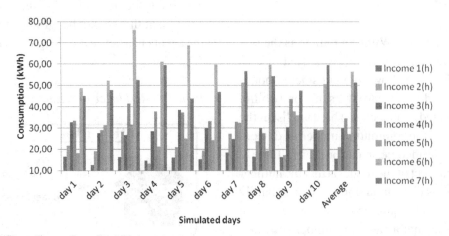

Table 9. simulation results of the economic consumers in summer season

Incomes	Average (kWh)	Standard Deviation
Income 1	15.70	1.66
Income 2	21.10	4.33
Income 3	29.76	3.78
Income 4	34.49	5.49
Income 5	26.99	6.43
Income 6	56.42	11.27
Income 7	51.38	5.87

Table 10. Simulation results of the economic consumers in winter season

Incomes	Average (kWh)	standard deviation
Income 1	18.50	2.52
Income 2	24.32	4.01
Income 3	27.86	5.56
Income 4	33.49	5.49
Income 5	37.58	5.79
Income 6	58,58	12.70
Income 7	51.20	7.28

- **Non-economic consumer in winter:** As shown in Figure 8 and Table 12, incomes had the following means and standard deviations. As expected, income 1 had the lowest average consumption (299.07 kWh) and income 7 had the highest average consumption (331.55 kWh).

Analysis of the produced simulation results shows that economic consumers of the income 1 in the summer season had the lowest consumption among all other consumers (51.38 kWh), and non-economic consumers of income 6 in the winter season had the highest consumption (331.55 kWh). However, we expected that income 7 had the highest consumption; this behavior can be explained by the following:

- The number of devices that are distributed according the different incomes are randomly generate, and the number of equipment for income 6 may be larger than for income 7, and so the time of use of the equipment.
- The consumption is different according to the capacity and technology used in the equipment.

Figure 6. Simulation results of the economic consumers in winter season. This figure shows the variations in the consumption of each income for each simulated day

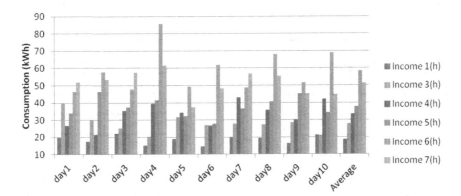

Figure 7. Simulation results of the non-economic consumers in summer season. This figure shows the variations in the consumption of each income for each simulated day

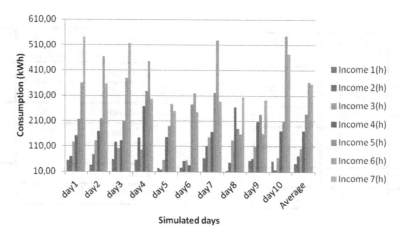

Figure 8. Simulation results of the non-economic consumers in winter season. This figure shows the variations in the consumption of each income for each simulated day

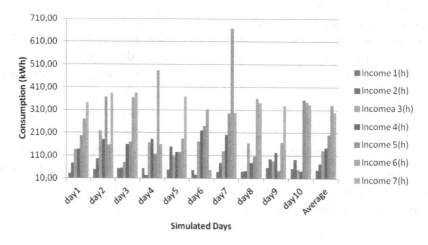

Table 11. Simulation result of non-economic consumers in summer season

incomes	average (kWh)	standard deviation
Income 1	43.60	17.55
Income 2	72.59	43,22
Income 3	102.25	34.16
Income 4	171.17	66.73
Income 5	238.48	52.12
Income 6	363.53	137.91
Income 7	356.29	111.98

Table 12. Simulation results of non-economic consumers in winter season

Incomes	average (kWh)	standard deviation
Income 1	46.71	17.55
Income 2	72.83	38.06
Income 3	131.47	51.49
Income 4	145.41	55.55
Income 5	202.03	109.50
Income 6	331.55	156.72
Income 7	299.07	109.66

FUTURE RESEARCH DIRECTIONS

As future work, we will leave to the user to set the definition of the number of times that each device will be connected. We intend to provide greater flexibility in the choice between economic or non-economic (from a certain percentage it will become economic), hybrid or non-economic profiles.

Another future work we envisage is to build consumers with different age groups, so the consumer will remain different time at home, varying according to their age.

FINAL REMARKS

The main motivation of this work was to enable the modeling of a scenario (home electricity usage) for which the authors could not find data of behavior online. This is extremely important as the electricity companies only have average consumption and can underestimate peak local electricity usage. The future research directions are toward the accuracy, and completeness of the model as a whole. This will enable tuning the model to reflect real human users, as demonstrated in the results. The use of the agent paradigm and NetLogo tool proved to be a powerful and versatile environment for simulating scenarios of electricity user profiles.

REFERENCES

Abushakra, B., & Claridge, D. (2001). Accounting for the occupancy variable in inverse building energy baselining models. In *Proceedings of the International Conference for Enhanced Building Operations (ICEBO)*, Austin, TX.

Azevedo, L. L., & Meneze, C. S. (2007). *Netplay – uma ferramenta para construção de modelos de simulação baseado em multiagente*. Paper presented at XVIII Simpósio Brasileiro de Informática na Educação, SBIE, Mackenzie.

Castro, R. (2004). *Análise de Decisões sob Incertezas para Investimentos e Comercialização de Energia Elétrica no Brasil* (Unpublished doctoral dissertation). Faculdade de Engenharia Elétrica da Universidade Estadual de Campinas.

Degelman, L. O. (2001). A model for simulation of daylighting and occupancy sensors as an energy control strategy for office buildings. In *Proceedings of the International Conference for Enhanced Building Operations (ICEBO)*.

Goldemberg, J., & Villanueva, L. D. (2003). Energia, meio ambiente e desenvolvimento (Trans. A. Koch, 2 ed.). São Paulo, Brazil: Editora da Universidade de São Paulo.

Hansen, A. M. D. (2000). *Padrões de Consumo de Energia Elétrica em Diferentes Tipologias de Edificações Residenciais* (Unpublished master dissertation). UFRGS, Porto Alegre.

Jinlong, O., & Kazunori, H. (2009). Energy-saving potential by improving occupants' behaviour in urban residential sector in Hangzhou City, China. *Energy and Building, 41*, 711–720. doi:10.1016/j.enbuild.2009.02.003

Klein, L., Kavulya, G., Jazizadeh, F., Kwak, J., Becerik-Gerber, B., & Tambe, M. (2011). *Towards optimization of building energy and occupant comfort using multi-agent simulation*. Paper presented at the International Symposium on Automation and Robotics in Construction.

Le, X. H. B., Kashif, A., Ploix, S., Dugdale, J., Mascolo, M. D., & Abras, S. (2010). *Simulating inhabitant behaviour to manage energy at home*. Paper presented at the International Building Performance Simulation Association. Conference, Moret-sur-Loing, France.

Martine, G. (2011). *Preparing for sustainable urban growth in developing areas. population distribution, urbanization, internal migration and development: An international perspective (Economic and Social Affairs)*. New York: United Nations Department of Economic and Social Affairs Population Division.

Raaij, W. F. V., & Verhallen, T. M. M. (1983). A behavioural model of residential energy use. *Journal of Economic Psychology*, *3*, 39–63. doi:10.1016/0167-4870(83)90057-0

Singh, M. P., Rao, A. S., & Georgeff, M. P. (1999). Formal methods in DAI: Logic-based representation and reasoning. In G. Weiss (Ed.), *Multiagent systems: A modern approach to distributed artificial intelligence* (pp. 331–376). Cambridge, MA: The MIT Press.

Wilensky, U. (1999). *NetLogo*. Retrieved January 14, 2014 from http://ccl.northwestern.edu/netlogo/

Wooldridge, M. (2002). *An introduction to multiagent systems*. Chichester, UK: Wiley.

ADDITIONAL READING

Anderson, J. R., & Bothell, D., & Byrne, M.D., & Lebiere, C. (2004). An integrated theory of the mind, Int. Journal of Psychological Review.

ANEEL. (2002). ANEEL, Retrieved December 14, 2012 from http://www.aneel.gov.br/cedoc/aren2008325.pdf.

ANEEL. (2002). Energia no Brasil e no mundo, Atlas de Energia Elétrica do Brasil. www.aneel.gov.br/arquivos/pdf/livro_atlas.pdf. Retrieved December, 2012.

Axelrod, R. (1996). *The complexity of cooperation: agent-based models of competition and collaboration*. Princeton, NJ: Princeton Univ. Press.

Dimuro, G. P., Costa, A. C. R., & Palazzo, L. A. M. (2005). Systems of exchange values as tools for multi-agent organizations. *Journal of the Brazilian Computer Society*, *11*(1), 3150. doi:10.1007/BF03192369

Dong, B., & Andrews, B. (2009). Sensor-based occupancy behavioral pattern recognition for energy and comfort management in intelligent buildings. 11th International Building Performance Simulation Association (IBPSA) Conference.

Energia (2012). Consumo de Energia. Retrieved January, 14, 2013 from http://www.ebanataw.com.br/ roberto/energia/ener15.htm

Ha, D. L., Ploix, S., Zamai, E., & Jacomino, M. (2006). A home automation system to improve household energy control, 12th IFAC Symposium on Information Control Problems in Manufacturing, St Etienne, France.

Henricksen, K. (2003). A Framework for Context-Aware Pervasive Computing Applications. PhD thesis, School of Information Technology and Electrical Engineering, University of Queensland.

Kashif, A., Ploix, S., Dugdale, J., & Le, X. H. B. (2012). *Simulating the dynamics of occupant behaviour for power management in residential buildings*. Energy and Buildings International Journal.

Masoso, O. T., & Grobler, L. J. (2010). The dark side of occupants' behaviour on building energy use. *Energy and Building*, *42*(2), 173–177. doi:10.1016/j.enbuild.2009.08.009

Newsham, G. (1994). Manual control of window blinds and electric lighting: implications for comfort and energy consumption. *Indoor Environment*, *3*, 135–144. doi:10.1177/1420326X9400300307

Parker, D., & Kirkpatrick, C. (2005). Privatisation in developing countries: a review of the evidence and the policy lessons. *The Journal of Development Studies*, *41*(4), 513–541. doi:10.1080/00220380500092499

Pires, J. C. L. (2000). Desafios da reestruturação do setor elétrico brasileiro. BNDES. Discussion Paper, 76.

POF. (2009). Pesquisas de Orçamentos Familiares 2008- 2009, despesas, rendimentos e condições de vida. Retrieved January 14, 2012 from http://www.ibge.gov.br/home/estatistica/pesquisas/pesquisa_resultados.php?id_pesquisa=25

Russel, S., & Norvig, P. (2003). *Artificial Intelligence: A modern approach* (2nd ed.). Pearson Education.

Sapkota, P. (2010). Modeling Diffusion Using an Agent-Based Approach. PhD thesis, University of Toledo.

Seryak, J., & Kissock, K. (2000). Occupancy and behavioural affects on residential energy use. American solar energy society, Austin, Texas.

Tisue, S., & Wilensky, U. (2004). Netlogo: A simple environment for modeling complexity. International Conference on Complex Systems, Boston.Zhang, Tao, Siebers, Peer-Olaf, Aickelin,Uwe (2011).

KEY TERMS AND DEFINITIONS

Agents: An agent is an entity that performs a set of operations which have been entrusted by a user or another program with some degree of independence or autonomy, and performing these operations, employs some knowledge of the goals or desires of the user.

Consumers Profile: Are profiles that are organized according to the income of consumers, these vary according to the values of the IBGE.

Electric Power: Is the rate at which electric energy is transferred by an electric circuit. The SI unit of power is the watt, one joule per second. Electric power is usually produced by electric generators, but can also be supplied by chemical sources such as electric batteries.

IBGE: Brazilian Institute of Geography and Statistics, or IBGE, for short, is a public foundation of the Brazilian federal government created in 1934 and installed in 1936 with the name of the National Statistics Institute.

Income: According to classical economics, it is the remuneration of the factors of production: wages (remuneration of labor), rents (payment of land cost), interest and profits (return on capital).

Multi-Agents System: Is a computerized system composed of multiple interacting intelligent agents within an environment. Multi-agent systems can be used to solve problems that are difficult or impossible for an individual agent or a monolithic system to solve.

NetLogo: Is a multi-agent programmable modeling environment. Tens of thousands of students, teachers and researchers use it worldwide.

Chapter 15
Agents' Risk Relations in a Strategic Tax Reporting

Nuno Trindade Magessi
Universidade de Lisboa-LabMag, Portugal

Luis Antunes
Universidade de Lisboa-LabMag, Portugal

ABSTRACT

Tax evasion is a classic problem in the field of economics and has been intensively studied over the last few decades. So far, research has been focused, and reasonably followed, on extensions from the original model developed by Alligham and Sandmo (1972). This chapter has taken the initiative to analyse and discuss the behaviour of taxpayers and the relation with risk when they act strategically. In this sense, the authors propose to replicate and discuss the three main conceptual functions of the brain (expressed by Spinoza) when agents do their strategic options concerning tax evasion risk. Output results demonstrate a tendency for strategic taxpayers to first react in detriment of structured and complex reasoning. The assumption, commonly used in tax evasion literature, that taxpayers are exclusively rational, is liable of being refuted. Even the strategic taxpayers are reluctant to follow only their reason.

INTRODUCTION

The first element, which constitutes the actual being of the human mind, is the idea of some particular thing actually existing. (In Ethics, Spinoza, 1677)

Tax evasion has been intensively studied in many scientific fields like economics, psychology and artificial intelligence. The decision to evade or comply to taxes is individual, and each agent has his/her own reasons to choose either behaviour.

One key factor in this decision is the position each agent has towards risk. In this case, the risk of being caught evading taxes. This factor is particularly important when agents act strategically.

Acting strategically, it means that agents are rational and "put strategic thinking into practice" (Olson, 1965). Strategic thinking involves the integration of several types of mental skills and techniques, as well as certain habits and attitudes, in the context of defining the problem to be solved from an initially ambiguous situation to solving it. There is an element of risk in strategic problem

DOI: 10.4018/978-1-4666-5954-4.ch015

solving because complexity causes uncertainty (Loehle,1996). Agents reason strategically about the advantages and disadvantages of alternative courses of action and choose the path which is more feasible to maximise their utility (Olson,1965; Cowell,1990). Therefore, agents activate more their logic reasoning instead of reacting based on intuitions, feelings or simple heuristics, when they report their income.

These rational actions and reactions can be seen as organised in a game, following the principles of interactive decision theory (Aumann, 2008). In the specific case of tax evasion, strategic taxpayers play several rounds against tax authority (Lucena & Gaspar,1987; Bernasconi,1998). Strategic taxpayers compare the opportunity of having extra benefits coming from underreporting income against the risk of being audited by inspectors. On the other hand, the tax authority has to guarantee the collection of taxes conditioned by a budget.

The interaction among agents could be played several times until the tax authority becomes satisfied with the tax report. In some countries, where the tax system enables information asymmetry among agents, this phenomena happens frequently. For example, taxpayers report eight times in the same year, trying to cheat tax authorities. These multiple reports are adjustments done to the original report after tax authorities reject it. These behaviours exemplify the action after reasoning about the pros and cons of taking risk on tax evasion, versus reaction to opponent position inside the game between taxpayers and tax authority. Taxpayers act or react to the policies implemented by tax authority and to the benefits allowable by underreporting. Reaction and reasoning are two of the mind functions presented by Spinoza. (Spinoza, 1677) Spinoza argued that mind has three major conceptual functions: reaction, reasoning and reflection. Reflection, in tax evasion, occurs when taxpayers begin to imitate each other, based on empathetic feelings.

So, it is important to figure out if taxpayers use these mind faculties when they face risk in a tax evasion context. If so, does a strategic taxpayer reacts after reasoning about risk or reacts before judgement about the risk itself. Are strategic taxpayers merely rational, as was described above? Which of the conceptual mind functions inducts more tax evasion?

To tackle this problem, we decided to integrate the reasoning behind the interactive decision theory into a multi-agent system, in order to build a model that exposes tax evasion phenomena and respective intrinsic characteristics about risk. Our main goal was to represent a heterogeneous society where distinct agents can interact each other and take their positions about tax evasion using their risk attitude. This simulation is very important, since analyses the influence of each mind function in the decision to comply or evade.

In section 2, we review the most relevant literature, making the case for our approach. In section 3, we outline the specificities of problem and its related concepts. Section 4 describes the model we propose, and the thinking process behind the corresponding abstract game. In section 5 we analyse our results and discuss the future impact and developments of research on the strategic tax reporting. Finally, on section 6, we draw out our conclusions.

REVISITING THE LITERATURE

Tax evasion modelling was firstly brought by the famous model from Allingham and Sandmo (1972) or by the model of Srinivasan (1973) introduced one year later. Both models were sustained upon the neoclassical economic theory. Models were suiting the work done about economic crime (Becker,1968). According to both authors, a taxpayer chooses what amount of his income he might ascribe within the concealed gains and the losses of being found. This model follows a portfolio choice approach and revealed some problems since forecasts a much higher percentage of tax evasion than what really is. For instance, the probability of audit together with the level of applied penalties were extremely low and hence inducing evasion. However, this is not what truly happens (Alm et al., 1992). In this sense, confirming these evidences, the research of the last two decades could be resumed as successive endeavours to extended the known model for tax compliance. All consecutive models have been built under agents individual choice (Levi, 1988). For example, the model outlined by Corchon (1984) and Telser (1987), which was also extended by Lucena and Gaspar (1989). The purpose of the last study was to include the sequential structure induced in tax evasion game under the circumstance of taxpayer reporting. The authors had focused the debate on the possibility of pooled mixed strategies.

Many were the studies focusing the core of research, in measuring and justify the ethics of economic agents. Studies described morale as a kind of implicit motivation, like a predisposition to pay taxes, subject to a superior conduct in society (Braithwaite & Ahmed, 2005). Such studies continue to insist to illustrate tax morale as a main reason for taxpayers to decide to comply on tax reports. For that, researchers subdued the phenomena into a dependent variable belonging to a multiple set of regression models. In order to obtain input data for their models, they typically design a survey to collect the data they want. The acquired effects are commonly uncertain, establishing connections among tax moral, socio demographic and ideological variables (Braithwaite & Ahmed, 2005).

After all these developments, researchers began to understand that standard economic methodology was insufficient to describe this social atrocity to societies (Kirchler, 2008). In consequence, they suggested to start studying tax evasion through cognitive perspective and social interactions, with incurrence's on regulation. Essentially, it was included experimental methodology to describe behavioural matters in economics. More recently, a niche of studies started to use an agent based models to recreate tax evasion at an aggregated

level. Those studies had the objective to include other dimensions in tax evasion research, like social interdependency. Therefore, researches were not only confined to the level of prevention. The first attempts happened with the studies of Mittone and Pattelli (2000) where they included imitation. Davis et al., (2003) enforces that agents social behaviour is the main cause to justify tax compliance. TCS model is the indictment of the previous ones, since it keeps agents composed by a large number of attributes and becomes more intricate in calculating the auditory rate (Torgler & Frey, 2007). The advantage is to enable the frame between the model outcomes and effective data.

In 2005, we can find the work called by the EC* series (Antunes et al., 2006). EC* models were built progressively with new features being added sequentially to the standard economic model. Authors also brought the concept of imitation as one possible behaviour for agents. They also check that under certain conditions, the ethical attitude of taxpayers is more relevant to compliance than the perception they have about tax system. Even so, the inclusion of inspectors with autonomy in terms of decision making, acquired great relevance (Balsa et al., 2006). They moreover suggest that indirect taxes are unpaid because of the collusion among interests between purchasers and sellers.

One year later, an emerged NACS model place the main objective into verifying the effect of a social structure, composed by a set of agents, in tax compliance behaviour (Korobow, 2007). The author used the Moore neighbourhood structure, where each taxpayer has neighbours around him that affect his choices and decision making. Other model with similar characteristics appeared, which was adapted, by agents, in the ISING physical model to tax compliance, substituting the particles, that interact in distinct paths relying on the temperature (Zacklan et al., 2009). In this case, taxpayers behaviour depends from others taxpayers actions, on their neighbourhood relations.

On the other hand, the TAXSIM model, integrates four sorts of agents complemented with some innovative factors like the degree of satisfaction with public services as was described as one of main reasons to not comply (Szabó et al., 2008). The degree of satisfaction depends from the previous experiences of each agent, influenced by his social network.

More recently, Bloomquist (2011) verified tax compliance for small business and interpreted as an evolutionary and coordinated game. He calibrated the model with real data from behavioural experiments. Finally, a different algorithm was built, based on four different decisional mechanisms: expected utility maximization, social network structure, decisional heuristics, heterogeneity of tax motivations and morale (Miguel et al., 2012).

In terms of risk, Bernasconi (1998) had established orders of risk aversion to tax evasion. His work demonstrated that is not only the "excess of risk aversion" the unique cause for the portfolio choice approach to be criticized. He argued that what influences the observed tax evasion rate in portfolio choice approach is the fact that misses the distinction between orders of risk aversion.

Psychology also gave its contribute. In situations of risk, like games, individuals have tendency to follow prospect theory. (Kahneman et al, 1979) Prospect theory is a behavioural economic theory that describes the way individuals chose between probabilistic alternatives that involve risk, where the probabilities of outcomes are known. The theory states that individuals make decisions based on the potential value of losses and gains rather than the final outcome. and that people evaluate these losses and gains using certain heuristics. The model is descriptive: it tries to model real-life choices, rather than optimal decisions. Kahneman (2002) also defended the duality of individual's mind. He argued that our minds are composed by two systems: system I and system II. System I is automatic, intuitive and fast, related to heuristics and emotions. System II, is deliberative, slow and based in rules. It is used to analyse complex things, through complex reasoning that activates our algorithmic mind (Stanovich, 2008). This perspective contrasts with what Spinoza defended in sixteen century, the three conceptual functions of mind (Spinoza, 1677). However both authors indentified in individuals different behaviours for reasoning and reaction.

As it can be seen, it has being used multiple perspectives to study the phenomena. Social simulation, through the use of multi-agents methodology, has been creating positive expectations about the future of this field of knowledge, independently of the existent literature. This happen because the biggest problem of other methodologies is the incapacity of integrate all involved perspectives.

STRATEGIC BEHAVIOUR AND RISK ON TAX EVASION

As we can see, there are several studies using agent based systems in tax evasion phenomena, but none of them treat the specific case when taxpayers act and react strategically, defying tax authorities to gamble. Of course, not all taxpayers adopt a strategic behaviour and we are conscious of that, but strategic taxpayers are indeed a preponderant group, taking account their relation with risk and the influence they have on society.

When taxpayers play against inspectors they simply want to maximize their wealth towards the minimum possible risk of being caught. Bernasconi (1998) had introduced risk and respective orders. to explain how the portfolio choice fails in predicting evasion amount. However, he doesn't explain the specific case of strategic taxpayers. In a game context, social and organizational aspects emerge, from the multitude of strategies being played, revealing forms of power among agents (Castelfranchi, 2003). Bloomquist (2011) and his interesting model with a lot of factors had missed the role of risk on taxpayer decision. For example, on EC* series the probability of being caught is randomly generated, based on a pre-defined inspection probability. But in reality, individuals conceive a perception about the probability of being inspected and they don't know the real probability. Fundamentally, the strategic taxpayers who adopt complex and logic reason. They collect data and do calculus regarding the possibility of being caught. In this sense, all taxpayers who think about cheating tax authorities have an implicit and subjective relation with risk, which need to be expressed . They can be risk averse and reluctant to take a risky position in the game or risk seekers and consequently entering in an enthusiastic way searching for an opportunity in the game.

In terms of game theory, Corchon (1984) and Lucena et al. (1987) brought us the case when agents played mixed strategies. The aim of their modelling was to highlight the interdependence between the taxpayer and inspector working for tax authority, providing scope for a sequential structure arising from its interaction. Unfortunately, both authors had developed a simple model using the assumption of rationality, homogeneity and risk neutrality of players. These studies had adopted only game theory, as approach, and entered in controversy. Its authors had considered a society with homogeneous agents. So, they extrapolated that the whole society will follow the interaction between one taxpayer and an inspector. In those cases, agents take their decisions similarly to what other players do, which unfits with reality. Second, because taxpayers are not only rational, and even strategic players as we will demonstrate. Agents like individuals, also use their intuitions or emotions to decide (Kahneman, 2002; Damasio, 2004)

Utility theory have problems well known described by artificial community since 1950s (Simon,1955). This theory fails to account the agent's will. In this case, strategic taxpayers will act and react depending on their own motivations and risk profile. Freedom of option is the key point of agent autonomy, because choice is not only about calculations or search, rather, it is about interest and motivation. The notion of rationality that we will use "can be described as individual, situated, and multi-varied" (Antunes et al, 2006). Our goal is make agent decision stand-

ing on a multi-dimensional notion of value, which provides a referential for decisions, instead of a single measure of marginal utility. Consequently, taxpayers and tax authority decisions can better be assess and adjust to metal mechanisms. Our argue is the option of take or not take the risk must be sufficiently adaptive to the problem and context mutations.

Third, no one is neutral to a risk that needs his own decision. If individuals are neutral to the risk, it means they are indifferent to the risk and consequently not being affected by it. The same authors had assumed a transversal tax rate to whole taxpayers. For us it is wrong doing this presumption, since authors had biased the reasoning of agents since the beginning. In this situation, taxpayers with high income lose part of their incentive to evade because the rate is transversal to the entire system. Instead taxpayers with low income are self-motivated to evade, since they have the same rate as the ones with higher income. So results are deceiving right from the beginning. Naturally, the biased reasoning will influence agents decision, teasing an adulteration of the conclusions drawn by these authors. This income gap is one of the components that influence the thinking process of taxpayers and consequently their decisions, which must not be neglected.

Another important aspect is the fact that literature holds back the essential features of mind, behind decision making. Transposing Spinoza (1677) thoughts to our problem, taxpayers react automatically to the relevant conditions established in environment, then they think intensively and make calculus about what is going to happen. They formalize the position to be held by each players in the game. Finally, reflect occurs under imitation. Mittone et al. (2000) had recognized the existence of imitators in tax evasion but considered under the perspective that agents are utility maximisers. Imitation is a behaviour adopted by agents to observe and replicate other agents behaviour. It is also a form of learning through social interaction where agents transfer information between them.

In this sense, this approach contrasts with the assumption of all agents are rational, defended by economists and used to modelling tax evasion. Antunes et al. (2006) had also used imitators as a class of taxpayers. Unfortunately, according their model, imitators imitate other taxpayer's behaviour under ethic dimension. It was out of scope the concept of risk.

Therefore, the importance of the existent dynamic among mind functions is evident on the relation established by taxpayers with risk. The official reporting made by a taxpayer precedes the tax authority's task of inspection, which determines an associated risk to his decision. This launch the issue about the plenitude of rationality for strategic taxpayers.

3Rs Perspective – Reaction, Reasoning and Reflection

As it was demonstrated above, strategic taxpayers with their intrinsic characteristics in decision-making were never considered on a multi-agent model. On the other hand, they were analyzed in works that used the theory of games which have revealed many critics. One of them is the assumption that all agents are homogeneous in their decisions. The relation with the risk should also be criticized, since those studies assume that agents are neutral to the risk. An assumption many times cited in literature, where utility functions are used, but without correspondence to reality. No one is indifferent to risk. If someone is indifferent to a specific risk it means that risk will not affect this person.

Model Description

In this sense, we developed a model that we called 3Rs, which brings together the capacity of agents to react, rationalise and reflect about the inherent conditions of risk in tax evasion. In this sense,

we solve the issue by providing the integration of implicit reasoning on interactive decision, where mixed strategies are adopted, inside a multi-agent based system (MABS). The main goal of the 3Rs is to understand what is the principal function of the mind in influencing decision about tax evasion. Taxpayers have to make a decision about evading or complying by comparing benefits and incurred risk. Taxpayers will be influenced by social interaction done under the perceived risk and risk aversion.

Methodology

An MABS is a most adequate method to build a model to reproduce tax reporting phenomena and inherent behaviour of agents. It includes parameters as social networks, social influence, heuristics and biases in the perception of the tax system, heterogeneity of tax motivations and tax morale among agents. Even other features that may generate complex social dynamics. In our case, the method is the more appropriated since allows us to bring heterogeneity to strategic taxpayers in terms of relation with risk. Those factors have not been integrated until very recently in the classical econometric models that aimed to explain the observed levels of tax compliance and tax morale.

Parameters

The 3Rs model presented here is empirically calibrated using the basic features of Portuguese tax system as well as the indicators typically described in literature which give us the capacity to reproduce the behaviour of agents. Some relevant setup parameters include total number of taxpayers, proportion of risk seekers, risk averters and imitators, the levels of income and consequent tax rates, underreport percentage, the probability of reporting high or low income, fine rates and audit costs.

Agents

Agents represent strategic taxpayers, programmed as possessing certain common attributes. Agents are divided in three classes: risk averters, seekers and imitators. While risk averters and seekers are predefined during all simulation, imitators can change their risk profile. Agents receive their annual income and have the obligation to report it to tax authorities. Income is divided in two levels: high and low income. Globally, lower income is more representative than higher income. Agents have capacity to perceive risk since they know the penalties and have capacity to generate subjective judgements about auditory probability. They also have a level of risk aversion, a capacity to react to others decisions, a reasoning to establish how do they react and capacity to imitate what they learn with other players. The perception and aversion of risk for each agent class follows an exponential distribution generated by a random engine. The probability of being audit, in risk averters point of view, is higher than the probability of risk seekers, in terms of mean. The same assumption was adopted to risk aversion where risk averter have a higher aversion level of being caught. Agents are embedded in a rich social network whose characteristics can also be adjusted to different experimental configurations. The imitation is build through the concept of neighbourhood. Agents adjust their decision through the number of agent-neighbours, classified as risk seekers or risk averters, and the closest distance among them. Implicitly the mechanism links their perception and aversion of risk. So each agent is embedded into a social network, with a mix of equal and diverse links or contacts, which locally became his own source of information about tax evasion behaviour. Taxpayers may be inspected and caught with a consequent payment of fines and recursive interest rate.

Decisional Algorithm

The decisional algorithm for each agent includes four types of mechanisms. These elements are constrictions for the action along a deliberative process that generates the decision related to tax evasion:

1. **Opportunity:** To evade, due to the inherent opportunity costs in the market;
2. **Reaction:** Strategic taxpayers react according the conditions established by tax authority, and vice versa;
3. **Rational choice:** Strategic taxpayers maximises their wealth having in mind his knowledge about the tax rates, calculating the probability of being caught if he evades, and the fines amount;
4. **Social influence:** Once the decision has been made, the behaviour of agent is sensitive to the perceived risk of other agents in his/her social network;

In order to establish the reasoning behind the decision making and taking account that taxpayers play against inspectors the best approach is to use interactive decision theory and consequently obtained the reaction functions.

In our model and for simplification, there are only two possible levels of income that a taxpayer may have: a high level of income y_H or a low level of income y_L. Taxpayers will pay distinct tax rates, t_H for high income and t_L for low income. Let us now operate within the reasoning framework of this issue. In the first moment, taxpayer confirms whether he has high or low income. This is private knowledge to which the taxman has no access. Therefore, we are in the presence of asymmetric information between taxpayers and inspectors. A taxpayer has a high level of income y_H, with a probability p_H or a low level of income y_L, with probability p_L, which means $1-p_H$.

In the second moment of the reason, taxpayer decides if he/she is going to report a high income r_H, or a low income r_L. In the third instance of the reason, inspectors decide, based on the obtained declaration, whether if they should review the taxpayer or not. Finally, the player's payoffs are realized.

Logically, a linear schedule is assumed. If the taxpayer is audited and found to be underreporting, he has to pay the tax liability due on his true income plus a fine, designated by f and an interest rate for delay - ir. When the taxpayer faces an audit he incurs a non-pecuniary loss of λ - Lucena (1989). If taxpayers are not caught they can take a benefit from an opportunity cost - oc. On other hand, the tax collecting agency incurs in an audit cost, c_H for a high level of income or c_L for a low level of income (where $c_H > c_L$). Both costs are rates applied to each income level. The tax authority's net revenue is given by tax revenue, plus fines and interests, less cost of auditing. The reasoning system could be represented as it is in the Cowell (1987) and Lucena and Gaspar (1989) models.

After the taxpayer has chosen the level of income and upon reception of a tax declaration, the tax collecting authority can make its decision on whether or not to audit this tax report. If the declared income is high r_H, the taxpayer is audited with probability q_H or if he declared a low income, his audit probability is q_L.

It is practical to start by talking about the taxpayer's problem, similarly to the approach of Lucena and Gaspar (1989). Since the taxpayer recognizes the realization of his own income, it is important to face this problem in different stages, separately.

When the taxpayer has high income y_H, he has to choose the probability of reporting high income, r_H, denoted by ph_H. Therefore the taxpayer's expected payoff is thus linear in ph_H and combined high income taxpayer's payoff and low income taxpayer's payoff. The coefficient is:

High income taxpayer's payoff

$$ph_H \left\{ q_H \left[(1-t_H)y_H - \lambda \right] + (1-q_H)\left[(1-t_H)y_H \right] \right\} \tag{1}$$

Lower income taxpayer's payoff

$$(1-ph_H)$$
$$\begin{bmatrix} q_L \left[y_H - t_L y_L - f - \lambda - (t_H y_H - t_L y_L)(1+ir)^n \right] + \\ (1-q_L)(y_H - t_L y_L)(1+oc)^n \end{bmatrix} \tag{2}$$

where $ph_L = 1 - ph_H$;

And therefore ph_H must be settled, assuming a value between 0 and 1. Instead, when the taxpayer has low income y_L, he also has to choose the probability of declaring high income, r_H, which is denoted as pl_H. So, pl_H must, as was shown above, assume a value between 0 and 1. If it is assumed that $\lambda < (t_H y_H - t_L y_L)$ it is easy to conclude that over the relevant range $(q_H, 1-q_H) \in [0,1]$ and $pl_H = 0$. That is to say, when the taxpayer has low income it is optimal for him to declare that he has low income.

To discover the function of reaction in mixed strategies, we could start by discussing the problem from the tax collecting agency's side. Inspectors have to choose the probability of auditing when receiving a high income declaration, q_H and the probability of auditing when receiving a low income report q_L. For the first of these cases, the authority payoff is:

Tax authority payoff for high income reported

$$\left[q_H \left(t_H y_H - c_H y_H \right) + (1-q_H) t_H y_H \right] \tag{3}$$

where $ph_H = 1$ would not be optimal.

For this, it was already established that $pl_H = 0$. The above expression is equivalent to: $t_H y_H - q_H c_H y_H$, which in reality is maximized over the relevant range when $q_H = 0$. This result shows that it is never optimal for the tax authority to audit those who report high incomes.

It has therefore been established that low income taxpayers never have conditions to report less since they receive the minimum of income ($pl_L = 1$) and that the tax collecting agency never audits anyone who reports high income ($q_H = 0$). But, high income taxpayers may underreport and to dissuade this behaviour, the tax collecting agency may audit a fraction of those false reporting. At this phase, we must now consider the case of the tax authority when receiving a low income report. For this, it is useful to introduce some additional notation: calling $p_{L/H}$ the probability of someone who reports low income r_L being in reality a high income individual; and $p_{H/H}$ the probability of someone who reports r_H being of a high income type. It is easy to see that, given that $ph_L = 0$ may be simplified in the above expressions:

$$p_{L/H} = \frac{p_H \left(1 - ph_H\right)}{p_H \left(1 - ph_H\right) + \left(1 - p_H\right)} \qquad (4)$$

$$1 - p_{L/H} = \frac{\left(1 - p_H\right)}{p_H \left(1 - ph_H\right) + \left(1 - p_H\right)} \qquad (5)$$

$$p_{H/H} = 1 \qquad (6)$$

$$1 - p_{H/H} = 0 \qquad (7)$$

Consequently the expected payoff, for the tax collecting agency, may now be written as:

$$q_L \left[\begin{matrix} p_{L/H} \\ \left[t_L y_L + f + \left(t_H y_H - t_L y_L\right)\left(1 + ir\right)^n - c_H y_H\right] + \\ \left(1 - p_{L/H}\right)\left(t_L y_L - c_L y_L\right) \end{matrix} \right] + \left(1 - q_L\right) t_L y_L, \qquad (8)$$

when $0 < q_L < 1$.

This equation may be written as:

$$-q_L t_L y_L + q_L p_{L/H}$$
$$\left[\left(t_H y_H - t_L y_L\right)\left(1 + ir\right)^n + f - \left(c_H y_H - c_L y_L\right)\right] \qquad (9)$$

Using pl_H determined above and since it was established that $q_H = 0$, the condition that allows taxpayers with high incomes to play mixed strategies becomes:

$$-q_H \lambda + q_L \left(f + \lambda\right) + \left(y_H - t_L y_L\right)\left(1 + oc\right)^n -$$
$$q_L \left[y_H - t_L y_L - \left(t_H - t_L\right)\left(1 + ir\right)^n\right] +$$
$$q_L \left(y_H - t_L y_L\right)\left(1 + oc\right)^n \qquad (10)$$

Which results in:

$$q_L = \frac{\left(y_H - t_L y_L\right)\left(1 + oc\right)^n}{\left[y_H - t_L y_L - \left(t_H y_H - t_L y_L\right)\left(1 + ir\right)^n + \left(y_H - t_L y_L\right)\left(1 + oc\right)^n + f + \lambda\right]}.$$

On the other hand, based on q_L estimated above, the condition that is compatible with the inspector playing mixed strategies is:

$$p_{L/H}\left[\begin{matrix}\left(t_H y_H - t_L y_L\right)\left(1 + ir\right)^n + \\ f - \left(c_H y_H - c_L y_L\right)\end{matrix}\right] - t_L y_L = 0 \qquad (11)$$

Rearranging and using the fact that $ph_L = 0$, it could be written that:

$$ph_H = \frac{p_H\left[\begin{matrix}\left(t_H y_H - t_L y_L\right)\left(1 + ir\right)^n + \\ f - \left(c_H y_H - c_L y_L\right)\end{matrix}\right] - t_L y_L}{p_H\left[\left[\begin{matrix}\left(t_H y_H - t_L y_L\right)\left(1 + ir\right)^n + \\ f - \left(c_H y_H - c_L y_L\right)\end{matrix}\right]\right] - t_L y_L}$$

As we can see, the probability of strategic taxpayers with high income report the true income is dependent from the tax income gap, interest rate applied into default, the gap between auditory costs and fine. On the other hand, tax authority is dependent from gap tax income, interest rate, opportunity cost, fine and pecuniary amount.

Environment

Our model simulates the dynamics in a simplified virtual environment in which tax authority, each time turn, proceeds to collect taxes and implements a inspection policy imposing fines on non-compliers. The simulated environment has the sufficient flexibility to add other relevant attributes to agents and different policies to tackle tax evasion.

System Dynamics

Our model simulates the dynamics in a simplified virtual environment in which tax authority, each time turn, proceeds to collect taxes and implements a inspection policy imposing fines on non-compliers.The simulated environment has the sufficient flexibility to add other relevant attributes to agents and different policies to tackle tax evasion.

Results

The 3R model allows us to observe how different mechanisms may yield, from given initial conditions to different outputs in terms of aggregate level of tax evasion in society. As we can see, after thousands of runs and doing variations on parameters, that tax evasion starts to increase until reach some maximum level depending from what parameter had changed. Then tax evasion begins to slowdown until reach a stable value with reduced oscillation (see Figure 1-4).

Results also demonstrate a higher variability on tax evasion with an increase of taxed income gap. It means under these circumstances, taxpayers are more sensible to this gap variation which brings high dynamic to the model. Consequently, society reveals more instability than status quo in terms of tax evasion, demonstrating high intensity of the three functions of mind in working on. It also reveals a greater level of tax evasion which suggests that as greater is the differential between both levels of income, the greater will be tax evasion. In this sense, governments should implement policies to avoid high dispersion of taxpayer's income scales.

In terms of risk aversion, an increase causes less variability in the model, this means more consensus among taxpayers. It also reduce the

Figure 1. "Status quo" simulation. This simulation was done using parameters that reflect the current situation in Portugal

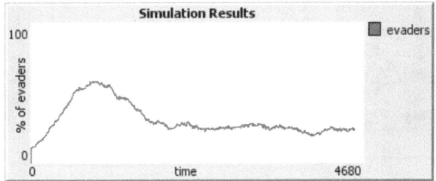

Figure 2. Tax income gap increase. Simulation represents an increase in the differential between tax amounts of income levels, maintaining other parameters static.

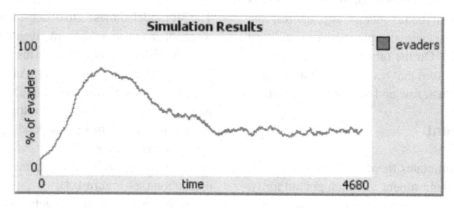

Figure 3. Opportunity cost increase. Simulation represents an increase in opportunity cost parameter, maintaining other parameters static.

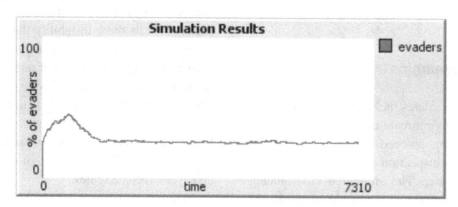

Figure 4. Risk aversion increase. Simulation represents an increase in risk aversion parameter for each taxpayer type, maintaining other parameters static.

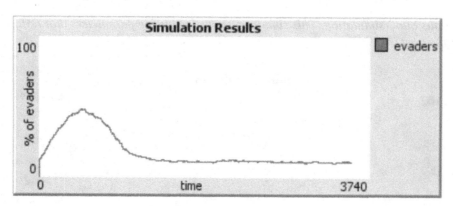

level of tax evasion in society. Instead, opportunity cost causes a great and immediate reaction from taxpayers, increasing tax evasion suddenly.

Figure 5 shows that perceived risk has been overtaken by calculated risk generated from the reason of agents and associated to interaction. This happens despite the fact that perceived risk by risk seekers had preponderance, presenting a first tendency to evade. This evidence appears also when we compare the audit rate in society with the agent's perceived rate generated by the system and the calculated rate towards interactive decision. We see that the effective audit rate coming up from the system dynamics has tendency to approach asymptotically the calculated rate by taxpayer's reasoning.

These results suggest that taxpayers first react instantaneously and only after think. Imitation reflects the "laziness" of imitators for reasoning attending the seduction of benefits to evade. This interesting result is in consonance with what Spinoza defended. Agents used the three mind functions. The results are also consistent with the findings of Kahneman, in which taxpayers conduct their decisions mainly by their intuitions instead of reason. Only after some interactions in society they start to reason about risk. This evidence goes against the economic perspective of tax evasion literature where strategic taxpayers are assumed as being completely rational agents.

FUTURE RESEARCH DIRECTIONS

As a result of this study, many questions arise for further research. The first one is knowing what kind of impact there would be if we added several tax categories to the game. Please note that only two levels of income were used in this study. However, it is important to clarify whether this segmentation influences or not the evasion system and consequently determines definition of fiscal policies. The second issue is to know how is the relation between risk aversion and perceived risk. In this case, it is important to clarify how risk aversion and consequent feelings, like fear, influence the tax evasion perception.

CONCLUSION

The strategic taxpayers behaviour under tax evasion is not a new concept. The literature has demonstrated the existing game, basically when taxpayers realize the ineffectiveness of the tax system and defend their own interests. This is

Figure 5. Comparison of distinct risk perspectives. Simulation compares all audit probabilities in the system.

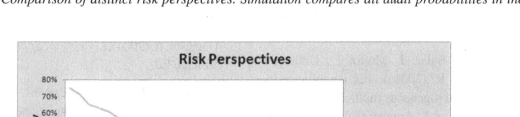

reflected on decision, which is not an arbitrary behaviour made by taxpayers, but constitutes a complex and rational mechanism. Third, because tax authority will develop policies to minimise the number of audited taxpayers.

So the main objective of this article was to analyze through a multi-agent system if and how the three functions of mind expressed by Spinoza interact with risk in order to influence tax evasion in society. We showed that strategic taxpayers firstly react according to their own perceived risk combined with wealth maximisation in deterrence of reasoning and reflection. Reasoning and consequent calculated risk change the course of tax evasion and breaks the tendency given by intuitions. Consequently, the developed model confirms what was discovered by psychology. Agents first react to the risk based on simple heuristics and only after they ignite the complex reasoning which refutes the assumption of literature that strategic agents are uniquely rational.

REFERENCES

Alligham, M., & Sandmo, A. (1972). Income tax evasion: A theoretical analysis. *Journal of Public Economics, 3*, 171–179.

Alm, J., McClelland, G. H., & Schulze, W. D. (1992). Why do people pay taxes? *Journal of Public Economics, 48*, 21–48. doi:10.1016/0047-2727(92)90040-M

Antunes, L., Balsa, J., Moniz, L., Urbano, P., & Palma, C. R. (2006a). Tax compliance in a simulated heterogeneous multi-agent society. In J. S. Sichman, & L. Antunes (Eds.), *MABS 2005. LNCS (LNAI)* (Vol. 3891). Heidelberg, Germany: Springer. doi:10.1007/11734680_11

Aumann, R. J. (2008). Game theory. In S. N. Durlauf, & L. E. Blume (Eds.), *The new Palgrave dictionary of economics* (2nd ed.). London: Macmillan. doi:10.1057/9780230226203.0615

Balsa, J., Antunes, L., Respício, A., & Coelho, H. (2006), Autonomous inspectors in tax compliance simulation. In *Proceedings of the 18th European Meeting on Cybernetics and Systems Research.*

Becker, G. (1968). Crime and punishment: An economic approach. *The Journal of Political Economy, 76*, 169–217. doi:10.1086/259394

Bernasconi, M. (1998). Tax evasion and orders of risk aversion. *Journal of Public Economics, 67*, 123–134. doi:10.1016/S0047-2727(97)00051-0

Bloomquist, K. (2011). Tax compliance as an evolutionary coordination game: An agent-based approach. *Public Finance Review, 39*, 25. doi:10.1177/1091142110381640

Braithwaite, V., & Ahmed, E. (2005). A threat to tax morale: The case of Australian higher education policy. *Journal of Economic Psychology, 26*(4). doi:10.1016/j.joep.2004.08.003

Castelfranchi, C. (2003). The micro-macro constitution of power. Understanding the Social II: Philosophy of Sociality. *ProtoSociology Journal, 18*, 208–265.

Corchon, L. (1984). *A note on tax evasion and the theory of games.* Madrid, Spain: Mimeo.

Cowell, F. (1987). The economics of tax evasion. In J. D. Hey, & P. J. Lambert (Eds.), *Surveys in the economics of uncertainty*. Oxford, UK: Basil Blackwell.

Damásio, A. (2004). *Looking for Spinoza.* London: Vintage Ed.

Davis, J. S., Hecht, G., & Perkins, J. D. (2003). Social behaviours, enforcement and tax compliance dynamics. *Accounting Review, 78*, 39–69. doi:10.2308/accr.2003.78.1.39

Kahneman, D. (2012). *Fast and slow, Two ways of thinking* (Portuguese Ed.). Brazil: Objetiva.

Kirchler, E. (2007). *The economic psychology of tax behaviour*. Cambridge, UK: Cambridge University Press. doi:10.1017/CBO9780511628238

Korobow, A., Johnson, C., & Axtell, R. (2007). An agent based model of tax compliance with social networks. *National Tax Journal, 60*(3), 589–610.

Levi, M. (1988). *Of rule and revenue*. Berkeley, CA: The University of California Press.

Lohele, C. (1996). *Thinking strategically: Power tools for personal and professional advancements*. Cambridge, UK: Cambridge University Press. doi:10.1017/CBO9780511525308

Lucena, D., & Gaspar, V. (1989, February). *Strategic tax reporting* (Working Paper 112. FEUNL. Retrieved from from http://fesrvsd.fe.unl.pt/WP-FEUNL/WP1989/wp112.pdf

Miguel, F., Noguera, J., Llàcer, T., & Tapia, E. (2012). Exploring tax compliance: An agent based simulation. In K. G. Troitzsch, M. Möhring, & U. Lotzmann (Eds.), *Proceedings of 26th European Conference on Modelling and Simulation*. ECMS.

Mittone, L., & Patelli, P. (2000). Imitative behaviour in tax evasion. In B. Stefansson, & F. Luna (Eds.), *Economic simulations in swarm: Agent-based modelling and object oriented programming* (pp. 133–158). Amsterdam, The Netherlands: Kluwer. doi:10.1007/978-1-4615-4641-2_5

Olson, M. (1965/1971). *The logic of collective action: Public goods and the theory of groups* (Revised Ed.). Cambridge, MA: Harvard University Press.

Simon, H. (1955). A behavioral model of rational choice. *The Quarterly Journal of Economics, 69*, 99–188. doi:10.2307/1884852

Spinoza, B. (2009). *Ethica ordine geometrico demonstrata* [The ethics]. Radford, VA: Wilder Publications. (Original work published 1677)

Srinivasan, T. (1973). Tax evasion: A model. *Journal of Public Economics*, 339–346. doi:10.1016/0047-2727(73)90024-8

Stanovich, K. E., & West, R. F. (2008). On the relative independence of thinking biases and cognitive ability. *Journal of Personality and Social Psychology, 94*, 672–695. doi:10.1037/0022-3514.94.4.672 PMID:18361678

Szabó, A., Gulyás, L., & Tóth, I. J. (2008). *TAXSIM agent based tax evasion simulator*. Paper presented at the 5th European Social Simulation Association Conference (ESSA 2008).

Telser, L. (1987). *A theory of efficient cooperation and competition*. Cambridge, UK: Cambridge University Press. doi:10.1017/CBO9780511528378

Torgler, B., & Frey, B. (2007). Tax morale and conditional cooperation. *Journal of Comparative Economics, 35*, 136–159. doi:10.1016/j.jce.2006.10.006

Zaklan, G., Westerhoff, F., & Stauffer, D. (2009). Analysing tax evasion dynamics via the Ising model. *Journal of Economic of Coordination and Interaction, 4*, 1–14. doi:10.1007/s11403-008-0043-5

ADDITIONAL READING SECTION

Christiansen, V. (1980). Two Comments on Tax Evasion. *Journal of Public Economics, 13*, 389–401. doi:10.1016/0047-2727(86)90012-5

Cowell, F. (1981).... *Taxation and Labour Supply with Risky Activities Economica, 48*, 365–379.

Cowell, F. (1985). Tax Evasion with Labour Income. *Journal of Public Economics*. doi:10.1016/0047-2727(85)90036-2 PMID:12267542

Damásio, A. (2003). *Ao Encontro de Espinosa: As Emoções Sociais e a Neurologia do Sentir*. Lisboa: Europa-América.

Greenberg, J. (1984). Avoiding Tax avoidance: A (Repeated) Game theorectic Approach. *Journal of Economic Theory*, *32*, 1–13. doi:10.1016/0022-0531(84)90071-1

Harsanyi, J. (1973). Games with Randomly Distributed Payoffs: a New Rationale for mixed strategies Equilibrium Points. *International Journal of Game Theory*, *2*, 1–23. doi:10.1007/BF01737554

Harsanyi. J and R. Selten(1988) A General Theory of Equilibrium Selection in Games, MIT Press

Reinganum, J. F., & Wilde, L. (1986). Equilibrium verification and Reporting Policies in a Model of Tax Compliance. *International Economic Review*, *27*(3), 739–760. doi:10.2307/2526692

Reinganum, J. F., & Wilde, L. L. (1985). Income Tax Compliance in a Principal-Agent Framework. *Journal of Public Economics*, *26*, 1–18. doi:10.1016/0047-2727(85)90035-0

Sanchez, I. (1988). *Principal-Agent Models of Income Tax Compliance Mimeo*. Madrid.

KEY TERMS AND DEFINITIONS

Reaction: Human or animal skilled behaviour in response to a stimulus. The brain function takes place in the instincts of primitive brain, fundamentally in the amygdale.

Reason: Express relations with things, intellect, analytical, and critical. Reason is not "lazy" but intentional, i.e. selective to what an individual is interested on. It is located in the cerebral cortex.

Reflect: Empathetic feelings, musing on the whole. It is located in the frontal lobes of the brain.

Risk: It is an adverse effect resulting from an event or an activity, rather than an opportunity for desired outcomes.

Risk Aversion: It is an attitude of reluctance when humans are exposed to risk.

Risk Perception: It is the recognition by people of the seriousness of risk.

Tax Evasion: It is a social phenomena where a taxpayer underreports his truly income.

Chapter 16
Knowledge–Based Externalities and Geographical Clusters:
An Agent–Based Simulation Study

Nunzia Carbonara
Politecnico di Bari, Italy

ABSTRACT

Agglomeration economies are positive externalities associated with the co-location of firms within a bounded geographic area. Traditionally, these agglomerative advantages have been expressed in terms of pecuniary externalities and they have been identified as one of the key sources of geographical cluster (GC) competitive advantage. However, in the last years the basics of competition are changed and the ability of firms to create new knowledge is more crucial for success rather than the efficiency in production. This has shifted the attention of scholars on the role of knowledge and learning in GCs. In line with these studies, this chapter suggests that agglomeration economies are related to both pecuniary externalities and knowledge-based externalities. The latter are benefits that co-located firms can gain in terms of development of knowledge. To investigate whether knowledge-based externalities affect geographical clustering of firms, an agent-based model is developed. By using this model, a simulation analysis is carried out.

INTRODUCTION

Geographical clusters (GCs) are concentrations of interconnected companies and institutions in particular fields (Porter, 1998). These systems of firms (including also Marshallian and dynamic industrial districts) have been extensively investigated in the literature. Different aspects have been observed, and some notions and models have been developed aimed at identifying the sources of

competitive advantage, such as the agglomeration economies concept introduced by Marshall (1920) and further formalized by Krugman (1991); the flexible specialization production model conceptualized by Piore and Sabel (1984); the industrial atmosphere notion conceived by Marshall (1919); and the *innovative milieux notion* developed by the GREMI (Maillat et al., 1993).

Referring to agglomeration economies, these are positive externalities (benefits) resulting from

DOI: 10.4018/978-1-4666-5954-4.ch016

the co-location of economic activities and motivating firms to geographically cluster. In fact, the spatial concentration of firms generates several benefits, such as: knowledge spillovers among competitors; industry demand that creates a pool of specialized labor; and industry demand that creates a pool of specialized input providers (Marshall, 1920). For Krugman (1991), the benefits of agglomeration in essence depend on three factors: i) substantial increasing returns to scale, both at the level of single firm (internal economies) and the industry (external economies); ii) sufficiently low transport costs; and iii) large local demand.

According to the geographical economics literature, firms tend to geographically cluster when agglomeration economies exist[1], which consist mainly of *pecuniary* externalities (Krugman, 1991), because they gain from the reduction of production cost and/or the increase of the production efficiency. Thus, GCs are cost efficient spatial configurations and their source of competitive advantage is based on cost reduction.

More recently strategic management literature has highlighted the limit associated with a competitive strategy based only on two sources of competitive advantage (cost reduction and differentiation) and has recognized the importance of knowledge as a fundamental factor in creating economic value and competitive advantage for firms (Grant, 1997; Leonard-Barton, 1995). What a firm knows, how it uses what it knows, and how fast it can develop new knowledge are key aspects for firm success (Prusak, 1997; Hamel and Prahalad, 1994). Therefore, knowledge is a key asset for competing firms and learning is a key process, because it increases the firm's cognitive capital, i.e. the firm's knowledge stock.

In the last years, some scholars have analyzed the role of knowledge in GCs and proposed a knowledge-based theory of GCs (Malmberg & Maskell, 2004; Maskell, 2001b; Tallman et al., 2004). Some works have investigated the nature of knowledge circulating in GCs, the knowledge transfer and creation processes embedded in GCs,

and the learning processes activated by firms in GCs (Albino and Schiuma, 2003; Albino et al., 2005). These are particularly effective in GCs, because proximity among firms largely enhances them (Baptista, 2000; Maskell, 2001a, Boshma, 2005).

These studies conceptualize GCs as venues of enhanced knowledge creation and they suggest that agglomeration economies are based on *knowledge-based* externalities (Lorenzen & Maskell, 2004; Maskell, 2001a). In this view, the very reason why a GC exists is to create a competitive advantage for the collective, as well as for individual firms, by enhancing individual firms' knowledge creation efforts (Arikan, 2009). In fact, the theory holds that geographic proximity increases not only the frequency of interactions between cluster firms but also the effectiveness of knowledge exchanges so as facilitating knowledge creation within GCs. Thus, firms can capture benefits from co-location not only in terms of lower costs or improved efficiency in production but also in terms of increased knowledge stocks.

The aim of this chapter is to contribute to the debate about the role of *knowledge-based* externalities in the process of geographical clustering of firms.

Could *knowledge-based* externalities explain the process of geographical clustering of firms? Do they are the very driving force of this process?

To address these questions, it is assumed that *knowledge-based* externalities are due to the existence within the GC of two processes of external learning (Malerba, 1988, 1992): learning by imitation and learning by interaction, and that the effectiveness of these learning processes is positively influenced by the geographical, cognitive, and organizational proximities among firms.

Such an assumption is built on recent studies that have highlighted the existence of relationship between the different dimensions of proximity, namely geographical, cognitive, and organizational, and the effectiveness of external learning processes (Boschma, 2004; Boshma, 2005; Cohendet & Llerena, 1997; Cohen & Levinthal, 1990).

To pursue this issue, the agent-based simulation is used as research methodology. Recently, some scholars have recognized that GCs are complex adaptive systems, pointing out the benefits coming from the use of complexity science tools in the study of GCs (Albino et al., 2005; Lane, 2002). In addition, agent-based simulation is a valuable approach to build new theories, concepts, and knowledge about some processes (Carley & Gasser, 2000).

An agent-based model is developed, where the agents (firms), located into a grid (geographical space), interact, learn, and develop their stock of knowledge. The aim of the agent is to maximize the value of its competitive advantage, defined as a higher knowledge stock than competitors. To do this, the agent can move within the grid looking for new positions that increase their competitive advantage.

The simulation allows observing whether the agents tend to geographically cluster, namely assume a stable spatial configuration where they are arranged in groups of close agents.

The chapter is organized as follows. In the next section a brief summary of the theoretical background is provided. Successively the agent-based model of the process of geographical clustering of firms driven by *knowledge-based* externalities is presented. Then the simulation analysis is carried out to study the emergence of geographical clusters and finally the results are discussed.

THEORETICAL BACKGROUND

To develop a theory of agglomeration economies based on knowledge externalities, it is needed to refer to different bodies of knowledge that allow understanding how firms can gain benefits by co-location and how they learn.

Similarly to the economic geography studies that develop the concept of agglomeration econo-

mies to describe the benefits that firms obtain by locating near each other, this study focuses on a new source of externalities, namely knowledge-based externalities, to explain the advantages of the co-localization of firms and the clustering processes. In particular, while the pioneering concept of "externalities" identifies static economies of agglomeration that are based on efficiency gains, this study focuses on dynamic agglomeration economies that highlights the central role of learning and knowledge creation (Ernst, 2002).

The need to turn the attention on these knowledge externalities is motivated by recent studies on strategic management highlighting that competitiveness is more and more related to the ability of firms to upgrade continuously their knowledge base (Porter, 1998), rather than simply to obtain static efficiency.

The knowledge externalities are then defined as benefits for co-located firms in terms of development of their knowledge stock due to learning processes.

To better investigate the central role of the learning processes in the agglomeration economies, we refer to recent contributions in the field of the regional studies that have analyzed the innovation and learning processes activated at a regional level (Maskell, 2004; Malberg e Maskell, 2004; Shaver et al., 2000; Tallman, 2004). These studies have highlighted that different and intertwined dimensions of proximity affect the external learning processes (Malerba, 1988). In particular, Boschma (2005) identifies five dimensions of proximity: cognitive, organizational, geographical, social, and institutional. Knoben and Oerlemans (2006) in a recent literature review consider also other two dimensions of proximity, namely cultural and technological. In a recent study Albino et al. (2007) have analyzed the role played by proximity dimensions as a communication resource that can be exploited by firms and regions for sustaining their competitive advantage, by increasing the effectiveness of the external learning processes and their innovative capability. This chapter focuses on three dimensions of proximity, namely cognitive, organizational, and geographic, and for each of them the effects on the external learning processes is analyzed.

Geographical proximity is defined as the spatial or physical distance between two firms. The literature has recently claimed that firms that are spatially concentrated benefit from knowledge externalities (Maskell, 2001a). Short distances in fact enable information contacts and facilitate the exchange of tacit knowledge. The larger the distance between firms, the less the intensity of these positive externalities. This may even be true for the exchange of codified knowledge, because its interpretation and assimilation may still require tacit knowledge and, thus, spatial closeness (Howells, 2002). Too much geographical proximity may also have negative impact on learning and innovation due to the problem of lock-in, meaning a lack of openness and flexibility (Boshma, 2005).

However, some authors have noticed that external learning processes to take place require some level of cognitive proximity. With the notion of cognitive proximity, it is meant the similarity of the knowledge stocks of two firms (Boschma, 2004). Firms sharing the same knowledge stock and expertise may learn from each other. However, too much cognitive proximity may have negative impact on learning and innovation. In fact, some cognitive distance should be maintained to enhance learning because knowledge building often requires dissimilar, complementary bodies of knowledge (Cohendet & Llerena, 1997).

Cognitive proximity also influences the firm absorptive capacity, namely the firm capacity to absorb new knowledge. In particular, it is facilitated by cognitive proximity between firms. Therefore, it depends on the knowledge stocks of interacting firms that should be enough close (Cohen and Levinthal, 1990).

Organizational proximity is defined as the extent to which relations are shared in an inter-organizational and intra-organizational arrangements. This involves the rate of autonomy and the degree of control that can be exerted in organizational arrangements (Boschma, 2004). Organizational proximity is believed to be beneficial for learning and innovation. However, too much organizational proximity may produce specific and immutable exchange relationships or a closeness of the organizational structure towards external sources of knowledge, negatively affecting learning and innovation processes. On the other hand, too little organizational proximity creates a lack of control increasing the opportunistic behaviors.

Finally, referring to the organizational learning studies as well as the recent contribution in the field of innovation economics, among the different types of external learning processes, those that strongly characterize GC are learning by interaction and learning by imitation (Malmberg & Maskell, 1999).

Processes of learning by interaction are deliberately activated by firms when they are involved within networks of formal and established relationships. These are based on the continuous exchange of information and knowledge among complementary firms, among firms and customers, and among firms and universities/research centers.

Learning by imitation is concerned with the gathering and reproduction of knowledge elsewhere created. In this process different knowledge channels can be used, such as the consultation of scientific and technical publications, the examination of suppliers, customers, and competitors, as well as the participation at events (e.g. conferences, trade-fairs). Both the external learning processes are based on knowledge spillovers which can be intentional and unintentional (Torre & Gilly, 2000).

THE AGENT-BASED MODEL OF GEOGRAPHICAL CLUSTERING

The process of geographical clustering of firms based on *knowledge-based* externalities is investigated by means of an agent-based simulation model. The main advantage in the use of this simulation technique is that it allows studying the process of geographical clustering of firms as an emergent behavior of the system. This means that GCs will emerge as the spontaneous result of the firm location decisions and the interactions among firms.

In the next subsections first the main hypotheses of the model are presented and then the model in terms of agents, environment, interactions among agents, and measures, is defined. The computational implementation of the model is made by using the software *NetLogo*.

Assumptions

The model is based on the following assumptions.

Firms are engaged in location choices. Geographical relocation is costless and instantaneous. In this way the location decision only depends on the incentives caused by agglomeration externality.

Agglomeration economies are only based on *knowledge-based* externalities, which consist in the development of the firm's knowledge stock due to two learning processes, namely learning by imitation and learning by interaction. No other sources of knowledge creation are considered, such as for example research and development activities or external (to the GC) source of knowledge.

The level of knowledge stock developed by the two learning processes is affected by three different dimensions of proximity, namely geographical, cognitive, and organizational proximities.

The firm competitive success is directly proportional to its knowledge stock. Therefore, the higher the knowledge stock, the more successful the firm.

Agents and Environment

The agent of the model corresponds to the single firm. It is modeled as an object located into a grid that represents the physical space in which agents move. The grid is a matrix 50x50, therefore for each agent 2500 positions are available and each

position can be occupied by an agent at a time. The grid is a virtual representation of the real world and as such represents the physical space in which firms can agglomerate and form a cluster. Considering the number of agents (N = 30), the dimension of the virtual space (the grid) can widely contain one or more clusters, so that, to some extent, it can be considered as the dimension of the real space potentially available for firms that choose new locations.

The number of agents (N) into the grid is defined as population.

Each agent *i* is characterized by two dynamic attributes:

- The position occupied at a given instant time within the grid $P_{i,t}(x,y)$,
- The value of accumulated knowledge stock at a given instant time $K_{i,t}$

The knowledge stock is modeled as a scalar number. This means that firm is considered as repository of knowledge that can indefinitely increase (Krogh & Vicari, 1992; Vicari, 1991). No difference between tacit and codified knowledge is considered.

The goal of each agent is to maximize its fitness that is influenced by the position of the agent within the grid. Therefore, during the simulation agents move looking for new position with higher fitness. The fitness measures the competitive advantage (*CA*) that the agent takes in a given position. Based on the general definition of competitive advantage as a superior performance than competitors, the agent maximizes its fitness when possesses a knowledge stock higher than the other agents.

The agent possesses a mental model that represents its view of external world, namely what agent knows about the other agents. Each agent knows the knowledge stock accumulated by the other agents and their position into the grid. It is assumed that agents know these values without errors.

Actions

Learning. Agents are continuously engaged in learning activities, i.e. learning by imitation and learning by interaction with all the other agents of population. Each agent activates $N-1$ learning relations at each step. Each learning relation between the agent i and the agent j determines, in each instant time t, a development of the knowledge stock of the agent i due to imitation ($\Delta K_{ij,t,imitation}$) and interaction ($\Delta K_{ij,t,interaction}$) with the agent j.

The effectiveness of learning processes is influenced by geographical, cognitive, and organizational proximities between the two interacting agents. In particular, it is assumed that the values of $\Delta K_{ij,t,imitation}$ and $\Delta K_{ij,t,interaction}$ decrease with the geographical distance between agents, according with the following functions:

$$\Delta K_{ij,t\,imitation}\left(\text{geographical\_prox.}\right) = \left(\frac{d_{max} - d_{ij}}{d_{max}}\right)^{\beta_{imitation}}$$

(1)

$$\Delta K_{ij,t\,interaction}\left(\text{geographical\_prox.}\right) = \left(\frac{d_{max} - d_{ij}}{d_{max}}\right)^{\beta_{interaction}}$$

(2)

where:

d_{ij} is the geographical distance between the agents i and j;

d_{max} is the maximum possible geographical distance between the agents i and j;

$\beta_{imitation}$ is a parameter that determines the influence of the geographical proximity on the process of learning by imitation;

$\beta_{interaction}$ is a parameter that determines the influence of the geographical proximity on the process of learning by interaction.

Based on the literature on learning organization (Badaracco, 1991; Dogson, 1993), it is assumed that, for the same geographical proximity, the de-

velopment of the knowledge stock due to learning by interaction is higher than the development of the knowledge stock due to learning by imitation, therefore in the model it is fixed: $\beta_{interaction} > \beta_{imitation}$.

As regard the cognitive proximity, it is assumed that the development of the knowledge stock of the agent i due to imitation and interaction with the agent j increases with the cognitive distance between agents, according with the following functions:

$$\Delta K_{ij,timitation}\left(\text{cognitive\_prox.}\right) = \left(K_{j,t} - K_{i,t}\right)$$
if $K_i < K_j$

(3)

$$\Delta K_{ij,timitation}\left(\text{cognitive\_prox.}\right) = 0$$

if $K_{i,t} \geq K_{j,t}$

(4)

$$\Delta K_{ij,t\,interaction}\left(\text{cognitive\_prox.}\right) = \left|K_{i,t} - K_{j,t}\right|$$

(5)

where $K_{i,t} - K_{j,t}$ is the cognitive distance between the agents i and j;

Equation 4 means that an agent does not imitate agents with a lower knowledge stock.

As regard the organizational proximity, it is considered that it positively affects both learning processes in the same way, according to the following function:

$$\Delta K_{ij,timitation/interaction}\left(\text{organizational\_prox.}\right) = \delta * \left(1 + p_{organizational_{ij}}\right)$$

(6)

where:

$p_{organizational_{ij}}$ represents the organizational proximity between the agents i and j.

$p_{organizational_{ij}} = 0$ if agents i and j are not linked by a cooperative relationship that facilitates the knowledge sharing and the knowledge exchange.

$p_{organizational_{ij}} = 1$ if agents i and j are linked by a cooperative relationship that facilitates the knowledge sharing and the knowledge exchange.

For each couple of agents, the value of the organizational proximity (1 or 0) is assigned randomly.

δ is a parameter that determines the influence of the organizational proximity on the processes of learning by interaction and by imitation. The value of the parameter is fixed equal to 0,5 to moderate the influence of the organizational proximity on the processes of learning by interaction and by imitation and then take into account the effect of the organizational lock-in.

The final expressions of the total knowledge stock of the agent i, developed by imitation ($\Delta K_{ij,t,imitation,total}$) and interaction ($\Delta K_{ij,t,interaction,total}$) with the agent j in each instant time t, are obtained by considering the combined effects of proximities but also by considering the effect of the absorptive capacity (Cohen and Levinthal, 1990). The latter, is defined as follows:

$$ac_{ij} = \frac{K_{i,t}}{K_{j,t}} \text{ if } K_{i,t} \leq K_{j,t} \tag{7}$$

$$ac_{ij} = \frac{K_{j,t}}{K_{i,t}} \text{ if } K_{i,t} > K_{j,t} \tag{8}$$

Therefore the values of $\Delta K_{ij,t,imitation,total}$ and $\Delta K_{ij,t,interaction,total}$ are given by the following functions:

$$\Delta K_{ij,t imitation,total} =$$
$$\gamma \left(K_{j,t} - K_{i,t} \right) * ac_{ij} * \left(\frac{d_{max} - d_{ij}}{d_{max}} \right)^{\beta_{imitation}} * \delta \left(1 + p_{organizational_{ij}} \right)$$
$$\text{if } K_{i,t} < K_{j,t} \tag{9}$$

$$\Delta K_{ij,t imitation,total} = 0 \text{ if } K_{i,t} \geq K_{j,t} \tag{10}$$

$$\Delta K_{ij,t int eraction,total} =$$
$$\alpha \left| K_{j,t} - K_{i,t} \right| * ac_{ij} * \left(\frac{d_{max} - d_{ij}}{d_{max}} \right)^{\beta_{int eraction}} * \delta \left(1 + p_{organizational_{ij}} \right),$$
$$\forall \left(K_{i,t}, K_{j,t} \right) \tag{11}$$

where:

α is the firm's propensity to create new knowledge through learning by interaction;
γ is the firm's propensity to create new knowledge through learning by imitation.

Developing knowledge stock: As a consequence of the two learning processes (learning by imitation and learning by interaction), each agent develops its knowledge stock. At each step t, the value of $K_{i,t}$ is updated by adding the quantity of knowledge stock resulted from the learning by imitation and learning by interaction. In particular, the knowledge stock of the agent i is updated as follows:

$$K_i(t+1) =$$
$$K_i(t) +$$
$$\sum_{j \neq i} \Delta K_{ij,t int eraction,total} + \sum_{j \neq i} \Delta K_{ij,t imitation,total} \tag{12}$$

According to this function, the knowledge stock of each agent is updated on the basis of: 1) the agent knowledge stock at step t, $K_i(t)$; 2) the incoming knowledge flow due to the interaction at the step t with the other agents

$$\sum_{j \neq i} \Delta K_{ij,t int eraction,total}$$

and 3) the incoming knowledge that the agent can acquire at the step t through learning by imitation

$$\sum_{j\neq i} \Delta K_{ij,t\,imitation,total} \cdot$$

Notice that while the incoming knowledge flow due to the interaction is always non-zero, the third term of the equation 12

$$\sum_{j\neq i} \Delta K_{ij,t\,imitation,total}$$

is equal to zero for the agent with maximum knowledge stock.

*Choosing the new position*L At each step t, each agent i selects a position into the grid among the possible adjacent cells (Figure 1). The selected position is the one that maximizes the development of $CA_i(t)$, calculated as follows:

$$CA_i(\mathrm{t}) = \sum_{j\neq i} \Delta K_{ijt\,interaction,total} +$$
$$\sum_{j\neq i} \Delta K_{ijt\,imitation,total} - \sum_{j\neq i} \Delta K_{ji,t\,imitation,total}$$

$$(13)$$

Figure 1. Possible new positions of the agent into the grid

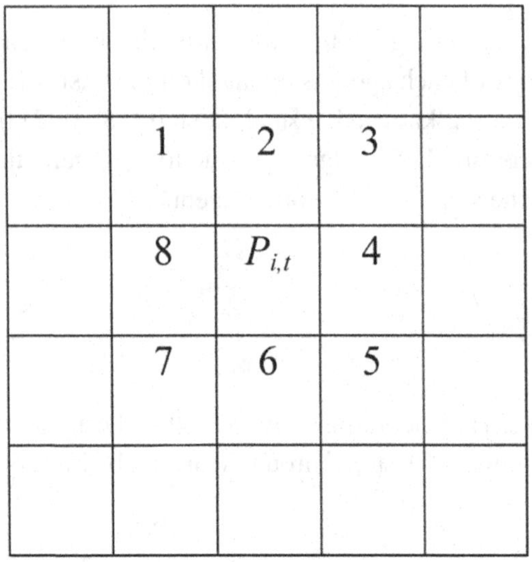

	1	2	3	
	8	$P_{i,t}$	4	
	7	6	5	

where:

$$-\sum_{j\neq i} \Delta K_{ij,t\,interaction,total}$$

is the incoming knowledge flow for agent i due to the interaction at the step t with each other agents j;

$$\sum_{j\neq i} \Delta K_{ij,t\,imitation,total}$$

is the incoming knowledge flow that the agent i can acquire at the step t by imitating each other agents j;

$$\sum_{j\neq i} \Delta K_{ji,t\,imitation,total}$$

is the outcoming knowledge flow for agent i due to the imitation of each other agents j at the step t;

Therefore, the competitive advantage is increased by the new knowledge acquired through learning by interaction and by imitation, but it is also decreased by the outcoming flow of knowledge due to imitation processes carried out by agents with a lower knowledge stock (knowledge spill-over).

Agent, at each step t, computes the value of $CA_{i,t}$ for nine positions, namely the eight adjacent positions and the position occupied by itself, and then chooses the new position that assures the highest value.

Moving in the selected position: At each step the agent moves into the new selected position.

Measures

The emergence of a spatial cluster. Starting from a randomly spatial distribution of the agents within the grid, a spatial cluster of agents will emerge when the agents that move within the grid by searching their preferred position will assume a stable position and will be arranged in groups of two or more than two agents. In this situation agents have no incentive to change their position. On the contrary, a clustering behavior does not emergence when agents continuously move within the grid and/or assume a stand-alone stable position.

Description of the spatial clusters. Once spatial clusters are emerged, it is interesting to have measures that describe their characteristics. To this aim, at the end of simulation, first the number of clusters has been measured and then, for each clusters, the following variables have been assessed:

- The average knowledge stock of cluster ($K_{average}$);
- The highest knowledge stock of cluster ($K_{highest}$);
- The lowest knowledge stock of cluster (K_{lowest}).

Sequencing of the Events and Simulation Steps

The initialization of the simulation involves the creation of the specified number of agents and the assignment of characteristics to each agent, namely the starting position into the grid (randomly assigned) and the starting value of the knowledge stock (randomly assigned according to a uniform distribution).

After initialization, the simulation is updated according to the following steps:

- Compute for the agent i the value of CA_i for all possible new positions included the current one;
- Choose the position that maximizes CA_i;
- Move agent i into the new position;
- Update the value of K_i;
- Repeat actions (a) through (d) until all agents have gone through that process;

- Repeat steps (a) through (d) for as many simulated time steps as specified;
- Compute the measures.

The number of simulation time steps is defined by assuming a value enough great to assure the emergence of spatial clusters (100 steps).

Experimental Settings

The model above is used to study the process of geographical clustering of firms based on *knowledge-based* externalities.

In order to observe whether agents tend to cluster, the simulation experiment has been conducted on the base-line model, characterized by 30 agents randomly positioned within the grid, with starting knowledge stock ($K_{i,0}$) randomly assigned from a uniform distribution with mean ($K_{i,0}$) equal to 100 and standard deviation (*St.dev* $K_{i,0}$) equal to 5. The other values assigned to the parameters in the base-line model are reported in Table 1.

Then, to test the robustness of the model and to assess the impact that changes in the model parameters will have on the simulation results, a sensitivity analysis has been conducted by varying the values of the model parameters, i.e. increasing and/or decreasing their initial value, *coeteris paribus*. In particular, has been evaluated the influence on the characteristics of the emerging clusters exerted by the following parameters:

- Number of agents;
- Distribution of the starting knowledge stock;
- The different propensity of firms to create new knowledge through learning by interaction or learning by imitation;
- Geographical proximity;
- Organizational proximity.

Table 1. Values of the parameters in the experimental settings

Parameter	Values										
	Ex1	*Ex2*	*Ex3*	*Ex4*	*Ex5*	*Ex6*	*Ex7*	*Ex8*	*Ex9*	*Ex10*	*Ex11*
N	30	20	40	30	30	30	30	30	30	30	30
$K_{i,0}$	100	100	100	100	100	100	100	100	100	100	100
St.dev $K_{i,0}$	5	5	5	2,5	10	5	5	5	5	5	5
α/γ	1	1	1	1	1	0	0,5	2	1	1	1
$\beta_{imitation}$	2,5	2,5	2,5	2,5	2,5	2,5	2,5	2,5	5	2,5	2,5
$\beta_{interaction}$	2	2	2	2	2	2	2	2	4	2	2
Org. agreements	50%	50%	50%	50%	50%	50%	50%	50%	50%	0%	100%

Thus, the simulation plan consists in 11 experimental settings. Experiment 1 (*Ex1*) corresponds to the base-line model (Table 1). All the other experiments (*Ex2-Ex11*) are obtained by modifying the values of the following parameters:

- The number of agent in the model (value of N);
- The standard deviation of the starting knowledge stock (St.dev $K_{i,0}$);
- The ratio between the firm's propensity to create new knowledge through learning by interaction (α) and the firm's propensity to create new knowledge through learning by imitation (γ);
- The values of the influence of the geographical proximity on the process of learning by imitation ($\beta_{imitation}$) and the influence of the geographical proximity on the process of learning by interaction ($\beta_{interaction}$);
- The percentage of inter-organizational agreements (*Org.agreements*).

In all the experiments the simulation time is equal to 100 steps and the number of replications is 100. The replication differs in the starting spatial configurations of agents within the grid. Notice that the number of replications assures a reasonable compromise between computational time and the ability to distinguish significant statistical differences among results in different settings (t-test).

SIMULATION RESULTS

Simulation results are shown in Table 2 where the mean and standard deviation of the measures are calculated over the 100 replications. To compare the means of the measures calculated in the baseline model *(Ex1)* with those calculated in the experiments obtained by modifying the values of the parameters *(Ex2-Ex11)* the Student's t-test has been adopted. The *t* values reported in Table 2 prove the statistical significance of the results.

The first important result is that the possibility to increase the knowledge stock motivates firms to geographically cluster. In fact, by running the base-line model it has been observed at the end of simulation the formation of one spatial cluster of agents and the same result is achieved in all the other experiments regardless the experiment with α/γ =0 *(Ex6)*. In this case, where the only learning process is learning by imitation (α = 0; γ ≠ 0), agents with a greater knowledge stock are not motivated to be part of a cluster because the knowledge is transferred from them to those agents with a lower knowledge and not in the opposite way (knowledge spill-over). Then, they continuously move far from the other agents to keep their competitive advantage. On the contrary, agents with a lower knowledge stock continuously follow the most competitive agents because they gain advantage being close to them and by imitating their knowledge.

Table 2. Simulation results

Experimental Settings	Number of Cluster	$K_{average}$		$K_{highest}$		K_{lowest}	
		Mean	Std	Mean	Std	Mean	Std
Ex1 – Baseline model	1	115.7	2.2	156.2	16.3	106.2	1.1
Ex2 (N = 20)	1	110.0	2.2	131.4	7.9	102.8	1.3
t value		*3.47*		*3.34*		*4.58*	
Ex3 (N = 40)	1	128.2	5.7	216.7	25.2	111.1	2.3
t value		*7.18*		*6.20*		*7.01*	
Ex4 – (*St.dev* $K_{i,0}$ = 2,5)	1	106.1	1.1	127.9	8.2	103.6	0.5
t value		*9.92*		*7.23*		*3.51*	
Ex5 – (*St.dev* $K_{i,0}$ = 10)	1	126.8	7.8	220.2	42.4	107.3	3.4
t value		*18.0*		*16.91*		*10.94*	
Ex6 – (α/γ =0)	0	98.9	0.3	111.2	3.4	92.6	2.9
t value		*15.68*		*18.96*		*9.50*	
Ex7 – (α/γ =0.5)	1	105.4	1.4	122.1	6.8	96.2	1.6
t value		*14.32*		*5.1*		*5.62*	
Ex8 – (α/γ =2)	1	163.6	15.5	461.8	85.4	125.1	5.2
t value		*16.9*		*17.8*		*11.4*	
Ex9 – ($\beta_{imitation}$ = 5; $\beta_{interaction}$ = 4)	1	111.4	1.7	144.2	10.9	102.4	0.4
t value		*11.8*		*3.34*		*2.9*	
Ex10 – (*Org. agreements = 0%*)	1	110.0	1.7	129.0	12.3	99.8	1.1
t value		*5.5*		*7.2*		*6.4*	
Ex11 – (*Org. agreements = 100%*)	1	122.0	2.4	173.1	15.5	109.8	1.1
t value		*3.47*		*4.58*		*2.30*	

t Value is calculated by using Student t-test with a = 0.05 (t_{crit} = 1.64).

The Influence of the Number of Agents

To analyze the influence of the number of agents, the results achieved by running the base-line model (*Ex1*) have been compared to those of the experiments with N = 20 (*Ex2*) and N = 40 (*Ex3*).

The number of agents influences the characteristics of the emergent cluster. In particular, as N increases, the average knowledge stock of the cluster increases. That means that a greater number of firms within a GC increases the number of both strong and weak ties among firms and individuals and as a consequence favors the processes of learning by interaction and by imitation. The

positive effect on the learning processes due to a greater number of firms is also confirmed by the trend measured for the highest knowledge stock of cluster.

The Influence of the Distribution of the Starting Knowledge Stock

To analyze the influence of the distribution of the starting knowledge stock, the results achieved by running the base-line model (*Ex1*) have been compared to those of the experiments with *St.dev* $K_{i,0}$ = 2,5 (*Ex4*) and *St.dev* $K_{i,0}$ = 10 (*Ex5*).

Results show that a greater cognitive heterogeneity of the GC firms increases the average knowledge stock of the cluster. This is due to the positive effect of the cognitive distance on the learning processes. However, it is interesting to notice that the average knowledge stock of the cluster does not increase in proportion to the standard deviation of the starting knowledge stock, given that the absorptive capacity of firms decreases when the cognitive distance increases.

The Influence of the Learning Processes

To analyze the influence of the two considered learning processes, the results achieved by running the base-line model (*Ex1*) have been compared to those of the experiments with $\alpha/\gamma = 0$ (*Ex6*), $\alpha/\gamma = 0,5$ (*Ex7*), and $\alpha/\gamma = 2$ (*Ex8*).

Results show that when the learning processes are due more by interaction than by imitation (*Ex8*) the knowledge stock of the cluster increases. In particular, the highest knowledge stock of cluster greatly increases (approximately 200%) in comparison with the same result achieved in the base-line model. This is explained by the fact that for the GC firms with a superior knowledge stock the benefits of learning by interaction are greater than the disadvantages resulting by the knowledge spill-over when $\alpha/\gamma = 2$.

The Influence of the Geographical Proximity

To study the influence of the geographical proximity, the results achieved by running the base-line model (*Ex1*) have been compared to those of the experiment with $\beta_{imitation} = 5$ and $\beta_{interaction} = 4$ (*Ex9*).

Results show that the geographical proximity among firms positively affects the development of knowledge stock, by favoring both the creation of strong and weak ties among individuals and firms, by increasing the knowledge spill-over, and by favoring the knowledge transfer. In fact, the average knowledge stock of the cluster is greater for the base-line model than for the experiment 9,

where the effect of the physical distance d_{ij} on the knowledge developed by each agent by imitation and by interaction is lower than in the base-line model, given that the values of the parameters $\beta_{imitation}$ and $\beta_{interaction}$ are higher.

The Influence of the Organizational Proximity

To study the influence of the geographical proximity, the results achieved by running the base-line model (*Ex1*) have been compared to those of the experiments with *Org. agreements = 0%* (*Ex10*) and with *Org. agreements = 100%* (*Ex11*).

Results show that when the percentage of inter-organizational agreements increases the average knowledge stock of the cluster increases. According to this outcome, a higher level of control within the GC, resulting by a greater formalization and hierarchization of the inter-firm relationships, favors the learning processes within the GC.

CONCLUSION

This study explores the concept of *knowledge-based* externalities in agglomeration economies, namely knowledge-based benefits that co-located firms can gain and that motive them to geographically cluster.

In particular, the chapter aims at investigating whether the geographical clustering of firms can be driven by *knowledge-based* externalities.

To pursue this aim, the agent-based simulation has been used as research methodology. Firstly, an agent-based model has been developed, where agents (firms) tend to maximize their competitive advantage, defined in terms of higher knowledge stock, by choosing new locations within the grid (the geographical space). The development of the knowledge stock depends both on the effectiveness of processes of learning by interaction and learning by imitation and on the agent's absorptive capacity. The effectiveness of the two learning processes is influenced by geographical, cognitive, and organizational distances among agents. The agent's absorptive capacity depends on the stocks of knowledge of the interacting agents. By simulating the developed agent-based model it has been observed that agents geographically cluster.

To test the robustness of the simulation results, a sensitivity analysis has been conducted by changing the values of the model parameters, i.e. increasing and/or decreasing their initial value, *coeteris paribus*.

Results have shown that a geographical cluster of agents emerges in all the experiments regardless in the experiment where the firm's propensity to create new knowledge through learning by interaction is equal to zero. This outcome is coherent with the behavior of a real system of leader and follower firms, in which the followers imitate the leaders in order to bridge the gap in the competitive advantage. In this case, leader firms are not motivated to cluster with the followers, because they will lose their competitive advantage given that the knowledge is transferred from them to the followers (knowledge spill-over) and not in the opposite way. Then, leader firms continuously move far from the followers to keep their competitive advantage. On the contrary, follower firms continuously follow the most competitive firms because they gain advantage being close to them and by imitating their knowledge.

REFERENCES

Albino, V., Carbonara, N., & Giannoccaro, I. (2005). Industrial districts as complex adaptive systems: Agent-based models of emergent phenomena. In C. Karlsson, B. Johansson, & R. E. Stough (Eds.), *Industrial clusters and inter-firm networks*. Northampton, MA: Edward Elgar Publ.

Albino, V., Carbonara, N., & Messeni Petruzzelli, A. (2007). Proximity as a communication resource for competitiveness: A rationale for technology clusters. *International Journal of Learning and Intellectual Capital, 4*(4), 430–452. doi:10.1504/IJLIC.2007.016337

Albino, V., & Schiuma, G. (2003). New forms of knowledge creation and diffusion in the industrial district of Matera-Altamura-Santeramo. In F. Belussi, G. Gottardi, & E. Rullani (Eds.), *The technological evolution of industrial districts*. Boston: Kluwer Academic Pub. doi:10.1007/978-1-4615-0393-4_19

Arikan, A. T. (2009). Interfirm knowledge exchanges and the knowledge creation capability of clusters. *Academy of Management Review, 34*(4), 659–676. doi:10.5465/AMR.2009.44885776

Baptista, R. (2000). Do innovations diffuse faster within geographical clusters? *International Journal of Industrial Organization, 18*, 515–535. doi:10.1016/S0167-7187(99)00045-4

Bartik, T. J. (1985). Business location decisions in the United States: Estimates of the effects of unionization, taxes, and other characteristics of states. *Journal of Business & Economic Statistics, 3*(1), 14–22.

Boschma, R. (2004, June). *Does geographical proximity favour innovation?* Paper presented at the 4th Congress on Proximity Economics, Marseilles, France.

Boschma, R. (2005). Proximity and innovation: A critical assessment. *Regional Studies, 39*(1), 61–75. doi:10.1080/0034340052000320887

Brusco, S. (1990). The idea of the industrial district: Its genesis. In G. Becattini, F. Pyke, & W. Sengenberger (Eds.), *Industrial districts and Inter-firm co-operation in Italy*. Geneva, Switzerland: International Institute for Labour Studies.

Camagni, R. P. (1989). Cambiamento tecnologico, Milieu locale e reti di imprese: una teoria dinamica dello spazio economico. *Economia e politica industriale, 64*, 209-236.

Carley, K. M., & Gasser, L. (2000). Computational organizational theory. In G. Weiss (Ed.), *Multiagent systems. A modern approach to distributed artificial intelligence*. Cambridge, MA: The MIT Press.

Carlton, D. W. (1983). The location and employment choices of new firms: An econometric model with discrete and continuous endogenous variables. *The Review of Economics and Statistics, 65*, 440–449. doi:10.2307/1924189

Cohen, W., & Levinthal, D. (1990). Absorptive capacity: A new perspective on learning and innovation. *Administrative Science Quarterly, 35*, 128–152. doi:10.2307/2393553

Cohendet, P., & Llerena, P. (1997). Learning, technical change, and public policy: How to create and exploit diversity. In C. Edquist (Ed.), *Systems of innovation. Technologies, institutions and organizations*. London: Pinter.

David, P., & Rosenbloom, J. (1990). Marshallian factor market externalities and the dynamics of industrial location. *Journal of Urban Economics, 28*, 349–370. doi:10.1016/0094-1190(90)90033-J

Ernst, D. (2002). Global production networks and the changing geography of innovation systems. Implications for developing countries. *Economics of Innovation and New Technology, 11*(6), 497–523. doi:10.1080/10438590214341

Grant, R. M. (1997). The knowledge-based view of the firm: implications for management in practice. *Long Range Planning, 30*(3), 450–454. doi:10.1016/S0024-6301(97)00025-3

Hamel, G., & Prahalad, C. K. (1994). *Competing for the future*. Boston: Harvard Business School Press.

Head, K., Ries, J., & Swenson, D. (1995). Agglomeration benefits and location choice: Evidence from Japanese manufacturing investment in the United States. *Journal of International Economics, 38*, 223–247. doi:10.1016/0022-1996(94)01351-R

Howells, J. R. L. (2002). Tacit knowledge, innovation and economic geography. *Urban Studies (Edinburgh, Scotland), 39*, 871–884. doi:10.1080/00420980220128354

Knoben, J., & Oelremans, L. A. G. (2006). Proximity and inter-organizational collaboration: A literature review. *International Journal of Management Reviews, 8*, 71–89. doi:10.1111/j.1468-2370.2006.00121.x

Krogh, G., & Vicari, S. (1992). L'approccio autopoietico all'apprendimento strategico sperimentale. *Economia e politica industriale, 74/76*.

Krugman, P. R. (1991). *Geography and trade*. Cambridge, MA: MIT Press.

Lane, D. (2002). Complexity and local interactions: Towards a theory of industrial districts, complexity and industrial districts. In A. Q. Curzio, & M. Fortis (Eds.), *Complexity and industrial clusters*. Heidelberg, Germany: Physica-Verlag. doi:10.1007/978-3-642-50007-7_5

Leonard-Barton, D. (1995). *Wellsprings of knowledge*. Boston: Harvard Business School Press.

Lipparini, A. (1998). L'apprendimento relazionale. *Sviluppo & Organizzazione, 166*.

Lipparini, A., & Lorenzoni, G. (1996). Le organizzazioni ad alta intensità relazionale. Riflessioni sui processi di learning by interacting nelle aree ad alta concentrazione di imprese. *L'Industria, 4*.

Lorenzen, M., & Maskell, P. (2004). The cluster as a nexus of knowledge creation. In P. Cooke, & A. Piccaluga (Eds.), *Regional economies as knowledge laboratories* (pp. 77–92). London: Edward Elgar.

Maillat, D., Quevit, M., & Senn, L. (Eds.). (1993). *Réseaux d'Innovation et Milieux Innovateurs: Un Pari pour le Déeveloppement Régional*. Neuchâtel, Switzerland: EDES.

Malerba, F. (1988). Apprendimento, innovazione e capacità tecnologica. *Economics and Politics*, 58.

Malerba, F. (1992). Learning by firms and incremental technical change. *The Economic Journal*, *102*(413), 845–859. doi:10.2307/2234581

Malmberg, A., & Maskell, P. (1999). The competitiveness of firms and regions. Ubiquitification and the importance of localized learning. *European Urban and Regional Studies*, 6, 9–25. doi:10.1177/096977649900600102

Malmberg, A., & Maskell, P. (2004). The elusive concept of localization economies: Towards a knowledge-based theory of spatial clustering. In G. Grabher, & W. W. Powell (Eds.), *Networks*. Cheltenham, UK: Edward Elgar.

Marshall, A. (1919). *Industry and trade*. London: Macmillan.

Marshall, A. (1920). *Principles of economics*. London: Macmillan.

Maskell, P. (2001a). Knowledge creation and diffusion in geographical clusters. *International Journal of Innovation Management*, *5*(2), 213–237. doi:10.1142/S1363919601000373

Maskell, P. (2001b). Towards a knowledge-based theory of the geographical cluster. *Industrial and Corporate Change*, *10*, 921–943. doi:10.1093/icc/10.4.921

Maskell, P. (2004). A knowledge-based theory of the geographical cluster. In S. Breschi, & C. A. Montgomery (Eds.), *Resource-based and evolutionary theories of the firm — Towards a synthesis*. Boston: Kluwer.

Piore, M., & Sabel, C. F. (1984). *The second industrial divide*. New York: Basic Books.

Porter, M. (1998). Clusters and the new economics of competition. *Harvard Business Review*, *76*(6), 77–90. PMID:10187248

Prusak, L. (1997). *Knowledge in organizations*. Washington, DC: Butterworth-Heinemann.

Rauch, J. E. (1993). Does history matter only when it matters little? The case of city-industry location. *The Quarterly Journal of Economics*, *108*, 843–867. doi:10.2307/2118410

Romer, P. M. (1986). Increasing returns and long-run growth. *The Journal of Political Economy*, *94*(5), 1002–1037. doi:10.1086/261420

Saviotti, P. P. (1996). *Technological evolution, variety and the economy*. Cheltenham, UK: Edward Elgar.

Shaver, J. M., & Flyer, F. (2000). Agglomeration economies, firm heterogeneity, and foreign direct investment in the United States. *Strategic Management Journal*, *21*, 1175–1193. doi:10.1002/1097-0266(200012)21:12<1175::AID-SMJ139>3.0.CO;2-Q

Tallman, S., Jenkins, M., Henry, N., & Pinch, S. (2004). Knowledge, clusters, and competitive advantage. *Academy of Management Review*, *29*(2), 258–271.

Torre, A., & Gilly, J. P. (2000). On the analytical dimension of proximity dynamics. *Regional Studies*, *34*(2), 169–180. doi:10.1080/00343400050006087

Vicari, S. (1991). *L'impresa vivente – Itinerario in una diversa concezione*. Milano, Italy: Etaslibri.

ADDITIONAL READING

Albino, V., Carbonara, N., & Giannoccaro, I. (2003). Cooperation and competition within industrial districts: An agent-based computational approach. *Journal of Artificial Societies and Social Simulation*, 6(4).

Albino, V., Carbonara, N., & Giannoccaro, I. (2006). Innovation within Industrial Districts: An Agent-Based Simulation Model. *International Journal of Production Economics*, *104*(1), 30–45. doi:10.1016/j.ijpe.2004.12.023

Albino, V., Carbonara, N., & Giannoccaro, I. (2007). Supply chain cooperation within Industrial Districts: A simulation analysis. *European Journal of Operational Research*, *177*(1), 261–280. doi:10.1016/j.ejor.2005.12.007

Audretsch, D., & Vivarelli, M. (1994). Small firms and spillovers: Evidence from Italy. *Small Business Economics*, *8*, 249–258. doi:10.1007/BF00388651

Axelrod, R. (1997). Advancing the art of simulation in social sciences. In R. Conte, R. Hegselmann, & P. Terna (Eds.), *Simulating Social Phenomena*. Berlin: Springer. doi:10.1007/978-3-662-03366-1_2

Axelrod, R., & Tesfatsion, L. (2005). A guide for newcomers to agent-based modeling in the social sciences. In: K. L. Judd & L.Tesfatsion (Eds.), Handbook of Computational Economics, Vol.2: Agent-Based Computational Economics. Amsterdam: North-Holland.

Barney, J. B. (1991). Firm resources and sustained competitive advantage. *Journal of Management*, *17*, 187–198. doi:10.1177/014920639101700108

Boero, R., Castellani, M., & Squazzoni, F. (2004). Cognitive identity and social re_exivity of the industrial district _rms: Going beyond the. complexity effect. with agent-based simulation. In G. Lindemann, D. Moldt, & M. Paolucci (Eds.), *Regulated Agent-Based Social Systems*. Berlin: Springer. doi:10.1007/978-3-540-25867-4_4

Boero, R., & Squazzoni, F. (2002). Economic performance, Inter-firm relations and local institutional engineering in a computational prototype of Industrial Districts. *Journal of Artificial Societies and Social Simulation*, *5*(1).

Brenner, T. (2001). Simulating the evolution of localised industrial clusters—an identification of the basic mechanism. *Journal of Artificial Societies and Social Simulation*, *4*(3).

Brenner, T. & Weigelt, N. (2001). The evolution of industrial clusters simulating spatial dynamics. *Advances in Complex Systems*, *4*, 127.147.

Capello, R., & Faggian, A. (2005). Collective learning and relational capital in local innovation processes. *Regional Studies*, *39*(1), 75–87. doi:10.1080/0034340052000320851

Carbonara, N., & Giannoccaro, I. (2011). Interpreting the role of proximity on industrial district competitiveness using a complexity science-based view and systems dynamics simulation. *Journal of Geographical Systems*, *13*, 415–436. doi:10.1007/s10109-010-0128-2

Cooke, P. (2002). Regional innovation systems: general findings and some new evidence from biotechnology clusters. *The Journal of Technology Transfer*, *27*, 133–145. doi:10.1023/A:1013160923450

Cooke, P., Heidenreich, M., & Braczyk, H. (2004). *Regional Innovation Systems*. London: Routledge.

Epstein, J. M., & Axtell, R. (1996). *Growing Artificial Societies: Social Science from the Bottom Up*. Cambridge, MA: The MIT Press.

Etzkowitz, H., & Klofsten, M. (2005). The innovating region: toward a theory of knowledge-based regional development. *R & D Management*, *35*(3), 243–255. doi:10.1111/j.1467-9310.2005.00387.x

Feldman, M. P., & Audretsch, D. B. (1999). Innovation in cities: science-based diversity, specialization and localized competition. *European Economic Review*, *43*, 409–429. doi:10.1016/S0014-2921(98)00047-6

Fioretti, G. (2001). Information structure and behavior of a textile industrial district. *Journal of Artificial Societies and Social Simulation*, *4*(4).

Gilbert, N., & Terna, P. (2000). How to build and use agent-based models in social science. *Mind & Society*, *1*, 57–72. doi:10.1007/BF02512229

Glaeser, E., Kallal, H., Scheinkam, J., & Shleifer, A. (1992). Growth in Cities. *The Journal of Political Economy*, *100*, 1126–1152. doi:10.1086/261856

Grant, R. M. (1996). Toward a knowledge-based theory of the firm. *Strategic Management Journal*, *17*, 109–122.

Jacobs, J. (1969). *The economy of cities*. New York: Vintage.

Markusen, A. (1996). Sticky places in Slippery Space: A typology of Industrial Districts. *Economic Geography*, *72*(3), 293–313. doi:10.2307/144402

Otter, H. O., van der Veen, A., & de Vriend Abloom, H. J. (2001). Location behavior, spatial patterns, and agent-based modelling. *Journal of Artificial Societies and Social Simulation*, *4*(4).

Romer, P. M. (1986). Increasing returns and long-run growth. *The Journal of Political Economy*, *94*, 1002–1037. doi:10.1086/261420

Saxenian, A. (1996). *Regional Advantage. Culture and competition in Silicon Valley and Route 128*. Boston: Harvard University Press.

Zhang, J. (2003). Growing silicon valley on a landscape: an agent-based approach to high-tech industrial clusters. *Journal of Evolutionary Economics*, *13*, 529–548. doi:10.1007/s00191-003-0178-4

KEY TERMS AND DEFINITION

Absorptive Capacity: Is the ability of any individual and organization to acquire, assimilate, adapt, and apply new knowledge – that is to learn. Cohen and Levinthal (1990) suggest that absorptive capacity depends on a system's prior stock of related knowledge. For instance, investment in R&D activities not only provides new knowledge but also makes the system more able to acquire and assimilate related R&D output of other similar firms.

Agent-Based Modeling: Is a computational method that enables a researcher to create, analyze, and experiment with models composed of agents that interact within an environment. An agent-based model (ABM) is a class of computational models for simulating the actions and interactions of autonomous agents (both individual and collective entities such as organizations or groups) with a view to assessing their effects on the system as a whole.

Agglomeration Economies: Are those external economies from which a firm can benefit by being located at the same place as one or more other firms. A distinction is often made between two types of agglomeration economies: `urbanisationurbanization economies' and `localisationlocalization economies'. The term `urbanisationurbanization economies' relates to the general economies of regional and urban concentration that apply to all firms and industries in a single location. `LocalisationLocalization economies' are the specific economies that relate to firms engaged in similar or interlinked activities, leading to the emergence of spatial agglomeration of related firms (industrial districts, localisedlocalized industry clusters, etc).

Cognitive Proximity: Is generally defined in terms of common knowledge base and expertise among people. The term can be used for referring to a group of people that belong to a community of practice and therefore can interact easily despite large geographical distance.

External Economies or Externalities: Are the cost-saving benefits of locating near factors which are external to a firm, such as locally available skilled labourlabor, training, and research and development facilities.

Geographical Clusters: Encompass an array of linked industries and other entities important to competition. They include, for example, suppliers of specialized inputs such as components, machinery, and services, and providers of specialized infrastructure. Clusters also often extend downstream to channels and customers and laterally to manufacturers of complementary products and to companies in industries related by skills, technologies, or common inputs. Finally, many clusters include governmental and other institutions – such as universities, standards-setting agencies, think tanks, vocational training providers, and trade association – that provide specialized training, education, information, research, and technical support.

Industrial Districts: Are geographically defined production systems, characterized by a large number of small and medium-sized firms that are involved at various phases in the production of a homogeneous product family. These firms are highly specialized in a few phases of the production process, and integrated through a complex network of inter-organizational relationships.

Knowledge Economy: An economy where production and services are based on knowledge-intensive activities that contribute to an accelerated pace of technical and scientific advance, as well as rapid obsolescence. The key component of a knowledge economy is a greater reliance on intellectual capabilities than on physical inputs or natural resources.

Knowledge Spillovers: Include all the information exchange taking place informally between people working in the same or in unrelated industries. Such flows of information may concern the technology of products or processes, specific input requirements, or unsatisfied market needs. Knowledge spillovers can be voluntary or involuntary.

Organizational Proximity: Can be defined as the extent to which relations are shared in an organizational system, either within or between organizations.

ENDNOTES

[1] This concept has been supported by formal treatments of agglomeration economies. Examples of formal models showing that firms will geographically cluster when agglomeration economies exist include Romer (1986), David and Rosenbloom (1990), Krugman (1991), and Rauch (1993). Moreover, some empirical studies confirm that firms are more likely to locate new plants in regions with greater levels of similar industry activity (e.g., Carlton, 1983; Bartik, 1985; Head, Riesand Swenson, 1995).

Chapter 17

Towards a Multi-Agent-Based Tool for the Analysis of the Social Production and Management Processes in an Urban Ecosystem:
An Approach Based on the Integration of Organizational, Regulatory, Communication and Physical Artifacts in the JaCaMo Framework

Flávia Santos
Universidade Federal do Rio Grande—Brasil

Thiago Rodrigues
Universidade Federal do Rio Grande—Brasil

Henrique Donancio
Universidade Federal do Rio Grande—Brasil

Iverton Santos
Universidade Federal do Rio Grande—Brasil

Diana F. Adamatti
Universidade Federal do Rio Grande—Brasil

Graçaliz P. Dimuro
Universidade Federal do Rio Grande—Brasil

Glenda Dimuro
Universidad de Sevilla—Spain

Esteban De Manuel Jerez
Universidad de Sevilla—Spain

ABSTRACT

The SJVG-MAS Project addresses, in an interdisciplinary approach, the development of MAS-based tools for the simulation of the social production and management processes observed in urban ecosystems, adopting as case study the social vegetable garden project conducted at the San Jerónimo Park (Seville/Spain), headed by the confederation "Ecologistas en Acción." The authors aim at the analysis of the current reality of the SJVG project, allowing discussions on the adopted social management pro-

DOI: 10.4018/978-1-4666-5954-4.ch017

cesses, and also for investigating how possible changes in the social organization (e.g., roles assumed by the agents in the organization, actions, behaviors, (in)formal interaction/communication protocols, regulation norms), especially from the point of view of the agent's participation in the decision making processes, may transform this reality, from the social, environmental and economic point of view, then contributing for the sustainability of the project. The MAS was conceived as a multi-dimensional BDI-like agent social system, involving the development of five components: the agents' population, the system's organization, the system's environment, the set of interactions executed among agents playing organizational roles (e.g., communication protocols for reaching agreements) and the normative policy structure (internal regulation established by SJVG community). The aim of this chapter is to discuss the problems faced and to present the solution found for the modeling of SJVG social organization using JaCaMo framework. The chapter shows the integration of the considered dimensions, discussing the adopted methodology, which may be applied in several other contexts.

1. INTRODUCTION

A Multiagent System (MAS) is a set of computational intelligent, autonomous, capable of communicating and coordinating, pro-active and situated entities, perceiving its environment through sensors and acting on it using actuators (Wooldridge, 2002; Weiss, 1999; Russell & Norvig, 2010; Padgham & Winikoff, 2004).

The SJVG-MAS Project[1] (Santos et al., 2011; Santos, et al., 2012; Rodrigues, et al., 2013a; Santos, et al., 2013a; Santos et al., 2013b) addresses, in an interdisciplinary approach, the development of MAS-based tools for the simulation of the social production and management processes observed in urban ecosystems (Dimuro, 2009, 2010; Dimuro & Jerez, 2010a, 2010b, 2011)—a joint effort for interrelating knowledge, seeking collective interpretations, adopting as case study the current tendency of (re)approaching the countryside to the city through urban vegetable gardens. In particular, we are focusing the social vegetable garden project conducted at the San Jerónimo Park (Seville/Spain), headed by the confederation "Ecologistas en Acción" (EA)[2].

The San Jerónimo Vegetable Garden (SJVG) is an urban vegetable garden maintained by its own users. The harvest is ecological, the production is only for self-consumption, but people can exchange products and services. Then, the SJVG's social organization is characterized for allowing and promoting a lot of interactions and social exchanges between the participants. Nevertheless, the behaviors, interactions and communications are regulated by norms established by the community in assembly, under the supervision and coordination of the EA.

The general objective of the SJVG-MAS Project is to develop a MAS-based simulation tool for the analysis of the current reality of the SJVG project, allowing discussions on the adopted social management processes, and also for investigating how possible changes in the social organization (e.g., roles assumed by the agents in the organization, actions, behaviors, (in)formal interaction/communication protocols, regulation norms), especially from the point of view of the agent's participation in the decision making processes, may transform this reality, from the social, environmental and economic point of view, then contributing for the sustainability of the project.

Among the agent models commonly used in agent-based simulation of decision processes in complex environments, there are the ones of an intentional nature, whose behaviors can be explained by attributing certain mental attitudes to the agents, such as knowledge, beliefs, desires, intentions, obligations, commitments. See, e.g., the discussion presented in (Subagdja et al., 2009).

The BDI (Beliefs, Desires, Intentions) agent architecture describes the agent internal processing by a set of mental categories, defining a control architecture by which the agent, rationally, selects its action course (Rao & Georgeff, 1991, 1992; Rao, 1996).

The intentional character of the BDI model is adequate for the problem addressed in the SJVG-MAS Project, namely, the simulation of social production and management processes. Then, in order to take into account all the suitable characteristics of the SJVG social organization, we conceived our MAS as a multi-dimensional BDI-like agent social system, involving the development of five components:

1. The agents' population (where the system's decision-making processes happen),
2. The system's organization (which describes the allowed behaviors in the MAS),
3. The system's environment (where the agents interact),
4. The set of interactions executed among agents playing organizational roles (e.g., communication protocols for reaching agreements) and
5. The normative policy structure (constitutive and regulative internal norms established by SJVG community).

The last two dimensions (4 and 5) are particularly important here, since modifications in the interaction/communication/normative structures may directly affect the social processes under analysis in this project.[3]

A framework that currently offers high-level and modular facilities to develop the first three dimensions mentioned above (1, 2 and 3) is JaCaMo (Boissier et al., 2012), which is actually the synergic usage of three separate technologies: the Jason interpreter of an extended version of AgentSpeak language (Bordini et al., 2007), the CArtAgO framework (Ricci et al., 2012) and the MOISE+ model (Hubner, 2003; Hübner et al., 2010). The

first is used to develop the agents' population, the second allows the environment's programming and the last is an organizational model. All those MAS components are programmed/developed in a modular way and in a high-level of abstraction, making JaCaMo a rich and easy-use MAS development framework.

We remark that JaCaMo is neither a platform for running simulations, nor a framework for the development of the most common applications in Social Simulation, since it not based on a discrete event simulation engine and does not offer the tools necessary for the quantitative/qualitative analysis of simulations.

However, in this work, we aim at the development of a MAS for the analysis of the social production and management processes through the "simulation of the functioning" of a special kind of real-world social organization (namely, an urban ecosystem). By analyzing the effects of the variation on the normative policy, the structure of the organization, the restrictions on interactions or in the available environment resources, the cooperation (or not) between agents, the allowed decision making processes, the influence of moral agents (Coelho et al., 2014) etc., it is expected that new practices may be put to work on the current state of such organization. We are not interested in quantitative/statistical analysis, since we are providing tools for qualitative research-action methodologies (French & Bell, 1973).

With this objectives in mind, we noticed that the modularity provided by JaCaMo framework may help the modeling of real world organizations, especially when an interdisciplinary working group is involved, as in the SJVG-MAS Project. Moreover, this modular development facilitates modifications in the organization, which is really important for the analysis of the impact of those changes in the social production and management processes.

However, we faced three main problems when using JaCaMo as the development framework in the SJVG-MAS Project. First, we found that many organizational roles' behaviors are of a periodic nature, that is, periodic routines, in which a certain goal may be satisfied repeatedly, and this was not possible to have in the MOISE+ organizational model. Second, we realized that in JaCaMo there is not a native and modular way of defining the interactions allowed among agents, neither in the agent population nor in the organization dimension.[4]

Finally, we have to deal with the various kinds of internal norms established by SJVG community.

The aim of this chapter is to present the solution we have found for the modeling of SJVG social organization using JaCAMo framework, adopting our view of a 5-dimension MAS system, then providing solutions to the problems above mentioned, mainly based on the CArtAgO framework. The chapter shows the integration of such dimensions, discussing the adopted methodology, which may be applied in several other contexts. The chapter is organized as follows. In sections 2 and 3, the aspects of the social production and management processes in a Urban Ecosystem as well as case study in San Jerónimo Park (SJVG) (Seville/Spain) are presented. In section 4, the JaCaMo framework and its related tools are showed. Section 5 presents the model of the SJVG Social Organization using JaCaMo. Section 6 presents related work and additional reading. Section 7 is the Conclusion.

2. THE SOCIAL PRODUCTION AND MANAGEMENT PROCESSES IN AN URBAN ECOSYSTEM

In this section, we briefly discuss some multidisciplinary issues related to the social production and management processes in urban ecosystems, and the role of the MAS-based simulation tools in this context. For more details, see Santos, et al. (2012) and Dimuro (2009).

To face the different problems caused by the industrial society, it is demanding to adopt paradigms to deal with the new social agents and

conflicts that comes with the flexibility generated by the industrial civilization of the information era, including, obviously, themes related to the ecological and economic issues of this society (Touraine, 2005): a modification of the scientific reasoning leading to "thinking about the context and the complex" (Morin, 2010), i.e., unifying which was before compartmentalized, respecting the diversity and, at the same time, recognizing the unity, a thinking that does not isolate, but that considers the object of study for its relation with the social, economic, political, environmental surroundings, accepting the uncertainty of its actions.

When analyzing this complex thinking, considering an ecological and systemic point of view, an alternative for diminishing the actual social, environmental and economic degradation has appeared, pointing to the concept of sustainability. Although many authors estimate that the success of this "new" terminology is due to its own conceptual ambiguity (Naredo, 1996), it is possible to drive its application from a complex approach.

Considering the various discussions related to concept of sustainability[5], it is clear that sustainability does not refer to the type of human interaction with the world that preserves the environment for not compromising the natural resources of future generations. In fact, it is necessary to include the reflections of the social and urban ecology, which are concerned with, respectively, the holistic relation among the human beings and the environment—especially, how the human activity frequently causes great damages on the nature (Vieria & Bredariol, 1998) and the application of the scientific ecology, social and environmental simulation, artificial intelligence, multiagent systems, etc., in order to understand and to interpret the urban reality (Bettini, 1998; Gilbert & Troitzsch, 1999).

To repair environmental damages it is necessary to solve social and economic issues, which imply mental and behavioral changes, increasing the participation and involvement of citizens in the defense of their surroundings, and, then, allowing to establish a connection between the urban ecology and the social production and management of the habitat (Lobo, 1998; Ortiz, 2010; Pelli, 2010; Romero et al., 2004).

Then, transposing the sustainability from the theory to practice means to conceive the human being and the territory where the majority of the species develop themselves (i.e., the cities) as taking part of the nature, under the concept of "urban ecosystem" (Terradas, 2001; Dimuro & Jerez, 2011). So, an urban ecosystem is not a simple aleatory aggregation of spaces, but a total connected to networks with causes and effects; an habitat whose structure is coherent with the cultural paradigms and specific necessities of a certain group and context; a process of constant increment of information; a territory physically closed, but open to energy and resource flows.

The concept of social production and management processes of urban ecosystems may be understood as the generation of new physical or relational situations, by constructing, transforming or eliminating physical objects and/or relational objects with the objective of ensuring, in the new produced situations, the fulfillment of their social and environmental functions (Ortiz, 2010; Pelli, 2010; Pelli, 2007). This includes the citizen participation in the process of urban planning and transformation, articulating the different involved agents (government, institutions, technicians, citizens), forming a network structured and supported by mechanisms and tools that allow the equal distribution of power in the decision making, so that all agents can participate and dialogue actively in the whole process of a certain project, from its planning to its management. The social production and management of urban ecosystems contribute to the strengthening of community practices, to the increasing of responsibility for a collective project, to the exercise of democracy, to the development of more supportive actions, including both productive and economic issues, as well as environmental issues.

The San Jerónimo Vegetable Garden (SJVG), the main concern of the SJVG-MAS Project, is an example of an urban ecosystem located in Seville, Spain. The SJVG-MAS Project is developing a MAS-based simulation tool in order to analyze the social production and management processes that are specifically observed in the SJVG's social organization. We aim to contribute for the analysis of the actual reality of the SJVG experiment, providing resources to foment the discussions on the adopted methodology and to help the investigation of new possible ideas that may be applied in the context of the SJVG's organization, from the social, environmental and economic point of view, so helping for its sustainability.

3. THE URBAN VEGETABLE GARDEN OF THE SAN JERÓNIMO PARK (SJVG) (SEVILLE/SPAIN)

The San Jerónimo Urban Vegetable Garden—SJVG (in Spanish: Huerta San Jerónimo) is an initiative of the confederation "Ecologistas in Acción" (EA) in order to promote social participation in organic farming practices through the use of urban vegetable gardens to recreation, and conducting activities related to environmental education. The main feature is this urban ecosystem is a nonprofit, social urban vegetable garden, that is, the production is dedicated to its own participants.

The vegetable gardens are located in the San Jerónimo Park, occupying about 1.5 hectares, divided into 42 individual plots (of size around 75m²), assigned to gardeners of different ages, especially retirees. Although the "ownership" of each parcel is individual, the work in the garden is sometimes shared among other family members or even friends.

The EA confederation has a collective plot, allocated to its partners, and another plot that serves as a kind of "School Plot," where classes on organic crops are eventually taught.

The role of EA confederation is to oversee the work of the gardeners, providing technical support, and also controlling the use of chemical pesticides, which is strictly forbidden. The gardeners, in turn, to ensure their permanence in the project, must comply with a set of determinations established in the SJVG's Internal Regulation Norms, including, e.g., the previously mentioned requirement for organic farming and the forbiddance of selling or trading the products, but also other rules such as to keep the portion clean, to take care of the common areas, to attend the assemblies, to irrigate by dripping water, to collaborate with the operation of the facilities and infrastructures, to pay a monthly fee, among others.

A key feature of the project is the horizontality time to make decisions that are always taken in the SJVG Assemblies and established in the form of consensus among the community of gardeners and technicians of the EA confederation.

Besides the cultivation of individual plots, the SJVG project includes the care of a greenhouse for growing seedlings and a chicken coop. Linked to the chicken coop, the EA confederation has an interesting project of organic waste recycling called "Your waste worth an egg," where gardeners share the responsibility of feeding the chickens with organic debris on certain days, and in return, they receive eggs.

EA also performs some agreements with Sevilla Universty and/or other academic institutions and supports students in internships. Finally, depending on the annual budget, EA also carries out work with neighborhood schools through school vegetable gardens.

For many years, the SJVG project ran through an agreement with the City of Sevilla, which meant annual economic resources for the execution of the project. Those funds supported the payment for a technician of the EA confederation, the purchase of materials, seedlings, fertilizers, etc. However, since last year, this aid was withdrawn from the garden and the economic situation is very delicate. Currently, EA along with gardeners' community are studying some possibilities for self-financing, as the cultivation of a joint portion dedicated to planting seedlings for sale.

4. THE JACAMO FRAMEWORK AND RELATED TOOLS

JaCaMo is a multiagent systems development framework that combines three separate technologies: Jason (for programming autonomous agents), CArtAgo (for programming environment artifacts) e MOISE+ (for programming multi-agent organizations) (Boissier et. al, 2011, 2012).

In this section, we present the main features of these technologies that cover some of the levels of abstractions that are required for the development of sophisticated multiagent systems. We also present the MSPP framework for modeling public policies, which was built in the context of JaCaMo framework and was adapted for modeling the internal norms of the SJVG project.

4.1 JaCaMo Technologies

For the implementation of a MAS agent population, JaCamo provides *Jason* (Bordini et al., 2007), which is an Agent-Speak-L interpreter that provides a platform[6] to develop multiagent systems, based on BDI agent model.

There are many BDI *ad hoc* implementations systems, however an important characteristic of the Agent Speak-L language is its theoretic base. The AgentSpeak-L programming language is an elegant extension of logic programming to BDI architecture for agents. An AgentSpeak agent corresponds to the specification of a set of beliefs and plans that will form the initial knowledge base.

AgentSpeak-L distinguishes two types of goals: achievement goals and test goals. Achievement and test goals are predicates, such as beliefs, but they have fixed operators '!' and '?', respectively. Achievement goals express what the agent wants to achieve in an environment state, where the predicate associated with the goal is true. In fact, these objectives start the execution of subplans. A test goal returns the unification of a predicate test with an agent belief, or failure if the unification is not possible with the agent beliefs.

A triggering event defines which events may initiate the execution of a plan. An event can be internal, when generated by the execution of a plan if a subgoal needs to be achieved, or external, when generated by the perception of the environment.

Activating events are related to the addition and removal of mental attitudes (beliefs or goals). Add and remove mental attitudes are represented by fixed operators ('+') and ('-').

For the MAS environment implementation (and other facilities, that we will show in the next sections), JaCaMo provides the *CartAgO* (Common ARTifact infrastructure for AGents Open environments) (Ricci et al. 2012), which is a multiagent systems virtual environment development and simulation framework. Through this tool is possible to implement virtual environments as a computational layer encapsulating the facilities and non-autonomous services exploited by agents during runtime.

CartAgO is based on the Agents & Artefacts (A & A) meta-model to model multi-agent systems. This model introduces a high-level metaphor, based in the idea that human workers work in a cooperative way with its environment: agents are computational entities that do some type of goal-oriented task (analogous to human workers), and artifacts are the resources and tools dynamically created, handled and shared by agents to support their activities, both individual and collective (as in the human context).

Therefore is possible to develop artifacts that are instantiated in the environment, providing services to agents, and able to do communication with external services (e.g., (e.g., Web-services).[7]

Finally, for the modeling of the MAS organization, JaCaMo offers the *MOISE+* (Hubner et al., 2002; Hubner, 2003) organizational model, which encompasses the specification of three dimen-

sions: the structural, where roles, inheritance links and groups are defined; the functional, where a set of global plans are defined, with missions to achieve those goals; and the normative dimension that specifies which role has to commit to which mission.

In a Structural Specification (SS), individual, social and collective levels can be defined based on three concepts: roles (individual level—set of behavioral constraints that an agent accepts when joining a group), relationships between roles (social level—relations allowed between the roles) and groups (collective level—a set of agents with similar affinities and objectives).

The SS can be represented by a tuple:

$$ss = \left(RG, R_{ss}, C \right)$$

where:

RG is the set of specification of roots groups of ss;
R_{ss} is the set of all roles in the SS;
C is the inheritance relationship on roles of R_{ss}.

In the MOISE+ model, the Functional Specification—FE is composed by a collection of Social Schemes—ES, which is a set of goals structured by plans. The Global Targets represent the state of the world that is desired by the organization, different from a local goal since the latter is of a single agent.

In the formal specification of MOISE+ model, the set of all social schemes is denoted by SCH and a scheme *sch* is represented by the tuple

$$sch = \left(G, P, M, mo, nm \right),$$

where

G is the set of goals in the scheme;
P the set of plans that builds the goal decomposition tree;

M is the set of missions, that is, a set of global goals that can be bound to a role;

$mo:M \rightarrow P\left(g\right)$ is a function that determines the set of goals in each mission;

$nm:M \rightarrow N \times N$ determines the maximum and minimum number of agents that must commit to each mission.

A scheme is a global goal decomposition tree, whose root is the goal of the entire scheme. The decomposition is made by plans (denoted by the '=' operator), that point a way of achieving a role. For instance, on plan "g0=g1,g2,g3" the role g0 is decomposed in three plans, indicating that it will be achieved only if plans g1, g2 and g3 are also achieved.

The Normative Specification (NS) is where role missions are specified with permission or obligation type. This specification defines a permission (*per*) or an obligation (*obr*) related to a mission (*m*) that an agent with a role in the organization is committed with. They are defined as:orwhere

p determines that an agent with the role **p** can be committed with the mission **m**;

tc determines that temporal restrictions are established, i.e., there is a period (times) where the permission is valid, e.g., every day, every hour, etc.

Figure 1 shows the connection between SS and FS, specified by NS.

4.2 The MSPP Framework for Modeling Public Policies

The MSPP (Modeling and Simulation of Public Policies) framework (Costa & Santos, 2012) aims to support agent-based models for the various types of sequential and non-sequential models of public policy processes (Hill, 2009).

The MSPP framework consists of a set of programming schemes, classes and an API developed for the Jason-Cartago platform (Bordini et al., 2007; Ricci et al., 2012). Its purpose is to help the development of agent-based simulations of public policy processes operating on agent-based simulations of social, economical and environmental contexts.

In general, a policy is conceived as a set of principles that orient and/or conditioned decisions and actions of the agents that operate in a given context, especially in what concerns the uses of resources available in that context (Easton, 1965). A public policy in a given society, thus, is a policy concerning the uses of resources that are considered to be public in that society (Hill, 2009), usually being issued by the government of that society.

In the context of this simplified agent-based model of public policy process (MSPP framework), the public policy definition is:

A public policy is a set of norms and action plans, to be adopted and followed by both the government agents and the societal agents that operate in the social context of concern.

Figure 1. Normative specification: Linking SE and FS

Structural Specification: Roles, groups and links	Normative Specification	Functional Specification: Schemes social and missions

The toolkit also contains the following set of agent types:

- **Government:** An agent able to issue public policies (for simplicity, the government of the society can be modeled as a single agent);
- **Societal or social agents:** Those agents to which the public policy is generally addressed, presumably to solve a public issued identified in their social context;
- **Government agents:** Agents that operate as detectors and effectors for the government.

Six special kinds of government agents are also identified:

- **Norm enforcers:** Detector and effector agents that participate in the process of enforcement of the norms specified by the public policy:
- **Norm detectors:** Capture information concerning the agents' compliances to the policy norms;
- **Norm effectors:** Apply the sanctions prescribed by the norms to the agents that do not comply to them;
- **Environmental operators:** Agents that perform plans specified by the public policy, aiming at the direct control of aspects of the physical or social environment of the society, in the sense of performing actions that operationally interfere with the structure and/or the elements of those environments (e.g.: actions on physical objects, interferences on social relationships, etc.):
- **Environmental detectors:** Capture information concerning the state of the environment resources;
- **Environmental effectors:** Act on the environment resources, changing their features, allowing or blocking the other agents accesses to them, creating or removing resources, etc.

The MSPP framework was implemented on the Jason-CArtAgO platform. The essential concept is that of policy artifacts, i.e., CArtAgO artifacts that reify the public policies that are addressed to the government agents and societal agents of the society, so that, the components of public policies are concretely represented as artifacts in the environment of the society. Given our definition of public policy, the reification of public policies as policy artifacts amounts to the reification of norms and plans, so that norm artifacts and plan artifacts should be defined and instantiated in the CArtAgO platform, together with AgentSpeak program schemes that allow the agents of the society to handle them adequately.

5. MODELING THE SJVG SOCIAL ORGANIZATION IN JACAMO: THE INTEGRATION OF ORGANIZATIONAL, REGULATORY, COMMUNICATION AND PHYSICAL ARTIFACTS

In this section, we present our solution for the modeling of the SJVG social organization using JaCaMo framework, based on the integration of organizational, regulatory, communication and physical CartAgO artifacts.

Environment is a computational or physical space in which agents are situated, in which the notions of perceptions, actions and interactions are defined and developed, and so, the agent can perceive and act (Ricci et al., 2011). Physical Artifacts for the SJVG were developed using CArtAgO and represent the resources or tools that agents can instantiate dynamically, share and use as support in their daily activities in SJVG, and these activities can be individual or in group.

The social organization was firstly modeled using MOISE+. Figure 2 shows the structural model for the SJVG, where roles, groups and sub-groups, role relationships are specified. In this SS, we have specified the root group HSJ_Vegetable_Garden (SJVG project), and its sub-groups EA confederation and Parcel (plot for cultivation). The roles that can be assumed in these sub-groups are: gardener and auxiliary gardener, administration, secretary and EA technician. The relationships between these roles can be: authority (which is the case of the EA administration in relation to the secretary, technician and gardener), communications and compatibility (between auxiliary gardener and aspirant gardener).

However, as briefly pointed out in the Introduction, the social organization of SJVG is based on the performance of periodic routines by the organizational roles (see Figure 3), and also on periodic norms that regulate their behaviors. An example can be seen in Figure 3, where a "Gar-

dener to join the SJVG project has obligation to pay a fee monthly."

In the JaCaMo framework, the modeling of such role routines cannot be easily done, since there are no native tools in the platform that allow this kind of specification.

In the actual development of JaCaMo infrastructure, the allowed processes in the MAS organization, in terms of the goals that must be achieved, have to be described through the MOISE+ model. This tool presents a good abstraction level to specify these objectives, as well as the definition of a hierarchy between them. However, a periodic routine involves the achievement of periodic goals (e.g., in periods of one month, one

Figure 2. Structural specification of SJVG social organization

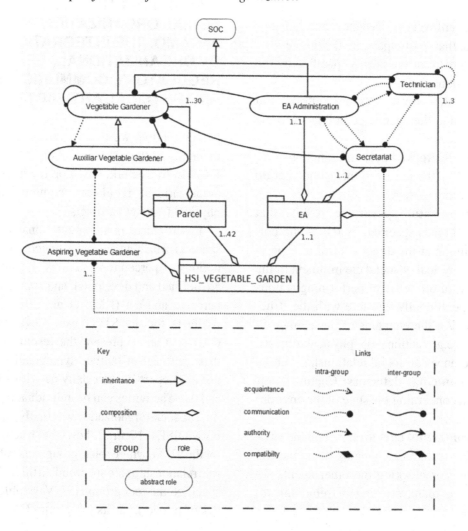

Figure 3. Periodic routines of a gardener

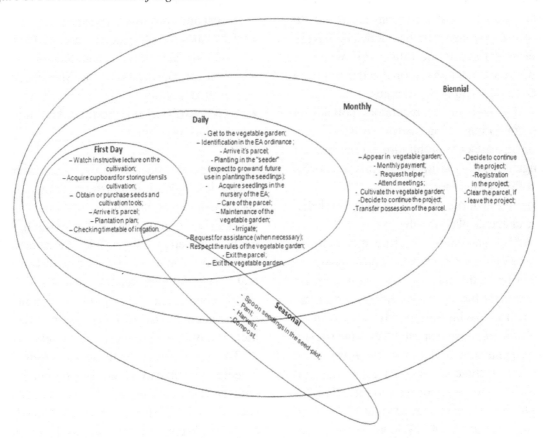

week, one day), and MOISE+ model does not have structures to do represent such periodicity.

Moreover, in social systems, there are situations in which norms must be applied, imposing sanctions over not allowed actions when the agents perform them. In SJVG, many behaviors subject to sanctions were identified, as the "sell garden's harvest"', "irrigate with hoses" and "use of chemicals in the garden," which are not allowed according to the SJVG's Internal Regulation Norms.

Another problem that we face in JaCaMo is that it does not have a native and modular way of defining the allowed interactions among agents, neither in the agent population nor in the organization dimension.

Therefore, considering that (1) there is not a direct way in MOISE+ for defining the periodicity of actions (in the achievement of goals), (2) there

is no direct mean to define norms in JaCaMO, their basic attributes (name, periodicity, applying role) and the sanctions, and (3) there is not a modular infrastructure for defining interactions via communication in JaCAMo, we present in the following section how we solve these problems, in the context of SJVG project.

5.1 Modeling Norms and the Regulatory Artifacts

Aiming to offer a modular way of describing periodic norms, simplifying our modeling of the social system comprised by the San Jerónimo garden, we extended the MSPP framework (Santos et al., 2012; Santos et al., 2013), adapting it to the case on internal regulation norms.

This tool complements the MOISE+ model, offering another abstraction layer. In MSPP framework, routines can be modeled, having the norms defined in the framework, while, in the MOISE+ model, the normalized actions are specified, constituting the routines.

For the modeling of regulatory policies of SJVG, four kinds of normative artifacts were developed: artifact of prohibition norms, artifact of obligation norms, artifact of permission norms and artifact of right norms.

Prohibition norms establishes the actions that the social agents playing roles in the SJVG organization (e.g., gardeners) are restrained to perform (e.g., in SJVG, "raising animals" is prohibited). On the other hand, the norms of obligation imposes obligations for the agents to perform certain actions, such as "paying the monthly fee." Norms of permission are those that establishes the society that the agents should check with the government agents (e.g., technicians, secretaries) whenever it is possible or not to perform a certain action, for example, there is a norm that says that "if you want to plant trees with a duty cycle greater than two years then it is necessary for the agent to request permission for that." Finally, there are the rules of right, which are regulations that establish for the social agent full power to execute the planned action whenever it does not infringe other norms.

The SJVG norms of the social organization are created through plans by the issuing EA agent. When EA agent execute those plans, actions contained in these plans create the norms through the corresponding normative artifact among the four types already mentioned. At the end of this creation, we have the sets of rules of prohibition, obligation, right or permission, and the agent responsible for issuing norms execute a "broadcast" (Jason action to disseminate message to all agents) so that the other agents begin to look for normative artifacts already containing its set of rules. This is illustrated in Figure 4.

Some examples of the four types of norms applied to modeling are presented below:

- Norm(n08, prohibited, sellProducts, seriousFault, seriousCumulative).
- Norm(n22, obligatory, monthlyPayment, seriousFault, seriousCumulative);
- Norm(n25, permission, useMachinery, permitted, nothing);
- Norm(n21, right, buildLocker, nothing, nothing);

Once agents receive the message sent by the issuing EA agent, it is transformed into a belief, and then the agent, through the operation "lookupartifact" (action provided by CArtAgO), looks for the normative artifact, adds the appropriate beliefs corresponding to each established norm (e.g., "+prohibited(createAnimals)") and ultimately continues observing this artifact through the operation "focus," in order to observe whenever there is any change in these rules or exclusion.

The government detector and/or effector agent (agent responsible for monitoring the compliance with the norms) and the social agents have knowledge (in their beliefs) of the norms issued by the EA agent, eventually verifying in the normative artifacts for any provided action or sanction. These agents acquire knowledge of the actions performed by the social agents through communication, i.e., the social agents inform the government detector and/or effector agent that performed action, and these, in turn, have the mission to verify with the normative artifacts if such action is a violation or not, according to the SJVG Regulation. Note that actions that are not in the SJVG Regulation are interpreted by the government detector and/or effector agent as legal actions, causing no sanctions to the agent who performs them.

Messages that social agents send to government agents have the feature: action (actionRealized, myName) where "action" indicates that this information is related to an action to be checked, "actionRealized" is the action that the agent has performed, and "myName" is the identification of the agent that performed the action, as the following example:

Figure 4. Norms and the regulatory artifacts

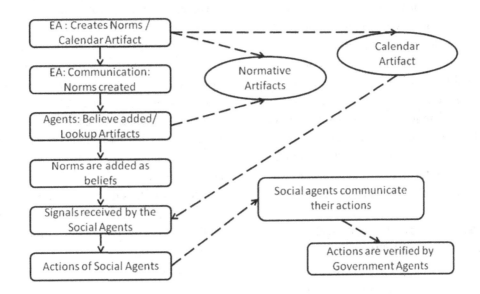

.send(detectorAgent, tell, action(cleanGarden, socialAgent)).

The action ."send" in this example is sent by the "socialAgent," communicating the detector agent that it has wiped his growing plot. This will be analyzed by the detector agent that verifies if the parameter "cleanGarden" indicates a prohibited action, but as it comes be to a regulated action of obligation, it does not cause any sanction. If the action is a violation to any prohibition, as below:

.send(detectorAgent, tell, action(sellProducts, socialAgent))

The detector agent, when receives the message, perceives that the action is a violation. Then, it looks in its belief base for the related penalties, notifying the violator agent, and applying the sanction by registering it in the artifact of penalty registration. Finally, the detector agent checks in the same penalty registration artifact if the agent is a recidivist violator. If so, and if the violator has more than three serious offenses cumulatively,

then this social agent is subjected to the SJVG assembly.

The assembly is convened by the detector/effector agent of the organization. This is to bring together all social agents to give opinions about the permanence of the violator agent in the social project. This is done through communication among agents, where the agent that detected the third recurrence of the violation summons the other agents for the meeting, using the action "broadcast" with parameters (tell, assembly (Agent)), where "assembly" represents the belief and "agent" the name of the violator. Once the voting agents receive this belief, they seek in their bases a value that previously was randomized between 0 and 1 so that they can give their vote in favor (value greater than 0.5) or not of excluding the violator agent of the SJVG project.[8] If the majority of voters opts for the violator removal, then the violator agent is expelled from the organization and this is done through the action ."kill_agent" (an action that is available in Jason).

Notice that the agents have the ability to qualify their own actions through the plans already inserted in the MSPP framework, and then they can opt for committing offenses whenever they have other more important goals for the moment. For example, an agent with financial problems can try to solve this problems selling cultivated products, thus committing a fault, according to SJVG Internal Regulation Norms.

The actions that social agents assume can be triggered by different ways, e.g., by communication with another agent, or by an established routine, or by a CArtAgO artifact that simulates a calendar with information regarding the time of planting, harvesting and cleaning the Garden.

5.2 Social Interactions and the Communication Artifacts

The communication is done by artifacts that allow modular specification of the possible interactions in the MAS, encapsulating the messages (Rodrigues et al., 2013b). Thus, it is possible to create new protocols and different ways of communication just creating the respective artifacts. The communication infrastructure offers the following resources:

- Communication among agents programmed in both AgentSpeak-L and Java languages;
- Communication among distributed agents and;
- Modular definition of communication protocols and other types of interaction, through their encapsulation within artifacts.

The communication infrastructure is composed by Communication Artifacts, which are divided into two groups: protocol artifacts, which encapsulate the logics of some communication protocol (a kind of communication that is, in general, more complex) and speech act artifacts, which execute simple speech acts. Communication is achieved by executing operations available on these artifacts. Since they operate as communications mediators,

their function is to route any message to its respective receivers and to supervise the order in which they are sent, if protocols are used.

The two basic classes of the communication infrastructure are: SpeechAct-Artifact and ProtocolArtifact. The former class defines the basic behavior of a speech act artifact, used for simpler communications. It manages the ongoing conversations that use artifacts of this type, storing the participants of the conversation as well as the message queues of each one.

The latter class defines the basic behavior of a protocol artifact, used for more complex communications. This class concentrates the details involved in a protocol-based conversation, such as the respective automata (used to control the protocol) and conversation states for each agent involved.

The speech act artifacts are used simply to send messages, while the protocol artifacts are used to define an authorized sequence of messages to send (that is, defining the protocol's execution flow). On the other hand, in the speech act artifacts, just the communication performatives are defined. If other types of communication are used (for example, when message exchanges are not used), the communication infrastructure still allows such scenario (for example, when considering implicit communication using the environment).

5.3 The Integration of the Artifacts

The JaCaMo framework integrates three agent-based platforms (Jason, CArtAgO, and Moise+) through a semantic relation among concepts of different dimensions of programming (namely, the agent population, the environment and the organization), all of them joined through a meta-model (CArtAgO), for obtaining a uniform and consistent programming model, in order simplify the combination of these dimensions for programming MAS (Boissier et al., 2011). In this work, we have also to integrate our proposed Regulatory and Communication dimensions.

The integration of the artifacts of SJVG model with the others components of the JaCaMo framework, shown in Figure 5, occurs through two default CArtAgO artifacts: GroupBoard and SchemeBoard. Both belong to the ora4mas.nopl package of CArtAgO framework. ORA4MAS consists in an artifact based infrastructure (based in CArtAgO), where the organizational elements are modeled as artifacts, as well as first-class entities of the system.

The artifact GroupBoard allows an agent to adopt an organizational role (adoptRole operation or leave an organizational role (leaveRole), as well as to add (addScheme) and remove a scheme (removeScheme). Their observable properties allow to know the current state of the groups defined in

the organization (if they are well formed or not) and the roles adopted by each agent.

The artifact SchemeBoard allows agents to commit to missions and to change the state of goals (after finished them). Likewise, it is possible to know which agent are committed to each mission and the state of each goal, through its observable properties.

The SJVG project is consisted by a virtual environment and the implementation considered three types of agents, as shown in Figure 5:

1. The agent "EA," which is responsible for creating the artifacts that will be used in the integration by the "Gardeners" agents.
2. The "Gardeners" use artifacts to achieve their goals and accomplish their tasks (routines);

Figure 5. Integration of the artifacts

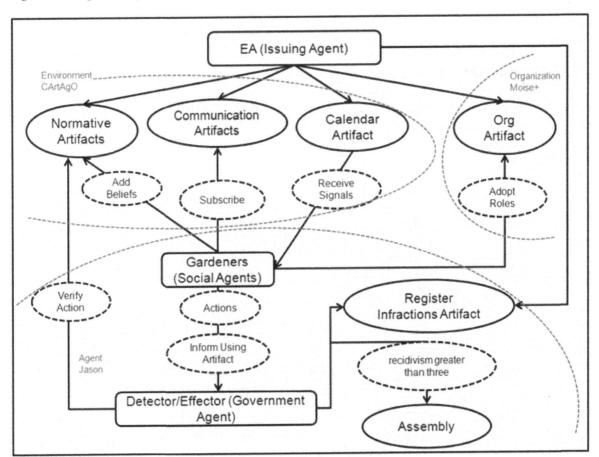

3. The "Admin" agents, which, in the environment, play the roles of technician and secretary.

The agents were implemented in Jason, the virtual environment with physical artifacts, normative and communication artifacts were implemented in CArtAgO framework and the organization model in the MOISE+ model.

5.4 Examples of Functioning Simulations of the SJVG Project [9]

In this section, we show just simple examples of a functioning simulations of the SJVG project. Since all dimensions were integrated through JaCaMo framework, it is allowed to an agent to assume a role in a specific group. For example the "Gardener" agent can assume the role of a "gardener" in the SJVG project by the "adoptRole" operation.

In Figure 6, a specific "Gardener" agent called "Cicero," through the operation lookupArtifact, search the artifact GroupBoard and then it adopts the role of "gardener" in the sub-group Parcel in SJVG (lines 11 and 12).

Observe that, in lines 15, 23, 27 and 32, the "social agents" add beliefs in their belief bases, as the confirmation of the creation of artifacts (makeArtifact operation), which is sent by the "EA" agent, through a .broadcast command.

The agents seek communication artifacts (line 16 and 17), the artifact calendar (which sends signals to agents about available actions in the virtual environment) (line 24), physical artifacts (line 28) and normative artifacts (line 33) by the lookupArtifact operation, which is performed for searching for an artifact by its name and identifier. Then, the agents can perform their actions with the use of these resources in the SJVG virtual environment.

Figure 6. Operations "lookupArtifact" and "adopteRole"

```
admin.asl    hsjV03.mas2j    ea.asl    *cicero.asl ⊠    genaro.as

10⊝ +org: true
11⊝          <- lookupArtifact("parcela_sgroup", GroupBoard);
12⊝          adoptRole(hortelao)[artifact_id(GroupBoard)];
13           focus(GroupBoard).
14
15⊝ +communication: true
16⊝          <- lookupArtifact("FIPARequestArtifact", ReqArt);
17⊝          lookupArtifact("FIPAInformArtifact", InfArt);
18⊝          subscribe[artifact_id(ReqArt)];
19⊝          subscribe[artifact_id(InfArt)];
20⊝          focus(ReqArt);
21           focus(InfArt).
22
23⊝ +calendary: true
24⊝          <- lookupArtifact("horta1", Calendary);
25           focus(Calendario).
26
27⊝ +physicals: true
28⊝          <- lookupArtifact("Pa", PaArt);
29⊝          focus(PaArt);
30           .println("Artefato Fisico: ", PaArt).
31
32⊝ +normasObrig: true
33⊝          <- lookupArtifact("normasObrig", NormasObrig);
34           focus(NormasObrig).
```

The focus operation is performed (lines 13, 20, 21, 25, 29, 34) so that the agent continues to observe changes that occur in those artifacts, or even deleting some in their environment.

In Figure 7, we show some examples of Normative Artifacts (obligation, permission, prohibition and right) that were developed from the set of rules established by the Confederation EA, in order to help agents to comply with the rules of the SJVG project. The norms are created through plans by the agent "EA" at the beginning of the simulation. Figure 7 shows the implementation of these plans by the agent, the actions contained in them and the creation of the norms through the normative artifacts.

In Figure 7 (line 63 of the implementation, in the top of the figure, and line 10 of the simulation, in the bottom of the figure), the norm "pagar mensalidade" (which means: to pay tuition') is mandatory and the non-compliance constitutes a cumulative serious misconduct.

This action is verified by the effector/detector agent (government agent "Admin"), which is responsible for monitoring the compliance with

Figure 7. Creating rules: Normative artifacts

the norms and check the normative artifacts to analyze if the performed action is in fact a violation.

After this verification, as shown in Figure 8, the agent "admin" search, in its belief base, for the adequate penalty and notify the offender their offense (lines 3 and 4), registering it in the "Penalty Registration (RP) artifact'' (line 23), in order to have the sanction applied to the agent who performed the prohibited action.

By checking the number of cumulative penalties recorded in the RP artifact, the government agent "Admin" may convene a meeting (assembly) of the agents participating in SJVG project (Figure 8, line 25), so they can vote with respect to the expulsion (or permanency) of the offending agent from the project. In the simulated example of Figure 8, the agent "Cicero" received 5 votes,

which, in this case, is sufficient to have it expelled from SJVG project (line 32).

Communication Artifacts must fulfill a function of mediating communication, that is, they forward messages to their recipients, according to protocols, overseeing the execution order of sending these messages. An example of the use of communication in the SJVG project is shown in Figure 9, where an agent called "lucas, playing the role of an auxiliary gardener, asks permission (through a request message to the government agent "admin") to cultivate trees in the garden (line 6). The agent "admin," in reply (using a message of type inform), informs that this action is not allowed (line 12).

Figure 8. Infringement of rules and assembly in SJVG

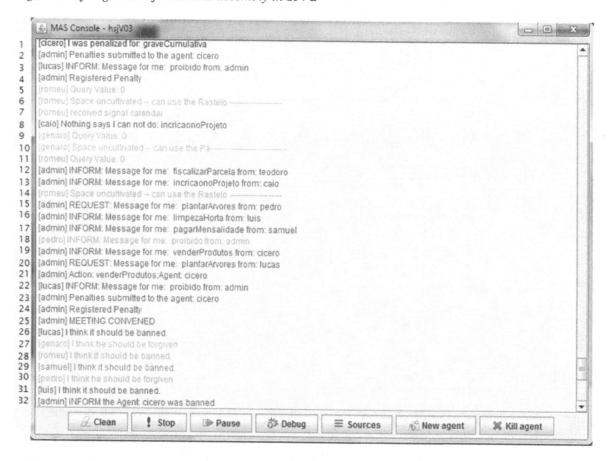

6. RELATED WORK AND ADDITIONAL READING

In the literature, we do not find any works where JaCaMo is used for the modeling of real-world-based systems, as our proposal. Some works present how JaCaMo infrastructure can be applied, using "toy examples" (Hubner et al., 2009) or "hypothetical examples" (Baldoni et al., 2010), in order to show the use of artifacts. Baldoni et al. (2010) presented an application of artifacts, showing how they are be flexible and reusable. However, concerning the modeling and simulation of (urban or not) ecosystems using multiagent systems, in general, artifacts are not used. In Alberti and Waddel (2000), agents and georeferenced data are used to propose a sustainable ecosystem, trying to explain how the metropolitan areas evolve. In Adamatti et al. (2005) and Koutiva and Makropoulos (2012), the multiagent approach is used to model urban water management.

Other models and tools developed in the context of SJVG-MAS Project are:

1. A hybrid BDI-Fuzzy model for the exchange of non-economical services, based on Piaget's theory of social exchanges (Farias et al., 2013);
2. The Modeling of Agent Periodic Routines in Agent-based Social Simulation using Colored Petri Nets (Silva et al., 2013)

Additional reading is recommended, mainly related to MAS organization modeling. See, for example, the book edited by V. Dignum (2009). In this book, for example, Coutinho et al. (2009) discuss the modeling of MAS organizations based on 4 dimensions (structural, interactive, functional and normative dimensions), Ferber et al. (2009) stress the importance of thinking a MAS in all aspects (agents, environment, interaction, organizations, institutions), proposing the MAS based on Quadrants (MASQ) meta-model.consifering two axes: interior/exterior dimension and individual/collective dimension.

Figure 9. Using communication artifacts

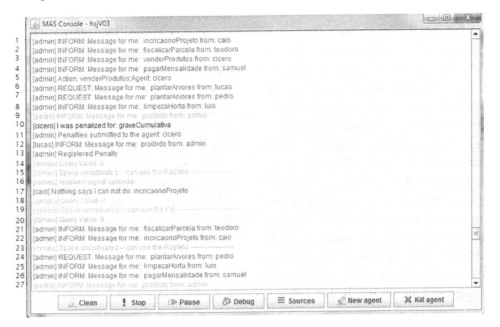

7. CONCLUSION

This chapter presented some developments towards the modeling of MAS-based tools for the simulation of the social production and management processes of an urban ecosystem, namely, the social organization of the San Jerónimo Vegetable Garden project, located in San Jerónimo Park (Seville, Spain), which is coordinated by the confederation "Ecologistas en Acción." Such social processes observed in the SJVG's project are characterized by the occurrence of a lot of interactions and social exchanges between the participants. Moreover, the periodic behaviors, interactions and communications are regulated by Internal Regulation Norms, established by the community in assembly, under the supervision and coordination of the EA confederation.

We conceived our MAS as a multi-dimensional BDI-like agent social system, composed by five integrated dimensions: (1) the population, (2) the organization, (3) the environment, (4) the set of interactions and the (5) normative policy. Notice that the two last dimensions are important here, since modifications in those dimensions may directly affect the social processes under analysis in this project.

Although JaCaMo is not a platform developed for performing simulations (as in the common sense usually adopted for the word simulation in the literature related to social simulation and MAS-based simulation), we decided to this framework for developing the MAS that "simulates" the SJVG functioning, since it presents high-level and modular facilities for the development of the first three dimensions mentioned above. We found that such modularity helped the modeling of this real world organization, especially facilitating the work of an interdisciplinary research group of the SJVG-MAS Project. Moreover, this modular development shall make easier doing modifications in the dimensions for the analysis of the

impact of those changes in the social production and management processes.

Although we have faced important problems when using JaCaMo framework (namely: (1) the impossibility of specifying directly periodicity in the MOISE+ model, (2) the impossibility of to define directly norms, their basic attributes (name, periodicity, applying role) and the sanctions, and (3) the inexistence of a modular infrastructure for defining interactions via communication), we found interesting modular solutions so that we could maintain our idea to have a 5-dimension MAS developed in JaCaMo.

The solutions we presented here are mainly based in the CartAgO framework, pointing also to the integration of organizational, normative, communication and physical artifacts.

The simple examples of the functioning simulations of the SJVG project showed how the SJVG community (and the researchers involved in this project) may use this tool to know and to analyze the current reality of the project. By modifying the current organization, roles or role behaviors, regulation, norms, physical resources, protocols, etc. it will be possible to analyze which management practices can contribute to the social production and to the sustainability of the project. Also, the agent behaviors may be sophisticated, so that other aspects may be observed, such us the influence of reputation, trust, etc. in the formation of groups in the presence of restrictions in the physical environmental (e.g., space for cultivation, seed storage, diseases in seedlings, etc.) and also the voting in assemblies.

Future work will be concerned with the improvement of the interface and the simulation of different scenarios for the analysis of the social production and management processes of SGVG project.

REFERENCES

Adamatti, D. F., Sichman, J. S., Bommel, P., Ducrot, R., Rabak, C., & Camargo, M. E. S. A. (2005). *JogoMan: A prototype using multi-agent-based simulation and role-playing games in water management.* Paper presented at CABM-HEMA-SMAGET, Bourg-Saint-Maurice, Les Arcs, France.

Alberti, M., & Waddell, P. (2000). An integrated urban development and ecological simulation model. *Integrated Assessment, 1,* 215–227. doi:10.1023/A:1019140101212

Baldoni, M., Baroglio, C., Bergenti, F., Boccalatte, A., Marengo, E., & Martelli, M. … Santi, A. (2010). MERCURIO: An interaction-oriented framework for designing, verifying and programming multi-agent systems. In N. Fornara & G. Vouros, (Eds.), Proc. of the 3rd Multi-Agent Logics, Languages, and Organisations Federated Workshops.

Bettini, V. (1998). *Elementos de Ecología Urbana.* Madrid: Editorial Trotta.

Boissier, O., Bordini, R., Hubner, J., Ricci, A., & Santi, A. (2011). *Multi-agent oriented programming with JaCaMo* (pp. 747–761). Amsterdam, The Netherlands: Elsevier.

Boissier, O., Bordini, R., Hubner, J., Ricci, A., & Santi, A. (2012). *JaCaMo project.* Retrieved from http://jacamo.sourceforge.net/

Bordini, R., Hubner, J., & Wooldridge, M. (2007). *Programming multi-agent systems in AgentSpeak using Jason.* Hoboken, NJ: Wiley.

Coelho, H., Costa, A. C., & Trigo, P. (2014). On agents intercations governed by morality. In D. Adamatti, G. P. Dimuro, & H. Coelho (Eds.), *Interdisciplinary applications of agent-based social simulation and modeling.* Hershey, PA: IGI Global.

Costa, A. C. R., & Santos, I. A. S. (2012). Toward a framework for simulating agent-based models of public policy processes on the Jason-CArtAgO platform. In *Proceedings of AMPLE@ECAI 2012: 2nd International Workshop on Agent-based Modeling for Policy Engineering, European Conference on Artificial Intelligence* (vol. 1, pp. 1-15). Montpellier, France: Université de Montpellier.

Coutinho, L., Sichman, J., & Boissier, O. (2009). Modeling dimensions for agent organization. In V. Dignum (Ed.), *Handbook of research on multi-agent systems: Semantics and dynamics of organizational models* (pp. 18–50). Hershey, PA: IGI Global. doi:10.4018/978-1-60566-256-5.ch002

Demazeau, Y. (1997). Steps towards multi-agent oriented programming. In *Proceedings of the First International Workshop on Multi-Agent Systems.* Boston.

Dignum, V. (Ed.). (2009). *Handbook of research on multi-agent systems: Semantics and dynamics of organizational models.* Hershey, PA: IGI Global. doi:10.4018/978-1-60566-256-5

Dimuro, G. (2009). *La producción y gestión social en ecosistemas urbanos: la agricultura urbana y periurbana en Sevilla* (Phd Thesis Proposal). Sevilla, Spain: Universidad de Sevilla.

Dimuro, G. (2010). Sistemas urbanos: el estado de la cuestión y los ecosistemas como laboratorio. *Arquitextos, 124,* 11.

Dimuro, G., & Jerez, E. (2010a). Comunidades en Transición: Hacia otras prácticas sostenibles en los ecosistemas urbanos. *Cidades Comunidades e Territórios, 20-21,* 87–95.

Dimuro, G., & Jerez, E. (2010b). La comunidad como escala d etrabajo en los ecosistemas urbanos. In *Proceedings of Ciencia y Tecnología, 20th Congreso de Ingeniería Sustentable y Ecologia Urbana, Buenos Aires, ISEU* (pp. 101—116). Palermo, Italy: Universidad de Palermo.

Dimuro, G., & Jerez, E. (2011). La comunidad como escala de trabajo en los ecosistemas urbanos. *Revista Ciencia y Tecnología, 10*, 101–116.

Easton, D. (1965). *A framework for political analysis*. Englewood Cliffs, NJ: Prentice-Hall.

Ecologistas en acción. (n. d.). Retrieved from http://www.ecologistasenaccion.org/

Farias, G. P., Dimuro, G. P., Dimuro, G., & Jerez, E. (2013). A fuzzy BDI-like agent model for exchanges of non-economic services. In *Proceedings of BRACIS 2013—Brazilian Conference on Intelligent Systems, Fortaleza*. (pp. 26-32). Los Alamitos, CA: IEEE.

Ferber, J., Stratulat, T., & Tranier, J. (2009). Towards an Integra approach of organizations in multi-agent systems. In V. Dignum (Ed.), *Handbook of research on multi-agent systems: Semantics and dynamics of organizational models* (pp. 51–75). Hershey, PA: IGI Global. doi:10.4018/978-1-60566-256-5.ch003

French, W. L., & Bell, C. (1973). *Organization development: Behavioral science interventions for organization improvement*. Englewood Cliffs, NJ: Prentice-Hall.

Gilbert, N., & Troitzsch, K. (1999). *Simulation for the social scientist*. Philadelphia: Open University Press.

Hill, M. (2009). *The public policy process* (5th ed.). London: Pearson Longman.

Hubner, J. (2003). *Um Modelo de Reorganização de Sistemas Multiagentes* (PhD Thesis). São Paulo, Brazil: USP.

Hübner, J., Boissier, O., Kitio, R., & Ricci, A. (2010). Instrumenting multi-agent organizations with organisational artifacts and agents. *Autonomous Agents and Multi-Agent Systems, 20*, 369–400. doi:10.1007/s10458-009-9084-y

Hubner, J., Bordini, R. H., Gouveia, G. P., Pereira, R. H., Picard, G., Piunti, M., & Sichman, J. S. (2009). Using Jason, Moise+, and CArtAgO to develop a team of cowboys. In J. Dix, M. Fisher, & P. Novák (Eds), *Proceedings of 10th International Workshop on Computational Logic in Multi-Agent Systems (CLIMA 2009)*, (pp. 203-207).

Hubner, J., Sichman, J., & Boissier, O. (2002). A model for the structural, functional, and deontic specification of organizations in multiagent systems. In *Proceedings of the Brazilian Symposium on Artificial Intelligence—SBIA 2002, Porto de Galinhas* (LNAI 2507, pp. 118–128). Berlin: Anais Springer.

Koutiva, I., & Makropoulos, C. (2012). Linking social simulation and urban water modeling tools to support adaptive urban water management. In *Proceedings of the International Environmental Modelling and Software Society (iEMSs)*.

Lobo, C. (1998). *Vivienda y Ciudad Posibles*. Bogotá, Columbia: Escala.

Morin, E. (2010). *Hacia el abismo? Globalización en el siglo XXI*. Madrid, Spain: Paidós.

Naredo, J. (1996). *Sobre el origen, el uso y el contenido del término sostenible*. Retrieved from http://habitat.aq.upm.es/cs/p2/a004.html

Ortiz, E. (2010). Derecho a la ciudad, producción social y gestión participativa del hábitat. La promoción de iniciativas comunitarias incluyentes en la Ciudad de México. *Hábitat y Sociedad, 1*, 55–70.

Padgham, L., & Winikoff, M. (2004). *Developing intelligent agent systems: A practical guide*. Chichester, UK: Wiley. doi:10.1002/0470861223

Pelli, V. (2007). *Habitar, participar, pertenecer. Acceder a la vivienda—incluirse en la sociedad*. Buenos Aires, Argentina: Nobuko.

Pelli, V. (2010). La gestión de la producción social del hábitat. *Hábitat y Sociedad, 39-54*.

Rao, A. (1996). AgentSpeak(L), BDI agents speak out in a logical computable language. In R. Hoe (Ed.), *Seventh European Workshop on Modelling Autonomous Agents in a Multi-Agent World,* (Lecture Notes in Computer Science, 1038) (pp. 42-55). Berlin: Springer.

Rao, A., & Georgeff, M. (1991). Modeling rational agents within a BDI-architecture. In R. Fikes & E. Sandewall (Eds.), *Proceedings of the 2nd International Conference on Principles of Knowledge Representation and Reasoning* (pp. 473-484). San Mateo: Morgan Kaufmann.

Rao, A., & Georgeff, M. (1992). An abstract architecture for rational agents. In *Proceedings of the 3rd International Conference on Principles of Knowledge Representation and Reasoning (KR'92)* (pp. 439-449). Morgan Kaufmann.

Ricci, A., Piunti, M., & Viroli, M. (2011). Environment programming in multi-agent systems: An artifact-based perspective. In *Proceedings of the Autonomous Agent Multi-Agent Systems.* Berlin: Springer.

Ricci, A., Santi, A., & Piunti, M. (2012). *Fonte: CArtAgO (Common ARTifact infrastructure for AGents Open environments).* Retrieved from http://cartago.sourceforge.net/

Rodrigues, H., Santos, I., Dimuro, G., Dimuro, G., Adamatti, D., & Jerez, E. (2013a). A MAS for the simulation of normative policies of the urban vegetable garden of San Jerónimo, Seville, Spain. In A. Brandão, R. Bordini, & J. Sichman (Eds.), *Anais do WESAAC 2013—VII Workshop-Escola de Sistemas de Agentes, seus Ambientes e Aplicações* (pp. 93-104). São Paulo, Brazil: USP.

Rodrigues, T. F., Costa, A. C. R., & Dimuro, G. P. (2013b). Communication infrastructure based on artifacts for the Jacamo platform. In *Proceedings of EMAS 2013—1st International Workshop on Engineering Multi-Agent Systems at AAMAS 2013* (pp. 1-15). Saint Paul: France.

Romero, G., Mesías, R., Enet, M., Oliveras, R., & García, L. (2004). *La participación en el diseño urbano y arquitectónico en la producción social del hábitat.* Mexico: CYTED.

Russell, S., & Norvig, P. (2010). *Artificial intelligence: A modern approach.* Upper Saddle River, NJ: Prentice Hall.

Santos, F., Dimuro, G., Rofrigues, T., Adamatti, D., Dimuro, G., Costa, A., & Jerez, E. (2012). Modelando a organização social de um SMA para simulação dos processos de produção e gestão social de um ecossistema urbano: o caso da horta San Jerónimo da cidade de Sevilla, Espanha. In J. Hubner, A. Brandão, R. Silveira, & J. Marchi (Eds.), *Anais do WESAAC 2012—VI Workshop-Escola de Sistemas de Agentes, seus Ambientes e Aplicções* (pp. 93-104). Florianópolis, Brazil: UFSC.

Santos, F., Rodrigues, H., Rodruigues, T., Dimuro, G., Adamatti, D., Dimuro, G., & Jerez, E. (2013a). Integrating CarTagO artifacts for the simulation of social production and management of urban ecosystems: The case of San Jerónimo Vegetable Garden of Seville, Spain. In A. Brandão, R. Bordini, & J. Sichman (Eds.), *Anais do WESAAC 2013—VII Workshop-Escola de Sistemas de Agentes, seus Ambientes e Aplicações* (pp. 93-104). São Paulo, Brazil: USP.

Santos, F., Rodrigues, H., Rodruigues, T., Dimuro, G., Adamatti, D., Dimuro, G., & Jerez, E. (2013b). Analyzing the problem of the modeling of periodic normalized behaviors in multiagent-based simulation of social systems: The case of the San Jerónimo Vegetable Garden of Seville, Spain. In B. Kamiñski & G. Koloch (Eds.), *Advances in Social Simulation: Proceedings of the 9th Conference of the European Social Simulation Association.* (1st ed., vol. 229, pp. 61-72). Berlin: Springer.

Santos, I., Rodrigues, T., Dimuro, G., Costa, A., & Jerez, E. (2011). Towards the modeling of the social organization of an experiment of social management of urban vegetable gardens. In *Proceedings of 2011 Workshop and School of Agent Systems, their Environment and Applications (WESAAC)* (pp. 98 -101). Los Alamitos, CA: IEEE.

Silva, C. E., Gonçalves, E. M. N., Dimuro, G. P., Dimuro, G., & Jerez, E. de M. Modeling agent periodic routines in agent-based social simulation using colored petri nets. In *Proceedings of 1st BRICS Countries Congress (BRICS-CCI) and 11th Brazilian Congress (CBIC) on Computational Intelligence, Porto de Galinhas*. Los Alamitos, CA: IEEE.

Subagdja, B., Sonenberg, L., & Rahwan, I. (2009). Intentional learning agent architecture. *Journal of Autonomous Agents and Multi-Agent Systems, 18*, 417–470. doi:10.1007/s10458-008-9066-5

Terradas, J. (2001). *Ecología urbana*. Barcelona, Spain: Rubes Editorial.

TILAB. (2003). *Fonte: JADE—Java Agent Development Framework*. Retrieved from http://jade.tilab.com/

Touraine, A. (2005). *Un nuevo paradigma para comprender el mundo de hoy*. Barcelona, Spain: Ediciones Paidós Ibérica S.A.

Vieria, L., & Bredariol, C. (1998). *Cidadania e política ambiental*. Rio de Janeiro, Brazil: Editorial Record.

Weiss, G. (1999). *Multiagent systems: A modern approach to distributed artificial intelligence*. Cambridge, MA: The MIT Press.

Wooldridge, M. (2002). *An introduction to multiagent systems*. Chichester, UK: Wiley.

World Commission on Environment and Development. (1987). *Our common future*. Oxford, UK: Oxford University Press.

KEY TERMS AND DEFINITIONS

Artifacts: In a computational context, the resources and tools dynamically created, handled and shared by agents to support their activities, both individual and collective, trying to simulate the human activities. In our chapter, there are 4 types of artifacts, each one to define a level of the social system: organizational, physical artifacts, normative and communication artifacts.

Public Policy: A set of norms and action plans, to be adopted and followed by both the government agents and the societal agents that operate in the social context of concern. In our chapter, we have reduce the idea of "government agents" to "management agents" in social systems. In our case study, these policies must be express in normative artifacts and can be analyzed by all agents in the social system.

Social Production and Management Processes: The social production of habitat, understood as the generation of new (physical or relational) situations by the construction, alteration or removal of physical objects—buildings, infrastructure pieces, housing complexes, cities, territorial fractions, networks—and / or relational objects—service systems, laws, codes and ordering and categorization norms—is seen as the slogan to ensure, in the new situations to be produced, compliance with specific functions (...), for the benefit of a particular user, or a social sector, or the society as a whole, often also for the benefit of the promoter of the action (Pelli, 2010).

ENDNOTES

[1] "SJVG-MAS Project: MAS-based tools for the simulation of the social production and management processes in urban ecosystems, the case of the San Jerónimo Urban Vegetable Garden of Seville" (FURG—Brazil, Universidad of Sevilla – Spain) has been developed under the context of the "RS-

SOC Project – Social Simulation Net of Rio Grande do Sul state, Brazil (UFRGS, FURG, UFPEL, UFSM, UNISINOS)," supported by FAPERGS. It is also partially supported by CNPq.

2   See *Ecologistas en acción* (n. d.).

3   The well-known Vowels Framework (De-mazeau, 1997) for the development of MAS establishes that four dimensions must be considered in a MAS, namely, Agents, Environment, Interactions and Organiza-tion, with the normative aspects being part of the Organization level. However, in this work, we decided to consider the normative structure separately, since those aspects are to be analyzed in an independent way by the specialists in their simulation scenarios.

4   A tool that helps this task and provides a set of services for communication is JADE (TILAB, 2003); however, it is an external resource and not a component of JaCaMo, not presenting the desired JaCaMo modularity.

5   See also the Brundtland Report, the docu-ment entitled "Our Common Future"—

World Commission on Environment and Development (1987), which defines Sustain-able Development as the one that satisfies the actual necessities, without compromising the capacity of the future generations of supplementing their own necessities.

6   Jason is implemented in Java (multi-plat-form) and is available as Open Source under the GNU LGPL license.

7   CartAgO is a Java-based, Open Source technology and is available in (Ricci et al. 2012) and includes an API based on the Java language for programming artifacts and runtime environment.

8   In future works, we intend that agents con-sult relevant information, e.g., the existent relationships with the violator agent, its antiquity in the project, its reputation and influence, etc.

9   In the figures of this example, some words are written in Portuguese, since they were specified by Brazilian specialists that studied the real SJVG's normative, organizational and physical structure.

Chapter 18
Building ABMs to Control the Emergence of Crisis Analyzing Agents' Behavior

Luca Arciero
Bank of Italy, Italy

Cristina Picillo
Bank of Italy, Italy

Sorin Solomon
Hebrew University of Jerusalem, Israel

Pietro Terna
University of Turin, Italy

ABSTRACT

Agent-based models (ABMs) are quite new in the modeling landscape; they emerged on the scene in the 1990s. ABMs have a clear advantage over other approaches: they create the capacity to manage learning processes in agents and discover novelties in their behavior. In addition to bounded rationality assumptions, ABMs share a number of peculiar characteristics: first of all, a bottom-up perspective is assumed where the properties of macro-dynamics are emergent properties of micro-dynamics involving individuals as heterogeneous agents who live in complex systems that evolve through time. To apply this framework to financial crisis analysis, a simplified implementation of the SWARM protocol (www. swarm.org), based on Python, is introduced. The result is the Swarm-Like Agent Protocol in Python (SLAPP). Using SLAPP, it is possible to focus on natural phenomena and social behavior. In the case of this chapter, the authors focus on the banking system, recreating the interactions of a community of financial institutions that act in the payment system and in the interbank market for short-term liquidity.

DOI: 10.4018/978-1-4666-5954-4.ch018

INTRODUCTION:
LITERATURE REVIEW[1]

... there is no general principle that prevents the creation of an economic theory based on other hypotheses than that of rationality (K. J. Arrow, 1987)

The *raison d'être* of Agent-based models (ABMs) lies in a vision of the world that is completely different from the conventional view of rational choice theory, which prevails in economics.

Beginning with Adam Smith's idea of the "invisible hand," the (minor) history of economic science may be represented in a stylized fashion as a progressive refinement of the rational agent hypothesis, which first materialized in profit (utility)-maximizing agents and, later, in the Lucas and Sargent rational expectation theory.

In the game theoretical strand of economic science, the rational agent paradigm translates into infinitely forward- and backward-looking agents that are usually endowed with common knowledge about their opponent's rational behavior.

Although infinitely rational, strategies elaborated by these agents may be proven as less successful than simpler strategies based on heuristics and shortcuts, as witnessed by the famous Axelrod tournament reported in Schellenberg (1996). Axelrod invited game theorists and behavioral economists to play an iterated prisoner's dilemma by submitting computer programs translating the strategies that they thought a player should follow during the game. A number of scholars joined the tournament: some of them presented complex software replicating forward- and backward-looking agents, and others submitted simple programs mimicking agents' behaviors with simpler rules, heuristics and shortcuts. The simplest of these programs was the one named "Tit for Tat," built by Anatol Rapoport, a famous psychologist. The artificial agent embedded in the Rapoport "Tit for Tat" program acted on a minimal decision tree (represented in four instructions), which led the

agent to cooperate at the first iteration and then to match the opponents' strategy: cooperate if the other cooperates, and defect if the opponent defects. Against every forecast, the Rapoport program won the tournament. Surprisingly, "Tit for Tat" emerged the winner in a second tournament in which the artificial agents embedded in the competing programs had been built to challenge "Tit for Tat" on the basis of complex decision trees. It was not the surprise effect that enabled "Tit for Tat" to overcome its opponents in the first tournament; Rapoport's artificial agent emerged as the most effective program, even though other artificial agents had been aware of its behavior.

The Rapoport "Tit for Tat" software history unavoidably recalls the concept of "bounded rationality," originally introduced by Nobel Laureate H. Simon in the 1950s as a "rational choice under computational constraints," whose specific ingredients are (1) the limited, sometimes fuzzy, information regarding possible alternatives to a specific problem and the related consequences at the agents' disposal; (2) the limited ability of the agents to elaborate the available pieces of information; and (3) the limited amount of time agents can spend deciding. Given these constraints, agents tend to adopt "satisficing" rather than optimizing behavior by relying on rules of thumb, heuristics and shortcuts to deliberately save resources (Simon, 1955).

The plausibility of the bounded rationality paradigm has been confirmed by a great deal of additional experimental evidence rooted in the seminal works of Daniel Kahneman, Amos Tversky, and their collaborators (who laid the foundation of an enormous body of literature on the topic). Among their main contributions (such as Tversky and Kahneman (1992)) was the discovery of the framing effects governing the decision processes of the agents whose choices do not depend on the contents of the choice but rather on the way that the decision problem is framed, i.e., the way the alternatives are presented.

Against this background, the need emerges for an approach that combines both complexity and simple heuristic rules in a balanced way.

A first alternative is experimental economics—whose initial applications date back to the 1950s, and which has been experiencing an ever-growing acceptance among academics—where real individuals are assigned cash incentives to maximize their expected profits to replicate the incentives operating in the real world and to draw inferences on market function.

To give an example of how experimental economics works, we choose, from among the thousands of experiments carried out thus far, an experiment developed by Cipriani and Guarino (2005), who set up an experiment based on the Glosten and Milgrom (1985) asymmetric information model to investigate the extent to which noise trading can be ascribed to trader irrationality in a laboratory financial market.

In the Cipriani and Guarino (2005) experiment, subjects receive private information on the value of an asset and trade it in sequence with a market maker. By observing the trader strategies and being aware of the model parameters, the authors estimate a structural model of sequential trading, finding that the noise in their experiment is due to the irrational use of private information accounts for 35 percent of decisions.

Experimental economics benefits from the presence of real subjects, who are given real cash incentives, in a model in which researchers can collect observational data that are not surrounded by confounding factors hiding the real world parameters. Experimental economics is not a panacea (Davis & Holt, 1993). Major drawbacks include the difficulty of replicating real incentives (people may exhibit different degrees of risk aversion in response to different amounts at stake) and a sort of selection bias (people cannot be forced to join an experiment). Other drawbacks include difficulties in designing and studying complex experiments close to real-world situations and iterating an

experiment several times with the same players to study learning mechanisms.

Against this backdrop, a possible solution is moving from real, human individuals to fictitious agents. These agents can be generated by software and can be assigned complex tasks, behavioral rules and proper incentives. The artificial behavior of these agents can be examined for a considerable amount of time.

In this vein, ABMs represent a suitable methodology for analyzing highly decentralized, highly parallel complex systems. Using an ABM with each agent (i.e., with each individual element of the system) is represented through a vector of attributes and a set of simple micro-level rules and heuristics governing the agent's behavior. Furthermore, the experiment design is under the complete control of the modeler, who decides how the virtual agents are defined and initialized.

A common feature of ABMs is the assumption of Simon's concept of bounded rationality, which can be subdivided into in a number of alternative options, as agents may vary greatly, exhibiting different degrees of sophistication. Reactive agents are the simplest agents because they are built and programmed to merely react to external stimuli, are unable to elaborate strategies, and usually have no memory, thus resembling the behavior of Pavlov's dog more than the behavior of a human. An early example of reactive agents can be found in the Gode and Sunder's "zero intelligent" agents[2] (1993), who post bids or offers in a double-auction model, comparing market prices with their reservation prices, without making any assumptions about the behaviors of the other agents. Even the models based on reactive agents have proved effective in reproducing real dynamics. The drawback of this approach is that the agents are too naive to adapt to unforeseen situations.

Deliberative agents lie opposite of reactive agents. Deliberative agents behave according to their knowledge about the external world and to their past experiences, and they elaborate strategies to achieve given targets[3]. These agents' ability to cope with uncertainty is not a free lunch: deliberative agents are likely to devote a (sometimes) unnecessary amount of time to elaborating and evaluating a set of alternative strategies, even in simple situations.

Hybrid agents involve a combination of the two approaches: they can respond to routine changes within the environment without elaborating complex, time-consuming strategies, but they maintain the ability to elaborate new strategies and plans when they are asked to cope with unprecedented situations.

Another attractive property of ABMs is the possibility of allowing them to modify their behavior through learning. "Reinforcement learning" techniques are widely used in ABM models, as they ensure that actions that provide profitable outcomes are "reinforced" and assigned a greater probability of being taken in the future. Other possible ways are the use of genetic algorithms or of learning of classifier systems (which are also commonly embedded in several ABMs to allow them to optimize and adapt their behavior).

Even though there is room for improving learning mechanisms in ABMs, agent-based simulation is a flexible tool for modeling system dynamics in the presence of learning mechanisms because, once created, agents may be forced to live for a certain period in a world where time and space are explicitly managed to evolve agents' behavior using parallel techniques.

In addition to bounded rationality assumptions, ABMs share a number of peculiar characteristics. First, a bottom-up perspective is assumed where the properties of macro-dynamics are emergent properties[4]—and not in equilibrium outcome, as in the neoclassical models—of micro-dynamics involving individual, heterogeneous agents living in complex systems that evolve through time. A further common feature of ABMs is the interaction among economic agents, which takes place in a direct and inherently non-linear fashion, as agents elaborate their decision on the basis of past choices made on their own and by other agents in the population.[5]

ABM models have become more and more effective since their initial applications [such as von Neumann's (1966) self-replicating machine and Conway's (Gardner, 1970) game of life], allowing the emergence of credible macro-level dynamics even when individuals are assigned simple rules and are assumed to be homogeneous.

An early and well-known example of the application of the ABM paradigm in the field of economics is the Santa Fe Artificial Stock Market, which was developed in the late 1990s. The Santa Fe Artificial Stock Market is a simple model reproducing trading dynamics with agents embedded with simple rules mapping the states of the world into buy or sell decisions. Despite its simplicity, this artificial market can replicate several features that resemble the statistical properties of real financial data: excess kurtosis of returns, little linear autocorrelation and persistent volatility (LeBaron et al., 1999). Applications of ABM to economic modeling span a broad range of research topics: from market design (Tesfatsion, 2011), technology diffusion (Gilbert et al., 2001) and the labor market (Neugart, 2008) to banking regulations (Westerhoff, 2008), central banks (Rapaport et al., 2009) and systemic risk. An example: Geanakoplos et al. (2012) created an ABM that reproduces the process leading to the formation and burst of the US real estate bubble, which played a crucial role in triggering the mortgage crisis. Running counterfactual analyses, the authors find that leverage (i.e., loan to value ratio), rather than low interest rates, was the main driver of the crisis.

As discussed in the case of experimental economics, we cannot refrain from highlighting the major limits and challenges that ABMs still face despite their growing popularity. Echoing Leo Tolstoy in Anna Karenina, "Happy families are all alike; every unhappy family is unhappy in its own way"[6], models are correct in only one way but may be wrong in several ways. In fact, when removing the hypothesis of rational choice, behavioral functions may be represented by an infinite number of plausible heuristics and shortcuts, inducing a sense of arbitrariness in the model (Rubinstein, 1998). Recently, there has been a great deal of work addressing the issue of ABM validation, proposing a number of different approaches to ABMs' empirical validation, among which the history-friendly approach, the indirect calibration approach and the Werker-Brenner (2004) approach may be considered the most influential (Windrum et al., 2007).

The history-friendly approach consists of calibrating the parameters and defining the behavioral rules embedded in the model to mimic specific actual features with a view to closely replicating the empirically observable history of a particular phenomenon. However, the indirect calibration approach and the Werker-Brenner approach avoid imposing ex-ante a set of restrictions on parameters; instead, they rely on empirical evidence to delimit specific sub-regions in the potential parameter space, where the model is able to give rise to actual statistical regularities or stylized facts.

Despite the efforts of ABM researchers, no approach has been recognized as a standard, universally agreed upon method for validating ABMs. Therefore, model validation still represents the greatest challenge that ABMs must face to be fully accepted by scholars.

Finally, to conclude this brief discussion of agent-based modeling, it is worth mentioning that ABMs still lack a unique, agreed upon protocol for building models. To shed light on this issue, in the next paragraph, we present the making of a large ABM based on the SLAPP protocol originally introduced by Terna (2010). (See http://eco83.econ.unito.it/terna/slapp/.)

FROM THE SLAPP PROTOCOL TO A CONCRETE APPLICATION

What is the Swarm Protocol, and Should We Care About It?

SLAPP, the Swarm-Like Protocol in Python, was used to build our simulation model. It comes from Swarm (Minar et al., 1996; Swarm can be accessed via www.swarm.org.) The Swarm project started at the Santa Fe Institute (first release: 1994) and represents a milestone in simulation.

Swarm has been highly successful; its protocol is the basis of several recently released tools, such as Repast, Ascape, NetLogo and StatLogo, and JAS. SLAPP is one of Swarm's most simplified reproductions, as it is written in Python (www.python.org). The original Swarm implementation was written in Objective C, a powerful language (which is the object-oriented merge of C and SmallTalk), which had a limited diffusion in the mid-1990s. Objective C is now quite popular; it is the base of the Mac OS X operating system. A second version of Swarm, with its main core always written in Objective C, but usable in Java, was released in the late 1990s. Swarm's popularity was limited by the beginning of the 2000s due to the lack of maintenance of its complex structure in the face of the new releases of the operating systems (also in the Linux case). JAS (sourceforge.net/projects/jaslibrary/) is similar to Swarm but is pure Java. SLAPP is similar to Swarm, with significant addenda, such as the original AESOP (Agents and Emergencies for Simulating Organizations in Python) layer, implemented in Python to take advantage of the simplicity of the language and its advanced internal structure, which has native powerful features.

According to Minar et al. (1996):

Swarm is a multi-agent software platform for the simulation of complex adaptive systems. In the Swarm system the basic unit of simulation is the swarm, a collection of agents executing a schedule of actions. Swarm supports hierarchical modeling approaches whereby agents can be composed of swarms of other agents in nested structures. Swarm provides object oriented libraries of reusable components for building models and analyzing, displaying, and controlling experiments on those models.

To summarize the paper of Minar et al. (1996) (1) Swarm defines a structure for simulations, a framework within which models are built; (2) Swarm's core commitment is creating a discrete-event simulation of multiple agents using an object-oriented representation; (3) to these basic choices, Swarm adds the concept of the *swarm*,

a collection of agents with a schedule of activity; and (4) the simulation of discrete interactions between agents stands in contrast to continuous system simulation, where simulated phenomena are quantities in a system of coupled equations. These are the key ideas of the ABM technique.[7]

We see the first step of the protocol in Figure 1, with a collection of bugs that need to be managed in a discrete-event simulation environment, following a schedule of actions. The *modelSwarm* contains the space where the bugs behave, the bugs and a clock.

The sequence that the protocol suggests is as follows: create the agents (or bugs, in our case) and then create the actions to be executed by the agents. In our case, we have a *class* or *set* named *Bug* (the initial capital letter is not mandatory but represents a useful convention), and from that class, we generate the required number of instances (named *aBug*) of the class. We place all of the generated instances into a collection, here

Figure 1. The basis of the Swarm protocol, with (1) the steps of the creation of the agents and of the schedule, (2) the model and (3) the collection of the agent to which we send the orders from the schedule.

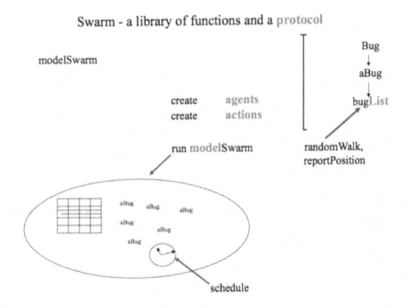

named *bugList*. For us, it is irrelevant that the formal name of each instance is always the same because the *list* will contain the information that is necessary to address each instance individually. After the creation of the agents, we prepare the actions to be taken (*randomWalk* and *reportPosition*) when the clock of the model, following the schedule, requires each action to be executed by each agent or by a specific agent. Using the collections, the code works with any number of agents because actions are addressed to the collection, which send the request to all of the collection's components. If a specific agent must act instead, the order is sent directly to that agent.

We have also to observe the behavior of our model. In Figure 2, we add a higher level of analysis by introducing an observer (*observerSwarm*), which contains the model and has objects (the model, the tools to observe it) and an independent schedule managed by a clock different from that of the model. It is normally not necessary to observe the model outcomes with the same granularity of the events occurring within the model itself.

In Figure 3, we add the probes as tools that allow us to look directly into the agents to inspect their data while the model is running. This tool is useful both for searching for errors in the code and for analytically evaluating the behavior of the components of the model. SLAPP does not currently have this capability (which is, instead, a pillar of the NetLogo agent-based platform).

A Concrete Application to the P&3M (Payments and Money Market Model)

Using an ABM and, in our case, SLAPP as preferred tool, we can focus both on natural phenomena and economic or social behaviors. For example, in the banking system case, we can recreate the interaction of a community of financial institutions that interact via both a payment system and an interbank market for short-term liquidity. Here, we show the importance of ABM for understanding potential systemic risk and the contagion effects arising from liquidity shortages.

Figure 2. We add a new layer, the observer, containing the model and the tools used to view it

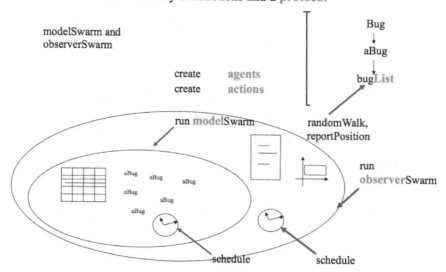

Figure 3. Via the probes, we can directly inspect the data of each agent

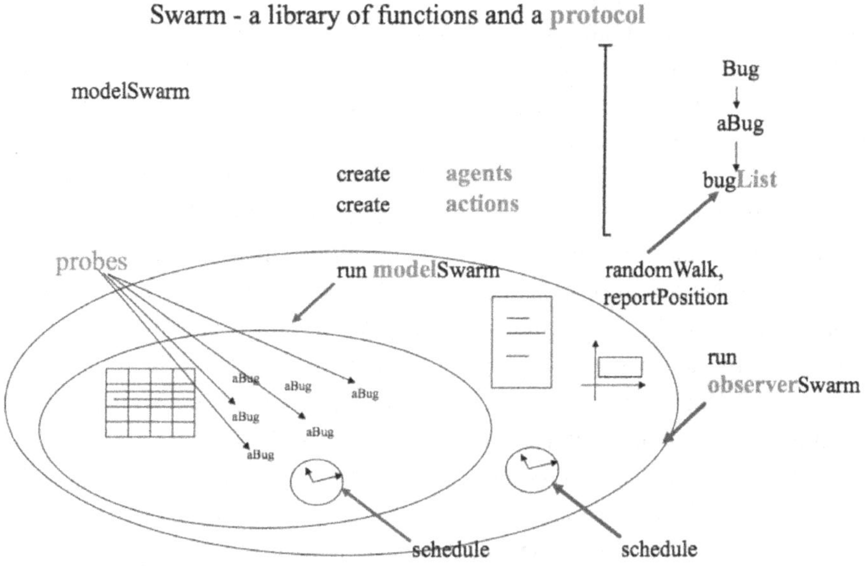

Modeling such a problem with an ABM is particularly attractive because the financial crisis has shown that securities and funding markets are potentially affected by sudden, (unexpected) deep modifications in agents' actions, which may be fruitfully analyzed through ABMs equipped with learning machines.

Quoting Tirole (2011) on market liquidity breakdowns (pp. 298–299), we can rely on authoritative advocacy to support our statement:

Market liquidity presumes that there are buyers (of assets, of securities) on the other side. As the recent crisis has demonstrated, this need not be the case. Commentators have accordingly mentioned the possibility of a "buyers' strike" a surprising concept for economists (...).

Before we enter into the details of the model, it is worth describing the institutional features of the environment under investigation. According to a consolidated definition (Bank for International Settlement, 2001), a payment system consists of a set of instruments, banking procedures and, typically, interbank funds transfer systems that ensure the circulation of money. In turn, interbank funds transfer systems (IFTS) are arrangements among banks and a settlement agent, typically central banks, that hold settlement accounts on behalf of participants and manage the settlement process of debiting and crediting the participants' account according to the payment instructions they submit to the system.

Currently, the majority of IFTS, which is hereafter referred to as a payment system, operates in a Real-Time Gross Settlement (RTGS) fashion, meaning that each payment submitted to the system is settled immediately in central bank money (cash), provided that sufficient liquidity is held in the participants' accounts.

The flows of incoming and outgoing payments create surplus or deficit of liquidity at the participant level, both on an intraday and a daily basis. On the intraday basis, liquidity deficits may prevent banks from executing payments with potential delay costs because their customers or other banks may perceive delaying banks as unreliable. Under certain stressful situations, banks delaying "critical" payments may bear enormous costs, as they may be perceived as illiquid, prompting other banks in the system to question their viability. Such questioning carries potential implications for systemic risk.

Banks commonly have a desired end-of-day level of cash in their accounts. This target comes from the reserve requirement regime imposed by central banks on commercial banks' monetary policy operations. This minimum reserve regime requires banks to hold in their central bank accounts a certain amount of cash in proportion to their short-term liabilities over a certain maintenance period. Thus, banks set intermediate daily desired end-of-day targets, with the growth of the average balance over the maintenance period in mind.

To manage their payment flows, banks may borrow and lend cash that they need not only on an intraday and daily basis in the interbank market (hereafter called the money market), usually on a bilateral, over-the-counter basis, but also on a multilateral basis, through screen-based electronic markets, as is the case of the e-MID Italian electronic exchanges for uncollateralized exchanges.

Our ABM model focuses on the liquidity management problem of commercial banks, which face a payment obligation that must be settled in an interbank fund transfer system under the intraday, end-of-day and multi-day constraints. This liquidity management problem can be solved by relying on the money markets.

The case presented closely resembles the Italian framework because Italian banks execute part of their trading in the money market through a screen-based multilateral market and settle their payment obligations through an RTGS system (the same RTGS system, TARGET2, is used in all of the countries in the Euro zone). From the model, some conclusions can be drawn about the design of mechanisms that aim to contain financial risk and to avoid contagion and cascading failures.

We introduce here a hybrid framework (see above). The agent-based model operates not only with the treasurers of the banks as agents but also with the interbank payment system as an agent within the model, moving payments around, with delays and failures determined by the treasurers. Payments create shortages and abundances of liquidity in banks by generating asks and bids in the money market, via a double auction system, as in a regular stock market. In this way, the model links both the behavior of the treasurers and the time distribution of the payments with the short-term movements of the interest rate.

Using SLAPP and ABM, we shift the focus on the concrete aspects of an actual banking system by recreating the interaction of two institutions (a payment system and a market for short-term liquidity) to investigate interest rate dynamics in the presence of delays in interbank movements. The delay problem is a crucial one because delays in payments can generate liquidity shortages that, in the presence of unexpected negative operational or financial shocks, can produce huge domino effects (Arciero et al., 2009). In this perspective, agent-based simulation is a magnifying glass for understanding reality.

We have two parallel and highly connected institutions: a RTGS, or Real Time Gross Settlement system, as described in Arciero and Impenna (2001); and an e-MID-like money market (electronic Market of Interbank Deposit, which is a standard double continuous auction market, with the special characteristic that asks and bids are identified by the name of the actor; see www.e-mid.it/?lang=uk). To avoid any misunderstanding, the asking agent requires a price, the interest rate, to lend money. On the contrary, the bidding agent offers a price for borrowing money. Considering the flow of interbank payments settled via the first institution, we simulate delays in payments and examine the emergent interest rate dynamics in the money market. In this type of market, the interest rate is the price. The behavior in this market is complicated by a few microstructures that will be investigated.

In Figure 4, we have a modified representation of the standard sequence diagram of the UML (Unified Modeling Language, www.uml. org) formalism that introduces time as the main actor in the sequence. Time, as the actor, is important because our model, and the related agents' behavior, is event driven. What are the events in our case? The events are the payments effectively recorded in a given time interval that come from actual interbank money movements

on a gross basis, i.e., without any clearing effects, as required by central banks all around the world (Angelini, 1998).

Events come from an archive of actual data and follow a time schedule that is sent to our simulated environment (we used artificial data to prepare the program; the code was applied to actual data only when running internally to the Bank of Italy). The treasurers of the banks, who receive payments or have to make payments via the RTGS system, bid prices with given probabilities to buy liquidity in the money market or ask prices to sell liquidity

Figure 4. A UML (Universal Modeling Language) representation of the actions taken by agents over time. Black arrow: a treasurer making a payment and bidding a price to obtain the money via the money market. Grey arrow: a treasure receiving a payment and asking a price to employ the money via the money market.

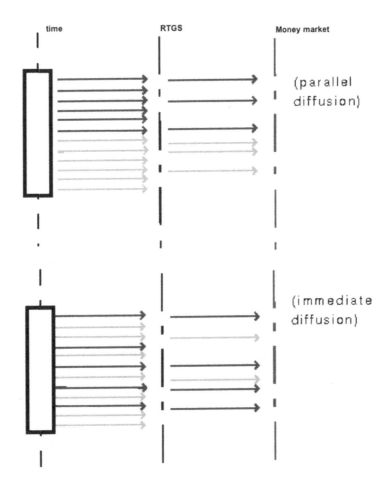

in the same market. Bid and ask probabilities can differ. The mechanism of bidding or asking on a probabilistic basis (if and only if a payment must be executed or has been received, as in Figure 4) is also related to the liquidity balance of the specific bank. As a consequence, the bid and ask mechanism is indirectly related to the whole set of financial movements of a given time period.

The different sequences of events (with their parallel or immediate diffusion, as in Figure 4) generate different lists of proposals into the double-auction money market that we analyze. Proposals are reported in logs: the log of the bid

proposals, according to decreasing prices (first listed: bid with the highest price); and the log of the ask proposals, according to increasing prices (first listed: ask with the lowest price). "Parallel" means that we are considering an actual situation in which all of the treasurers make the same kind of choices at the same time. "Immediate" means that we have a situation in which the treasurers are acting step by step, in a mixed way, both bidding and asking simultaneously.

In Figure 5, we discuss how a new price is proposed to the market when we consider the last executed price as a reference point and place

Figure 5. Viewing the last executed price, both in a parallel and immediate diffusion scheme

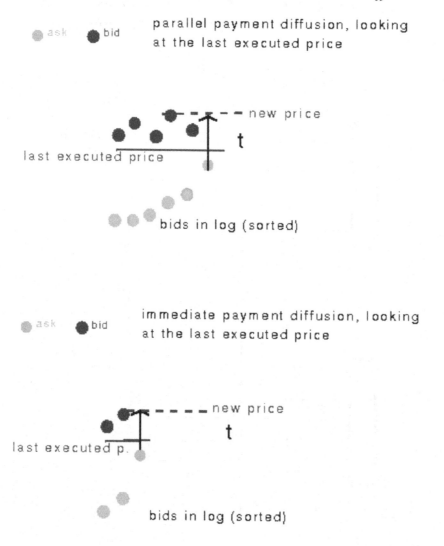

a price below it to obtain an easily matched ask position. In this case, both the cases of parallel proposals and immediate diffusion are expected to produce close results. In Figure 6, a new price is proposed to the market by considering the best proposal in the opposite log as a reference point and placing a price below it to obtain again, in a different way, an easily matched ask position. The cases of parallel proposals and immediate diffusion are now expected to produce different effects. As can be verified here, market microstructures are highly important in an ABM.

We see that, following the Swarm protocol, the *Model* is responsible for creating the agents as a class (*Banks*), each single agent (*aBank*) and the list of all agents (*BankList*). The protocol is also responsible for shaping the agents' actions. The time runs on an internal schedule of events based on a simulated clock. This clock triggers, at specific moments, the actions of the entire class of agents or of single agents. However, another schedule exists: that of the external *Observer*, who monitors the development of the actions and interactions within the *Model* and whose time does

Figure 6. Viewing the best proposal in the opposite market log, both in a parallel and immediate diffusion scheme

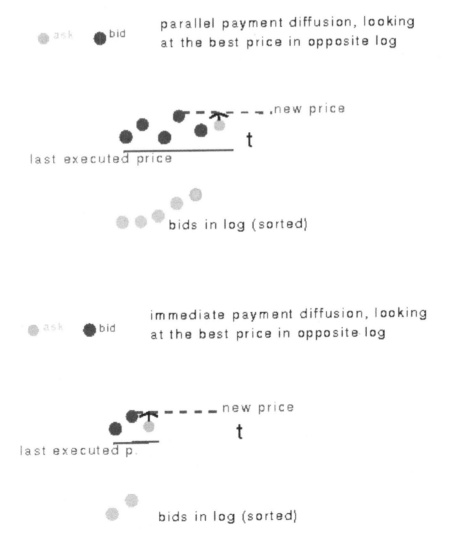

not necessarily elapse at the same speed as that of the *Model*. The *Observer* can stop the model execution. For example, the *Observer* can consider the interactions among the agents in a very specific instant of the simulation or run statistics on the simulated world up to that moment.

The *Observer* is also responsible for shaping the agents' characteristics (e.g., number, interconnectedness, level of required reserves, initial account balances) as well as determining the economic variables that condition the agents' behavior (monetary policy determinants, such as the interest rate and the level of the monetary aggregates).

Behavioral Rules within P&3M

Different layers of rules do coexist in the model. Following the SLAPP scheme and the ERA convention in Figure 7, we can introduce how rules are represented within the model. The main value of the Environment-Rules-Agents (ERA) scheme, introduced in Gilbert and Terna (2000), is that it keeps both the environment, which models the context by means of rules and general data, and the agents, with their private data, at different conceptual levels.

With the aim of simplifying the code design, external objects determine agent behavior. *Rule Masters*, for instance, can be interpreted as abstract

Figure 7. The Environment-Rules-Agents (ERA) scheme (Gilbert and Terna, 2000). See http://Web.econ. unito.it/terna/ct-era/ct-era.html for more details.

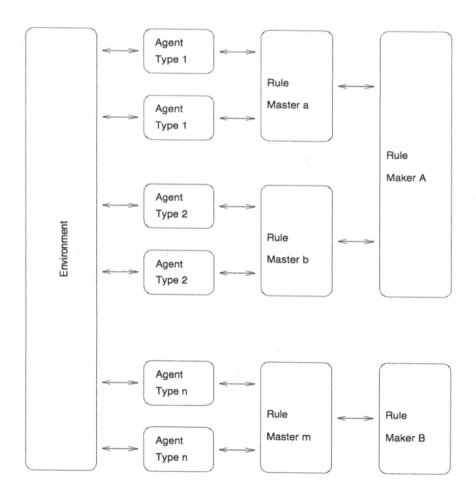

representations of the cognition of the agent. Production systems (sets of fixed rules), classifier systems, neural networks and genetic algorithms are all candidates for the implementation of *Rule Masters*.

We may also need to employ meta-rules, i.e., rules used to modify rules (for example, the training side of a neural network). The Rule Master objects are therefore linked to *Rule Maker* objects, whose role is to modify the rules mastering agent behavior, for example, by means of a simulated learning process.

P&3M general principles are embedded within the framework from which all of the possible behavioral rules of our banks stem. Examples of *Rule Maker* contents are compliance with the minimum reserve requirement, profit maximization, opportunity cost minimization, and payment timeliness versus delay in a repeated game perspective. From *Rule Makers*, any number of specific rules can be derived. The rules can affect all of the agents (profit maximization) or only a specific subset of agents (greedier banks versus more prudent banks). Additionally, the same rule can have different gradations, particularly regarding trade-offs (e.g., avoiding opportunity costs at any price versus a different intensity of tolerance, accepting opportunity costs against the costs of delaying payments or being forced to raise money on the interbank market to fulfill obligations).

How the Model Works

The starting principles of P&3M (Payments and Money Market Model) are in Arciero and Picillo (2012); a detailed presentation of the model is at http://eco83.econ.unito.it/terna/P&3M/P&3M. html; finally, the code can be obtained by contacting the corresponding author.

The model is fed either with exogenous real world data or artificially generated data. The model's parameters can be finely tuned either through an initial panel or input files. Banks are the agents: in each tick, all banks are asked to act in a random order, relying on prescheduled incoming and outgoing payments (actual data, when used, stem from the Italian RTGS system). The actions are based on empirical patterns inferred from the behavior of market participants on e-MID, the Italian electronic multilateral interbank money market platform, and on anecdotal evidence yielded during contacts with banks' treasurers. The schedule of the model is characterized by time breaks that represent the end of the day. In fact, the simulation embraces a *multiday* interval, mimicking the reserve requirement maintenance period. The single payment includes a progressive number, a start time and an end time, the sending and receiving bank, and the amount. When we use artificial data, a delay can be added to the starting time, assuming that the treasurer has the opportunity to evaluate whether to pay immediately or with a delay. The delay is defined as a random draw from a uniform distribution between zero and a plausible upper limit. The same effect could be introduced into the real world data by applying an *undelay*, assuming that the original due time of a payment is not always the one at which the transaction is really settled and may be a moment in time before the effective timestamp. Additionally, the *undelay* is a random draw from a uniform distribution.

The P&3M model manages situations in which a payment is due but the agent does not have enough liquidity on its account to settle it immediately. The payment will be bounced, delayed and resubmitted for settlement in the subsequent tick of the internal schedule, whereas the needed liquidity will be either supposed to flow in if the expected end-of-day balance exceeds the due amount or *purchased* on the interbank money market. To have a market clearing end-of-day, payments that cannot be fulfilled are dropped and settled via correspondent banking.

The parallelism of the different actions (1) determines the flow of payments and the smoothness of the functioning of the payment system, as in Figure 8; (2) populates the money market book;

Figure 8. The interest price dynamic (upper line), stock of due payments (intermediate line), and flow of received payments (lower line)

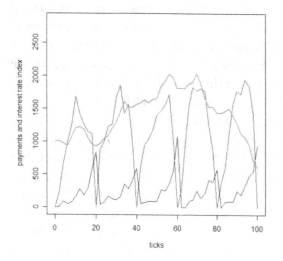

and (3) influences the interest rate dynamic. These aspects are captured by output reports generated by the P&3M model, both in terms of aggregate statistics that allow capturing the outcome of the complex interaction of the agents and their rules as well as in terms of micro-level indicators.

We show now an interesting case of the dynamics emerging from this simulation environment. This case occurs when the diffusion of the payment into the RTGS system is parallel and the operators consider the last executed price in the money market. The run reported in Figure 8 shows a non-trivial behavior of the interest rate. The dynamic is magnified here due to the dimension chosen for micro-movement in bids and asks. In these five days, we see a large movement of this time series as a consequence of significant delays in interbank payments. The simulation runs step by step, but we account for breaks in time to reproduce the end of each day (i.e., cleaning all the positions, etc.).

In Figure 8, we have the following: the interest price dynamic (upper line), stock of due payments (intermediate line), and flow of the received payments (lower line) in case of relevant delay in

payments (with a uniform random distribution between 0 and 90% of the available time until the time break). Time breaks (day changing) occur at 20, 40, … ticks.

By elaborating the interest rate series with the standard AR (autoregressive) and MA (moving average) techniques and directly connecting SLAPP to R (http://www.r-project.org), we find a typical AR(1) model in the graphs of the second row in Figure 9.

For the time being, the general principles have been designed as fixed and have been imposed by an external *god*. Future work will be focused on the introduction of a system of reinforced learning, where the agents will update the superior governing principles that can be emended and updated based on the experience yielded by the interaction with other agents within the environment.

Further research related to the technical functioning of the P&3M model will entail differentiating between "bland" and "tasty" agents. Bland agents are the simple, unspecific and basic agents whose behavioral rules operate in the background of the simulation. These actions are carved in the basic code implementing the SLAPP protocol. Tasty agents, the ones on which a researcher will focus, are subjects with specific predetermined skills and discretionary powers (acting capabilities). The rules governing the agents' actions operate in the foreground of the simulations in the sense that they are not fixed in the underlying code but rather are explicitly managed via scripts that can be *steered* by a researcher in an explicit way. These scripts will allow for the application of rules on different sets of agents with different numbers of elements. For example, the researchers will have the opportunity to decide whether an increased risk perception affects a specific kind of bank in any desired moment of the simulated days. From a technical point of view, this decision can be performed by creating an ad-hoc agent for each role in which a tasty agent is desired.

In this way, we have an artificial, but close to real, artifact that reproduces the interbank payment

Figure 9. The autocorrelation analysis of the interest rate data of Figure 8 (with the presence of delays in interbank payments). First row: raw data; lagged correlations among data; and the same, but as partial correlations. Second row: data first differences with lag 1; their lagged correlations; and their lagged partial correlations.

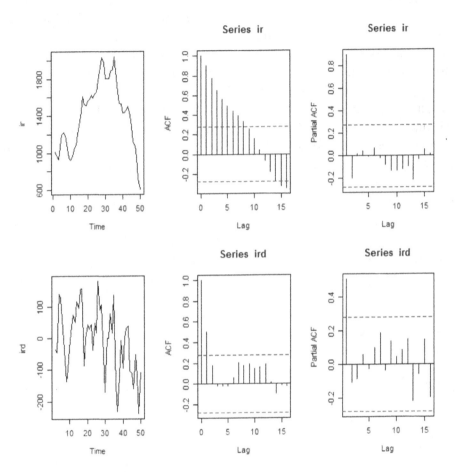

system and serves as an actual tool for policy analysis. For instance, the artifact can experiment with modifications in rules and control the daily behavior of the market, simulating the market while it evolves. Imagine having the ability to explore a set of possible realistic continuations of the payments and money market access in the middle of each day to fine-tune the interventions of the central bank in order to face potential liquidity issues. This simulation would be a non-trivial application of the model. Unfortunately, such an application is quite far from our present capabilities of the model.

A QUITE LONG CONCLUSION: INTEGRATING DIFFERENT TECHNIQUES

When managing the effects of emerging novelties in agent behavior, we must consider a research path that takes us from abstraction to realism. This means coping with complexity.

The standard economic approach compresses the complexity of reality into the mathematical structure of models based on ex-ante hypotheses arising from classic paradigms, such as rationality in behavior, thus ignoring interaction and sociality among real-world agents. The use of these models for individual and collective choices determines the ineffectiveness of corrective actions of policies. The first step in a pro-social direction is to bring the equations of the models to the level of individual agents (possibly with some degree of heterogeneity closer both to realism and to social dimension. Particularly in the presence of heterogeneity, doing so is a step ahead of pure numerical simulation but still too closely tied to the standard paradigm. If agents stylize their equations to operate (calculate) in a system with institutions (for example, a trading system), the model takes another step toward realism and usefulness. However, we believe that this type of achievement is insufficient.

Quoting Trichet (2010), the former president of the European Central Bank:

When the crisis came, the serious limitations of existing economic and financial models immediately became apparent. Arbitrage broke down in many market segments, as markets froze and market participants were gripped by panic. Macro models failed to predict the crisis and seemed incapable of explaining what was happening to the economy in a convincing manner. As a policy-maker during the crisis, I found the available models of limited help. In fact, I would go further: in the face of the crisis, we felt abandoned by conventional tools.

The consequence was that policy makers found very limited help and guidance in standard economic models. The policy makers used judgment and historical analysis, with an increasing number of risks. Thus, it is necessary to take a few steps ahead in new directions to offer new tools that can be used with the traditional ones.

Quoting Trichet:

(...) The atomistic, optimizing agents underlying existing models do not capture behavior during a crisis period. We need to deal better with heterogeneity across agents and the interaction among

those heterogeneous agents. We need to entertain alternative motivations for economic choices. Behavioral economics draws on psychology to explain decisions made in crisis circumstances. Agent-based modeling dispenses with the optimization assumption and allows for more complex interactions between agents. Such approaches are worthy of our attention.

We are now very close to the ABM perspective suggested above, mainly from the point of view of capturing unexpected actions and behavior. A large project awaits us: the construction of models that can compare in a parallel way to (1) the standard setting of the purely mathematical model; (2) equations that reproduce behavior in a decentralized way and with heterogeneity; and (3) agent interaction through institutions and rules vs. (4) the use of models that are completely based on agents, both with simple behavioral skills or arbitrarily complex ones. These skills are related to the structures of relationships, mutual influence, information, and learning capabilities.

From our perspective, it is crucial to introduce a capability for developing forms of *intelligent behavior* that allow agents to plan actions randomly or trivially in a starting phase, but in successive steps, to verify the effects of their behavior via ABMs as well as to use tools, such as artificial neural networks, to memorize the positive or negative effects of their choices. An alternative approach with genetic programming is another possibility.

While the elements listed above constitute a powerful and promising starting point for constructing a system of thinking and a corresponding system of acting, their integration into a solid, coherent basis is still a difficult and lengthy challenge. The unexpected and threatening recent collapse of the financial system has been an extreme incentive to base the steering of financial and economic systems on more scientific, systematic and commonly accepted procedures. To achieve this, we must fulfill a series of difficult syntheses.

1. **Integrate multi-agent methods into traditional macroeconomic thinking**: Recently, agent-based methods (also with statistical mechanics, phase transitions, percolation, multi-scale, localization, spatially extended stochastic processes) have been used by a number of groups, but the emphasis has been on the interactions between simple agents. The integration into those models of bi-directional feedback between agents' actions and macro-economic phenomena, entities and expectations has yet to be fully expressed and understood. In fact, the lack of top-down mechanisms in the initially proposed models was one reason why economists treated them with justified reservation. While including all of the relevant factors of the economic world in our models is an enormous and perhaps intimidating multi-disciplinary task, the formulation of agents is, in the long term, uniquely suited for expressing and incorporating such a collection of eclectic elements and for representing faithfully the ultimately human nature that underlies economic systems.

2. **Integrate the theoretical models with the data:** The neoclassical synthesis and the game theory methods used in economics are mathematically rigorous and allow one to express precisely a variety of ideas, methods and mechanisms. In fact, their conceptual crispness often impedes their contact with empirical reality, which has accidents, the subjectivity of human behavior and the related serendipity, and the extreme irregularity of (endogenous and exogenous) events. Maybe it is useful to remember that the statistical methods of statistical physics were designed to deal with elements that are full of *impurities* and to study the systemic effects of such *impurities*.

3. **The difficulty of applying precise mathematical theorems to imperfect, concrete reality has also complicated the** *application of academic results to policy and decision making***:** The results of research have been cast in a language and format that are not always familiar and or immediately relevant to practitioners. In the opposite direction, the flow of information from practitioners to academics has frequently been limited by a lack of detailed data on the financial and economic systems. Even today, data are scattered and not entirely publicly available, typically due to confidential constrain. However, recent events have incited the practitioners (private practitioners and regulators) to seek more contact with academics. From the academic side, the formulation of ideas into the language of individual agents and their specific actions is much more understandable and translatable to concrete decisions and policy[8]. Researchers' access to the details of individual financial and economic transactions and the tight feedback between modeling and real action is a promising and sine qua non condition for upgrading the degree of control one has over financial and economic phenomena.

This line of work can allow us to empirically verify the relevant feedback interactions between macro (institutional, emergent) and micro (individual agents) entities, which in turn can guide us in formulating models that theoretically represent empirical reality.

REFERENCES

Angelini, P. (1998). An analysis of competitive externalities in gross settlement systems. *Journal of Banking & Finance, 22*(1), 1–18. doi:10.1016/S0378-4266(97)00043-5

Arciero, L., Biancotti, C., D'Aurizio, L., & Impenna, C. (2009). Exploring agent-based methods for the analysis of payment systems: A crisis model for StarLogo TNG. *Journal of Artificial Societies and Social Simulation*.

Arciero, L., & Impenna, C. (2001). *Time pattern of payments in the Italian RTGS system: The effect of institutional financial variable* (Technical report). Banca d'Italia. Retrieved September 2013 from http://www.bancaditalia.it/sispaga/sms/sistemi/pag ingrosso/sistemi sistemi bi 5.pdf

Arciero, L., & Picillo, C. (2012). Analysing the large value payment systems: Need for an agent-based models complex approach. In B. Alexandrova-Kabadjova, S. Martinez-Jaramillo, A. L. Garcia-Almanza, & E. Tsang (Eds.), *Simulation in computational finance and economics: Tools and emerging applications*. Hershey, PA: IGI Global. doi:10.4018/978-1-4666-2011-7.ch005

Arrow, K. J. (1987). Rationality of self and others in an economic system. In R. M. Hogarth, & M. W. Reder (Eds.), *Rational choice* (pp. 201–217). Chicago: The University of Chicago Press.

Bank for International Settlement. (2003, March). *Glossary of terms used in payments and settlement system* (Report prepared by the Committee on Payment and Settlement Systems of the Central Banks of the Group of Ten Countries). Basel, Switzerland.

Becker, G. S. (1962). Irrational behaviour and economic theory. *The Journal of Political Economy, 70*, 1–13. doi:10.1086/258584

Cipriani, M., & Guarino, A. (2005). Herd behavior in a laboratory financial market. *The American Economic Review, 95*(5), 1427–1443. doi:10.1257/000282805775014443

Davis, D. D., & Holt, C. A. (1993). *Experimental economics*. Princeton, NJ: Princeton University Press.

eMID. (n. d.). Retrieved September 2013 from http://www.e-mid.it/?lang=uk

Gardner, M. (1970). The fantastic combinations of John Conway's new solitaire game life. *Scientific American, 223*, 120–123. doi:10.1038/scientificamerican1070-120

Geanakoplos, J., Axtell, R., Doyne Farmer, J., Howitt, P., Conlee, B., & Goldstein, J. et al. (2012). Getting at systemic risk via an agent-based model of the housing market. *The American Economic Review, 102*(3), 53–58. doi:10.1257/aer.102.3.53

Gilbert, N., Pyka, A., & Ahrweiler, P. (2001). Innovation networks – A simulation approach. *Journal of Artificial Societies and Social Simulation, 4*(3), 1–13.

Gilbert, N., & Terna, P. (2000). How to build and use agent-based models in social science. *Mind & Society, 1*(1), 57–72. doi:10.1007/BF02512229

Glosten, L. R., & Milgrom, P. R. (1985). Bid, ask and transaction prices in a specialist market with heterogeneously informed traders. *Journal of Financial Economics, 14*(1), 71–100. doi:10.1016/0304-405X(85)90044-3

Gode, D. K., & Sunder, S. (2004). Double auction dynamics: Structural effects of non-binding price controls. *Journal of Economic Dynamics & Control, 28*(9), 1707–1731. doi:10.1016/j.jedc.2003.06.001

Ladley, D. (2012). Zero intelligence in economics and finance. *The Knowledge Engineering Review, 27*(2), 273–286. doi:10.1017/S0269888912000173

LeBaron, B., Arthur, W. B., & Palmer, R. (1999). Time series properties of an artificial stock market. *Journal of Economic Dynamics & Control, 23*, 1487–1516. doi:10.1016/S0165-1889(98)00081-5

Minar, N., Burkhart, R., Langton, C., & Askenazi, M. (1996). The swarm simulation system: A toolkit for building multi-agent simulations. *SFI Working Paper, 06*(42). Retrieved September 2013 from http://www.santafe.edu/media/workingpapers/96-06-042.pdf

Neugart, M. (2008). Labor market policy evaluation with ACE. *Journal of Economic Behavior & Organization, 67*, 418–430. doi:10.1016/j.jebo.2006.12.006

Payments and money market model. (2011). Retrieved September 2013 from http://eco83.econ.unito.it/terna/P&3M/P&3M.html

Rao, A., & Georgeff, M. (1991). Modeling rational agents within a BDI-architecture. In *Proceedings of the 2nd International Conference on Principles of Knowledge Representation and Reasoning.* Morgan Kaufmann Publishers Inc.

Rapaport, O., Levi-Faur, D., & Miodownik, D. (2009). The puzzle of the diffusion of central-bank independence reforms: Insights from an agent-based simulation. *Policy Studies Journal: the Journal of the Policy Studies Organization, 37*, 695–716. doi:10.1111/j.1541-0072.2009.00331.x

Rubinstein, A. (1998). *Modeling bounded rationality.* Cambridge, MA: The MIT Press.

Schellenberg, J. A. (1996). *Conflict resolution: Theory, research and practice.* Albany, NY: State University of New York Press.

Simon, H. (1955). A behavioral model of rational choice. *The Quarterly Journal of Economics, 69*(1), 99–188. doi:10.2307/1884852

Terna, P. (2010). A new agent-based tool to build artificial worlds. In M. Faggini, & C. P. Vinci (Eds.), *Decision theory and choices: A complexity approach* (pp. 177–191). Heidelberg, Germany: Springer. doi:10.1007/978-88-470-1778-8_4

Tesfatsion, L. (2001). Structure, behavior, and market power in an evolutionary labor market with adaptive search. *Journal of Economic Dynamics & Control, 25*(3), 419–457. doi:10.1016/S0165-1889(00)00032-4

Tirole, J. (2011). Illiquidity and all its friends. *Journal of Economic Literature, 49*(2), 287-Đ325.

Trichet, J. C. (2010, 18 Nov). *Opening address at the ECB Central Banking Conference,* Frankfurt. Retrieved September 2013 from http://www.ecb.int/press/key/date/2010/html/sp101118.en.html

Tversky, A., & Kahneman, D. (1992). Advances in prospect theory: Cumulative representation of uncertainty. *Journal of Risk and Uncertainty, 5*(4), 297–323. doi:10.1007/BF00122574

Von Neumann, J. (1966). *The theory of self-reproducing automata.* Champaign, IL: University of Illinois Press.

Werker, C., & Brenner, T. (2004). *Empirical calibration of simulation models* (Papers on Economics and Evolution 2004-10). Max Planck Institute of Economics, Evolutionary Economics Group.

Westerhoff, F. (2008). The use of agent based financial market models to test for the effectiveness of regulatory policies. [Journal of Economics and Statistics]. *Zeitschrift für Nationalökonomie und Statistik, 228*, 195–227.

Windrum, P., Fagiolo, G., & Moneta, A. (2007). Empirical validation of agent-based models: Alternatives and prospects. *Journal of Artificial Societies and Social Simulation, 10*(2), 8–22.

ADDITIONAL READING

Allan, R. J. (2010). *Survey of agent based modelling and simulation tools. Technical report.* Science & Technology Facilities Council.

Angelini, P. (2002). Are Banks Risk-Averse? Timing of the Operations in the Interbank Market. *Journal of Money, Credit and Banking, 32*(3), 54–73.

Arciero, L. (2012). Evaluating the impact of shock in the supply of overnight unsecured money market funds on the TARGET2-Banca d'Italia functioning: a simulation approach, *Rivista Bancaria - Minerva Bancaria, Istituto di Cultura Bancaria Francesco Parrillo,* issue 2-3, June.

Ashcraft, A. B., & Darrell, D. (2007). Systemic Illiquidity in the Federal Funds Market. *The American Economic Review, 97*(2), 221–225. doi:10.1257/aer.97.2.221

Axelrod, R. (1997). Advancing the Art of Simulation in the Social Sciences. In R. Conte, R. Hegselmann, and P. Terna, editors, Simulating Social Phenomena, volume 456 of Lecture Notes in Economics and Mathematical Systems, pages 21-40. Springer, Berlin.

Axelrod, R., & Tesfatsion, L. (2005). A guide for newcomers to agent-based modeling in the social sciences. In K. L. Judd and L. Tesfatsion, editors, *Handbook of Computational Economics,* volume 2, pages 1647-1658. North-Holland. URL http://www.econ.iastate.edu/tesfatsi/GuidetoABM.pdf.

Axtell, R. (2000). *Why Agents? On the Varied Motivations for Agent Computing in the Social Sciences.* In Proceedings of the Workshop on Agent Simulation: Applications, Models and Tools. Argonne National Laboratory, IL. URL http://www.brookings.edu/~/media/Files/rc/reports/2000/11technology axtell/agents.pdf.

Bank for International Settlement (1997). *Real-time Gross Settlement Systems.* Report prepared by the Committee on Payment and Settlement Systems of the Central Banks of the Group of Ten Countries, Bank for International Settlements, Basle.

Boero, R., Bravo, G., Castellani, M., & Squazzoni, F. (2010). Why bother with what others tell you? an experimental data-driven agent-based model. *Journal of Artificial Societies and Social Simulation, 13*(3),6. ISSN 1460-7425. URL http://jasss.soc.surrey.ac.uk/13/3/6.html.

Bonabeau, E. (2002). Agent-based modeling: Methods and techniques for simulating human systems. *Proceedings of the National Academy of Sciences of the United States of America, 99*(Suppl. 3), 7280–7287. doi:10.1073/pnas.082080899 PMID:12011407

Borrill, P. L., & Tesfatsion, L. (2010). *Agent-based modeling: The right mathematics for the social sciences?* Iowa State University, Department of Economics. URL http://econpapers.repec.org/RePEc:isu:genres:31674.

Cioffi-Revilla, C. (2010). Computational social science. *Computational Statistics, 2*(3), 259–271. doi:10.1002/wics.95

Cristelli, M., Pietronero, L., & Zaccaria, A. (2011). *Critical Overview of Agent-Based Models for Economics.* ArXiv e-prints. URL http://arxiv.org/abs/1101.1847.

Diehl, M. (2013). The Use of Simulations as an Analytical Tool for Payment Systems. In B. Alexandrova-Kabadjova, S. Martinez-Jaramillo, A. Garcia-Almanza, & E. Tsang (Eds.), *Simulation in Computational Finance and Economics: Tools and Emerging Applications* (pp. 29–45). Hershey, PA: Business Science Reference.

Fagiolo, G., & Roventini, A. (2012). Macroeconomic policy in dsge and agent-based models. *EconomiX*. URL http://www2.econ.iastate.edu/tesfatsi/MacroPolicyDSGEACE.FagioloRoventini2012.pdf.

Gaffeo, E., Gallegati, M., & Gostoli, U. (2012). *An agent-based proof of principle for walrasian macroeconomic theory*. Technical report, Cognitive and Experimental Economics Laboratory, Department of Economics, University of Trento, Italia, 2012. URL http://www-ceel.economia.unitn.it/papers/papero12 02.pdf.

Galbiati, M., & Soramäki, K. (2011). An agent-based model of payment systems. *Journal of Economic Dynamics & Control*, *35*(6), 859–875. doi:10.1016/j.jedc.2010.11.001

Gallegati, M., & Kirman, A. (2012). Reconstructing economics: Agent based models and complexity. *Complexity Economics*, *1*, 5–31. doi:10.7564/12-COEC2

Giansante, S. (2009). *Agent-based Economic (ACE) Modelling of Payments Media: Emergence of Monetary Exchange, Banking, Large Value Payment and Settlement Systems*, University of Essex, Centre for Computational Finance and Economic Agents (CCFEA), Ph.D Thesis.

Heijmans, R., & Heuver, R. (2013). Preparing Simulations in Large Value Payment Systems using Historical Data. In B. Alexandrova-Kabadjova, S. Martinez-Jaramillo, A. Garcia-Almanza, & E. Tsang (Eds.), *Simulation in Computational Finance and Economics: Tools and Emerging Applications* (pp. 46–68). Hershey, PA: Business Science Reference.

http://papers.ssrn.com/sol3/papers.cfm?abstract id=2173846.

http://users.uom.gr/~iliass/projects/NetLogo/Papers/Extending_NetLogo_SETN08_SVerlag_Camera_ready.pdf.

http://www.sciencedirect.com/science/article/pii/S1364815213001394.

Isaac, A. G. (2008). Simulating evolutionary games: a python-based introduction. *Journal of Artificial Societies and Social Simulation*, *11*(3), 8. http://jasss.soc.surrey.ac.uk/11/3/8.html

Isaac, A. G. (2011). The ABM template models: A reformulation with reference implementations. *Journal of Artificial Societies and Social Simulation*, *14*(2), 5. http://jasss.soc.surrey.ac.uk/14/2/5.html

Janssen, M. A., & Ostrom, E. (2006). Empirically based, agent-based models. *Ecology and Society*, *11*(2), 37.

Kirman, A. (2010). Learning in Agent-Based Models. *Eastern Economic Journal*, *37*(Issue 1), 20–27. doi:10.1057/eej.2010.60

Klee, E. (2010). Operational Outages and Aggregate Uncertainty in the Federal Funds Market. *Journal of Banking & Finance*, *34*(10), 2386–2402. doi:10.1016/j.jbankfin.2010.03.002

Kokkola, T. (2010). *The Payment System: Payments, Securities and Derivatives, and the Role of the Eurosystem*. European Central Bank.

Laine, T., Korpinen, K., & Hellqvist, M. (2013). Simulation Approaches to Risk, Efficiency, and Liquidity Usage in Payment Systems. In B. Alexandrova-Kabadjova, S. Martinez-Jaramillo, A. Garcia-Almanza, & E. Tsang (Eds.), *Simulation in Computational Finance and Economics: Tools and Emerging Applications* (pp. 69–83). Hershey, PA: Business Science Reference.

Laine, T., Korpinen, K., & Hellqvist, M. (2013). Simulation Approaches to Risk, Efficiency, and Liquidity Usage in Payment Systems. In B. Alexandrova-Kabadjova, S. Martinez-Jaramillo, A. Garcia-Almanza, & E. Tsang (Eds.), *Simulation in Computational Finance and Economics: Tools and Emerging Applications* (pp. 69–83). Hershey, PA: Business Science Reference.

LeBaron, B. (1998). Agent based computational finance: Suggested readings and early research. *Journal of Economic Dynamics & Control, 24*, 679–702. doi:10.1016/S0165-1889(99)00022-6

LeBaron, B., & Tesfatsion, L. (2008). Modeling macroeconomies as open-ended dynamic systems of interacting agents. *The American Economic Review, 98*(2), 246–250. doi:10.1257/aer.98.2.246

Leinonen, H., & Soramäki, K. (2003). *Simulating interbank payment and securities settlement mechanisms with the BoF-PSS2 simulator. Bank of Finland Discussion Papers, No 23/2003*. Suomen Pankki.

Manning, M., Nier, E., & Schanz, J. (2009). *The Economics of Large-Value Payments and Settlement: Theory and Policy Issues for Central Banks*. Oxford: Oxford University Press.

Markose, S., Alentorn, A., Millard, S., & Yang, J. (2011). *Designing large value payment systems: An agent-based approach* (University of Essex Economics Department Discussion Paper No. 700). Colchester: University of Essex.

McAndrews, J., & Trundle, J. M. (2001). New payment system designs: causes and consequences. *Bank of England Financial Stability Review, 11*, 127–136.

Müller, B., Bohn, F., Dreßler, G., Groeneveld, J., Klassert, C., & Martin, R. et al. (2013). Describing human decisions in agent-based models - odd+d, an extension of the odd protocol. *Environmental Modelling & Software, 48*, 37–48. doi:10.1016/j.envsoft.2013.06.003

North, M., & Macal, C. (2009). Agent-based modelling and systems dynamics model reproduction. *International Journal of Simulation and Process Modelling, 5*(3), 256–271. doi:10.1504/IJSPM.2009.031099

Sakellariou, I., Kefalas, P., & Stamatopoulou, I. (2008). *Enhancing NetLogo to simulate BDI communicating agents. Artificial Intelligence: Theories* (pp. 263–275). Models and Applications.

Sheppard, D. (1996). *Payment Systems. Handbooks in Central Banking, No 8*. London: Centre for Central Banking Studies, Bank of England.

P. Siebers, C. Macal, J. Garnett, D. Buxton, and M. Pidd. Discrete-event simulation is dead, long live agent-based simulation! Journal of Simulation, 4(3),204,Äì210, 2010.

N. Smith. Development as Division of Labor: Adam Smith Meets Agent-Based Simulation.

Spaanderman, J. J. (2012). A central bank perspective on liquidity management, *Journal of Financial Market Infrastructures*, Volume 1/Number 2, Winter 2012/13 (65–78).

Summers, B. J. (1994). *The Payment System: Design, Management, and Supervision*. International Monetary Fund.

URL http://groups.forestry.oregonstate.edu/fpf/system/files/Janssen%20and%20Ostrom%202006.pdf.

Vriend, N. J. (1999). *Was Hayek an ace?* http://citeseerx.ist.psu.edu/viewdoc/summary?doi=10.1.1.140.5808.

Windrum, P., Fagiolo, G., & Moneta, A. (2007). Empirical validation of agent-based models: Alternatives and prospects. *Journal of Artificial Societies and Social Simulation, 10*(2), 8. http://jasss.soc.surrey.ac.uk/10/2/8.html

KEY TERMS AND DEFINITIONS

eMID (Electronic Market for Interchange Deposits): The money market; see details and explanations at eMID (n. d.).

P&3M (Payments and Money Market Model): The specific agent-based simulation program introduced here.

SLAPP (Swarm-Like Agent-Based Protocol): The general shell we use here to develop the models. (Retrieved September 2013 from http://eco83.econ.unito.it/terna/slapp)

RTGS: Both as a payment system and as a source of data, the Real Time Gross Settlement System; see Arciero & Impenna (2001).

ENDNOTES

[1] The opinions expressed are those of the authors and do not necessarily reflect the views or the opinions of the Banca d'Italia.

[2] The Zero Intelligent approach precedes the advent of the ABM, which was originally introduced by the Nobel Laureate G. Becker in 1962. For an extensive review of the Zero Intelligence approach for the analysis of financial market, see Ladley (2004).

[3] The BDI model (Belief, Desire, Intention) introduced by Rao and Geogeff (1991) is perhaps the most popular paradigm for deliberative agents. BDI agents interpret the macro changes occurring within the environment, record the information acquired and act proactively.

[4] See also Chapter 1.

[5] See also Chapter 16.

[6] Translated by Constance Black Garnett (1862-1946) in 1917.

[7] See also Chapter 9.

[8] See also Chapters 7 and 8.

Compilation of References

Abdulhai, B., & Abdelgawad, H. (2009). Towards fully integrated adaptive urban traffic control. In I. L. AlQadi, T. Sayed, A. Alnuaimi & E. Masad, (Eds.), *Efficient transportation and pavement systems: Characterization, mechanisms, simulation, and modeling: Proceedings of the 4th International Gulf Conference on Roads, Doha, Qatar*, (pp. 17-31).

Abrahamson, E., & Rosenkopf, L. (1993). Institutional and competitive band wagons: Using mathematical modeling as a tool to explore innovation diffusion. *Academy of Management Review, 21*(1), 254–285. doi:10.5465/AMR.1996.9602161572

Abrahamson, E., & Rosenkopf, L. (1997). Social network effects on the extent of innovation diffusion: A computer simulation. *Organization Science, 8*(3), 289–309. doi:10.1287/orsc.8.3.289

Abushakra, B., & Claridge, D. (2001). Accounting for the occupancy variable in inverse building energy baselining models. In *Proceedings of the International Conference for Enhanced Building Operations (ICEBO)*, Austin, TX.

Achen, C. H. (2006). Evaluating political decision-making models. In R. Thomson, F. N. Stokman, C. Achen, & T. König (Eds.), *The European Union decides*. Cambridge, UK: Cambridge University Press. doi:10.1017/CBO9780511492082.011

Adamatti, D. F., Sichman, J. S., Bommel, P., Ducrot, R., Rabak, C., & Camargo, M. E. S. A. (2005). *JogoMan: A prototype using multi-agent-based simulation and role-playing games in water management*. Paper presented at CABM-HEMA-SMAGET, Bourg-Saint-Maurice, Les Arcs, France.

Adamatti, D., Sichman, J., & Coelho, H. (2009). An analysis of the insertion of virtual players in GMABS methodology using the Vip-JogoMan prototype. *Journal of Artificial Societies and Social Simulation, 12*(3).

Agha, G. (1986). *Actors: A model of concurrent computation in distributed systems*. Cambridge, MA: MIT Press.

Alberti, M., & Waddell, P. (2000). An integrated urban development and ecological simulation model. *Integrated Assessment, 1*, 215–227. doi:10.1023/A:1019140101212

Albino, V., Carbonara, N., & Giannoccaro, I. (2005). Industrial districts as complex adaptive systems: Agent-based models of emergent phenomena. In C. Karlsson, B. Johansson, & R. E. Stough (Eds.), *Industrial clusters and inter-firm networks*. Northampton, MA: Edward Elgar Publ.

Albino, V., Carbonara, N., & Messeni Petruzzelli, A. (2007). Proximity as a communication resource for competitiveness: A rationale for technology clusters. *International Journal of Learning and Intellectual Capital, 4*(4), 430–452. doi:10.1504/IJLIC.2007.016337

Albino, V., & Schiuma, G. (2003). New forms of knowledge creation and diffusion in the industrial district of Matera-Altamura-Santeramo. In F. Belussi, G. Gottardi, & E. Rullani (Eds.), *The technological evolution of industrial districts*. Boston: Kluwer Academic Pub. doi:10.1007/978-1-4615-0393-4_19

Albin, P. S. (1975). *The analysis of complex socioeconomic systems*. Lexington, MA: Lexington Books.

Alligham, M., & Sandmo, A. (1972). Income tax evasion: A theoretical analysis. *Journal of Public Economics, 3*, 171–179.

Alm, J., McClelland, G. H., & Schulze, W. D. (1992). Why do people pay taxes? *Journal of Public Economics*, *48*, 21–48. doi:10.1016/0047-2727(92)90040-M

Andrelini, L. (1999). Communication, computability and common interest games. *Journal of Games and Economic Behaviour*, *27*, 1–37. doi:10.1006/game.1998.0652

Andrighetto, G., Campenni, M., Conte, R., & Paolucci, M. (2007). On the immergence of norms: A normative agent architecture. In *Proceedings of AAAI Symposium, Social and Organizational Aspects of Artificial Intelligence,* Washington DC.

Angelini, P. (1998). An analysis of competitive externalities in gross settlement systems. *Journal of Banking & Finance*, *22*(1), 1–18. doi:10.1016/S0378-4266(97)00043-5

Antunes, L., Balsa, J., Moniz, L., Urbano, P., & Palma, C. R. (2006a). Tax compliance in a simulated heterogeneous multi-agent society. In J. S. Sichman, & L. Antunes (Eds.), *MABS 2005. LNCS (LNAI)* (Vol. 3891). Heidelberg, Germany: Springer. doi:10.1007/11734680_11

Antunes, L., Balsa, J., Urbano, P., & Coelho, H. (2010). Exploring Context permeability in multiple social networks. In K. Takadama, C. Cioffi-Revilla, & G. Deffuant (Eds.), *Simulating Interacting agents and social phenomena* (Vol. 7, pp. 77–87). Japan: Springer. doi:10.1007/978-4-431-99781-8_6

Antunes, L., Nunes, D., Coelho, H., Balsa, J., & Urbano, P. (2009). Context switching versus context permeability in multiple social networks. *Progress in Artificial Intelligence*, *5816*, 547–559. doi:10.1007/978-3-642-04686-5_45

AnyLogic. (2013). AnyLogic® multimethod simulation software. Retrieved from http://www.anylogic.com/

Arciero, L., & Impenna, C. (2001). *Time pattern of payments in the Italian RTGS system: The effect of institutional financial variable* (Technical report). Banca d'Italia. Retrieved September 2013 from http://www.bancaditalia.it/sispaga/sms/sistemi/pag ingrosso/sistemi sistemi bi 5.pdf

Arciero, L., Biancotti, C., D'Aurizio, L., & Impenna, C. (2009). Exploring agent-based methods for the analysis of payment systems: A crisis model for StarLogo TNG. *Journal of Artificial Societies and Social Simulation.*

Arciero, L., & Picillo, C. (2012). Analysing the large value payment systems: Need for an agent-based models complex approach. In B. Alexandrova-Kabadjova, S. Martinez-Jaramillo, A. L. Garcia-Almanza, & E. Tsang (Eds.), *Simulation in computational finance and economics: Tools and emerging applications.* Hershey, PA: IGI Global. doi:10.4018/978-1-4666-2011-7.ch005

Arciero, L., Picillo, C., Solomon, S., & Terna, P. (2014in press). Building ABMs to control the emergence of crisis analyzing agents' behavior. In D. F. Adamatti, G. P. Dimuro, & H. Coelho (Eds.), *Interdisciplinary applications of agent-based social simulation and modeling.* Hershey, PA: IGI Global.

Arikan, A. T. (2009). Interfirm knowledge exchanges and the knowledge creation capability of clusters. *Academy of Management Review*, *34*(4), 659–676. doi:10.5465/AMR.2009.44885776

Arregui, J., Stokman, F. N., & Thomson, R. (2006). Compromise, exchange and challenge in the European Union. In R. Thomson, F. N. Stokman, C. H. Achen, & T. König (Eds.), *The European Union decides.* Cambridge, UK: Cambridge University Press. doi:10.1017/CBO9780511492082.006

Arregui, J., Stokman, F., & Thomson, R. (2004). Bargaining in the European Union and shifts in actors' policy positions. *European Union Politics*, *5*(1), 47–72. doi:10.1177/1465116504040445

Arrow, K. J. (1987). Rationality of self and others in an economic system. In R. M. Hogarth, & M. W. Reder (Eds.), *Rational choice* (pp. 201–217). Chicago: The University of Chicago Press.

Arthur, W. B. (1996). *Asset pricing under endogenous expectations in an artificial stock market* (Doctoral dissertation). Brunel University, London.

Arthur, W. B. (1994, May). Inductive Reasoning and Bounded Rationality. *The American Economic Review*, *84*(2), 406–411.

Arthur, W. B., Durlauf, S., & Lane, D. (1997). *The economy as a complex evolving system II.* Menlo Park, CA: Addison-Wesley.

Aumann, R. J. (2008). Game theory. In S. N. Durlauf, & L. E. Blume (Eds.), *The new Palgrave dictionary of economics* (2nd ed.). London: Macmillan. doi:10.1057/9780230226203.0615

Axelrod, R. (1997). Advancing the art of simulation in the social sciences. In R. Conte, R. Hegselmann, & P. Terna (Eds.), *Simulating social phenomena* (pp. 21–40). Berlin: Springer-Verlag. doi:10.1007/978-3-662-03366-1_2

Axelrod, R. (1997). The dissemination of culture: A model with local convergence and global polarization. *The Journal of Conflict Resolution, 41*(2), 203–226. doi:10.1177/0022002797041002001

Axelrod, R. (2007). Simulation in social sciences. In J. Rennard (Ed.), *Handbook of research on nature-inspired computing for economics and management*. Hershey, PA: IGI Global.

Axelrod, R., & Tesfatsion, L. (2006). *A guide for newcomers to agent-based modeling in the social sciences. Handbook of computational economics* (Vol. 2, pp. 1647–1659). Amsterdam, The Netherlands: Elsevier.

Axtell, R. L. (2007). What economic agents do: How cognition and interaction lead to emergence and complexity. *The Review of Austrian Economics, 20,* 105–122. doi:10.1007/s11138-007-0021-5

Axtell, R., & Epstein, J. M. (1996). *Growing Artificial Societies*. Cambridge, Mass.: MIT Press.

Axtel, R., Epstein, J. M., & Young, H. P. (2004). Social dynamics. In *Social dynamics, economic learning and social evolution series*. Cambridge, MA: MIT Press.

Azevedo, L. L., & Meneze, C. S. (2007). *Netplay – uma ferramenta para construção de modelos de simulação baseado em multiagente*. Paper presented at XVIII Simpósio Brasileiro de Informática na Educação, SBIE, Mackenzie.

Bagni, R., Berchi, R., & Cariello, P. (2002). A comparison of simulation models applied to epidemics. *Journal of Artificial Societies and Social Simulation, 5*(3).

Baldoni, M., Baroglio, C., Bergenti, F., Boccalatte, A., Marengo, E., & Martelli, M. … Santi, A. (2010). MERCURIO: An interaction-oriented framework for designing, verifying and programming multi-agent systems. In N. Fornara & G. Vouros, (Eds.), Proc. of the 3rd Multi-Agent Logics, Languages, and Organisations Federated Workshops.

Balsa, J., Antunes, L., Respício, A., & Coelho, H. (2006), Autonomous inspectors in tax compliance simulation. In *Proceedings of the 18th European Meeting on Cybernetics and Systems Research*.

Bank for International Settlement. (2003, March). *Glossary of terms used in payments and settlement system* (Report prepared by the Committee on Payment and Settlement Systems of the Central Banks of the Group of Ten Countries). Basel, Switzerland.

Baptista, R. (2000). Do innovations diffuse faster within geographical clusters? *International Journal of Industrial Organization, 18,* 515–535. doi:10.1016/S0167-7187(99)00045-4

Barabási, A.-L., Albert, R., & Jeong, H. (2000). Scale-free characteristics of random networks: The topology of the world-wide Web. *Physica A: Statistical Mechanics and its Applications, 281*(1-4), 69–77. doi:10.1016/S0378-4371(00)00018-2

Barabási, A. L., & Albert, R. (1999). Emergence of scaling in random net-works. *Science, 286,* 509–512. doi:10.1126/science.286.5439.509 PMID:10521342

Bartik, T. J. (1985). Business location decisions in the United States: Estimates of the effects of unionization, taxes, and other characteristics of states. *Journal of Business & Economic Statistics, 3*(1), 14–22.

Basch, D. (2012). *Some fresh Twitter stats (as of July 2012, dataset included)*. Retrieved from http://diegobasch.com/some-fresh-twitter-stats-as-of-july-2012

Becker, G. (1968). Crime and punishment: An economic approach. *The Journal of Political Economy, 76,* 169–217. doi:10.1086/259394

Becker, G. S. (1962). Irrational behaviour and economic theory. *The Journal of Political Economy, 70*, 1–13. doi:10.1086/258584

Beck, N., Gleditsch, K. S., & Beardsley, K. (2006). Space is more than geography: Using spatial econometrics in the study of political economy. *International Studies Quarterly, 50*(1), 27–44. doi:10.1111/j.1468-2478.2006.00391.x

Beisbart, K., & Norton, J. D. (2012). Why Monte Carlo Simulations Are Inferences and Not Experiments. *International Studies in the Philosophy of Science, 26*(4), 403–422. doi:10.1080/02698595.2012.748497

Bennett, R. J., & Payne, D. (2000). *UK local and regional development agencies data: Renegotiating power under labour*. Aldershot, UK: Ashgate.

Bentham, J. (2007). *Introduction to the principles of morals and legislation*. New York: Dover Publications. (Original work published 1823)

Bergenti, F., Franchi, E., & Poggi, A. (2011). Selected models for agent-based simulation of social networks. In *3rd Symposium on Social Networks and Multiagent Systems (SNAMAS 2011)* (pp. 27-32).

Bergenti, F., Franchi, E., & Poggi, A. (2012). *Enhancing social networks with agent and Semantic Web technologies. Collaboration and the Semantic Web: Social networks, knowledge networks, and knowledge resources* (pp. 83–100). Hershey, PA: IGI Global. doi:10.4018/978-1-4666-0894-8.ch005

Bergenti, F., Franchi, E., & Poggi, A. (2013). Agent-based interpretations of classic network models. *Computational & Mathematical Organization Theory, 19*(2), 105–127. doi:10.1007/s10588-012-9150-x

Bernasconi, M. (1998). Tax evasion and orders of risk aversion. *Journal of Public Economics, 67*, 123–134. doi:10.1016/S0047-2727(97)00051-0

Bernstein, M. S., Bakshy, E., Burke, M., & Karrer, B. (2013). Quantifying the invisible audience in social networks. In *ACM SIGCHI Conference on Human Factors in Computing Systems (CHI 2013)* (in press).

Berry, C., Hobbs, B., Meroney, W., O'Neill, R., & Stewart, W. R. Jr. (1999). Understanding how market power can arise in network competition: a game theoretic approach. *Utilities Policy, 8*(3), 139–158. doi:10.1016/S0957-1787(99)00016-8

Berry, F. S., & Berry, W. D. (2006). Innovation and diffusion models in policy diffusion. In P. A. Sabatier (Ed.), *Theories of the policy process* (pp. 223–260). Boulder, CO: Westview Press.

Bettini, V. (1998). *Elementos de Ecología Urbana*. Madrid: Editorial Trotta.

Bickman, L., & Rog, D. J. (2009). *The Sage Handbook of Applied Social Research* (2nd ed.). Newbury Park: Sage.

Binmore, K. (2009). *Rational Decisions. Gorman Lectures in Economics*. Princeton, N.J.: Princeton University Press.

Bishop, S., Helbing, D., Lukowicz, P., & Conte, R. (2011). FuturICT: FET flagship pilot project. *Procedia Computer Science*. Retrieved from http://papers.ssrn.com/sol3/papers.cfm?abstract_id=1895523

Blanchart, E., Cambier, C., Canape, C., Gaudou, B., Ho, T.-N., & Ho, T.-V. et al. (2011). EPIS: A grid platform to ease and optimize multi-agent simulators running. In Y. Demazeau, M. Pechoucek, J. M. Corchado, & J. Bajo P'erez (Eds.), *Advances on practical applications of agents and multiagent systems* (Vol. 88, pp. 129–134). Berlin, Heidelberg, Germany: Springer. doi:10.1007/978-3-642-19875-5_17

Bloomquist, K. (2011). Tax compliance as an evolutionary coordination game: An agent-based approach. *Public Finance Review, 39*, 25. doi:10.1177/1091142110381640

Boehmke, F. J., & Witmer, R. (2004). Disentangling diffusion: The effects of social learning and economic competition on state policy innovation and expansion. *Political Research Quarterly, 57*(1), 39–51.

Boissier, O., Bordini, R., Hubner, J., Ricci, A., & Santi, A. (2012). *JaCaMo project*. Retrieved from http://jacamo.sourceforge.net/

Boissier, O., Bordini, R., Hubner, J., Ricci, A., & Santi, A. (2011). *Multi-agent oriented programming with JaCaMo* (pp. 747–761). Amsterdam, The Netherlands: Elsevier.

Bonabeau, E. (2002). Agent-based modeling: methods and techniques for simulating human systems. *Proceedings of the National Academy of Sciences of the United States of America, 99*, 7280–7287. doi:10.1073/pnas.082080899 PMID:12011407

Bonoli, G. (2001). Political institutions, veto points, and the process of welfare state adaptation. In P. Pierson (Ed.), *The new politics of the welfare state* (pp. 238–264). Oxford, UK: Oxford University Press. doi:10.1093/0198297564.003.0009

Bordini, R., Hubner, J., & Wooldridge, M. (2007). *Programming multi-agent systems in AgentSpeak using Jason.* Hoboken, NJ: Wiley.

Boschma, R. (2004, June). *Does geographical proximity favour innovation?* Paper presented at the 4th Congress on Proximity Economics, Marseilles, France.

Boschma, R. A. (2005). Proximity and innovation: A critical assessment. *Regional Studies, 39*(1), 61–74. doi:10.1080/0034340052000320887

Boutilier, C., Dearden, R., & Goldszmidt, M. (1995). Exploiting structure in policy construction. *Proceedings of the, IJCAI-95*, 1104–1111.

Bowles, S., Gintis, H., & Osborne, M. (2005). *Unequal chances: Family background and economic success.* Princeton, NJ: Princeton University Press.

Boyd, D. M., & Ellison, N. B. (2008). Social network sites: Definition, history, and scholarship. *Journal of Computer-Mediated Communication, 13*(1), 210–230. doi:10.1111/j.1083-6101.2007.00393.x

Braithwaite, V., & Ahmed, E. (2005). A threat to tax morale: The case of Australian higher education policy. *Journal of Economic Psychology, 26*(4). doi:10.1016/j.joep.2004.08.003

Bratman, M. E. (1999). *Intention, plans, and practical reason.* Stanford, CA: Center for the Study of Language and Information.

Braun, D., & Gilardi, F. (2006). Taking Galton's problem seriously. Towards a theory of policy diffusion. *Journal of Theoretical Politics, 18*(3), 298–322. doi:10.1177/0951629806064351

Braun, D., Gilardi, F., Fueglister, K., & Luyet, S. (2007). Ex pluribus unum: Integrating the different strands of policy diffusion theory. *Politische Vierteljahresschrift, 38*, 39–55.

Briegel, R., Ernst, A., Holzhauer, S., Klemm, D., Krebs, F., & Martínez Piñánez, A. (2012). Social-ecological modelling with LARA: A psychologically well-founded lightweight agent architecture. *International Congress on Environmental Modelling and Software 2012.* Leipzig.

Briot, J.-P., Vasconcelos, E., Adamatti, D., Sebba, V., Irving, M., Barbosa, S., et al. (2008, July). Computer-based support for participatory management of protected areas: The SimParc project. In *Proceedings of 28th Congress of Computation Brazilian Society (CSBC '08),* Belém, Brazil.

Brooks, S. M. (2005). Interdependent and domestic foundations of policy change: The diffusion of pension privatization around the world. *International Studies Quarterly, 49*(2), 273–294. doi:10.1111/j.0020-8833.2005.00345.x

Brooks, S. M. (2007). When does diffusion matter? Explaining the spread of structural pension reforms across nations. *The Journal of Politics, 69*(3), 701–715. doi:10.1111/j.1468-2508.2007.00569.x

Brusco, S. (1990). The idea of the industrial district: Its genesis. In G. Becattini, F. Pyke, & W. Sengenberger (Eds.), *Industrial districts and Inter-firm co-operation in Italy.* Geneva, Switzerland: International Institute for Labour Studies.

Buchegger, S., & Datta, A. (2009, February). A case for P2P infrastructure for social networks-opportunities & challenges. In *Wireless On-Demand Network Systems and Services, 2009. WONS 2009. Sixth International Conference on* (pp. 161-168). IEEE.

Buchegger, S., Schiöberg, D., Vu, L. H., & Datta, A. (2009, March). PeerSoN: P2P social networking: Early experiences and insights. In *Proceedings of the Second ACM EuroSys Workshop on Social Network Systems* (pp. 46-52). ACM.

Buckingham Shum, S., Aberer, K., Schmidt, A., Bishop, S., Lukowicz, P., Anderson, S., … Helbing, D. (2012). Towards a global participatory platform. Democratising open data, complexity science and collective intelligence. *The European Physical Journal, 214*(1).

Bueno de Mesquita, B. (1994). Political forecasting: An expected utility method. In B. Bueno de Mesquita, & F. N. Stokman (Eds.), *European community decision making. Models, comparisons, and applications.* New Haven, CT: Yale University Press.

Bunn, D., & Oliveira, F. (2003). Evaluating individual market power in electricity markets via agent-based simulation. *Annals of Operations Research, 19*(2), 57–77. doi:10.1023/A:1023399017816

Burkhart, R., Langton, C., & Askenazi, M. (1996, June). The swarm simulation system: A toolkit for building multi-agent simulations. Santa Fe, AZ: Santa Fe Institute.

Byagowi, A. (2012). Agent based modeling project demonstration [Video]. Retrieved from https://http://www.youtube.com/watch?v=LS559iCNXjQ

Byagowi, A., Mohaddes, D., & McLeod, R. D. (2012). Accidental emergence within an agent based model simulation of agent interactions in an emergency situation. In Q. Mehdi, A. Elmaghraby, I. Marshall, R. Moreton, R. Ragade, B. G. Zapirain, J. Chariker, M. ElSaid, R. Yampolskiy & N.L. Zhigiang, (Eds.), *2012 17th International Conference on Computer Games (CGAMES)* (pp. 189-193). Los Alamitos, CA: IEEE Computer Society.

Camagni, R. P. (1989). Cambiamento tecnologico, Milieu locale e reti di imprese: una teoria dinamica dello spazio economico. *Economia e politica industriale, 64*, 209-236.

Camerer, K. (1995). Individual decision making. In J. H. Kagel, & A. E. Ross (Eds.), *Handbook of experimental economics.* Princeton, NJ: Princeton University Press.

Camerer, K. (2003). *Behavioural game theory: Experiment in strategic interaction.* Princeton, NJ: Princeton University Press.

Camerer, K., & Weber, M. (1992). Recent developments in modelling preferences: Uncertainty and ambiguity. *Journal of Risk and Uncertainty, 5*(4), 325–370. doi:10.1007/BF00122575

Cao, X. (2010). Networks as channels of policy diffusion: Explaining worldwide changes in capital taxation, 1998-2006. *International Studies Quarterly, 54*(3), 823–854. doi:10.1111/j.1468-2478.2010.00611.x

Carbonara, N. (2014 in press). Knowledge-based externalities and geographical clusters: An agent-based simulation study. In D. F. Adamatti, G. P. Dimuro, & H. Coelho (Eds.), *Interdisciplinary applications of agent-based social simulation and modeling.* Hershey, PA: IGI Global.

Carley, K. M., Fridsma, D. B., Casman, E., Yahja, A., & Altman, N., C., L.-C., Kaminsky, B., & Nave, D. (2006). Biowar: Scalable agent-based model of bioattacks. *IEEE Transactions on Systems, Man, and Cybernetics. Part A, Systems and Humans, 36*(2), 252–265. doi:10.1109/TSMCA.2005.851291

Carley, K. M., & Gasser, L. (2000). Computational organizational theory. In G. Weiss (Ed.), *Multiagent systems. A modern approach to distributed artificial intelligence.* Cambridge, MA: The MIT Press.

Carlsson, H., & Van Damme, E. (1993). Global games and equilibrium selection. *Econometrica, 61*, 989–1018. doi:10.2307/2951491

Carlton, D. W. (1983). The location and employment choices of new firms: An econometric model with discrete and continuous endogenous variables. *The Review of Economics and Statistics, 65*, 440–449. doi:10.2307/1924189

Cascalho, J. (2007). *The role of attributes for mental states architectures* (PhD Thesis) (in Portuguese). University of Açores, Portugal.

Castelfranchi, C. (2000). The invisible (left) hand. For a pessimistic theory of the invisible hand and spontaneous social order: A critical homage to F. von Hayek (Invited talk). *Artificial Economics.* Retrieved from http://www.academia.edu/823483/For_a_Pessimistic_Theory_of_the_Invisible_Hand_and_Spontaneous_Order

Castelfranchi, C. (2012). *Simulation-based, reactive, and situated new social-planning. Hints for a manifesto.* (Preliminary version presented at ICAART 2012). Retrieved from http://www.academia.edu/1009698/Simulation-based_Reactive_and_Situated_new_Social-Planning._Hints_for_a_Manifesto

Castelfranchi, C. (2013). Making visible the invisible hand - The mission of social simulation. In Interdisciplinary applications of agent-based social simulation and modeling. Open Agent Based Modeling (OpenABM) Consortium.

Castelfranchi, C., Dignum, F., Jonker, C. M., & Treur, J. (2000). Deliberative normative agents: Principles and architectures. In *Proceedings of 6ᵗʰ ATAL Conference (1999), Intelligent Agents VI*, (LNCS 1757). Berlin: Springer.

Castelfranchi, C. (1993). Discredito dell'idea di piano e progetto e ruolo della scienza cognitive. *Il Mulino, 5*(1), 159–166.

Castelfranchi, C. (1998). Emergence and cognition: Towards a synthetic paradigm in AI and cognitive science. In H. Coelho (Ed.), *Progress in artificial intelligence - IBERAMIA 98* (pp. 13–26). Berlin: Springer. doi:10.1007/3-540-49795-1_2

Castelfranchi, C. (1998). *Simulating with cognitive agents: The importance of cognitive emergence multi-agent systems and agent-based simulation* (pp. 26–44). Lecture notes in computer scienceBerlin: Springer. doi:10.1007/10692956_3

Castelfranchi, C. (2000). Per una teoria pessimistica della mano invisibile e dell'ordine spontaneo. [For a pessimistic theory of the invisible hand and spontaneous social order] In S. Rizzello (Ed.), *Organizzazione, informazione e conoscenza. Saggi su F.A. von Hayek*. Torino, Italy: UTET.

Castelfranchi, C. (2001). The theory of social functions. Challenges for multi-agent-based social simulation and multi-agent learning. *Journal of Cognitive Systems Research, 2*, 5–38. doi:10.1016/S1389-0417(01)00013-4

Castelfranchi, C. (2003). The micro-macro constitution of power. *Understanding the Social II: Philosophy of Sociality. ProtoSociology Journal, 18*, 208–265.

Castelfranchi, C. (2013). *Goaldirectness. Encyclopedia of philosophy and the social sciences*. Thousand Oask, CA: SAGE.

Castelfranchi, C. (2014in press). Making visible the invisible hand. The mission of social simulation. In D. F. Adamatti, G. P. Dimuro, & H. Coelho (Eds.), *Interdisciplinary applications of agent-based social simulation and modeling*. Hershey, PA: IGI Global.

Castelfranchi, C. (in press). Making visible the invisible hand. The mission of social simulation. In D. Adanatti, G. Dimuro, & H. Coelho (Eds.), *Interdisciplinary applications of agent-based social simulation and modelling*. Hershey, PA: IGI Global.

Castelfranchi, C., Conte, R., & Diani, M. (1994). Paradossi cognitivi della democrazia e limiti all'azione del cittadino. *Parolechiave, 5*, 33–63.

Castelfranchi, C., Falcone, R., & Piunti, M. (2006). *Agents with anticipatory behaviours: To be cautious in a risky environment*. ECAI.

Casti, J. L. (1997). *Would-be worlds: How simulation is changing the frontiers of science*. New York: John Wiley & Sons, Inc.

Castle, C. J. E., & Crooks, A. T. (2006). *Principles and concepts of agent-based modelling for developing geospatial simulations* (Working Paper Series, 110). University College London. Retrieved from http://discovery.ucl.ac.uk/3342/

Castro, R. (2004). *Análise de Decisões sob Incertezas para Investimentos e Comercialização de Energia Elétrica no Brasil* (Unpublished doctoral dissertation). Faculdade de Engenharia Elétrica da Universidade Estadual de Campinas.

Cederman, L.-E., & Gleditsch, K. S. (2004). Conquest and regime change: An evolutionary model of the spread of democracy and peace. *International Studies Quarterly, 48*(3), 603–629. doi:10.1111/j.0020-8833.2004.00317.x

Chandak, A., & Browne, J. C. (1983). Vectorization of discrete event simulation. In *Proceedings of the 1983 International Conference on Parallel Processing* (pp. 359).

Choquet, G. (1953). Theory of capacities. *Ann. Inst. Fourier (Grenoble), 5*, 131–295. doi:10.5802/aif.53

Churchland, P. (2011). *Braintrust: what neuroscience tells us about morality*. Princeton, NJ: Princeton University Press.

Cilliers, P. (2001). Boundaries, hierarchies and networks in complex systems. *International Journal of Innovation Management, 05*(02), 135–147. doi:10.1142/S1363919601000312

Cioffi-Revilla, C. (2002). Invariance and universality in social agent-based simulations. *Proceedings of the National Academy of Sciences of the United States of America, 99*, 7314–7316. doi:10.1073/pnas.082081499 PMID:12011412

Cipriani, M., & Guarino, A. (2005). Herd behavior in a laboratory financial market. *The American Economic Review*, *95*(5), 1427–1443. doi:10.1257/000282805775014443

Clark, A. (1998). *Being there: Putting brain, body, and world together again*. Cambridge, MA: The MIT Press.

Coakley, S., Gheorghe, M., Holcombe, M., Chin, S., Worth, D., & Greenough, C. (2012). Exploitation of high performance computing in the FLAME agent-based simulation framework. In *IEEE 14th International Conference on High Performance Computing and Communication 2012 (HPCC-ICESS)* (pp. 538–545). doi:10.1109/HPCC.2012.79

Coelho, H., & Costa, A. R. (2009). On the intelligence of moral agency. In L. S. Lopes, N. Lau, P. Mariano & L. M. Rocha (Eds.), *New trends in artificial intelligence: Proceedings of the Encontro Português de Inteligência Artificial (EPIA-2009)*, (pp. 439-450). Aveiro, Portugal.

Coelho, H., Costa, A. R., & Trigo, P. (2010). Decision taking for agent moral conducts. In *Proceedings of INFORUM2010*, University of Minho, Braga, Portugal.

Coelho, H., Costa, A. R., & Trigo, P. (2010). On the operationality of moral-sense decision making. In *Proceedings of the Brazilian Workshop on Social Simulation (BWSS2010), SBIA Congress*, São Bernardo, Brazil.

Coelho, H., Costa, A. C., & Trigo, P. (2014). On agents intercations governed by morality. In D. Adamatti, G. P. Dimuro, & H. Coelho (Eds.), *Interdisciplinary applications of agent-based social simulation and modeling*. Hershey, PA: IGI Global.

Cohen, B. (2008). *The bittorrent protocol specification*. Retrieved from http://www.bittorrent.org/beps/bep_0003.html

Cohendet, P., & Llerena, P. (1997). Learning, technical change, and public policy: How to create and exploit diversity. In C. Edquist (Ed.), *Systems of innovation. Technologies, institutions and organizations*. London: Pinter.

Cohen, W., & Levinthal, D. (1990). Absorptive capacity: A new perspective on learning and innovation. *Administrative Science Quarterly*, *35*, 128–152. doi:10.2307/2393553

Collier, N., & North, M. (2012). Parallel agent-based simulation with repast for high performance computing. *SIMULATION: Transactions of the Society for Modeling and Simulation International*, 1-21.

Collier, N., & North, M. (2011). Repast HPC: A platform for large-scale agent-based modeling. In W. Dubitzky, K. Kurowski, & B. Schott (Eds.), *Large-scale computing* (pp. 81–109). Hoboken, NJ: John Wiley & Sons, Inc. doi:10.1002/9781118130506.ch5

Comfort, J. C. (1984). The simulation of a master-slave event set processor. *Simulation*, *42*(3), 117–124. doi:10.1177/003754978404200304

Conte, R., Andrighetto, G., Campennì, M., & Paolucci, M. (2007). Emergent and immergent effect in complex social systems. In *Proceedings of AAAI Symposium, Social and Organizational Aspects of Intelligence*. Washington.

Conte, R., Gilbert, N,. Bonelli, G., Cioffi-Revilla, C., Deffuant, G., Kertesz, J. … Helbing, D. (2012). Manifesto of computational social science. *The European Physical Journal*, *214*(1).

Conte, R., & Castelfranchi, C. (1995). *Cognitive and social action*. London: UCL Press.

Conte, R., & Castelfranchi, C. (1996). Simulating multi-agent interdependencies. A two-way approach to the micro-macro link. In U. Mueller, & K. Troitzsch (Eds.), *Microsimulation and the social science (Lecture notes in economics)*. Berlin: Springer Verlag. doi:10.1007/978-3-662-03261-9_18

Conte, R., Gilbert, N., Bonelli, G., Cioffi-Revilla, C., Deffuant, G., & Kertesz, J. et al. (2012). Manifesto of computational social science. *The European Physical Journal. Special Topics*, *214*(1), 325–346. doi:10.1140/epjst/e2012-01697-8

Conte, R., Hegselmann, R., & Terna, P. (Eds.). (1997). *Simulating social phenomena (Lecture Notes in Economics and Mathematical Systems)*. Berlin: Springer.

Conzelmann, G., North, M., Boyd, G., Cirillo, R., Koritarov, V., Macal, C., et al. (2004). Agent-based power market modeling: Simulating strategic market behaviour using an agent-based modeling approach. In *Proceedings of the 6th IAEE European Conference on Modeling in Energy Economics and Policy*, Zurich, Switzerland.

Corchon, L. (1984). *A note on tax evasion and the theory of games*. Madrid, Spain: Mimeo.

Cordasco, G., Chiara, R., Mancuso, A., Mazzeo, D., Scarano, V., & Spagnuolo, C. (2011). A framework for distributing agent-based simulations. Euro-Par 2011: Parallel Processing Workshops, 7155, 460-470. Berlin: Springer.

Cordasco, G., De Chiara, R., Scarano, V., Carillo, M., Mancuso, A., Mazzeo, D., et al. (2011). *D-Mason: Distributed multi-agent based simulations toolkit*. Retrieved from https://sites.google.com/site/distributedmason/

Corrêa, M., & Coelho, H. (1998). From mental states and architectures to agents´ programming. In *Proc. of the 7ᵗʰ Iberoamerican Congress on Artificial Intelligence (IBERAMIA98)*, Lisbon, Portugal (LNAI 1484, pp. 64-85). Berlin: Springer-Verlag.

Corrêa, M., & Coelho, H. (2010). Abstract mental descriptions for agent design. *Intelligent Decision Technologies*, *4*(2), 115–131.

Costa, A. C. R., & Santos, I. A. S. (2012). Toward a framework for simulating agent-based models of public policy processes on the Jason-CArtAgO platform. In *Proceedings of AMPLE@ECAI 2012: 2nd International Workshop on Agent-based Modeling for Policy Engineering, European Conference on Artificial Intelligence* (vol. 1, pp. 1-15). Montpellier, France: Université de Montpellier.

Costa, A. R., & Dimuro, G. (2007). A basis for an exchange value-based operational notion of morality for multiagent systems. In J. Neves, M. Santos & J. Machado (Eds.), *Proceedings of EPIA2007* (LNAI 4874, pp. 580-592). Berlin: Springer.

Costa, A. R., & Dimuro, G. (2009). *Moral values and the structural loop (Revisiting Piaget´s model of normative agents)*. PUC Pelotas Working Report.

Cousins, J. B., & Earl, L. M. (1992). The case for participatory evaluation. *Educational Evaluation and Policy Analysis*, *14*, 397–418.

Coutinho, L., Sichman, J., & Boissier, O. (2009). Modeling dimensions for agent organization. In V. Dignum (Ed.), *Handbook of research on multi-agent systems: Semantics and dynamics of organizational models* (pp. 18–50). Hershey, PA: IGI Global. doi:10.4018/978-1-60566-256-5.ch002

Cowell, F. (1987). The economics of tax evasion. In J. D. Hey, & P. J. Lambert (Eds.), *Surveys in the economics of uncertainty*. Oxford, UK: Basil Blackwell.

Cutillo, L. A., Molva, R., & Strufe, T. (2009). Safebook: A privacy-preserving online social network leveraging on real-life trust. *Communications Magazine*, *47*(12), 94–101. doi:10.1109/MCOM.2009.5350374

da Fonseca Feitosa, F. (2010). Urban Segregation as a Complex System. An Agent-Based Simulation Approach. Bonn.

Damásio, A. (2004). *Looking for Spinoza*. London: Vintage Ed.

Dasgupta, P. (2000). Trust as a commodity? In D. Gambetta (Ed.), *Trust: Making and breaking cooperative relations* (pp. 49–72). Oxford, UK: Department of Sociology, University Oxford.

David, P., & Rosenbloom, J. (1990). Marshallian factor market externalities and the dynamics of industrial location. *Journal of Urban Economics*, *28*, 349–370. doi:10.1016/0094-1190(90)90033-J

Davis, D. D., & Holt, C. A. (1993). *Experimental economics*. Princeton, NJ: Princeton University Press.

Davis, J. P., Eisenhardt, K., & Bingham, C. B. (2007). Developing theory through simulation methods. *Academy of Management Review*, *32*(2), 480–499. doi:10.5465/AMR.2007.24351453

Davis, J. S., Hecht, G., & Perkins, J. D. (2003). Social behaviours, enforcement and tax compliance dynamics. *Accounting Review*, *78*, 39–69. doi:10.2308/accr.2003.78.1.39

Day, C., & Bunn, D. (2001). Divestiture of generation assets in the electricity pool of England and Wales: A computational approach to analyzing market power. *Journal of Regulatory Economics*, *19*(2), 123–141. doi:10.1023/A:1011141105371 .

de Fonseca Feitosa, F., Bao Le, Q., & Vlek, P. L. (2011, March). Multi-agent simulator for urban segregation (MA-SUS): A tool to explore alternatives for promoting inclusive cities. *Computers, Environment and Urban Systems, 35,* 104–115. doi:10.1016/j.compenvurbsys.2010.06.001

Dean, J. S., Gumerman, G. J., Epstein, J. M., Axtell, R. L., Swedlund, A. C., Parker, M. T., & McCarroll, S. (2000). Understanding Anasazi culture change through agent-based modeling. In T. A. Kohler, & G. G. Gumerman (Eds.), *Dynamics in human and primate societies: Agent-based modeling of social and spatial processes* (pp. 179–205). New York: Oxford University Press, USA.

Deffeyes, K. S. (2010). *When oil peaked.* New York: Hill and Wang Press.

Deffuant, G., Neau, D., Amblard, F., & Weisbuch, G. (2000). Mixing beliefs among interacting agents. *Advances in Complex Systems, 3*(01n04), 87–98.

Deffuant, G., Amblard, F., Weisbuch, G., & Faure, T. (2002). How can extremism prevail? A study based on the relative agreement interaction model. *Journal of Artificial Societies and Social Simulation, 5*(4), 1.

Deffuant, G., Huet, S., & Amblard, F. (2005). An individual-based model of innovation diffusion mixing social value and individual benefit. *American Journal of Sociology, 110*(4), 1041–1069. doi:10.1086/430220

Degelman, L. O. (2001). A model for simulation of daylighting and occupancy sensors as an energy control strategy for office buildings. In *Proceedings of the International Conference for Enhanced Building Operations (ICEBO).*

DeGroot, M. H. (1974). Reaching a consensus. *Journal of the American Statistical Association, 69*(345), 118–121. doi:10.1080/01621459.1974.10480137

Dehghani, M., Tomai, E., Forbus, K., & Klenk, M. (2008). An integrated reasoning approach to moral decision-making. In *Proceedings of 23th AAAI Conference on Artificial Intelligence* (pp. 1280-1286).

Demazeau, Y. (1997). Steps towards multi-agent oriented programming. In *Proceedings of the First International Workshop on Multi-Agent Systems.* Boston.

Dignum, F., Kinny, D., & Sonenberg, L. (2001). *From desires, obligations and norms to goals.* The Netherlands: Utrecht University.

Dignum, V. (Ed.). (2009). *Handbook of research on multi-agent systems: Semantics and dynamics of organizational models.* Hershey, PA: IGI Global. doi:10.4018/978-1-60566-256-5

Dimuro, G. (2009). *La producción y gestión social en ecosistemas urbanos: la agricultura urbana y periurbana en Sevilla* (Phd Thesis Proposal). Sevilla, Spain: Universidad de Sevilla.

Dimuro, G. P., Rocha, A. R., & Gonçalves, L. V. (2010). Recognizing and learning observable social exchange strategies in open societies. In *Proceedings of the Brazilian Workshop on Social Simulation (BWSS2010),* São Bernardo do Campo, Brazil.

Dimuro, G., & Jerez, E. (2010b). La comunidad como escala d etrabajo en los ecosistemas urbanos. In *Proceedings of Ciencia y Tecnología, 20th Congreso de Ingeniería Sustentable y Ecologia Urbana, Buenos Aires, ISEU* (pp. 101—116). Palermo, Italy: Universidad de Palermo.

Dimuro, G. (2010). Sistemas urbanos: el estado de la cuestión y los ecosistemas como laboratorio. *Arquitextos, 124,* 11.

Dimuro, G., & Jerez, E. (2010a). Comunidades en Transición: Hacia otras prácticas sostenibles en los ecosistemas urbanos. *Cidades Comunidades e Territórios, 20-21,* 87–95.

Ding, L., & Khandelwal, A. (2012). OWL 2 Web ontology language – Quick reference guide (2nd Ed.). W3C Recommendation, W3C.

Dobbin, F., Simmons, B., & Garrett, G. (2007). The global diffusion of public policies: Social construction, corecion, competition or learning? *Annual Review of Sociology, 33,* 449–472. doi:10.1146/annurev.soc.33.090106.142507

Dongarra, J. J., & van der Steen, A. J. (2012). High-performance computing systems: Status and outlook. *Acta Numerica, 21,* 379–474. doi:10.1017/S0962492912000050

Dubois, D., Willinger, M., & Van Nguyen, P. (2011). Optimization incentive and relative riskiness in experimental stag-hunt games. *International Journal of Game Theory, 41,* 369–380. doi:10.1007/s00182-011-0290-x

Duffy, J. (2006). Agent-based models and human subject experiments. In L. Tesfatsion, & K. Judd (Eds.), *Handbook of computational economics* (Vol. 2). Amsterdam, The Netherlands: Elsevier.

Easton, D. (1965). *A framework for political analysis.* Englewood Cliffs, NJ: Prentice-Hall.

EC. (2009). *European directive, 2009/72/EC (EUR-Lex. europa.eu).* Retrieved from http://eur-lex.europa.eu/

Ecologistas en acción. (n. d.). Retrieved from http://www.ecologistasenaccion.org/

Eichberger, J., & Kelsey, D. (2011). Are the treasures of game theory ambiguous? *Economic Theory, 48,* 313–339. doi:10.1007/s00199-011-0636-4

Elkink, J. A. (2011). The international diffusion of democracy. *Comparative Political Studies, 44*(12), 1651–1674. doi:10.1177/0010414011407474

Elkins, Z., Guzman, A. T., & Simmons, B. (2006). Competing for capital: The diffusion of bilateral investment treaties, 1960$,Äì$2000. *International Organization, 60*(4), 811–846. doi:10.1017/S0020818306060279

Ellemers, N., Spears, R., & Doosje, B. (2002). Self and social identity. *Annual Review of Psychology, 53*(1), 161–186. doi:10.1146/annurev.psych.53.100901.135228 PMID:11752483

Ellsberg, D. (1961). Risk, ambiguity and the savage axioms. *The Quarterly Journal of Economics, 75,* 643–669. doi:10.2307/1884324

Elzinga, K., & Mills, D. (2011). The Lerner index of monopoly power: Origins and uses. *The American Economic Review, 101*(3). doi:10.1257/aer.101.3.558

eMID. (n. d.). Retrieved September 2013 from http://www.e-mid.it/?lang=uk

Emmeche, C. (1997). Aspects of complexity in life and science. *Philosophica, 59*(1), 41–68.

Epstein, J. M. (1999). Agent-based computational models and generative social science. *Complexity, 4*(5), 41–60. doi:10.1002/(SICI)1099-0526(199905/06)4:5<41::AID-CPLX9>3.0.CO;2-F

Epstein, J. M. (2002). Modeling civil violence: An agent-based computational approach. *Proceedings of the National Academy of Sciences of the United States of America, 99*(Suppl 3), 7243–7250. doi:10.1073/pnas.092080199 PMID:11997450

Epstein, J. M. (2006). *Generative Social Science. Studies in Agent-Based Computational Modeling.* Princeton, Oxford: Princeton University Press.

Epstein, J. M. (2008). Why model? *Journal of Artificial Societies and Social Simulation, 11*(4), 12.

Epstein, J. M., & Axtell, R. (1996). *Growing artificial societies.* Cambridge, MA: MIT Press.

Epstein, J. M., & Axtell, R. (1996). *Growing artificial societies: Social science from the bottom up.* Washington, DC/Cambridge, MA: Brookings Institution Press/MIT Press.

Erdős, P., & Rényi, A. (1959). On random graphs. *Publ. Math. Debrecen, 6,* 290–297.

Ernst, D. (2002). Global production networks and the changing geography of innovation systems. Implications for developing countries. *Economics of Innovation and New Technology, 11*(6), 497–523. doi:10.1080/10438590214341

Esping-Andersen, G. (1990). *The three worlds of welfare capitalism.* Princeton, NJ: Princeton University Press.

Everett, M., & Borgatti, S. P. (2005). Ego network betweenness. *Social Networks, 27*(1), 31–38. doi:10.1016/j.socnet.2004.11.007

Fan, Z., Qiu, F., Kaufman, A., & Yoakum-Stover, S. (2004). GPU cluster for high performance computing. In *Proceedings of the 2004 ACM/IEEE conference on Supercomputing (SC '04)* (pp. 47). IEEE Computer Society.

Farago, J., Greenwald, A., & Hall, K. (2002). Fair and Efficient Solutions to the Santa Fe Bar Problem. *Proceedings of the Grace Hopper Celebration of Women in Computing 2002.*

Farias, G. P., Dimuro, G. P., Dimuro, G., & Jerez, E. (2013). A fuzzy BDI-like agent model for exchanges of non-economic services. In *Proceedings of BRACIS 2013—Brazilian Conference on Intelligent Systems, Fortaleza.* Los Alamitos, CA: IEEE.

Ferber, J., Stratulat, T., & Tranier, J. (2009). Towards an Integra approach of organizations in multi-agent systems. In V. Dignum (Ed.), *Handbook of research on multi-agent systems: Semantics and dynamics of organizational models* (pp. 51–75). Hershey, PA: IGI Global. doi:10.4018/978-1-60566-256-5.ch003

Flache, A., & Hegselmann, R. (2001). Do irregular grids make a difference? Relaxing the spatial regularity assumption in cellular models of social dynamics. *Journal of Artificial Societies and Social Simulation*, 4(4).

Fogel, D. B., Chellapilla, K., & Angeline, P. J. (1999, July). Inductive Reasoning and Bounded Rationality Reconsidered. *IEEE Transactions on Evolutionary Computation*, 3(2), 142–146. doi:10.1109/4235.771167

Folcik, V., An, G., & Orosz, C. (2007). The basic immune simulator: An agent-based model to study the interactions between innate and adaptive immunity. *Theoretical Biology & Medical Modelling*, 4(1), 39. doi:10.1186/1742-4682-4-39 PMID:17900357

Forrester, J. W. (1968). Priciples of Systems (2nd preliminary ed.). Cambridge, Mass., and London: MIT Press/Wright Allen.

Fosca, G., Pedreschi, D., Pentland, A., Lukowicz, P., Kossmann, D., Crowley, J., Helbing, D. (2012). A planetary nervous system for social mining and collective awareness. *The European Physical Journal*, 214(1).

Foster, I., Zhao, Y., Raicu, I., & Lu, S. (2008). Cloud computing and grid computing 360-degree compared. In *Grid Computing Environments Workshop, 2008. GCE'08* (pp. 1–10). doi:10.1109/GCE.2008.4738445

Franchi, E. (2012a, August). A domain specific language approach for agent-based social network modeling. In *Advances in Social Networks Analysis and Mining (ASONAM), 2012 IEEE/ACM International Conference on* (pp. 607-612). IEEE.

Franchi, E. (2012b). Towards agent-based models for synthetic social network generation. In *Virtual and networked organizations, emergent technologies and tools* (pp. 18–27). Berlin: Springer. doi:10.1007/978-3-642-31800-9_3

Franchi, E., & Poggi, A. (2011). Multi-agent systems and social networks. In *Business social networking: Organizational, managerial, and technological dimensions* (pp. 84–97). Hershey, PA: IGI Global. doi:10.4018/978-1-61350-168-9.ch005

Franchi, E., & Tomaiuolo, M. (2013). Distributed social platforms for confidentiality and resilience. In L. Caviglione, M. Coccoli, & A. Merlo (Eds.), *Social network engineering for secure Web data and services* (pp. 88–114). Hershey, PA: IGI Global. doi:10.4018/978-1-4666-3926-3.ch006

Franco, M. I., Costa, A. R., & Coelho, H. (2009). Exchange values and social power supporting the choice of partners. *Revista Pueblos y Fronteras Digital*, No. 9.

Franco, M. I. (2008). *Interaction mechanism among agents: Construction and evaluation of social exchanges*. Brazil: Universidade Federal do Rio Grande do Sul. (in Portuguese)

French, J. P. R. J. (1956). A formal theory of social power. *Psychological Review*, 63, 181–194. doi:10.1037/h0046123 PMID:13323174

French, W. L., & Bell, C. (1973). *Organization development: Behavioral science interventions for organization improvement*. Englewood Cliffs, NJ: Prentice-Hall.

Freyne, J., Coyle, L., Smyth, B., & Cunningham, P. (2010). Relative status of journal and conference publications in computer science. *Communications of the ACM*, 53(11), 124–132. doi:10.1145/1839676.1839701

Friedman, T. L. (2008). *Hot, flat, and crowded: Why we need a green revolution and how it can renew America*. New York: Farrar, Straus and Giroux Press.

Friesen, M., Gordon, R., & McLeod, B. (2013). Exploring emergence within social systems with agent based models. In Interdisciplinary applications of agent-based social simulation and modeling. Open Agent Based Modeling (OpenABM) Consortium.

Friesen, M. R., Gordon, R., & McLeod, R. D. (2014). Exploring emergence within social systems with agent based models. In *Interdisciplinary applications of agent-based social simulation and modeling*. Hershey, PA: IGI Global.

Fudenberg, D., & Levine, D. (1998). *The theory of learning in games*. London: MIT Press.

Fujimoto, R. M. (1990). Parallel discrete event simulation. *Communications of the ACM*, *33*(10), 30–53. doi:10.1145/84537.84545

Fujimoto, R. M. (2000). *Parallel and distributed simulation systems*. Hoboken, NJ: John Wiley & Sons.

Gabriel, S., Zhuang, J., & Kiet, S. (2004). A Nash-Cournot model for the North American natural gas market. *In Proceedings of the 6th IAEE European Conference: Modelling in Energy Economics and Policy.*

Galam, S. (1997). Rational group decision making: A random field Ising model T = 0. *Physica A: Statistical Mechanics and its Applications, 238*(1), 66–80.

Galán, J. M., Izquierdo, L. R., Izquierdo, S. S., Santos, J. I., del Olmo, R., López-Paredes, A., & Edmonds, B. (2009). Errors and artefacts in agent-based modelling. *Journal of Artificial Societies and Social Simulation, 12*(1).

Ganghof, S. (2003). Promises and pitfalls of veto player analysis. *Swiss Political Science Review, 9*(2), 1–25. doi:10.1002/j.1662-6370.2003.tb00411.x

Gardner, M. (1970). The fantastic combinations of John Conway's new solitaire game life. *Scientific American, 223*, 120–123. doi:10.1038/scientificamerican1070-120

Gaston, M. E., & desJardins, M. (2005). Agent-organized networks for dynamic team formation. In *Proceedings of the Fourth International Joint Conference on Autonomous Agents and Multiagent Sytems* (pp. 230–237).

Geanakoplos, J., Axtell, R., Doyne Farmer, J., Howitt, P., Conlee, B., & Goldstein, J. et al. (2012). Getting at systemic risk via an agent-based model of the housing market. *The American Economic Review, 102*(3), 53–58. doi:10.1257/aer.102.3.53

Gelernter, D. H. (1992). *Mirror worlds: Or the day software puts the universe in a shoebox...how it will happen and what it will mean*. Oxford, UK: Oxford Univ. Press.

Georgalos, K. (2013). *Playing with ambiguity: An agent based model of vague beliefs in games. Interdisciplinary applications of agent-based social simulation and modeling. Open Agent Based Modeling (OpenABM)*. Consortium.

Gerritsen, C. (2011). *Using ambient intelligence to control aggression in crowds*. Retrieved from http://www.computer.org/csdl/proceedings/wi-iat/2011/4513/03/4513c053-abs.html

Gibbons, R. (1992). *Game theory for applied economists*. Princeton, NJ: Princeton University Press.

Gilardi, F. (2005). The institutional foundations of regulatory capitalism: The diffusion of independent regulatory agencies in Western Europe. *The Annals of the American Academy of Political and Social Science, 598*(1), 84–101. doi:10.1177/0002716204271833

Gilardi, F. (2010). Who learns from what in policy diffusion processes? *American Journal of Political Science, 54*(3), 650–666. doi:10.1111/j.1540-5907.2010.00452.x

Gilardi, F., Fueglister, K., & Luyet, S. (2009). Learning from others: The diffusion of hospital financing reforms in OECD countries. *Comparative Political Studies, 42*(4), 549–573. doi:10.1177/0010414008327428

Gilbert, N. (1998). *The simulation of social processes* (Unpublished).

Gilbert, G. N. (1995). Emergence in social simulation. In G. N. Gilbert, & R. Conte (Eds.), *Artificial societies: The computer simulation of social life*. London: UCL Press.

Gilbert, G. N. (2008). *Agent-based models*. Los Angeles, CA: Sage.

Gilbert, N. (1997). A simulation of the structure of academic science. *Sociological Research Online, 2*(2). doi:10.5153/sro.85

Gilbert, N. (2008). *Agent-based models (No. 153)*. London: Sage.

Gilbert, N., & Conte, R. (Eds.). (1995). *Artificial societies. The computer simulation of social life*. London: UCL Press.

Gilbert, N., & Doran, J. (Eds.). (1994). *Simulating societies: The computer simulation of social phenomena*. London: UCL Press.

Gilbert, N., Pyka, A., & Ahrweiler, P. (2001). Innovation networks – A simulation approach. *Journal of Artificial Societies and Social Simulation, 4*(3), 1–13.

Gilbert, N., & Terna, P. (2000). How to build and use agent-based models in social science. *Mind & Society*, *1*(1), 57–72. doi:10.1007/BF02512229

Gilbert, N., & Troitzsch, K. G. (2005). *Simulation for the social scientist*. New York, NY: McGraw-Hill International.

Gilboa, I. (1987). Expected utility with purely subjective non-additive probabilities. *Journal of Mathematical Economics*, *16*, 65–88. doi:10.1016/0304-4068(87)90022-X

Gilboa, I. (2009). *Theory of decision under uncertainty (Econometric Society Monograph Series)*. New York: Cambridge University Press. doi:10.1017/CBO9780511840203

Gjoka, M., Kurant, M., Butts, C. T., & Markopoulou, A. (2010). Walking in Facebook: A case study of unbiased sampling of OSNs. In *2010 Proceedings IEEE INFOCOM*. New York: IEEE.

Gleditsch, K. S., & Ward, M. D. (2006). Diffusion in the international context of democratization. *International Organization*, *60*(4), 911–933. doi:10.1017/S0020818306060309

Glosten, L. R., & Milgrom, P. R. (1985). Bid, ask and transaction prices in a specialist market with heterogeneously informed traders. *Journal of Financial Economics*, *14*(1), 71–100. doi:10.1016/0304-405X(85)90044-3

Gode, D. K., & Sunder, S. (2004). Double auction dynamics: Structural effects of non-binding price controls. *Journal of Economic Dynamics & Control*, *28*(9), 1707–1731. doi:10.1016/j.jedc.2003.06.001

Goldemberg, J., & Villanueva, L. D. (2003). Energia, meio ambiente e desenvolvimento (Trans. A. Koch, 2 ed.). São Paulo, Brazil: Editora da Universidade de São Paulo.

Goldstone, R. J., Popat, R., Fletcher, M. P., Crusz, S. A., & Diggle, S. P. (2012). Quorum sensing and social interactions in microbial biofilms. In G. Lear, & G. D. Lewis (Eds.), *Microbial biofilms: Current research and applications* (pp. 1–24). Norfolk, UK: Caister Academic Press.

Goldstone, R. L., & Janssen, M. A. (2005). Computational models of collective behavior. *Trends in Cognitive Sciences*, *9*(9), 424–430. doi:10.1016/j.tics.2005.07.009 PMID:16085450

Gordon, R. (2000). The emergence of emergence: A critique of design, observation, surprise!. *Rivista di Biologia/Biology Forum*, *93*(2), 349-356.

Gordon, R., Björklund, N. K., Smith, R. J., & Blyden, E. R. (2009). Halting HIV/AIDS with avatars and havatars: A virtual world approach to modelling epidemics. BMC Public Health, 9(Suppl 1: OptAIDS Special Issue), S13 (16 pages).

Gordon, R., & Drum, R. W. (1994). The chemical basis for diatom morphogenesis. *International Review of Cytology*, *150*, 243–372, 421–422. doi:10.1016/S0074-7696(08)61544-2

Gotts, N. M., & Polhill, J. G. (2010). Size matters: Large-scale replications of experiments with FEARLUS. *Advances in Complex Systems*, *13*(4), 453–467. doi:10.1142/S0219525910002670

Graffi, K., Gross, C., Mukherjee, P., Kovacevic, A., & Steinmetz, R. (2010, August). LifeSocial. KOM: A P2P-based platform for secure online social networks. In *2010 IEEE Tenth International Conference on Peer-to-Peer Computing (P2P)*, (pp. 1-2). IEEE.

Granovetter, M. (1978). Threshold models in collective behavior. *American Journal of Sociology*, *83*(6), 1420–1443. doi:10.1086/226707

Grant, R. M. (1997). The knowledge-based view of the firm: implications for management in practice. *Long Range Planning*, *30*(3), 450–454. doi:10.1016/S0024-6301(97)00025-3

Gray, V. (1973). Innovation in the states: A diffusion study. *The American Political Science Review*, *67*(4), 1174–1185. doi:10.2307/1956539

Greene, J., Sommerville, R., Nystrom, L., & Darley, J. (2001). An fMRI investigation of emotional engagement in moral judgment. *Science*, *293*(5537), 2105–2108. doi:10.1126/science.1062872 PMID:11557895

Green, J., & Haidt, J. (2002, December). How (and where) does moral judgment work? *Trends in Cognitive Sciences*, *6*(12). PMID:12200171

Grimm, V., Berger, U., Bastiansen, F., Eliassen, S., Ginot, V., & Giske, J. et al. (2006). A standard protocol for describing individual-based and agent-based models. *Ecological Modelling, 198*(1–2), 115–126. doi:10.1016/j.ecolmodel.2006.04.023

Grimm, V., Berger, U., DeAngelis, D. L., Polhill, J. G., Giske, J., & Railsback, S. F. (2010). The ODD protocol: A review and first update. *Ecological Modelling, 221*(23), 2760–2768. doi:10.1016/j.ecolmodel.2010.08.019

Grossback, L. J., Nicholson-Crotty, S., & Peterson, D. A. M. (2004). Ideology and learning in policy diffusion. *American Politics Research, 32*(5), 521–545. doi:10.1177/1532673X04263801

Guba, E., & Lincoln, Y. (1989). Fourth generation evaluation. *Journal of Artificial Societies and Social Simulation*.

Gunasekara, C. (2012). Mobile users' trajectory patterns in Manitoba Province. Retrieved from http://www.youtube.com/watch?v=cOJZKzy0XBY

Hacker, J. S. (2004). Review article: Dismantling the health care state? Political institutions, public policies and the comparative politics of health reform. *British Journal of Political Science, 34*, 693–724. doi:10.1017/S0007123404000250

Haeusermann, S., & Palier, B. (2008). The politics of employment-friendly welfare reforms in post-industrial economies. *Socio-economic Review, 6*(3), 559–586. doi:10.1093/ser/mwn011

Haidt, J., & Kesebir, S. (2010). *Handbook of social psychology*. Hoboken, NJ: John Wiley.

Halevy, Y. (2007). Ellsberg revisited: An experimental study. *Econometrica, 75*(2), 503–536. doi:10.1111/j.1468-0262.2006.00755.x

Hallerberg, M., & Basinger, S. (1998). Internationalization and changes in tax policy in OECD countries: The importance of domestic veto players. *Comparative Political Studies, 31*(3), 321–352. doi:10.1177/0010414098031003003

Hamel, G., & Prahalad, C. K. (1994). *Competing for the future*. Boston: Harvard Business School Press.

Hamill, L., & Gilbert, N. (2009). Social circles: A simple structure for agent-based social network models. *Journal of Artificial Societies and Social Simulation, 12*(2), 3.

Hannappel, M., & Troitzsch, K. G. (2012). Demographic and educational projection. Building an event-oriented microsimulation model with CoMicS II. In K. G. Troitzsch, M. Möhring, & U. Lotzmann, *Shaping reality through simulation. 26th European Conference on Modelling and Simulation, May 29–June 1, 2012, Koblenz, Germany* (S. 613–618). Koblenz: ECMS.

Hansen, A. M. D. (2000). *Padrões de Consumo de Energia Elétrica em Diferentes Tipologias de Edificações Residenciais* (Unpublished master dissertation). UFRGS, Porto Alegre.

Harsanyi, J., & Selten, R. (1995). *A general theory of equilibrium selection for games*. Cambridge, MA: MIT Press.

Harsanyi, J., & Selten, R. (1998). A general theory of equilibrium selection for games with complete information. *Journal of Games and Economic Behavior, 8*, 91–122. doi:10.1016/S0899-8256(05)80018-1

Hauser, F., Huber, J., & Kirchler, M. (2009). Comparing laboratory experiments and agent-based simulations: The value of information and market efficiency in a market with asymmetric information. In C. Hernández, M. Posada, & A. López-Paredes (Eds.), *Artificial economics: The generative method in economics* (pp. 199–210). Berlin: Springer-Verlag. doi:10.1007/978-3-642-02956-1_16

Hauser, M. D. (2006). *Moral minds: How nature designed our sense of right and wrong*. New York: Ecco/Harper Collins.

Hayek, F. (1988). *Conoscenza, Mercato, Pianificazione* (Anthology of Hayek's writings, including The Use of Knowledge in Society[). Bologna, Italy: Il Mulino.]. *The American Economic Review*, 1945.

Hayek, F. A. (1967). The result of human action but not of human design. In *Studies in philosophy, politics and economics*. London: Routledge & Kegan.

Hazen, R. M. (2011). (In preparation). The emergence of patterning in life's origin and evolution. *The International Journal of Developmental Biology*.

Head, K., Ries, J., & Swenson, D. (1995). Agglomeration benefits and location choice: Evidence from Japanese manufacturing investment in the United States. *Journal of International Economics, 38*, 223–247. doi:10.1016/0022-1996(94)01351-R

Hegselmann, R. (2009). Moral dynamics. In R. A. Meyers (Ed.), *Encyclopedia of complexity and systems sciences* (pp. 5677–5692). Berlin: Springer. doi:10.1007/978-0-387-30440-3_338

Hegselmann, R., & Krause, U. (2002). Opinion dynamics and bounded confidence: Models, analysis and simulation. *Journal of Artificial Societies and Social Simulation, 5*(3), 2.

Hegselmann, R., & Will, O. (2013). From small groups to large societies: How to construct a simulator? *Biological Theory, 8*(2), 185–194. doi:10.1007/s13752-013-0110-6

Helbing, D., & Balietti, S. (2012). Agent-based modeling. In D. Helbing (Ed.), *social self-organization (Understanding complex systems)* (pp. 25–70). Berlin: Springer. doi:10.1007/978-3-642-24004-1_2

Helbing, D., Yu, W., & Rauhut, H. (2011). Self-organization and emergence in social systems: modeling the coevolution of social environments and cooperative behavior. *The Journal of Mathematical Sociology, 35*(1-3), 177–208. doi:10.1080/0022250X.2010.532258

Helleboogh, A., Vizzari, G., Uhrmacher, A., & Michel, F. (2007). Modeling dynamic environments in multi-agent simulation. *Journal of Autonomous Agents and Multi-Agent Systems, 14*(1), 87–116. doi:10.1007/s10458-006-0014-y

Hey, J. D., Lotito, G., & Maffioletti, A. (2010). The descriptive and predictive adequacy of theories of decision making under uncertainty/ambiguity. *Journal of Risk and Uncertainty, 41*(2), 81–111. doi:10.1007/s11166-010-9102-0

Hey, J. D., & Pace, N. (2011). *The explanatory and predictive power of non two-stage-probability theories of decision making under ambiguity (Discussion Papers 11/22)*. Department of Economics, University of York.

Hill, M. (2009). *The public policy process* (5th ed.). London: Pearson Longman.

Hill, R., Carl, R., & Champagne, L. (2006). Using agent simulation models to examine and investigate search theory against a historical case study. *Journal of Simulation, 1*(1), 29–38. doi:10.1057/palgrave.jos.4250003

Holland, J. (1998). *Emergence: From chaos to order*. Cambridge, MA: Perseus Books.

Holme, P., & Kim, B. (2002). Growing scale-free networks with tunable clustering. *Physical Review E: Statistical, Nonlinear, and Soft Matter Physics, 65*(2), 2–5. doi:10.1103/PhysRevE.65.026107

Hommes, C. H. (2006). Heterogeneous agent models in economics and finance. In L. Tesfatsion, & K. Judd (Eds.), *Handbook of computational economics* (Vol. 2). Amsterdam, The Netherlands: Elsevier.

Horty, J. F. (1994, February). Moral dilemmas and non-monotonic logic. *Journal of Philosophical Logic, 23*(1), 35–65. doi:10.1007/BF01417957

Howells, J. R. L. (2002). Tacit knowledge, innovation and economic geography. *Urban Studies (Edinburgh, Scotland), 39*, 871–884. doi:10.1080/00420980220128354

Hubner, J. (2003). *Um Modelo de Reorganização de Sistemas Multiagentes* (PhD Thesis). São Paulo, Brazil: USP.

Hubner, J., Bordini, R. H., Gouveia, G. P., Pereira, R. H., Picard, G., Piunti, M., & Sichman, J. S. (2009). Using Jason, Moise+, and CArtAgO to develop a team of cowboys. In J. Dix, M. Fisher, & P. Novák (Eds), *Proceedings of 10th International Workshop on Computational Logic in Multi-Agent Systems (CLIMA 2009)*, (pp. 203-207).

Hubner, J., Sichman, J., & Boissier, O. (2002). A model for the structural, functional, and deontic specification of organizations in multiagent systems. In *Proceedings of the Brazilian Symposium on Artificial Intelligence—SBIA 2002, Porto de Galinhas* (LNAI 2507, pp. 118–128). Berlin: Anais Springer.

Hübner, J., Boissier, O., Kitio, R., & Ricci, A. (2010). Instrumenting multi-agent organizations with organisational artifacts and agents. *Autonomous Agents and Multi-Agent Systems, 20*, 369–400. doi:10.1007/s10458-009-9084-y

Hybinette, M., Kraemer, E., Xiong, Y., Matthews, G., & Ahmed, J. (2006). SASSY: A design for a scalable agent-based simulation system using a distributed discrete event infrastructure. In *Proceedings of the 36th Conference on Winter Simulation (Monterey, California)* (pp. 926–933).

Icosystem Corporation. (2013). *The game*. Retrieved from http://www.icosystem.com/labsdemos/the-game

Ilachinski, A. (2000). Irreducible semi-autonomous adaptive combat (ISAAC): An artificial-life approach to land combat. *Military Operations Research, 5*(3), 29–46. doi:10.5711/morj.5.3.29

Isaak, A. G. (2008). Simulating evolutionary games: A Python-based introduction. *Journal of Artificial Societies and Social Simulation, 11*(3), 8.

ITEM-game. (2013). *Investment and trading in electricity markets*. Retrieved from http://www.item-game.org/

Izquierdo, L. R., Izquierdo, S. S., Galán, J. M., & Santos, J. I. (2013). Combining Mathematical an Simulation Approaches to Understand the Dynamics of Computer Models. In B. Edmonds, & R. Meyer (Eds.), *Simulating Social Complexity. A Handbook* (pp. 235–271). Heidelberg: Springer. doi:10.1007/978-3-540-93813-2_11

Jackson, M. O. (2010). *Social and economic networks*. Princeton, NJ: Princeton University Press.

Jager, W., & Amblard, F. (2004). Uniformity, bipolarization and pluriformity captured as generic stylized behavior with an agent-based simulation model of attitude change. *Computational & Mathematical Organization Theory, 10*, 295–303. doi:10.1007/s10588-005-6282-2

Jang, M.-W., & Agha, G. (2005). Adaptive agent allocation for massively multi-agent applications. In T. Ishida, L. Gasser, & H. Nakashima (Eds.), *Massively Multi-Agent Systems I: First International Workshop MMAS 2004* (pp. 25–39). Kyoto, Japan: Springer, Berlin.

Jang, M.-W., & Agha, G. (2006). Agent framework services to reduce agent communication overhead in large-scale agent-based simulations. *Simulation Modelling Practice and Theory, 14*(6), 679–694. doi:10.1016/j.simpat.2005.10.002

Jinlong, O., & Kazunori, H. (2009). Energy-saving potential by improving occupants' behaviour in urban residential sector in Hangzhou City, China. *Energy and Building, 41*, 711–720. doi:10.1016/j.enbuild.2009.02.003

Kaelbling, L. P., Littman, M. L., & Cassandra, A. R. (1998). Planning and acting in partially observable stochastic domains. *Artificial Intelligence, 101*(1-2), 99–134. doi:10.1016/S0004-3702(98)00023-X

Kahneman, D. (2012). *Fast and slow, Two ways of thinking* (Portuguese Ed.). Brazil: Objetiva.

Kastener, S. L., & Rector, C. (2003). International regimes, domestic veto-players, and capital controls policy stability. *International Studies Quarterly, 47*(1), 1–22. doi:10.1111/1468-2478.4701001

Kermack, W. O., & McKendrick, A. G. (1927). Contribution to the mathematical theory of epidemics. In *Proceedings of the Royal Society of London Series a-Containing Papers of a Mathematical and Physical Character, 115*(772), 700-721.

Ketter, W., Collins, J., Reddy, P., Flath, C., & de Weerdt, M. (2011). The power trading agent competition. In ERIM Report Series No. ERS-2011-011-LIS, (Vol. 2). SSRN.

Khan, I., & McLeod, R. D. (2012). Managing Hajj crowd complexity: Superior throughput, satisfaction, health, & safety. *Kuwait Chapter of Arabian Journal of Business and Management Review, 2*(4), 45–59.

Kil Lee, C., & Strang, D. (2006). The international diffusion of public-sector downsizing: Network emulation and theory-driven learning. *International Organization, 60*(4), 883–909.

Kirchler, E. (2007). *The economic psychology of tax behaviour*. Cambridge, UK: Cambridge University Press. doi:10.1017/CBO9780511628238

Klein, L., Kavulya, G., Jazizadeh, F., Kwak, J., Becerik-Gerber, B., & Tambe, M. (2011). *Towards optimization of building energy and occupant comfort using multi-agent simulation*. Paper presented at the International Symposium on Automation and Robotics in Construction.

Knight, F. H. (1921). Risks, uncertainty and profit. Boston: Houghton-Mifflin.

Knoben, J., & Oelremans, L. A. G. (2006). Proximity and inter-organizational collaboration: A literature review. *International Journal of Management Reviews, 8*, 71–89. doi:10.1111/j.1468-2370.2006.00121.x

Koesrindartoto, D., Sun, J., & Tesfatsion, L. (2005). An agent-based computational laboratory for testing the economic reliability of wholesale power market designs. In *Proceedings of the IEEE Power Engineering Conference* (pp. 931–936). San Francisco, CA.

Koesrindartoto, D. (2002). *Discrete double auctions with artificial adaptive agents: A case study of an electricity market using a double auction simulator (Technical report). Dep. of Economics.* Iowa University.

Kohler, T. A., Gumerman, G. J., & Reynolds, R. J. (2005). Simulating ancient societies. *Scientific American*, *293*, 76–84. doi:10.1038/scientificamerican0705-76 PMID:16008305

Kohler, T. A., & Gummerman, G. J. (Eds.). (2001). *Dynamics of human and primate societies: agent-based modeling of social and spatial processes.* New York: Oxford University Press.

Kollman, K., Miller, J. H., & Page, S. E. (1992). Adaptive parties in spatial elections. *The American Political Science Review*, *86*(4), 929–937. doi:10.2307/1964345

Kollman, K., Miller, J. H., & Page, S. E. (1998). Political parties and electoral landscapes. *British Journal of Political Science*, *28*, 139–158. doi:10.1017/S0007123498000131

König, A., Möhring, M., & Troitzsch, K. G. (2003). Agents, Hierarchies and Sustainability. In F. Billari, & A. Prskawetz (Eds.), *Agent-Based Computational Demography* (pp. 197–210). Heidelberg: Physica. doi:10.1007/978-3-7908-2715-6_11

Korobow, A., Johnson, C., & Axtell, R. (2007). An agent based model of tax compliance with social networks. *National Tax Journal*, *60*(3), 589–610.

Koutiva, I., & Makropoulos, C. (2012). Linking social simulation and urban water modeling tools to support adaptive urban water management. In *Proceedings of the International Environmental Modelling and Software Society (iEMSs).*

Krause, U. (1997). In U. Krause, & M. Stöckler (Eds.), *Soziale Dynamiken mit vielen Interakteuren. Eine Problemskizze in Modellierung und {S}imulation von {D}ynamiken mit {V}ielen {I}nteragierenden {A}kteuren* (pp. 37–51). Modus, Universität Bremen.

Krogh, G., & Vicari, S. (1992). L'approccio autopoietico all'apprendimento strategico sperimentale. *Economia e politica industriale, 74/76.*

Krugman, P. R. (1991). *Geography and trade.* Cambridge, MA: MIT Press.

Kumar, R., Novak, J., & Tomkins, A. (2010). Structure and evolution of online social networks. In *Link mining: Models, algorithms, and applications* (pp. 337–357). New York: Springer. doi:10.1007/978-1-4419-6515-8_13

Kurowski, K., de Back, W., Dubitzky, W., Gulyás, L., Kampis, G., & Mamonski, M. et al. (2009). Complex system simulations with qoscosgrid. In *Computational Science--ICCS 2009* (pp. 387–396). Berlin: Springer. doi:10.1007/978-3-642-01970-8_38

Ladley, D. (2012). Zero intelligence in economics and finance. *The Knowledge Engineering Review*, *27*(2), 273–286. doi:10.1017/S0269888912000173

Lan, C., & Pidd, M. (2005). High performance simulation in quasi-continuous manufacturing plants. In M. E. Kuhl, N. M. Steiger, F. B. Armstrong, & J. A. Joines (Eds.), *Proceedings of the 2005 Winter Simulation Conference* (pp. 1367–1372). Picataway, NJ.: IEEE Computer Society Press.

Landes, W., & Posner, R. (1981). Market power in antitrust cases. *Harvard Law Review*, *94*(5), 937–996. doi:10.2307/1340687

Lane, D. (2002). Complexity and local interactions: Towards a theory of industrial districts, complexity and industrial districts. In A. Q. Curzio, & M. Fortis (Eds.), *Complexity and industrial clusters.* Heidelberg, Germany: Physica-Verlag. doi:10.1007/978-3-642-50007-7_5

Law, A. M. (2007). *Simulation modeling and analysis* (4th ed.). New York: McGraw-Hill.

Lazer, D., Pentland, A., Adamic, L., Aral, S., Barabási, L., & Brewer, D. et al. (2009). Computational social science. *Science*, *23*, 721–723. doi:10.1126/science.1167742 PMID:19197046

Le, X. H. B., Kashif, A., Ploix, S., Dugdale, J., Mascolo, M. D., & Abras, S. (2010). *Simulating inhabitant behaviour to manage energy at home.* Paper presented at the International Building Performance Simulation Association. Conference, Moret-sur-Loing, France.

LeBaron, B., Arthur, W. B., & Palmer, R. (1999). Time series properties of an artificial stock market. *Journal of Economic Dynamics & Control*, *23*, 1487–1516. doi:10.1016/S0165-1889(98)00081-5

Lehrer, K. (1975). Social consensus and rational agnoiology. *Synthese, 31*(1), 141–160. doi:10.1007/BF00869475

Leonard-Barton, D. (1995). *Wellsprings of knowledge.* Boston: Harvard Business School Press.

Lerner, A. (1934). Concept of monopoly and the measurement of monopoly power. *The Review of Economic Studies, 14*(1), 157–175. doi:10.2307/2967480

Levi-Faur, D. (2005). The global diffusion of regulatory capitalism. *The Annals of the American Academy of Political and Social Science, 598*(1), 12–32. doi:10.1177/0002716204272371

Levi, M. (1988). *Of rule and revenue.* Berkeley, CA: The University of California Press.

Lindenberg, E. B., & Ross, S. A. (1981). Tobin's q ratio and industrial organization. *The Journal of Business, 54*, 1–31. doi:10.1086/296120

Lipparini, A. (1998). L'apprendimento relazionale. *Sviluppo & Organizzazione, 166.*

Lipparini, A., & Lorenzoni, G. (1996). Le organizzazioni ad alta intensità relazionale. Riflessioni sui processi di learning by interacting nelle aree ad alta concentrazione di imprese. *L'Industria, 4.*

Littman, M. L. (1994). *The witness algorithm: Solving partially observable Markov decision processes (Technical Report: CS-94-40).* Providence, RI: Brown University.

Liu, L., Mackin, S., & Antonopoulos, N. (2006). Small world architecture for peer-to-peer networks. In *Proceedings of the 2006 IEEE/WIC/ACM international Conference on Web Intelligence and Intelligent Agent Technology* (pp. 451–454). Washington, DC: IEEE Computer Society. doi:10.1109/WI-IATW.2006.123

Liu, B., Ghosal, D., Chuah, C.-N., & Zhang, H. M. (2012). Reducing greenhouse effects via fuel consumption-aware variable speed limit (FC-VSL). *IEEE Transactions on Vehicular Technology, 61*(1), 111–122. doi:10.1109/TVT.2011.2170595

Li, X., Mao, W., Zeng, D., & Wang, F. (2008). Agent-based social simulation and modeling in social computing. In C. C. Yang, H. Chen, M. Chau, K. Chang, S. Lang, & P. S. Chen et al. (Eds.), *Intelligence and security informatics. LNCS 5075* (pp. 401–412). Berlin: Springer. doi:10.1007/978-3-540-69304-8_41

Lobb, C. J., Chao, Z., Fujimoto, R. M., & Potter, S. M. (2005). Parallel event-driven neural network simulations using the Hodgkin-Huxler neuron model. In *Proceedings of the 19th Workshop on Principles of Advanced and Distributed SImulation* (pp. 16–25). New York, NY: ACM Press.

Lobo, C. (1998). *Vivienda y Ciudad Posibles.* Bogotá, Columbia: Escala.

Lohele, C. (1996). *Thinking strategically: Power tools for personal and professional advancements.* Cambridge, UK: Cambridge University Press. doi:10.1017/CBO9780511525308

Lopes, F., & Coelho, H. (Eds.). (in press). *Negotiation and argumentation in multi-agent systems, fundamentals, theories, systems and applications.* Bentham Books.

Lorenzen, M., & Maskell, P. (2004). The cluster as a nexus of knowledge creation. In P. Cooke, & A. Piccaluga (Eds.), *Regional economies as knowledge laboratories* (pp. 77–92). London: Edward Elgar.

Lucas, P., & Payne, D. (2013). Usefulness of agent-based simulation to test collective decision-making models. In Interdisciplinary applications of agent-based social simulation and modeling. Open Agent Based Modeling (OpenABM) Consortium.

Lucas, P., & Payne, D. (2014). Usefulness of agent-based simulation to test collective decision-making models. In D. Adamatti, G. Dimuro, & H. Coelho (Eds.), *Interdisciplinary applications of agent-based social simulation and modeling.* Hershey, PA: IGI-Global.

Lucena, D., & Gaspar, V. (1989, February). *Strategic tax reporting* (Working Paper 112. FEUNL. Retrieved from from http://fesrvsd.fe.unl.pt/WPFEUNL/WP1989/wp112.pdf

Lukeman, R., Li, Y.-X., & Edelstein-Keshet, L. (2009). A conceptual model for milling formations in biological aggregates. *Bulletin of Mathematical Biology, 71*(2), 352–382. doi:10.1007/s11538-008-9365-7 PMID:18855072

Luke, S., Cioffi-Revilla, C., Panait, L., Sullivan, K., & Balan, G. (2005). Mason: A multiagent simulation environment. *Simulation, 81*(7), 517–527. doi:10.1177/0037549705058073

Lunneborg, C. E. (2005). Jonckheere–Terpstra Test. In Encyclopedia of Statistics in Behavioral Science (S. DOI: doi:10.1002/0470013192.bsa324). New York: Wiley.

Luyet, S. (2013). From meso decisions to macro results: An agent- based approach of policy diffusion. In Interdisciplinary applications of agent-based social simulation and modeling. Open Agent Based Modeling (OpenABM) Consortium.

Luyet, S. (2011). *Policy diffusion: An agent-based approach.* Lausanne, Switzerland: University Of Lausanne.

Lysenko, M., & D'Souza, R. M. (2008). A framework for megascale agent based model simulations on graphics processing units. *Journal of Artificial Societies and Social Simulation, 11*(4), 10.

Macal, C. M., & North, M. J. (2007). Agent-based modeling and simulation: Desktop ABMS. In *Proceedings of the 39th Conference on Winter Simulation: 40 years! The best is yet to come* (pp. 95–106). Piscataway, NJ: IEEE Press. Retrieved from http://portal.acm.org/citation.cfm?id=1351542.1351564

Macal, C. M., & North, M. J. (2010). Tutorial on agent-based modeling and simulation. *Journal of Simulation, 4*, 151–162. doi:10.1057/jos.2010.3

Macedo, L. F. K., Dimuro, G., Aguiar, M. S., Costa, A. C. R., Mattos, V. L. D., & Coelho, H. (2012, October). Analyzing the evolution of social exchanges strategies in social preference-based MAS through an evolutionary spatial approach of the ultimatum game. In *Proceedings of the Third Brazilian Workshop on Social Simulation.* Curitiba, Brazil: IEEE Press.

Magessi, N. T., & Antunes, L. (2013). Agent's risk relation on strategic tax reporting game. In Interdisciplinary applications of agent-based social simulation and modeling. Open Agent Based Modeling (OpenABM) Consortium.

Maillat, D., Quevit, M., & Senn, L. (Eds.). (1993). *Réseaux d'Innovation et Milieux Innovateurs: Un Pari pour le Déeveloppement Régional.* Neuchâtel, Switzerland: EDES.

Malatesta, E. (1891). *L'Anarchia.* Retrieved from http://www.marxists.org/archive/malatesta/1891/xx/anarchy.htm

Malerba, F. (1988). Apprendimento, innovazione e capacità tecnologica. *Economics and Politics*, 58.

Malerba, F. (1992). Learning by firms and incremental technical change. *The Economic Journal, 102*(413), 845–859. doi:10.2307/2234581

Malmberg, A., & Maskell, P. (1999). The competitiveness of firms and regions. Ubiquitification and the importance of localized learning. *European Urban and Regional Studies, 6*, 9–25. doi:10.1177/096977649900600102

Malmberg, A., & Maskell, P. (2004). The elusive concept of localization economies: Towards a knowledge-based theory of spatial clustering. In G. Grabher, & W. W. Powell (Eds.), *Networks.* Cheltenham, UK: Edward Elgar.

March, J. G., & Olsen, J. P. (2009). *The logic of appropriateness* (Arena Centre for European Studies Working Papers WP 04/09). University of Oslo, Norway.

Marinacci, M. (2000). Ambiguous games. *Games and Economic Behavior, 31*(2), 191–219. doi:10.1006/game.1999.0739

Marshall, A. (1919). *Industry and trade.* London: Macmillan.

Marshall, A. (1920). *Principles of economics.* London: Macmillan.

Martin, C. W. (2009). *Conditional diffusion: Smoke free air legislation and tobacco taxation policies in the United States 1970-2006.* Retrieved from http://www.polsci.org/martin/downloads/Martin_ConditionalDiffusion.pdf

Martine, G. (2011). *Preparing for sustainable urban growth in developing areas. population distribution, urbanization, internal migration and development: An international perspective (Economic and Social Affairs).* New York: United Nations Department of Economic and Social Affairs Population Division.

Mascarenhas, S. F. (2009). *Creating social and cultural agents* (MS.C. Thesis). Instituto Superior Tecnico, Universidade Tecnica de Lisboa, Portugal.

Maskell, P. (2001a). Knowledge creation and diffusion in geographical clusters. *International Journal of Innovation Management, 5*(2), 213–237. doi:10.1142/S1363919601000373

Maskell, P. (2001b). Towards a knowledge-based theory of the geographical cluster. *Industrial and Corporate Change, 10*, 921–943. doi:10.1093/icc/10.4.921

Maskell, P. (2004). A knowledge-based theory of the geographical cluster. In S. Breschi, & C. A. Montgomery (Eds.), *Resource-based and evolutionary theories of the firm — Towards a synthesis*. Boston: Kluwer.

Mason . (n.d.). Retrieved from http://cs.gmu.edu/~eclab/projects/mason/

Massaioli, F., Castiglione, F., & Bernaschi, M. (2005). OpenMP parallelization of agent-based models. *Parallel Computing, 31*(10), 1066–1081. doi:10.1016/j.parco.2005.03.012

Merton, R. K. (1988). The Matthew effect in science, II. Cumulative advantage and the symbolism of intellectual property. *Isis, 79*, 606–623. doi:10.1086/354848

Meseguer, C. (2004). What role for learning? The diffusion of privatisation in OECD and Latin American countries. *Journal of Public Policy, 24*(3), 299–325. doi:10.1017/S0143814X04000182

Meseguer, C. (2005). Policy learning, policy diffusion, and the making of a new order. *The Annals of the American Academy of Political and Social Science, 598*(1), 67–82. doi:10.1177/0002716204272372

Meseguer, C. (2006a). Learning and economic policy choices. *European Journal of Political Economy, 22*, 156–178. doi:10.1016/j.ejpoleco.2005.06.002

Meseguer, C. (2006b). Rational learning and bounded learning in the diffusion of policy innovations. *Rationality and Society, 18*(1), 35–66. doi:10.1177/1043463106060152

Meseguer, C., & Gilardi, F. (2009). What is new in the study of policy diffusion? A critical review. *Review of International Political Economy, 16*(3), 527–543. doi:10.1080/09692290802409236

Miguel, F., Noguera, J., Llàcer, T., & Tapia, E. (2012). Exploring tax compliance: An agent based simulation. In K. G. Troitzsch, M. Möhring, & U. Lotzmann (Eds.), *Proceedings of 26th European Conference on Modelling and Simulation*. ECMS.

Mikhail, J. (2007). Universal moral grammar: Theory, evidence and the future. *Trends in Cognitive Sciences, 11*(4). doi:10.1016/j.tics.2006.12.007 PMID:17329147

Miller, J. H., & Page, S. E. (2009). *Complex adaptive systems: An introduction to computational models of social life*. Princeton, NJ: Princeton University Press.

Minar, N., Burkhart, R., Langton, C., & Askenazi, M. (1996). The swarm simulation system: A toolkit for building multi-agent simulations. *SFI Working Paper, 06*(42). Retrieved September 2013 from http://www.santafe.edu/media/workingpapers/96-06-042.pdf

Mithen, S., & Reed, M. (2002). Stepping out: A computer simulation of hominid dispersal from Africa. *Journal of Human Evolution, 43*(4), 433–462. doi: doi:10.1006/jhev.2002.0584 PMID:12393003

Mittone, L., & Patelli, P. (2000). Imitative behaviour in tax evasion. In B. Stefansson, & F. Luna (Eds.), *Economic simulations in swarm: Agent-based modelling and object oriented programming* (pp. 133–158). Amsterdam, The Netherlands: Kluwer. doi:10.1007/978-1-4615-4641-2_5

Moffat, J., Smith, J., & Witty, S. (2006). Emergent behaviour: Theory and experimentation using the MANA model. *Journal of Applied Mathematics and Decision Sciences, 2006*, 13. doi:10.1155/JAMDS/2006/54846

Monahan, G. E. (1983). A survey of partially observable Markov decision processes: Theory, models and algorithms. *Management Science, 28*, 1–16. doi:10.1287/mnsc.28.1.1

Montañola-Sales, C., Rubio-Campillo, X., Casanovas-Garcia, J., Cela-Espín, J. M., & Kaplan-Marcusán, A. (2014). Large-scale social simulation, dealing with complexity challenges in high performance environments. In D. F. Adamatti, G. P. Dimuro, & H. Coelho (Eds.), *Interdisciplinary applications of agent-based social simulation and modeling*. Hershey, PA: IGI Global.

Morin, E. (2010). *Hacia el abismo? Globalización en el siglo XXI*. Madrid, Spain: Paidós.

Mota, F., Santos, I., Dimuro, G., & Rosa, V. (2014). Agent-based simulation of electric energy consumers: The NetLogo tool approach. In *Interdisciplinary applications of agent-based social simulation and modeling*. Hershey, PA: IGI Global.

Murphy, J. T. (2011). Computational social science and high performance computing: A case study of a simple model at large scales. In *Proceedings of the 2011 Computational Social Science Society of America Annual Conference*.

Myerson, R. B. (1991). *Game theory*. Cambridge, MA: Harvard University Press.

Nardin, L. G., & Sichman, J. S. (2011). Simulating the impact of trust in coalition formation: A preliminary analysis. In G. P. Dimuro, A. C. da Rocha Costa, J. Sichman, D. Adamatti, P. Tedesco, J. Balsa, & L. Antunes (Ed.), *Advances in Social Simulation, Post-Proceedings of the Brazilian Workshop on Social Simulation* (pp. 33-40). IEEE Computer Society.

Nardin, L. G., Rosset, L., & Sichman, J. (2013). Scale and topology effects on agent-based simulation: A trust-based coalition formation case study. In Interdisciplinary applications of agent-based social simulation and modeling. Open Agent Based Modeling (OpenABM) Consortium.

Nardin, L. G., Rosset, L. M., & Sichman, J. S. (2014). Scale and topology effects on agent-based simulation: A trust-based coalition formation case study. In *Interdisciplinary applications of agent-based social simulation and modeling*. Hershey, PA: IGI Global.

Naredo, J. (1996). *Sobre el origen, el uso y el contenido del término sostenible*. Retrieved from http://habitat.aq.upm.es/cs/p2/a004.html

Neugart, M. (2008). Labor market policy evaluation with ACE. *Journal of Economic Behavior & Organization, 67*, 418–430. doi:10.1016/j.jebo.2006.12.006

Newman, M. E. J. (2010). *Networks: An introduction. New York*. USA: Oxford University Press. doi:10.1093/acprof:oso/9780199206650.001.0001

North, M. J., Howe, T. R., Collier, N. T., & Vos, J. R. (2007, January). A declarative model assembly infrastructure for verification and validation. In *Advancing social simulation: The first world congress* (pp. 129-140). Japan: Springer.

North, M. J., Macal, C. M., Aubin, J. S., Thimmapuram, P., Bragen, M., & Hahn, J. et al. (2010). Multiscale agent-based consumer market modeling. *Complexity, 15*(5), 37–47.

North, M., Collier, N., & Vos, J. (2006). Experiences creating three implementations of the Repast agent modeling toolkit. *ACM Transactions on Modeling and Computer Simulation, 16*, 1–25. doi:10.1145/1122012.1122013

Nowak, M. A., & May, R. M. (1992). Evolutionary games and spatial chaos. *Nature, 359*, 826–829. doi:10.1038/359826a0

Nunes, D. (2012). *Exploration, design and analysis of social spaces for social simulation models* (MSc Dissertation). University of Lisbon, Portugal.

Nunes, D., & Antunes, L. (2012a). Consensus by segregation - The formation of local consensus within context switching dynamics. In *Proceedings of the 4th World Congress on Social Simulation, WCSS 2012*.

Nunes, D., & Antunes, L. (2012b). Parallel execution of social simulation models in a grid environment. In *Proceedings of the 13th International Workshop on Multi-Agent Based Simulation, MABS 2012*. Retrieved from http://www.Webcitation.org/67vbjSGuB

Nunes, D., & Antunes, L. (2013). Social space in simulation models. In Interdisciplinary applications of agent-based social simulation and modeling. Open Agent Based Modeling (OpenABM) Consortium.

Nunes, D., Antunes, L., & Amblard, F. (2013). Dynamics of relative agreement in multiple social contexts. In L. M. Correia, L. P. Reis, & J. M. Cascalho (Ed.), *Proceedings of the 16th Portuguese Conference on Artificial Intelligence* (pp. 456–467). Berlin: Springer. doi:10.1007/978-3-642-40669-0_39

O'Sullivan, D. B. (2000). *Graph-based cellular automaton models of urban spatial processes* (PhD Dissertation). University of London.

Olson, M. (1965/1971). *The logic of collective action: Public goods and the theory of groups* (Revised Ed.). Cambridge, MA: Harvard University Press.

OMIP. (2013). *Iberian electricity market operator.* Retrieved from www.omip.pt

Onggo, B., Montañola-Sales, C., & Casanovas-Garcia, J. (2010). Performance analysis of parallel demographic simulation. In *Proceedings of the 24th European Simulation and Modelling Conference,* (pp. 142-148). Hasselt, Belgium: Eurosis-ETI.

OpenSocial and Gadgets Specification Group. (2012). *Open social specifications.* Retrieved from http://docs.opensocial.org/display/OSD/Specs

Orcutt, G. H., Merz, J., & Quinke, H. (1986). *Microanalytic Simulation Models to Support Social and Financial Policy. Information Research and Resource Reports* (Vol. 7). Amsterdam: North-Holland.

Ortiz, E. (2010). Derecho a la ciudad, producción social y gestión participativa del hábitat. La promoción de iniciativas comunitarias incluyentes en la Ciudad de México. *Hábitat y Sociedad, 1,* 55–70.

Osborne, A., & Dvorak, J. (1984). *Hypergrowth: The rise and fall of Osborne Computer Corporation.* Berkeley, CA: Idthekkethan Pub. Co.

Ostrom, T. (1988). Computer Simulation: The Third Symbol System. *Journal of Experimental Social Psychology, 24,* 381–392. doi:10.1016/0022-1031(88)90027-3

Owens, J. D., Luebke, D., Govindaraju, N., Harris, M., Krüger, J., Lefohn, A. E., & Purcell, T. J. (2007). A survey of general-purpose computation on graphics hardware. *Computer Graphics Forum, 26,* 80–113. doi:10.1111/j.1467-8659.2007.01012.x

Ozel, B. (2012). Collaboration structure and knowledge diffusion in Turkish management academia. *Scientometrics, 93*(1), 183–206. doi:10.1007/s11192-012-0641-9

Pacheco, P. S. (1997). *Parallel programming with MPI.* San Francisco: Morgan Kaufmann Publishers Inc.

Padgham, L., & Winikoff, M. (2004). *Developing intelligent agent systems: A practical guide.* Chichester, UK: Wiley. doi:10.1002/0470861223

Paglieri, F., Tummolini, L., Falcone, R., & Miceli, M. (Eds.). (2012). *The goals of cognition: Essays in honour of Cristiano Castelfranchi.* College Publications.

Paolucci, M., Kossman, D., Conte, R., Lukowicz, P., Argyrakis, P., Blandford, A., … Helbing, D. (2012). Towards a living earth simulator. *The European Physical Journal, 214*(1).

Parker, J. (2007). A flexible, large-scale, distributed agent based epidemic model. In S. G. Henderson, B. Biller, M.-H. Hsieh, J. Shortle, J. D. Tew, & R. R. Barton (Eds.), *Proceedings of the 39th Conference on Winter Simulation, Washington, DC,* (pp. 1543–1547). Piscataway, NJ, USA: IEEE Press.

Parry, H. (2012). Agent based modeling, large scale simulations. In R. A. Meyers (Ed.), *Computational complexity* (pp. 76–87). New York: Springer. doi:10.1007/978-1-4614-1800-9_5

Parry, H. R., & Bithell, M. (2012). Large scale agent-based modelling: A review and guidelines for model scaling. In *Agent-based models of geographical systems* (pp. 271–308). Berlin: Springer. doi:10.1007/978-90-481-8927-4_14

Pastor-Satorras, R., & Vespignani, A. (2001). Epidemic spreading in scale-free networks. *Physical Review Letters, 86*(14), 3200. doi:10.1103/PhysRevLett.86.3200 PMID:11290142

Pavon, J., Arroyo, M., Hassan, S., & Sansores, C. (2008). Agent-based modelling and simulation for the analysis of social patterns. *Pattern Recognition Letters, 29*(8), 1039–1048. doi:10.1016/j.patrec.2007.06.021

Payments and money market model. (2011). Retrieved September 2013 from http://eco83.econ.unito.it/terna/P&3M/P&3M.html

Pelechano, N., Allbeck, J. M., & Badler, N. I. (2007). Controlling individual agents in high-density crowd simulation. In *Proceedings of the 2007 ACM SIGGRAPH/Eurographics Symposium on Computer Animation* (pp. 99–108). Aire-la-Ville, Switzerland.

Pelli, V. (2010). La gestión de la producción social del hábitat. *Hábitat y Sociedad, 39-54.*

Pelli, V. (2007). *Habitar, participar, pertenecer. Acceder a la vivienda—incluirse en la sociedad.* Buenos Aires, Argentina: Nobuko.

Pereira, D. R., Gonçalves, L. V., Dimuro, G. P., & Rocha, A. R. (2008). Towards the self-regulation of personality-based social exchanges in multiagent systems. In G. Zaverucha & A. L. da Costa (Eds.), *Advances in AI, Proceedings of the Brazilian Workshop on Social Simulation (BWSS2008),* Salvador (Baía) (LNAI 5249). Berlin: Springer.

Pereira, L. M., & Saptawijaya, A. (2007). Moral decision making with ACORDA. In *Proceedings from the 14th International Conference on Logic for Programming Artificial Intelligence and Reasoning (LPAR'07).*

Pereira, L. M., & Saptawijaya, A. (2009). *Computational modelling of morality* (Working Report).

Perfitt, T., & Englert, B. (2010, May). Megaphone: Fault tolerant, scalable, and trustworthy p2p microblogging. In *2010 Fifth International Conference on Internet and Web Applications and Services (ICIW),* (pp. 469-477). IEEE.

Perumalla, K. S. (2006). Parallel and distributed simulation: Traditional techniques and recent advances. In *Simulation Conference, 2006. WSC 06. Proceedings of the Winter* (pp. 84–95).

Perumalla, K. S., & Aaby, B. G. (2008). Data parallel execution challenges and runtime performance of agent simulations on GPUs. In *Proceedings of the 2008 Spring Simulation Multiconference* (pp. 116–123).

Perumalla, K. (2010). Computational spectrum of agent model simulation. In S. Cakaj (Ed.), *Modeling simulation and optimization - Focus on applications* (pp. 185–204). InTech.

Pesendorfer, W. (1995). Design innovation and fashion cycles. *The American Economic Review,* 771–792.

Pezzulo, G. (2011). Grounding procedural and declarative knowledge in sensorimotor anticipation. *Mind & Language, 26*(1), 78–114. doi:10.1111/j.1468-0017.2010.01411.x

Pierson, P. (2001). Post-industrial pressures on the mature welfare states. In P. Pierson (Ed.), *The new politics of the welfare state* (pp. 80–104). Oxford, UK: Oxford University Press. doi:10.1093/0198297564.003.0004

Piore, M., & Sabel, C. F. (1984). *The second industrial divide.* New York: Basic Books.

Polhill, G., Izquierdo, L. R., & Gotts, N. M. (2005). The ghost in the model (and other effects of floating point arithmetic). *Journal of Artificial Societies and Social Simulation, 8*(1).

Popper, K. R. (1963). *Conjectures and Refutations: the Growth of Scientific Knowledge.* London: Routledge.

Porter, M. (1998). Clusters and the new economics of competition. *Harvard Business Review, 76*(6), 77–90. PMID:10187248

Poza, D., Galán, J. M., Santos, J. I., & López-Paredes, A. (2010). An agent based model of the Nash demand game in regular lattices. In Balanced automation systems for future manufacturing networks (IFIP Advances in Information and Communication Technology, vol. 322), (pp. 243–250). Berlin: Springer.

Prietula, M. J., Carley, K. M., & Gasser, L. (Eds.). (1998). *Simulating organizations: computational models of institutions and groups.* Cambridge, MA: MIT Press.

Prusak, L. (1997). *Knowledge in organizations.* Washington, DC: Butterworth-Heinemann.

Quinn, A. J., & Bederson, B. B. (2011). Human computation: A survey and taxonomy of a growing field. In *CHI-2011, Proceedings of the SIGCHI Conference on Human Factors in Computing Systems* (pp. 1403-1412).

Raaij, W. F. V., & Verhallen, T. M. M. (1983). A behavioural model of residential energy use. *Journal of Economic Psychology, 3,* 39–63. doi:10.1016/0167-4870(83)90057-0

Ramchurn, S., Vytelingum, P., Rogers, A., & Jennings, N. R. (2012). Putting the 'smarts' into the smart grid: A grand challenge for artificial intelligence. *Communications of the ACM, 55*(4), 86–97. doi:10.1145/2133806.2133825

Rand, W., & Wilensky, U. (2007). *NetLogo El Farol model.* Northwestern University, Center for Connected Learning and Computer-Based Modeling. Evanston, IL: http://ccl.northwestern.edu/netlogo/models/ElFarol.

Randolph, G. M., & Tasto, M. T. (2012). Special interest group formation in the United States: Do special interest groups mirror the success of their spatial neighbors? *Economics and Politics, 24*(2), 119–134. doi:10.1111/j.1468-0343.2012.00394.x

Rand, W., & Rust, R. T. (2011). Agent-based modeling in marketing: Guidelines for rigor. *International Journal of Research in Marketing, 28*(3), 181–193. doi:10.1016/j.ijresmar.2011.04.002

Rao, A. (1996). AgentSpeak(L), BDI agents speak out in a logical computable language. In R. Hoe (Ed.), *Seventh European Workshop on Modelling Autonomous Agents in a Multi-Agent World,* (Lecture Notes in Computer Science, 1038) (pp. 42-55). Berlin: Springer.

Rao, A., & Georgeff, M. (1991). Modeling rational agents within a BDI-architecture. In R. Fikes & E. Sandewall (Eds.), *Proceedings of the 2nd International Conference on Principles of Knowledge Representation and Reasoning* (pp. 473-484). San Mateo: Morgan Kaufmann.

Rao, A., & Georgeff, M. (1992). An abstract architecture for rational agents. In *Proceedings of the 3rd International Conference on Principles of Knowledge Representation and Reasoning (KR'92)* (pp. 439-449). Morgan Kaufmann.

Rapaport, O., Levi-Faur, D., & Miodownik, D. (2009). The puzzle of the diffusion of central-bank independence reforms: Insights from an agent-based simulation. *Policy Studies Journal: the Journal of the Policy Studies Organization, 37,* 695–716. doi:10.1111/j.1541-0072.2009.00331.x

Rauch, J. E. (1993). Does history matter only when it matters little? The case of city-industry location. *The Quarterly Journal of Economics, 108,* 843–867. doi:10.2307/2118410

Reid, R. G. B. (2007). *Biological emergences: Evolution by natural experiment.* Cambridge, MA: MIT Press.

Research Computing Support Group. (n. d.). *Website.* Retrieved from http://www.rcsg.rice.edu/sharecore/bluegenep/

Reuillon, R., Leclaire, M., & Rey, S. (2013). OpenMOLE, a workflow engine specifically tailored for the distributed exploration of simulation models. *Future Generation Computer Systems, 29*(8), 1981–1990. doi:10.1016/j.future.2013.05.003

Ricci, A., Piunti, M., & Viroli, M. (2011). Environment programming in multi-agent systems: An artifact-based perspective. In *Proceedings of the Autonomous Agent Multi-Agent Systems.* Berlin: Springer.

Ricci, A., Santi, A., & Piunti, M. (2012). *Fonte: CArtAgO (Common ARTifact infrastructure for AGents Open environments).* Retrieved from http://cartago.sourceforge.net/

Richmond, P., Walker, D., Coakley, S., & Romano, D. (2010). High performance cellular level agent-based simulation with FLAME for the GPU. *Briefings in Bioinformatics, 11*(3), 334–347. doi:10.1093/bib/bbp073 PMID:20123941

Richter, C., & Sheble, G. (1998). Genetic algorithm evolution of utility biding strategies for the competitive market price. *IEEE Transactions on Power Systems, 13*(1), 256–261. doi:10.1109/59.651644

Riley, S. (2007). Large-scale spatial-transmission models of infectious disease. *Science, 316*(5829), 1298–1301. doi:10.1126/science.1134695 PMID:17540894

Roccas, S., & Brewer, M. B. (2002). Social identity complexity. *Personality and Social Psychology Review, 6*(2), 88–106. doi:10.1207/S15327957PSPR0602_01

Rodrigues, H., Santos, I., Dimuro, G., Dimuro, G., Adamatti, D., & Jerez, E. (2013a). A MAS for the simulation of normative policies of the urban vegetable garden of San Jerónimo, Seville, Spain. In A. Brandão, R. Bordini, & J. Sichman (Eds.), *Anais do WESAAC 2013—VII Workshop-Escola de Sistemas de Agentes, seus Ambientes e Aplicações* (pp. 93-104). São Paulo, Brazil: USP.

Rodrigues, T. F., Costa, A. C. R., & Dimuro, G. P. (2013b). Communication infrastructure based on artifacts for the Jacamo platform. In *Proceedings of EMAS 2013—1st International Workshop on Engineering Multi-Agent Systems at AAMAS 2013* (pp. 1-15). Saint Paul: France.

Rogers, E. M. (2003). Diffusion of Innovations (5th Ed.). New-York: Free Press.

Rogers, E. M., Medina, U. E., Rivera, M. A., & Wiley, C. J. (2005). Complex adaptive systems and the diffusion of innovations. *The Innovation Journal: The Public Sector Innovation Journal, 10*(3), Article 29.

Romero, G., Mesías, R., Enet, M., Oliveras, R., & García, L. (2004). *La participación en el diseño urbano y arquitectónico en la producción social del hábitat.* Mexico: CYTED.

Romer, P. M. (1986). Increasing returns and long-run growth. *The Journal of Political Economy, 94*(5), 1002–1037. doi:10.1086/261420

Ronald, E. M. A., & Sipper, M. (2001). Surprise versus unsurprise: Implications of emergence in robotics. *Robotics and Autonomous Systems, 37*(1), 19–24. doi:10.1016/S0921-8890(01)00149-X

Ronald, E. M. A., Sipper, M., & Capcarrère, M. S. (1999). Design, observation, surprise! A test of emergence. *Artificial Life, 5*(3), 225–239. doi:10.1162/106454699568755 PMID:10648952

Rosenkopf, L., & Abrahamson, E. (1999). modeling reputational and informational influences in threshold models of bandwagon innovation diffusion. *Computational & Mathematical Organization Theory, 5*(4), 361–384. doi:10.1023/A:1009620618662

Roth, A., & Erev, I. (1995). Learning in extensive-form games: Experimental data and simple dynamic models in the intermediate term. *Games and Economic Behavior, 8*, 164–212. doi:10.1016/S0899-8256(05)80020-X

Rousseau, D., & Van Der Veen, A. M. (2005). The emergence of shared identity. *The Journal of Conflict Resolution, 49*(5), 686–712. doi:10.1177/0022002705279336

Rousseau, J. J. (1755). *Discourse on inequality.* Holland: Marc-Michel Rey.

Rubinstein, A. (1998). *Modeling bounded rationality.* Cambridge, MA: The MIT Press.

Rubio, X., & Cela, J. M. (2010). Large-scale agent-based simulation in archaeology: An approach using high-performance computing. In *Proceedings of the 38th Annual Conference on Computer Applications and Quantitative Methods in Archaeology,* (pp. 153-159). Granada, Spain.

Rubio-Campillo, X. (2013). *Pandora: An hpc agent-based modelling framework.* Retrieved from https://github.com/xrubio/pandora/

Rubio-Campillo, Xavier, Cela, J. M., & Hernández-Cardona, F. X. (2012). Simulating archaeologists? Using agent-based modelling to improve battlefield excavations. *Journal of Archaeological Science, 39*(2), 347–356. doi:10.1016/j.jas.2011.09.020

Rudas, T. (2008). Probability Theory in Statistics. In T. Rudas (Ed.), *Handbook of Probability. Theory and Application* (pp. 69–84). Los Angeles: Sage. doi:10.4135/9781452226620.n5

Russell, S., & Norvig, P. (2010). *Artificial intelligence: A modern approach.* Upper Saddle River, NJ: Prentice Hall.

Sahneh, F. D., Chowdhury, F. N., & Scoglio, C. M. (2012). On the existence of a threshold for preventive behavioral responses to suppress epidemic spreading. *Scientific Reports, 2*.

Sakoda, J. M. (1971). The checkerboard model of social interaction. *The Journal of Mathematical Sociology, 1*(1), 119–132. doi:10.1080/0022250X.1971.9989791

Santos, F., Dimuro, G., Rofrigues, T., Adamatti, D., Dimuro, G., Costa, A., & Jerez, E. (2012). Modelando a organização social de um SMA para simulação dos processos de produção e gestão social de um ecossistema urbano: o caso da horta San Jerónimo da cidade de Sevilla, Espanha. In J. Hubner, A. Brandão, R. Silveira, & J. Marchi (Eds.), *Anais do WESAAC 2012—VI Workshop-Escola de Sistemas de Agentes, seus Ambientes e Aplicções* (pp. 93-104). Florianópolis, Brazil: UFSC.

Santos, F., Rodrigues, H., Rodruigues, T., Dimuro, G., Adamatti, D., Dimuro, G., & Jerez, E. (2013a). Integrating CarTagO artifacts for the simulation of social production and management of urban ecosystems: The case of San Jerónimo Vegetable Garden of Seville, Spain. In A. Brandão, R. Bordini, & J. Sichman (Eds.), *Anais do WESAAC 2013—VII Workshop-Escola de Sistemas de Agentes, seus Ambientes e Aplicações* (pp. 93-104). São Paulo, Brazil: USP.

Santos, F., Rodrigues, H., Rodruigues, T., Dimuro, G., Adamatti, D., Dimuro, G., & Jerez, E. (2013b). Analyzing the problem of the modeling of periodic normalized behaviors in multiagent-based simulation of social systems: The case of the San Jerónimo Vegetable Garden of Seville, Spain. In B. Kamiński & G. Koloch (Eds.), *Advances in Social Simulation: Proceedings of the 9th Conference of the European Social Simulation Association.* (1ˢᵗ ed., vol. 229, pp. 61-72). Berlin: Springer.

Santos, I., Rodrigues, T., Dimuro, G., Costa, A., & Jerez, E. (2011). Towards the modeling of the social organization of an experiment of social management of urban vegetable gardens. In *Proceedings of 2011 Workshop and School of Agent Systems, their Environment and Applications (WESAAC)* (pp. 98 -101). Los Alamitos, CA: IEEE.

Santos, F., Rodrigues, T., Donancio, H., Santos, I., Adamatti, D. F., & Dimuro, G. P. et al. (2014). Multi-agent-based simulation of the social production and management processes in a urban ecosystem: An approach based on the integration of organizational, regulatory, communication and physical artifacts in the JaCaMo framework. In *Interdisciplinary applications of agent-based social simulation and modeling.* Hershey, PA: IGI Global.

Sarin, R., & Wakker, P. (1992). A simple axiomatization of nonadditive expected utility. *Econometrica, 60,* 1255–1272. doi:10.2307/2951521

Savage, L. J. (1954). *The foundations of statistics.* New York: Wiley.

Saviotti, P. P. (1996). *Technological evolution, variety and the economy.* Cheltenham, UK: Edward Elgar.

Sawyer, R. K. (2003, February). Artificial societies: Multi agent systems and the micro-macro link in sociological theory. *Sociological Methods & Research.* doi:10.1177/0049124102239079

Sawyer, R. K. (2005). *Social emergence: Societies as complex systems.* Cambridge, UK: Cambridge University Press. doi:10.1017/CBO9780511734892

Schellenberg, J. A. (1996). *Conflict resolution: Theory, research and practice.* Albany, NY: State University of New York Press.

Schelling, T. C. (1971). Dynamic models of segregation. *The Journal of Mathematical Sociology, 59*(2), 143–186. doi:10.1080/0022250X.1971.9989794

Schelling, T. C. (1978). *Micromotives and macrobehavior.* New York: W. W. Norton.

Scheutz, M., Schermerhorn, P., Connaughaton, R., & Dingler, A. (2006). SWAGES: An extendable distributed experimentation system for large-scale agent-based ALife simulations. In *Proceedings of the 10th International Conference on the Simulation and Synthesis of Living Systems.*

Schultz, D. M. (2010). Rejection rates for journals publishing in the atmospheric sciences. *Bulletin of the American Meteorological Society, 91*(2), 231–243. doi:10.1175/2009BAMS2908.1

Schuster, S., & Gilbert, N. (2004). Simulating online business models. In *Proceedings of the 5th Workshop on Agent-Based Simulation (ABS-04)* (pp. 55–61).

Shadbolt, N.Y., Shoham, & Tennenholtz, M. (1995). On social laws for artificial agent societies: Offline design. *Journal of Artificial Intelligence, 73*(1-2).

Shaver, J. M., & Flyer, F. (2000). Agglomeration economies, firm heterogeneity, and foreign direct investment in the United States. *Strategic Management Journal, 21,* 1175–1193. doi:10.1002/1097-0266(200012)21:12<1175::AID-SMJ139>3.0.CO;2-Q

Shipan, C. R., & Volden, C. (2006). Bottom-up federalism: The diffusion of antismoking policies from U.S. Cities to states. *American Journal of Political Science, 50*(4), 825–843. doi:10.1111/j.1540-5907.2006.00218.x

Shipan, C. R., & Volden, C. (2008). The mechanisms of policy diffusion. *American Journal of Political Science, 52*(4), 840–857. doi:10.1111/j.1540-5907.2008.00346.x

Shoham, Y., & Leyton-Brown, K. (2009). *Multiagent systems.* New York: Cambridge University Press.

Shub, C. M. (1978). On the relative merits of two major methodologies for simulation model construction. In *WSC '78 Proceedings of the 10th conference on Winter simulation, 1,* (pp. 257-264). IEEE Press.

Silva, C. E., Gonçalves, E. M. N., Dimuro, G. P., Dimuro, G., & Jerez, E. de M. Modeling agent periodic routines in agent-based social simulation using colored petri nets. In *Proceedings of 1st BRICS Countries Congress (BRICS-CCI) and 11th Brazilian Congress (CBIC) on Computational Intelligence, Porto de Galinhas*. Los Alamitos, CA: IEEE.

Silva, V. T., Hermoso, R., & Centeno, R. A. (2009). Hybrid reputation model based on the use of organizations. In J. F. Hubner, E. Matson, O. Boissier & V. Dignum (Eds.), Coordination, Organizations, Institutions and Norms (COIN2008) in Agent Systems IV, (LNCS 5428, pp. 111-125). Berlin: Springer.

Simmons, B., Dobbin, F., & Garrett, G. (2006). Introduction: The international diffusion of liberalism. *International Organization, 60*(4), 781–810. doi:10.1017/S0020818306060267

Simmons, B., & Elkins, Z. (2004). The globalization of liberalization: policy diffusion in the international political economy. *The American Political Science Review, 98*(1), 171–189. doi:10.1017/S0003055404001078

Simon, H. A. (1954). Bandwagon and underdog effects and the possibility of election predictions. *Public Opinion Quarterly, 18*(3), 245–253. doi:10.1086/266513

Simon, H. A. (1955a). A behavioral model of rational choice. *The Quarterly Journal of Economics, 69*(1). doi:10.2307/1884852

Simulating the past to understand human behavior (Simul-Past). (n.d.). Retrieved from http://www.simulpast.es

Singh, M. P., Rao, A. S., & Georgeff, M. P. (1999). Formal methods in DAI: Logic-based representation and reasoning. In G. Weiss (Ed.), *Multiagent systems: A modern approach to distributed artificial intelligence* (pp. 331–376). Cambridge, MA: The MIT Press.

Skinner, B. F. (1965). *Science and human behavior*. New York, NY: Free Press.

Snijders, T. A. B. (2011). Statistical models for social networks. *Annual Review of Sociology, 37*(1), 131–153. doi:10.1146/annurev.soc.012809.102709

Song, H., Liu, C. C., & Lawarrée, J. (1999). Decision making of an electricity supplier's bid in a spot market. In *Proceedings of the Power Engineering Society Summer Meeting, vol. 2* (pp. 692–696). IEEExplore.

Sousa, J., Trigo, P., & Marques, P. (2012). Investment and trading in electricity markets (ITEM). Seminar course. In *Proceedings of the 9th International Conference on the European Energy Market (EEM'12)*.

Spinoza, B. (2009). *Ethica ordine geometrico demonstrata* [The ethics]. Radford, VA: Wilder Publications. (Original work published 1677)

Srinivasan, T. (1973). Tax evasion: A model. *Journal of Public Economics*, 339–346. doi:10.1016/0047-2727(73)90024-8

Stanovich, K. E., & West, R. F. (2008). On the relative independence of thinking biases and cognitive ability. *Journal of Personality and Social Psychology, 94*, 672–695. doi:10.1037/0022-3514.94.4.672 PMID:18361678

Stokman, F. N., & Van den Bos, J. M. M. (1992). A two-stage model of policy making, the political consequences of social networks. In G. Moore, & J. A. Whitt (Eds.), *Research and Society* (Vol. 4). Greenwich, CT: JAI Press.

Stokman, F. N., & Van Oosten, R. (1994). The exchange of voting positions: An object-oriented model of policy networks. In B. Bueno de Mesquita, & F. N. Stokman (Eds.), *European Community decision making. Models, comparisons, and applications*. New Haven, CT: Yale University Press.

Stroud, D. (2008). Social networking: An age-neutral commodity — Social networking becomes a mature web application. *Journal of Direct. Data and Digital Marketing Practice, 9*(3), 278–292. doi:10.1057/palgrave.dddmp.4350099

Subagdja, B., Sonenberg, L., & Rahwan, I. (2009). Intentional learning agent architecture. *Journal of Autonomous Agents and Multi-Agent Systems, 18*, 417–470. doi:10.1007/s10458-008-9066-5

Swank, D. (2005). Policy diffusion, globalization, and welfare state retrenchment in 18 capitalist countries, 1976-2001. Paper presented at the American Political Science Association Annual Meeting, Washington, DC.

Swank, D. (2006). Tax policy in an era of internationalization: Explaining the spread of neoliberalism. *International Organization*, *60*(4), 847–882. doi:10.1017/S0020818306060280

Swank, D., & Steinmo, S. (2002). The new political economy of taxation in advanced capitalist democracies. *American Journal of Political Science*, *46*(3), 642–655. doi:10.2307/3088405

Swan, L. S., Gordon, R., & Seckbach, J. (Eds.). (2012). *Origin(s) of design in nature: A Fresh, interdisciplinary look at how design emerges in complex systems, especially life*. Dordrecht, The Netherlands: Springer. doi:10.1007/978-94-007-4156-0

Sweeney, L. B., & Meadows, D. (2010). *The systems thinking playbook*. White River Junction, VT: Chelsea Green Publishing.

Szabó, A., Gulyás, L., & Tóth, I. J. (2008). *TAXSIM agent based tax evasion simulator*. Paper presented at the 5th European Social Simulation Association Conference (ESSA 2008).

Szemes, G. L. G. G. K., & de Back, W. (2010). GridABM - templates for distributed agent based simulation. In *Open Grid Forum 28*. Munich, Germany.

Tallman, S., Jenkins, M., Henry, N., & Pinch, S. (2004). Knowledge, clusters, and competitive advantage. *Academy of Management Review*, *29*(2), 258–271.

Tang, Y., Perumalla, K. S., Fujimoto, R. M., Karimabadi, H., Driscoll, J., & Omelchenko, Y. (2005). Optimistic parallel discrete event simulations of physical systems using reverse computation. In *Proceedings of the 19th Workshop on Principles of Advanced and Distributed Simulation* (pp. 26–35). New York, NY: ACM Press.

Telser, L. (1987). *A theory of efficient cooperation and competition*. Cambridge, UK: Cambridge University Press. doi:10.1017/CBO9780511528378

Terna, P., Arciero, L., Picillo, C., & Solomon, S. (2013). Building ABMs to control the emergence of crisis analyzing agents' behaviour. In Interdisciplinary applications of agent-based social simulation and modeling. Open Agent Based Modeling (OpenABM) Consortium.

Terna, P. (2010). A new agent-based tool to build artificial worlds. In M. Faggini, & C. P. Vinci (Eds.), *Decision theory and choices: A complexity approach* (pp. 177–191). Heidelberg, Germany: Springer. doi:10.1007/978-88-470-1778-8_4

Terradas, J. (2001). *Ecología urbana*. Barcelona, Spain: Rubes Editorial.

Tesfatsion, L. (2001). Structure, behavior, and market power in an evolutionary labor market with adaptive search. *Journal of Economic Dynamics & Control*, *25*(3), 419–457. doi:10.1016/S0165-1889(00)00032-4

Tesfatsion, L. (2002). Agent-based computational economics: Growing economies from the bottom up. *Artificial Life*, *8*(1), 55–82. doi:10.1162/106454602753694765 PMID:12020421

Tesfatsion, L. (2006). Agent based computational economics: A constructive approach to economic theory. In L. Tesfatsion, & K. Judd (Eds.), *Handbook of computational economics* (Vol. 2). Amsterdam, The Netherlands: Elsevier. doi:10.1016/S1574-0021(05)02016-2

The European Graduate School. (n. d.). *Carl Micham: Quotes*. Retrieved from http://www.egs.edu/faculty/carl-mitcham/quotes

Thimmapuram, P., Veselka, T., Vilela, S., Pereira, R., & Silva, R. (2008). Modeling hydro power plants in deregulated electricity markets: Integration and application of EMCAS to VALORAGUA. In *Proceedings of the 4th International Conference on the European Electricity Market (EEM-08)*.

Thomson, R. (2011). *Resolving controversy in the European Union*. Cambridge, UK: Cambridge University Press. doi:10.1017/CBO9781139005357

Thomson, R., Stokman, F. N., Achen, C. H., & Konig, T. (2006). *The European Union decides*. Cambridge, UK: Cambridge University Press. doi:10.1017/CBO9780511492082

Thomson, R., Stokman, F. N., & Torenvlied, R. (2003). Models of collective decision-making: Introduction. *Rationality and Society*, *15*(1), 5–14. doi:10.1177/1043463103015001037

TILAB. (2003). *Fonte: JADE—Java Agent Development Framework*. Retrieved from http://jade.tilab.com/

Timm, I. J. (2005). Large scale multiagent simulation on the grid. In *Proceedings of 5th IEEE International Symposium on Cluster Computing and the Grid* (pp. 334–341). IEEE Computer Society. doi:10.1.1.90.2116

Tirole, J. (2011). Illiquidity and all its friends. *Journal of Economic Literature, 49*(2), 287-Đ325.

Tisue, S., & Wilensky, U. (2004, May). Netlogo: A simple environment for modeling complexity. In *International Conference on Complex Systems* (pp. 16-21).

Torgler, B., & Frey, B. (2007). Tax morale and conditional cooperation. *Journal of Comparative Economics, 35*, 136–159. doi:10.1016/j.jce.2006.10.006

Torre, A., & Gilly, J. P. (2000). On the analytical dimension of proximity dynamics. *Regional Studies, 34*(2), 169–180. doi:10.1080/00343400050006087

Touraine, A. (2005). *Un nuevo paradigma para comprender el mundo de hoy*. Barcelona, Spain: Ediciones Paidós Ibérica S.A.

Travers, J., & Milgram, S. (1969). An experimental study of the small world problem. *Sociometry, 32*(4), 425–443. doi:10.2307/2786545

Treuille, A., Cooper, S., & Popović, Z. (2006). Continuum crowds. *ACM Transactions on Graphics (TOG) - Proceedings of ACM SIGGRAPH 2006, 25*(3), 1160–1168.

Trichet, J. C. (2010, 18 Nov). *Opening address at the ECB Central Banking Conference*, Frankfurt. Retrieved September 2013 from http://www.ecb.int/press/key/date/2010/html/sp101118.en.html

Trigo, P., & Coelho, H. (2009). Agent inferencing meets the Semantic Web. In Progress in Artificial Intelligence, EPIA-09 (Lecture Notes in Artificial Intelligence, vol. 5816, pp. 497–507). Berlin: Springer-Verlag.

Trigo, P. (2014). Multi-agent economically motivated decision-making. In D. Adamatti, G. Dimuro, & H. Coelho (Eds.), *Interdisciplinary applications of agent-based social simulation and modeling*. Hershey, PA: IGI-Global.

Trigo, P., Marques, P., & Coelho, H. (2010). (Virtual) agents for running electricity markets. *Journal of Simulation Modelling Practice and Theory, 18*(10), 1442–1452. doi:10.1016/j.simpat.2010.04.003

Trindade Magessi, N., & Antunes, L. (2014). Agent's risk relation on strategic tax reporting game. In D. Adamatti, G. Dimuro, & H. Coelho (Eds.), *Interdisciplinary applications of agent-based social simulation and modeling*. Hershey, PA: IGI-Global.

Troitzsch, K. (2013). Analysing simulation results statistically: Does significance matter? In Interdisciplinary applications of agent-based social simulation and modeling. Open Agent Based Modeling (OpenABM) Consortium.

Tsebelis, G. (2002). *Veto players: How political institutions work*. Princeton, NJ: Princeton University Press.

Tversky, A., & Kahneman, D. (1992). Advances in prospect theory: Cumulative representation of uncertainty. *Journal of Risk and Uncertainty, 5*(4), 297–323. doi:10.1007/BF00122574

Tyson, P. (2007). Everyday examples of emergence. Retrieved from http://www.pbs.org/wgbh/nova/nature/emergence-examples.html

Urbig, D., Lorenz, J., & Herzberg, H. (2008). Opinion dynamics: The effect of the number of peers met at once. *Journal of Artificial Societies and Social Simulation, 11*(2).

Van den Bos, J. (1991). *Dutch EC policy making. A model-guided approach to coordination and negotiation*. Amsterdam, The Netherlands: Thela Thesis.

Van Dinther, C. (2008). Agent-based simulation for research in economics handbook on information technology. In S. Detlef, C. Weinhardt, & F. Schlottmann (Eds.), *Finance international handbooks information system*. Berlin: Springer. doi:10.1007/978-3-540-49487-4_18

Van Noorden, R., & Tollefson, J. (2013). Brazilian citation scheme outed. *Nature, 500*(7464), 510–511. doi:10.1038/500510a PMID:23985850

Vaughn, R. L., Muzi, E., Richardson, J. L., & Würsig, B. (2011). Dolphin bait-balling behaviors in relation to prey ball escape behaviors. *Ethology, 117*(10), 859–871. doi:10.1111/j.1439-0310.2011.01939.x

Vicari, S. (1991). *L'impresa vivente – Itinerario in una diversa concezione*. Milano, Italy: Etaslibri.

Vieria, L., & Bredariol, C. (1998). *Cidadania e política ambiental*. Rio de Janeiro, Brazil: Editorial Record.

Vigueras, G., Lozano, M., Perez, C., & Ordua, J. M. (2008). A scalable architecture for crowd simulation: Implementing a parallel action server. In *Proceedings of the 37th International Conference on Parallel Processing (ICPP. 2008)* (pp. 430–437). doi:10.1109/ICPP.2008.20

Vigueras, G., Orduña, J., & Lozano, M. (2010). A GPU-based multi-agent system for real-time simulations. In Y. Demazeau, F. Dignum, J. Corchado, & J. Pérez (Eds.), *Advances in practical applications of agents and multiagent systems* (Vol. 70, pp. 15–24). Berlin: Springer. doi:10.1007/978-3-642-12384-9_3

Visudhiphan, P., & Ilic, M. (2002). On the necessity of an agent-based approach to assessing market power in the electricity markets. In *Proceedings of the International Symposium on Dynamic Games and Applications*, Saint-Petersburg, Russia.

Vogt, W. P. (1993). Dictionary of Statistics and Methodology. A Nontechnical Guide for the Social Sciences. Newbury Park: 1993.

Volden, C. (2006). States as policy laboratories: Emulating success in the children's health insurance program. *American Journal of Political Science*, *50*(2), 294–312. doi:10.1111/j.1540-5907.2006.00185.x

Volden, C., Ting, M. M., & Carpenter, D. P. (2008). A formal model of learning and policy diffusion. *The American Political Science Review*, *102*(3), 319–332. doi:10.1017/S0003055408080271

Von Neumann, J. (1966). *The theory of self-reproducing automata*. Champaign, IL: University of Illinois Press.

Vuze. (2012). *Vuze software*. Retrieved from http://www.vuze.com/.

Wang, F., Turner, S., & Wang, L. (2005). Agent communication in distributed simulations. In P. Davidsson, B. Logan, & K. Takadama (Eds.), *Multi-agent and multiagent-based simulation* (Vol. 3415, pp. 11–24). Berlin: Springer. doi:10.1007/978-3-540-32243-6_2

Wang, X., Yao, Z., & Loguinov, D. (2009). Residual-based estimation of peer and link lifetimes in P2P networks. [TON]. *IEEE/ACM Transactions on Networking*, *17*(3), 726–739. doi:10.1109/TNET.2008.2001727

Watts, C., & Gilbert, N. (2011). Does cumulative advantage affect collective learning in science? An agent-based simulation. *Scientometrics*, *89*, 437–463. doi:10.1007/s11192-011-0432-8

Watts, D. J., & Strogatz, S. (1998). Collective dynamics of small-world networks. *Nature*, *393*(6684), 440–442. doi:10.1038/30918 PMID:9623998

Weidlich, W. (1972). The Use of Statistical Models in Sociology. *Collective Phenomena*, *1*, 51–59.

Weidlich, W., & Haag, G. (1983). *Concepts and Models of a Quantitative Sociology. The Dynamics of Interacting Populations*. Berlin, Heidelberg: Springer. doi:10.1007/978-3-642-81789-2

Weisbuch, G. (2004). Bounded confidence and social networks. *The European Physical Journal B - Condensed Matter and Complex Systems, 38*(2), 339–343.

Weiss, G. (1999). *Multiagent systems: A modern approach to distributed artificial intelligence*. Cambridge, MA: The MIT Press.

Wellman, M. (2006). Methods for empirical game-theoretic analysis. In *Proceedings of the 21st national conference on Artificial Intelligence, vol. 2 of AAAI'06* (pp. 1552–1555). Boston, MA.

Werden, G. (1998). Demand elasticities in antitrust analysis. *Antitrust Law Journal, 66*, 363–414.

Werker, C., & Brenner, T. (2004). *Empirical calibration of simulation models* (Papers on Economics and Evolution 2004-10). Max Planck Institute of Economics, Evolutionary Economics Group.

Westerhoff, F. (2008). The use of agent based financial market models to test for the effectiveness of regulatory policies. [Journal of Economics and Statistics]. *Zeitschrift für Nationalökonomie und Statistik, 228*, 195–227.

Whitehead, D. (2008). The El Farol Bar Problem Revisited: Reinforcement Learning in a Potential Game. University of Edinburgh, Edinburgh School of Economics. ESE Discussion Papers 186.

Wiegel, V. (2006). Building blocks for artificial moral agents. In *Proceedings of EthicalALife06*. Workshop.

Wijedasa, S., Gunasekara, C., Laskowsk, M., Friesen, M. R., & McLeod, R. D. (2013, 4 January). Smartphone and vehicular trajectories as data sources for agent-based infection spread modelling. *Health Systems*. doi:10.1057/hs.2012.1025

Wikipedia. (2013a). Compartmental models in epidemiology. Retrieved from http://en.wikipedia.org/wiki/Compartmental_models_in_epidemiology

Wikipedia. (2013b). Ant mill. Retrieved from http://en.wikipedia.org/wiki/Ant_mill

Wikipedia . (2013c). Emergence. Retrieved from http://en.wikipedia.org/wiki/Emergence

Wilensky, U. (1999). *NetLogo*. Retrieved January 14, 2014 from http://ccl.northwestern.edu/netlogo/

Windrum, P., Fagiolo, G., & Moneta, A. (2007). Empirical validation of agent based models: Alternatives and prospects. *Journal of Artificial Societies and Social Simulation*, *10*(2), 8–22.

Wittek, P., & Rubio-Campillo, X. (2012). Scalable agent-based modelling with cloud HPC resources for social simulations. *Cloud Computing Technology and Science (CloudCom), 2012 IEEE 4th International Conference on* (pp. 355-362). IEEE Computer Society.

Wittek, P., & Rubio-Campillo, X. (2013). Social simulations accelerated: Large-scale agent-based modeling on a gpu cluster. In *GPU Technology Conference*. San Diego, CA.

Wolfram, S. (2001). *A New kind of science*. Champaign, IL: Wolfram Media.

Wooldridge, M. (2002). *An introduction to multiagent systems*. Chichester, UK: Wiley.

World Commission on Environment and Development. (1987). *Our common future*. Oxford, UK: Oxford University Press.

Xu, T., Chen, Y., Zhao, J., & Fu, X. (2010, June). Cuckoo: Towards decentralized, socio-aware online microblogging services and data measurements. In *Proceedings of the 2nd ACM International Workshop on Hot Topics in Planet-scale Measurement* (pp. 4). ACM.

Xu, T., Chen, Y., Fu, X., & Hui, P. (2011). Twittering by cuckoo: Decentralized and socio-aware online microblogging services. *ACM SIGCOMM Computer Communication Review*, *41*(4), 473–474.

Yariv, L., & Jackson, M. O. (2008). Diffusion, strategic interaction, and social structure. In Benhabib, Bisin, & Jackson (Eds.), *Handbook of social economics*. Elsevier. Retrieved from http://www.hss.caltech.edu/~lyariv/Papers/DiffusionChapter.pdf

Yoginath, S. B., & Perumalla, K. S. (2008). Parallel vehicular traffic simulation using reverse computation-based optimistic execution. In *Proceedings of the 22nd Workshop on Principles of Advanced and Distributed Simulation* (pp. 145–152). Piscataway, NJ.

Zaklan, G., Westerhoff, F., & Stauffer, D. (2009). Analysing tax evasion dynamics via the Ising model. *Journal of Economic of Coordination and Interaction*, *4*, 1–14. doi:10.1007/s11403-008-0043-5

Zambrano, E. (1. (2004, May). The Interplay between Analytics and Computation in the Study of Congestion Externalities: The Case of the El Farol Problem. *Journal of Public Economic Theory*, *6*(2), 375–395. doi:10.1111/j.1467-9779.2004.00170.x

Zeigler, B. P. (1976). *Theory of Modelling and Simulation*. New York, London, Sydney, Toronto: John Wiley and Sons.

Zhang, Y., Theodoropoulos, G., Minson, R., Turner, S., Cai, W., Xie, Y., & Logan, B. (2005). Grid-aware large scale distributed simulation of agent-based systems. In *Proceedings of the 2005 European Simulation Interoperability Workshop*.

Ziliak, S. T., & McCloskey, D. N. (2007). *The Cult of Statistical Significance. How the Standard Error Costs Us Jobs, Justice and Lives*. Ann Arbor: University of Michigan Press.

Zimmerman, R. D., Thomas, R. J., Gan, D., & Murillo-Sánchez, C. (1999). A Web-based platform for experimental investigation of electric power auctions. *Decision Support Systems*, *24*, 193–205. doi:10.1016/S0167-9236(98)00083-9

Zittrain, J. (2008). *Ubiquitous human computing* (Oxford Legal Studies Research Paper No. 32/2008). Retrieved from http://papers.ssrn.com/sol3/papers.cfm?abstract_id=1140445

About the Contributors

Diana Francisca Adamatti is associate professor at Universidade Federal do Rio Grande, Brazil. She received her PhD from Escola Politécnica da Universidade de São Paulo, Brazil (2007). She has an MSc from Universidade Federal do Rio Grande do Sul (2003) and BSc from Universidade de Caxias do Sul (2000), both in Brazil. Her research areas are Multiagent Systems, Trust and Natural Research Management.

Gracaliz Pereira Dimuro graduated in Civil Engineering (1980) at Universidade Católica de Pelotas, and has a M.Sc. degree (1992) and a Ph.D. degree (1998) in Computer Science, all from UFRGS. His current research interests are Agent and Multiagent Systems, Social Agent-based Simulation, Soft and Evolutionary Hybrid Agent Models, Fuzzy Logic and Systems. She is a research fellow of CNPq, member of the board of the Brazilian Society of Computational and Applied Mathematics (SBMAC), member of the editorial board of the journal Trends in Computational and Applied Mathematics (TEMA), member of the Special Committee of Artificial Intelligence (CEIA) of the Brazilian Computer Society (SBC), and advises graduate thesis at FURG.

Helder Coelho is full professor of Lisbon University, ECAI Fellow, Member of the Portuguese Academy of Engineering.

* * *

Luis Antunes holds a position as auxiliary professor in the University of Lisbon, and head of the Group of Studies in Social Simulation. His current research themes are motivation and action in a multi-agent setting, social dissemination through context permeability, and collective building of adaptive ontologies for use in the semantic web.

Luca Arciero is a senior economist at the Market and Payment System Oversight Directorate of the Bank of Italy, currently with the Wholesale Markets and Payment Systems Division. His research interests lie in payment system, money and government bond market. He is currently pursuing research on agent based modeling applied to the analyses of settlement systems. He has published papers and book contributions on payment system economics. In the academic field he has held lectures at the Universities of Tor Vergata, Torino and Siena. He graduated in Statistics and Economics from the University of Rome "La Sapienza" and obtained a M.Sc in Economics from the University of London.

Tibérius O. Bonates holds a PhD in Operations Research from Rutgers University and works primarily with combinatorial optimization, mathematical programming and artificial intelligence. He is currently a Professor of Industrial Mathematics at the Federal University of Ceará, Brazil.

Silvia Botelho is graduated at Eng Elétrica from Universidade Federal do Rio Grande do Sul (1991), master's at Computer Science from Universidade Federal do Rio Grande do Sul (1996) and ph.d. at Informática e Telecomunicações from Centre National de la Recherche Scientifique (2000). Has experience in Computer Science, Robotic and Automation for energy, oil and gas applications.

Nunzia Carbonara is Associate Professor in Management Engineering at the Polytechnic of Bari (Italy).

Josep Casanovas-Garcia is a full professor in Operations Research, specializing in Simulation systems. He is one of the founders of the Barcelona School of Informatics (FIB) where he had acted as its Dean from 1998 to 2004. He also is the director of the inLab FIB (Barcelona informatics school laboratory), an institution that has been very active in technology transfer to business. One of his recent projects has been the cooperation in the creation of simulation environments for people and vehicle flow in the new airport of Barcelona. He has led several EU funded projects in the area of simulation and operations research and is a strong advocate of the knowledge and technology transfer function between the university and society.

Cristiano Castelfranchi is full professor of General Psychology ("Cognitive Science") at the University of Siena (retired); former Director of the Institute of Cognitive Sciences and Technologies of the Italian National Research Council; Professor of Psychology at UNINETTUNO Telematic University, and at the LUISS University of Rome. Cognitive scientist, with a background in linguistics and psychology, active in the Multi-Agent Systems, the Social Simulation, and the Cognitive Science communities. Program chair of the First International Joint Conference on Autonomous Agents and Multi-Agent Systems—AAMAS-2002. Award as "fellows" of the ECCAI, for "Pioneering work in the field", 2003. "Mind and Brain" award 2008. Most influential paper award IFMAAS 2013. Research fields of interest include cognitive approach to communication (semantics and pragmatics); cognitive agent theory and architecture; multi-agent systems; agent-based social simulation; social cognition and emotions; cognitive foundations of complex social phenomena (dependence, power, cooperation, norms, organization, social functions, etc.).

José Mª Cela is the director of the Computer Applications in Science & Engineering department at the Barcelona Supercomputing Center (BSC), he is also associated professor of the Universitat Politècnica de Catalunya (UPC) - BarcelonaTech. He has participated more than 20 R+D projects and he has published more than 40 papers in international journals and conferences. His research is related with the parallelization and optimization of numerical simulations, mainly in PDEs solvers, inverse problem simulations, ab-initio molecular dynamics codes, plasma physics codes and different types of optimization codes (non linear optimization, stochastic optimization, etc.).

Antônio Carlos da Rocha Costa is adjunct professor at the Centro de Ciências Computacionais of the Universidade Federal do Rio Grande (FURG), head of the Graduate Programme in Computer Engineering.

Glenda Dimuro is an architect and PhD student at Universidad de Sevilla. Works primarily with Social Production of Habitat and urban agriculture.

Henrique Donâncio is currently an undergraduate student in Computer Engineering at the Universidade Federal do Rio Grande (FURG).

Enrico Franchi received from the University of Parma a B.Sc. in Mathematics and Computer Science, a M.Sc. in Computer Science and a Ph.D. in Information Technologies under the supervision of Prof. Agostino Poggi. His main interests are related to Multi-Agent and distributed systems, social networks, artificial intelligence and software engineering. He is currently investigating the mutual relationships between social networks and multi-agent systems, with a special regard to simulations.

Gabriel Franklin is graduated in Law at the Universidade Federal do Ceará (2009). Since 2011 he has independently researched Philosophy of the Mind and Cognitive Science, with emphasis on Artificial Intelligence and its application to Social Science.

Marcia Friesen is an associate professor in Design Engineering at the University of Manitoba, and Director of the Internationally-Educated Engineers Qualification Program. She holds a Bachelor degree in Agricultural Engineering, Master of Education, and a Ph.D. in Biosystems Engineering. Her research scope includes professional practice and engineering culture, foreign credentials recognition, agent-based modeling for healthcare applications, and mHealth development.

Konstantinos Georgalos is a PhD candidate in Economics at the University of York. His work focuses on Decision Theory under Ambiguity, and more specifically on the axiomatic foundations of dynamic non-Bayesian models in both individual and strategic decision making. In his research he is using experimental economics methods as well as agent based computational models. Konstantinos holds a Master in Economics (M.Sc. 2011) from the Toulouse School of Economics. He also holds a Master of Philosophy (M.Phil. 2010) in Economics awarded by the University of Athens Doctoral Program in Economics UADPhilEcon. His Bachelor in Economics was awarded by the Athens University of Economics and Business.

Richard Gordon is a retired Professor and itinerant scientist. His present appointments are as Adjunct Professor in the Department of Obstetrics & Gynecology at Wayne State University, and Director of the Embryogenesis Center at the Gulf Specimen Marine Laboratory in Panacea, Florida. His primary research interest is the question of how embryos build themselves. He also works on diatom motility, morphogenesis and use for gasoline secreting solar panels, origin of life, search and destroy approaches to premetastasis cancer using low dose computed tomography, HIV/AIDS prevention using condoms, and the changing 3D structure of the genome during cell differentiation. He started Books With Wings, which sends books to the universities of Afghanistan.

Adriana Kaplan is the Director and Chair of Knowledge Transfer at the Department of Social Anthropology, Universitat Autònoma of Barcelona (UAB) in Spain, and Principal Investigator of the Interdisciplinary Group for the Prevention and Study of Harmful Traditional Practices. Professor Kaplan lectures on Medical Anthropology and Gender and Development Studies throughout Spain, Europe, Africa, and Mexico. She is also the Executive Director of the NGO, Wassu Gambia Kafo. Principally, her fieldwork has been in West Africa concerning health, nutrition, reproductive, and sexual health. She leads the Transnational Observatory on Applied Research and Knowledge Transfer on Female Genital Mutilation in Gambia and Spain as well as the training of health professionals and students on FGM. Additionally, Professor Kaplan has published books and articles on FGM and co-directed the documentary Initiation without Mutilation.

Pablo Lucas is a Lecturer in Entrepreneurship and International Business (Innovation) at the University of Essex, with research focused on Agent-Based Modelling and Social Network Analysis. His areas of interest include: computational social science, research methods and design of experiments. His education include reading for a Bachelor of Science in Computer Science (BSc) focused on evolutionary networks, a Master of Philosophy (MPhil) and a Doctor of Philosophy (PhD) focused on agent-based simulation.He is also a research fellow at the Maastricht School of Management, the Netherlands and the Geary Institute, University College Dublin, Ireland.

Stéphane Luyet is currently a researcher at the Institute of Preventive and Social Medicine of the Lausanne University Hospital. He holds a master degree in economics from the University of Fribourg (Switzerland) and a Ph.D. in political science from the University of Lausanne (Switzerland). His research scope includes policy diffusion, agent-based modeling, health care systems in international comparison, geographical implementation of health care activities and substitution treatment for dependent persons.

Nuno Trindade Magessi is a researcher and PhD Student in Cognitive Science at Universidade de Lisboa, MSc(2008) in Statistic and Information Management at Universidade Nova Lisboa and graduated in Management(2000) at Nova School of Business and Economics. Research topics: Risk, Cognitive Modelling, Artificial Economics, Neuroeconomics, Social simulation, Multiagent Systems and Fuzzy logic.

Esteban de Manuel Jerez is an architect and Professor at Univesidad de Sevilla. Director of the research group ADICI. Director of Hábitat and Society Journal.

Robert (Bob) McLeod is a full professor in Electrical and Computer Engineering at the University of Manitoba in Canada. His main research interests are in agent based modeling ranging from applications in epidemiology to social networks. He is also a proponent of improving the utility of agent based models through the incorporation of real human movement and proximity data collected through noninvasive cellular telephony technologies.

Fernanda Pinto Mota graduated in Conmputer Engineering (2011) at Universidade Federal do Rio Grande and is a master student in Computer Engineering at Universidade Federal do Rio Grande.

Cristina Montañola-Sales is a PhD student at the Statistics and Operations Research Department and research assistant at inLab FIB in Universitat Politècnica de Catalunya (UPC) - BarcelonaTech. She is currently doing her research on agent-based modelling applied to demographics in a parallel environment in the Department of Computer Applications in Science and Engineering from Barcelona Supercomputing Center (BSC). She holds a MSc in Computer Science from UPC. Her research interests include agent-based modelling, computer simulation and high-performance computing.

Luis Gustavo Nardin is a Computer Engineering PhD student at University of São Paulo - Brazil, from where he has obtained his Master's degree and a specialization in Software Engineering. He has obtained his undergraduate degree in Computer Engineering from the University São Francisco. He has experience in multiagent systems, more particularly reputation, regulation and multiagent-based simulation. Currently his main focus of research is related to regulation mechanisms of normative multiagent systems and he is working as Research Fellow at Institute of Cognitive Sciences and Technologies (CNR/ISTC) in the GLODERS project.

Davide Nunes is a PhD student at the University of Lisbon. He is currently a researcher at the Laboratory of Agent Modelling (LabMAg) and works in the Group of Studies in Social Simulation (GUESS). His current research interests are social simulation, evolutionary computation, and distributed adaptive approaches to build adaptive ontologies for use in the semantic web.

Diane Payne is Director of the Dynamics Lab at the Geary Institute in University College Dublin. Before joining UCD, she worked at the University of Cambridge and Trinity College,Dublin and completed her PhD training in the ICS School at the Rijksuniversiteit Groningen, Netherlands. She has published many books and journal articles and has led a range of research projects. At UCD she has also established and coordinates a thematic doctoral training programme (CSCS PhD) in the field of Computational Social Science.

Cristina Picillo is Economist at the Market and Payment System Oversight Directorate of the Bank of Italy, currently working at the Wholesale Markets and Payment Systems Division. Her research interests lie in payment systems, financial and money markets, with publications in the latter field. She graduated in Economics of Financial Markets and International Institutions from University "Tor Vergata" in Rome and obtained a MSc in Money and Finance from the University of Brescia.

Thiago F. Rodrigues is graduated in Computer Engineering at the Universidade Federal do Rio Grande (FURG) in 2012 and is currently a master Student at Universidade Federal do Rio Grande do Sul (UFRGS).

Vagner Rosa holds a Ph.D (2010) and a M.Sc(2005). degree in Computer Science from Universidade Federal do Rio Grande do Sul (UFRGS – Porto Alegre/RS – Brazil) and BS (2002) degree Computer Engineering from Universidade Federal do Rio Grande (FURG – Rio Grande/RS – Brasil). He is Professor at FURG since 2006. His main research is in digital and embbeded systems. His research also includes robotic systems modelling and integration (hardware and software), Real-time systems, Image Processing and Computer Vision for feature localization, Image and Video compression (hardware and software) Agent-based social simulation and Social Networks for environmental monitoring.

Luciano Menasce Rosset is an undergraduate student at the University of São Paulo - Brazil. He participates in researches at the Inteligent Technics Laboratory at the Politechnic School, working on multiagent social simulations.

Xavier Rubio-Campillo is a researcher in Computer Applications in Science and Engineering Department at Barcelona Supercomputing Center (BSC). He holds a PhD on social science didactics from University of Barcelona and a MSc in Computer Science from Universitat Pompeu Fabra. His current work is focused on the development of large scale social science and humanities simulation in distributed environments. He is the BSC coordinator inside Simulpast, a project designed to introduce simulation into archaeological research. He is the project manager of Pandora, an open source platform for HPC social simulations.

Flavia Santos is graduated in Computer Science at the Universidade Catolica de Pelotas (UCPEL) in 2010 and M.Sc. in Computational Modeling at Universidade Federal do Rio Grande (FURG) in 2013.

Iverton Santos is a Bachelor of Computer Science (2011) and a Master of Computational Modelling (2013).

Jaime Simão Sichman has received his PhD degree from the Institut National Polytechnique de Grenoble (INPG), France. He has published more than 160 papers in national and international conferences and journals. He is member of the editorial board of the Journal of Artificial Societies and Social Simulation (JASSS), Computación y Sistemas, Iberoamerican Journal of Artificial Intelligence and the Knowledge Engineering Review. He was the SBIA/IBERAMIA General Chair (2000), Program Co-Chair (2006), and AAMAS Tutorial Chair (2007) and Program Co-Chair (2009). With other colleagues, he was one of the founders of the Multi-Agent-Based Simulation (MABS) and the Coordination, Organization, Institutions and Norms in Agent Systems (COIN) workshop series. His main research focus is multi-agent systems, more particularly social reasoning, organizational reasoning, multi-agent-based simulation, reputation and trust, and interoperability in agent systems. Currently, he is an Associated Professor at University of São Paulo, Brazil.

Sorin Solomon holds a PhD in theoretical physics from the Weizmann Institute of Science (1984). He is a professor at the Racah Institute of Physics of the Hebrew University of Jerusalem and was previously a Bantrell Research Fellow at Caltech and held a Career Development Chair at the Weizmann Institute of Science. He coordinated the Lagrange Interdisciplinary Laboratory for Excellence in Complexity in Turin, Italy, and a few EU projects in complexity. He authored more than 200 publications and books including 'Microscopic Simulation of Financial Markets From Investor Behavior To Market Phenomena.' Princeton University Press 2000 and "Cracking the ad code" Cambridge University Press 2009. Among the prizes he was awarded are Bantrell Prize Fellowship, J.F. Kennedy Prize for Scientific Research, Weizmann Fellowship, Keren Kayemet Prize, Levinson Prize for Scientific Research, St Francis Xavier prize. He is a foreign member Member of the Academy of Romanian Scientists.

Pietro Terna (born in 1944) is full professor of Economics at the University of Torino (Italy). His recent works are in the fields (i) of artificial neural networks and economic and financial modeling and (ii) of social simulation with agent based models, where he has been pioneering the use of Swarm. He is currently developing a new Python based version both of Swarm, named SLAPP (Swarm-Like Agent Protocol in Python). He is teaching both an advanced course on Simulation Models for Economics and an introductory one, on Microeconomics. He teaches the course of Economic simulation for the students of the PhD School of Economics of the University of Torino. He is the author of numerous papers in journals and collective volumes, published in Italy and abroad, and co-author of a book on application of artificial neural networks to economics and finance.

Michele Tomaiuolo received a M.Eng. in Computer Engineering and a PhD in Information Technologies from the University of Parma. Currently he is an assistant professor at the Department of Information Engineering, University of Parma. He has given lessons on Foundations of Informatics, Object-Oriented Programming, Software Enigineering, Computer Networks, Mobile Code and Security. He participated in various research projects, including the EU funded @lis TechNet, Agentcities, Collaborator, Comma, and the national project Anemone. His current research activity is focused on peer-to-peer social networking, with attention to security and trust management, multi-agent systems, semantic web, rule-based systems, peer-to-peer networks.

Paulo Trigo is an adjunct professor at the Instituto Superior de Engenharia de Lisboa (ISEL) where he has been teaching in the fields of artificial intelligence, semantic web and information systems. His research interests include: distributed artificial intelligence, autonomous multi-agent planning and learning, simulation and decision-making, semantic web approaches and, more recently, computer vision. He holds a degree in Computer Science (from University of Lisbon) focused on natural language processing, a Master degree (from Instituto Superior Técnico) in Electrical Engineering and Computer Science focused on computer supported cooperative work and a PhD in Computer Science / Artificial Intelligence (from University of Lisbon) focused on multi-agent hierarchical planning and learning.

Klaus G. Troitzsch is professor emeritus of computer applications in the social sciences. He took his master and doctoral degrees in political science from the University of Hamburg, Germany. From 1979 till 2012 he was a member of the University of Koblenz-Landau, where he created a study program in computer applications in the social sciences, ranging from statistical methods and social simulation to e-government. He organised several conferences, workshops and summer schools in computational social science, published plenty of articles and book chapters, edited and co-edited conference proceedings and wrote several books, among them "Simulation for the Social Scientist", co-authored with Nigel Gilbert. As a member of the editorial board of the Journal of Artificial Societies and Social Simulation he is responsible for its Forum. He participated in several EU FP6 and FP7 projects devoted to agent-based modelling and coordinated several TEMPUS projects liaising with universities in Eastern Europe and Middle Asia.

Index